POLITICS AND POLICY
IN STATES
&
COMMUNITIES

POLITICS AND POLICY IN STATES & COMMUNITIES

Sixth Edition

JOHN J. HARRIGAN

Hamline University

LONGMAN

An imprint of Addison Wesley Longman, Inc.

New York • Reading, Massachusetts • Menlo Park, California • Harlow, England
Don Mills, Ontario • Sydney • Mexico City • Madrid • Amsterdam

Executive Editor: Pamela A. Gordon
Acquisitions Editor: Peter Glovin
Associate Editor: Jessica Bayne
Marketing Manager: Suzanne Daghlian
Project Coordination and Text Design: York Production Services
Cover Designer: Kay Petronio
Cover Photo: Artville, photographer David Wasserman
Full Service Production Manager: Valerie Zaborski
Manufacturing Manager: Hilda Koparanian
Electronic Page Makeup: York Production Services
Printer and Binder: The Maple-Vail Book Manufacturing Group
Cover Printer: Coral Graphic Services, Inc.

Library of Congress Cataloging-in-Publication Data

Harrigan, John J.
    Politics and policy in state and communities/by John J.
Harrigan. —6th ed.
        p.   cm.
    Includes bibliographical references and indexes.
    ISBN 0-321-01352-2
    1. State Governments—United States.   2. Municipal government—
United States.   3. Local government—United States.   I. Title.
JK2443.H37   1997
320.973—dc21   97-31719
                                                            CIP

ISBN 0-321-01352-2

1234567890—MA—00999897

Contents

Preface   *xi*

Chapter 1 ◇ **INTRODUCTION TO STATE
AND COMMUNITY POLITICS**   **1**

Introduction   1
Rejuvenation of State and Local Government   3
What Matters in State and Community Politics   4
The Plan of This Book   13
Summary   13
Key Terms   14
References   14

Chapter 2 ◇ **THE CONSTITUTIONAL ENVIRONMENT
OF STATE AND LOCAL GOVERNMENTS**   **17**

Introduction   17
State Constitutions   18
Problems with State Constitutions   19
The Model State Constitution   23
The Politics of Constitutional Reform   23
Constitutional Reform and Social Change   28
Summary   31
Key Terms   31
References   32

Chapter 3 ◇ **THE INTERGOVERNMENTAL FRAMEWORK
FOR STATE AND COMMUNITY POLITICS**   **34**

Introduction   34
The Evolution of Federalism   36
Other Intergovernmental Politics   48
East–West Conflict   51
Intergovernmental Impact on State
    and Local Political Economies   55
Summary   57
Key Terms   58
References   59

Chapter 4 ◇ **FINANCIAL CONSTRAINTS ON STATE
AND LOCAL GOVERNMENT**   **62**

Introduction   62

How State and Local Governments Spend Your Money 65
Where State and Local Revenue Comes From 67
Conflicts and Issues in State and Local Finance 78
State–Community Finance and the Political Economy 84
Summary 86
Key Terms 87
References 88

Chapter 5 ◇ CHANNELS OF CITIZEN INFLUENCE:
PARTICIPATION, PUBLIC OPINION,
AND INTEREST GROUPS 91

Introduction 91
Political Participation 92
Public Opinion 102
Interest Groups 105
Conclusion: A Comparison of Public Opinion
and Interest Groups 115
Summary 117
Key Terms 117
References 118

Chapter 6 ◇ CHANNELS OF CITIZEN INFLUENCE:
THE BALLOT BOX, PARTIES,
AND DIRECT ACTION 122

Introduction 122
The Ballot Box 122
Political Parties 127
Direct Democracy 138
Direct Action 139
Social Change and the Ballot Box 144
Conclusion 145
Summary 145
Key Terms 146
References 147

Chapter 7 ◇ THE INSTITUTIONS OF LOCAL GOVERNMENT 151

Introduction 151
Different Types of Local Government 152
The Organization of Counties and Cities 157
The Evolution of Reform-Style City Politics 163
The Metropolitan Challenge 170
Social Change and Local Government 175
Conclusion 176
Summary 176
Key Terms 177
References 178

Chapter 8 ◇ **THE DYNAMICS OF COMMUNITY POLITICS**   182

Introduction   182
Theories of Community Power   183
Who Governs in the Age of Urban Restructuring?   188
Mayors and the Quest for Leadership   194
Mayors and the Challenge of Social Conflict   198
Mayoral Leadership and the Urban Political Economy   204
Summary   206
Key Terms   207
References   207

Chapter 9 ◇ **STATE LEGISLATURES AND PUBLIC POLICY**   212

Introduction   212
Legislative Functions   213
Legislative Structure:
    How Organization Affects Policymaking   219
Legislative Process: How Legislators Make Policy   224
Legislative Reform: Improving Legislative
    Performance   226
Summary   232
Key Terms   233
References   234

Chapter 10 ◇ **GOVERNORS AND THE CHALLENGE
OF EXECUTIVE LEADERSHIP**   239

Introduction   239
The Demand for Strong Executives   240
Executive Leadership at the State Level:
    Making Governors Stronger   242
Exercising Leadership: Governors' Styles   249
Governors' Careers   252
Other State Executives   255
Governors and Public Conflict   258
Summary   261
Key Terms   262
References   263

Chapter 11 ◇ **ADMINISTRATORS AND
THE IMPLEMENTATION OF POLICY**   267

Introduction   267
Tension Between Administrators and Executives   268
Managing Personnel for Better
    Policy Implementation   269
Social Conflict in the Public Workforce   273
Reorganizing and Reengineering Bureaucracy   279

Budgeting as a Device for Improving
   Executive Management 282
Political Economy and Reengineering
   for Greater Productivity 284
Summary 287
Key Terms 287
References 288

Chapter 12 ◇ **COURTS, CRIME, AND CORRECTIONS
IN AMERICAN STATES** 292

Introduction 292
Public Policy and the Courts 294
Court Organization and Procedure 295
Politics in American Courts 297
Courts and Social Conflict: Coping with Crime 302
Political Values and Conflicts over
   Criminal Justice Policy 308
Summary 317
Key Terms 318
References 319

Chapter 13 ◇ **POVERTY AND SOCIAL WELFARE POLICIES** 324

Introduction 324
Poverty as a Social Problem 326
Political Values and Poverty 333
State, Local, and Federal Roles in Social Welfare Policy 336
The Major Social Welfare Programs 340
Health-Care Policies: The Intergovernmental System
   in Practice 346
Reforming Social Welfare 349
Welfare Reform, Social Conflict,
   and the Political Economy 354
Summary 356
Key Terms 357
References 358

Chapter 14 ◇ **EDUCATION** 363

Introduction 363
State, Local, and Federal Roles in Education 365
Political Values and Public Education 369
Education and Social Conflict 371
Reforming Public Education 382
Education and the Political Economy 385
Summary 387
Key Terms 387
References 388

Chapter 15 ◇ **INFRASTRUCTURE POLICIES:
TRANSPORTATION, HOUSING,
AND COMMUNITY DEVELOPMENT**   **393**

Introduction   393
Transportation   394
Housing and Community Development   404
Political Values and the Social Consequences
    of Infrastructure Policy   416
Summary   418
Key Terms   419
References   420

Chapter 16 ◇ **REGULATING THE ENVIRONMENT**   **425**

Introduction   425
Environmental Regulation   427
Does the Pollution Control System Work?   438
Social Conflict and the Environment:
    Environmental Justice   439
Summary   444
Key Terms   445
References   446

Chapter 17 ◇ **STATE AND COMMUNITY ECONOMIC
DEVELOPMENT POLICIES**   **449**

Introduction   449
The Changing Climate for State
    and Community Economics   450
Strategies for Economic Development   454
Political Combat Strategies   462
Issues in the Search for Economic Development   464
Social Conflict and the Competition
    for Economic Development   466
Summary   468
Key Terms   469
References   469

Appendix: Career Prospects in State and Local Government   473
Name Index   485
Subject Index   495

Preface

In the closing years of the twentieth century, Americans are turning increasingly to state and community governments for leadership on the great domestic problems facing the nation. They are doing so in part because the federal government has abdicated leadership in so many areas of domestic policy over the past two decades, and there was no other governmental arena to which to turn. But they are doing so also because of four vital threads that have woven through the fabric of American domestic politics in recent years:

- The unprecedented rejuvenation of state and local governments over the past quarter century.
- The unprecedented role that state and community governments play today in the political economy and in promoting economic development.
- The never-ending ideological conflict over the public issues that dominate state and community politics.
- The emergence of explosive social conflicts over ethnicity, gender, and sexual preference.

These four themes play important roles in *Politics and Policy in States and Communities.* Examples of the four themes abound.

Item: A quarter century ago, as we shall see, state government was decried as "dullsville" and local government as a "lost world." So complete has been the rejuvenation of state and local government in the past two decades that these complaints no longer ring true. Today the talk is of rejuvenating government and, as we shall see, of "reinventing" government. Some of the most exciting political leaders around the nation are emerging from state politics. (President Bill Clinton, for example, came to prominence as governor of Arkansas, and Republican senator Richard Lugar came to the Senate from the mayor's office in Indianapolis).

Item: States and municipalities have gone into the economic development business in a big way in recent years. They seek to stimulate business activity to create more jobs, attract new industries, and keep existing ones. This has sparked an intense interstate and interregional competition for corporate investment dollars. When General Motors decided to build a factory to manufacture a new automobile called the Saturn, over half the states offered packages to GM in their competition to get the site of the new Saturn plant.

Item: Barely a quarter century ago, a prominent scholar published a book lamenting the end of ideology. Today ideology is alive and well in state and community politics. Too alive, in some people's judgment. On virtually every major domestic issue area (education, social welfare, crime, infrastructure, regulation) political leaders divide themselves into a variety of ideological positions on the left-right spectrum, which we shall examine shortly.

◇ CONCEPTUAL THEMES

Rejuvenation of state and local government, the role of those governments in state political economies, and the influence of political ideology in state and community politics are the unifying themes of this book. Rejuvenation of state and local government is particularly the dominant theme for Chapters 2 through 12, which deal with the institutions and processes of state and local politics. Political ideology is most relevant in the material for Chapters 13 through 16, which deal with the major policy areas confronting state and local governments (crime, education, social welfare, infrastructure, and regulation). The object of examining the ideological aspect of these issue areas is twofold: (1) to help the reader better understand his or her own value orientations toward these issues and (2) to provide conceptual tools that the reader can use to evaluate these issues as they arise in the reader's own community. The theme of political economy is relevant in several chapters of the book but nowhere more directly than in Chapter 17, on the role that state and local governments play in promoting economic development. Finally, today's great social conflicts over ethnicity and gender will surface in a great many chapters ranging from legislative representation in Chapter 9 to affirmative action in Chapter 11.

◇ IMPORTANT FEATURES OF THIS EDITION

- A separate chapter (17) on economic development policy. So important has economic development politics become that a special chapter is devoted specifically to it. Especially useful in this chapter is a set of analytical questions the reader can use to assess proposed economic development projects in his or her own state.
- A unique appendix on career prospects in state and community government and politics. This appendix gives students a guide to numerous career possibilities in state and local politics as well as some references for exploring different careers. This is especially helpful given today's demand that the college curriculum be relevant to the workplace.
- End-of-chapter glossaries. Important terms are defined in glossaries at the end of each chapter, where they can easily be found by the reader.
- Up-to-date coverage of recent developments in state and community politics. These include the legislative term limitation movement, casino gambling, and recent changes in health care policy, among others.

◇ TEACHING FEATURES OF THIS BOOK

This book contains numerous pedagogical features that aid the instructor in teaching the course and help the student in learning the material:

- "You Decide" exercises. These are boxed case studies that ask the reader to respond to lively issues that range from deciding welfare eligibility in a complicated case to applying comparable worth to a particular situation.

- Chapter previews and summaries. Chapter previews give the reader a brief outline of the major issues in each chapter. The end-of-chapter summaries seek to wrap up the most important points.
- Highlight boxes in each chapter. These are short, boxed case studies that seek to illustrate important points made in the body of the text.
- A comprehensive *Instructor's Manual*. This manual provides: (1) chapter outlines, (2) twenty-five to thirty multiple-choice questions for each chapter, (3) suggested classroom exercises to promote discussion of key issues and topics, (4) proposed research projects designed to have the student investigate how well the chapter's assertions apply to his or her state or community, (5) a career exploration exercise tied to the book's Appendix, (6) a film guide, and (7) study guides that can be given to the student. The two-page study guide for each chapter can be duplicated and distributed to the class as an aid for mastering the material of the course. Each contains (a) learning objectives for the chapter, (b) identification terms that the student should understand, and (c) mastery questions for which the student should be able to outline answers.
- Detailed footnotes that the reader can use as a guide to basic literature on research topics.

◇ ACKNOWLEDGMENTS

For me it is exciting to write and teach about state and local politics, because it is a topic that is directly involved in people's daily lives and one that has changed dynamically over the past decade. If some of that excitement rubs off on some of the student users of this text, I have many people to thank. First, there are the many users of the earlier editions of the book. They will see retained the approaches they responded to positively in the earlier editions and will note substantial additions in this edition to accommodate changing events and perspectives. Additionally and more directly, I am greatly indebted to the following reviewers who read part or all of the manuscript and gave me their invaluable comments: Beverly A. Cyler, Penn State Harrisburg; Donald C. Williams, Western New England College; Richard K. Scher, University of Florida; Albert J. Nelson, University of Wisconsin-La Crosse; Ann Lin, University of Michigan; Richard Saeger, Valdosta State University. But most of all my appreciation is to Sandy for her support.

John J. Harrigan

POLITICS AND POLICY
IN STATES
&
COMMUNITIES

1

INTRODUCTION TO STATE AND COMMUNITY POLITICS

Chapter Preview

Chapter 1 introduces the central concerns of state and community government today and outlines the plan of this book. In this chapter, we will discuss in turn:

1. How state and local government responsibilities have increased in recent decades.
2. How state and local governments have reformed and rejuvenated themselves to handle their new responsibilities.
3. What conflicts arise in states and communities as those governments seek to carry out their responsibilities.
4. How state and local governments have become increasingly concerned with political economy and the politics of economic development.

◇ INTRODUCTION

State and local governments affect our lives much more directly than does the national government in Washington. Most of the governmental services we receive are delivered by state or local units, not by Washington. That includes most of the federal government's domestic services, such as public housing, Medicaid and most forms of public welfare. Many people feel they can influence what goes on in their city hall or state capitol much more than they can influence what goes on in Washington. For most of us, Washington seems very far away, with most of its money being spent elsewhere, in somebody else's neighborhood, somebody else's state, or somebody else's country. State and local governments spend their money locally, and their projects are literally carried out before our eyes, sometimes in our own neighborhoods.

Not only do state and community governments have a more direct impact on our lives than does the government in Washington, but their role in domestic policy is steadily growing. This growth is illustrated in Figure 1-1, which shows that growth of state and local government expenditures since midcentury has outstripped the growth of federal governmental spending, the gross domestic product (or GDP, the most common measure of the nation's economic output), and inflation, as measured by change in the consumer price index (CPI).

This growing role was pushed on the states in part because the federal government during the 1980s abdicated leadership in tackling some of our most pressing domestic problems, such as air and water pollution, massive poverty, deteriorating public school systems, and dreaded toxic wastes seeping into the drinking water and contaminating the ocean beaches. During these years of neglect, groups concerned about these problems, finding little support for their

Figure 1-1 GROWTH IN THE PUBLIC SECTOR

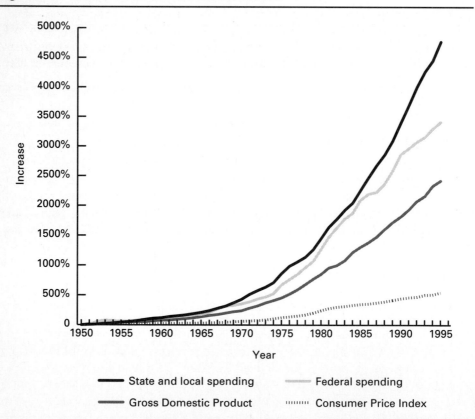

Sources: Bureau of the Census, *Statistical Abstract of the United States: 1996* (Washington, D.C.: U.S. Government Printing Office, 1996), pp. 303, 330, 443, 483; *Statistical Abstract: 1987*, pp. 250, 416, 463; *Statistical Abstract: 1984*, pp. 272; *Statistical Abstract: 1971*, pp. 305, 396.

concerns in Washington, D.C., began turning their attention to the states instead. The most imaginative leadership on some of these national problems today is coming not from the national capital in Washington, but from the state capitals.

The years of domestic neglect were possible in no small measure because domestic problems for most of the past forty years were overshadowed by America's great Cold War conflict with the Soviet Union. When choices had to be made in the federal budget, Cold War fears over national security usually ensured that it was not the military but federal programs for the environment, education, social welfare, and other domestic problems that got the axe. There are still dangerous challenges to America's security, but the Cold War is over, and nothing on the international horizon poses a threat of that magnitude. With the Cold War gone, it is more difficult to ignore any longer the scores of domestic problems that were given low priority during the years of neglect. As national attention turns to these issues, state and community governments have been playing ever-growing roles and have been reasserting their historic role as the laboratories of democracy.[1]

As states move to the forefront on domestic issues, they find themselves with difficult choices to make. Which public services should be emphasized? At what levels? Who should receive these services? Who should pay for their cost? And how should the great burden of regulating the environment, the economy, health, and safety be divided among the three levels of government (national, state, and local)?

◇ REJUVENATION OF STATE AND LOCAL GOVERNMENT

If these great tasks had been handed to the states a generation ago, in the 1960s, the states probably would not have been up to the task. In those years, scholars and journalists usually viewed state and community governments as incompetent at best. State governments were described as "sick,"[2] and state legislatures were caricatured as "horse-and-buggy" institutions.[3] States for the most part shirked their responsibilities for dealing with urban problems.[4] And as states ignored their growing urban problems in the 1950s and 1960s, the federal government picked up much of the slack with a vast expansion of social services and domestic programs. Journalists and social scientists increasingly turned their attention to Washington or to the central city, largely ignoring state government as "Dullsville."[5]

Today, these charges no longer ring true. State and community governments have profoundly rejuvenated themselves in recent years. With few exceptions, there has been a broad upgrading of the professionalism and competence of the governors, legislatures, courts, and public bureaucracies. The ability of states to cope with domestic problems has been further enhanced by more effective revenue collection systems.[6] According to the Advisory Commission on Intergovernmental Relations, this transformation of state government capability in such a short time "has no parallel in American history."[7]

By the early 1990s, the predominant buzzword for this reformist impulse was "reinventing government." This term, taken from a book by David Osborne and Ted Gaebler[8] represents the idea that governments at all levels should become more flexible, decentralized, entrepreneurial, and consumer oriented in their quest to provide public services. The 1990s are turning out to be a time when the demands for services by state and local governments are great, but the financial resources for meeting those demands are scarce. The advocates of reinventing government hope that their entrepreneurial, decentralized approach will rebuild public confidence in government by making governments more effective and possibly less costly. The prospects for this happening is a theme we will examine throughout this book.

◇ WHAT MATTERS IN STATE AND COMMUNITY POLITICS

The big question about this rejuvenation of the past decade, of course, is, for what purpose? What is the proper role of government in a democratic society? What problems should government tackle? And in tackling those problems, what should be the proper distribution of responsibility between the states and the federal government?

These are not easy questions to answer, however, because every major interest grouping in society has a different answer. And the clash between these various interests about the purpose of government is at the heart of what state and community politics is about. As states and communities move to the forefront of American domestic politics, they become the battleground for dealing with society's most contentious issues.

Should, for example, teenage girls be permitted to obtain legal abortions without consulting their parents? Should each state be permitted to decide this issue for itself? Or should the will of the federal government prevail on all fifty states?

What we are going to see, as we explore the proper role of state and community governments, is that certain facets of our political system matter a great deal to the ability of state and community governments to discharge their responsibilities. Five of these matters are going to gain our attention throughout this book.

Political Economy Matters

One of the things that matters most to a state's ability to perform its responsibilities effectively is the **political economy** (the interaction between economic conditions and public economic policy). Public revenues to provide good schools, for example, will be more plentiful if the state has a dynamic growing economy. And a state's ability to produce a dynamic growing economy is in part influenced by policies adopted by the state. The community of East St. Louis, Ill., offers a case in point. Jonathan Kozol has described what he calls "savage inequalities" in that city's schools. Delapidated buildings. Outdated books. Insufficient modern instructional technology such as computers. And abysmally unsafe environments where school children run a high risk of drugs, abuse, teen pregnancy, and vio-lence.[9] East St. Louis endures these deplorable conditions for its children in no small measure because the city's coal mining economy has been on the skids for decades. For East St. Louis, the inability to use the powers of government to rekindle the economy results in a school system of savage inequalities.

Ideology Matters

More than political economy is involved in the plight of East St. Louis, however. Ideology also matters. That community is part of the state of Illinois, which, in addition to impoverished East St. Louis, has some of the most richly endowed public schools in the nation. Should some of Illinois's wealth be used to reduce the savage inequalities afflicting the people of East St. Louis? To argue yes is to argue an ideological position favoring **redistributive policies.** These types of policies serve people at the lower end of the income scale but are financed by revenue collected disproportionately from people at the middle and upper ends of the income scale.*

Not everybody agrees that public services should be redistributive, and there are ways to ensure that they are not. The first is to minimize government's role and let it provide the least amount of services. A second is to provide only the services that disproportionately benefit the middle and upper classes—higher education, public freeways, redevelopment of big-city central-business districts, and support for the arts. A third is to finance public services through regressive taxes rather than through progressive taxes. (A *regressive tax* takes a bigger percentage of poor people's income than it takes from high-income people. A *progressive tax* does the opposite.) Progressive and regressive taxes are discussed more fully in Chapter 4.

People on the left, or liberal, end of the **ideological spectrum** generally sup-port the expanding of government services for low-income people and paying for these services out of a progressive tax system. This system redistributes in-come from the rich to the poor. In contrast, people on the right, or conservative, end of the ideological spectrum support minimal government services and re-gressive tax systems. This leads to distributive policies; that is, people receive about as much in government services as they pay in taxes. Ideological differ-ences are illustrated in Figure 1-2, which shows that the overwhelming majority of people are middle of the road or lean just slightly away from center.

Redistributive policies usually draw their greatest support from groups rep-resenting people low on the socioeconomic scale. These include labor unions (which may want more jobs), welfare rights organizations (which may want higher welfare benefits), minority groups (which may want higher expenditures on health and educational services), the elderly (who may want better trans-portation services for senior citizens), and groups for other specific categories of people, such as the poor, the handicapped, or the mentally disturbed.

---

*Redistribution can also work in the opposite direction—taking from the poor and giving to the well-off. As the term is used in this book, however, redistribution means taking from the well-off and giving it to the not-so-well-off.

Figure 1-2   THE IDEOLOGICAL SPECTRUM

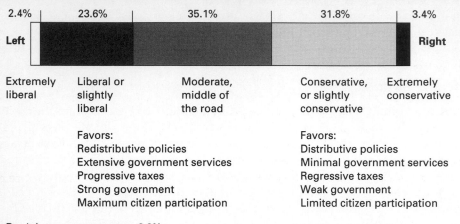

2.4%	23.6%	35.1%	31.8%	3.4%
Left				Right

Extremely liberal	Liberal or slightly liberal	Moderate, middle of the road	Conservative, or slightly conservative	Extremely conservative

	Favors:		Favors:	
	Redistributive policies		Distributive policies	
	Extensive government services		Minimal government services	
	Progressive taxes		Regressive taxes	
	Strong government		Weak government	
	Maximum citizen participation		Limited citizen participation	

Don't know + no answer = 3.9%

Sources: James Allan Davis, *General Social Surveys, 1972–1994* [machine-readable data file.] Principal Investigator, James A. Davis; Senior Study Director, Tom W. Smith. NORC ed. (Chicago: National Opinion Research Center, producer, 1994, Storrs, Conn.: Roper Center for Public Opinion Research, University of Connecticut, distributor).

Opposition to redistributive policies usually comes from interest groups representing people who expect to see their taxes rise as a result of higher expenditures—chambers of commerce (which may fear potential tax increases), business groups (which may fear that higher taxes will erode the business climate), and ad hoc taxpayers associations (which may resent potential tax increases, welfare expenditures, or higher salaries for public employees).

Redistributive policies also pose problems for the advocates of reinventing government, whom we discussed earlier. At the core of the idea of reinventing government is the desire to make government more efficient, more cost effective. But is cost-effectiveness the highest goal of government? When it conflicts with other values, which value should prevail? If you turn to the box labeled "You Decide," you will find an exercise asking you to sort out some of the tradeoffs between efficiency and other values such as effectiveness, justice, equity, and public order.

Citizens Matter: You Matter

If the states are truly becoming laboratories of democracy, then citizens will have to play an important role in shaping public policies. And certainly there are ample opportunities to do this. One way is for you to run for and win elective office. There are 7,000 state legislative positions and tens of thousands of other elective offices. Thus, virtually anyone seriously interested in government can get elected to *some* office if he or she does the right things and persists long enough. In addition, citizens can influence policy through interest groups, political parties, and political movements, a topic that we will discuss in Chapters 5 and 6. With a little

luck and a lot of persistence, the average citizen *can* affect what his or her governments do. Nearly all college students could, if they seriously pursued that goal
for a number of years, become important figures in their state or community.

Although state and local political systems are sufficiently open that the ener-
getic citizen can realistically aspire to elective office and the average college
graduate can realistically aspire to a position of considerable influence, there is a
great danger that less ambitious citizens will be reduced to being passive consumers of public services. This possibility raises important questions about
whether states and communities are truly laboratories of democracy. What role
does the average citizen really play in state and community governance? Are
these governments really as close to the people as they are said to be in American political mythology? And how much citizen participation can take place and
still permit effective governance? These are important issues that will surface repeatedly throughout this book.

Political Culture Matters

East St. Louis suffers its savage inequalities also in part due to its **political culture,** the citizens' attitudes, beliefs, and expectations about what governments
should do, who should participate, and what rules should govern the political
game.[10] Some political cultures may place very strict limits on what a state or local government can do, whereas other political cultures may allow their governments considerable freedom.

Daniel Elazar has described three state political cultures—the individualistic, the moralistic, and the traditionalistic.[11] These three cultures differ sharply in
the way they view the purpose of government and the role of the average citizen. The **individualistic political culture** believes government exists primarily
to distribute favors to government supporters and to regulate the economic marketplace so that everyone can freely pursue his or her own self-interest. It also
believes politics exists primarily to help politicians make a living and get ahead.
The individualist culture favors large bureaucracies because they offer opportunity for providing services for voters and patronage jobs for political party
workers. But it does not expect the average citizen to participate much, beyond
voting for candidates selected by professional politicians.

The **moralistic political culture,** in contrast, believes government exists to
achieve moral goals that are in the public interest. It gives governments a
broader role, permitting them to initiate new programs even if there is no public
pressure for them, as long as the programs can be justified as being in the public
interest. The moralistic culture places a high value on citizen participation and
expects public officials to follow higher standards of ethical conduct than the individualistic culture expects. The moralistic culture also favors large bureaucracies because they are believed to enhance political neutrality in the provision of
services. Unlike the individualistic culture, however, the moralistic culture rejects a patronage system of employment (government jobs given to political supporters) and favors a merit system, in which people are hired and promoted on
the basis of their qualifications and job performance.

YOU DECIDE

Is Efficiency the Answer to the Problem of Governance?

As state and local governments find their budgets squeezed by strong demonds for services and reduced financial resources to provide those services, critics have begun to demand that governments become more efficient and increase their productivity. Efficiency, in this sense, refers to providing more public services without increasing their cost.

This drive for greater efficiency draws support from a mounting body of evidence that there are wide disparities in the efficiency of state and local governments around the nation. A comparison of city-run water-meter readers in Chicago with privately run meter-readers in Indianapolis found that Chicago's meter-reading costs were more than four times as high as those of Indianapolis. If Chicago meter-readers could become as efficient as those in Indianapolis, Chicago residents would be getting more for their tax dollars.

But is efficiency always the highest value to be sought in delivering public services? Sometimes the value of efficiency conflicts with the value of *effectiveness.* Public school systems, for example, could probably handle more pupils for fewer dollars by increasing pupil–teacher ratios by 50 percent. But this increased efficiency might actually decrease teaching effectiveness and learning.

Efficiency can also conflict with *justice.* Judges might devise routines to process more civil and criminal cases each day, but such speed might result in hastily considered outcomes: guilty persons might be let off and innocent persons punished; or inequitable decisions might be made in divorce and child custody suits.

There are even circumstances where increasing efficiency today can lead to greater *public disorder* tomorrow. Local welfare departments, for another example, might lower the cost of caring for disturbed children in treatment centers by reducing the amount of time each child is permitted to spend in such centers. In one sense, this would increase the department's efficiency by increasing the number of children being treated per dollar. But sending disturbed children back to their home environments before they are ready might well exacerbate their problems, and thus possibly increase future assaults and vandalism.

The **traditionalistic political culture** believes government exists to preserve the social order. It permits governments to initiate new programs only if they serve the interests of the governing elites. It limits political participation to the few appropriate elites. Political parties are less important than family or social ties. And bureaucracy is viewed negatively as a force for depersonalizing government. The traditionalistic culture rejects the merit system of employment.

Elazar traces these three political cultures in historical development. The moralistic culture is traced to the colonial New England Puritans and the Scandinavian and German Protestants. As these peoples migrated across the northern states to the west, they imposed their cultural values on those regions. The individualistic culture is traced to nineteenth-century European immigration, especially of Catholics, and to the rise of the business centers in the mid-Atlantic states of New Jersey, New York, Pennsylvania, and Delaware. The traditionalistic culture is traced to the plantation economy of the South.

Combinations of these cultures predominate in the states where the westward migration of population caused these peoples to move, as shown in the

In short, the way that state and local governments provide services reflects such societal values as efficiency, effectiveness, justice, equity, and public order.

We all have opinions about such matters. What is your opinion? This exercise lets you decide that for yourself. On each of the issues discussed here, indicate the value (efficiency, effectiveness, justice, equity, or public order) that you consider most important, least important, and moderately important.

	MOST IMPORTANT VALUE	MODERATELY IMPORTANT VALUE	LEAST IMPORTANT VALUE
Water-meter reading			
Garbage collection			
Pupil–teacher ratios			
Criminal cases (e.g., robbery)			
Civil cases (e.g., divorce)			
Length of treatment for disturbed children			

Are there any patterns to your answers and those of your classmates? Does this exercise give you any insight into your own feelings about these issues? On the basis of these reflections, how would you respond to someone arguing for efficiency as the highest value in the delivery of governmental services? Agree totally? Agree partially? Disagree totally?

Sources: For meter-reading data: E. S. Savas, "Municipal Monopolies versus Competition," *Improving the Quality of Urban Management,* vol. 8, Urban Affairs Annual Reviews, ed. Willis D. Hawley and David Rogers (Beverly Hills, Calif.: SAGE Publications, 1974), p. 483.

map of Figure 1-3. Thus the moralistic culture is most strongly rooted along the northern tier of states following a stream of New England migrants in that direction. The individualistic culture is most strongly rooted in the mid-Atlantic and the lower Great Lakes states of Illinois, Indiana, Ohio, and Pennsylvania; and the traditionalistic culture is most strongly embedded in the South.

Although Elazar cautions us not to identify particular states as completely dominated by a single political culture, different combinations of cultures lead some states to develop peculiar political styles. This can be seen most clearly in the Midwest. In the moralistic states of Michigan, Wisconsin, and Minnesota, an **issue-oriented politics** developed, whereas in the individualistic states of Illinois, Indiana, and Ohio, a **jobs-oriented politics** developed.[12] In issue-oriented states, the Democratic party is strongly allied with organized labor, and it promotes liberal policies such as civil rights, public welfare, strong worker-protection legislation, and progressive taxes. The Republican party draws its greatest strength from rural areas, the suburbs, and the business community, and it is ideologically opposed to the Democrats on most of these issues.

Figure 1-3   DISTRIBUTION OF POLITICAL CULTURE IN THE UNITED STATES

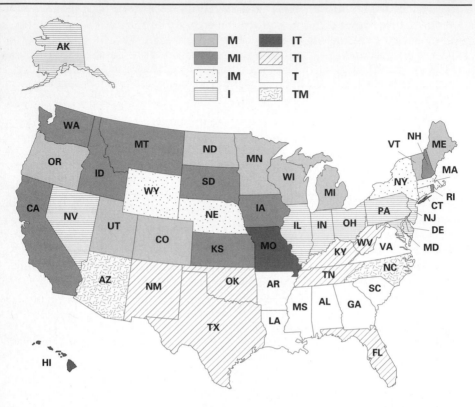

M = Moralistic; I = Individualistic; T = Traditionalistic

Source: Map from *American Federalism: A View from the States,* 3rd ed. by Daniel Elazar. Copyright © 1984 by Harper & Row, Publishers, Inc. Reprinted by permission of Addison-Wesley Educational Publishers, Inc.

In contrast to these three issue-oriented states, Ohio, Indiana, and Illinois developed a jobs-oriented politics consistent with their dominant individualistic cultures. Rather than fighting over issues, Republicans and Democrats in these states fight mostly over who will get to distribute the benefits of government to their supporters. All three states traditionally had extensive patronage employment in which government workers got jobs because they supported the winning political party. In the jobs-oriented system, when government changes hands, large numbers of public employees are replaced by new employees who belong to the party that is coming to power. Graft and political corruption are much more extensive in Illinois, Indiana, and Ohio than they are in Michigan, Wisconsin, or Minnesota. Politics is viewed as much dirtier. These states have not provided the progressive reform movement leadership provided by their three northern neighbors. And whereas political machines have pretty much withered away in the moralistic, issue-oriented states, machine-style politics is still alive where politics is individualistic and jobs oriented, especially in Chicago.

What impact does political culture have on the politics and policies of the different states? Research into this question has produced several conclusions. First, citizen participation in politics is highest in the moralistic cultures and lowest in the traditionalistic cultures.[13] This is due in great measure to the fact that moralistic states facilitate participation by having more lenient requirements for voter registration and voting in elections than do traditionalistic states, and that the institutions of government are more open to citizen input than they are in traditionalistic states.[14]

Second, numerous studies have found that political culture influences the kind of policies adopted by states. Moralistic states tend to pursue more redistributive policies than do the traditionalistic states, but this may be because the moralistic states are also more affluent.[15] In a number of other policy areas, political culture was found to have an independent influence. States with a traditionalistic culture are much less likely to have lenient divorce legislation than moralistic states,[16] and traditionalistic states also tend to spend less money on government programs than do moralistic or individualistic states.[17] Moralistic states are much more likely to engage in a broad scope of governmental activity, to pursue innovative government programs, and to spend more money on welfare and economic development policies.[18] When traditionalistic states do spend money on economic development, they tend to spend it in different ways than do moralistic states. Whereas moralistic states tend to spend more of their development dollars trying to create new industries or restructuring old ones, traditionalistic states are more inclined to spend dollars trying to keep existing plants in the state or enticing out-of-state firms to build branch plants.[19]

A third important impact of political culture on state politics is that moralistic states do indeed have higher ethical standards of public conduct than other states.[20] Public officials in moralistic states are convicted for corrupt behavior much less frequently than are public officials in individualistic and traditionalistic states.[21]

Finally, although Elazar's theory of political culture has been a powerful concept for understanding the variations in politics and policy from one state to another, it is not clear *how* or by what mechanism the political cultures have this impact.[22] Attempts to use public opinion surveys to categorize people into the moralistic, traditionalistic, or individualistic types have been inconclusive.[23]

It also is unlikely that states in the future will continue to fit as neatly into Elazar's three categories as they have in the past.[24] Since Elazar formulated this theory three decades ago, population migrations have led to a dynamic mixing of cultures that will possibly create new types and combinations of cultures. There has been a heavy migration of people from the individualistic and moralistic regions to the South and Southwest, leading to a very turbulent mixing of cultural values in those regions. The South in particular appears to be becoming much less traditionalistic. And the Southwest is, in a sense, becoming the new melting pot of the nation. It has absorbed substantial inmigration of peoples from all three political cultures. It is absorbing millions of Latin American immigrants who are leaving their imprint on the political culture. And the substantial number of Asian immigrants has influenced local culture, especially on the West Coast. As a consequence of these changes, the three political cultures outlined here will almost certainly evolve into something reflecting the growing diversity of American society.[25]

Social Conflict Matters

A final issue that matters greatly to state and community governments is the growing tendency to balkanize American politics. The Balkans are a region of South-Central Europe torn apart periodically over the years by hatreds and bloody warfare between uncompromising ethnic-religious groups. Like the Balkans, the United States also contains many diverse ethnic, religious, economic, and ideological groups. But unlike the Balkans, most of these groups historically expressed a commitment to the broader whole of American society and eventually grew to tolerate one another. Government itself was pledged to a constitutional principle of treating all people equally under the law. No society, of course, is ever able to treat all people with perfect equality, and in America the principle of equality under the law was especially violated in regard to African Americans and Native Americans. But the existence of the principle of equal treatment under the law at least was a beacon of hope that kept the nation striving for greater equality and helped hold all the diverse elements of society together. People believed in America as a melting pot that would melt all the diverse elements into a new American whole.

Today, this notion of America as a melting pot sounds archaic in the face of bitter social conflicts based on gender, racial differences, ideological differences, and class discrepancies. The eminent historian Arthur M. Schlesinger, Jr., has written about the *Disuniting of America*.[26] Spokespersons emerge among the various ethnic groups, religious beliefs, ideological causes, and economic groups. Many of them have legitimate claims on society and press their claim in highly moralistic rhetoric that frequently condemns the majority of Americans as sexist, racist, or homophobic, and frequently, according to Schlesinger, they play fast and loose with historical accuracy. Other people react adversely to being labeled as sexist or racist or homophobic. Others deny government the legitimacy to collect taxes from them and hole up in mountain retreats or organize armed citizen militias. And still others are so convinced of the nobility of their cause that they feel justified in destroying property and breaking laws that bind the rest of their fellow citizens. At times, America's many diverse peoples seem to be moving more toward the hatred and uncompromising postures of the Balkans than they are toward mutual tolerance under one nation.

These social conflicts matter to states and communities because those governments must establish policies that will satisfy the conflicting demands of different racial, cultural, and classes of people. Furthermore, states and communities must find ways to satisfy these demands in the face of political–economic forces that are concentrating wealth at the top of the social ladder and inhibiting government from playing its traditional redistributive role. In this environment, the myth of the melting pot is not likely to get reestablished. And the great danger is that the balkanization of social conflict will gradually erode the foundations of state and community governments themselves.

◇ THE PLAN OF THIS BOOK

State and local governments, then, are highly relevant to our lives. They directly affect how well we live. Sometimes they give benefits to us, and other times they tax us to pay for services that other people receive. Whether these benefits and taxes are redistributive is an issue that deeply touches our own personal values about the role of government and about the kind of society in which we want to live. Whether we can influence what these governments do is a direct challenge to our belief in democracy. And whether our governments can cope with the social conflicts of the day will greatly affect the quality of our lives.

In order to discuss these important aspects of state and local government in as orderly a way as possible, the first group of chapters examines the constraints or limitations within which state and local governments operate. Chapter 2 studies the constitutional constraints. Chapter 3 analyzes how federalism has evolved into an elaborate intergovernmental system. State and local governments are no longer autonomous. Each governmental unit is limited by actions of the federal government and by actions of other governments at the state and local levels. Chapter 4 examines the financial constraints on state and local governments. State and local governments can provide only as many services as they can pay for. And deciding which of their citizens will pay for what services is a difficult political question.

The next four chapters study the political processes. Chapter 5 looks at public opinion and interest groups, Chapter 6 at political parties and elections, Chapter 7 at forms of local government, and Chapter 8 at the dynamics of community politics.

The next four chapters discuss the state-level policymaking institutions—the legislatures (Chapter 9), the executives (Chapter 10), the administrative apparatus (Chapter 11), and the courts (Chapter 12). A primary concern of these chapters is to show the impact of the reformist movement on the organization and policies of these institutions as well as the nature of political conflicts that surround these institutions.

The final group of chapters examines several policy areas—poverty and welfare (Chapter 13); education (Chapter 14); infrastructure policies regarding housing, community development, and transportation (Chapter 15); regulatory policies toward the environment, energy, and the economy (Chapter 16); and the politics of economic development (Chapter 17).

SUMMARY

1. Recent years have seen a dramatic reform and rejuvenation of state and local governments in the United States.

2. One of the major additions to state and local government responsibilities during the recent period of rejuvenation has been responsibility for state and local political economies.
3. As state and local governments carry out their responsibilities, they become focal points for important political conflicts, especially conflicts over political ideology and group benefits.
4. Because of budget squeezes and administrative reform movements, state and local governments are increasingly assessed by the value of efficiency in their delivery of public services. The "You Decide" exercise in this chapter presents a situation in which efficiency as a value is compared to other values in the assessment of government's effectiveness.
5. As state and local governments become increasingly central to our lives, it also becomes increasingly important to have an effective system of citizen participation in order to keep government accountable to the people.

KEY TERMS

Ideological spectrum   The traditional left-right spectrum, in which liberal (or left-leaning) ideological positions are on the left side of the spectrum and conservative (or right-leaning) ideological positions are on the right side.

Individualistic political culture   A viewpoint that believes government exists to distribute favors and believes politics should be dominated by professional politicians.

Issue-oriented politics   A politics characterized by a liberal–conservative split between political parties as they compete over the direction of public policy.

Jobs-oriented politics   A politics characterized by competition over the power to control a patronage apparatus and to distribute benefits to political followers.

Moralistic political culture   A viewpoint that believes government should seek to achieve moral goals in the public interest. Places a high value on citizen participation.

Political culture   People's attitudes, beliefs, and expectations about what governments should do, who should participate, and what rules should govern the political game.

Political economy   The interaction between public policy and economic growth.

Redistributive policies   Policies that provide extensive public services for people on the low end of the income scale and finance those services with revenues collected from people at the middle and upper ends of the income scale.

Traditionalistic political culture   A viewpoint that believes government's purpose is to preserve the existing social order.

REFERENCES

1. David E. Osborne, *Laboratories of Democracy* (Cambridge, Mass.: Harvard Business School Press, 1988).
2. Charles Press and Charles Adrian, "Why Our State Governments Are Sick," *Antioch Review* 24, no. 2 (1964): 154–165.
3. James Nathan Miller, "Our Horse-and-Buggy State Legislatures," *Reader's Digest* (May 1965): 49–54.
4. Roscoe C. Martin, *The Cities and the Federal System* (New York: Atherton Press, 1965), pp. 45–47.
5. Coleman Ransone, "Scholarly Revolt in Dullsville: New Approaches to the Study of State Government," *Public Administration Review* 26, no. 4 (December 1966): 343–352.

6. See David C. Nice, "Revitalizing the States: A Look at the Record," *National Civic Review* 72, no. 7 (July–August 1983): 371–376; Ann O'M. Bowman and Richard C. Kearney, *The Resurgence of the States* (Englewood Cliffs, N.J.: Prentice-Hall, 1986); Carl E. Van Horn, *The State of the States* (Washington, D.C.: Congressional Quarterly Press, 1989).

7. Advisory Commission on Intergovernmental Relations, *In Brief: State and Local Roles in the Federal System* (Washington, D.C.: U.S. Government Printing Office, 1981), p. 3. Also see Advisory Commission on Intergovernmental Relations, *The Question of State Governmental Capability: An Authoritative Catalogue of State Action to Modernize State Governments in Recent Decades,* Report A-98 (Washington, D.C.: U.S. Government Printing Office, 1986).

8. David E. Osborne and Ted Gaebler, *Reinventing Government: How the Entrepreneurial Spirit Is Transforming the Public Sector* (Reading, Mass.: Addison-Wesley, 1992).

9. Jonathan Kozol, *Savage Inequalities: Children in America's Schools* (New York: Crown Pub., 1991).

10. Lucian Pye defines political culture as the "set of attitudes, beliefs, and sentiments that give order and meaning to the political process." See his "Political Culture," *International Encyclopedia of the Social Sciences,* vol. 12 David L. Sills, ed. (New York: Macmillan, 1968), p. 218.

11. Daniel J. Elazar, *American Federalism: A View From the States,* 2nd ed. (New York: Thomas Y. Crowell, 1972), Ch. 4, especially pp. 100–101.

12. John Fenton, *Midwest Politics* (New York: Holt, Rinehart & Winston, 1966).

13. This was recently found in a survey of Illinois residents. See Ellen B. Dran, Robert B. Albritton, and Mikel Wyckoff, "Surrogate Versus Direct Measures of Political Culture: Explaining Participation and Policy Attitude in Illinois," *Publius* 21, no. 2 (Spring 1991): 15–30. Numerous earlier studies also confirmed the higher participation rates of people in the moralistic culture. Ira Sharkansky, "The Utility of Elazar's Political Culture: A Research Note," *Polity* 2, no. 1 (Fall 1969): 66–83. This pattern of participation rates was also found in another study that was generally supportive of Elazar's theory on the geographic dispersion of the cultures. See Timothy D. Schlitz and R. Lee Rainey, "The Geographic Distribution of Elazar's Political Subcultures Among the Mass Population: A Research Note," *Western Political Quarterly* 31, no. 3 (September 1978): 410–415. In support of Elazar's theory, see Robert L. Savage, "Looking for Political Subcultures: A Critique of the Rummage-Sale Approach," *Western Political Quarterly* 34, no. 2 (June 1981): 331–336.

14. Eric B. Herzik, "The Legal-Formal Structuring of State Politics: A Cultural Explanation," *Western Political Quarterly* 38, no. 3 (September 1985): 413–423.

15. Sharkansky, "The Utility of Elazar's Political Culture."

16. Gillian Dean, "The Study of Political Feedback Using Non-Recursive Causal Models: The Case of State Divorce Policies," *Policy Studies Journal* 8, no. 6 (Summer 1980): 920–927.

17. David Young Miller, "The Impact of Political Culture on Patterns of State and Local Government Expenditures," *Publius* 21, no. 2 (Spring 1991): 83–100.

18. Charles A. Johnson, "Political Culture in American States: Elazar's Formulation Examined," *American Journal of Political Science* 20, no. 3 (August 1976): 491–509.

19. Keith Boeckelman, "Political Culture and State Economic Development Policy," *Publius* 21, no. 2 (Spring 1991): 49–81.

20. John G. Peters and Susan Welch, "Politics, Corruption, and Political Culture: A View from the State Legislatures," *American Politics Quarterly* 6, no. 3 (July 1978): 345–356.

21. See Ibid. and David C. Nice, "Political Corruption in the American States," *American Politics Quarterly* 11, no. 4 (October 1983): 507–517.

22. David Lowery and Lee J. Sigelman, "Political Culture and State Public Policy: The Missing Link," *Western Political Quarterly* 35, no. 3 (September 1982): 376–384.

23. For a pessimistic attempt to do this see Peter F. Nardulli, "Political Subcultures in the American States: An Empirical Examination of Elazar's Formulation," *American Politics Quarterly* 18, no. 3 (July 1990). For a survey of Illinois residents that was able to classify people into the types, see Dran, Albritton, and Wyckoff, "Surrogate Versus Direct Measures of Political Culture," pp. 15–30.

24. One attempt to update Elazar's categorization through 1980 found several states that no longer fit Elazar's original classification. Only two states, for example, were able to be labeled moralistic, whereas Elazar had originally put nine states into that group. See David R. Morgan and Sheilah S. Watson, "Political Culture, Political System Characteristics, and Public Policies Among the American States," *Publius* 21, no. 2 (Spring 1991): 31–48.

25. One study, for example, finds ten versions of regional subcultures. See Joel Lieske, "Regional Subcultures of the United States," *The Journal of Politics* 55, no. 4 (November 1993): 888–913.

26. Arthur M. Schlesinger, Jr. *The Disuniting of America* (New York: Norton, 1992).

2

THE CONSTITUTIONAL ENVIRONMENT OF STATE AND LOCAL GOVERNMENTS

Chapter Preview

Chapter 2 outlines the constitutional and cultural environments within which state and local politics take place. In this chapter, we will discuss in turn:

1. The constitutional framework for state and community politics.
2. The criticisms of state constitutions.
3. The politics of constitutional reform.
4. The relevance of state constitutions to contemporary social conflict.

◇ INTRODUCTION

State constitutions exert a powerful influence on our lives. They have become deeply enmeshed in some of the social conflicts mentioned in Chapter 1. Consider, for example:

- Colorado, in 1992, approved a constitutional amendment so controversial that its supporters and opponents could not even agree on a neutral description. Supporters of the amendment said that it prohibited special privileges for gays and lesbians. Opponents said that it prohibited legislation that would protect gays and lesbians from discrimination.
- Gay rights activists charged that this new Colorado constitutional provision violated the federal constitution, and in 1996, the U.S. Supreme Court struck down the Colorado amendment.
- In 1996, California voters faced a proposed constitutional amendment that would, if passed, threaten the legality of many affirmative action provisions already in California law.

- Hawaii courts, in 1996, were considering a ruling that would legalize gay marriages under Hawaii's constitution. Under the full faith and credit clause of the U.S. constitution, all states are obliged to recognize the legitimacy of marriages in other states. Would this Hawaii court ruling mean that any other state, Mississippi, for example, or North Dakota, would be obliged to recognize gay marriages even though legislation permitting gay marriages had not been passed by their legislatures, or any other legislature for that matter?
- Going back to the "savage inequalities" in East St. Louis mentioned in Chapter 1, several state courts ruled that their state constitutions required a redistribution of school funding, thus forcing upon legislatures and governors the difficult task of accomplishing this goal. Unfortunately for East St. Louis, Illinois was not one of those states.

This chapter provides a context for examining the proper role of state constitutions and judges in resolving these bitter social conflicts. First, we will look at state constitutions, problems with those constitutions, and the constitutional reform movement. A guiding theme of this analysis will be that state constitutions have slowly been moving from a positive law tradition to a higher law tradition of constitutionalism. Finally, we will examine the growing importance of state constitutions in coping with our contemporary social conflicts.

◇ STATE CONSTITUTIONS

A constitution establishes the structure of government and prescribes the fundamental rules of the game of politics. Constitutions may be unwritten (as in the case of Great Britain) or written (as in all fifty American states). Because the constitution outlines government structures and the basic rules of the political game, it is the **fundamental law** of a state and takes precedence over the **statutory laws,** that is, the laws passed by the legislature. If the statutory laws contradict the constitution, judges may declare them unconstitutional and not enforce them in the courts. This feature of constitutional government is called **judicial review.** It is because of judicial review that judges today are playing such a prominent role in issues such as gay marriages in Hawaii, gay rights in Colorado, and savage inequalities in the schools of East St. Louis.

The notion that the constitutional law is superior to the statutory law is called the higher law tradition of constitutionalism.[1] Under this tradition, the constitution is supposed to be a brief charter that sets the framework of government and prescribes the basic civil liberties of the citizens. Because the constitution is seen as higher law, it is deliberately made difficult to amend. It is meant to "endure for ages to come" as the Supreme Court stated in one of its most famous decisions.[2] The U.S. Constitution has all these elements. It is brief, succinct, embarrassingly vague in many places (could anyone, for example, provide a universally acceptable definition of the phrase "due process of law"), and difficult to amend. Congress is slow to initiate new amendments to that document, even when powerful public pressures clamor for amendment. In the early 1990s, there was strong public pressure for a proposed constitutional amendment that would overturn a recent Supreme Court ruling that had protected burning of the American flag as a form of free speech. Speaking against the proposed amendment, Senator David Durenburger (R, Minn.) gave a classic higher law argument: "The Constitution is a document for the ages, not a tool for dealing with the politics of the moment. . . . We should not tinker with the Constitution—even for such a critical reason as this—when we have evidence that statutory changes will do the job."[3]

◇ PROBLEMS WITH STATE CONSTITUTIONS

In contrast to this higher law tradition, most state constitutions historically followed a different tradition, a positive law tradition of constitutionalism. Under the positive law tradition, it is considered quite proper for the constitution to contain policy details that the higher law tradition would provide for by statute rather than by constitutional amendment. The practical consequences of these two traditions is illustrated in Table 2-1, which compares the federal and state constitutions. The federal constitution is concise and well written, and it focuses on prescribing the fundamental law. In contrast, state constitutions are typically long, poorly written, and full of petty details. The state constitutions have been

Table 2-1 DIFFERENCES BETWEEN THE FEDERAL AND STATE CONSTITUTIONS

	Federal	The Average State Constitution
Length	About 8,700 words	About 30,000 words
Frequency of amendments	Seldom. Only sixteen amendments since 1800.	Frequent. The average state passes at least one amendment every two years.
Focus	Broad focus on setting fundamental law, with emphasis on the structure of government, the powers of government, and citizens' rights.	Narrow focus on details that might be better left to ordinary statutory law.
Legal theory	The federal government possesses only those powers specified in the Constitution.	The state governments possess any powers that are not specifically prohibited.
Supremacy	The Constitution is the supreme law of the land.	State constitutions are subordinate to the federal Constitution and to federal law.

criticized as archaic documents reflecting the biases of 100 years ago. For example, Mississippi's constitution provides a religious test for public officeholders and also regulates dueling.[4] In addition, reformers say that many state constitutions place too many restrictions on state legislatures, create fragmented executive branches and inefficient court systems, and hamper the operations of local governments.[5]

Too Long and Too Detailed

Although the U.S. Constitution has only about 8,700 words, the average state constitution has 30,000. Alabama's, with about 174,000 words, is the longest. Such excessive length makes the document very difficult to understand. Accompanying this excessive length is excessive detail, or **super legislation,** as it has been sometimes called.[6] Super legislation refers to provisions in a constitution that most reformers think should be left to statutory law. California's constitution, for example, regulates the length of wrestling matches, while New York's determines the location of certain ski trails, and the constitutions in Arkansas and Kansas contain so-called right-to-work provisions that inhibit labor unions from building their memberships. Because these provisions are written into the constitution itself, they become super legislation that is more difficult to adapt to changing times and changing popular majorities than is statutory legislation.

Because of these considerations, reformers advocate shorter constitutions that deal only with the fundamental structures of government. States with the weakest political parties tend to be the states with the longest constitutions.[7] When political parties are weak, it is easier for specific interests to get favorable provisions written into constitutions.

Legislative Restrictions

Many constitutions put such rigid restrictions on the state legislatures that those bodies find it difficult to establish state policies. The most significant restrictions are the ones on finance and taxation powers of the legislatures. Most constitutions limit the amount of debt the state may incur. Nebraska, for example, puts a $100,000 debt limit on most government construction projects. To build something larger than that (except for highways or university facilities) requires a constitutional amendment.[8] All constitutions restrict the classification of property taxes. They typically exempt some property (such as church-owned property) from taxation and place other property in special categories that the legislatures cannot change.

Not only do most constitutions limit the state's debt and restrict the legislature's ability to raise taxes, they also earmark certain revenues (those raised from specific taxes) to be spent only in specific **dedicated funds** (funds set aside for specific activities). One of the most important **earmarked revenues** is the state gasoline tax, most of which goes directly into a highway users' fund. This fund can be spent only for highway maintenance or construction. The revenues from fishing and hunting licenses are often earmarked for conservation and natural resources.

Why earmark funds? Because, say its advocates, legislatures cannot be trusted to keep their commitments. Legislators serve at the will of the people and can easily turn their back on important programs if public opinion shifts in another direction. In 1989, for example, the Maryland legislature committed itself to a significant expansion in university funding and dramatically increased appropriations for that purpose. Two years later, however, this enthusiasm for higher education waned, and appropriations dropped back to what they had been two years earlier.[9] If university funding had been earmarked in the constitution, it would not have been as easy for the state to back away from its commitment. It can be very difficult for a public body to keep a sustained, decades-long commitment to a project if it has to rely on annual appropriations. It is unlikely, for example, that the Interstate Highway System, which took forty years to build and was built almost solely on earmarked state and federal gasoline taxes, would be as extensive as it is today if it had had to rely upon annual appropriations.

The trouble, however, say critics, is that earmarking is little more than a shell game.[10] Earmarking revenues for Maryland's higher education program would not guarantee higher funding in future years. Knowing that the earmarked revenues were guaranteed, future legislatures could easily shift some of the nonearmarked revenues out of higher education to some other purpose. In fact, this has been a common practice with lottery revenues. Several states in the 1980s persuaded their residents to pass constitutional amendments adopting lotteries, on the promise that the lottery revenues would be earmarked for public education. Illinois, for example, earmarked 100 percent of its lottery revenue to public education. In 1988, this amounted to $524 million. But an analysis of the Illinois finance system found that as lottery revenues began flowing into the education system, funding from other sources immediately began to drop off.[11]

Not only are earmarked revenues criticized as a highly sophisticated shell game, but they also weaken the normal procedures of democratic accountability. Earmarked revenues and dedicated funds restrict the legislature's ability to oversee the services delivered by the departments that receive the earmarked funds.

Earmarked revenues and dedicated funds also inhibit the legislature's ability to alter policy priorities. Since the earmarked revenues roll in to the dedicated fund perpetually, the legislature cannot do its job of providing a forum for debate on whether the program ought to be reduced in scope or altered significantly.

This, of course, was exactly the case with the Interstate Highway System. Started in 1956, the bulk of the system was completed by 1970, with the uncompleted remainder being predominantly the central-city portions. Finishing off those portions led to enormous social conflict. Inner city, often minority, neighborhoods had to be torn out to make way for the freeways, public transit systems deteriorated in virtually every city in the country, and a perception was growing that the new freeways were speeding up the decline of the central cities themselves. Furthermore, by 1970 the Interstate Highway System had become the single largest public works project in human history, and it was doing more than any other single phenomenon to shape the sprawling pattern of today's typical metropolitan areas. Despite these major issues, it was impossible for most state legislatures to debate whether or not it might be good public policy to alter the original 1956 Interstate Highway plans in order to create a transportation system less heavily dependent on freeways and automobiles.

This debate was impossible because 90 percent of the money came from the earmarked federal gasoline tax and only 10 percent from state funds; this was a deal too good for most legislators to pass up. If you had been a suburban legislator in 1970, it is conceivable that you might have been able to talk your constituents into scaling back freeway construction if they were going to have to provide the funds for it themselves and if you had a proposal for a better and less costly method of easing their traffic congestion problems. But it would have been impossible to convince them of that when 90 percent of the costs were going to be paid by motorists in the rest of the country and when your constituents themselves would lose this gift from the rest of the country if the funds were not spent on new freeway construction.

Too much earmarked revenue and too many dedicated funds can prevent the legislature from carrying out its major role of establishing the state's policy priorities. Although there has been a general decline in reliance on earmarking over the past few decades, the average legislature still lacks control over a fifth of its budget because of earmarked funds.[12] In Alabama, that figure is 89 percent,[13] rendering that state's legislature almost impotent to set budget priorities.

Fragmented Executive Branches

Most state constitutions provide numerous independent administrative agencies and departments that are not directly accountable to the governor or to the legislature. The typical state constitution also provides for several independently elected state officials. Consequently, the executive power is fragmented into many different offices, making it harder for the governor to provide strong leadership. Political reformers prefer that the state executive branch be modeled after the business corporation. In the corporation, all administrative units are ultimately accountable to a chief executive, who in turn, answers to a policy-making board of directors. By analogy the governmental reformers view the governor as the corporate chief executive and the legislature as the policy-making board of directors. Reformers want state executive power to be integrated and accountable to a limited number of policymakers.

Inefficient Court Systems

The typical court system is not integrated. Rather, it comprises dozens of courts that are independent of each other. No one body ensures the enforcement of high judicial standards. The procedures by which cases are given to one court rather than another are unclear and confusing. In civil cases when one person sues another, conflict or confusion over which court has jurisdiction can delay the case. In criminal cases when a person is tried for breaking the law, the fragmented court systems are not tied into the correctional system; law enforcement, adjudication, and corrections are not integrated. This compounds the already difficult task of creating a corrections system that actually corrects the antisocial behavior of criminals.

Hamstrung Local Governments

Most constitutions restrict how much debt local governments can incur, and this often limits their ability to provide public services efficiently. Many state constitutions prescribe the type of governments for localities, making it impossible for residents to choose the type of government they want. In sum, local governments are legally creatures of the state and possess only those powers that the state constitutions and legislatures permit them to have. Reformers advocate giving local governments more financial flexibility, giving local officials enough authority to meet their responsibilities, and giving local residents a form of home rule that would allow them to choose the type of local government they want.

◇ THE MODEL STATE CONSTITUTION

A number of reformers have called for the systematic overhauling of the worst state constitutions. These constitutional reformers come from various places— the National Municipal League, the Council of State Governments, public administration specialists, and citizen groups such as the League of Women Voters. The ideal sought by these reformers is a constitution similar to the **model state constitution** drafted by the National Municipal League.[14] The model constitution is short, stems from the higher law tradition of constitutionalism rather than the positive law tradition. It is short and deals in fundamental principles of government instead of specific legislative details. It provides a bill of rights to protect the civil liberties of its citizens. Rather than a large number of elected executive offices, it permits only the governor and lieutenant governor to be elected, with the other state officials being appointed by the governor. The legislature is granted considerable authority and flexibility as the chief policymaking and taxing body in the state. In short, as Figure 2-1 shows, the model state constitution is the exact opposite of the typical state constitution, which is subject to the five criticisms just outlined.

◇ THE POLITICS OF CONSTITUTIONAL REFORM

In later chapters, we will see that constitutional reform has not always improved governments as much as expected. For now it is sufficient simply to understand the reformist critique of state constitutions: unreformed constitutions create an inefficient, anachronistic governmental structure that is unable to respond effectively to the needs of the late twentieth century. Reformers urge that the constitutions be changed. Practical politicians attempt to get around the more cumbersome constitutional restrictions in several ways.

Figure 2-1   THE MODEL STATE CONSTITUTION

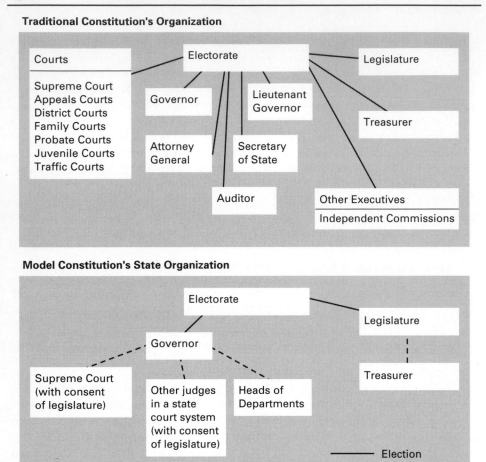

Traditional Constitution's Organization

Electorate

Courts

Supreme Court
Appeals Courts
District Courts
Family Courts
Probate Courts
Juvenile Courts
Traffic Courts

Governor

Lieutenant
Governor

Legislature

Treasurer

Attorney
General

Secretary
of State

Auditor

Other Executives

Independent Commissions

Model Constitution's State Organization

Electorate

Governor

Legislature

Supreme Court
(with consent
of legislature)

Other judges
in a state
court system
(with consent
of legislature)

Heads of
Departments

Treasurer

———— Election
- - - - Appointment

In contrast to the traditional constitution's large number of elected offices and the fragmentation of authority, the Model State Constitution concentrates responsibility in the governor and legislature.

Source: Adapted from *Model State Constitution,* 6th ed. (New York: National Municipal League, 1963).

Circumvention and Interpretation

Many restrictive constitutional provisions are simply circumvented. For example, although some state constitutions require that a proposed law be read aloud three times in the legislature before it can be approved, this rigid requirement is regularly circumvented by having the presiding officer read only the title of each bill. Critics say such circumvention encourages disrespect for the constitution and the law without changing outmoded constitutional provisions. The "You

Decide" on p. 26 gives you an opportunity to decide if a typical practice of loading many topics into a single law amounted to constitutional circumvention.

The most common way of adjusting rigid constitutional language to the needs of the times is by filing lawsuits that require the courts to interpret the constitution. Judicial interpretation does not change the wording of the constitution, but it changes the way in which the constitution is applied. Kentucky's constitution, for example, limits state salaries to $12,000 per year. This may have been a reasonable sum in 1949 when it was last changed by constitutional amendment, but it is quite unreasonable today. Kentucky courts got around this limit, however, by a so-called rubber dollar ruling that permitted the dollar limit to be adjusted for inflation.[15]

Amendment

Amending a constitution is a two-step process requiring, first, initiation and then ratification. The most common procedure for initiation is for both houses of the legislature to pass the amendment by a simple majority (although some states require a three-fifths or a two-thirds majority). Fourteen states permit citizens to put a constitutional amendment directly on the ballot if they can gather enough signatures on a petition.

Ratification usually requires a majority vote of all those people voting on the amendment. But some states make amendments difficult to pass by either requiring passage in two sessions of the legislature in order to initiate the amendment, limiting the number of amendments that may be put on the ballot in any election, or requiring more than a simple majority vote for initiation or ratification.

Constitutional Conventions

Constitutions can also be completely rewritten by **constitutional conventions.** Unlike the federal Constitution, which has never been rewritten, the fifty state constitutions have been rewritten ninety-five times since independence in 1776. Louisiana, with eleven, leads in the number of constitutional rewritings. The great bulk of constitutional rewritings took place in three relatively short periods, periods of great national turbulence. Following the Declaration of Independence in 1776 and the Revolutionary War, ten constitutions were revised. The second turbulent period was the one immediately preceding and following the Civil War, when fifty-two constitutional revisions occurred. And the third period took place from the 1960s to the early 1980s when eleven constitutions were rewritten. This recent flurry of constitutional revision seems to have come to an end, however, since there are currently no constitutional conventions meeting and even the number of ordinary constitutional amendments has dropped off since the 1970s.[16]

The process of rewriting a constitution requires several steps, which in turn take several years to carry out. First, a constitutional convention must be called. In some states, the legislature can call the convention whenever it wants.

In most states, however, the legislature must vote to have a referendum on the question of whether a convention should be held. If the legislature approved

YOU DECIDE

Constitutional Circumvention

A common criticism of state legislatures is that they frequently lump many unrelated items together in one law. This enables legislative leaders to write into law some pet provisions that would most likely be voted down if voted on individually. To curb this practice in Minnesota, the Minnesota Constitution stipulates that "No law shall embrace more than one subject, which shall be embraced in its title." The title of one law passed by the Minnesota legislature in 1982 embraced the following:

Collection of taxes

Distribution of campaign funds

Interest rate limits on municipal bonds

Provisions to withhold income tax refunds from child support debtors

Requiring registration of rental housing in Minneapolis

Provisions for residential energy credits

Sale of unstamped cigarettes to members of Indian tribes

Lease and sale of equipment by local governments

Eligibility for property tax refunds

Restrictions on tax increment financing

Issuance of bonds to promote tourism

Allowing one county a levy for fire protection purposes

Allowing another county to exceed its levy limitation

Providing for lease of hydroelectric power

In your view, is the inclusion of all these topics in one law consistent with the constitutional provision that a law embrace no more than one subject? Or is this a circumvention of the quoted constitutional provision? If you were a state Supreme Court justice being asked to determine whether the topics listed here did violate the state constitutional provision, how would you decide?

To see how the Minnesota Supreme Court ruled, see the Highlight box on p. 27.

Source: Minnesota Laws, 1982, ch. 523, An Act Relating to the Financing of Government in this State.

---

the referendum in 1999, for example, the second step would be putting the question of a constitutional convention on the general election ballot for voter approval in 2000. The third step would be for the legislature in its 2001 session to provide for holding the convention and electing the delegates. The fourth step would be the elections and convention. These would take place in 2001 and 2002. The fifth and most crucial step would be ratification by the voters at the 2002 general election. If approved, the new constitution would take effect in 2003. Thus, the very shortest period for completely rewriting the constitution would be four years. Because of the time and difficulty it takes to establish a constitutional convention, about half the states require that a call for a convention be periodically put on the ballot. Illinois, for example, requires that this question be

HIGHLIGHT

Constitutional Circumvention: Ruling

In 1986, the Minnesota Supreme Court struck down as unconstitutional a law, similar to the one on p. 26, that embraced many different subjects.

---

put before the voters every 20 years. When last asked, in 1990, if they wanted a new constitutional convention, a majority of Illinois voters said no.

When constitutional conventions are held these days, they usually are non-partisan. The delegates usually are elected on ballots that do not identify their party affiliation; and once the convention starts, the delegates tend to perceive themselves as "idealistic statesmen" concerned about the good of the state as a whole rather than as representatives of a political party.[17] Delegates are now more likely than in the past to accept the higher law rather than the positive low tradition of constitutionalism.[18]

Conventions today also are usually limited to making proposals on only specified constitutional provisions. Although an unlimited convention can do a more thorough job of overhauling the constitution, the more radically the constitution is revised, the less likely it is to be approved by the voters.[19] Because of this, constitutional reformers tend to prefer more limited reforms that have a better chance of being adopted. Slightly more than half of the constitutional conventions since 1960 have been limited in scope.

One of the most successful unlimited constitutional conventions in recent years was Hawaii's, held in 1978. It put curbs on state expenditures, provided for open meetings of the state legislature, created an intermediate appellate court, added a privacy provision to the state Bill of Rights, and replaced all male gender words with words having no reference to gender. One of the most note-worthy features of Hawaii's new constitution is the way in which its provisions were approved by the voters. Incorporated into 34 proposals were 116 changes so that the voters could vote separately on each proposal. Submitted to the voters in 1980, all 34 proposals passed.[20]

The ease of getting Hawaii's new constitution adopted by the voters, how-ever, was extraordinary. In recent years, North Dakota, Arkansas, Maryland, New Mexico, and New York have all held extensive constitutional conventions only to have the proposed constitution rejected by the voters.

Constitutional Revision Commissions

Another approach to broad constitutional change is the **constitutional revision commission.** This commission may be either a preparatory commission or a study commission. The study commission meets, studies the constitutional problems, and proposes a number of changes to the legislature. Utah has found such commissions to be so useful that in 1977 it created a permanent Constitutional Revision Commission to propose changes on a regular basis. In contrast to the study commission, which reports to the legislature, the constitutional preparatory commission actually conducts the background work for a constitutional convention. Since the convention meets for a very limited period, it needs as much prior preparation as possible. New Hampshire created a constitutional study commission in 1983 that held public hearings in different locations throughout the state to consider proposals for change. With this groundwork laid, a limited constitutional convention was held the following year. It put ten proposed changes before the voters, six of which were accepted.[21]

Although constitutional study commissions have become very useful and popular, they are not without their drawbacks. One drawback lies in the fact that many state constitutions prohibit amendments dealing with more than one specific subject. Thus, for example, it becomes constitutionally impossible to use a simple amendment to reorganize the entire executive branch. One proposal to remedy this has been the **gateway amendment,** which changes the constitution so that subsequent amendments can cover more than one subject and can pass with a smaller majority.

◇ CONSTITUTIONAL REFORM AND SOCIAL CHANGE

As we saw at the beginning of this chapter, our state constitutions are deeply enmeshed in the nation's various social conflicts. Throughout most of the twentieth century, state constitutional law took a back seat to federal constitutional law in dealing with dramatic social change. Nowhere was this more true than in the example of the civil rights movement of the 1950s and 1960s, which successfully broke the system of racial segregation in the South. Civil rights advocates had no success challenging segregation under state law because the constitutions of the southern states permitted segregation. Consequently, civil rights advocates used the federal courts to charge that segregation practices violated several provisions of the U.S. Constitution, especially the equal-protection clause, the due process clause, and the commerce clause. In this way, they were fully in keeping with the higher law tradition of constitutionalism. As a result of this history, we grew accustomed to thinking of the federal constitution and the federal courts as more progressive than state constitutions and state courts when dealing with issues of social change.

Expanding State Bills of Rights

Today, however, this perception is no longer accurate. Two developments in particular are putting state constitutional law in the forefront of issues dealing with contemporary social conflict. First, because of widespread constitutional reform, most states have reduced the most glaring constitutional weaknesses identified earlier. With the issue of legal segregation settled and constitutional reformers increasingly adopting the higher law tradition of constitutionalism, states began expanding their bills of rights to include many provisions not found in the federal Constitution. Some of this is summarized in Table 2-2, which outlines selected provisions from bills of rights in twenty states.

Table 2-2 STATE BILL OF RIGHTS PROVISIONS NOT FOUND IN THE FEDERAL CONSTITUTION

Environmental Rights Provisions

Massachusetts	Right to clean air and water and freedom from excessive noise.
Hawaii	All public natural resources are held in trust by the state for the benefit of the people.
Virginia	The state's natural oyster beds shall not be leased, rented, or sold but shall be held in trust for the benefit of the people.
California	People shall have the right to fish upon and from public lands and waters.
Washington	State's waters shall be deemed a public use.

Economic Rights Provisions

Hawaii	Public employees may organize for collective bargaining.
Florida	Public employees may not strike.
New York	Workers on public works projects shall be paid no less than the prevailing wage of the locality.
Louisiana	People have the right to own and enjoy private property.
New York	Human labor is not a commodity or an article of commerce.

Natural Rights Provisions

Montana	Human dignity is inviolable.
New Hampshire	Upon entering society, people surrender some natural rights in order to ensure the protection of society.

Provisions Related to Racial and Cultural Relations

N. Carolina	Secret political societies shall not be tolerated.
Alabama S. Carolina	Prohibits marriages between whites and blacks.
Alaska	Public schooling shall always be conducted in English.
Colorado	Prohibits the assignment or transportation of a pupil to a public school for purposes of achieving racial balance.

Criminal Justice Provisions

Michigan	Death penalty prohibited.
Georgia	Prohibits whipping as a punishment for crime.

Other Provisions

Arizona	No child under age shall be employed during public school hours.
N. Carolina	Atheists guaranteed the right to hold public office.
Tennessee	Persons may not be forced to perform any service to the public on their religion's day of rest.
Idaho	Prohibits the registration or licensing of firearms.

Source: Mark L. Glasser and John Kincaid, "Selected Rights Enumerated in State Constitutions," *Intergovernmental Perspective* 17, no. 4 (Fall 1991): 35–44.

We can make several observations about Table 2-2. First, the provisions relating to environmental rights, economic rights, and natural rights have no parallel in the federal Constitution. To declare, as Virginia does, that the state's oyster beds shall not be leased or sold protects that natural resource from being sold off in a way that no provision of the U.S. Constitution protects U.S. held natural resources from being sold off to private developers. The natural rights provisions from Montana and New Hampshire also grab one's attention. The New Hampshire provision is so grounded in the philosophy of natural law and natural rights that it reads almost as though it came directly out of Thomas Hobbes's *Leviathan.* In the U.S. Constitution, the only allusion to natural rights does not come until the Ninth Amendment, which admits that people may have rights in addition to those specifically mentioned in the Constitution.

Although most of the bill of rights provisions in Table 2-2 lean in a liberal direction, it is obvious that not all of them do. This is especially true of Florida's prohibiting public employees from striking and Idaho's prohibition on the licensing and registration of firearms.

Some of the provisions, especially the antimiscegenation provisions in Alabama and South Carolina, are clearly unenforceable because they violate the federal Constitution. Some others, such as the environmental rights in Massachusetts, the private property right in Louisiana, and the human labor right in New York, are so vague that it is hard to envision how they would be enforced. In sum, however, the overall impact of state bills of rights today is to expand the notion of rights and liberties far beyond what the federal Constitution guarantees.

Trends in Constitutional Interpretation

A second development relating state constitutions to contemporary social change comes from changing trends in how judges interpret constitutions. We saw that a key component in the success of the civil rights movement of the 1950s and 1960s was the willingness of liberal federal judges to make progressive interpretations of the U.S. Constitution. In recent years, however, federal judges have become less liberal. Republicans have controlled the presidency for twenty of the past twenty-eight years (through 1996); and they appointed a large number of conservative judges to the federal courts. As the federal courts slowly became less venturesome in tackling difficult social issues, state courts became more so.[22] This is especially the case regarding issues of civil liberties. Four states, for example, include a right to privacy in their bill of rights.[23] A number of state courts have taken up the slack as the U.S. Supreme Court has backed off from the civil libertarian posture it advanced during the 1960s and 1970s. Constitutional law in California and Oregon now provides much more expansive protection of freedom of speech than does federal constitutional law. New York and some other states now have more expansive protections of defendants' rights in some areas.[24] Indeed, eighteen states have broader protections against sex discrimination than does the federal Constitution.[25]

In sum, the general principle evolving is that state courts may not set lower standards for human rights than those established under U.S. constitutional law, but they may set higher standards if they choose. We can expect to see state constitutional interpretations also continue to touch on social conflict issues such as those discussed at the beginning of this chapter—gay rights, gay marriages, affirmative action, inequalities in funding public schools, and others.

SUMMARY

1. Under the higher law tradition of constitutionalism, a constitution is viewed as fundamental law that takes precedence over statutory laws.
2. The state constitutions have been heavily criticized for five weaknesses: They are too long and too detailed. They place too many restrictions on state legislatures. They create ineffective, fragmented executive branches. They create outmoded, ineffective court systems. They hamstring local governments.
3. The National Municipal League has drafted a model state constitution that it encourages the states to adopt.
4. Many detailed constitutional provisions are evaded through circumvention or judicial interpretation.
5. The two major strategies for overhauling state constitutions are constitutional conventions and constitutional revision commissions. Although a fifth of the states have rewritten their constitutions since 1965, the majority of constitutional conventions are not successful in getting their new constitutions adopted by the voters. Limited conventions have been more successful at getting their constitutions adopted than have unlimited conventions.
6. Both bills of rights of state constitutions and judicial interpretation of state constitutions are becoming increasingly important in the struggles over the nation's contemporary social conflicts.

KEY TERMS

Constitutional convention   A convention that drafts a new constitution and proposes it to voters for ratification.

Constitutional revision commission   A commission appointed by the legislature to study the constitution and make recommendations for change. The revision commission may be either a study commission (which presents its results to the legislature) or a preparatory commission (which presents its results to the constitutional convention).

Dedicated fund   A portion of a budget set aside for a specific purpose.

Earmarked revenues   Revenues raised from specific sources (such as gasoline taxes) that can only be spent for related purposes (such as transportation).

Fundamental law   The law of a constitution.

Gateway amendment   A constitutional amendment that makes it easier to pass future constitutional amendments.

Judicial review   The power of courts to determine the constitutionality of acts of other government actors.

Model state constitution   A proposal for constitutions advanced by the National Municipal League that would concentrate authority in the governor and legislature and would reduce the number of elected executives.

Statutory law   A law enacted by a legislature.

Super legislation   Detailed provisions of a constitution that should more properly be a part of statutory law.

REFERENCES

1. John J. Carroll and Arthur English, "Traditions of State Constitution Making," *State and Local Government Review* 23, no. 3 (Fall 1991): 103–108.
2. *McCulloch v. Maryland* 4 L.Ed. 579 (1819).
3. Carroll and English, "Traditions of State Constitution Making," p. 103.
4. *The Wall Street Journal,* August 19, 1986, p. 50.
5. This agenda for reform appears in a number of critiques. The one relied on most heavily here is: Committee for Economic Development (1968). A more recent summary of the constitutional reform agenda can be found in Advisory Commission on Intergovernmental Relations, *The Question of State Government Capability,* Report A-98 (Washington, D.C.: U.S. Government Printing Office, 1985), pp. 35–44.
6. Lawrence M. Friedman, "An Historical Perspective on State Constitutions," *Intergovernmental Perspective* 13, no. 2 (Spring 1987): 10.
7. David C. Nice, "Interest Groups and State Constitutions: Another Look," *State and Local Government Review* 20, no. 1 (Winter 1988): 21–26. Also see Lewis A. Froman, Jr., "Some Effects of Interest Group Strength in State Politics," *The American Political Science Review* 60, no. 4 (December 1966): 956.
8. A. B. Winter, "The State Constitution," in *Nebraska Government and Politics,* Robert D. Miewald, ed. (Lincoln: University of Nebraska Press, 1984), p. 15.
9. Jim Rosapepe and Christopher Zimmerman, "The Case for Earmarking," *State Legislatures* 17, no. 9 (September 1991): 22–24.
10. Ronald K. Snell, "The Trouble with Earmarking," *State Legislatures* 17, no. 2 (February 1991): 33–35.
11. Ibid., p. 35.
12. Steven D. Gold, "The Pros and Cons of Earmarking," *State Legislatures* 13, no. 6 (July 1987): 30.
13. Snell, "The Trouble with Earmarking," p. 35.
14. National Municipal League, *Model State Constitution,* 6th ed. (New York: National Municipal League, 1963).
15. Thomas Parrish, "Kentucky's Fourth Constitution a Product of the 1890 Times," *State Government: CQ's Guide to Current Issues and Activities,* Thad L. Beyle, ed. (Washington, D.C. Congressional Quarterly Press, 1991), p. 47. Also see Carl Chelf, "The Kentucky Constitution," in *Kentucky Government and Politics,* Joel Goldstein, ed. (Bloomington, Ind.: Tichenor Publishing, 1984), p. 29.
16. Janice C. May, "State Constitutions and Constitutional Revision: 1988–89 and the 1990s," *The Book of the States: 1990–91* (Lexington, Ky.: Council of State Governments, 1990), pp. 20–39. May writes that constitutional revision in the late 1980s had declined to "its lowest level in 40 and even 50 years," p. 20.
17. Wayne R. Swanson, Sean A. Kelleher, and Arthur English, "Socialization of Constitution Makers: Political Experience, Role Conflict, and Attitude Change," *Journal of Politics* 34 (February 1972): 183–198.
18. Carroll and English, "Traditions of State Constitution Making," p. 106. The authors discovered this in their survey of delegates to Arkansas's constitutional conventions of 1970 and 1980.
19. Albert L. Sturm, *Trends in State Constitution Making: 1966–1972* (Lexington, Ky.: Council of State Governments, 1973). Of fourteen constitutional conventions from 1966 to 1975 described in *The Book of the States,* five were limited to specific subject matters, and all five were successful in getting all or most of their suggested provisions adopted by the voters (Louisiana, Rhode Island, Tennessee, New Jersey, Pennsylva-

nia). Of the nine states with unlimited constitutional conventions, the new constitutions were adopted by only three states (Montana, Illinois, and Hawaii). See *The Book of the States: 1974–75* (Lexington, Ky.: Council of State Governments, 1974). Also see the editions for 1972–73, 1970–71, and 1968–69.

20. Norman Meller and Richard H. Kosaki, "Hawaii's Constitutional Convention—1978," *National Civic Review* 69, no. 5 (May 1980): 48–257.
21. Friedman, "An Historical Perspective on State Constitutions," pp. 9–13.
22. Mark L. Glasser and John Kincaid, "Selected Rights Enumerated in State Constitutions," *Intergovernmental Perspective* 17, no. 4 (Fall 1991): 31–34.
23. Stanley M. Mosk, "The Emerging Agenda in State Constitutional Law," *Intergovernmental Perspective* 13, no. 2 (Spring 1987): 19–22.
24. Steven Pressman, "Protecting Rights in State Courts," *Editorial Research Reports*, May 27, 1988, pp. 278–279.
25. John Kincaid and Robert F. Williams, "The New Judicial Federalism: The States' Lead in Rights Protection," *The Journal of State Government* (April–June, 1992): 50–52.

THE INTERGOVERNMENTAL FRAMEWORK FOR STATE AND COMMUNITY POLITICS

Chapter Preview

In the previous chapter, we saw how constitutions limit what state and community governments can do. In this chapter, we examine the limiting impact of federalism, or intergovernmental relations, as it is increasingly being called. We shall discuss in turn:

1. The federal division of powers between the national and state governments.
2. The constitutional evolution from dual federalism through cooperative federalism to creative or New Federalism.
3. Other intergovernmental politics.
4. Intersectional rivalries.
5. The implications of competitive federalism for state–community political economies.

Let us begin with a look at a major shock delivered to the system of federalism in 1994 and 1995.

◇ INTRODUCTION

In 1994, for the first time in forty years, the Republican party won control of both houses of Congress and a majority of the state governorships. They ran for election in 1994 promising "A Contract for America," which they then attempted to put into practice when they took office the following year. When Democratic President Bill Clinton vetoed some portions of the Contract and successfully negotiated compromises on others, the stage was set for a knock down, drag out battle in the following year's presidential election over the issues raised in the Contract.

At issue was nothing less than the fundamental division of powers between the federal and state governments as they had evolved over the previous sixty years. Congressional Republicans sought to strip the federal government of its primary policy-making powers in a wide array of domestic public issues and turn those responsibilities over to the states. These responsibilities ranged from welfare to environmental protection to civil rights enforcement to the regulation and control of abortion.

The battle over these issues went to the heart of one of the most basic principles of government in America—federalism. **Federalism** is a form of government that divides authority between a government at the national level and other governments at the state level. Federalism is distinguished from unitary **government** (such as that of Great Britain), in which all governmental authority resides at the national level, and confederacy (such as the Confederate States of America, 1861–1865), in which individual states have the ultimate authority. In the United States, the term *federalism* refers to the national government.

These important definitions do not do justice, however, to the turmoil that the 1994 Republican victories brought to the federalism debate. Led by Speaker of the House of Representatives Newt Gingrich (R, Ga.), the Republicans sought to reverse a series of decades-old arrangements that had put the federal government in the driver's seat for setting national policy on virtually every important issue of American domestic politics ranging from welfare to civil rights to environmental protection. These efforts are still ongoing. If successful, they could ultimately create a completely new stage of federalism, "competitive federalism," in which there might not even be national policies in these areas. Instead, each state would set its own policies, and states would compete with one another over these policies.

1994 was not the first time that the nation threatened to come unglued over issues of federalism.

- In 1832, John C. Calhoun got a South Carolina convention to proclaim the Nullification Ordinances. Calhoun argued that the U.S. Constitution was a compact between the state governments rather than a charter from the people. This **compact theory** proposed that any state could nullify a law of Congress. At issue was a high tariff being considered by Congress. Although the tariff would protect the industries of the Northeast from imported competition, it would hurt the South's ability to export cotton and agricultural products to Europe. In reaction to the Nullification Ordinances, the northeasterners compromised, and the South won a moderate tariff that would not damage its export economy.
- From 1861 to 1865, in order to keep eleven southern states in the Union, the nation fought its bloodiest war, a war that claimed half a million lives. As a result, the southern slave economy was destroyed, the economic dominance of the North was established, and the South's status as an underdeveloped region was determined for at least the next two generations.

- In the 1930s, the basic structure of federalism was fundamentally changed as the nation faced the Great Depression, its sharpest challenge since the Civil War. As the Depression took its toll in the wake of the 1929 stock market crash, unemployment rates climbed to 25 percent, millions of people lost their homes and their life's savings, and cities across the land were plagued by wandering bands of unemployed workers who had become hobos. Thousands of World War I veterans set up a camp across from the nation's capitol in Washington, D.C., while they lobbied unsuccessfully with Congress for the early payment of a bonus they had been promised. The U.S. Army rode through their camp, burned their shacks, evicted them from the city, and put them back on the roads again. The states lacked the resources to cope with the economic catastrophe, and the federal government, under the prevailing view of **dual federalism** lacked the authority. Finally, under the New Deal presidency of Franklin D. Roosevelt, the federal government claimed new authority for itself to establish a welfare state, regulate business, and stimulate the economy. These actions created a new **cooperative federalism** arrangement that put the federal government in the driver's seat for steering the nation in a new direction.

It is precisely this cooperative federalism arrangement that was being called into question by Newt Gingrich and his colleagues in 1994–1995.[4] The "You Decide" exercise below gives you a chance to determine how power should be distributed among the three levels of government.

◇ THE EVOLUTION OF FEDERALISM

Federalism today is very different from federalism in 1787, when the Constitution was written. Federalism has evolved through different stages,[1] which have led us from a dual-federalism concept of state-national relations through cooperative federalism to current attempts to establish a competitive or New Federalism. At issue in these concepts is the question raised in the accompanying "You Decide" exercise. How should power be divided among the federal, state, and local governments?

Dual Federalism: Pre-1937

Before 1937, **dual federalism** was the prevailing view of the relations between the state and national governments. Each level of government was viewed as having its own separate source of authority and areas of responsibility.[2] The states were not supposed to interfere in foreign affairs, for example, because that was seen as a federal responsibility, and the federal government was not supposed to intervene in areas of state responsibility.

Federal Government Responsibilities

Under this arrangement, the federal government had only those powers delegated to it by the Constitution. Included among those **delegated powers** (or

YOU DECIDE

How Should Power Be Divided Among the Federal, State, and Local Governments?

Here is an illustration of three empty glasses. Each glass has a scale from 0 to 100, with 0 meaning empty or no power, and 100 meaning full or all of the power. If you had 100 units of power to distribute between the federal, state, and local levels of government, how many units of power would you put in each?

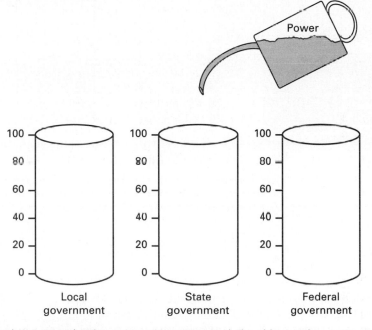

To see how a sample of American citizens responded to this question, see p. 38.

enumerated powers) are the powers to coin money, to regulate foreign and interstate commerce, to establish a post office, to declare war, and to provide for the defense and general welfare of the United States. This delegated powers limitation on the federal government, however, is partially undone by the clause that grants Congress the power to make all laws "necessary and proper for carrying into execution" the enumerated powers. Loose constructionists argue that this **necessary-and-proper clause** gives the federal government implied powers to act even if such actions have not been specifically enumerated.

Strict and loose constructionists clashed in the very first presidential administration. Secretary of the Treasury Alexander Hamilton (a loose constructionist) wanted Congress to establish a national bank, arguing that such a bank would promote the general welfare of the nation. Secretary of State Thomas Jefferson (a

HIGHLIGHT

Dividing Power Among Governments

When Americans were asked to fill each level of government's glass with power, they gave 30 percent of the power to the local glass, 31 percent to state glass, and 39 percent to the federal glass.

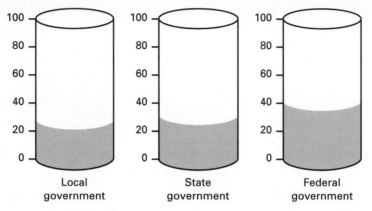

Local	State	Federal
government	government	government

Source: Advisory Commission on Intergovernmental Relations, *Changing Public Attitudes on Government and Taxes: 1991* (Washington, D.C.: Advisory Commission on Intergovernmental Relations, 1991), pp. 14–15.

strict constructionist) objected to the proposal since the Constitution did not specifically give Congress the authority to charter banks. Hamilton prevailed, and the bank was established for a period to end in 1808.

In 1811, a second national bank was chartered. The state of Maryland charged that Congress had no authority to issue such a charter and placed a tax on that bank's operations within Maryland's state boundaries, hoping to drive the bank out of the state. The U.S. Supreme Court held that the necessary-and-proper clause did indeed authorize Congress to charter the bank, and Maryland's tax on it violated the **national supremacy clause.** As a result of this court case, *McCulloch v. Maryland* (1819), the powers of the federal government were expanded, and it became impossible for the states to tax the federal government.[3]

A third constitutional clause that would eventually facilitate the expansion of the federal government's power is the **commerce clause.**[4] In a very early interpretation, the Supreme Court ruled that the authority to regulate interstate commerce belongs exclusively to Congress. However, it was not until the catastrophe of the Great Depression of the 1930s that Congress was able to use the commerce clause and necessary-and-proper clause powers to make substantial inroads into areas of state responsibility. Until that time, the states, by and large, enjoyed great latitude to set their own public policies without federal interference.

In future years, these constitutional clauses (necessary and proper, national supremacy, and commerce) would serve as a potent force for expanding federal power over the states.

State Government Responsibilities   The states enjoyed this freedom from federal interference because of the strict construction interpretation of the Constitution that prevailed during most of the nineteenth and early twentieth century. This interpretation held that whereas the federal government has only those powers delegated to it, the Tenth Amendment of the Constitution reserves all other powers "to the states respectively, or to the people." Accordingly, these are called the **reserve powers.** In practice, dual federalism and the reserve powers gave the states and their local governments primary responsibilities over most domestic matters. They administered and still administer the election process; conduct most court trials; operate the public school systems; and maintain most of our public services, such as streets, sewers, water supply, public recreational facilities, and public health facilities.

State supremacy in these areas began to break down starting in the 1930s when Congress responded to the Great Depression with a broad array of laws that started the national welfare system and established federal regulatory control over much of the economy. Congress based its authority to pass these laws on the Constitution's commerce clause, which gives Congress exclusive authority to regulate interstate commerce. For the first four years of the New Deal, the Supreme Court struck down much of this legislation as unconstitutional. But the Court finally capitulated in 1937 and acknowledged that Congress's commerce powers gave it extensive powers to regulate the economy.[5]

Cooperative Federalism: 1933–present

As the federal government's policy-making role grew in the 1930s, it led to a new arrangement called **cooperative federalism** because the three levels of government (federal, state, and local) now began working cooperatively on programs to cope with the nation's domestic problems. In time, however, the federal government came to dominate many key aspects of the new federal partnership. This dominance came through four devices: (1) grants-in-aid, (2) federal court orders, (3) preemptive legislation, and (4) unfunded mandates.

The Grant-in-Aid System   The major device for implementing cooperative federalism is the grant-in-aid. A **grant-in-aid** is a federal payment to a state or local government for some activity, such as building and maintaining the Interstate Highway System. As shown in Table 3-1, there are two types of federal grants to state and local governments—categorical grants and block grants. A third type, general revenue sharing, existed from 1972 to 1986. It gave about $5 billion yearly to state and local governments to spend as they saw fit, but this program was eliminated in a set of budget cuts in 1986.

Categorical Grants   A **categorical grant** is a federal payment to a state or local government to carry out a specific activity. The Interstate Highway Program, for

Table 3-1   TYPES OF FEDERAL AID

Type of Aid	Percent of Total
Categorical grants (e.g.: Interstate Highway Program)	87.7%
Block grants (e.g.: Education Block Grant)	10.5
General revenue sharing	0
Other general assistance	1.8
	100.0%

Source: Office of Management and Budget, *Special Analyses of the Budget of the United States Government: FY 1990* (Washington, D.C.: U.S. Government Printing Office, 1989), p. H-25.

example, provides federal funds to states to build the Interstate Highway System. Federal funds under this categorical grant cannot be used for any purpose not specified in the program. The grants usually have extensive federal guidelines stipulating in minute detail how the programs should be administered. They also contain matching provisions that require the recipient governments to match a certain percentage of the federal grant. In the Interstate Highway Program, a state has to contribute only $10 for every $90 contributed by the federal government.

Categorical grants are either project grants, formula grants, or open-ended reimbursements. In a **project grant** (for example, the Urban Development Action Grant, which funds community construction projects), a state or local agency makes a grant application to some federal agency, which has considerable discretion to decide who gets the money. In a **formula grant** (for example, the Interstate Highway program), the aid is distributed automatically to state or local governments according to a formula drawn up by Congress. In an **open-ended reimbursement** program (for example, unemployment compensation, which gives short-term cash grants to workers who have lost their jobs), states and communities are reimbursed for whatever expenses they incur implementing the federal share of the program. These programs are open-ended because their costs vary greatly with the economy, rising in times of recession but dropping in periods of economic boom. Most federal aid is now dispensed by open-ended reimbursements.

Block Grants   In contrast to the categorical grant, which can be used only for a very specific purpose, a **block grant** is one that can be used for a wider variety of purposes and has far fewer federal guidelines on how programs are to be administered. Most block grants have been formed through the consolidation of several specific categorical grants. For example, in 1981 Congress consolidated thirty-eight specific educational categorical grants into one education block grant that increased state flexibility and responsibility for administering federal education dollars.

Because of this greater flexibility, state and local elected officials generally prefer block grants to categorical grants.[6] There are currently fourteen block grant programs, twelve of them established during the 1980s.[7]

By 1996, the federal government was spending $237 billion on grants-in-aid each year. Because most of these grants-in-aid had matching features, states were also forced to spend money to meet the policy goals established by Congress. This had the inevitable effect of shifting substantial power to set policy goals from the states to the federal government.

Federal Court Orders As cooperative federalism began to mature, the Supreme Court and other federal courts increasingly issued orders to states to undertake actions to meet national policy goals. The landmark precedent was probably *Brown* v. *Board of Education*[8] (1954) in which the Supreme Court ordered states to begin desegregating their public schools. Another landmark decision came in 1973, the Supreme Court made it unconstitutional for states to prohibit abortion in the first three months of pregnancy.[9] For more than a decade during the 1970s and 1980s, federal courts took over the administration of schools in South Boston in order to implement desegregation there.[10] The Supreme Court required states to reapportion their state legislatures on the basis of one person, one vote.[11] In 1988, the Court further eroded state power when it upheld a Congressional law denying highway grants to states that refused to adopt a twenty-one-year-old minimum drinking age.[12] And in 1985, the Court forced state and local governments to pay their employees according to wage and hour standards set by the federal government rather than by the states.[13] This last decision was especially damaging to states' rights because the Supreme Court explicitly rejected the states' contention that their reserve powers protected them from federal interference in handling their own management–employee relations.[14] While increasingly likely to uphold federal laws that restricted states, the Supreme Court also grew increasingly willing to strike down state laws as unconstitutional. The number of such decisions grew from 3.6 per year before 1932 to 17.2 per year in the 1970s and 1980s.[15]

Preemptive Legislation The latter years of cooperative federalism also saw a dramatic increase in preemptive laws passed by Congress. A preemptive law is a federal law that actually displaces a state law on the same subject. Most federal environmental protection laws, for example, take precedence over corresponding state laws. From the beginning of the nation's history up to 1969, Congress had preempted only 206 state laws. In the next 22 years, it preempted more than 233.[16] Much preemptive legislation is pushed by big businesses that prefer uniformity in the regulations they obey rather than separate regulatory standards in each of the fifty states.[17]

A high-profile preemption case arose after California and Arizona in 1996 adopted legislation that allows the use of marijuana for medical purposes. The Clinton administration swiftly introduced a federal bill that will, when passed by Congress, make federal laws outlawing marijuana preempt the new laws in California and Arizona.

Unfunded Mandates Finally, the latter years of cooperative federalism also saw a dramatic increase in the congressional practice of requiring states to carry out certain activities without providing the funds to carry out those activities. This is the practice of unfunded mandates. The 1990 Americans with Disabilities Act (ADA), for example, required all public buildings to install push-button door openers for handicapped people, and it required public bus companies to provide transit services for people in wheel chairs. Carrying out these unfunded federal mandates required the expenditure of billions of dollars that were not provided by Congress. The state of Ohio calculated that complying just with the mandates of the ADA would cost $430 million. The bill for all other federal mandates would run to $390 million per year, much of which was to fund Ohio's matching portion of the Medicaid program.[18] The sum total of mandates has been extensive. During the 1980s and early 1990s, state or local governments were required by federal law, among other things, to raise the minimum drinking age from eighteen to twenty-one, remove asbestos from public schools, implement stricter water pollution regulations, establish programs to protect workers against certain dangerous chemicals, and make reports on measures to protect more than 150 new endangered species.[19] As the costs for these mandated expenditures go up, the ability of state and local governments to set their own policy priorities among other programs goes down.[20]

The Centralizing Effects of Cooperative Federalism   As can be seen from this short review, cooperative federalism gradually drew more and more power from the states and transferred it to the federal government. By the 1980s, the combined impact of grants-in-aid, federal court orders, preemptive legislation, and unfunded mandates had for all practical purposes put the federal government in command of national policymaking on the most serious and visible areas of domestic public policy. In some respects, the states were being increasingly reduced to becoming administrative units responsible for carrying out the national government's will. Critics complained that cooperative federalism had become coercive federalism.[21]

Competitive Federalism: 1980–present

Criticisms of Cooperative Federalism   The most dramatic expansion of federal power took place in the 1960s and 1970s. The federal government increasingly claimed power to set policies in controversial issues such as abortion, affirmative action hiring plans, admissions' policies for graduate and professional schools, environmental protection, occupational safety, and the establishment of legislative districts that were guaranteed to have minority representatives. As federal intrusion grew, a backlash to that intrusion gained strength. The backlash was part philosophical and part political.

Philosophical Backlash   To some critics, the federal system has become too complicated to function well and to enable citizens to exercise democratic control over them. If one looked at any specific government program, it was becoming impossible to decide who was responsible for what. Consider the case of the child protection program, a program in which federal grants are given to local governments to combat child abuse and child neglect by parents and other adults. The key official fighting child abuse is the child-protection worker:

> Usually employed and paid by the local county welfare department, the child pro-
> tection worker is financed partly from county funds, partly from state funds, and
> partly from federal welfare grants. Although a county employee, the child protection
> worker functions as an official of many different governments, acting as a federal of-
> ficer when getting a client to apply for federally funded food stamps or AFDC, and
> as a state officer when investigating a complaint about a violation of state laws pro-
> hibiting abuse of children. When bringing a client to a mental health center in a
> county hospital, the worker functions as a county officer; because the center is
> funded by a federal program, however, the worker also functions as a federal officer.
> When the worker investigates a complaint that a city family lets its infant crawl on a
> floor strewn with the feces of family pets, he or she is acting as a city officer, con-
> cerned both with the ordinance on health and the ordinance on the number of pets
> permitted in a home. When the worker follows up on court orders that abusing par-
> ents continue with family counseling, he or she is serving as an officer of the court.
> When the worker visits a man in jail who has sexually abused his daughter, to see
> whether he is taking part in the counseling program there, he or she is serving in part
> as a state corrections officer. The child protection worker may also act as a negotiator
> with several other local governments and private agencies; for example, he or she
> may negotiate with local school districts to get clients into special programs, or with
> neighboring counties to purchase services for clients that the worker's own county
> does not provide, or with private agencies, foster homes, halfway houses, or church
> groups to get their resources applied to clients.[22]

In short, this county-hired social worker acts partly as an agent of the federal government, partly as an agent of the state, and partly as an agent of the county. This example shows that we have come a long way from the single two-layered division of powers in dual federalism where one level of government had clear areas of responsibility. We have evolved a complex administrative apparatus with so many checks and balances that the competing actors in any given program are in danger of working at cross purposes. A rich body of scholarly and journalistic literature developed in the 1960s and 1970s suggested that the public might be served better if the complexity were reduced.[23]

From these philosophical perspectives, the nation badly needed to sort out responsibilities on a pragmatic basis. To reduce complexity and improve program administration, it was essential to decide what functions could best be done at the federal level and which could be done best by state and local governments.[24]

Political Backlash   The most potent complaints, however, were the political ones. Many people simply objected to the substance of what the federal government was doing. Since most of the federal initiatives in the environment, civil rights, and other policy areas were imposed by liberal Democrats in Congress, political opposition began to grow among conservative Republicans. Many of these complaints found expression by Ronald Reagan when he ran for the presidency in 1980 on the promise to "get the federal government off your backs."[25] Reagan struck a responsive chord with this pledge not only among conservative Republicans but with many young, working-class white men who perceived, rightly or wrongly, that much of the federal prodding for race-based employment and college admissions policies were at fault for their own declining economic welfare.[26] Some of this feeling was captured by an angry white firefighter in Chicago who complained to newspaper reporters about Democratic support for race norming tests that made it harder for whites than blacks to be hired in the Chicago fire department. "The guys they are stepping on are middle-class white Americans, and we are leaving in droves for the Republican Party."[27] As these developments took place, support for a powerful, coercive, liberally oriented cooperative federalism began to dissipate.

Public opinion polls began noting that it was not only young, white, male voters who were losing confidence in the federal government. If public confidence is the blood supply that brings life to a government body, the federal government today is suffering a massive hemorrhage. The Advisory Commission on Intergovernmental Relations conducts an annual survey in which it tries to measure public support for different levels of government. The most recent findings, shown in Figure 3-1, illustrate the problem of the federal government.

As Figure 3-1 shows, most people express less confidence in the federal government than in state or local governments, and they believe that it is the level of government that wastes the most of their tax money.[28] Twenty years earlier, the federal government scored much better on these questions.

Figure 3-1   SUPPORT FOR THE FEDERAL GOVERNMENT

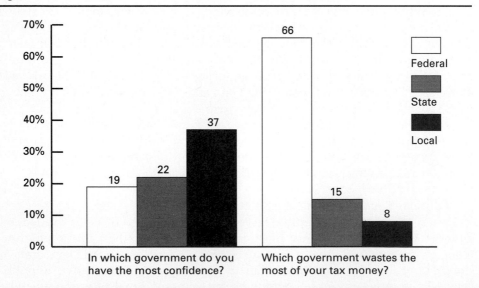

Source: Advisory Commission on Intergovernmental Relations, Changing Public Attitudes Toward Government and Taxes.

Reagan's New Federalism   Given the hemorrhage of public support for the federal government and the ability of Republicans to capture at least one branch of government in fourteen of the past sixteen years, it is not surprising that these years saw two frontal assaults on cooperative federalism. The first assault came in 1981 when the Reagan administration (1981–1989) proposed a **New Federalism** in which, the president proclaimed: "It is my intention to curb the size and influence of the federal establishment."[29] The key to this curbing of the federal government was devolution or spinning off the federal government's responsibilities to state and local governments and to the private sector. Devolution had three components: the budget, regulation, the private sector.

Budgetary Devolution   Reagan sought to spin off substantial federal budgetary responsibilities to state and local governments by consolidating seventy-seven categorical grants into nine new block grants, which would be administered by the states with minimal federal strings attached, and by making severe budget cutbacks in social service programs in an effort to shift more of the burden for these services onto the states. He also sought from Congress, but failed to get, a *Great Swap,* under which the federal government would assume all responsibility for Medicaid, a very expensive and rapidly growing program of health care for the indigent, the elderly, and people on welfare. In exchange, the states would take over responsibility for Food Stamps, Aid to Families with Dependent Children (AFDC), and forty-three other categorical programs.

The important point about these complicated proposals is that they were the most significant attempts to date to reverse federal dominance of the federal-fiscal partnership that has existed since the 1930s. The original intent of the Reagan administration was to cut the total amount of federal grants almost in half, which would have consequently cut much of the federal government's ability to set budget priorities for the states.

Although Reagan scored stunning successes on his block grant and social services cutback proposals, Congress rejected his Great Swap proposal. As satirized in the cartoon local officials resisted taking over these new responsibilities from the federal government. Many of them viewed poverty and welfare as national problems, and for years they had urged the federal government to assume full financial responsibility for the major welfare programs. Reagan's Great Swap proposal to devolve Food Stamps and AFDC onto the states directly contradicted this goal. Against opposition from the states, Reagan succeeded in cutting federal grants-in-aid back to $86 billion in 1982. Despite this reduction, federal aid continued to grow and by 1991 had reached $152 billion.

Regulatory Devolution   A second aspect of Reagan's New Federalism was regulatory devolution. Between 1965 and 1980, there was a virtual explosion of federal laws, administrative agency rules, and court orders that put the sharpest regulation in American history on several aspects of the economy,

**Isn't it wonderful, Orville? And after we thought
he'd be whisked off to Washington forever?**

The Reagan administration's New Federalism sought to turn more governmental responsibility over to state and local governments. As this cartoon suggests, however, not all local and state officials were pleased with the prospect.

Source: C.P. Houston, *The Houston Chronicle,* 1981.

ranging from environmental protection to antidiscrimination and occupational health and safety. Because these new regulations added to the cost of doing business, American business leaders bitterly resented many of them. Thus the Carter administration (1977–1981) took some early steps toward deregulation by phasing out federal controls over the price of petroleum and natural gas and deregulating the airline industry. President Reagan made further reductions of federal regulatory activities and sought legislation that would shift major regulatory responsibilities to the states, especially in environmental protection. Under Reagan, the Environmental Protection Agency cut back sharply the number of regulations it issued.

Devolution to the Private Sector   When the Reagan administration cut funds for social programs in the early 1980s, it called on the private sector to take up the slack. In cutting social expenditures, for example, Reagan argued that some federally funded programs providing food and shelter for the destitute could be replaced by volunteers from churches and nonprofit organizations. The heart of his proposals for tackling urban problems was to create so-called *urban enterprise zones.* These would be city neighborhoods in which taxes and regulatory restrictions (such as occupational safety and minimum wages) would be relaxed for companies that moved facilities into those neighborhoods and created jobs there. This reliance on the private sector to accomplish public goals did not, of course, initiate with Reagan. But he pushed for this objective more strongly than any other recent president.

Assessing the New Federalism Did Reagan's New Federalism achieve his goal of returning more power and authority to the states and communities?

On balance, it seems to have achieved a partial victory. He temporarily capped the growth rate of most domestic social programs, reduced the number of federal grant-in-aid programs, got nine new block grants passed, terminated general revenue sharing, and provoked an ongoing debate over the sorting out of federal from state and local responsibilities. Furthermore, because of the huge budget deficits built up during the Reagan–Bush years, there was little room for his successors in the White House to expand the federal government's domestic policy role. In a speech to the nation's governors, Reagan said that he hoped:

> history will record that [I] not only talked about the need to get the federal govern-
> ment off the backs of the states but that [I] did, in fact, fight the use of federal grant-
> in-aid dollars . . . and sought to return power and responsibility to the states, where
> they belong.[30]

Nevertheless, Reagan's victories were only partial victories. Most of his accomplishments came in his first two years when Republicans controlled the U.S. Senate. However, Democrats regained control of Congress in 1985, Reagan's influence was weakened by scandals in the administration, and Reagan's successor, George Bush, was much less ideologically adamant about curbing federal regulation. With Bush's assistance, the Clean Air Act was rewritten in 1991 and it put substantial federal restrictions in place on the environment. Funding for social programs began to rise again, and grew to record numbers in subsequent years.[31]

In sum, the New Federalism of the Reagan and Bush administrations did not dismantle the federal government's domestic policy machine, but it did reduce the machine's abilities to advance the liberal agenda that had dominated federal policymakers during the 1960s. Ironically, despite the attempt of New Federalism to impose conservative social policies on the nation, many states have liberalized their own social service expenditures to make up for the federal budget cutbacks. One study examined the responses of fourteen states to federal cuts in social services. Of the fourteen states, thirteen either increased their own expenditures to make up for the federal cuts or adopted stronger policy-making roles than they had previously had.[32] The net result of New Federalism has been less spending on social services and welfare, but it clearly did not bring about the extensive reduction in the overall size and scope of government in welfare and domestic policy that had originally been envisioned by Reagan.

Competitive Federalism The second assault on New Federalism was launched by Republicans in the House of Representatives when they took control there in 1985 and sought to enact the Contract for America, on which they had campaigned the previous year. One of their first acts was legislation that restricted the federal government's ability to impose new unfunded mandates on the states and localities. Additionally, they passed a block grant program that gave the states responsibility for AFDC, a major cash assistance program for poor, single-parent families. As of this writing, they are also proposing that the nation's two largest public health programs, Medicare and Medicaid, be turned over to the states for implementation. How much of this agenda will eventually work its way into law is impossible to say at this writing. If the whole agenda passes, however, it will significantly reduce the federal government's ability to set national policy goals for social welfare and health care.

This agenda of the House Republicans is being labeled competitive federalism because it seeks to invigorate competition between the states in the provision of public services. In theory, the hope is that competition between the states will improve public services. Political scientist Paul Peterson, however, raises some questions about this assumption. To Peterson, it is conceivable that interstate competition might improve delivery of distributive services such as education, public safety, or transportation, which are distributed somewhat evenly to all members of society. He doubts, however, whether interstate competition will improve redistributive services such as social welfare or regulatory services such as environmental protection. Interstate competition in these areas will most likely reduce the levels of social services and weaken the enforcement of environmental regulations.[33]

◇ OTHER INTERGOVERNMENTAL POLITICS

Federalism refers to the relationship between the national and the state governments. In addition, there are so many other ways in which governments interact with each other that scholars use the term **intergovernmental relations** (IGR) to refer to this phenomenon. Two of these patterns of interaction deserve notice. They are the role of local governments in the IGR system and the patterns of politics among states.

Local Governments in the IGR System

The evolution of cooperative federalism has had the long-term effect of eroding local autonomy. In federal and local relations this has taken the form of weakening the general-purpose local governments. In state and local relations, a long-term centralization process has eroded much local autonomy.

Federal and Local Relations   Until the 1930s, the federal government had little direct involvement with local governments. To cope with the Great Depression, as we saw, the federal government gave grants-in-aid directly to cities. This practice expanded during the 1960s and 1970s. City governments became very dependent on federal funds to ward off economic recessions and on federal employment funds to hire public service workers. When federal aid was cut back during the Reagan administration's New Federalism years, many cities were forced to make severe cutbacks and to raise their own taxes and fees.

State and Local Relations   Communities rely strongly on the states for their legal authority. City governments are creatures of the state, and the legal principle known as **Dillon's Rule** holds that city governments' powers must be interpreted very narrowly. Because of Dillon's Rule, cities are usually permitted to exercise only those powers granted to them by their state constitutions or their state legislatures. Boulder, Colorado, relearned this lesson the hard way in 1982 when the Supreme Court struck down that city's attempt to regulate cable television.[34]

Probably the most visible impact states have on local governments is financial. State governments provide general and categorical aids to local governments. They determine how much debt local governments can have, and they limit how much local governments may increase their property taxes from year to year.

Although local autonomy has generally eroded in the twentieth century, it must not be concluded that local politics are irrelevant. Local communities remain as the key political bases of state legislators, congresspersons, and, in some instances, statewide officials. Local leaders are able to call on their elected officials or congresspersons to exert influence on the administration of national policies.

Interstate Politics

Some interstate relationships are required by the U.S. Constitution. The Supreme Court has jurisdiction over legal conflicts between states. The full-faith-and-credit clause requires each state to recognize the official acts of other states. Thus, people divorced in one state do not find their divorce nullified when they cross into another state. The privileges-and-immunities clause prohibits a state from discriminating against nonresidents.

In addition to these clauses, the Constitution also contains a rendition clause that requires governors to return fugitives from justice to the state from which they fled. If a governor refuses to return a fugitive, however, the Supreme Court is unlikely to intervene. Florida, for example, once refused to return to Missouri a man who had stolen a chimpanzee from the St. Louis Zoo but had left behind in the chimp's cage enough money to pay for the animal. Missouri could hardly complain about Florida's reluctance to cooperate in this case, however, because Missouri itself annually refuses about a half-dozen rendition requests from other states.[35]

The most popular mechanism for resolving interstate problems is probably the *interstate compact*. This is an agreement made by two or more states and ratified by Congress. Interstate compacts are commonly used to settle problems in corrections, education, transportation, or natural-resources management. The most famous interstate compact is the one that created the Port Authority of New York and New Jersey in 1921 to regulate and develop transportation facilities. This Authority quickly developed bridges, tunnels, commuter railroads, bus terminals, airports, and, more recently, the World Trade Center.

Rising Regionalism

One significant interstate development in recent years has been the resurgence of sectional rivalries. The best-known regional rivalries are the sunbelt–frostbelt and the East–West ones. At the heart of these conflicts, as shown in Figure 3-2, has been the long-term demographic and economic decline of the midwestern and northeastern **frostbelt** states in comparison with the more rapidly growing **sunbelt** and western states. The problem is especially acute in the midwestern

Figure 3-2 SUNBELT AND FROSTBELT PROSPERITY: 1980–1995

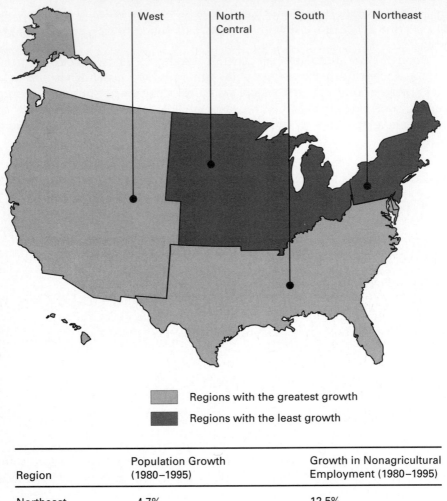

| | Regions with the greatest growth |
| | Regions with the least growth |

Region	Population Growth (1980–1995)	Growth in Nonagricultural Employment (1980–1995)
Northeast	4.7%	12.5%
North Central	5.0	24.1
South	21.9	39.6
West	30.7	36.9
United States	15.7	28.9

Source: Calculated from Bureau of the Census, *Statistical Abstract of the United States: 1996* (Washington, D.C.: U.S. Government Printing Office, 1996), pp. 28, 418.

(North Central) region, whose economies were severely hampered by the decline of industrial manufacturing.

Northerners argue that their economic problems are compounded by the way in which federal expenditures are spread around the country. The residents of each state pay income taxes to the federal government. The federal government then spends money in the states so that each state's economy may receive from the federal expenditures either more or less money than its residents send to the federal government in taxes. In order to determine which states actually make out best from this arrangement, the Tax Foundation calculated the amount of expenditures that the federal government spent in each state in 1994 for each dollar that the state's taxpayers sent to Washington in federal taxes. New Mexico made out best from this viewpoint since it received $1.88 in federal expenditures for each dollar of taxes that New Mexicans sent to Washington in taxes. Connecticut made out the worst since it received only 66 cents for each tax dollar that Connecticut taxpayers sent to Washington.

Table 3-2 also shows that the frostbelt states made out worse than the rest of the nation from this fiscal arrangement. Fifty-nine percent of frostbelt states paid more in taxes than they received in federal expenditures, compared to 18 percent for sunbelt states and 30 percent for the rest of the states. This pattern has existed for many years, and it led some vocal frostbelt leaders to charge that they were not getting a fair deal from fiscal federalism.

To improve their share of fiscal federalism, frostbelt leaders began to form multistate associations. The Northeast Coalition of Governors and the Northeast–Midwest Coalition of Congressional Members, in particular, sought to get a greater share of federal grants-in-aid spent in their regions. In response to these frostbelt initiatives, southerners reacted by forming their lobbying organization, the Southern Growth Policies Board. Southerners respond to northern complaints about the distribution of federal expenditures by pointing out that their rapid growth in recent decades has imposed numerous costs on them, such as substantial investments made in public construction projects for roads and schools to handle the rapidly expanding population. Nor has the prosperity gap between the South and the rest of the nation been closed. Per capita income in the average southern states lags far behind the rest of the nation.[36]

◇ EAST–WEST CONFLICT

Western concerns attracted national attention in July 1979 when the Nevada Legislature passed a resolution demanding that 49 million acres of federal land in Nevada be turned over to the state. Termed the **Sagebrush Rebellion,** the idea quickly spread and similar legislation was introduced in other western states where the federal government was a big land owner.[37] Three issues prompted this Sagebrush Rebellion, and they are likely to remain important in western politics. These are land, energy, and water.

Land Issues

Land is an issue because the federal government owns over half of the land in five western states and over a third of the land in ten states. Until 1976, the fed-

Table 3-2   FEDERAL EXPENDITURES PER DOLLAR OF TAXES: 1994

Frostbelt States		Sunbelt States		Rest of the Nation	
Connecticut	.66	Texas	.97	Nevada	.77
New Jersey	.70	California	.97	Oregon	.93
Delaware	.71	N. Carolina	.98	Washington	.93
Illinois	.75	Florida	1.03	Colorado	1.01
New Hampshire	.76	Georgia	1.04	Wyoming	1.04
Minnesota	.80	Tennessee	1.12	Idaho	1.11
Michigan	.82	Arizona	1.17	Utah	1.12
Wisconsin	.82	Kentucky	1.21	Hawaii	1.21
New York	.82	S. Carolina	1.25	Alaska	1.32
Indiana	.87	Arkansas	1.26	Montana	1.36
Ohio	.91	Oklahoma	1.26		
Vermont	.94	Louisiana	1.33		
Massachusetts	.97	Alabama	1.37		
Pennsylvania	1.00	Virginia	1.39		
Nebraska	1.02	W. Virginia	1.51		
Kansas	1.04	Mississippi	1.69		
Rhode Island	1.05	N. Mexico	1.88		
Iowa	1.09				
Maryland	1.28				
S. Dakota	1.29				
Missouri	1.33				
Maine	1.34				
N. Dakota	1.55				

Each figure represents the amount of dollars that the federal government spends in each state for each dollar of taxes collected in that state. In Connecticut, for example, the federal government spends sixty-six cents for each dollar of taxes that it collects from Connecticut taxpayers.

Source: Tax Foundation, *Tax Features,* 39, no. 6 (July–August, 1995): 2.

eral government leased its land mostly for traditional uses such as mining, logging, and grazing livestock. This arrangement changed with the federal Land Policy and Management Act of 1976, which sought to protect the environmental quality of these federally owned lands. Ten-year leases were replaced by one-year leases, and the tenants were required to file environmental impact statements indicating how their use of the land would affect the overall environment. When the Bureau of Land Management sought to carry out those provisions, it sparked a strong reaction from traditional users (such as ranchers and mining companies), who sought to get the federal government "off our backs."

The land issue in the West is only partly a conflict between the western states and the federal government. It is also a conflict between the New West and the Old West. Old West interests seek to use the land primarily for ranching, farming, and mining, which are called "dominant" traditional uses. New West interests want to use the land for industrial development, urbanization, intensified energy exploration, and recreation, which are called "multiple uses." Under its 1976 mandate, the Bureau of Land Management is managing the land for "multiple uses" rather than for "dominant" traditional uses, a situation that angers Old West interests. Bureau of Land Management officials also resist turning the federal land over to the states for fear that the states will not protect the environmental quality of the land as it is used for more industrial and urban purposes. Many of these complaints were put to rest by the Reagan administration, which clamped down on the regulatory efforts of the Bureau of Land Management[38] and slowly began increasing the sale of federal lands.[39]

Energy Issues

Energy issues are also prominent in the Sagebrush Rebellion. Most of the nation's energy-producing areas are found in the West. Only twelve states produce as much energy as they consume each year, and all but two of those are west of the Mississippi River.[40]

The disproportionate concentration of energy resources in a few states creates a serious issue for intergovernmental politics. When the acute energy shortages of the 1970s produced an **energy crisis,** oil, coal, and natural gas companies responded by dramatically expanding their energy explorations. Each coal-mining site or energy-processing plant brought in new people who needed houses, schools, and public services while they worked in the energy production enterprises. To pay for these services, some energy-producing states drastically increased their **severance taxes** (the tax on resources extracted from the ground). Louisiana, for example, sharply increased its tax on natural gas that was piped out of state, and Montana increased its coal tax to 30 percent of the value of coal that was mined. Energy-consuming states bitterly complained that these increases were a blatant attempt by energy-producing states to gouge the rest of the country by exporting their tax burdens. In 1981 the Supreme Court voided the Louisiana tax on natural gas because it exempted Louisianans,[41] but the Court let stand the Montana tax because it fell on Montanans as well as non-Montanans.[42]

By the mid-1980s, the energy shortage was replaced by an energy glut, and the price of oil fell by 50 percent. This development eased greatly the financial problems of energy-consuming states, but it wreaked financial havoc on much of the West. Some of the energy boomtowns created a decade earlier faced the prospect of becoming ghost towns still burdened with the task of paying for the school buildings, water systems, and other public facilities they built to accommodate their then-growing populations. Some of them no longer have the population and tax base required to raise the needed revenues. States such as Texas and Oklahoma that relied heavily on energy taxes to expand their public facilities in the 1970s suddenly in the mid-1980s found their tax base shrinking as the price of oil dropped. By the 1990s, however, oil prices improved and the economic prospects of these states began to look better.

Water Issues

Although the West is energy-rich, it is water-poor. The West traditionally has sought to meet its water needs through federally sponsored projects that dammed up rivers and moved large volumes of water huge distances through long aqueducts to growing urban populations. Some urban locations became overdeveloped in relation to their water supply. They have depended greatly on fertility funded projects to pipe water heading 9 miles into the cities.

   Because of urbanization, industrialization, and the desire to exploit natural resources, many competing interests want access to scarce western water rights. One proposal for allocating water resources is to let the marketplace determine the allocation by selling water as most other commodities are sold. But there appears to be little support for this proposal.[43] A survey of legislators and the public in four western states found no support for re-allocating existing water supplies among competing users.[44] Rather, they wanted to increase the water supply. In 1980, Arizona passed legislation that sought simultaneously to increase water supplies and to decrease consumption through conservation.[45] Crucial to this plan is the Central Arizona Project, a huge system of aqueducts to pipe water hundreds of miles away into Arizona at a cost to federal taxpayers of $180 million per year.

The water problems inherent in development of the sunbelt are graphically portrayed here by the frostbelt cartoonist Jerry Fearing.

Source: Jerry Fearing, *St. Paul Pioneer Press,* January 18, 1981.

Several questions arise for interregional water politics. From how far can water actually be transported to the West? From the Mississippi River? From the Great Lakes? Even if such feats were technologically possible, would they make sense as public policy? Will nonwestern states be willing to pay the costs for projects that will benefit mainly the West? Worried about this possibility, the Great Lakes states in 1985 adopted the Great Lakes Charter, which sets up a plan for managing the use and diversion of Great Lakes' waters.[46]

The Scope of Intergovernmental Conflict in the West

One of the most important aspects of these political conflicts has been their expansion from the state level to the federal level. State governments have been unable to resolve the competition for use of land and water, so some of the interests have turned to the federal government. As these interests looked to Washington for help, the Bureau of Land Management played a stronger role as mediator of multiple versus dominant land uses. But it was just this role that helped precipitate the Sagebrush Rebellion. And under the Reagan administration, the Bureau of Land Management became less aggressive than it had been in earlier years.

◇ INTERGOVERNMENTAL IMPACT ON STATE AND LOCAL POLITICAL ECONOMIES

It is apparent from our review here that federalism and intergovernmental relations have important consequences for the ability of state and local governments to deliver public services and facilitate economic growth in their private sectors. Two of these consequences are very important: (1) the forces for interregional conflict, and (2) the strengths and weaknesses of the intergovernmental system in dealing with regional and state diversity.

Cooperation Versus Conflict

Underlying much of what occurs in intergovernmental politics is the fact that the states and regions differ widely in their economic resources and assets. The West has an abundance of energy resources, but it is the nation's driest region and lacks the water to develop its resources. The Northeast and Midwest regions have the most extensive network of factories and productive capacity, but they have been hit hard in recent years by foreign competition. The South has benefited immensely from population and economic growth in recent years, but it is still the poorest region.

Not only are there disparities in assets among regions, there are also dramatic disparities within regions. The sunbelt includes impoverished rural Mississippi as well as dynamic growth centers in Texas and Florida. The northeastern–midwestern frostbelt includes not only Detroit, whose unemployment rates exceeded 20 percent during the early 1980s, but also one of the nation's highest concentrations of dynamic high-technology industry in the Boston suburbs near Harvard University and the Massachusetts Institute of Technology.

These disparities in economic assets create forces both for cooperation and for conflict among the states. Interstate cooperation has been enhanced by the emergence of regionally based economies. States are still the dominant political units for dealing with local economies, but states have been forced to band together to cope with economies that overlap state boundaries. The Great Lakes, for example, are an economic asset to eight different states, and there are many questions on managing water rights, navigation rights, and other matters that force the Great Lakes states into cooperation. Similar overarching economic interests exist in other regions also. Hence the devices of cooperation discussed earlier are used more and more frequently; they include interstate compacts, regional commissions, and regional lobbying groups such as the Southern Growth Policies Board and the Northeast–Midwest Coalition.

Working against interstate cooperation, however, are other forces leading the states into conflict with each other. The widespread desire for economic growth sometimes leads states into destructive bidding wars to offer unreasonable concessions to companies to expand in their states. These bidding wars involve extensive tax concessions; the promise of low tax rates; minimal regulation of the environment, health, and safety; promises to keep down costly welfare services; and the promise to enact right-to-work laws that make it difficult for unions to organize employees.

Free market competition is, of course, one of the basic values of the American culture, and it has the benefits of promoting greater efficiency and a wider variety of products. But an unbridled competition between cities and states to attract industry also has seriously unhealthy consequences. Because economic resources and assets are not evenly divided across the country, most places will make out poorly while a few places will prosper handsomely. In the 1980s, for example, increasing numbers of cities entered the competition to entice service industries and high-technology industries in computers, software, biomedical engineering, and genetics. A critical resource needed for this strategy to succeed, however, is a major research university such as Harvard or MIT outside of Boston or the University of California and Stanford near that state's famous Silicon Valley, which had an early start in making silicon chips for computers. Nearly two-thirds of all scientific articles published in this country are produced in just thirteen states.[47] These states are in a much better position to attract high-technology industry than are the other thirty-seven states. States without major research universities to provide personnel and other attractions to high-technology companies could well invest large sums of money into the competition and get very little payoff.[48]

Unbridled bidding wars for industry might also drastically weaken the ability of states to carry out their constitutional responsibilities to raise revenues for public services and to regulate the public health, safety, and environment. A state or city that gives away too many tax concessions to attract new industries may find itself financially strapped for police, fire, education, welfare, and other services. Or neighboring states may find themselves being played off against each other by a major industry threatening to relocate out of state. For years, for example, Oregon found itself in a weak position for forcing paper mills to clean up the pollution they dumped into the Columbia River, because the companies threatened to move their operations into neighboring states.[49] Federal action was needed to enforce environmental regulation.

In light of these experiences, it seems that one likely consequence of competitive federalism will be to weaken environmental protection regulation and to reduce overall expenditures for social services.[50] Social services are essentially redistributive services that take taxes from middle- and upper-income people and redistribute them through social services to lower-income and poor people. If states are put in competition over social services, there will be a natural tendency to hold taxes down by keeping social service expenditures as low as possible. This is because no state will want to look more profligate than its neighbor. Environmental regulations are likely to be weakened for the same reasons. If business corporations think regulations are too rigid in one state, they will threaten to move their operations to states where the regulations are more lax. In order to prevent that from happening, each state will have a powerful incentive to promote weak rather than strong environmental regulations.

SUMMARY

1. The Constitution divides authority between the national and state governments. The national government possesses those powers delegated to it by the Constitution. All other powers not otherwise forbidden are reserved to the states or to the people.
2. Although the federal government is restricted to exercising only delegated powers, some constitutional provisions have permitted the Supreme Court to make a loose constructionist interpretation of those delegated powers. The most significant constitutional clauses are the necessary-and-proper clause, the national-supremacy clause, and the commerce clause.
3. Although the states are given the reserved powers, a number of constitutional provisions put limits on the states' exercise of those powers. The most significant constitutional clauses are the commerce clause, the equal-protection clause, and the due-process clause.
4. Federalism evolved from dual federalism to cooperative federalism and competitive federalism. The major mechanisms for cooperative federalism have been grants-in-aid, court orders, preemptive legislation, and mandates.
5. President Reagan sought a New Federalism in the 1980s that would devolve federal responsibilities to the states and the private sector for many social services and for much governmental regulation. He succeeded in obtaining nine new block grants. His banner was picked up by House Republicans in 1995 with their Contract for America.
6. In addition to state and national relations, there are also several other forms of intergovernmental relations: local and national, local and state, local and local, and state and state. Over the long term, the changes in intergovernmental relations have caused local autonomy to decline. The major instrument of state-to-state relations is the interstate compact.
7. Two patterns of interregional conflicts are sunbelt–frostbelt and East–West.

8. State and community political economies are greatly affected by contemporary inter-governmental relations. Fiscal federalism redistributes income from the richer states to the poorer states. The competition for economic growth often pits regions, states, and communities against each other. The Contract for America passes competitive federalism seems likely to weaken environmental regulation and to reduce overall welfare expenditures.

KEY TERMS

Block grant   A grant that can be used for a much wider variety of purposes than a cate-gorical grant. Usually created by consolidating several categorical grants into a sin-gle grant.

Categorical grant   A grant-in-aid given for a specific purpose. Also called *categorical aid*.

Commerce clause   The provision in Article II, Section 8, of the Constitution that grants Congress the authority to control interstate and international commerce.

Compact theory The theory of John C. Calhoun that the U.S. Constitution was a compact between the state governments rather than a charter from the people.

Cooperative federalism   The theory of federalism in which federal and state levels of government cooperate in differing programs in areas previously considered reserved to the states. The opposite of *dual federalism.*

Delegated powers   See *enumerated powers.*

Dillon's Rule   The principle that city government powers must be interpreted very narrowly.

Dual federalism   The concept of federalism in which the state and national levels of government have separate areas of authority. Popular until the 1930s. Distinct from *cooperative federalism.*

Due-process clause   The provision of the Fifth and Fourteenth Amendments that pro-tects a person from deprivation of life, liberty, or property without due process of law.

Energy crisis   A situation in the 1970s when petroleum and natural gas sources were scarce, and prices for them increased precipitously.

Enumerated powers   The powers specifically granted to Congress by the Constitution. Also called *delegated powers.*

Equal-protection clause   The provision of the Constitution's Fourteenth Amendment that forbids any state to deny any person in its jurisdiction the equal protection of the laws.

Federalism   A formal division of authority between a national government and state governments.

Formula grant   A grant-in-aid in which the funds are dispensed automatically according to a formula specified by Congress.

Frostbelt   The Northeast and Midwest.

General revenue sharing   A program in which the federal government turned funds over to local governments to use as they saw fit with very few federal guidelines on how the money is to be spent.

Grant-in-aid   A federal payment to a state or local government to carry out some activ-ity or run some program.

Intergovernmental relations   A term used for contemporary federalism in which many different layers of government interact with each other in a complex system.

National-supremacy clause   The provision in Article VI of the Constitution that makes the Constitution and all legislation passed under its authority the supreme law of the land.

Necessary-and-proper clause The clause in Article I, Section 8, of the Constitution that gives Congress power to pass all laws necessary and proper for carrying into execution the enumerated powers.

New Federalism Attempts by the Nixon and Reagan administrations to turn federal responsibilities over to the states, usually through general revenue sharing and block grants. The Reagan administration added the concept of "devolution" and sharp cutbacks in federal aid to states and communities.

Open-ended reimbursement A grant-in-aid in which the federal government automatically reimburses state or local governments for the federal share of whatever program funds are spent. Applies only to entitlement programs, such as unemployment compensation, in which the funds spent will vary greatly with economic conditions.

Project grant A grant-in-aid in which the recipient government has to make an application to the granting agency and the granting agency has considerable discretion in deciding which applicants will receive the grant.

Reserve powers The powers reserved to the states or to the people of the United States by the Tenth Amendment to the Constitution.

Sagebrush Rebellion The rebellion of many states in the West against federal ownership and management of significant amounts of western land.

Severance tax A tax levied on natural resources extracted from the earth.

Sunbelt The South and Southwest.

REFERENCES

1. See Deil S. Wright, "Intergovernmental Relations: An Analytical Overview," *Annals of the American Academy of Political and Social Science* 416 (November 1974): 5.
2. See Daniel J. Elazar, *The American Partnership* (Chicago: University of Chicago Press, 1962), p. 20.
3. *McCulloch v. Maryland,* 4 L.Ed. 579 (1819).
4. *Gibbons v. Ogden,* 6 L.Ed. 23 (1824).
5. *National Labor Relations Board v. Jones and Laughlin Steel Corp.,* 300 U.S. 1 (1937).
6. For the position of the National Governors' Association supporting the consolidation of categorical grants into block grants, see "Governors' Bulletin," no. 80–20 (Washington, D.C.: National Governors' Association, May 16, 1980).
7. For an excellent history of the origins and development of block grants, see Timothy J. Conlan, "The Politics of Federal Block Grants from Nixon to Reagan," *Political Science Quarterly* 99, no. 2 (Summer 1984): 247–270.
8. *Brown v. Board of Education,* 347 U.S. 483 (1954); 349 U.S. 294 (1955).
9. *Roe v. Wade,* 410 U.S. 113 (1973).
10. *The New York Times,* December 28, 1988, p. 1; March 1, 1989, p. 8.
11. *Baker v. Carr,* 369 U.S. 186 (1962); *Reynolds v. Simms,* 377 U.S. 533 (1964).
12. *South Dakota v. Dole,* 483 U.S. 203 (1987).
13. *Garcia v. San Antonio Metropolitan Transit Authority,* 469 U.S. 528 (1985).
14. See John Kincaid, "Constitutional Federalism: Labor's Role in Displacing Places to Benefit Persons," *PS: Political Science and Politics* 26, no. 2 (June 1993): 172–177.
15. David M. O'Brien, "The 'Rehnquist Court' and Federal Preemption: In Search of a Theory," *Publius: The Journal of Federalism* (1994).
16. Advisory Commission on Intergovernmental Relations, *Federal Statutory Preemption of State and Local Authority* (Washington, D.C.: Advisory Commission on Intergovernmental Relations, 1992).

17. Ellen Perlman, "The Gorilla that Swallowed State Laws," *Governing* (August 1994): 46–48.
18. Philip M. Dearborn, "Assessing Mandate Effects on State and Local Governments," *Intergovernmental Perspectives* (Summer–Fall 1994): 23.
19. *The New York Times,* May 21, 1990, p. A11.
20. *The New York Times,* March 24, 1992, p. 1.
21. Thomas R. Dye, "Federalism: A Return to the Future," *Madison Review* 1, no. 1 (Fall 1995): 2.
22. John J. Harrigan, *Political Change in the Metropolis,* 5th ed. (New York: HarperCollins College Publishers, 1993), pp. 256–257.
23. See Edward C. Banfield, "Making a New Federal Program: Model Cities, 1964–1968," in *Policy and Politics in America,* Allan P. Sindler, ed. (Boston: Little, Brown and Co., 1973), pp. 160–198; Martha Derthick, *New Towns in Town: Why a Federal Program Failed* (Washington, D.C.: Urban Institute, 1972); Paul R. Dommel, "Distribution Politics and Urban Policy," *Policy Studies Journal* 3, no. 4 (June 1975): 370–374; Jeffrey L. Pressman and Aaron B. Wildavsky, *Implementation* (Berkeley, Calif.: University of California Press, 1973); Helen W. Smookler, "Administrative Hara-Kiri: Implementation of the Urban Growth and New Community Development Act," *Annals of the American Academy of Political and Social Science* 422 (November 1975), pp. 133–137.
24. David B. Walker, "The Federal Role in the Federal System: A Troublesome Topic," *National Civic Review* 72, no. 1 (January 1983): 6–23.
25. Ronald Reagan, "Inaugural Address," January 20, 1981 and speech to the National Governors Association, August 8, 1988.
26. Tom Kenworthy and Thomas B. Edsell, "The Voices of Those Who Think Civil Rights Have Gone Too Far," *Washington Post National Weekly,* June 10–June 16, 1991, p. 14.
27. Ibid.
28. *Washington Post National Weekly,* March 27–April 2, 1995, p. 37.
29. Ronald Reagan, "Inaugural Address," January 20, 1981.
30. Ronald Reagan, speech to the National Governors Association, August 8, 1988.
31. Spending on federal grants grew from $154 billion in 1991 to $236 billion in 1996. *Statistical Abstract of the United States: 1996,* p. 300.
32. Richard P. Nathan and Fred C. Doolittle, "The Untold Story of Reagan's 'New Federalism,'" *Public Interest,* no. 77 (Fall 1984): 96–105.
33. Paul E. Peterson, "Who Should Do What? Divided Responsibilities in a Federal System," *Brookings Review* 13, no. 2 (Spring 1995): 6–11.
34. *Community Communications Company, Inc.* v. *City of Boulder,* 102 S.Ct. 835 (1982).
35. Richard J. Hardy and Michael P. McConachie, "Missouri in the Federal System," *Missouri Government and Politics,* Richard J. Hardy and Dohm, eds. (Columbia, Mo.: University of Missouri Press, 1985), p. 10.
36. *Statistical Abstract of the United States: 1996,* p. 453.
37. See *The National Journal,* November 11, 1979, p. 1928.
38. See *The New York Times,* February 14, 1983, p. 1, and June 18, 1982, p. 11. State complaints were not totally put to rest, however. Alaskans, in particular, got upset in the 1980s when the amount of National Park land was expanded in that state; See *The New York Times,* August 4, 1986, p. 1.
39. Frank J. Popper, "The Timely End of the Sagebrush Rebellion," *The Public Interest,* 76 (Summer 1984): 61–73.
40. They are Kentucky and West Virginia. *National Journal,* March 22, 1980, p. 469.
41. *Maryland* v. *Louisiana,* 451 U.S. 725 (1981).
42. *Commonwealth Edison* v. *Montana,* 453 U.S. 609 (1981).

43. *The New York Times,* May 12, 1986, p. 9.
44. John C. Pierce, "Conflict and Consensus in Water Politics," *Western Political Quarterly* 32, no. 3 (September 1979): 307–317.
45. Michael F. McNulty and Gary C. Woodward, "Arizona Water Issues: Contrasting Economic and Legal Perspectives," *Arizona Review* 32, no. 2 (Fall 1984): 1–13.
46. Larry Morandi, "Not For Sale," *State Legislatures* 13, no. 1 (January 1987): 16–19.
47. Michael Gianturco, "Who's Got the Best Science?" *Forbes* October 14, 1991, p. 202.
48. See Aaron S. Gurwitz, "The New Faith in High Tech," *The Wall Street Journal,* October 27, 1982.
49. Council on Environmental Quality, *Environmental Quality Annual Report: 1973* (Washington, D.C.: U.S. Government Printing Office, 1973), pp. 43–71.
50. Peterson, "Who Should Do What? Divided Responsibilities in a Federal System," 6–11.

4

FINANCIAL CONSTRAINTS ON STATE AND LOCAL GOVERNMENT

Chapter Preview

Chapter 4 examines the financial constraints on state and local governments. State fiscal policies affect state economic conditions and vice versa. The overall economic trend in a region sharply affects how much money states and communities can spend on public services. And at the same time, state and community fiscal policies also affect how vibrant their economy is. We shall examine these relationships in this chapter by asking:

1. For what purposes do state and local governments spend your money?
2. How do state and community governments raise their revenues?
3. What major conflicts and issues concern states and communities as we enter the twenty-first century?
4. What is the importance of the political economy in state and community finances?

Let us begin this excursion into state and community finances with a look at one of the most symbolically important events of the last two decades—Proposition 13 in California.

◇ INTRODUCTION

One of the most important events in recent American politics took place on June 6, 1978. California voters that day struck terror into the hearts of most California state and local officials and a good many other public officials around the country by overwhelmingly passing an initiative* called **Proposition 13.** This vote cut

---

*The *initiative* is a device in some states that enables voters to pass laws directly without having to go through the state legislature.

local government property tax revenues by over $6 billion and gave property owners a 57 percent tax relief. Immediately after the proposition passed, tax or expenditure limitation movements gathered steam in virtually every state, ushering in an era of financial tightfistedness. More than any other event, the passage of Proposition 13 separates the period of governmental expansion (1960s and 1970s) from the contemporary period of general governmental retrenchment (1978 to the present).[1]

Government officials could not have been surprised by the victory of Proposition 13, however. Resentment against high taxes and government spending had been building throughout the 1970s. When voters were given the chance to vote on bond issues or school budgets, they often defeated them.[2] A speculative real estate boom had driven up California home prices dramatically, and most real estate taxes went up even faster. In contrast to the property tax squeeze on homeowners, the California State treasury by 1978 had built up a surplus of over $5 billion, although the state legislators disagreed on how to use it to provide property tax relief.

At that point, retired businessmen Howard Jarvis and Paul Gann took matters into their own hands. With very little effort or expense, they quickly gathered 1.2 million signatures on a petition to place on the June 1978 ballot a constitutional amendment initiative that:[3]

1. Reduced the maximum property tax rate to 1 percent of the 1975–1976 assessed value of the property.
2. Limited future assessment increases to 2 percent per year, except when ownership changes, at which point the property can be reassessed at current market value.
3. Barred the state legislature from raising any state taxes to make up for those cuts unless the new taxes pass by a two-thirds majority vote.

From the average taxpayer's viewpoint, Proposition 13 was an unmitigated success. He or she received a substantial property tax reduction. The spirit that led to Proposition 13 also helped limit future state tax increases.[4] Furthermore, the immediate decimation of local public services that had been resoundingly predicted by critics of Proposition 13 never occurred, because the state had a huge $5 billion surplus, which it distributed to local governments to help make up for the Proposition 13 cuts.[5] California voters appeared to have gotten exactly what their critics said was impossible—tax reduction without public service reductions, or to use the critics' imagery, something for nothing, a free lunch.[6]

Seldom can you get something for nothing in the long run, however, and when California's big budget surpluses disappeared in the 1980s, the costs of Proposition 13 became apparent. Governmentally, the main cost was an eventual sharp reduction in most public services. Within a decade, class size in California schools rose to the largest among the states, and California dropped from number twenty-one in per-pupil funding of schools to number thirty-five.[7] In per capita spending for highway maintenance, California's rank fell to number fifty. Comparable cutbacks were felt in welfare and other public services.[8] Politically, the increased reliance on state funding led to a shift in power from local officials to the state capitol in Sacramento.[9] And socially, the tax reduction benefits were not distributed evenly across the population. Older, upper-middle-income people who had bought their homes before 1975 got substantial benefits, whereas renters and young people who bought their homes after 1978 received much less. By the tenth anniversary of Proposition 13, recent home buyers were paying three to four times the tax rate of the pre-Proposition 13 homeowners.[10]

In fact, the biggest winners were not homeowners at all, but corporations. A lower-middle-income homeowner saved a few hundred dollars, but Standard Oil Corporation, for example, saved an estimated $13.1 million. The ten largest utilities and railroads saved $400 million.[11]

Since these corporations do not buy and sell their property as often as individuals do, they would not have to worry about being reassessed every time they bought. The long-term effect of Proposition 13 was clear (but apparently irrelevant to most voters). It would shift the property tax burden from corporations to homeowners. Praised by conservatives it was condemned by liberals.[12]

In 1994, the fiscally conservative magazine *Money* sponsored a seminar on the legacy of Proposition 13 and concluded that the restrictions of Proposition 13 had produced a disaster for the ability of the state and local governments to provide public services. The deterioration of public services prompted growing numbers of affluent Californians to turn their back on the state's public sector and look to private schools to educate their children and private guards to police their neighborhoods.[13]

Although it may look bad in retrospect, the victory of Proposition 13 in 1978 bolstered fiscal conservatives to push for other **tax or expenditure limitation (TEL) movements** around the nation. Other states with statewide initiative provisions, such as Iowa, Michigan, and Oregon, soon saw similar measures put before their voters. Although few of these had the dramatic results of Proposition 13, Massachusetts' 1980 Proposition 2½ had a large impact. By limiting a community's property tax revenue to 2.5 percent of the full value of taxable property, it gave Massachusetts homeowners a $1.3 billion tax reduction.[14]

After the passage of Massachusetts' Proposition 2½ however, the tax-cutting movement seemed to wither, as state and local governments began to face a **budget retrenchment** challenge. Budget surpluses, which were quite common in the 1970s, began disappearing in the 1980s, as the economic recessions (of 1980–1982) and cutbacks in federal grants-in-aid began to make themselves felt. Instead of being able to vote themselves tax cuts, citizens in most states saw their taxes begin to rise to cover revenue shortfalls. Even Californians, who started the TEL movement in 1978, voted in 1990 to ease up on the lid they had placed on state spending.

In sum, the few short years since the passage of Proposition 13 changed the intellectual climate within which public services are offered and revenues raised to pay for them. In the current era of fiscal constraint, public officials find it much more necessary than previously to ask where revenues will come from before they enact new programs or expand existing ones. To understand the dynamics of this new climate, this chapter addresses the following.

1. What services should state and local governments offer? That is, for what purposes should these governments spend their money?
2. Where should government money come from? The property tax? Sales tax? Income tax? Entrepreneurial activities? Other sources?
3. What is meant by the variety of technical terms used in the discussion of Proposition 13 and other government finances—terms like *assessed valuation, mill rates, market value, property tax relief, circuit breaker, tax burden, tax effort,* and others?
4. How should the tax burden be distributed? For example, if a state lets most of its services be provided by local governments and paid for by local property taxes, who gets stuck with the biggest share of the taxes? The rich? The poor? Businesspeople? The elderly? The young? Or you?

◇ HOW STATE AND LOCAL GOVERNMENTS SPEND YOUR MONEY

State and local governments spend a lot of money. We saw in Chapter 1 (Figure 1-1, p. 2) that state and local government spending since midcentury rose faster than either federal government expenditures or the economy as a whole. The major index of national economic growth is the gross domestic product (GDP). As Figure 1-1 shows, state and local government spending has risen nearly 3,400 percent since 1950, while the GDP rose at a little over half that rate (1,816 percent).

Why Costs Have Gone Up

There are several explanations for these rapid increases in state and local expenditures. First is inflation. In the quarter century from 1965 to 1993, the purchasing power of the dollar declined to 24 cents.[15] Rising government expenses may anger many people; but in practical terms, just to maintain the same levels of services that existed a quarter century ago, governments today have to spend four times as many dollars as they spent then.

However, citizens and interest groups are not content with simply maintaining the same level of services; this trend is a second explanation for the rise of government spending. During the entire post–World War II period, Americans have demanded more services in education, health care, transportation, law enforcement, housing, and other areas. Each increase in services meant an increase in dollars spent and employees hired. The number of state and local employees has approximately doubled since the mid-1960s, compared to an increase of less than 20 percent in federal employment.[16] Most of this rapid increase in employment occurred at the local level. The growth in the number of government employees also helped stimulate government spending, as those employees in turn became a growing source of demands for more spending.[17]

Where Your Money Goes

Half the money spent by state and local governments goes for just three services: public education, public welfare, public health. But Figure 4-1 shows that states

Figure 4-1 WHERE STATE AND LOCAL GOVERNMENTS SPEND YOUR
MONEY: 1992

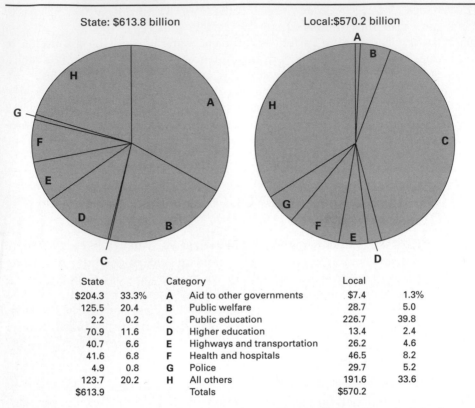

State: $613.8 billion   Local:$570.2 billion

State		Category	Local	
$204.3	33.3%	A Aid to other governments	$7.4	1.3%
125.5	20.4	B Public welfare	28.7	5.0
2.2	0.2	C Public education	226.7	39.8
70.9	11.6	D Higher education	13.4	2.4
40.7	6.6	E Highways and transportation	26.2	4.6
41.6	6.8	F Health and hospitals	46.5	8.2
4.9	0.8	G Police	29.7	5.2
123.7	20.2	H All others	191.6	33.6
$613.9		Totals	$570.2	

Note: These are direct expenditures for 1992. Local expenditures include aid from the federal government and state governments. State expenditures include aid from the federal government.

Source: Bureau of the Census: *Significant Features of Fiscal Federalism: 199,* p. 78.

spend their money slightly differently than do local governments. For states, the
single biggest expenditure is for aid to local governments, followed by welfare,
education, transportation, health services (including medical aid for the poor),
and the other purposes shown in Figure 4-1. States also spend considerable
amounts of money on insurance trust fund payments for such items as public
employee pension benefits, workers' compensation payments, and unemployment compensation payments. However, since most of these trust fund expenditures are covered by employee and employer contributions to the trust funds,
they are not a direct drain on the tax dollar.

For local governments, the single largest expenditure is for public education,
followed by utility systems and the other purposes shown in Figure 4-1. However, utility systems, like the states' trust fund expenditures, also generate offsetting revenues and thus are not a direct cost to the taxpayer.

Table 4-1   DESIRED LEVEL OF TAXES AND SERVICES

	"Considering all government services on the one hand and taxes on the other, which of the following comes closest to your view?"					
	1975	**1977**	**1979**	**1980**	**1982**	**1986**
Keep taxes and services about where they are	45%	52%	46%	45%	42%	51%
Decrease services and taxes	38	31	39	38	36	31
Increase services and taxes	5	4	6	6	8	9
No opinion	12	13	9	11	14	9

Source: Advisory Commission on Intergovernmental Relations, *Changing Public Attitudes on Governments and Taxes: A Commission Survey: 1988,* Report S-1 (Washington, D.C.: U.S. Government Printing Office, 1988), pp. 60–61.

Conflict over Expenditures

In the Proposition 13 battle described earlier, two aspects of these expenditure patterns became the subjects of bitter conflict. First, the architects of Proposition 13 complained that the expenditures were simply too high. They argued that state and local budgets included so much fat and waste that they could easily be cut back. The level of government spending is a key issue in the conflict between liberals and conservatives. Conservatives are much more inclined than liberals to cut government expenditures. Table 4-1 shows that about a third to two-fifths of the public at large consistently agreeing with this conservative position. About half of the public consistently wants to keep services and taxes as they are. And only a small minority wants to increase spending and taxes.

If the level of spending is the first key conflict between liberals and conservatives, the second is over the purposes for which money should be spent. Continually faced with limited resources, state and local leaders must regularly set priorities among government programs. The "You Decide" exercise asks you to take a shot at setting priorities among competing public purposes. And Table 4-2 shows how the public at large reacted to the same task. Note how much peoples' priorities were affected simply by changing the program labels for item number 4. The people questioned in August were asked to respond to a category called "public welfare programs," but in the September survey that term was relabeled "aid to the needy." In contrast to "public welfare," which was the program people most wanted to cut, "aid to the needy" fared much better, ranking only a few percentage points behind the most favored programs (public safety and schools).

◇ WHERE STATE AND LOCAL REVENUE COMES FROM

In general, state and local governments have four sources of revenue: taxes, intergovernmental aid, charges on services or enterprises they operate, and borrowing. Figure 4-2 shows that the revenue sources for state governments differ

YOU DECIDE

Cutting Budgets

Suppose the budgets of your state and local governments have to be curtailed. Which of these programs would you cut most severely? Put a number 6 by that program. Then rank the rest of the programs in priority, from 1 (the one with the least cuts) to 5 (the one with the most cuts).

Public safety (fire, police, criminal justice) _____

Public schools (kindergarten through twelfth grade) _____

Tax-supported colleges and universities _____

Aid to the needy _____

Streets and highways _____

Parks and recreation _____

To compare your choices with those of the American public, see Table 4-2.

significantly from those for local governments. Local governments rely heavily on state and federal aid, property taxes, and charges levied on services (such as parking meters and sewer fees). State governments place little reliance on property taxes. They rely most heavily on aid from the federal government, income taxes, sales taxes, and insurance trust fund revenues.

Conflict over Revenue Sources

The revenue sources of a government strongly affect the distribution of the tax burden. **Tax burden** is the total amount of taxes paid as a percentage of a person's income. A **progressive tax** system is one that increases the tax burden for upper-income people while reducing it for lower-income people. A **regressive tax** system increases the tax burden for lower-income people while reducing it for upper-income people. In short, progressive taxes are based on the ability to pay. Some states have very progressive tax systems, and others have very regressive ones, as will be shown at the end of this chapter.

Taxation as a Revenue Source

Few of us like to pay taxes, but we dislike some taxes more than others. Table 4-3 shows that for the past quarter century, the most unpopular taxes have been the federal income tax and the local property tax.

Table 4.2   POPULAR CANDIDATES FOR BUDGET CUTS

"If the budgets of your state and local governments have to be curtailed, which of these parts would you limit most severely?"

	August 1981		September 1981	
	Percent	Rank	Percent	Rank
1. Public safety (fire, police, criminal justice)	4%	1	3%	1
2. Public schools (kindergarten—12th grade)	7	2	3	1
3. Tax-supported colleges and universities	10	4	24	5
4. Public welfare programs	39	6	xx	
Aid to the needy	xx		7	3
5. Streets and highways	9	3	10	4
6. Parks and recreation	24	5	45	6
7. None of these or don't know	9		10	

Note: xx = choice not offered.

Source: Advisory Commission on Intergovernmental Relations, *Changing Public Attitudes on Government and Taxes: 1981,* Report S-10 (Washington, D.C.: U.S. Government Printing Office, 1981), p. 2.

Evaluating the Major Taxes   In order to evaluate taxes, we need to go beyond public opinion about them. Table 4-4 provides six criteria for evaluating taxes— equity, yield, certainty, administrative convenience, economic effect, and appropriateness. *Equity* has various meanings,* but it will be used here to mean taxation based on the ability to pay. *Yield* means how much money a tax will raise; closely akin to the concept of yield is the *certainty* that the tax can be counted on to yield the same amount year after year. *Administrative convenience* refers to how difficult it is to collect the tax. *Economic effect* refers to the consequences the tax can have on the economy that surrounds the government levying it. Finally, *appropriateness* refers to the level of government that gets the best use out of the tax.

  Property Tax   A person's **property tax** is based on two factors—the assessed value of the real estate property and the tax rate, which local governments levy on property. The assessed value is determined periodically by an assessor. Your house, for example, may have a taxable assessed value of $100,000.

---

*Economists distinguish between vertical equity, horizontal equity, and equity in relation to benefits received from the tax. *Vertical* equity refers to whether the tax is based on the ability to pay. *Horizontal* equity refers to levying the same tax rate on all persons within the same taxable class. For example, if identical houses on the same block have different property taxes, that violates horizontal equity. Equity *in relation to benefits received* refers to whether the value of benefits a person receives from paying a tax equals the amount of the tax paid.

Figure 4-2 **WHERE STATE AND LOCAL GOVERNMENTS GET THEIR REVENUES: 1991**

State: $744.2 billion   Local: $647.9 billion

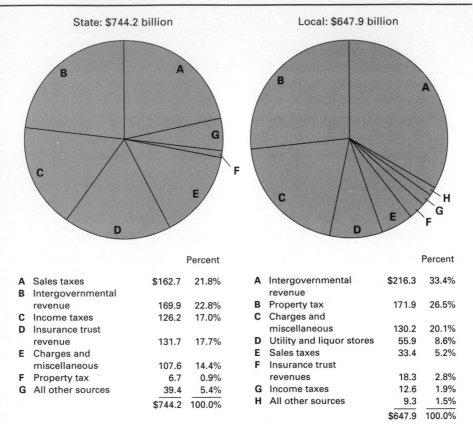

		Percent				Percent
A	Sales taxes	$162.7	21.8%	**A**	Intergovernmental revenue	$216.3	33.4%
B	Intergovernmental revenue	169.9	22.8%	**B**	Property tax	171.9	26.5%
C	Income taxes	126.2	17.0%	**C**	Charges and miscellaneous	130.2	20.1%
D	Insurance trust revenue	131.7	17.7%	**D**	Utility and liquor stores	55.9	8.6%
E	Charges and miscellaneous	107.6	14.4%	**E**	Sales taxes	33.4	5.2%
F	Property tax	6.7	0.9%	**F**	Insurance trust revenues	18.3	2.8%
G	All other sources	39.4	5.4%	**G**	Income taxes	12.6	1.9%
		$744.2	100.0%	**H**	All other sources	9.3	1.5%
						$647.9	100.0%

Source: Bureau of the Census, *Statistical Abstract of the United States: 1994* (Washington, D.C.: U.S. Government Printing Office, 1994), p. 307.

Table 4-3 **THE WORST TAX FROM THE PUBLIC'S VIEWPOINT**

"What do you think is the worst tax—that is, the least fair?"

	1972	1975	1978	1981	1984	1988	1991	1994
Federal income tax	19%	28%	30%	36%	36%	33%	26%	27%
State income tax	13	11	11	9	10	10	12	7
State sales tax	13	23	18	14	15	18	19	14
Local property tax	45	29	32	33	29	28	30	28
Do not know	11	10	10	9	10	11	14	12

Source: Advisory Commission on Intergovernmental Relations, *Changing Public Attitudes on Governments and Taxes: A Commission Survey,* Report S-23 (Washington, D.C.: U.S. Government Printing Office, 1994), p. 1.

Table 4-4 CRITERIA FOR EVALUATION TAXES

Criterion	Property Tax	Income Tax	Sales Tax
Equity	Most regressive, but regressivity can be reduced	Most progressive	Regressive, but regressivity can be reduced
Yield and certainty	High yield; the most certain	Yield depends on other variables; least certain	High yield; less certain than property tax, more certain than income tax
Administrative convenience	Most costly	Least costly	Less costly than property tax; possibly more costly than income tax
Economic effect	Associated with no incentives for improving property; fiscal disparities	Useful for controlling economy's growth	Incentive for saving and investing
Appropriateness	Best for local	Best for federal and state	Best for state

If the tax rate is 2 percent, then your property tax will be $2,000 ($100,000 × 2% = $2,000). If your home's value and the tax rate each go up by only 10 percent this year, your total taxes will go up by 21 percent ($110,000 × 2.2% = $2,420). This combined effect was one of the things that drove up Californians' property taxes in the 1970s and led to the Proposition 13 tax revolt.

Property taxes receive their heaviest criticism on the criteria of equity, administrative convenience, and economic effect. The property tax is not based on the ability to pay. You must pay that $2,420 next year whether you get a big salary increase or whether you lose your job. Most states have taken four measures either to make the tax more equitable or to shift the tax burden off certain kinds of property. First is the **circuit breaker,** which limits how much of your income can be taken in property taxes. If the state sets a 4 percent limit, then your property taxes cannot exceed 4 percent of your income. If they do exceed that amount, the circuit breaker protects you by giving you a tax deduction or credit to reimburse you.

In addition to the circuit breaker, most states have *homestead* and *senior citizens' credits.* Your taxes will be lower for a building that you make your home than for a building in which you operate a business. Many states have adopted a special credit for senior citizens that freezes their property taxes once they retire.

States also grant *exemptions* to certain property, such as nonincome-producing church property or property used for charitable purposes. Finally, states shift the property tax burden by creating different property tax *classifications*. Farmland usually is classified in a lower bracket than land in a city.

Although the property tax has historically been considered regressive, circuit breakers, credits, and exemptions have made the property tax much more equitable than it was ten or twenty years ago. Economists and tax experts are consequently beginning to view the property tax more positively.[18]

The other criteria on which property taxes are heavily criticized are administrative convenience and economic effect. The need to hire assessors, create boards of appeal, process complaints about assessments, and make fair assessments of different kinds of property can make the property tax difficult and costly to administer. And, as will be shown in the special case of schools, property taxes breed fiscal disparities between communities. The same $100,000 house might have taxes twice as high in one municipality as in a neighboring community.

Property taxes score high on the criteria of yield and certainty. This is because the property tax is the most certain of all the taxes. It will bring in exactly as much money as the assessors project. Nobody can escape it. Property taxes not paid this year must be paid next year, and if you go too long without paying them, the government will sell your property for the amount of back taxes you owe. Finally, the property tax is the most appropriate at the local level. It provides a stable source of revenue for funding basic local services such as police protection, street maintenance, and building code enforcement, among others.[19]

Income Taxes   Forty-three states levy personal income taxes.* State income taxes score highest on the criteria of equity, administrative convenience, and economic effect. They have the greatest chance of taxing people on their ability to pay, especially in states that use a graduated income tax. In these states, the rate goes from a very small percentage for low-income residents to higher percentages for people with higher incomes. The income tax is easy to administer since it is collected automatically by employers. However, some administrative costs are incurred in auditing returns and in trying to discourage tax evasion. It is a very positive tool for influencing the overall economy since tax rates can be manipulated to stimulate or retard growth rates. However, this works much more successfully at the federal level than at the state level.

On the questionable side, the yield from state income taxes is unstable because it depends on several factors—the rate of inflation, the rate of unemployment, the tax rates, and the amount of tax money lost because of credits, deductions, exemptions, and loopholes. The income tax is therefore the least certain of all taxes. During years of economic boom, income tax revenues often exceed estimates, giving the state treasury a surplus. When the economy has a recession, however, income tax revenues lag behind forecasts, and a treasury deficit results.

The income tax works best at the federal and state levels. Many cities (New York City, for example) impose a small income tax on people who live or work there. But cities that impose an income tax risk driving residents and employers out of the city and into suburbs that levy no such tax.

---

*The states with no income tax are: Alaska, Florida, Nevada, South Dakota, Texas, Washington, and Wyoming.

In addition to the personal income tax, forty-six states charge a corporate income tax, which in many respects is even more controversial than the personal income tax. Critics complain that the corporate tax can create an unfriendly environment for business and that it is simply a personal tax in disguise since corporations pass the tax on to their customers. Supporters of the corporate income tax argue that corporations should pay their share of the cost of government just as citizens do.

Sales Tax   Forty-five states levy a general **sales tax.*** This tax scores negatively only on the criterion of equity. Mississippi, for example, has a 6 percent sales tax on all retail items. This tax is traditionally considered regressive because it inherently takes a higher percentage of the incomes of poor people than it takes from rich people. Some states seek to reduce this regressivity by granting tax credits and exempting certain categories of purchases, such as food, clothing, medicines, and textbooks. Since poor people spend a greater percentage of their income on food and clothing than do the wealthy, these exemptions help shift the tax burden from the poor onto the higher-income groups in those states. Current thinking, however, argues that progressivity could be best achieved if no exemptions were granted and a circuit-breaker income tax credit were given to poor people.

On all the other criteria, the sales tax scores high. It generally produces a high yield, although this yield is reduced if the states grant a lot of exemptions in order to make it less regressive. Sales tax revenues are much less certain than those from the property tax but much more certain than those from the income tax. Sales tax revenues fluctuate with changes in the national economy, but not nearly as much as revenue from income taxes. The sales tax is easy and inexpensive to administer since it is collected by retailers, who send their tax receipts to the state tax office. In theory, its economic effect is to encourage people to save and invest since it taxes retail purchases.

Finally, sales taxes work best at the state level. Many local governments do impose local sales taxes. However, if these are too high or too inconvenient, shoppers go to neighboring communities to shop.

Other Tax Sources   In addition to the three major taxes, state and local governments rely on a number of other taxes (see Figure 4-2). Major among these other taxes are motor fuel taxes, alcohol and tobacco taxes, and severance taxes. About three-fifths of the states levy **severance taxes** on industries that extract (that is, "sever") natural resources such as timber, ore, coal, and natural gas. But few states rely on severance taxes for more than 10 percent of their tax revenue. The "Highlight" on p. 74 shows the importance of severance taxes to Alaska.

The beauty of severance taxes is that they *export* the tax burden to people in other states who buy the natural resources. One state's beauty, however, is another state's beast, as Louisiana and Montana discovered when other states protested bitterly in the late 1970s when Louisiana raised its severance tax on natural gas and Montana raised its tax on coal. The U.S. Supreme Court struck

---

*The states without a general sales tax are: Alaska, Delaware, Montana, New Hampshire, and Oregon.

HIGHLIGHT

Alaska Uses Its Oil and Gas Income

Severance taxes tend to be a very unstable source of revenue, as can be seen in the case of Alaska. Following the discovery of huge oil and natural gas reserves in the 1970s, Alaska became the biggest user of severance taxes. By the 1980s, oil and gas revenues amounted to $1.4 billion per year, nearly 80 percent of all the state's tax revenues.

To safeguard against the day when the oil and gas stop flowing, Alaskans in 1976 approved a Permanent Fund, which now receives 10 percent of all the oil and gas royalties. By 1988, the Permanent Fund had reached $8 billion, an enormous surplus for a state whose population is barely 500,000 people. So big was this surplus, in fact, that Alaska abolished its income tax, raised salaries for state officials, initiated numerous economic development projects, and began sending each resident an annual check that started out at $400 and by 1987 had reached $675.

By the mid-1980s, however, the worldwide oil shortages of just a few years earlier had turned into an oil glut. Oil prices plummeted from over $30 per barrel to under $12 per barrel in 1986 before rebounding to the lower twenties. Alaskans were suddenly faced with scarcity rather than abundance. Although continuing the annual check to each resident, the state was forced to cancel a number of economic development projects, reduce state aids to local governments, and begin talk of reinstating the income tax.

In 1990, oil prices shot back up in the wake of Iraq's invasion of Kuwait, and once again Alaska's oil revenues rebounded.

Sources: *The New York Times,* November 29, 1977, p. 11; June 5, 1981, p. 7; June 18, 1982, p. 11; March 17, 1983, p. 1; April 8, 1986, p. 1; February 21, 1987, p. 5; March 29, 1988, p. 13; *State Legislatures* 12, no. 10 (November–December 1986): 8; Bureau of the Census, *State Government Tax Collections in 1986* (Washington, D.C.: U.S. Government Printing Office, 1987), p. 3; *State Legislatures* 16, no. 10 (November–December, 1990): 5.

---

down Louisiana's tax because it exempted Louisianans.[20] The Court upheld Montana's 30 percent coal tax, however, because the tax had to be paid by Montanans as well as by others.[21] In these two cases, the Court seemed to be saying that it would not interfere with a state's severance taxes unless that state was blatantly using such taxes to export the tax burden to other states; this is just what Louisiana was doing when it exempted its residents from its new gas tax.

Tax-Base Breadth One final concern today is **tax-base breadth.** If too many people are exempted from the tax base (through property tax classification, income tax loopholes, sales tax exemptions, or untaxed so-called underground transactions such as getting paid in cash to paint your neighbor's house), then the tax base is narrow, which has a number of consequences. Principally, states relying on a narrow tax base tend to have a much more volatile flow of tax revenue than do states with a broader tax base, and they also need to have higher tax rates on the smaller number of people and businesses that pay the taxes. The traditional reason for narrowing the tax base has been to achieve progressivity or some other *social good* (see pp. 68, 75). But current thinking asserts that progressivity could be obtained just as easily by broadening the tax base and providing income tax credits for low-income people.

Entrepreneurial Sources of Revenue

In addition to taxes, state and local governments operate enterprises that generate revenue. At the state level, about 17 percent of all revenue is raised from insurance programs. These include workers' compensation, unemployment compensation, and public employee retirement funds. The monies contributed to these programs by workers and employers are kept in large trust funds run by the state. The interest from these funds is earmarked for the benefits of the programs. States collect another 14 percent of their revenue from state-owned liquor stores and from charges for college tuition, highway tolls, and public hospitals and health facilities.

At the local level, the major entrepreneurial sources of revenue are public utilities (bus companies, power plants, water supply companies). Local governments also earn substantial revenues from fees for sewer service, garbage collection, parking facilities, building permits, franchises, and the use of publicly owned facilities, such as golf courses, tennis courts, and swimming pools. Municipalities also have licensing powers and can tax commercial establishments such as movie theaters, bars, restaurants, sports arenas, and hotels. In the tight budget environment that has prevailed since Proposition 13, many communities doubled and tripled the fees and charges they collect in order to cover revenue shortfalls.

If local governments can raise money by charging fees and running profit-making enterprises and if state governments can run lotteries at a profit, we might ask, why they do not run more and more enterprises until their profits are such that they do not need to levy taxes at all? The answer seems to be that, in a capitalist economy, governments traditionally run only certain kinds of enterprises. Economists distinguish between private goods to be distributed by private companies and public goods to be distributed by governments. One of three criteria can be used to make this distinction.[22] First, some public goods are **social goods,** which are goods (such as a city's unpolluted drinking water supply) that nobody can be excluded from and that cannot be divided up among the users so that what is used by one person is unavailable to be used by another. In contrast, a dinner at your favorite restaurant is a private good. People unwilling to pay the price are excluded, and the portion consumed by one customer is no longer available to be used by another. Thus, social goods are nonexclusive and nondivisible, in contrast to private goods, which are exclusive and divisible.

A second criterion for distinguishing public from private goods is that of merit. **Merit goods** are those (such as minimal public health care and free public education) that society judges all citizens should have, whether or not they can personally afford them.

Finally, the criterion of **externalities** can be used to distinguish between public and private goods. Private economic activities produce certain external costs that are not reflected in the purchase price of the good. The construction of a major shopping center, for instance, requires police protection, streets, and storm sewers, costs not borne by the shopping center owners or passed on to the consumers. Although the costs are external to the shopping center, they are nevertheless real and somebody must pay them. They are paid by the neighboring local governments.

"When I grow up, I hope to win the lottery."

Opponents of the state-run lottery dislike the state's involvement in promoting the attitude satirized in this cartoon.

Source: Drawing by Mulligan; Copyright © 1984, The *New Yorker* Magazine, Inc.

Following these criteria, the economist argues that governments normally engage in entrepreneurial activity only when that activity involves a good that cannot be produced by private entrepreneurs. The goods that cannot be produced profitably by private entrepreneurs are the social, merit, and external goods.

Intergovernmental Aid as a Revenue Source

As was shown in Figure 4-2, intergovernmental aid is the largest source of revenue for both state and local governments. In 1995, the federal government provided $228 billion in aid to the states and localities. As a percentage of state and local revenue, federal aid peaked in 1978, declined during the 1980s and has been rising since then.[23]

Federal Aid   Federal aid has a number of important financial consequences. First, it was one of the major reasons for the rapid increase in state and local expenditures during the 1970s.[24] Second, much federal aid has been channeled into human services programs, and this has forced state and local budgets to provide more money for programs such as Medicaid, AFDC,* and other social services. Third, since much federal aid is deliberately used to get state and local governments to carry out federal objectives, federal aid has the effect of determining how state and local governments will spend their money. This is especially true for the states' matching portion of federal categorical grants (see p. 76).[25] Finally, when federal aid was cut back during the 1980s, many states and communities found themselves severely strapped to meet the obligations they had taken on.

State Aid to Local Governments   State aid to local governments follows the same pattern as federal aid. Some aids are **categorical aids.** Others are similar to revenue sharing in that they simply support local budgets and give local governments great discretion in spending the money. In the education sector, for example, states finance public schools primarily through categorical aids and foundation aids. The foundation aids are based on a per-pupil amount that the state contributes to each local school district.

In contrast to the overall budget support provided by the foundation aids, educational categorical aids are aimed at specific program objectives, such as transportation, aiding children with special learning disabilities, and providing special assistance to children from low-income backgrounds.

The biggest complaint local officials have about state aid is probably over mandating. Many state programs are *mandated* (required) by state law, and most have matching-fund provisions. This forces local governments to adopt the program but does not provide all the finances for it. The local governments thus must either raise local taxes or, if that is impossible, cut other programs to pay for the state-mandated programs. Because local governments may not cut programs mandated by the federal or state government, mandating has contributed to the declining autonomy of local governments discussed in Chapter 3.

Borrowing as a Revenue Source

If state and local governments had to finance every operation on a pay-as-you-go basis, it would become impossible for them to function in today's world. They need to borrow money to build school buildings, universities, and prisons, or install sewer systems or water purification projects. All these large construction projects are referred to as **capital expenditures** and are financed by long-term debt. State and local governments also borrow money on a short-term basis to meet immediate payroll or other obligations, when they have not yet received the taxes levied to pay for those obligations. This short-term borrowing is accomplished through **revenue-anticipation notes** or **tax-anticipation notes.**

Long-term borrowing is accomplished by selling bonds. The person who buys a $5,000 municipal bond actually lends the city $5,000. The city pledges to repay the $5,000 and to pay a fixed amount of interest.

---

*Medicaid is a program that provides health care to poor people. AFDC (Aid for Families with Dependent Children) provides cash payments for the care of dependent children in low-income, single-parent families.

A **general-obligation bond** puts the full faith and credit of the issuing agency behind it. The issuing government guarantees that it will use its taxing powers to pay off the bonds. These bonds become in effect a charge against the property of all homeowners in the jurisdiction. For this reason, general-obligation bonds usually require approval by a voter referendum. Because these bonds are backed by the taxing power of the government, they are very safe; and because their interest is exempt from federal income taxes, they usually pay very low interest rates.

Distinct from general-obligation bonds are **revenue bonds.** These are not guaranteed by the taxing power of the issuing government. Rather, they are paid off from the revenue earned by the facility for which they were issued. Toll bridges, toll roads, convention centers, industrial parks, and municipally owned athletic stadiums are common examples of projects financed by revenue bonds. Interest on these bonds is exempt from federal income taxes. Since the bonds are slightly riskier than general-obligation bonds, they carry a slightly higher interest rate. A special type of revenue bond is the **Industrial Development Revenue Bond** (IDRB), through which a city uses its tax-exempt status to raise money for commercial development projects. IDRBs will be discussed more fully in Chapter 17.

◇ CONFLICTS AND ISSUES IN STATE AND LOCAL FINANCE

As should be apparent from the discussion up to this point, state and local finances are highly politicized. If there is a major shift in the expenditure or revenue patterns of these governments, some people win and others lose. These conflicts are probably most apparent in three specific problems affecting state and local finance during the 1990s: (1) the special problem of property taxes and the public schools, (2) the regressivity or progressivity of the tax burden, and (3) attempts to reform state tax structures.

The Special Problem of Property Taxes and Public Schools

The biggest portion of most people's property tax bill supports public schools. The amount of money the local school district can raise is based directly on the assessed valuation of property within its boundaries. Assume that school districts A and B have the same number of pupils. School district A has a large shopping center, a number of commercial and manufacturing establishments, and many expensive homes. District B, in contrast, has no large shopping center or commercial or manufacturing establishments. It has only small supermarkets and gas stations, and it has few expensive homes. School district B has a much lower total assessed valuation than does district A. To provide the same level of educational services as those provided in district A, the residents in district B will have to pay a much higher property tax rate. If the district B homeowners are less affluent than the district A homeowners, which is likely since they live in

HIGHLIGHT

Legalized Gambling as a Way to Reduce Direct Taxes on Citizens

With the fiscal stress of recent years, it is not surprising that states have increasingly looked to legalized gambling as a revenue source. Nevada is the most extensive user of gambling taxes, collecting almost 20 percent of its tax revenue from them. Only two states prohibit all gambling.

Lotteries have become the most widespread form of state-sanctioned gambling since New Hampshire started its lottery in the 1960s. Thirty-seven states currently have lotteries, which raise over $23 billion per year in state revenues, about 3 percent of all state revenues.

Casino gambling has also been spreading, with casinos now existing in 10 states and on nearly 200 Indian reservations. Whereas the main argument for lotteries is tax revenue, casino gambling is usually promoted as a tool for economic development and job growth. This was the case in New Jersey, where casino gambling was sold in the mid-1970s as a surefire means to revitalize the decaying Atlantic City. In fact, Atlantic City has gained very little from the casinos despite the creation of 42,000 jobs there. Most of the jobs went to suburban commuters, and Atlantic City itself has continued to deteriorate. Property values escalated along the beach where the casinos are located, but the rest of the city shared very little in the growth of casino gambling.

In contrast to Atlantic City, where casino gambling did little for overall economic development, there is reason to think that gains from Indian reservation casinos may be more widespread. Under federal statutes, if state law permits any form of gambling within its borders, then it cannot prohibit Indian tribes from opening gambling houses on their reservations. By 1994, these activities were bringing $2.7 billion in revenue into the impoverished reservations. This provided jobs for many Indians, significant cash distributions to tribal members, and some investment in other development enterprises on the reservations.

In addition to lotteries and casinos, many other forms of gambling can also raise state revenue. Bingo is permitted in all but five states. The next most popular form of legalized gambling is horse racing. Other forms of legalized betting include numbers games, sports betting, off-track betting, dog racing, and jai alai. If all states were to adopt all these forms of gambling, then—some people project—state gambling revenues would rise sharply. To keep this projection in perspective, however, we must also recognize the possibility that expansion to all types of legalized gambling could simply increase the competition between the types for existing customers, in which case the take would fall short of projections.

By the mid-1990s, a backlash was starting to emerge against the rapid spread of gambling. With nearly $500 billion wagered in 1994 and $40 billion in government revenues, gambling had become a very big business. Lobbyists were beginning to show up in state capitols in efforts to legalize further gambling opportunities. And political action committees with gambling ties made large contributions to campaigns for gambling referendums. The potential for corruption between the gaming industry and state licensing officials bothers an increasing number of critics.

Sources: George Sternlieb and James Hughes, *Atlantic City Gamble* (Cambridge, Mass.: Harvard University Press, 1984), Charles Clotfelter and Philip Cook, *Selling Hope* (Cambridge, Mass.: Harvard University Press, 1989); Henry C. Cashen and John C. Dill, "The Real Truth About Indian Gaming and the States," *State Legislatures* 18, no. 3 (March 1992): 23–26; Pam Greenberg, "Not Quite the Pot of Gold," *State Legislatures* 18, no. 12 (December 1992): 24–27; Steven D. Gold, "If It's Not a Miracle, It's a Mirage," *State Legislatures* 20, no. 2 (February 1994): 30. *New York Times,* December 18, 1995, p. A-8. *Washington Post National Weekly,* March 11–18, 1996, p. 6.

cheaper houses, they may be unable to pay higher taxes. In that case, their children will get fewer educational services. This will mean a higher pupil–teacher ratio, older textbooks, fewer extracurricular activities, and fewer course offerings. The term given to this situation is **fiscal disparities.** Especially within metropolitan areas, communities have large disparities in property tax rates and in the level of public services.

Critics look to the states to alleviate fiscal disparities. One obvious way to do this is to shift the financing burden from the local property tax to the state income and sales taxes. By financing schools from the state level, the burden is borne throughout the state, and the fiscal disparities are evened out. In the past decade, the states have assumed increasing shares of the cost of public education.

Like many political movements, the movement to shift the education tax burden from the local to the state level got kicked off in California. In 1971, that state's Supreme Court, in *Serrano* v. *Priest,* ruled that financing public education through local property taxes violated both the California and the federal constitutions.[26] Despite this decision, the California legislature failed to implement it well until voters passed Proposition 13. Another important conflict over fiscal disparities took place in Texas, where residents of a tax-poor school district in San Antonio asked the federal courts to strike down the property tax as a basis for funding Texas schools. However, the U.S. Supreme Court, in *Rodriguez* v. *San Antonio School District,* decided that the Constitution did not preclude property taxes as the method for funding local schools. The Supreme Court did agree that fiscal disparities in public education should be eliminated, but felt that this action should come from the states. In 1989, the Texas Supreme Court ruled that the fiscal disparities among school districts violated the state constitution and ordered the Texas legislature to find an equitable system of finance.[27] A tax sharing plan was adopted in 1993.

The most dramatic conflict over fiscal disparities occurred in New Jersey, which in the 1970s had neither a statewide income tax nor a sales tax. The New Jersey Supreme Court, in its *Robinson* v. *Cahill* decision in 1973, ordered the legislature to find an alternative to the property tax for funding the public schools.[28] Not until three years later, when the state supreme court ordered all the schools closed until a new funding plan was devised, did the legislature agree upon and pass an income tax that would meet the court's requirements.

Even with the new plan for increased state funding, extreme fiscal disparities among school districts persisted. In 1990, the New Jersey Supreme Court ordered the state to raise the spending levels of the 28 poorest districts (all in the central cities) up to the state average.[29] Democratic Governor Jim Florio did just that by enticing the legislature to approve a plan that would finance the increased state aid through a $1 billion increase in state income taxes. Voter disenchantment with this solution was swift and harsh. Voters dealt a stunning blow to the Democrats by giving the Republicans control over the legislature and then turning Florio out of the governorship in favor of Christine Todd Whitman who promised to undo the plan and give New Jersians a billion-dollar, 30 percent cut in their income taxes. To finance the tax cut without corresponding cuts in services, Whitman pushed a two-year wage freeze on state employees, juggled the state's pension fund, and rescheduled New Jersey's bonded indebtedness.[30]

While New Jersey has been floundering in its efforts to reduce its reliance on property taxes for schools, Michigan totally revamped its school funding system. In 1993, the Michigan legislature scrapped its traditional use of property taxes to fund the public schools, thus giving homeowners a huge property tax reduction. To compensate for this multibillion-dollar loss of revenue, the legislature called a referendum for a constitutional amendment that forced voters to choose between two options. One would replace the lost property tax revenue by boosting the state income tax from 4.6 to 6 percent, and the other would make a comparable increase in the state sales tax from 4 to 6 percent. In 1994, the voters resoundingly voted for the sales tax option and thus made Michigan the only state to move from heavy reliance on property taxes in funding schools to the total elimination of property taxes in the funding system.[31]

Shifting the Tax Burden

The hottest tax controversy, not surprisingly, is over the distribution of the **tax burden.** How heavy will it be, and who will bear the brunt of it? Figure 4-3 estimates the progressivity of state and local taxes in each state. It compares the percent of income paid in taxes (that is, the tax burden) of the poorest 20 percent of the people to the richest 1 percent. By any reasonable definition of the term *progressive,* the richest 1 percent ought to pay a higher percent of their income in taxes (that is, their tax burden) than the poorest 20 percent. But in the average state, the tax burden of the poor is 1.8 times as high as it is for the rich. Nevada is the most regressive, with its poor people paying 5.6 times the tax burden of the rich. And in only three states are taxes progressive (Vermont, Delaware, and Hawaii).

The most direct way to shift the tax burden in a progressive manner is to adopt the graduated income tax. Not surprisingly, none of the five most regressive states has a personal income tax. But imposing or even increasing the income tax often draws strong opposition from upper-middle-income earners, as the case of New Jersey's 1990 income tax increase shows. These taxpayers get hit the hardest by graduated income taxes, and they also tend to be the most active and influential participants in state politics. Even when graduated income taxes are adopted, it is difficult to keep their graduations meaningful. Through a process called **bracket creep,** inflation pushes people into higher tax brackets, so that eventually middle-income earners pay the same rate as high-income earners. To avoid this, some states adopted **indexation** of their income taxes so that tax brackets go up to match inflation.

In no small measure, the tax or expenditure limitation (TEL) movements discussed at the beginning of this chapter must be seen as a revolt of the haves against the have nots.[32] Combined with the federal grant-in-aid reductions of the early Reagan years, the TELs sought to shift the tax burden from upper- and upper-middle-income people to lower-middle- and lower-income people. They sought to do this by putting a lid on government expenditures for social welfare purposes, increasing the use of user fees for public services, and reducing the ability of states to export their tax burdens to the federal treasury through the use of grants-in-aid.

Figure 4-3 PROGRESSIVITY OF STATE AND LOCAL TAXES

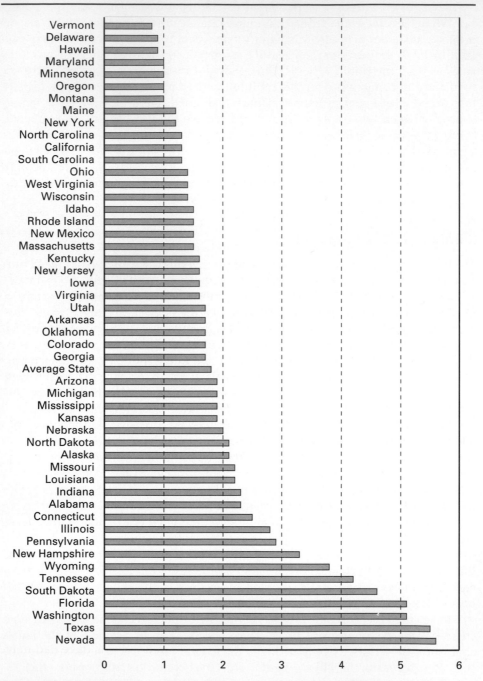

States with a progressive tax structure have a ratio lower than 1. Regressive states have a ratio higher than 1. Thus in Nevada, the tax burden of the poorest 20 percent of taxpayers is 5.6 times as great as the tax burden of the richest 1 percent of taxpayers. In Vermont, by contrast, the tax burden of the poorest group is only 80 percent of that of the richest group.

Source: Based on *A Far Cry From Fair* (Washington, D.C.: Citizens for Tax Justice, 1991).

Looking back on those events, however, it appears that the revolt of the haves against the have nots was only partially successful. Although reliance on federal aid dropped markedly, so did reliance on regressive property taxes. And this was accompanied by an increased reliance on the more progressive personal income tax, as well as on severance taxes.[33]

State Tax Reform

The years since Proposition 13 have witnessed extreme turmoil in state tax systems due to the tax limitation movements, the deep recessions of 1980–1982, federal aid cutbacks, significant tax changes at the federal level, interstate competition to reduce taxes in order to create a more attractive business climate, and another recession in 1990–1991. Most states responded to Proposition 13 by enacting some form of tax or expenditure limitation after 1978. Next they were forced to raise taxes to make up for revenue shortfalls caused by the recessions of 1980 to 1982 and the federal grant-in-aid cutbacks. Then as the economy rebounded in the mid-1980s, most states reduced taxes once again. Throwing another ingredient into the pot, Congress in 1986 dramatically cut the federal income tax rates, eliminated the federal deductibility of state sales taxes, and sharply restricted the use of tax-favored economic-development tools. These actions by Congress forced the states once again to reform their tax structures anew.

These reforms were dominated by two major concerns: (1) reducing reliance on the personal income tax and (2) broadening the tax base.[34] States wanted to reduce reliance on the personal income tax, because it made revenue collection vulnerable to economic slowdowns. And by broadening the tax base, tax reformers meant to eliminate a number of tax exemptions and deductions that had been built into state tax structures in order to ease the tax burden on certain groups of people.

This thrust toward broadening the tax base and reducing reliance on income taxes is not politically neutral. It has an inherent bias toward regressivity. This was indicated by a study the American Federation of State, County, and Municipal Employees (AFSCME) conducted of the round of state tax reforms that followed the federal tax changes of 1986.[35] AFSCME studied income tax changes in the forty states (plus the District of Columbia) with broad-based income taxes and found that these changes had moved in a regressive direction in twenty-one states and in a progressive direction in only seventeen. One of the states AFSCME found to have become more regressive was Wisconsin, whose tax reforms had so closely followed the model of broadening the tax base.

Having examined one of the most turbulent periods of fiscal reform in American history, we must note how little impact those reforms have had in reducing overall spending by state and local governments. In 1970, state and local government taxes amounted to $11.30 per $100 of personal income. By 1987, after TELs, fiscal restraint, initiatives, and referendums, that figure stood at $11.50.[36]

How could the TELs, the federal cutbacks, the fiscal restraint, and the voter initiatives against government growth over such a long period have had such little affect? Scholars have spent considerable energy studying this question, and

"We therefore feel that a person should be taxed
according to his inability to do anything about it."

The reality of tax reform is probably not quite as bad as the cynical viewpoint expressed
in this cartoon. But no one would doubt that some people are better able to protect themselves from the tax burden than are others.

Source: Dunagin's People by Ralph Dunagin. © 1980 Tribune Media Services. All rights reserved.
Reprinted with permission.

two answers seem to predominate. First, despite citizen disapproval of government growth in the abstract, virtually every major public service has citizen
groups that want to protect it and see it grow. In this kind of environment, the
mark of a successful politician is to preserve the service quite openly but to hide
the tax increases necessary to pay for it. Second, politicians are able to do this because the revenue structures are so diverse and so complicated that citizens cannot keep track of every move to escalate some revenues (user fees, for example)
to make up for tax reductions in other areas (the property tax reductions of
Proposition 13, for example).[37]

◇ STATE–COMMUNITY FINANCE AND THE POLITICAL ECONOMY

The ability of states and communities to finance their public services is tightly
interwoven with the overall economy within which they operate. Revenue raising is easiest, obviously, when the economy is booming, most people have jobs,
and tax collection is relatively simple. Holding down expenditures is easier in
low-inflation periods than in periods of high inflation because the cost of government purchases and payrolls will not escalate so rapidly. We shall use the

term *political economy* to refer to this reciprocal relationship between government and the economy.

The Impact of Economic Trends

In the 1990s, national economic trends are both a plus and a minus for state fiscal systems. On the plus side has been the low inflation of recent years. On the minus side is the simple fact that the national economy has been growing much more slowly than it did in earlier decades. The gross domestic product grew at a real annual rate (that is, adjusted for inflation) of 3.8 percent in the 1960s but only 2.8 percent in the 1970s, 2.9 percent in the 1980s, and 2.0 percent in the first half of the 1990s, giving the 1990s the slowest growth rate of any decade since the Great Depression of the 1930s.[38]

Regional Economic Dislocations

In addition to the prospects for slower economic growth, the national economy affects each region of the country differently. In the 1970s, the industrial economies of the Northeast and Midwest were devastated by escalating energy prices and a rising tide of good-quality, cheaply priced imported manufactured goods. During the same period, the Southwest prospered from the energy boom and, not being dependent on heavy manufacturing, was only marginally affected by foreign competition in manufactured products.

In the 1980s, these situations partially reversed. Energy-producing states of the Southwest, such as Texas and Oklahoma, were badly hit by the petroleum glut and the 50 percent drop in oil prices in 1986.[39] The Northeast, in the meantime, staged a vibrant recovery. The Midwest, still staggering from its industrial losses, fell into the worst agricultural depression in fifty years. By the mid-1990s, these patterns seemed staged for another reversal. The Northeast had gone through a deep recession, while Midwestern agriculture and manufacturing were booming. California, meanwhile, was badly hit by the end of the Cold War and resulting cutbacks in defense industries. The state lost an estimated 750,000 jobs between 1990 and 1992. This loss of jobs brought a sharp reduction in state tax collections, and a bitter conflict broke out in 1992 between the Republican governor and Democratic legislature on how to make up for this shortfall of state revenues. For two months, the state was unable to issue checks to pay its bills, and state workers received their pay in the form of warrants or IOUs. When the budget conflict was finally resolved, there were substantial cuts in welfare services and state aids to local government combined with significant increases in college tuitions and fees for other public services.[40]

The Impact of International Economics

These domestic and regional economic trends are much more closely tied to the international economy than they have ever been in the past. Consider, for example, the economic fate of oil states and states based on heavy manufacturing.

During the 1970s, state governments in the oil patch saw their revenues sky-rocket as oil prices rose. Then in the mid-1980s, their revenues plummeted as oil prices dropped. In great measure their revenues were driven not by their state economies but by the success or failure of OPEC (Organization of Petroleum Exporting Countries) in controlling the price of oil. And the governors of Oklahoma and Alaska recognized this fact in 1988 when they traveled to an OPEC meeting in Europe to urge that organization to stabilize oil production and prices.[41] The tax revenues of the industrial states were also affected by such esoteric facts as the exchange rate of the dollar. When the value of the dollar falls, as it does periodically, those states see their revenues increase, because American industrial production soars when the dollar falls. The cheaper dollar makes it easier to export American manufactured goods.

Federal Budget Cutbacks

In real dollars (that is, adjusted for inflation), federal aid to state and local governments peaked in the late 1970s. Given the severe pressures on the federal government to curb its budget deficits, there seems to be no likelihood in the immediate future of significant increases in federal aid to state and local governments.

Interstate Tax Competition

There is today an intense competition among states to maintain an attractive tax climate in order to attract high-income in-migrants and foster business expansion. Many state leaders fear their states will not attract new businesses, or even keep existing businesses, if their tax rates are too much higher than those of neighboring states. The bottom line is that states feel powerful pressures to make tax concessions to large corporations and major league athletic teams in order to keep them from moving out of state. Whether these efforts actually succeed in stimulating economic development is a question we will tackle in Chapter 17.

SUMMARY

1. The experience of Proposition 13 in California introduces some important questions about state and local finances. What services should state and local governments offer? On what sources of revenue should these governments rely? How should the tax burden be distributed? How can property tax relief best be implemented?
2. Since 1950, state and local government expenditures and employment rose much faster than the gross national product or federal government expenditures.
3. The major state government expenditures are for insurance trust benefits, higher education, welfare, highways, and aid to local government. The major local government expenditures are for education, health, welfare, and public safety.
4. State governments get over half their revenues from federal aid, sales taxes, and income taxes. Local governments get about 60 percent of their revenues from state and federal aid and from property taxes.

5. Six criteria for evaluating taxes are equity, yield and certainty, administrative convenience, economic effect, and appropriateness.
6. In deciding what kinds of entrepreneurial activities are proper for governments in capitalist societies, economists have presented the criteria of social goods, merit goods, and externalities.
7. In borrowing money, governments rely on general obligation bonds and revenue bonds.
8. Key problems for state and local finance during the 1990s are the special problem of property taxes and public schools, shifting the tax burden, tax reform, and the interplay between public fiscal policy and economic development.

KEY TERMS

Bracket creep The phenomenon of a person's being boosted into a higher income tax bracket by inflation.

Budget retrenchment The phenomenon of governments having to raise taxes and cut back expenditures in order to balance their budgets.

Capital expenditure Expenditure for buildings and other fixed equipment.

Categorical aid A grant-in-aid for a specific purpose. Also called *categorical grant*.

Circuit breaker A device that limits the amount of income that can be taken in property taxes.

Externalities Costs that are not borne directly by the buyers or sellers of a particular product, for example, air pollution produced by automobiles but whose cleanup costs are not included in the price of cars.

Fiscal disparities The situation in which neighboring governmental jurisdictions vary widely in their ability to raise revenue. One jurisdiction may have a substantial property tax base, whereas a neighboring one has a meager tax base.

General-obligation bond A government bond that is backed by the taxing authority of the issuing government.

Indexation The practice of adjusting income tax brackets to rise with the cost of living. Also refers to the practice of making benefit levels in certain programs adjustable for inflation.

Industrial Development Revenue Bond A revenue bond issued by a government to enable a particular company or a collection of companies to raise funds to develop a site by selling bonds with the tax and interest rate advantages of government bonds.

Merit goods Goods that society judges all citizens should have as a matter of right.

Progressive tax A tax that takes a higher percentage of the income of upper-income people than it does of lower-income people.

Property tax A tax levied on real estate.

Proposition 13 An initiative proposition in 1978 that cut California property taxes by 60 percent.

Regressive tax A tax that takes a higher percentage of the income of lower-income people than it does of upper-income people.

Revenue-anticipation note A short-term note a government uses to borrow money to make payments that will come due before a next revenue payment comes in. The note is payed off from the proceeds of the next revenue payment.

Revenue bond A public bond that is payed off from revenue earned by the facility that was built with the bond's proceeds.

Sales tax A tax levied on retail sales.

Severance tax A tax levied on natural resources extracted from the earth.

Social goods Goods whose benefits are nondivisible and nonexclusive. Their enjoyment by one person does not prevent their enjoyment by others.

Tax-anticipation note A short-term note a government uses to borrow money to make payments that will come due before a next tax payment comes in. The note is paid off from the proceeds of the next tax payment.

Tax-base breadth The broadness or narrowness of the base on which a tax is levied.

Tax burden The total amount of taxes paid as a percentage of a person's income.

Tax or expenditure limitation (TEL) movement The movement of the late 1970s and early 1980s to put legal or constitutional limits on the amount of money a government can raise or the amount of money it can spend.

REFERENCES

1. From 1954 to 1978, expenditures for all states increased at an annual rate of 4.9 percent and local expenditures at an annual rate of 4.2 percent. Over the four-year period following the passage of Proposition 13 (1978–1982), state expenditures *declined* at an annual rate of 0.4 percent and local expenditures *declined* at an annual rate of 2.1 percent (figures adjusted for inflation and population changes). See John Shannon and Susannah E. Calkins, "Federal and State–Local Spending Go Their Separate Ways," Advisory Commission on Intergovernmental Relations, *Intergovernmental Perspective* 8, no. 4 (Winter 1983): 24.
2. See *The New York Times,* November 6, 1975, p. 1.
3. See Joan C. Baratz and Jay H. Moskowitz, "Proposition 13: How and Why It Happened," *Phi Delta Kappan* (September 1978).
4. In the two decades prior to Proposition 13, state taxes in California increased at an annual rate of 3.5 percent. In the three years following Proposition 13, the rate of increase dropped to .7 percent. Steven D. Gold, "State Tax Increases in 1983: Prelude to Another Tax Revolt," *National Tax Journal* 37 (March 1984): 14.
5. Terry Christensen and Larry N. Gerston, *The California Connection: Politics in the Golden State* (Boston: Little, Brown and Co., 1984), p. 217.
6. On the "something for nothing" concept, see Jack Citrin, "Do People Want Something for Nothing? Public Opinion on Taxes and Government Spending," *National Tax Journal* 32 (supplement) (1979): 113.
7. United States Bureau of the Census, *Statistical Abstract of the United States: 1994* (Washington, D.C.: 1994), p. 186.
8. Jerry Hagstrom and Neal R. Peirce, "The Quake Didn't Quit," *National Journal,* May 28, 1988, pp. 1413–1416.
9. See Robert Lindsey, "California Agencies Begin to Feel Tax Revolt," *The New York Times,* April 21, 1986, p. 11.
10. Edmund L. Andrews, "The Curse of California's Proposition 13," *The New York Times,* June 17, 1988, p. 27.
11. See *Time,* June 19, 1978, p. 16.
12. See *The New Republic,* June 3, 1978, p. 6.
13. *Money,* August 1994, p. 5.
14. Sherry Tvedt, "Enough Is Enough! Proposition 2½ in Massachusetts," *National Civic Review* 70, no. 10 (November 1981): 527–533.
15. United States Bureau of the Census, *Statistical Abstract of the United States: 1994* (Washington, D.C.: 1994), p. 487.
16. Advisory Commission on Intergovernmental Relations, *Significant Features of Fiscal Federalism: 1994, Vol. 2 Revenues and Expenditures* (Washington, D.C.: Advisory Commission on Intergovernmental Relations, 1994), M 190-II, p. 11.

17. James C. Garand tested five possible explanations for government growth in the fifty states. In thirty-eight of the fifty he found that the extent of government employment had a larger impact on government spending than the other four variables (party control, intergovernmental aid, reliance on corporate taxes and withholding taxes, and Wagner's law that traces government growth to industrialization). The second most important variable was the extent of intergovernmental aid. See Garand's "Explaining Government Growth in the U.S. States," *American Political Science Review* 82, no. 3 (September 1988): 837–849.

18. See Henry J. Aaron, *Who Pays the Property Tax? A New View* (Washington, D.C.: Brookings Institution, 1975); James A. Maxwell and J. Richard Aronson, *Financing State and Local Government,* 3rd ed. (Washington, D.C.: Brookings Institution, 1977).

19. Ronald K. Snell, "The Tax the Public Loves to Hate," *State Legislatures* 17, no. 12 (December 1991).

20. *Maryland* v. *Louisiana,* 451 U.S. 725 (1981).

21. *Commonwealth Edison* v. *Montana,* 453 U.S. 609 (1981).

22. These arguments are taken from Richard Musgrave, *Fiscal Systems* (New Haven, Conn.: Yale University Press, 1969), Ch. 1.

23. *Statistical Abstract of the United States: 1984,* p. 278; *1995,* p. 302.

24. Susan B. Hansen, "Extraction: The Politics of State Taxation," *Politics in the American States: A Comparative Analysis,* 4th ed., Virginia Gray, Herbert Jacob, and Kenneth N. Vines, eds. (Boston: Little, Brown and Co., 1983), p. 433.

25. On the consequences of federal grants, see David C. Nice, *Federalism: The Politics of Intergovernmental Relations* (New York: St. Martin's Press, 1987), pp. 57–60.

26. *Serrano* v. *Priest,* 5 Cal. 3d 584 (1971).

27. *Rodriguez* v. *San Antonio School District,* 411 U.S. 59 (1973). On the 1989 Texas Supreme Court ruling, see *The New York Times,* October 3, 1989, p. 1.

28. For background on this case, see Richard Lehne, *The Quest for Justice: The Politics of School Finance Reform* (New York: Longman, 1978) and Margaret E. Goertz, *Money and Education in New Jersey: The Hard Choices Ahead* (Princeton, N.J.: Education Policy Research Institute, Educational Testing Service, 1981), pp. 3, 31.

29. *The New York Times,* June 6, 1990, p. 1.

30. On Whitman see Neil Upmeyer, "The Time Bomb in Governor Whitman's Tax Cut," *The New York Times,* January 3, 1996, p. A-11.

31. William Celis III, "Michigan Votes for Revolution in Financing Its Public Schools," *The New York Times,* March 17, 1994, p. A-1; "Centralizing Educational Responsibility in Michigan and Other States," *National Tax Journal* (September 1995): 417–428.

32. Robert Kuttner, *Revolt of the Haves* (New York: Simon and Schuster, 1980).

33. David Lowery, "After the Tax Revolt: Some Positive If Unintended Consequences," *Social Science Quarterly* 67, no. 4 (December 1986): 736–766. Lowery made this discovery in comparing the mixtures of state and local revenue sources in 1976–1977 to those of 1981–1982.

34. Ronald K. Snell, "Our Outmoded Tax Systems," *State Legislatures* 20, no. 6 (August 1994): 17–22.

35. *Public Employee* 53, no. 4 (May–June 1988): 9; *Saint Paul Pioneer Press Dispatch,* April 10, 1988, p. 6-A; *State Legislatures* 14, no. 6 (July 1988): 21.

36. Steven D. Gold, "Tax Revenues Soar and Tumble," *State Legislatures* 15, no. 4 (May–June 1989): 30.

37. For empirical tests of fiscal illusion theory, see David Lowery, "Electoral Strength and Revenue Structures in the American States: Searching for the Elusive Fiscal Illusions," *American Politics Quarterly* 15, no. 1 (January 1987): 5–46; and Elaine B. Sharp

and David Elkins, "The Impact of Fiscal Limitations: A Tale of Seven Cities," *Public Administration Review* 47, no. 4 (September–October 1987): 385–392.

38. *Statistical Abstract of the United States: 1995*, p. 451.

39. For an assessment of the impact of falling oil prices on the Texas budget, see *The New York Times*, January 4, 1983, p. 9. On oil-producing states generally, see *The New York Times*, April 8, 1986, p. 1.

40. *Washington Post National Weekly*, September 7–13, 1992, p. 33.

41. See *Barron's*, January 23, 1989.

5

CHANNELS OF CITIZEN INFLUENCE: PARTICIPATION, PUBLIC OPINION, AND INTEREST GROUPS

Chapter Preview

If democracy is to have any meaning, there must be channels through which ordinary citizens can influence government policies. This chapter examines three of these channels. We shall discuss in turn:

1. The patterns of political participation and the attempts to increase participation of the poor and the racial minorities.

2. The influence of public opinion on government and public policy.

3. Interest groups—their types, tactics, and patterns of influence.

Let us begin with an incident that illustrates how important it is to one's well-being to understand how to use the channels of citizen influence.

◇ INTRODUCTION

In 1967 and 1968, the village of Weston, Illinois, and seventy-one surrounding farms were removed to make way for a large atom smasher in the form of an enormous underground ring two miles in diameter. The needed properties were donated to the Atomic Energy Commission (now called the Nuclear Regulatory Commission) by the state of Illinois, which used its power of eminent domain to buy the Westonites' houses. In purchasing the homes, state officials used pressure tactics that got most of the homeowners and farmers to sell their property to the state at a price far below what they could have received had they consulted one another, hired lawyers, maintained a united front, and confronted the state as an adversary.

According to a critical study of Weston, the residents of that town unwittingly helped bring about their own financial losses and the demise of their village by not being skeptical enough about the project when it was first proposed and by trusting political leaders who either let them down or proved incapable of defending their interests.[1] The residents also faced a hostile county board of commissioners that was unsympathetic to the village because it was perceived as an undesirable working- and lower-middle-class community in the middle of one of the nation's richest counties. The atom smasher would bring in upper-middle-class professionals and scientists as residents; the Westonites could move elsewhere.

Interestingly, at the same time that Weston was being considered as the site for the atom smasher, the nearby upper-income suburb of Barrington was also being considered as the site. Barrington residents effectively communicated with their political leaders that they did not want the atom smasher near Barrington, and they immediately organized such strong local opposition to the project that the Atomic Energy Commission quickly decided against placing the atom smasher near Barrington.

The tale of Weston and Barrington lays bare one of the starkest truths of American democracy: People who know how to participate in government and who have the means to do so are able to protect their self-interest. People who do not know how to do this or who lack the means find themselves at the mercy of persons who may not understand their circumstances and who often have little sympathy for them.

The outcome of Weston and Barrington also raises some important questions about the channels of political participation. Why did the channels work so well for the residents of Barrington and so poorly for Weston? We might ask the same question more generally. How do the channels of participation work, and who benefits from them? In order to deal with this question, this chapter will first explore the patterns of political participation and then examine two channels of citizen influence—public opinion and interest groups. The following chapter, Chapter 6, will examine three other channels of citizen influence—political parties, elections, and direct democracy.

◇ POLITICAL PARTICIPATION

Political participation is activity that seeks to influence the selection of government officials or actions that these officials take.[2] Political participants can be classified as gladiators and spectators, to use the terminology of Lester Milbrath.[3] **Spectators** compose the 50 to 60 percent of the population that votes regularly and displays political support through activities such as flying the flag and attending patriotic events. The **gladiators** do these things that spectators do, plus they invest time and money in political activity. Table 5-1 shows that the more demanding a political activity is the fewer the participants. About two-

Table 5-1 HIERARCHY OF POLITICAL PARTICIPATION

Spectator Activities Requiring Little Initiative	Percent Saying They Did That Activity
Member of one or more organizations	69.7
Voted in 1992	68.6
Ever contributed money to a group	63.2
Read a newspaper every day	49.6

Gladiator Activities Requiring Greater Initiative	
Ever worked with others to solve some local community problem	33.2
Ever contacted a local government official about a problem	32.7
Ever worked for a political party or candidate in an election	25.6
Ever contributed to a political candidate or a political cause	21.4
Attended a political meeting in the last three or four years	19.5
Ever contacted government officials on behalf of a group	18.1
Ever picketed in a labor strike	9.5
Ever took part in a civil rights demonstration	4.3

Source: James Allan Davis and Tom W. Smith, *General Social Surveys, 1972–1994* [machine-readable data file]. Principal investigator, James A. Davis; director and co-principal investigator, Tom W. Smith, NORC ed. Chicago: National Opinion Research Center, Producer, 1994; Storrs, Conn.: The Roper Center for Public Opinion Research, University of Connecticut, Distributor.

thirds of the people report having voted in the previous presidential election or contributing money to a group, but fewer than a fifth said that they ever contacted a government official or attended a political meeting in the previous three or four years. Furthermore, fewer people vote, join groups, or otherwise engage in politically related activities today than in the recent past.

Given the importance of effective participation to a meaningful democracy, there are several questions we want to raise about these patterns to political participation. In what ways do the participators differ from the nonparticipators? Why do some people avoid participating in the public life of their communities? Why has participation declined over time? And do the patterns of participation make any difference to the success of America's state and community political systems?

Who Participates?

The standard measure of political participation is the percentage of eligible voters who turn out on election day. The most pronounced pattern to voter turnout is its systematic association with either upper-status people or people with

Table 5-2   THE SOCIOECONOMIC BASE TO PARTICIPATION

	Percentage of Eligible Voters Who Voted in the 1992 Presidential Election
Income	
Poorest third	57%
Middle third	68
Richest third	79
By education	
Did not complete high school	50
Completed twelve years of school	67
Some college or more	82
By race	
Black	67
White	70
By organizational membership	
No memberships	44
One or two memberships	73
Three or more memberships	80
By church attendance	
Infrequent	63
Frequent (at least two or three times per month)	77
By Democratic or Republican party attachment	
Independent, or weak attachment	56
Strong, or moderate attachment	76
All eligible voters	64

Source: James Allen Davis; *General Social Surveys, 1972–1994* [machine-readable data file]. Principal investigator, James A. Davis; director and co-principal investigator, Tom W. Smith. NORC ed. (Chicago: National Opinion Research Center, producer, 1994; Storrs, Conn.: Roper Public Opinion Research Center, University of Connecticut, distributor.)

strong organizational ties. In all the social categories shown in Table 5-2, voter turnout is higher among the upper socioeconomic levels than among the lower socioeconomic levels. This difference is even more pronounced among the gladiators. The gladiator positions shown in Table 5-1 are held overwhelmingly by people with college degrees; and research on elective officeholders consistently shows that elected officials tend to be slightly above the average socioeconomic level of their constituents.

At the bottom of Milbrath's hierarchy of participation are what he calls the *apathetics,* those people who rarely vote or engage in the other forms of conventional participation. However, a much less biased term for them would be *nonparticipants*, since many nonvoters regularly engage in a variety of activities that either support the political system or place demands on it. They work, obey laws, pay taxes, use public services, collect benefits from government programs, raise families, send their children to school, serve in the armed forces, support the national economy through their purchases, and do a variety of other things that are politically relevant. They are apathetic only in the sense that they do not engage in the very narrow range of conventional gladiator and spectator political activities. And there are many reasons why they abstain.

Why Do Some People Not Participate?

Table 5-2 shows that the nonparticipants tend to be heavily concentrated among poor people, those who do not belong to organizations, and those with little education. Raymond Wolfinger and Steven Rosenstone sorted out the relative association of various socioeconomic variables with nonvoting and concluded that education was the most important of these variables.[4] Thus, poor people vote less often than middle-class people not because they are poor but because they have much less education. Less-educated people are more likely than middle-class people to lack the confidence and the communications skills needed to engage in community organizing, campaign work, and lobbying. They are less knowledgeable about political issues and candidates than college-educated people are, and they are less likely to have internalized a **sense of civic duty,** the belief that they have a community obligation to vote and take part in community affairs.[5]

One form of political participation is not explained very fully by socioeconomic status, however: the contacting of local or state officials about neighborhood problems. This is especially so in neighborhoods with serious needs. In such neighborhoods, people of low socioeconomic status are just as likely to bring their complaints to local officials as are people of higher status.[6]

For most forms of political activity, however, the poor and undereducated have the lowest participation rates, and this is one of the great paradoxes of American society. If poor people are most in need of governmental benefits and if political participation is a way of gaining those benefits, why then do the poor not participate more actively? Three explanations have been advanced: (1) individual psychological and skill barriers, (2) legal and political barriers, and (3) lack of organizations to mobilize them.

Psychological Factors Play a Part   Psychological and skill barriers prevent poor people's participation. As just indicated, the poor often lack the self-confidence that comes with education. They do not work in the highly verbal or analytical occupations that businesspeople, union organizers, lawyers, doctors, or other professionals do. Thus, persuasion tactics, organizing activities, and seeking cooperative solutions to common problems do not become second nature to the poor as they do to the more educated. If poor people attend a city council meeting and clash with an articulate lawyer, for instance, they are very likely to lose the argument and come away with bruised egos. Repeated experiences such as this reduce one's **sense of political efficacy,** a term used by political scientists to describe a person's belief that one's participation in politics can have some impact. Voting research has demonstrated that the lower a person's sense of political efficacy, the less likely that person is to vote.[7]

How the various psychological factors affect participation is rather complicated. Using voter turnout as a measure of participation, Arthur Hadley divided nonvoters into six different types,[8] five of which result from psychological factors. First, the largest group of nonvoters are the *positive apathetics*, about 35 percent of his sample of nonvoters. These people are contentedly involved in their jobs and family lives and perceive politics as irrelevant. Second, about 13 percent of the nonvoters are the *bypassed*, people who have such low levels of information that they do not bother to participate. A third category of nonvoters, about 6 percent, is composed of the *naysayers*, those who have philosophically rejected voting. Fourth are the *cross-pressured*, about 5 percent of the nonvoters. They choose not to vote so that they can escape the pressures of the forces pushing them to vote Democratic and the contrary pressures pushing them to vote Republican.

A fifth category of nonvoters (about 22 percent of Arthur Hadley's sample) is the *political impotent*, who has an extremely low sense of political efficacy. The political impotents do not think that they can influence political outcomes. Anthony Downs applies a form of cost–benefit analysis to explain this form of nonvoting.[9] With thousands of voters in a typical legislative race, for example, an individual's chance to affect the outcome is negligible. If a person thinks the material circumstances of his or her life will be the same no matter who wins, even the minimal cost of taking a few minutes to stop at the polling place may outweigh the apparently nonexistent benefits, especially if one has no sense of civic duty to nag the conscience.

Legal and Practical Factors Play a Part   The sixth category of nonvoter found by Hadley was the *physically disenfranchised.* Composing about 18 percent of nonvoters, these people are knowledgeable and have a relatively high sense of civic duty. Yet they either do not meet voter registration requirements or physical or health reasons keep them from going to the polls.

Historically, there were many legal barriers to voting. In colonial times, property requirements were common, but these have now been stripped away. Until the passage of the Nineteenth Amendment to the Constitution in 1920, most states denied women the right to vote. And until the ratification of the Twenty-Sixth Amendment in 1971, few states permitted eighteen-year-olds to vote.

The most enduring and pervasive voting discrimination was that against racial minorities prior to the passage of the Voting Rights Act of 1965. The historical experience of the racial minorities—especially blacks before 1965—best illustrates how legal impediments have been used to deny the vote to large minority groups.

Although the Fifteenth Amendment (1870) guaranteed racial minorities the right to vote, southern states applied a number of discriminatory devices that nullified the Fifteenth Amendment in practice. The *poll tax* reduced turnout among minorities and the poor because it had to be paid each election year, and it accumulated for every year it was not paid. In a short time, one could owe a considerable amount of money just to exercise the right to vote. The poll tax was finally prohibited by the Twenty-Fourth Amendment in 1964. Many states also required voters to pass *literacy tests* before being allowed to register, but these were usually conducted in a blatantly discriminatory fashion. In some instances, blacks with graduate degrees were failed on the test. In other instances, black applicants would be given obtuse passages of the state constitution to interpret. Some states, such as Oklahoma, had a *grandfather clause,* which exempted people from the literacy test if they had a grandfather who had voted in 1866. This obviously was designed to exempt whites but not blacks from the literacy test, and it was struck down by the Supreme Court in 1915. Other states, such as Texas, had *white primaries.* Blacks were allowed to vote in the general election but not in the primary election of the Democratic party. Because Texas was a one-party Democratic state, the Democratic primary really determined who got elected to office. The white primary was struck down by the Supreme Court in 1944.[10] When black voters became numerous enough to determine local elections, local communities often changed their boundaries or gerrymandered election districts to dilute the impact of black voters. The most flagrant case of this was Tuskegee, Alabama, which in the 1950s changed its boundaries from the shape of a square to a twenty-eight-sided polygon in order to dilute black voting in city elections. This practice was struck down by the Supreme Court in 1960.[11]

The key that finally enabled racial minorities to enter the electorate as full citizens was the **Voting Rights Act of 1965.** This law and its amendments of 1970, 1975, and 1982 set up provisions for eliminating the literacy test, placing federal registrars and poll watchers in counties with the worst records of voting discrimination, and requiring federal government approval before changes in the voting laws could take effect (see the "Highlight" on p. 99). The results of this act have been dramatic. Since 1965, the number of black voters and black officeholders has increased not only in the South but throughout the country. In 1969, only 1,185 black officials had been elected throughout the United States; by 1993, this number had increased sevenfold to 7,984.[12] As we will discuss in Chapter 9, the Voting Rights Act has become a major issue in drawing boundaries for state legislative districts and city councils.

Ironically, as the more recent legal barriers to voting were overcome, there was a decrease in the percentage of eligible voters who actually turned out and voted. This has led some critics to push for relaxing voter registration requirements and holding elections on Sundays instead of workdays. Wolfinger and Rosenstone estimate that voter turnout would increase by 9 percent if all states relaxed their registration laws to the level of the most lenient states.[13] In this spirit, Oregon instituted a mail-in election in 1995. The state mailed out ballots to all registered voters. If this practice catches fire, you will not even have to go to the polls anymore. Just return the ballot through the mail. In 1993, Congress passed the Motor Voter Bill, which requires each state to register people to vote when they apply for their driver's licenses. Two states (Minnesota and

There's an old saying that "You can't fight city hall." In fact, as this cartoon suggests, sometimes you can. And sometimes you win.

Source: Drawing by Levin; copyright © 1980, The *New Yorker* Magazine, Inc.

Wyoming) allow voters to register at the polling places on election day, whereas one state (North Dakota) has no registration requirement at all. Not surprisingly, these four states (Oregon, Minnesota, Wyoming, and North Dakota) were among the top seven in voter turnout in the 1994 elections.[14]

Mobilizing Organizations Play a Part   A third factor reducing political participation, especially among the poor, is the lack of organizations to mobilize them. Among working-class people, labor unions, for example, make strenuous efforts to mobilize their members to participate.

The importance of union-organizing activities was seen in a study comparing West Virginia counties with neighboring Virginia counties of a similar economic character. The West Virginians voted much more regularly than the Virginians. The reason for this was that unions had organized the West Virginia coal

HIGHLIGHT

The Voting Rights Act

1. *A Triggering Formula*
   The provisions of the act would apply to any state, county, or municipality that had (a) used a literacy test for voter registration in 1964 and (b) experienced less than a 50 percent turnout in the 1964 presidential election. This was called the triggering formula.

2. *Voting Examiners*
   The Department of Justice was authorized to use federal voting examiners to register people in any jurisdiction identified by the triggering formula.

3. *Literacy Tests*
   The Justice Department was authorized to suspend literacy tests in any jurisdiction identified by the triggering formula.

4. *Preclearance Requirement*
   Voting laws, municipal boundaries, and election districts could not be changed in any community identified by the triggering formula unless the change was cleared in advance by the Justice Department or a three-judge district court panel in Washington, D.C. The object of this provision is to prevent dilution of the minority vote by gerrymandering election districts or by annexing substantial white subdivisions.

5. *Enforcement Machinery*
   The act gave the Attorney General considerable authority to prosecute violations and stipulated fines and imprisonment for convictions.

---

miners in the early twentieth century and those miners had developed the habit of participation. In Virginia, in contrast, politics were dominated by an extremely conservative political organization called the Byrd Machine, which discouraged participation because it thrived on lower voter turnouts.[15]

The key role that an organization can play in mobilizing people to participate in politics is seen in New York City's public employee union, District Council 37, a 110,000-member affiliate of the American Federation of State, County and Municipal Employees (AFSCME—pronounced Aff-smee).[16] Because the leaders of Council 37 understood that they needed an activist membership in order to enhance the union's influence, the union energetically promoted both gladiator and spectator activities. To produce more gladiators, Council 37 organized election campaign classes and lobbying classes that trained union members how to engage effectively in local politics. As a result, the union generated a core of 150–200 activists, many of whom could be counted on regularly to run telephone banks, organize campaign contributions, conduct political meetings, and find people to do precinct work on behalf of union-endorsed candidates. The union also organized special women's programs and encouraged the involvement of union members in neighborhood groups that would tackle community problems such as education, crime, employment, and housing. At the spectator level, the union's efforts resulted in an extraordinary 85 percent of its membership registered to vote (compared to about 68 percent for the general population) and two-thirds of the members voting often or fairly often in local primary elections. These extraordinary levels of participation are even more astounding because many of the union's members are poorly paid and poorly educated health-care workers, who, as Table 5-2 shows, typically do not vote. The bottom line of these participatory efforts was not only to give the union leaders more influence in city politics but to give rank-and-file members influence upon the union leaders and on city politics as well.

What makes District Council 37 stand out is that its high level of membership participation is so extraordinary. As we will see shortly, the last fifty years have seen a decline in the types of intermediary associations, such as unions and other groups, that stimulate citizen activity. Not only do many groups stimulate activity, but from a very early age, they help their members develop participatory skills that stick with them as adults.[17]

Why Does Participation Matter?

Participation matters because peoples' declining willingness to invest time and energy in public affairs weakens the ability of states and communities to deal effectively with their public problems. Nowhere is this seen more starkly than in the slow deterioration of our once great, thriving, metropolitan centers—from Boston in the Northeast to Los Angeles in the Southwest.

On the face of it, this statement might seem absurd because most of our metropolitan centers teem with advocacy groups, and there seems to be no shortage of group leaders screaming into television cameras about some outrage they are committed to correcting. But consider the following perspectives offered by three perceptive observers of the political scene.

The Propensity for Exit, Not Voice   As we will see in Chapters 7 and 8, many of our metropolitan centers are plagued with drugs, crime, unemployment, spreading poverty, and erosion of public services such as schools, public safety, and public recreation. People who become dissatisfied with these developments have two basic options, according to Albert O. Hirschman,[18]—exit or voice. Voice is the option of fighting to protect the stability of one's neighborhood. This is a political option that requires people to work together—even when they disagree with one another—to solve their common problems. Exit is the option of looking elsewhere for one's services. If you are very affluent, you can afford to substitute private services for deteriorating public services. Send your children to private schools; join the YMCA or some private recreational club; hire private security forces to protect your block or your street. Obviously, only the very affluent can afford to do all these things. However, even middle-class people can exit from the city's problems by moving to a safer, more pleasant environment in the suburbs. As increasing numbers of people exercise the exit option, central city neighborhoods lose an important category of people who have the financial resources and personal skills to help protect the safety and integrity of the neighborhood.

Bowling Alone and the Decline of Social Capital   Compounding the consequences of the exit strategy is a long-term decline in what Robert Putnam calls "social capital," the "networks, norms, and trust—that enable participants to act together more effectively to pursue shared objectives."[19] Over the last three decades, there have been membership declines of 25 to 50 percent in community groups as diverse as PTAs, Elk clubs, unions, and even bowling leagues. Although the number of bowlers has gone up, participation in bowling leagues has gone down, hence Putnam's provocative phrase, "bowling alone." As fewer people engage in the public lives of their communities, these communities see their social capital decline. Fewer people belonging to fewer community groups means that fewer people step forward to confront community problems, and fewer groups serve as intermediaries between government and individual people. As more and more people absorb themselves in their private pursuits, fewer people tend to the public sphere.

Professionalizing Politics   Finally, as large numbers of people exit the problems of the central city and large numbers of people disengage from community life generally, public affairs get increasingly handled by professionals. Traditional American politics by part-time amateurs has given way to public problem-solving by experts, leaving most people functioning primarily as clients outside the problem-solving process. These clients sometimes donate checks to large interest groups whom they favor, but few clients have any face-to-face involvement with other people in resolving public problems. The result, according to Harry Boyte, is a population that has been socialized to make moralistic judgments about politics as sleazy, immoral, and corrupt. In reality, successful politics requires different interests to compromise with each other in order to achieve common goals. But compromise is a dirty word in the minds of people brought up to disengage from politics and to view politics essentially in personal and moralistic terms.[20] In this sense, declining participation contributes to the emergence of a political system where it becomes increasingly difficult to solve problems through compromise.

It would be unrealistic to expect too much in the way of political participation from average people. After all, most of us have our hands full simply raising our families and building our careers, and there is not a whole lot of time left over to become gladiators on very many fronts. But the growing number of people who *never* act as gladiators and seldom engage in spectator activities raises disturbing issues about the quality of democracy in most of the nation's communities. A community can tolerate some people following the exit option and still thrive. However, if everybody follows the exit option, the community will wither. Our communities can survive a period where more people bowl alone, to use Putnam's phrase, but if *nobody* joins a league or a Lion's club or a labor union or a PTA, then the community does indeed lose social capital and that will hinder its abilities to confront its problems. Finally, in the complicated world that we inhabit, some professionalization of politics is inevitable. But democracy cannot survive if *everybody* leaves decision making to the professionals. In short, some level of gladiator activity by ordinary people is essential if our states and communities are to have a meaningful democracy. And the declining participation of people in these activities over the past generation poses disturbing questions.

What Are the Channels of Participation?

Much of the rest of this chapter and the next is devoted to exploring the various ways in which people participate in the political process. Political scientists identify *linkages* between the individual citizen and the governing officials. These linkages can be thought of as channels through which individuals have input into the governing process. The major channels to be examined in these two chapters are (1) public opinion, (2) interest groups, (3) political parties, (4) elections, and (5) direct democracy. For any of these channels to serve as effective means of allowing citizens to influence government policy, two conditions must prevail. The channels themselves must effectively influence government policy, and the channels must be responsive to citizen demands.

◇ PUBLIC OPINION

Public opinion refers to peoples' views on politically relevant issues.[21] If democracy has any meaning at all, there must be some correlation between public opinion and government policy. By this criterion, how democratic are the American states?

Fifteen years ago, the preponderant research would have concluded, not very! Most research until that time had concluded that a state's per-capita income and its level of economic development had a bigger impact on the kind of policies it adopted than did any political factors, including public opinion.[22] Recent research, however, has found that public opinion has a much greater impact on public policy than previously thought. Researchers have found a consistency between preferences expressed in public opinion polls and public policies on about two-thirds of all public opinion preferences. They have also identified many instances (but not all) in which public opinion directly influences policy outcomes.[23] One team of researchers used *New York Times*/CBS telephone surveys from 1976 to 1982 to rank each state on an index of political ideology (see Figure 5-1). When this index was correlated with eight different policy outcomes (such as welfare expenditures, consumer policies, legalized gambling policy, and

---

One of the strongest variables affecting the overall direction of policies in a state is the degree of conservatism or liberalism of the population. This graph ranks the states and the District of Columbia according to an index of political ideology, ranging from the District of Columbia at the most liberal and Idaho at the most conservative. Each state's ranking is calculated from the percentage of that state's respondents who identified themselves as liberal, moderate, or conservative in a series of surveys conducted by *The New York Times*/CBS Poll between 1976 and 1982. Note that the most liberal states are concentrated in the Northeast and along the southern Pacific coast, whereas the conservative and most conservative states are found in and around the Old Confederacy.

Source: Adapted from Gerald C. Wright, Jr., Robert S. Erikson, and John P. McIver, "Measuring State Partisanship and Ideology with Survey Data," *Journal of Politics* 47, no. 2 (May 1985): 469–489. By permission of the authors and the University of Texas Press.

Figure 5-1 STATE IDEOLOGY INDEX

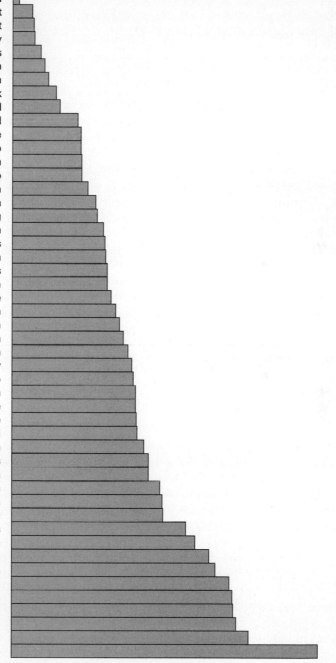

Extent of conservatism

tax progressivity), the researchers found that public opinion had a greater impact on public policy than did economic variables such as per-capita income or level of education. In short, states with the most liberal populations also have the most liberal policies, and states with the most conservative populations have the most conservative policies.[24]

Does Public Opinion Influence Policy?

In Theory   Basically, three theoretical models describe how public opinion can influence public policy.[25] The first model is the *rational activist* model,[26] which holds that people choose their legislators rationally on the basis of their issue positions. However, there is very little evidence in support of the rational activist model since voters seldom know the candidates' stands on a range of issues.[27] A second model is the *role-playing* model, in which the legislators play the delegate role of finding out what their constituents want before voting on critical issues.[28] Although some evidence exists that local leaders can accurately predict public opinion on specific issues,[29] there is very little evidence that this knowledge affects the decisions of these local officials.[30] The third model is a *sharing or consensus* model. In this view, the legislators share the same values that their constituents hold. When the legislators cast their votes, they automatically bring the values of their constituents to bear on the policy questions before the legislature. Legislators' policy decisions reflect popular opinion not because they fear voter retaliation but because they share that opinion.[31]

In Practice   Given these theoretical models, is there any evidence showing how, in practice, public opinion affects policy? Four important generalizations can be made. First, the policies adopted by a state appear to be influenced to some extent by how liberal or how conservative a state's population is. Figure 5-1 graphs the extent of conservatism of each state's population as expressed in public opinion surveys. Studies correlating state policy outcomes with this index tend to find a strong relationship.[32] For example, states at the conservative end of this index (Idaho, North Dakota, Mississippi, and Oklahoma) are not usually the standard bearers for liberal policies on abortion, welfare spending, or civil rights. Conversely, the four states at the liberal end of the spectrum (Vermont, Connecticut, New Jersey, and Massachusetts) do tend to have more liberal policies in these issue areas. The correlations are far from perfect, but a pattern exists. What people think makes a difference on public policies that get adopted.

A second link between public opinion and public policy is that public opinion has its strongest impact on issues that are highly visible and emotional. This can be seen most clearly in the history of the civil rights movement. A study of the relationship between the voting of congresspersons and the attitudes of their constituents during the 1950s found civil rights to be an issue on which congressional voting most strongly reflected constituents' opinions.[33] An attempt to correlate public opinion in the states with policy outputs found the strongest corr lations in the area of prohibiting racial discrimination in public accommodations.[34] Where public opinion was strongly against this, it was difficult to enact.

A third generalization concerns the **intensity problem.** When an issue is visible and emotional, public opinion is often sharply divided. Some constituents feel more intensely about the issue than do others. On gun control, for example, an individual legislator may find that two-thirds of the constituents favor stricter controls but are not excited about it. The other one-third may oppose tighter controls vociferously and may agitate for the defeat of legislators who support those controls. Since the minority feels much more intensely about its position than does the majority, the legislator will lose votes by going along with the majority public opinion. Anne Hopkins found that gun permit legislation typically was not passed until more than 70 percent of people supported it.[35]

A fourth generalization is that some parts of the public have more influence on public policy than do others. Legislators identify **attentive constituents** in their districts[36] who are politically aware, especially those who hold office at the local level. The legislators not only respect the opinion of these constituents but actively seek their advice. These attentive constituents have more effect on public policy than does the public at large.

Finally, it is important to keep in mind that finding a correlation between public opinion and public policy, does not always tell us which caused which. Comparing 1930s survey data with later public policy changes, Robert Erikson studied public opinion on capital punishment and argued that public opinion preceded the public policy. That is, states with the strongest antideath-penalty feelings in the 1930s were the first states to abandon capital punishment in later decades.[37] However, examples can also be found where the policy shapes opinion. Scholars have noted, for example, that public opinion on foreign policy tends to change in response to the government's policies.[38]

In summary, public opinion's influence on public policy cannot be ignored. It is difficult for legislators to enact policies that violate deeply held values of a substantial majority of the population. Public values help establish the overall boundaries within which policymakers have much discretion but outside of which they cannot act decisively. On the day-to-day operations of government that are less visible and less emotional than civil rights or gun control, policymakers find themselves responding more to other channels of influence than to public opinion.

◇ INTEREST GROUPS

A second conventional channel of citizen influence is the political **interest group,** any organization that tries to influence government decisions. Interest groups are sometimes confused with political parties, but the two differ in several respects. Interest groups do not run candidates for office. It is true that candidates are *endorsed* by interest groups, such as labor unions, gun clubs, environmental groups, and business associations, but the candidates are *not nominated* by interest groups. They are nominated by political parties (in partisan elections), and they appear on the ballot with their party designation. Interest groups also do not organize the government once the election is over. Parties do. The legislature (except for Nebraska's) is formally divided between the Republican and Democratic parties, not a series of interest groups. Finally, whereas parties represent geographic entities, interest groups usually represent functional entities.

Kinds of Interest Groups

There are many different interest groups. Traditionally, the five interest groups that dominated state politics were business, labor, education, farmers, and local government groups.[39] But this dominance has been challenged by a dramatic expansion of interest groups over the past two decades. The explosion in interest group activity can be seen in the fact that the number of organizations registered to lobby before state legislatures increased from an average of 195 per state in 1975 to more than 600 per state in 1990.[40] Table 5-3, relying on a recent, exhaustive study of interest groups in the fifty states, lists the fifteen groups most frequently listed as influential in state politics. This table shows four broad categories of groups: economically motivated groups (business and labor), professional groups, public agency groups, and ideological groups.

Economically Motivated Groups   First, and most influential on state policy-making, are the economically motivated groups, groups that have a direct economic interest in government policy. Government policies will either cost or save their members' money. Business and labor are the most obvious examples. Table 5-3 shows that of the groups that were consistently ranked as among the most effective in influencing state politics, most were economically motivated business or labor groups.

Business groups tend to focus on state taxation and spending policies. They seek to minimize business taxes and to channel government spending into areas that will benefit the business community. The business groups identified as most influential were general business groups, such as chambers of commerce, and organizations representing specific industries such as bankers, manufacturers, utilities, and farmers.

Labor organizations are also economically motivated. Their main purpose is to improve the working conditions and economic status of their members. But unions also have fought for social welfare policies generally that have served a broad cross section of people regardless of whether they are union members. Indeed, organized labor has stood out in twentieth-century American history as the single most effective force behind the promotion of programs ranging from Social Security and unemployment compensation to Medicare and Medicaid. And the tens of millions of people who draw benefits from these programs owe their benefits in no small measure to the past effectiveness of the labor movement.

In contrast to its influential past, organized labor is unlikely to operate with comparable effectiveness in future years. During the 1980s, unions came under their sharpest attack in fifty years. The decline of the manufacturing sector of the American economy saw corresponding declines in the membership of industrial

Table 5-3   MOST INFLUENTIAL INTEREST GROUPS IN THE STATES

Interest Represented	Category of Group	Number of States in Which Group Ranks at Highest Level of Effectiveness
School teachers	Labor	43
General business organizations (chambers of commerce, etc.)	Business	37
Bankers associations	Business	21
General farm organizations (mainly state farm bureaus)	Business	14
Traditional labor organizations (mostly the AFL-CIO)	Labor	22
Utility companies and associations (electric, gas, telephone)	Business	23
Manufacturers	Business	20
Lawyers	Professional	26
General local government organizations (municipal leagues, county organizations, etc.)	Public agency groups	16
Doctors	Professional	22
Individual banks and financial institutions	Business	14
State employees	Labor	18
Insurance trade associations	Business	21
Realtors	Business	17
Health care groups other than doctors	Business	15

Source: Adapted from Clive S. Thomas and Ronald J. Hrebenar, "Interest Groups in the States," *Politics in the American States: A Comparative Analysis,* 6th ed. Virginia Gray, Herbert Jacob, eds. (Washington, D.C.: CQ Press, 1996), p. 149. Used by permission of the CQ Press.

unions such as the United Auto Workers (UAW) and the United Steel Workers (USW)[41] (although *total* union membership has remained stable). These problems were compounded by the hostile Reagan and Bush administrations, which appointed antiunion people to head agencies that are very important to organized labor, such as the National Labor Relations Board (NLRB), which oversees collective bargaining elections and adjudicates worker–employer disputes. Under its antiunion leadership in the 1980s, the NLRB followed a practice of delaying and hindering collective bargaining elections and tilting toward management when adjudicating fair labor practice grievances.[42] But the strongest obstacle facing workers has been the renewed hard line that corporations have taken recently in dealing with unions. Often refusing to negotiate with unions, employing union-busting consulting firms to stymie union organizing activities, and engaging in unfair labor practices such as firing union organizers, corporations have placed severe roadblocks in the way of successful unionization in the past decade.[43]

As traditional labor unions in the private sector have lost influence over the past generation, government employee unions have gained influence. When legislators and knowledgeable observers in states are asked to identify the most powerful interest groups in their states, time and again they cite public employee unions, especially teachers' associations and state employee associations. The most important of these associations are the NEA (National Education Association), the AFT (American Federation of Teachers), and AFSCME (American Federation of State, County, and Municipal Employees). The fifty-state interest group study found that teachers' organizations rank as the most effective interest groups in forty-three of the fifty states.[44]

Professionally Motivated Groups The second most influential category of interest group is the *professionally motivated group*, whose primary purpose is to provide services to its members. The state medical association, for example, might distribute medical journals to members, or it might sponsor conferences on important medical issues. Although the primary purpose of these groups is to further the professional concerns of their members, the groups do not hesitate to press for economic advantages as well. Thus doctors' groups are very vocal on issues such as state policy toward health maintenance organizations, and trial lawyers are very vocal on issues such as automobile insurance, an area from which many trial lawyers derive a fair amount of income. The fifty-state study found that doctors' and lawyers' groups were the professional groups ranked as the most influential in the states.

Public Agency Groups A third category of interest groups is the public agency group, an organization of public agencies. The seven most prominent are the Council of State Governments, the United States Conference of Mayors, the National Governors' Association, the National Conference of State Legislatures, the National Association of County Officials, the National League of Cities, and the International City Management Association. These groups provide opportunities for public officials to exchange ideas, to lobby collectively at the regional and national levels, and to get up-to-date information about the latest developments and concepts that affect their own public agency.

Ideological Groups A final category of interest group is the ideological group, such as the Sierra Club, the Audubon Society, Common Cause, and similar organizations that claim to represent a public interest not represented by the economic or professionally motivated interest groups. Because they claim to represent the public interest ideological groups are frequently called **Public Interest groups.** The Sierra Club, for example, is an aggressive group devoted to conserving the environment. Unlike a labor union or a medical association, the ideological group offers its members no direct economic or professional benefits; rather, members are attracted by an ideological concern—protecting the environment, in the case of the Sierra Club. The most relevant ideological groups for college students are the Public Interest Research Groups (PIRGs), established on college campuses by Ralph Nader in the 1970s. Many PIRGs are supported by student fees collected by the colleges and passed on directly to the local or state PIRG. The PIRG then uses the funds to hire students to research social issues, prepare position papers, and lobby for these issues before the state legislatures and other public agencies. The PIRGs usually lobby for liberal and environmental causes.

Finally, some groups overlap into more than one category. Racial minority groups, women's groups, and gay rights groups are examples. To the extent that they promote civil rights and civil liberties for all citizens, they function as ideological groups. To the extent that they promote policies aimed at the economic advancement of their own members, however, they function as economically motivated groups.

Interest Group Political Tactics

The most common political tactics of interest groups are *public relations, electioneering,* and *lobbying.* **Public relations** probably absorbs more time than any other interest group activity. The objective normally is to create a favorable climate within which the interest group can operate. Public electric companies, for example, frequently run public relations campaigns designed to counter the attacks of environmentalists who charge the utilities with polluting the atmosphere with their power plants.

Electioneering is the tactic of trying to elect legislators who are sympathetic to your point of view. Thus, farmers' groups are partial to rural-based candidates for office, business groups lean toward conservative candidates, labor unions favor economic liberals, and teachers' associations unite behind candidates who support public employee collective bargaining and more expenditures for public schools.

Whereas business groups tend to make the most effective use of public relations tactics, labor unions and teachers' associations are probably most skilled at electioneering, especially in the Northeast and Midwest and on the West Coast, where union membership is very large. Unions endorse candidates, collect campaign contributions from their members, and donate these contributions to the endorsed candidates. Their most effective electioneering asset, however, lies in their large and active memberships. Teachers, in particular, are accustomed to persuading people and to organizing their activities. Thus, they have many skills that are useful in an election campaign. Additionally, they perceive a direct benefit to themselves from electing candidates who favor collective bargaining and greater expenditures for public schools. As a consequence, they contribute a disproportionate number of people to deliver campaign literature, make telephone calls, organize coffee parties, set up fund-raising parties, and plan campaign strategies.

As a counter to union electioneering, business corporations and independent professionals such as doctors and lawyers are increasingly relying on the **political action committee (PAC)** to influence the electoral process. A PAC collects money to use as a campaign contribution in an effort to get friendly people elected to public office. Many states prohibit unions or corporations from directly contributing money to campaigns. But unions or corporations can legally set up a PAC that will collect money from potential contributors. In this way, the PAC can effectively give the union or corporation political influence without violating the law. An estimated 12,000 PACs are active in the states.[45]

Individual contributions to PACs tend to be quite small, averaging about $14 to union PACs and $160 to business PACs.[46] But when these sums are multiplied by tens of thousands of contributors, they give PACs enormous clout in campaign finance. PAC contributions as a percentage of all campaign fund-raising has grown steadily since the mid-1970s, when federal legislation stimulated the growth of PACs. A study of PAC contributions in four states with reliable data found considerable variation in candidate's dependence on PAC money. Legislative candidates in Colorado and Minnesota relied on PACs for only about one-fourth of their campaign funds, but PACs provided more than 50 percent of campaign funds to legislative candidates in Missouri and Washington.[47] As is true of congressional campaign contributions, most PAC money for state legislative races goes to incumbent legislators and to legislative leaders. PAC leaders look on their contributions as ensuring their access to the lawmakers.

As the role of PACs in elections has grown, political reform groups such as Common Cause have pushed the states to limit the amount of money a PAC may contribute to a campaign. Today, most states have adopted some limit on PACs,[48] but few observers expect the influence of PACs to decline. Nor, in the view of some observers, *should* PACs be prohibited from making campaign contributions. The nation's foremost observer of campaign contributions has argued vigorously that PACs dramatically expand the number of people contributing to the campaigns and perform a number of other positive roles in the democratic process.[49]

Lobbying is the tactic of trying to influence the legislature or some other governmental body. Lobbying is done directly by interest groups, by individuals, and by professional lobbyists who make a career of representing the interests of various groups before the legislature. This year it may be the electrical contractors' association seeking to prevent a change in the state's building codes; next year it may be the savings and loan association trying to fend off a challenge from commercial banks. Such lobbying is often defensive in nature, seeking to prevent new legislation that might undo some existing privilege or right.

The fifty-state interest group study identified five types of lobbyists.[50] First are the *contract lobbyists;* these are people who are paid a fee by one or many clients to look after those clients' interests before the legislature and state regulatory bodies. Extremely effective contract lobbyists can command fees of $100,000 or more, but the vast majority earn far less than that. Instead of paying for a contract lobbyist, many larger organizations (such as the state education association) prefer to have their own *in-house lobbyists.* These are regular employees of the organization who carry titles such as government relations officer and spend most of their work time on lobbying and governmental relations activities. Third are the *government legislative liaisons.* Like the in-house lobbyists, they are regular employees of a government organization and spend their work day furthering the interests of their organization before the legislature and other governmental bodies. Also, like the in-house lobbyists, they call themselves by titles such as legislative liaison officer rather than lobbyist. A fourth type of lobbyist is the *citizen or cause lobbyist*. They are often volunteers or highly committed representatives of environmental organizations, organizations for the handicapped, or other cause groups. Finally, a small number of *hobbyist lobbyists* exist. These are individual citizens who stalk the legislative corridors pushing for some pet project or policy proposal.

Lobbyists have the reputation of wheeler-dealers who get what they want by wining and dining legislators and making under-the-table payoffs of one sort or another. Unfortunately, this type of activity was widespread at one time. Lobbyists in the early history of Wyoming, for example, set up card tables outside the legislative chambers where they paid off legislators for voting properly.[51]

Today, by contrast, lobbying has become highly sophisticated. The most important resource of the professional lobbyist today is information about issues before the legislature. Effective lobbying firms often supplement the presentation of information to legislative committees with elaborate media campaigns to build up public opinion for the lobbyist's position and also with detailed grass roots campaigns aimed at putting pressure on legislators from constituents in their own districts. National public relations firms have emerged to help corporations react to legislative developments in each state. Proctor & Gamble, for example, contracts with a public relations firm to track key phrases in bills that are introduced in legislatures each year. This enables the company to review 3,000 bills each year in the various states. Of these, the company instructs its local lobbyists to take a position on two or three hundred.[52] The goal of tracking the process of bills through legislatures is often defensive in nature. The lobbying group wants to protect some favorable piece of law from being altered. AFL-CIO lobbyists in Oregon, for example, once got a legislative committee to delete from a civil rights bill a phrase that would have prohibited denying anyone a job because of membership or nonmembership in any organization. The quick-witted lobbyists realized that this wording would have outlawed Oregon's union shop.[53]

Lobbyists also seek to link their highly sophisticated information presentations with local grass roots support. The California Association of Realtors, for example, maintains a "legislative tree" that lists any personal, professional, or social connections that individual realtors in the state may have with specific legislators.[54] In this way, the Association is not limited to making a formal presentation to a legislative committee. It can enlist the support of an individual realtor who has some personal link to a key legislator.

The professionalization of lobbying does not mean that money has lost its importance. But the money is more likely to come in the form of a campaign contribution of some sort than it is in the form of an implicit bribe. Campaigning for state office is becoming increasingly expensive, and political action comittees, as we saw earlier, are assuming a growing role in campaign finance. Just how much difference a campaign contribution makes on a legislator's vote is very difficult to calculate. Many lobbyists feel that it does make a difference, so they arrange for contributions to legislators whom they think will be important to them. One long-time lobbyist in California was quoted:

> If everything else is equal and your opposition has a significant advantage in contributions, you are going to lose. It has to be equal on the merits, but I've seen votes change because of money.[55]

Finally, despite the widespread belief that PAC contributions corrupt the legislators who accept them, most of the evidence for this belief is sporadic and anecdotal. Some campaign contributions certainly are little more than vote-buying exercises. But most scholarly studies seeking to tie campaign contributions to legislative voting patterns have failed to find any systematic link.[56]

Do Interest Groups Affect Public Policy?

How much influence interest groups have on public policy is difficult to determine. We can approach the problem, however, by asking: (1) What resources can interest groups bring to bear on influencing public policy? (2) In which states are

Of course daddy loves us, why do you ask?

Source: Jerry Fearing, *St. Paul Dispatch*, April 27, 1971.

interest groups the strongest? and (3) How effective have states been in regulating the influence of lobbying groups?

The Resources for Interest Group Influence   Some groups have more of the resources leading to strength than others. Three of the most important resources are size of membership, quality of the leadership, and status.

Size of the membership can be a source of interest group strength. Cities and states with large labor union memberships, for example, usually have public policies that are pro-union.[57] The size of groups is important because their members are a source of campaign contributions, campaign workers, and potential lobbyists during the legislative session.

Although large memberships can be an asset for group influence, they can also weaken its influence if the group's policy positions become too broad or vague. Chambers of commerce, for example, seek to represent the business community in general and thus must avoid certain specific issues that might alienate significant businesses. In contrast, a trade association such as a Savings and Loan Association League can target its efforts to issues that concern its members. Some scholars argue that the large membership groups tend to win symbolic benefits for their members, whereas the small membership groups tend to win tangible benefits.[58]

The leadership and cohesion of an interest group is also an important power resource. The AFL-CIO is powerful in the Northeast and Midwest not only because of its size but also because it enjoys capable leadership. Some observers argue that group leadership over the long term tends to gravitate into the hands of a small circle of staff and self-perpetuating leaders. Roberto Michels called this the **iron law of oligarchy**.[59] Groups have a tendency to become less democratic and more oligarchic over time.

Finally, the status of a group also affects its level of influence. In a Republican-dominated state, business groups are likely to have more status than labor unions and to get a better reception among legislators. In a Democratic-controlled legislature of the Northeast or Midwest, however, the reverse may often be true.

State Differences in Interest Group Strength   In addition to a group's resources and tactics, interest group influence is determined by the overall political and economic environments of the states. Table 5-4 lists the states along a range from those dominated by interest groups to those in which interest groups are subordinated to other political institutions such as the governor, the legislature, the political parties, and the bureaucracy. In the interest-group-dominated states, policymaking is pretty much dominated by the interest groups. At the other extreme, where no states are found, interest group influence on policy would be subordinated to the other political institutions. In the middle of the range, the complementary states are those in which interest groups clearly have an important influence on public policy, but an influence that is shared more or less equally with the legislature, the governor, the bureaucracy, the political parties, and other institutions of the state's political system.

The pattern shown in Table 5-4 is not a random one. With a few exceptions (such as Florida), the states with dominant interest group systems tend to have

Table 5-4 COMPARATIVE INTEREST GROUP STRENGTH
IN THE STATES

Strong ← States Where the Overall Impact of Interest Groups Is: → Weak

Dominant (7)	Dominant/ Comple- mentary (20)	Comple- mentary (18)	Comple- mentary/ Subordinate (5)	Subordinate (0)
Alabama	Alaska	Colorado	Delaware	
Florida	Arizona	Connecticut	Minnesota	
Illinois	Arkansas	Indiana	Rhode Island	
Iowa	California	Iowa	South Dakota	
Kansas	Georgia	Maine	Vermont	
Kentucky	Hawaii	Maryland		
Louisiana	Idaho	Massachusetts		
Mississippi	Michigan			
Montana	Missouri			
Nebraska	New Jersey			
Nevada	New Hampshire			
New Mexico	New York			
Ohio	North Carolina			
Oklahoma	North Dakota			
Oregon	Pennsylvania			
South Carolina	Utah			
Tennessee	Washington			
Texas	Wisconsin			
West Virginia				
Wyoming				

Source: Adapted from Clive S. Thomas and Ronald J. Hrebenar, "Interest Groups in the States," *Politics in the American States: A Comparative Analysis,* 6th ed. Virginia Gray and Herbert Jacob, eds. (Washington, D.C.: CQ Press, 1996), p. 152. Used by permission of the CQ Press.

less complex economic systems than do the states with weak interest groups. That is, strong-interest-group states tend to have lower per-capita incomes, lower population densities, lower levels of education among the adult population, and less industrialized economies and are more likely to have state economies dominated by a single industry.[60] The weak-interest-group states also tend to have stronger political parties, although that relationship is not nearly as pronounced as it was two decades ago. The weak-interest-group states additionally tend to have stronger governors and more professional legislatures than the strong-interest-group states. In general, one could safely conclude that the more diversified a state's economy is, the more affluent is its population, and the stronger its political party system and governing institutions, the less likely that state Is to be dominated by a single interest group or a single combination of groups.

Interest Group Regulation

How effective have the states been in regulating interest groups to curb the growing influence of PACs and minimize corrupt practices? Not very! seems to be the answer. Following the Watergate scandals in Washington, D.C. (1972–1974), most states passed laws to limit campaign contributions, force the disclosure of the names of contributors, and require the registration of lobbyists. From all appearances, these laws have been easy to circumvent. Michigan, for example, forbade any PAC or lobbying firm to contribute more than $250 to a legislative campaign for a specific legislative seat or $450 to a state senate seat. In fact, however, multi-client lobbying firms easily get around this limit by contributing to targeted legislators in the names of the firms' clients. A firm with fifty clients might easily give a legislator over $5,000 by donating as little as $100 in the name of each client.[61] Lobbyist regulation laws have been equally easy to circumvent. California passed one of the most stringent lobbying regulation acts in 1974, requiring lobbyists to register with the Secretary of State and make detailed reports on their income and expenditures. Despite these seemingly strict provisions, one California analyst commented, it "has not significantly altered lobbyist activity in Sacramento [the capital], although wining and dining has been drastically curtailed."[62]

The most extensive study of state interest group politics to date indicates that lobbying regulations have weakened since the post-Watergate reform days.[63] Where lobbying practices are honest, noncorrupt, and aboveboard, that desirable situation seems to stem more from a broad climate of a moralistic culture in the state than from specific laws to regulate lobbying behavior.[64]

◇ CONCLUSION: A COMPARISON OF PUBLIC OPINION AND INTEREST GROUPS

Table 5-5 summarizes the preceding discussion. Public opinion and interest groups are rated as channels of political participation by their policy impact, the ease through which a citizen can use the channel to affect public policy, and the responsiveness of the channels.

For policy impact, public opinion is a very weak channel of citizen input. Public opinion does not have a direct effect on most issues that governments face. Public opinion is most effective on visible and highly emotional issues. As discussed earlier, there is some evidence that elected public officials share a consensus of values with the majority of their constituents. By contrast, interest groups exert a very strong influence on public policy, although their influence varies from state to state.

In the ease with which an outsider can use the channel to affect public policy, public opinion is paradoxically the least effective. Outsiders can manipulate public opinion only when they have a charismatic appeal and only

Table 5-5   PUBLIC OPINION AND INTEREST GROUPS AS CONVENTIONAL CHANNELS OF POLITICAL PARTICIPATION

Channel	Policy Impact	Ease Through Which an Outsider Can Use This Channel to Change Public Policies	Most Responsive to Whom?	Least Responsive to Whom?
Public opinion	Very weak, except for visible and emotional issues; unreliable	Very difficult (except when a charismatic candidate manipulates an emotional issue)	Vocal minorities	Poor and unorganized people
Interest groups	Very strong, especially on the day-to-day, unemotional issues that give tangible benefits to particular groups	Difficult, but possible	Existing institutions; members of the interest groups	Poor and unorganized people

when the issue is visible and emotional. Most established interest groups are not accessible to manipulation by outsiders. Yet if enough outsiders feel strongly enough about a policy, they are free to organize their own interest group. In the environmental politics of the 1970s, many environmentalists formed ad hoc interest groups, which exerted influence on environmental policymaking.

Finally, and most important from the point of view of representative democracy, Table 5-5 examines the responsiveness of these channels. Public opinion and interest groups as channels of political participation are most responsive to the middle- and upper-middle classes, to people who participate, to the gladiators, and to such existing institutions as unions, corporations, and professional associations. Neither of these conventional channels is particularly responsive to the demands or needs of the poor and the unorganized.

To place interest groups and public opinion in a broader comparative context, we need to examine the other channels of political influence. We will do this in the next chapter.

SUMMARY

1. Several patterns of participation arise in conventional political activities. Participation is concentrated among a small part of the population and is disproportionately an upper-status and middle-status phenomenon. This is especially true for demanding gladiator activities. Poor people do not participate nearly as much as do affluent people. To explain these patterns of participation, scholars have focused on psychological and skill barriers among the poor, political barriers, the lack of mobilizing organizations, and the indifference of the governing institutions to the demands of the poor.
2. Three models try to explain the impact of public opinion on public policy—the rational activist model, the role-playing model, and the sharing or consensus model. Public opinion appears to have its strongest voice in issues that are visible and emotional. In deciding how much importance to attach to public opinion on a given issue, legislators have to cope with the intensity of voters' reactions. Policymakers also tend to be more responsive to their attentive constituents than they are to constituents in general. Even when public policy does correlate with public opinion, it often is not possible to know which one caused the other.
3. Interest groups are organizations that try to influence government decisions. A distinction can be drawn between economically motivated groups, professionally motivated groups, public interest groups, and ideological groups. Interest groups engage in a variety of tactics to influence government decisions—public relations, electioneering, and lobbying.

KEY TERMS

Attentive constituent   The constituent, often a local official, who is aware of a legislator's activity and voting behavior in the legislature.

Electioneering   The interest group tactic of trying to get favorable people elected to the legislature.

Gladiator   A person very active in political activities, campaigning, contributing to campaigns, and lobbying.

Intensity problem   The legislators' problem in deciding whether they should support the legislative preferences of a small minority that feels very intensely about an issue or the majority that feels much less intensely about it.

Interest group   Any organization of people who try to influence government decisions.

Iron law of oligarchy   The tendency of groups to become less democratic over time and to fall under the dominance of a small group of leaders.

Lobbying   The interest group tactic of trying to influence a decision of the legislature or some other governmental body.

Political action committee (PAC)   A group that collects money from various sources and uses it to make campaign contributions and to try to influence election outcomes.

Political participation   Individual or group activity that seeks to influence the selection of government officials or the actions that those officials take.

Public interest group   An interest group that claims to represent the public interest.

Public opinion   The general population's views on politically relevant issues.

Public relations   The use of the media to create a favorable public opinion.

Sense of civic duty   One's belief that one has a community obligation to vote and take part in community affairs.

Sense of political efficacy   One's belief that one's participation in politics can have some effect.

Spectator   A person whose main political activity is voting and observing politics.

Voting Rights Act of 1965   This law was very effective in striking down the legal barriers that had prevented the majority of racial minorities in the South from registering and voting.

REFERENCES

1. The tale of Weston is described and analyzed in Theodore J. Lowi et al., *Poliscide* (New York: Macmillan, 1976).
2. Sidney Verba and Norman Nie, *Participation in America* (New York: Harper & Row, 1972), p. 2.
3. See Lester W. Milbrath and M. L. Goel, *Political Participation: How and Why Do People Get Involved in Politics?* 2d ed. (Chicago: Rand McNally, 1977), pp. 19–21. Also see Robert Lane, *Political Life: Why People Get Involved in Politics* (Glencoe, Ill.: Free Press, 1959).
4. Raymond E. Wolfinger and Steven J. Rosenstone, *Who Votes?* (New Haven, Conn.: Yale University Press, 1980), pp. 23–30.
5. The importance of a sense of civic duty to voting is discussed in the work of William Riker and Peter Ordeshook, "A Theory of the Calculus of Voting," *American Political Science Review* 62, no. 1 (March 1968): 25–42.
6. This was the major finding of Elaine B. Sharp's study of citizen-contacting in Kansas City, Missouri, in 1982–1983. See her "Citizen Demand Making in the Urban Context," *American Journal of Political Science* 28, no. 4 (November 1984): 654–670.
7. Angus Campbell et al., *The American Voter* (New York: Wiley, 1960), Ch. 4.
8. Arthur T. Hadley, *The Empty Polling Booth* (Englewood Cliffs, N.J.: Prentice-Hall, 1978), pp. 67–103.
9. Anthony Downs, *An Economic Theory of Democracy* (New York: Harper & Row, 1957), Ch. 14.
10. *Smith* v. *Allwright*, 321 U.S. 649 (1944).
11. *Gomillion* v. *Lightfoot*, 364 U.S. 339 (1960).

12. Bureau of the Census, *Statistical Abstract of the United States: 1995* (Washington, D.C.: U.S. Government Printing Office, 1995), p. 287.
13. Wolfinger and Rosenstone, *Who Votes?* p. 73.
14. *Statistical Abstract of the United States, 1995*, p. 290. For an assessment of the relative impacts of various registration devices, see Stacy L. Rhine, "Registration Reform and Turnout Changes in the American States," *American Politics Quarterly* 23, no. 4 (October 1995): 409–426.
15. Gerald W. Johnson, "Research Note on Political Correlates of Voter Participation: A Deviant Case Analysis," *American Political Science Review* 65, no. 3 (September 1971): 768–776. One study found that black voting increased when outside organizers and federal registrars appeared. See Lester M. Salamon and Stephen Van Evera, "Fear, Apathy, and Discrimination: A Test of Three Explanations of Political Participation," *American Political Science Review* 67, no. 4 (December 1973): 1288–1307.
16. Bernard Bellush and Jewell Bellush, *Union Power and New York: Victor Gottbaum and District Council 37* (New York: Praeger Publishing, 1984), Ch. 13.
17. Henry E. Brady, Sidney Verba, and Kay Lehman Schlozmann, "Beyond SES: A Resource Model of Political Participation," *American Political Science Review* 89, no. 2 (June 1995): 271–294.
18. Albert O. Hirschman, *Exit, Voice and Loyalty: Responses to Decline in Firms, Organizations and States* (Cambridge, Mass.: Harvard University Press, 1970).
19. Robert Putnam, "Tuning In, Tuning Out: The Strange Disappearance of Social Capital in America," *PS: Political Science and Politics* 27, no. 4 (December 1994): 664–683.
20. Harry Boyte, "Civic Education as Public Leadership Development," *PS* (December 1993): 763–769.
21. M. Margaret Conway and Frank B. Feigert, *Political Analysis: An Introduction*, 2d ed. (Boston: Allyn and Bacon, 1976), p. 130.
22. Thomas R. Dye was one of the most persistent and influential advocates of this view. See his *Politics, Economics, and the Public: Policy Outcomes in the American States* (Chicago: Rand McNally and Company, 1966). Dye, in this book, does not directly test public opinion as a possible independent variable; rather, he uses measures such as interparty competition and voter turnout, which presumably reflect public opinion partially.
23. On the consistency between public policy and public opinion preferences, see Benjamin I. Page and Robert Y. Shapiro, "Effects of Public Opinion on Policy," *American Political Science Review* 77, no. 1 (March 1983): 175–191; and Alan D. Munroe, "Consistency Between Public Preferences and National Policy Decisions," *American Politics Quarterly* 7, no. 1 (January 1979): 3–20. For instances when public opinion has influenced policy outcomes, see Robert Weissberg, *Public Opinion and Popular Government* (Englewood Cliffs, N.J.: Prentice-Hall, 1976), p. 137.
24. Gerald C. Wright, Jr., Robert S. Erikson, and John P. McIver, "Measuring State Partisanship and Ideology with Survey Data," *Journal of Politics* 47, no. 2 (May 1985): 469–489. The validity of this measure of political ideology was affirmed by Thomas M. Holbrook-Provow and Steven C. Poe who found high correlations between this measure and four other measures of ideological leaning in the states. See their "Measuring State Political Ideology," *American Politics Quarterly* 15, no. 3 (July 1987): 399–414.
25. Robert Erikson, "The Relationship Between Public Opinion and State Policy: A New Look Based on Some Forgotten Data," *American Political Science Review* 20, no. 1 (February 1976): 25–37.
26. Norman R. Lutbeg, *Public Opinion and Public Policy*, rev. ed. (Homewood, Ill: Dorsey Press, 1974), p. 4.

27. Warren E. Miller and Donald E. Stokes, "Constituency Influence in Congress," *American Political Science Review* 57, no. 1 (March 1963): 15–56.

28. Lutbeg, *Public Opinion and Public Policy,* 8.

29. Roberta S. Sigel and H. Paul Friesema, "Urban Community Leaders' Knowledge of Public Opinion," *Western Political Quarterly* 18, no. 1 (December 1965); 881–895.

30. See Kenneth Prewitt, "Political Ambitions, Volunteerism, and Electoral Accountability," *American Political Science Review* 64, no. 1 (March 1970:) pp. 5–17.

31. David R. Morgan, "Political Linkage of Public Policy: Attitudinal Congruence Between Citizens and Officials," *Western Political Quarterly* 26, no. 2 (June 1973): 219–223. Eric Uslaner and Ronald E. Weber, "U.S. State Legislators' Opinions and Perceptions of Constituency Attitudes," *Legislative Studies Quarterly* 4 (November 1979): 563–585.

32. Kim Quaile Hill and Angela Hinton-Andersson, "Pathways of Representation: A Causal Analysis of Public Opinion-Policy Linkages," *American Journal of Political Science* 39, no. 4 (November 1995): 924–935.

33. Miller and Stokes, "Constituency Influence in Congress," pp. 45–56.

34. Ronald E. Weber and William R. Shaffer, "Public Opinion and American State Policy Making," *Midwest Journal of Political Science* 16, no. 4 (November 1972): 683–699.

35. Anne H. Hopkins, "Opinion Publics and Support for Public Policy in the American States," *American Journal of Political Science* 18, no. 1 (February 1974): 167–177.

36. G. R. Boynton, Samuel C. Patterson, and Ronald D. Hedlund, "The Missing Links in Legislative Politics: Attentive Constituents," *Journal of Politics* 31, no. 3 (August 1969): 700–721.

37. Erikson, "The Relationship Between Public Opinion and State Policy," pp. 25–37.

38. See Weissberg, *Public Opinion and Popular Government,* pp. 159–162.

39. L. Harmon Zeigler, "Interest Groups in the States," in Virginia Gray, Herbert Jacob, and Kenneth N. Vines, eds., *Politics in the American States: A Comparative Analysis,* 4th ed. (Boston: Little, Brown and Co., 1983): 99.

40. David Lowery and Virginia Gray, "The Density of State Interest Group Systems," *Journal of Politics* 55, no. 1 (February 1993): 191–206

41. Between 1968 and 1989, USW membership dropped from 1,120,000 to 421,000 and UAW membership dropped from 1,473,000 to 771,000. *Statistical Abstract of the United States: 1971,* p. 234; *Statistical Abstract of the United States: 1995,* p. 443.

42. Jack Barbash, "Trade Unionism from Roosevelt to Reagan," *Annals of the American Academy of Political and Social Science,* no. 473 (May 1984): 21.

43. Michael Goldfield, "Labor in American Politics: Its Current Weaknesses," *Journal of Politics* 48, no. 1 (February 1986): 2–29.

44. Clive S. Thomas and Ronald J. Hrebenar, "An Overview of Interest Group Activity in the States," *Comparative State Politics Newsletter* 8, no. 6 (December 1986): 6.

45. Clive S. Thomas and Ronald J. Hrebenar, "Political Action Committees in the States: Some Preliminary Findings," a paper presented at the American Political Science Association annual convention. Washington, D.C.: September 1991.

46. Larry Sabato, *PAC Power: Inside the World of Political Action Committees* (New York: Norton, 1984), pp. 197–198.

47. James D. King and Helena S. Robin, "PACs and Campaign Finance in National and State Elections," *Comparative State Politics* 16, no. 4 (August 1995): 32–44.

48. Candace Romig, "Placing Limits on PACs," *State Legislatures* 10, no. 2 (January 1984): 22.

49. Herbert E. Alexander, "The Case for PACs," a Public Affairs Council monograph (Los Angeles: Calif. The Public Affairs Council, 1983).

50. Clive S. Thomas and Ronald J. Hrebenar, "Interest Groups in the States," in *Politics in the American States: A Comparative Analysis*, 5th ed. (Glenview, Ill.: Scott, Foresman, 1990), p. 149.

51. Clive S. Thomas and Ronald J. Hrebenar, "The Wheeler Dealer Lobbyist: An Endangered Species in States Capitals?" *Comparative State Politics* 13, no. 2 (April 1992): 32.

52. Randy Welch, "Lobbyists, Lobbyists All Over the Lot," *State Legislatures* 15, no. 2 (February 1989): 21.

53. L. Harmon Zeigler and Harvey J. Tucker, *The Quest for Responsive Government: An Introduction to State and Local Politics* (North Scituate, Mass.: Duxbury Press, 1978), p. 117.

54. John C. Syer and John H. Culver, *Power and Politics in California*, 4th ed. (New York: Macmillan, 1992), p. 63.

55. Ibid., p. 63.

56. Jay K. Dow and James Endersby, "Campaign Contributions and Legislative Voting in the California Assembly," *American Politics Quarterly* 22, no. 3 (July 1994): 334–353.

57. See Weber and Shaffer, "Public Opinion and American State Policy Making," pp. 683–699.

58. This argument is especially made by Thomas R. Dye and L. Harmon Zeigler in their *The Irony of American Democracy: An Uncommon Introduction to American Politics*, 4th ed. (North Scituate, Mass.: Duxbury Press, 1978), pp. 209–210.

59. Roberto Michels, *Political Parties: A Sociological Study of the Oligarchical Tendencies of Modern Democracy*, trans. Eden Paul and Cedar Paul (New York: Free Press, 1962).

60. Sarah McCally Morehouse, *State Politics, Parties and Policy* (New York: Holt, Rinehart & Winston, 1981), pp. 108–113, 491–492.

61. William P. Browne and Delbert J. Ringquist, "Michigan Interests: The Politics of Diversification," in *Interest Group Politics in the Midwestern States*, Clive S. Thomas and Ronald J. Hrebenar, eds. (Salt Lake City: University of Utah Press, forthcoming).

62. Michael J. Ross, *California: Its Government and Politics* (North Scituate, Mass.: Duxbury Press, 1979), p. 66.

63. Thomas and Hrebenar, "Comparative Interest Groups in the American West," *The Journal of State Government* 59, no. 3 (September to October 1986): 131.

64. This was the conclusion reached by observers of interest groups in Iowa and North Dakota. See Charles W. Wiggins and Keith E. Hamm, "Iowa: Interest Group Politics in an Undistinguished Place," a paper presented at the 1987 meeting of the Midwest Political Science Association, Chicago, April 1987, pp. 5–6. Also see another paper presented at the 1987 meeting: Theodore B. Pedeliski, "Interest Groups in North Dakota: Constituency Coupling in a Moralistic Political Culture," pp. 26–28.

6

CHANNELS OF CITIZEN INFLUENCE: THE BALLOT BOX, PARTIES, AND DIRECT ACTION

Chapter Preview

This chapter explores the efficacy with which various channels of citizen input enable citizens to influence the actions of state and local governments. Examined in turn are:

1. The election process.
2. Political parties.
3. Direct democracy devices, such as initiative, referendum, and recall.
4. Direct action tactics, such as protests, demonstrations, and sit-ins.

Let us begin by discussing how election systems operate.

◇ INTRODUCTION

The ultimate test of democracy is whether people can effectively influence their government through the electoral process. At the national level most people can expect to influence events only indirectly and in very small ways. Washington, for most of us, is very far away. State capitols and city halls, however, are much closer. It is at the state and local levels of government that democracy would seem to have the best prospects for success. How effective the electoral channels of influence are will be examined in this chapter.

◇ THE BALLOT BOX

In a representative democracy such as that in the United States, the election process is the central means by which people are expected to hold the government accountable.

Elections are regulated by the states and generally administered by local governments. In all states, you must meet minimal requirements in order to vote. You must be a United States citizen, eighteen years of age, and a resident of your state for a given period. Except for North Dakota, all states also require you to register in order to vote.

Except for the Nebraska Legislature and most judgeships, state elections use a partisan ballot on which the political party of each candidate is indicated near his or her name, so you know whether you are voting for a Democrat, a Republican, or a member of another party.

At the local level there is a much wider variety of election systems. In general, local election systems can be categorized as either *reformed* or *unreformed*. A **reformed election system** tends to have nonpartisan, at-large elections, which are held at times separate from state or national elections. In nonpartisan elections, the ballots do not list the party designation of the candidates. In at-large elections, city council members are elected from the entire city. They are distinguished from **ward elections,** or **district elections,** in which the council members are elected from neighborhood areas usually called *wards* (sometimes *districts*). Reformed elections also protect against voter fraud by voter registration, voting machines, election judges from all parties and factions, and safeguards in counting the ballots. An **unreformed election system,** in contrast, tends to be partisan, ward rather than at-large, and held at the same time as statewide elections, and lacks effective protection against voter fraud. Reformed election systems predominate in suburbs and in the Far West. Unreformed election systems predominate in the central cities of the East, the Midwest, and the South.

One consequence of reformed election systems is reduced voter turnout. Most of the reform devices slightly increase the difficulty of voting. Since nonvoting tends to be highest among the poor, one inevitable bias of reformed election systems is to reduce the influence of poor people in the election process.[1] These considerations are discussed more fully in Chapter 7.

Elections as Instruments of Accountability

Do elections hold governing officials accountable to the voters? Two general propositions can be made. First, elections are instruments of **retroactive accountability;** they hold public officials accountable after the fact. They are not instruments of **proactive accountability** because they do not usually give mandates for the winners to carry out a specific policy line. Rather they let the voters judge candidates on past performance.[2] Voters simply do not know enough about the issue positions of legislative or gubernatorial candidates to choose one set of policies over another. The winners will have to face reelection two or four years later, and at that time the voters make a retroactive judgment about whether they are dissatisfied enough to replace the incumbent.

Second, contrary to what one would think intuitively, the available evidence suggests that elections are better instruments of accountability at the state level than they are at the local level. Kenneth Prewitt interviewed over 400 city council members in the San Francisco area and discovered that most of them really did not worry about getting defeated at the polls if they angered their constituents.[3] A fourth of them got their council positions through appointment rather than election. During elections, voter turnout was so small that the average candidate could win by getting the vote from as little as 6 to 8 percent of the population. Once in office, 80 percent were reelected when they chose to run. The offices had low salaries, and few council members cared to run for higher office. In short, they were community volunteers doing a civic duty, not professional politicians attempting to build a career. We can call this phenomenon **volunteerism.** These voluntary public officials followed their own judgments and the judgments of trusted associates. Despite the election process, the council members were in practice unaccountable to the majority. Joseph Schlesinger has written, "No more irresponsible government is imaginable than one of high-minded men unconcerned for their political futures."[4] That is, the volunteer does not have to worry about displeasing the majority, because he or she has little to lose if ousted from office. Even when the volunteer is ousted, he or she is replaced by another volunteer, who also has no compelling reason to worry about majority opinion. At best the majority can hope to make its will felt only in fits and starts when voters occasionally rise in rebellion against occasional unpopular decisions. Usually, this occurs retroactively, as when a neighborhood group is upset by the cost of installing sewers or sidewalks or some other public amenity and votes out the local council members at the next election. By this time, however, the unpopular action has usually been accomplished and cannot be reversed. The problem of holding local elected officials accountable to the majority is also complicated by the fact that most local governments are severely constrained by state and federal regulations in what they can do (see Chapters 7 and 8).

In contrast to local-level elections, state-level elections provide more opportunity for accountability to the voters. Although people do not follow state affairs any more closely than they follow local ones,[5] state elections have higher turnout rates than local elections, and this suggests that state officials represent a broader spectrum of the population than do local officials. State legislators, as one study found, more often share the public policy preferences of the majority of the population than do state agency heads or party leaders.[6] Finally, the governor is usually the most visible state official and, as such, is an "easy target of discontent" when things do not seem to be going well in a state.[7] This can occur when people perceive their state economy is lagging in growth. When this happens, governors tend to see downturns in their public opinion ratings and their vote totals at reelection time.[8] Governors are even more likely to become targets of discontent if they pushed for an unpopular increase in state sales or income taxes.[9] Few governors were taught this lesson more brutally than New Jersey's James Florio who was voted out of office in 1994 after raising the state income tax by $1 billion in order to improve funding for impoverished school districts in the state.[10]

Elections as Channels of Citizens Input

Related to the issue of elections as instruments of accountability is the question of whether citizens can use the election process as a means to get the government to enact favorable policies. This is especially important for low-income people, who—as we saw in Chapter 5—have lower voter turnouts than do middle-income people. If more low-income people voted, could they get more favorable policies and programs from government?

Early research on this question during the 1960s was not very encouraging.[11] Attempts to correlate each state's voter turnout rate with different policy outcomes (such as spending for education or public welfare) found that increases in voter turnout had no effect on the amount of money spent on services for the poor. Nor did turnout appear to affect whether the state is controlled by Democrats (who presumably would be more favorable to low-income voters) or by Republicans. One study estimated that even if voter turnout were increased by 10 percent (which would be a big increase), the increase would make only a marginal difference in the vote outcome for Democrats and Republicans. It would increase the net Democratic vote by only 0.3 percent.[12]

In contrast to these early studies, a more recent analysis compared the states by how well low-income voters were represented at the polling place on election day. Low-income people consistently received better welfare-type benefits in the states where they had the best voter turnout. Where their turnout was poor, they fared badly.[13]

What was true for low-income voters was also true for other categories of people. When a distinctive category of people goes from practically no voter turnout to a relatively high turnout, one notices that the political system does indeed become more responsive to their concerns. Quantum leaps in voter turnout for distinct categories of people happened twice in this century—following the Nineteenth Amendment's enfranchisement of women in 1920 and following enfranchisement of racial minorities after the Voting Rights Act of 1965. Enfranchisement enabled them to take on gladiator roles (see Chapter 5), which previously had been reserved for white males. Also, in both cases, the emergence of increasing numbers of minorities and women into gladiator roles was followed by the emergence of public policies aimed at their concerns. In the case of women, this development included such issues as abortion, affirmative action programs, and antirape and anti-wife-abuse measures. In the case of minorities, we have seen the emergence of bilingual programs, affirmative action programs, and social welfare programs, because disproportionate numbers of minorities live in poverty and benefit from such programs.

In sum, the right to vote does not necessarily give a particular category of people a great deal of influence in public policymaking, but the absence of the right to vote virtually ensures that their influence will be minimal. How influential they can make their voice depends on several factors in addition to the right to vote—whether they are united, whether their leaders can mobilize them to vote, whether their leaders are effective, and whether the political system has the resources to meet their demands.

Financing State and Local Elections

"The mother's milk of politics!" That is how the late Jesse Unruh of California once described money's role in politics. And an apt description it is. A lot of money is needed to produce the bumper stickers, put out the brochures, hire the pollsters, buy the advertisements, pay for the television time, and do all the other things necessary to run an effective campaign today. A governor's race can easily cost over $2 million, and a state legislative race, $100,000. Candidates for the Texas governorship spent $50 million in 1990,[14] and Tom Hayden spent $1.8 million winning a California legislative race in 1982.[15]

Where this money comes from is vitally important. Since big contributors will logically expect to gain access to the candidates they support, the public at large has a key interest in seeing who the contributors are, in broadening the contribution base as much as possible, and in limiting the potential for corrupting relationships between contributors and candidates.

Reform Provisions In the wake of the Watergate scandal in Washington (1972–1974), many states enacted campaign finance legislation, and all states now have some campaign regulation. The most common provisions are disclosure of contributors (fifty states), limits on campaign contributors (thirty-nine states), and limits on campaign expenditures (nine states). Twenty states provide some public funding for campaigns. Eleven offer an income tax checkoff provision whereby taxpayers can earmark a portion of their income taxes to a public campaign fund. And seven states provide either income tax credits or income tax deductions for a portion of campaign contributions.[16] Minnesota offers a cash refund for the first $50 of a person's campaign contribution, meaning that every adult in the state could, if they wanted, contribute $50 to their favorite candidate and get every penny of the contribution back. (The following "You Decide" exercise gives you a chance to examine the incentives it would take to get you to contribute.)

Goals of Reform Three essential goals underlie these elaborate provisions. First, the financial disclosure requirements are intended to let voters know if the candidates themselves have any potential conflicts of interest between their governmental responsibilities and either their sources of income or their campaign contributions. Some citizens, for example, might want to vote against candidates who obtain most of their campaign funds from labor unions; other voters might want to do the opposite. In either case, campaign finance disclosure helps the voter make a more informed choice. Second, the contribution limits aim to reduce the influence of wealthy contributors. If each state legislative candidate is limited to accepting no more than $5,000 from a single contributor (as is the case for congressional campaigns), that candidate is less likely to be bankrolled by a single faction or group. Third, the public financing provisions are designed to give the average voter an incentive to make campaign contributions, in the hope that such contributions will offset the influence of PACs and wealthy individuals.

Does Campaign Finance Reform Work? How well have the finance reforms worked? Better, no doubt, than campaign funding regulation before Watergate. Not nearly as well, however, as the reformers had hoped. Implementation has been plagued with problems. Reliance on PACs continues to grow in the states as it does in Washington (see Chapter 5). The principal problem, however, is the difficulty reformers have in keeping up with the ingenuity of campaign contributors and fund-raisers in finding new avenues to exceed contribution limits when reformers close down old avenues. Texas, for example, has legislation that prohibits corporations from making direct campaign contributions. To get around this restriction, the Republican National Committee in 1980 arranged for the transfer to Texas of direct corporate contributions raised in Missouri, whose law permitted such contributions. Although these transfers were legal, they clearly violated the intent of Texas reformers to shut down direct corporate contributions in that state.[17]

Another major implementation problem lies in the underfunding and understaffing of the watchdog agencies set up to enforce campaign finance laws. Out of twenty-six such agencies established by the early 1980s, only four (Connecticut, New Jersey, Florida, and California) have systematically sought to levy fines or impose other punishments on campaign law breakers. And even those few agencies are underfunded. New Jersey's Election Law Enforcement Commission, for example, faced the task of monitoring the activities of 187 PACs and all the state election campaigns in the 1987–1988 election cycle with a staff that employed only two auditors and only one field investigator.[18] The fundamental problem in beefing up the regulatory strength of these agencies is that the agencies rely for their budget and authority on the very people they oversee, the legislators. When watchdog agencies get tough about exercising their authority, legislatures tend to cut their budgets.[19]

Despite these obstacles in the way of campaign finance reform, a resurgence of reform has been taking place in recent years.[20] As noted earlier (p. 126) several states enacted provisions ranging from expenditure limitations to income tax check-offs that let voters earmark a dollar of their income taxes to a public fund that helps finance state elections. In New Jersey's experience, nearly a third of taxpayers do this every year which provides a substantial base for public funding of the governor's race.[21]

◇ POLITICAL PARTIES

The great contribution that political parties make to democracy is that they nominate candidates for public elective office, help those candidates win elections, and organize the government once the election is over. Increasingly, however, parties have been losing their ability to control these functions. We can see this decline of ability by examining the political party as a **tripartite organization:** the party in its organization, the party in the electorate, and the party in government.[22]

Party Organization

Party organization refers to the structures and people that nominate the party's candidates for office and seek to get them elected. The party structure, or organization, is divided into semi-independent units at different levels of government

YOU DECIDE

What Would It Take to Get You to Contribute?

The integrity of the democratic process is undermined to the extent that campaign finance is left to wealthy individuals, interest groups, and political action committees. Few Americans ever contribute to political campaigns. The democratic process in most states would probably be healthier if more people contributed or if there were a broader base of contributions. As a student, you may not have the spare funds now to contribute to political causes. But a few years after graduation, your finances will stabilize, and you will find yourself with the discretionary income to support causes and candidates. Listed here are several steps proposed by various groups to encourage a broader range of participation in campaign finance. Assuming you had an extra $100, above and beyond your normal spending needs, what would it take to get you to contribute half of that $100 to a political campaign for a candidate or party of your choice?

	Yes	No
1. No special incentive needed. I would willingly contribute.	❏	❏

Rationale:_____

_____

	Yes	No
2. A state tax credit for one-half the contribution, so that the $50 contribution would actually cost me only $25.	❏	❏

Rationale:_____

_____

	Yes	No
3. A state tax credit for one-half the contribution and an additional federal tax credit for the other half so that the $50 contribution would actually cost me zero.	❏	❏

Rationale:_____

_____

	Yes	No
4. I would not contribute $50, but I would willingly earmark $1 of my state income tax refund to a public campaign fund distributed to the candidates of my party.	❏	❏

Rationale:_____

_____

(see Figure 6-1). The highest levels have traditionally exerted very little influence over the lower levels. The national convention's authority over the lower levels is limited to setting its own rules for seating each state's delegates. If two competing delegations both demand to be seated, the national convention must decide which delegation is legitimate.

The leading party organization officials are the state and the county chairpersons. Despite negative stereotypes of political party leaders, state chairper-

	Yes	No
5. I would not contribute $50 or earmark $1 of my state income tax refund for candidates of a particular party, but I would willingly earmark $1 of my state income tax refund to a public campaign fund distributed equally to all candidates of all parties.	❏	❏

Rationale:_____

_____

6. I would not make any of the aforementioned contributions, but I would support tax dollars from the general fund being spent on public funding of campaigns, with equal amounts going to all candidates for the office. To hold down the number of frivolous candidacies, candidates would have to get a minimum percentage of the vote.	❏	❏

Rationale:_____

_____

7. None of the aforementioned tax concessions or public funding proposals appeal to me, but I would contribute if it were likely to lead to an appointment to some public advisory commission for me.	❏	❏

Rationale:_____

_____

8. I would not contribute the $50, and I would not support any of the public funding or tax incentives listed.	❏	❏

Rationale:_____

_____

Having decided what incentives, if any, would be needed to get you to contribute under these ideal conditions in which you had a spare $100, what percentage of the people in your state do you think would support each of the eight options? What percentage of your classmates? How many of the options exist in your state? What are some of the advantages and disadvantages of each option?

---

sons are successful, well-educated people who often are attracted to politics because of their philosophical and ideological concerns. They administer the party organization and promote the party image.[23] If the state chairperson is the most significant party official, the county (legislative district in some states) is probably the most important level of party organization.

The precinct is the basic level of political organization. There is one precinct for each polling place. The precinct chairperson's job is to keep a list of all voters

Figure 6-1 POLITICAL PARTY ORGANIZATION

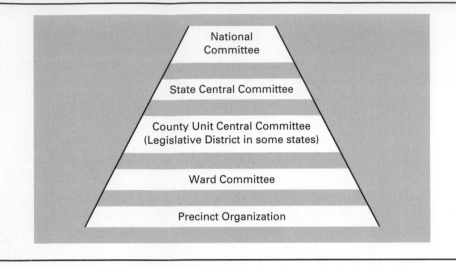

in the precinct, to identify which ones are Republicans, Democrats, or Independents, and to get the voters from his or her party to the polls on election day. The precinct chairperson is normally elected at the precinct caucus or mass meeting. In strong-machine cities, he or she is appointed by the ward leader.

Nominating Candidates   Perhaps the most important role of the party organization is the nomination of candidates for public office. Candidates are nominated through a combination of conventions and primary elections. The **nominating convention** is usually dominated by party activists, and it endorses candidates for the party nomination. In most states, however, the official nomination comes not from the convention but from the primary election. If no candidate gets enough votes to win endorsement at the convention or if the losing candidate at the convention thinks he or she can do better in the primary, then a **primary election** is held to determine the nominee. Connecticut has a **challenge primary.** The losing candidate at the convention can challenge the winner to a primary election only if the loser received at least 20 percent of the vote. Normally, the convention-endorsed candidates go on to win the primary election.[24] Sometimes, however, the party conventions fall under the control of ideological zealots who nominate extremist candidates who then lose in the follow-up primary. In Minnesota, for example, the Republican party convention in 1994 rejected the endorsement bid of the incumbent Republican governor and endorsed instead a conservative extremist who was then defeated by the governor in the ensuing primary.[25]

As Table 6-1 shows, there are four different types of direct primaries. In the twenty-seven **closed primary** states, only registered Democrats can vote in the Democratic primary and only registered Republicans can vote in that party's primary, although ten of these states permit you to change your party registra-

Table 6-1 TYPES OF PRIMARY ELECTIONS

Closed (Party registration required)	Semiclosed (Voters may register or change registration on Election Day)	Semiopen (Voters required to request party ballot publicly)	Open (Voter may vote in any party primary)	Blanket	Nonpartisan
Arizona	Colorado*	Alabama	Hawaii	Alaska§	Louisiana
California	Iowa†	Arkansas	Idaho	Washington	
Connecticut	Kansas*	Georgia	Michigan		
Delaware	Maine*	Illinois	Minnesota		
Florida	Massachusetts‡	Indiana	Montana		
Kentucky	New Hampshire‡	Mississippi	North Dakota		
Maryland	New Jersey*	Missouri	Utah		
Nebraska	Ohio†	South Carolina	Vermont		
Nevada	Rhode Island*	Tennessee	Wisconsin		
New Mexico	Wyoming†	Texas			
New York		Virginia			
North Carolina					
Oklahoma					
Oregon					
Pennsylvania					
South Dakota					
West Virginia					

Source: John F. Bibby and Thomas M. Holbrook, "Parties and Elections," *Politics in the American States:* 6th ed., Virginia Gray and Herbert Jacob, eds. (Washington, D.C.: CQ Press, 1996) p. 100. Used by permission of the CQ Press.

*Persons not previously voting in a primary may register with a party on election day.

†Party registration may be changed on election day.

‡Independents may change reistration on election day.

§Democratic party uses a blanket primary, and the Republican primary is restricted to Republicans or Independents.

tion as late as election day. In the **open primary** states, you can vote in either (but not both) the Republican or Democratic primary. Washington has the **blanket primary,** which allows you to vote in the Republican primary for some offices and the Democratic primary for other offices. Finally, Louisiana has a **nonpartisan** primary, in which the party affiliations of the candidates are not listed and the top two vote-getters become the nominees for the general election. If the top vote-getter receives more than 50 percent of the primary vote, however, he or she wins the office and no general election is held.

Party leaders frown on the open primary because it allows members of one party to cross over and vote for the weakest candidates in the other party's primary.[26] The open primary was given a boost in 1986 when the Supreme Court struck down state laws requiring a closed primary.[27] The Republican party of Connecticut had wanted to allow Independents to vote in its primary elections but was prevented from doing so by that state's closed primary law.

Electing the Party Nominees   The main value of the party to the nominated candidate is the party label. For all practical purposes, one cannot get elected to the governorship or the state legislature (except in Nebraska or Louisiana) unless one has been nominated by the Republican or Democratic party.

Whether the party organization will contribute much assistance beyond the party nomination varies greatly from state to state, depending on the strength or weakness of the state party system. Historically, the parties contributed a great deal, especially where the **political machines** dominated electoral politics, as under Chicago's legendary Mayor Richard J. Daley from 1955 to 1976. Daley controlled thousands of jobs in city government and obliged those jobholders to work for the machine's nominees at election time.[28] After Daley's death in 1976, the machine fell into disarray, and a succession of court decisions have made it increasingly difficult to maintain an army of party patronage workers.[29]

In most of the country, however, Chicago-style machine politics are a thing of the past. Victory in a statewide race, or even a big-city mayoral race, depends much less on an army of precinct workers making personal contact with voters than it does on television appearances, imaginative advertising in the media, favorable endorsements by influential interest groups and celebrities, and computerized information banks for direct mailings to target groups. These activities require the expertise of professional campaign management firms. To a great extent, these firms displaced the parties as campaign managers since the firms provide "all of the campaign services which could be provided by a party organization: fundraising, voter communications, scheduling, campaign events and appearances, voter canvassing and polling, and election-day staffing of polling places."[30]

Had the party organizations not responded to this challenge, they might well have become empty shells, with their nominating function usurped by interest groups and PACs. What the parties did was to adopt fundraising and campaign service functions that put the party organizations into an important *broker* position between potential contributors and candidates for the party endorsement. The Republicans discovered this new broker role first, and the Democrats followed suit. The national committees of both parties regularly make contributions to the state parties or, as the example of Texas and Missouri on p. 127 showed, they broker the exchange of so-called **soft money** from willing contributors to state party organizations.

State party organizations have emulated the brokerage role of the national parties. They coordinate PAC contributions to their parties' nominees. Further, as the recipients of soft money coming from the national parties, they often have the funds to provide media consulting, public opinion polling, and other campaign services to party nominees that the candidates themselves might not be able to afford.[31]

The most striking development in recent years has been the use of this brokering role by the political party leaders in the state legislatures. Forty states now have PACs run by the legislative parties or the legislative leaders. These PACs play a significant role in recruiting candidates, helping finance their campaigns, and providing them with valuable campaign services. California Assembly Speaker Willie Brown was probably the most accomplished at this. In 1992, he raised $5.3 million, which he used to help elect Democrats in targeted districts.[32] The ability to influence campaign funds of this magnitude necessarily strengthens the parties in state legislatures and contributes to party discipline.[33]

The net result of these developments today is a greatly transformed political party organization[34] that has access to huge sums of money. These sums and the influence they bring make the party organization the target of different ideological movements that seek to use the party as a tool to achieve their own political ends. In some states, such as California, Minnesota, and New Jersey, the political parties have become sharply polarized along ideological lines, with the Democratic organizations heavily influenced by the ideological left and the Republican organizations heavily influenced by the ideological right.

The Party in the Electorate

These changes in party organization have been accompanied by equally dramatic changes in the *party in the electorate,* which refers to the mass of people who identify themselves regularly as Republicans or Democrats. The most important change in the party in the electorate has been a weakening of political partisanship and a growing tendency of people to identify themselves as political Independents (see Figure 6-2) rather than as Democrats or Republicans.

A second important change has been a powerful growth of Republican strength in the South. Historically, the South was solidly Democratic, a reaction to the fact that it was the Republican party that had promoted the Civil War, ended slavery, and imposed a Reconstruction period on the South. Today, the South has become a competitive two-party region. In 1994, Republicans for the first time captured a majority of congressional seats in the South. These Republican candidates benefited from a growing Republican allegiance among southern whites. These Republican gains, however, have been partially offset by a growing electoral strength of black Democrats and a tendency of many whites to vote

Figure 6-2 TRENDS IN PARTY IDENTIFICATION

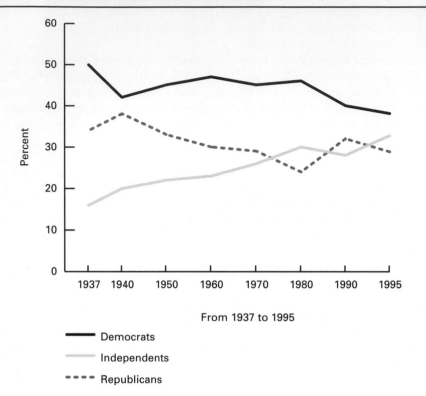

From 1937 to 1995

—— Democrats

—— Independents

■ ■ ■ ■ Republicans

Sources: The Gallup Poll: Public Opinion 1981 (Wilmington, Del.: Scholarly Resources, Inc., 1982), p. 128; *The Gallup Report,* no. 286 (July 1989), p. 2; *The Gallup Poll Monthly,* no. 322 (July 1992), p. 49.

a split ticket,[35] voting for Republican presidential candidates but for Democratic candidates in state races. Some southerners, in fact, report a dual partisanship, viewing themselves as Republicans in national elections but as Democrats in state and local elections.[36]

A third important development in the party in the electorate is a growing ideological polarization of the voting coalitions that support each party. Robert D. Brown and Gerald C. Wright studied public opinion surveys of the states from 1976 through 1988 and found that there was a strong ideological polarization between the parties in some states.[37] The most polarized states were Utah, California, and Connecticut, where large numbers of the people identified themselves as either liberal Democrats or conservative Republicans. The least polarized states were found in the South where far fewer people split along liberal–conservative lines. Brown and Wright also found that the more polarized a state's population was ideologically, the less it engaged in ticket splitting and the less likely it was to swing sharply back and forth between the parties by electing Democrats in one election and Republicans in another.

Amid these profound changes in the party in the electorate, there are also some important continuities with the past. Table 6-2 illustrates the most important of these continuities. The socioeconomic character of the Republican and Democratic voter coalitions continues to have the same class, racial, and religious split that it has had since the 1930s. In both education and income, upper-status people are more likely to be Republican. There are also key differences by race and religion. Blacks and Jews are more likely to be Democrat, whereas whites and Protestants (especially nonsouthern, white Protestants) are more likely to be Republican.

The Party in Government

The last component of the tripartite political party is the *party in government,* which refers to public officeholders such as governors and legislators. Figure 6-3 shows which states are most often controlled by Democrats or by Republicans

Table 6-2   THE SOCIAL BASIS OF PARTISANSHIP (1991)

	Percentage Republican	Percentage Democrat	Percentage Independent
Education			
College	35%	33%	32%
High school	28	36	36
Grade school	22	45	33
Income			
$75,000 and over	50	25	25
50,000–74,999	32	35	36
25,000–49,999	29	35	36
12,500–24,999	23	40	37
under $12,500	23	41	36
Race			
White	33	32	35
Black	6	71	23
Religion			
Protestant	32	36	32
Catholic	27	39	34
Jewish	19	55	26
Sex			
Male	30	34	36
Female	29	39	32

Source: James Allen Davis, *General Social Surveys, 1972–1994* [machine-readable data file]. Principal investigator, James A. Davis; director and co-principal investigator, Tom W. Smith (Chicago: National Opinion Research Center, producer, 1994, Storrs, Conn.: Roper Public Opinion Research Center, University of Connecticut, distributor).

Figure 6-3   1997–1998: WHO CONTROLS THE STATES?

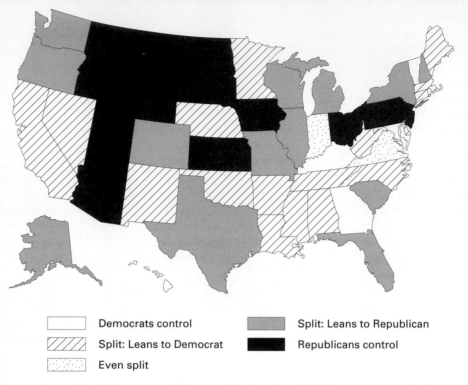

	Democrats control		Split: Leans to Republican
/////	Split: Leans to Democrat	■	Republicans control
::::::	Even split		

Democratic- or Republican-controlled states are those in which that party controls the governorship, the state Senate, and the state House of Representatives. Leaning states are those in which the party controls two of those three institutions. Nebraska has a nonpartisan, unicameral legislature, so it is listed as leaning to the party that controls the governorship.

and in which states the parties are most competitive. The division of state government into Democratic and Republican control raises two important questions: Does it make any difference in policy outcomes whether strong competition exists between the parties? Does it matter which party controls the government?

Two-Party Competition: Does It Make Any Difference?

According to American democratic theory, strong two-party competition ensures that the parties will be responsive to the needs of the majority of the voters. V. O. Key argued also that the parties' attempts to satisfy constituent needs would force the states with competitive parties to give more generous benefits than the states that lacked competitive parties.[38]

Contemporary political scientists have invested enormous time and energy studying whether two-party competition leads to more generous government benefits as V. O. Key had predicted. By comparing the level of government benefits provided by the competitive and the one-party states, two generalizations about competition and government benefits can be made. First, interparty competition is firmly based in the socioeconomic, regional, and organizational characteristics of a state. With few exceptions, two-party competition is the keenest in states that have large populations, high educational levels, substantial socioeconomic diversity, and strong political party organizations. With few exceptions, the one-party states tend to lack these characteristics.[39] Second, the two-party states provide more generous welfare benefits and educational benefits than do the one-party states. Early studies, especially those of Thomas R. Dye, attributed this to the greater wealth of the competitive states, not to their greater competitiveness.[40] More recent studies, however, have used increasingly sophisticated statistical tests and discovered that competition, especially when combined with high turnouts, did have an effect on education and welfare expenditures.[41]

Democrats or Republicans: Does It Make Any Difference?

Does it matter which party controls a state? In most states, the answer to that question clearly is yes. Two important differences exist between the parties. In many states, the party leaders differ sharply in ideology. A survey of Republican and Democratic delegates to the national conventions found that the party leaders differed from each other much more than did the party supporters. The Democratic voters were just slightly liberal, and the Republican voters just slightly conservative. In contrast, the Democratic leaders were very liberal, and the Republican leaders very conservative.[42] Even in a state such as Indiana, where political struggles are renowned for their lack of ideological content, researchers found sharp ideological differences between Republican leaders and Democratic leaders on issues such as support for prayer in public schools, lotteries, abortion, and nuclear power plants.[43]

Second, because Democratic leaders differ sharply from Republican leaders on issues and because Democrats draw their voting strength from different social groups than do Republicans (see Table 6-2), it is plausible to hypothesize that when Democrats control a state they will enact policies that Republicans would not enact. To some extent, this hypothesis is borne out by research. Robert Erikson traced the enactment of civil rights legislation outside the South.[44] He discovered that civil rights laws were three times as likely to get passed when the Democrats controlled the legislature as when it was controlled by Republicans or divided between Republicans and Democrats. Democratic governments also tend to spend more than Republican governments. However, Democrats in power do not make a state any more redistributive.[45] They do not take from the rich and divide it among the poor. Nevertheless, Democrats are more likely to enact less conservative policies than Republicans. For these reasons, it is important to know how the parties fare in their quest for control over state government. Figure 6-3 maps the breakdown of party control for

1997–1998. The strongest Democratic regions are the South, the Pacific Coast, the Midwest, and the Northeast. Republican strength shows up in the West and in New Hampshire.

◇ DIRECT DEMOCRACY

Direct democracy refers to the *initiative,* the *referendum,* and the *recall.* If an elected official becomes controversial and displeases voters, the **recall** provides a special election to determine whether that official should be removed before the term of office expires. If the legislature passes a controversial law, the **referendum** allows the voters to decide whether it should be repealed. If the legislature fails to pass a desired act, the **initiative** lets voters draft legislative proposals and, if they gather enough petition signatures, put these proposals on a ballot, where they can be decided directly by the people. The initiative, thus, is a political safety value that allows people to act directly when legislatures fail to act on hot issues. There is some evidence that the existence of this safety valve keeps the legislatures in touch with public preferences.[46]

Initiatives can be either direct or indirect. Under the *direct* initiative, people draft a bill and put it on the ballot. Not all petitions gain enough signatures to be put on the ballot, and almost two-thirds of those put on the ballot are rejected by the voters.[47] Under the *indirect* initiative, people also draft a bill, but it must be submitted first to the legislature. If the legislature does not act by the end of the legislative session, it goes on the ballot in the next general election.

Direct democracy came into existence at the start of the twentieth century and has been primarily a western phenomena. The seven states of California, Oregon, Washington, Colorado, North Dakota, Oklahoma, and Arizona account for 80 percent of all initiatives.[48] The initiative has become so popular in California that the process has run amok. Twenty-nine separate items were on the ballot in 1988 and another twenty-eight in 1990. To help the voter sort through these issues, the state publishes a voter's pamphlet. In 1990, that pamphlet ran to 222 pages,[49] giving the voters a prodigious reading assignment by any reckoning. When one group gets an initiative qualified for the ballot, it is not rare for opponents to place a contrary proposition on the same ballot. Thus in 1988 there were five different measures on automobile insurance. (Voters selected the one that gave them a 20 percent cut in automobile insurance rates.[50]) Also on the same ballot in 1988, Proposition 68 provided public funding for election campaigns, and Proposition 73 prohibited such funding. Voters passed both measures, which forced the courts to decide which law should prevail. The California Supreme Court opted for Proposition 73, because it received the most votes, but in the meantime, a federal court struck down portions of that law as unconstitutional.[51] Finally, the politics of initiative and referendum have in many ways been transformed from a safety valve for average citizens into an expensive contest between well-heeled interest groups. For the 1988 initiatives in California, for example, three times as much money was spent on initiative contests ($129 million) as the two gubernatorial candidates combined spent on the governor's election ($43.5 million).[52]

These problems have led many scholars to become disillusioned with the initiative. As the Highlight shows, direct democracy does not have a consistent ideological impact. The initiative process introduces an element of political instability and gives the legislators a reason to avoid action on controversial issues in the hope that they will be dealt with through an initiative.[53] From his research on referenda in Toledo, Ohio, Howard Hamilton asserts that direct democracy is governance by an active minority and that "minority may be far from a mirror image of the populace."[54] There is no way to balance the intense wishes of a minority with the less intense wishes of the majority. The rights of minorities seem bound to suffer. Raymond Wolfinger and Fred I. Greenstein sum up the conventional wisdom on direct democracy:

> Asking voters to pass judgment on substantive policy questions strains their information and interest, leading them to decisions that may be inconsistent with their own desires. The consequence is subversion of representative government and the exercise of undue influence by groups that can afford to gather the signatures to qualify a measure for the referendum ballot and then wage a publicity campaign that will have an impact on voters.[55]

Despite its shortcomings, direct democracy is not likely to be dropped where it exists. If anything, its use is growing. The 1980s saw more initiatives passed than any decade since the 1930s.[56] Two-thirds of Californians in a 1982 poll thought that people should vote on important issues directly rather than having them dealt with by the legislature, and two-thirds of Americans in a 1987 Gallup Poll favored a recall provision for members of Congress.[57] Proponents argue that the threat of an initiative victory will often lead the legislature to adopt a compromise bill before the initiative balloting begins. In California, for example, a 1976 initiative banning nuclear power plant construction prompted the legislature to impose a temporary ban on new nuclear plant construction and tighten safety restrictions on all plants.[58] Finally, supporters of direct democracy disagree with the charge in the cartoon on p. 141 that initiatives and referenda are dominated by big spenders.[59]

◇ DIRECT ACTION

Direct action is not an electoral activity. Rather, it is the attempt to influence public policy outcomes through the use of tactics such as citizen contacting, group protests, civil disobedience, labor strikes, rent strikes, sit-ins, and takeovers. *Citizen contacting* refers to communications of demands or grievances by citizens to public officials, both elective and appointive. *Protest* occurs when a group complains about something by staging a march down a main thoroughfare, confronting a mayor in his or her office, or even passing out leaflets in a shopping center. A common protest tactic during the 1960s was for groups of blacks to gather in a mayor's office and demand more jobs for black teenagers. *Civil disobedience* occurs when someone deliberately breaks a law for the purpose

HIGHLIGHT

Direct Democracy in Practice

Direct democracy is a two-edged sword that can have either liberal or conservative outcomes:

Liberal Outcomes	Conservative Outcomes
In 1996, Arizona and California voters approved the legislation of marijuana for medical purposes.	In 1996, California voters repealed the state's affirmative action programs.
In 1992, Oregon voters defeated an anti-gay initiative to amend the state constitution.	In 1992, Colorado voters approved an initiative that would prohibit the categorization of gays and lesbians as a protected class of people.
In 1986, voters in Massachusetts, Oregon, and Rhode Island defeated measures to outlaw abortion or to prohibit state funds for abortions.	In 1986, Vermont voters rejected a state Equal Rights Amendment.
In 1982, voters in eight states passed propositions calling for a freeze in nuclear weapons possessed by the United States and the USSR.	In 1982, voters in Arizona rejected a call for a nuclear freeze.
In 1978, voters in four states refused to set tax and spending limits on their state governments.	Voters in eleven states in 1978 set tax and spending limits on their state governments.
Colorado voters in 1976 refused to repeal the state Equal Rights Amendment and the state sales tax.	In 1978, voters in Miami, Saint Paul, and several other cities repealed gay rights sections of their cities' human rights ordinances.

of turning public opinion against the law. The most famous advocate of civil disobedience was Henry David Thoreau, who refused to pay taxes in support of the Mexican-American War and was jailed.

A *labor strike* occurs when a group of employees refuse to work until management agrees to collective bargaining or other demands. *Rent strike* refers to the refusal to pay rent until some grievance has been met. Tenants pay the rent to an escrow account held by an attorney until the landlord complies.

A *sit-in* is the tactic of people simply sitting in a place where they are not supposed to be until someone in charge responds to their demands. During the civil rights movement, the Student Nonviolent Coordinating Committee (SNCC) brought groups of black and white college students to lunchroom counters that were supposed to be segregated. The lunchroom business could not go on until the manager responded by serving the demonstrators or having them removed. When the demonstrators were convicted of violating the local segregation ordinances, they expanded the scope of the conflict to the federal courts, which usually declared the segregation ordinances unconstitutional.

. . . But for me, stuffing the ballot box is perfectly legal!

In the eyes of critics, direct democracy gives undue influence to well-organized and well-financed special interest groups, contrary to the theory that it returns influence to the average citizen.

Source: Reprinted by permission of Mike Keefe.

A *takeover* is similar to a sit-in. A group simply occupies a facility and refuses to give it up. This tactic was used by some antiwar demonstrators who took over college buildings in the late 1960s. At Columbia University, the demonstrators had to be removed by the New York City police.

These direct action tactics are normally used to achieve some broader goal, such as greater leverage for bargaining. By demonstrating in front of a city hall where they receive television and newspaper attention, the protesters can make the mayors and city councils uncomfortable and force the mayors to negotiate with the protest leaders. Another common objective is to change policies. Protesters often want more minority police or firefighters hired by the city. Antiabortion advocates often demonstrate for the purpose of pressuring state legislators not to liberalize state abortion laws, and women's movement groups often demonstrate for the opposite purpose.

A Successful Example of Direct Action in Practice

The most successful use of direct action tactics came with the civil rights movement, those thousands of isolated activities during the 1950s and 1960s that sought to overturn segregation laws and policies. Although civil rights activities had occurred for decades, they did not draw broad support from blacks and white liberals until the Montgomery bus boycott of 1955 (see the "High-

HIGHLIGHT

The Montgomery Bus Boycott

A critical point in the civil rights movement came late on an afternoon in 1955 when a black domestic maid, Rosa Parks, took a seat in the front of a Montgomery, Alabama, bus. A Montgomery ordinance, typical of other ordinances throughout the South, specified that blacks could sit only at the back of the bus. But the back seats were full that day, so Rosa Parks would have had to stand if she moved to the rear of the bus. She later stated that she had no intention of starting a bus boycott; she was simply too tired to ride home standing up. So she refused to move and was arrested.

The plight of Rosa Parks captured the imagination of Montgomery blacks, who began protesting against the arrest and the rear-of-the-bus rule. They joined a well-organized boycott designed to get the bus company to change its policy. A key figure in the boycott was Martin Luther King, Jr., then a young minister, who led much of the protest activity and went to jail himself for his demonstrations. Not only did the boycott get the company policy changed, the litigation following the boycott resulted in a federal court decision declaring all such bus segregation unconstitutional.

Source: *Gayle* v. *Browder*, 352 U.S. 903 (1956).

---

light" above). Encouraged by the success of Montgomery's bus boycott, black leaders organized other protest demonstrations and sit-ins that sought to desegregate other facilities, such as lunch counters, hotels, restaurants, libraries, schools, universities, rest rooms, and parks. A key strategy was expanding the scope of the conflict beyond local southern communities to the federal level, which culminated with the Civil Rights Act of 1964 and the Voting Rights Act of 1965. Perhaps the most successfully implemented feature of the 1964 act was the prohibition of racial discrimination in public accommodations, such as movies, theaters, hotels, and restaurants. The 1965 act extended the voting franchise to blacks throughout the South.

The civil rights movement did not eliminate all the inequities that blacks suffered and continue to suffer; nor did it end racial discrimination. However, it did give middle-class blacks access to mainstream facilities and institutions in American society that previously had been closed to them. In this respect, the civil rights movement was clearly the most successful use of direct action in the history of the United States.

What Does Direct Action Accomplish?

Two strong proponents of the notion that direct action forces governments to respond in some way to the grievances of the protesters are Frances Fox Piven and Richard Cloward.[60] Although a specific protest action may not lead to a specific policy change, Piven and Cloward argue, the repeated use of direct action tactics during the 1930s and the 1960s definitely produced policy benefits for working-class and poor people. During the 1930s, the policy benefits for working-class people centered on organized labor. The National Labor Relations Act of 1935 forced employers to bargain collectively with unions and to refrain from certain strike-breaking tactics. The 1930s also saw the introduction of a number of other labor programs, such as unemployment compensation and workers' compensation. During the 1960s, the policy benefits for the poor were AFDC, Food Stamps, Medicaid and health care, poverty programs, and a broad increase in the number of programs targeted at poor people.

Piven and Cloward argue that when the fear of lower-class insurrection passed, the political system once again contracted. Although the 1930s saw the federal government protect union-organizing activities, the next two decades saw numerous attempts to restrict the influence of unions. The 1960s saw a broad expansion in federal programs for the poor, but the 1970s saw the Model Cities program, the Office of Economic Opportunity, and several other innovations of the poverty program either discontinued or substantially cut back. In the view of Piven and Cloward, this historical record is evidence that governments expand benefits to lower-class people when those people use direct action to threaten rebellion, and governments restrict benefits when those people become peaceful.

Whether direct action is really as effective as Piven and Cloward believe is debatable. Arguing from historical trends is always dangerous. One could also use historical developments to argue that the most notable consequence of such direct actions as the draft riots of the Civil War, the ghetto revolts of the 1960s, or the labor disturbances of the early twentieth century was the direct, violent, and deadly repression of the participants.

In many respects, the most notable beneficiaries of direct action have been not the poor, but the upwardly mobile middle class. The civil rights movement was led by the black middle class, which derived most of the benefits from civil rights legislation. Benefits gained by labor strikes primarily go to people who already have jobs, and most of those people are above the poverty class.

Perhaps the most serious shortcoming of direct action tactics is their failure to lead to the creation of permanent institutions to represent the interests of the protesters. The most successful transition from direct action tactics to institution building occurred in organized labor. What began as movements by militant agitators during the 1880s was transformed in the 1930s into organized labor unions, which are officially recognized by the government and have the legal right to bargain collectively and to strike.

Most direct action movements, however, have not transformed themselves into permanent institutions, and this is especially true of the civil rights movement. After the Civil Rights Act of 1964 and the Voting Rights Act of 1965 were passed by Congress, most of the established civil rights organizations declined in membership and political impact.[61] The success of the civil rights movement and the growing voting power of blacks had broadened the political horizons of all black leaders. Middle-class blacks gained many new opportunities that they never had before; they could become business executives, mayors, members of Congress, academics, or anything else that was open to white middle-class people. But there is a shortage of permanent institutions to represent the economic interests of lower-class blacks very well.

◇ SOCIAL CHANGE AND THE BALLOT BOX

How do women, minorities, and the lower income fare in the battle of the ballot box? Since white men hold the majority of elected positions in the country, it would seem that women and minorities are at a big disadvantage. In fact, however, they fare quite well at the ballot box.

The National Women's Political Caucus studied success rates for female and male candidates in state legislative races from 1986 to 1992 and for Congress and governors from 1972 to 1992. When women ran as incumbents, they won more than 90 percent of the time, giving them the same success rate as men. When women ran against men for open seats, they won 55 percent of the time in state senate contests and 52 percent of the time in state house contests. When they ran as challengers in state senate contests, women beat male incumbents 17 percent of the time, compared to only 11 percent of the time that male challengers beat incumbent female senators.[62] Based on these results, women do as well as men in electoral contests, and may be doing even slightly better. Why then, do women only hold about a fourth of state legislative seats? The most likely reason is that up to the present, incumbents have more frequently been male than female. As increasing numbers of women compete in elections, their percent of officeholders will continue to rise in the future as it has in the past.

Although we do not have comparable studies for the electoral success of minorities, other statistics tell much the same story. The number of black elected officials in the nation more than quintupled from 1,469 in 1970 to 7,984 in 1993, and the number of Hispanic elected officials increased by two-thirds from 3,147 in 1985 to 5,459 in 1993.[63] Black members of the U.S. House of Representatives totaled thirty-nine by 1995, or 9 percent of the total membership. By comparison, blacks account for about 12.6 percent of the total U.S. population.

Although women and minorities have made dramatic gains at the ballot box in recent years, the same cannot be said for the low-income population. In fact, there is some reason to believe that they continue to lose influence. For example, voter turnout in presidential elections dropped twenty-seven percent among the poorest quintile of voters, compared to a drop of only one percent in the richest quintile of voters.[64]

Does it make any difference that turnout rates continue to fall among the lowest income groups of the population? Emphatically yes. If low-income people do not turn out at the polls, they do not give political support to legislators who might otherwise be inclined to help them. In states where low-income people have the best voter turnout rates, welfare benefits were above average. In states with the worst turnout rates among low-income people, welfare benefits were below average.[65]

In essence, the electoral impact of the contemporary social movements among women, minorities, and gay rights activists has been in keeping with the historical pattern of American immigrant politics. Americans traditionally organized themselves along ethnic and religious lines rather than class lines. Irish, Jewish, Italian, and other European immigrant politicians of the early twentieth century sought primarily their own upward mobility to the middle class rather than a social revolution that would demolish class boundaries. Immigrant machine politicians may have drawn their political support from the lower classes, and they certainly rewarded their supporters with as many favors and benefits as they could arrange, but they generally worked to carve out their own place in the existing social order.[66] Elected women and minority leaders today do the same. This is not to say that their work is unimportant, for they have broken down barriers against other women and other minorities. But their primary goals are gender based and ethnic based rather than class based. With the decline of organized labor, as discussed in the last chapter, and the splintering of the Democratic party into ideological and ethnic enclaves as discussed in this chapter, the lower- and lower-middle income populations have seen their electoral influence decline.

◇ CONCLUSION

One theme that has pervaded the past two chapters has been that state and local governments are more responsive to established institutions and to special interests than they are to the public interest, to the interests of isolated citizens who are unrepresented by existing institutions, or to the poorest part of the population. The conventional channels of citizen influence (public opinion, elections, political parties, and interest groups) tend to be dominated by large, economic-based institutions. These channels of citizen influence also are more capable of communicating middle-class concerns to the government than of transmitting concerns of either the poor or isolated individuals who do not speak for some specific interest.

In contrast to these conventional channels of political influence, the 1960s and 1970s saw significant use of the more unconventional tactics of direct action and independent political action. Many of the tactics of direct action and independent political action seem to depend on face-to-face contacts and the mass mobilization of people in relatively small communities, such as in a business establishment, a small town, a suburb, or a big-city neighborhood. Because these tactics seem most appropriate for community-level politics, we need to make a closer examination of such politics. Chapter 7 will examine the institutions of local government, and Chapter 8 will look into the dynamics of community politics.

SUMMARY

1. The election process is the most fundamental institution of democracy. However, elections were found to be very limited channels for citizen input to public policy for several reasons. Elections do not give mandates. At the local level, elected officials are not greatly concerned with the opinions of the mass of the electorate, since reelection is not a worry.
2. Political parties play roles in nominating candidates to office and in organizing the government once the election is over. The parties tend to be decentralized organizations, with the strongest units at the county and state legislative district levels. Recent years have seen a decline in people's tendency to identify as strong Democrats

or strong Republicans. Despite these declines, recent scholarship attributes more importance to interparty competition than was thought a decade earlier. The thrust of policymaking, as well, will depend on whether a state is controlled by the Republicans or the Democrats.

3. Direct democracy refers to the initiative, the referendum, and the recall. These controversial practices are most popular in the West. They can be used for either liberal or conservative causes.

4. Direct action strategies were extremely successful during the civil rights movement of the 1950s and 1960s. They have had more limited success, however, in trying to combat such complicated urban problems as slum housing. To be successful, direct action requires excellent leadership, sympathetic outsider political actors in the press and in government, and an ability to expand the scope of the conflict beyond the local level to the state and national levels.

5. The social movements of the past two decades have brought more electoral influence to women and minorities than they have to low- and moderate-income people.

KEY TERMS

Blanket primary   A primary election in which the ballot lists all the parties, enabling a voter to choose some Democrats and some Republicans.

Challenge primary   A primary election held only if the candidates receive a show of support in their party's nominating convention.

Closed primary   A primary election in which only identifiable party supporters may vote. Only Republicans may vote in the Republican primary, and only Democrats may vote in the Democratic primary.

Direct action   Such political tactics to influence public policy as group protests, civil disobedience, strikes, and sit-ins.

Direct democracy   The initiative, the referendum, and the recall as political devices.

District election   See *Ward election.*

Initiative   A political device that lets voters draft legislative proposals and, if they gather enough petition signatures, put their proposals on a ballot, where they can be decided directly by the people.

Nominating convention   A political party's convention for nominating candidates for public office.

Nonpartisan primary   A primary election in which the ballot does not list the nominees by party affiliation, and the nomination goes to the two candidates who get the most votes.

Open primary   A primary election in which anyone can vote, regardless of party affiliation.

Political machine   A tightly knit party organization that controls the party's nominations for public office and controls many patronage jobs.

Primary election   An election held to choose nominees to compete for public office in the general election.

Proactive accountability   The idea that elections give winners a mandate to establish a specific line of policy.

Recall   A political device that allows voters to remove from office, before his or her term ends, an official who has invoked popular displeasure.

Referendum   A political device for letting the voters decide whether a law just passed by a legislature should be repealed. Also a device for letting voters decide to approve municipal bond issues or to amend the constitution of a state.

Reformed election system   An election system characterized by nonpartisan, at-large elections.

Retroactive accountability The idea of holding someone accountable after the fact

Soft money The channeling of campaign contributions that might be illegal federally or in one state to a political party in a state where the contribution will not be illegal.

Tripartite organization The view of the political party as composed of three components: the party organization, the party in the electorate, and the party in government.

Unreformed election system An election system characterized by partisan, ward elections.

Volunteerism Refers to elected officials who look on themselves as community volunteers doing a civic duty rather than as professional politicians attempting to build a career. Common among suburban local officials.

Ward election An election in which city council members are elected from neighborhood units called wards or districts.

REFERENCES

1. For further discussion of this point, see John J. Harrigan, *Political Change in the Metropolis*, 4th ed. (Glenview, Ill.: Scott, Foresman, 1989), Ch. 4.
2. Gerald Pomper, *Elections in America: Control and Influence in Democratic Politics* (New York: Dodd, Mead, 1968), pp. 254–255.
3. Kenneth Prewitt, "Political Ambitions, Volunteerism, and Electoral Accountability," *American Political Science Review* 64, no. 1 (March 1970): 5–17.
4. Joseph A. Schlesinger, *Ambition and Politics* (Chicago: Rand McNally, 1966), p. 2.
5. M. Kent Jennings and Harmon Zeigler, "The Salience of American State Politics," *American Political Science Review* 64, no. 2 (June 1970): 523–535.
6. Eric M. Uslaner and Ronald E. Weber, "Representing People Who Have Interests," a paper presented at the 1980 meeting of the Midwest Political Science Association, Chicago, April 1980, pp. 19–20. Also see Uslaner and Weber, "U.S. State Legislators' Opinions and Perceptions of Constituency Attitudes," *Legislative Studies Quarterly* 4 (November 1979): 563–585.
7. Dick Kirschten, "The Targets of Discontent," *National Journal* 22, no 45, (Nov. 10, 1990): 2736–2742.
8. Randall W. Partin, "Economic Conditions and Gubernatorial Elections: Is the State Executive Held Accountable?" *American Politics Quarterly* 23, no. 1 (January 1995): 81–95.
9. Susan J. Kane and Richard F. Winters, "Taxes and Voting: Electoral Retribution in the American States," *Journal of Politics* 55, no. 1 (February 1993): 27–40. Kane and Winters studies 407 gubernatorial elections from 1957 through 1985.
10. See *The New York Times*, November 6, 1991, p. 1.
11. Thomas R. Dye, *Politics, Economics, and the Public: Policy Outcomes in the American States* (Chicago: Rand McNally, 1966), pp. 260–270.
12. Raymond E. Wolfinger and Steven J. Rosenstone, *Who Votes?* (New Haven, Conn.: Yale University Press, 1980), p. 85.
13. Kim Quaile Hill and Jan E. Leighley, "The Policy Consequences of Class Bias in State Electorates," *American Journal of Political Science* 36, no 2 (May 1992): 351–365.
14. Tommy Neal, "The Sky High Cost of Campaigning," *State Legislatures* 18, no. 5 (May 1992): 16–20; Thad Beyle, "Costs of the 1990 Gubernatorial Campaigns," *Comparative State Politics* 12, no. 5 (October 1991): 3–7.
15. Terry Christensen and Larry N. Gerston, *The California Connection: Politics in the Golden State* (Boston: Little, Brown and Co., 1984), pp. 33–37.
16. Herbert E. Alexander, *Financing Politics: Money, Elections, and Political Reform*, 4th ed. (Washington, D.C.: Congressional Quarterly Press, 1992), pp. 127–131.

17. Herbert E. Alexander, "Political Parties and the Dollar," *Society* 22, no. 2 (January–February 1985): 54.

18. Robert J. Huckshorn, "Who Gave It? Who Got It? The Enforcement of Campaign Finance Laws in the States," *Journal of Politics* 47, no. 3 (August 1985): 773–791. The information on New Jersey was provided by the agency director. See *The New York Times,* December 27, 1988, p. 7.

19. Herbert E. Alexander, *Reform and Reality: The Financing of State and Local Campaigns* (New York: The Twentieth Century Fund Press, 1991).

20. Herbert E. Alexander, "The Resurgence of Election Reform in the States and Cities," *Comparative State Politics Newsletter* 9, no. 6 (December 1988): 30–32. The seven states were Arizona, California, Florida, North Carolina, Ohio, Oregon, and Rhode Island.

21. Robert A. Cropf, "Public Campaign Financing in New Jersey," *Comparative State Politics* 13, no. 2 (April 1992): 1011.

22. Frank J. Sorauf and Paul Allen Beck, *Party Politics in America,* 6th ed. (Glenview, Ill.: Scott, Foresman, 1988), pp. 9–11.

23. Charles W. Wiggins and William L. Turk, "State Party Chairmen: A Profile," *Western Political Quarterly* 23, no. 2 (June 1970): 321–332.

24. A study of party endorsements in seven midwestern states from 1960 to 1990 found that party-endorsed candidates for governor won their primary elections 88 percent of the time and those for attorney general won 96 percent of the time. James P. Melcher, "Party Endorsements for Statewide Office," a paper presented at the Midwest Political Science Association convention, Chicago, Illinois, April 14–16, 1994.

25. James P. Melcher, "Party Endorsements in Minnesota in the Wake of the 1994 Elections: Reform Strikes Out," *Comparative State Politics* 16, no. 6 (December 1995): 1–13.

26. The extensiveness of such party crossover voting is, however, not really known. One study of presidential primaries in Wisconsin from 1968 to 1984 estimated such partisan crossover to be no more than 11 percent of the voters. More numerous were Independents who voted in Republican or Democratic primaries (about 34 to 39 percent of the total). The overwhelming majority of primary election voters were people who belonged to the party in whose primary they were voting. See Ronald D. Hedlund and Meredith W. Watts, "The Wisconsin Open Primary: 1968–1984," *American Politics Quarterly* 14, nos. 1 and 2 (January–April 1986): 55–74.

27. *Tashjian* v. *Republican Party of Connecticut* 107 S.Ct. 544 (1986).

28. A 1980 study estimated that the machine controlled 20,000 jobs. Price, *Bringing Back the Parties,* p. 23.

29. *Elrod* v. *Burns* 427 U.S. 347 (1976), *Branti* v. *Finkel* 445 U.S. 507 (1980), and *Rutan* v. *Republican Party of Illinois* 110 S.Ct. 2729 (1990).

30. Malcolm E. Jewell and David M. Olson, *American State Political Parties and Elections* (Homewood, Ill.: Dorsey Press, 1982), p. 181.

31. Advisory Commission on Intergovernmental Relations, *The Transformation of American Politics: Implications for Federalism* (Washington, D.C.: U.S. Government Printing Office, 1986), p. 115.

32. Cindy Simon Rosenthal, "Where's the Party?" *State Legislatures* 20, no. 6 (June 1994): 33.

33. Frank J. Sorauf, *Maney in American Elections* (Glenview, Ill.: Scott, Foresman, 1988), p. 268.

34. James L. Gibson, Cornelius P. Cotter, John F. Bibby, and Robert J. Huckshorn, "Whither the Local Parties? A Cross-Sectional and Longitudinal Analysis of the Strength of Party Organizations," *American Journal of Political Science* 29, no. 1 (February 1985): 139–161.

35. See Harold W. Stanley, "Southern Partisan Changes: Dealignment, Realignment or Both?" *Journal of Politics* 50, no. 1 (February 1988): 64–87. Stanley found that in 1952, barely 14 percent of southern whites called themselves Republican; by 1984, this had increased to almost 40 percent.

36. Charles D. Hadley, "Dual Partisan Identification in the South," *Journal of Politics* 47, no. 1 (February 1985): 255–268.

37. Robert D. Brown and Gerald C. Wright, "Elections and State Party Polarization," *American Politics Quarterly* 20, no. 4 (October 1992): 411–426.

38. V. O. Key, Jr., *Southern Politics in State and Nation* (New York: Knopf, 1949), Ch. 5.

39. Samuel C. Patterson and Gregory A. Caldeira, "The Etiology of Partisan Competition," *American Political Science Review* 78, no. 3 (September 1984): 691–707.

40. See especially Dye, *Politics, Economics, and the Public*, pp. 293–297; Richard E. Dawson and James A. Robinson, "Inter-Party Competition, Economic Variables, and Welfare Policies in the American States," *Journal of Politics* 25, no. 2 (May 1963): 265–289; Richard I. Hofferbert, "The Relation Between Public Policy and Some Structural and Environmental Variables in the American States," *American Political Science Review* 60, no. 1 (March 1966): 78–82.

41. Virginia Gray studied competition and policy over time and found that when the competition was unstable, two-party competition affected welfare policy outcomes. See Gray, "The Effect of Party Competition on State Policy, A Reformulation: Organizational Survival," *Polity* 7, no. 2 (Winter 1974): 248–263. Gerald C. Wright used a multiple regression of the logarithms of two-party competition and welfare expenditures and found a curvilinear rather than a linear relationship. That is, increasing the degree of competition did not affect policy outcomes until it became very competitive. Once competition approached the maximum possible level, it began to have significant effect on outcomes. See Wright, "Interparty Competition and State Welfare Policy: When a Difference Makes a Difference," *Journal of Politics* 37, no. 3 (August 1975): 796–803. Finally, Richard I. Hofferbert found that two-party competition combined with high voter turnouts produced higher expenditures for education and welfare. See Hofferbert, *The Study of Public Policy* (Indianapolis: Bobbs-Merrill, 1974), pp. 218–221.

42. Herbert McClosky, Paul J. Hoffmann, and Rosemary O'Hara, "Issue Conflict and Consensus Among Party Leaders and Followers," *American Political Science Review* 54, no. 2 (June 1960): 406–427. For a similar finding in relation to the 1980 national conventions, see *The New York Times*, August 13, 1980, p. B-2.

43. Robert X. Browning and William P. Shaffer, "Leaders and Followers in a Strong Party State," *American Politics Quarterly* 15, no. 1 (January 1987): 87–106.

44. Robert S. Erikson, "The Relationship Between Party Control and Civil Rights Legislation in the American States," *Western Political Quarterly* 24, no. 1 (March 1971): 178–182.

45. Richard Winters, "Party Control and Policy Change," *American Journal of Political Science* 20, no. 4 (November 1976): 597–636.

46. Elizabeth Gerber examined the passage of legislation requiring parental notification or parental consent before a minor could have an abortion. She compared the existence of such legislation to state-level public opinion surveys and found not only that the legislation was more likely to pass in states where it had popular support, but it was even more likely to pass in such states if they had the initiative. The potential threat of an initiative, thus, may have helped persuade legislators to pass the law. Elizabeth R. Gerber, "Legislative Response to the Threat of Popular Initiatives," *American Journal of Political Science* 40, no. 1 (February 1966): 99–128.

47. Richard Winters, "Party Control and Policy Change," *American Journal of Political Science* 20, no. 4 (November 1976): 597–636.
48. Charles M. Price, "The Initiative: A Comparative State Analysis and Reassessment of a Western Phenomenom," *Western Political Quarterly* 28, no. 2 (June 1975): 243–262.
49. John C. Syer and John H. Culver, *Power and Politics in California*, 4th ed. (New York: Macmillan, 1992), p. 157.
50. See *The New York Times*, November 11, 1988, p. 1; November 12, 1988, p. 6.
51. Syer and Culver, *Power and Politics in California*, p. 159.
52. Ibid., p. 156.
53. William J. Keefe and Morris S. Ogul, *The American Legislative Process: Congress and the States*, 3rd ed. (Englewood Cliffs, N.J.: Prentice-Hall, 1973), p. 258.
54. Howard D. Hamilton, "Direct Legislation: Some Implications of Open Housing Referenda," *American Political Science Review* 64, no. 1 (March 1970): 127, 131.
55. Raymond E. Wolfinger and Fred I. Greenstein, "The Repeal of Fair Housing in California: An Analysis of Referendum Voting," *American Political Science Review* 62, no. 3 (September 1968): 787.
56. David B. Magleby, "Taking the Initiative: Direct Legislation and Direct Democracy in the 1980s," *PS: Political Science and Politics* 21, no. 3 (Summer 1988): 603.
57. See Thomas E. Cronin, "Public Opinion and Direct Democracy," *PS: Political Science and Politics* 21, no. 3 (Summer 1988): 613–615.
58. Gladwin Hill, "Initiatives: A Score Card," *Working Papers for a New Society* 4, no. 4 (Winter 1977): 33–37.
59. John R. Owens and Larry L. Wade studied campaign spending for and against 708 ballot propositions in California between 1924 and 1984. They concluded that "Money has simply been overemphasized as a determinant of voting on direct legislation." See their "Campaign Spending on California's Ballot Propositions, 1924–1984: Trends and Voting Effects," *Western Political Quarterly* 39, no. 4 (December 1986): 688.
60. Frances Fox Piven and Richard A. Cloward, *Regulating the Poor: The Functions of Public Welfare* (New York: Random House, 1971).
61. On the decline of black civil rights interest groups since 1965, see Hanes Walton, Jr., *Black Politics: A Theoretical and Structural Analysis* (Philadelphia: Lippincott, 1972), pp. 140–160.
62. Cited in *State Legislatures* (December 1994): 5.
63. United States Bureau of the Census, *Statistical Abstract of the United States: 1995* (Washington, D.C.: U.S. Government Printing Office, 1995), p. 287.
64. Calculated from National Election Studies data preserved in Jan E. Leighley and Jonathan Nagler, "Socio-economic Class Bias in Turnout, 1964–1988. The Voters Remain the Same," *The American Political Science Review* 86, no. 3 (September 1992): 731. In the interest of accuracy, it must be noted that Leighley and Nagler draw the opposite conclusion from their reading of its data.
65. Kim Quaile Hill and Jan E. Leighley, "The Policy Consequences Class Bias in State Electorates," *American Journal of Political Science* 36, no. 2 (May 1992): 351–365.
66. John J. Harrigan, *Political Change in the Metropolis*, 5th ed. (New York: HarperCollins, Publishers, 1993), Chapter 3.

THE INSTITUTIONS OF LOCAL GOVERNMENT

Chapter Review

To understand how state and local governments affect our lives, we need to understand how local government is organized, why it is organized the way it is, and the biases inherent in its organization. We will cover these topics in this chapter by examining:

1. The different types of local governments and the functions they perform.
2. How cities and counties are organized.
3. How machine-style politics came to dominate cities in the nineteenth century but has faded since the midtwentieth century.
4. How reform-style politics emerged as a reaction to machine-style politics, and how reform-style politics has biases of its own.
5. How the metropolitan challenge has been confronted.

Let us begin with an overview of the types of local governments in the United States.

◇ INTRODUCTION

We each live in a community. It may be rural, small town, big city, or suburban, but in the last analysis, it is in a local place where the quality of our lives is determined and where we have our most visible contact with government. Those contacts might include the local schools, the local welfare department, local drinking water, local street maintenance, local public libraries, local police services, and so on. It is also to a local place that we usually develop out strongest emotional attachments. Few Los Angelenos, I would bet, spend much time worrying about the quality of life of the sprawling Los Angeles Consolidated Statistical Area (to use the cumbersome language of the U.S. Census Bureau). Rather,

151

they identify with, and show concern about, some smaller neighborhood or suburb where they happen to live—hard-pressed Watts, perhaps, or tony Beverly Hills. In fact, the United States during the twentieth century built up a nationwide collection of locally delivered public services that became the envy of the world—even most of the advanced industrialized world.

Today, our community public lives are under great pressure as a result of many forces over which local governments have little control. These include social change, international economic competition, growing divisiveness between the country's mosaic of ethno-religious and ideological groups, the fraying of stabilizing social institutions such as the family, and huge demographic migrations that have poured more than a hundred million people into the great suburban developments that seem to be sprawling beyond the ability of local governments to keep up.

In Chapters 7 and 8, we want to examine the local governments that try to cope with these pressures. We will begin with some groundwork in Chapter 7 by describing the institutions of local government. Then, in Chapter 8, we will turn to the dynamics of community politics.

Let us begin this excursion into community politics by focusing on (1) the different types of local government, (2) county and city organization, (3) the evolution of reform-style local government, and (4) the metropolitan challenge.

◇ DIFFERENT TYPES OF LOCAL GOVERNMENT

Local government structure is much more complicated than state government structure. Whereas the 50 states all have very similar constitutions, the 80,000 local governments have an array of structures. Some local governments (counties, municipalities, towns, and townships) have a general purpose and perform a variety of governmental functions. Others (school districts and special districts) have a single purpose and perform only one function.

Single-Purpose Local Governments

The two single-purpose local governments are the **school district** and the special district. As Table 7-1 shows, there has been a sharp decline in the number of school districts over the past half century. This decline resulted from the movement to consolidate school districts. School districts have been pressed to provide new educational services, costly laboratories, and expensive athletic equipment. Small rural school districts often cannot afford these services, and several small districts may find themselves pressured to consolidate into one large district. The trend of school district consolidation, however, has slowed down dramatically since 1982.

Although the number of school districts has declined, the number of non-school, single-purpose special districts has more than tripled since 1942. A **special district** is a government that provides a single service. In metropolitan areas, for example, often one special district is used to provide public transit

Table 7-1   NUMBER OF GOVERNMENTS IN THE UNITED STATES

	1942	1952	1962	1972	1982	1992
Counties	3,050	3,049	3,043	3,044	3,041	3,043
Municipalities	16,220	16,778	18,000	18,517	19,083	19,296
Townships and towns	18,919	17,202	17,142	16,991	16,748	16,666
School districts	108,579	67,346	34,678	15,781	15,032	14,556
Special districts	8,299	12,319	18,323	23,885	28,733	33,131
Total local governments	155,067	116,694	91,186	78,218	82,637	86,692
States	48	48	50	50	50	50
Federal	1	1	1	1	1	1
Total all governments	155,116	116,743	91,237	78,269	82,688	86,743

Note: The growth in local governments since 1972 is accounted for by the continuing proliferation of special districts combined with a dramatic slowdown in the rate of school district consolidations.

Source: Bureau of the Census, *Census of Governments: 1987* (Washington, D.C.: U.S. Government Printing Office, 1990), p. vi.; *Statistical Abstract of the United States: 1995* (Washington, D.C.: U. S. Government Printing Office, 1995), p. 297.

services, another to construct suburban hospitals, another to install sewer systems, another to provide water supply, and still another to handle housing and renewal activities.

Because the need for their services is so apparent, and their mode of operation so apparently businesslike, the number of special districts has proliferated, and, as Table 7-1 shows, they are still proliferating today. They do, however, create two serious problems—coordination and lack of accountability. Especially in metropolitan areas, where governmental coordination is important, the existence of too many special districts can threaten effective governance. Also, since their governing officials are more often appointed rather than elected, they are not very visible. Even when special-district officials are elected, the election turnouts are pitifully low. In some instances, the elections have not been held because nobody knew when they were scheduled or because nobody ran.[1] For all these reasons, special districts, in principle, present serious problems of accountability. Political reformers favor the consolidation of school districts, but they oppose the continuing growth in special districts.[2]

General-Purpose Local Governments

The general-purpose local governments are counties, municipalities, towns, townships, and villages. Although they are labeled general-purpose governments, they are not general purpose in the same sense that the state is a general-purpose government. They are much more limited in what they can do, and their grants of authority are much more specific.

The **county** is the basic administrative subdivision of the state, and its existence is often specified in the state constitution. It is responsible in most states for the local administration of some state services, including law enforcement, justice, welfare, roads, agricultural extension services, and, in some states, education. As a form of government, the county is strongest in the South and Southwest, where the historical rural character, low population density, and more elitist nature of local politics facilitated a form of government that covered large geographic areas and required less concentration of authority. Authority was dispersed through a large number of administrative agencies that had little to do with one another. There was little coordination among the county highway department, the county welfare department, and the county courts. Patronage was widespread, and the legislative board of commissioners made little attempt to control the departments. As the Highlight illustrates, this was precisely the way that many traditional county officials wanted to keep things.

In New England, the **town** rather than the county has been the predominant form of local government. Towns perform many of the same functions as counties, but they govern a much smaller geographic area, usually twenty to forty square miles,[3] which encompasses both urban and rural territory. The most distinctive feature of town government is the famous town meeting. This takes place once a year when the voters meet, establish the town budget for the following year, enact ordinances, and set the town policies. The town meeting has been proclaimed as America's unique contribution to direct democracy.[4] Be-

HIGHLIGHT

County Government: The Best That's Ever Been

The tension created between a rural-oriented county commissioner and a reform-oriented professional person is graphically illustrated in the following excerpts from a Texas university professor's interview with a prominent Harris County (Houston) commissioner, E. J. "Squatty" Lyons. Lyons expresses his scorn for modern techniques of public administration, from merit systems of personnel management to unity of command to home rule.

INTERVIEWER: One of the basic principles of organizational theory is that of unity of command, that organizations should be based on a single hierarchy with one official at the top to direct and coordinate the organization's activities. Does county government need a strong executive?

LYONS: You're talking about a dictatorship.

INTERVIEWER: Or the type of arrangement we have with the president and executive branch at the national level, or the strong-mayor system that Houston has.

LYONS: It's the strong-mayor system that makes Houston city government so . . . bad. You got thousands of employees and every one of them is the mayor's employee—you got dictatorship in Houston.

INTERVIEWER: Is the county administration too politicized? Would the adoption of a civil service system lead to more professional administration?

LYONS: How can you point to a civil service as such a great thing? You've got a perfect example in the city of Houston. I mean, officials just have one hell of a time keeping loyalty or anything else among employees. They sit back and say kiss my foot . . . and that's the biggest fun in the world, to tell the people who are signing your paycheck to kiss my foot.

INTERVIEWER: . . . [W]ould you favor a home-rule amendment to the constitution giving counties the authority to design their own governing structures?

LYONS: Now, people like that word *home rule* but it's a misnomer. . . . What it amounts to is boss rule. You put some big jackass up there [as county manager] who's been appointed by five or seven or nine people to run the show and the only way the taxpayer can get to that S.O.B. is to have enough influence with the majority of those who appointed him. . . . He can just ignore the individual citizen.

INTERVIEWER: What concluding statement would you like to make on behalf of county government?

LYONS: I like county government because you can vote for or against the man responsible for the specific service. . . . You can take your blackboard government. . . . You can draw up a plan where every S.O.B. who follows it is going to be a millionaire in twenty years. But you just don't get things done drawing on blackboards. People with their blackboard governments just don't know what they're talking about. It just doesn't work that way in practice.

Source: David Fairbanks, "County Government—The Best That's Ever Been: An Interview with E. J. 'Squatty' Lyons," Eugene W. Jones, et al.: *Practicing Texas Politics,* Fifth Edition. Copyright © 1986 by Houghton Mifflin Company. Used by permission.

tween town meetings, day-to-day operations are carried out by elected, part-time officials.

The **township** as a form of government exists primarily in the Midwest. Townships are primarily rural units of government. They perform at the local level many of the functions that the county performs at the countywide level. Thus a township constable performs local police functions that supplement those of the county sheriff. Townships are governed by a town meeting and township officers similar to those used in the New England towns. As township territory gets invaded by growing metropolitan populations, the territory is quite often annexed to suburbs or central cities, which are better able to provide the public services that the urban populations require.

The **municipality** is the form of government in cities. Most Americans live in municipalities. Unlike the counties, which are basic subdivisions of the state, municipalities (or city governments) only come into existence when they are incorporated by a charter. The charter prescribes the basic structure of city government and outlines its powers. The city charter has been a target of the political reform movement.

Local Charters

The legal authority for local government differs fundamentally from the legal authority for states. The U.S. Constitution reserves to the states all the governmental powers not given by the Constitution exclusively to the national government or reserved exclusively to the people. Local governments, on the other hand, are creatures of the state and have only those powers that are specifically given to them by the state constitution, the state legislature, or the state charter. If a city wants to do something not specified in the charter then the courts usually prohibit the city from action by applying **Dillon's Rule.** Dillon's Rule is named after Judge John Dillon, who established the principle of law that city governments' powers are very restricted. Cities may exercise only the powers specifically mentioned in their charter. Dillon wrote, "Any fair, reasonable, substantial doubt concerning the existence of power is resolved by the courts against the [city government], and the power is denied."[5]

The city charter spells out the precise powers that the local government possesses and determines how the government is to be organized. The charters fall into five categories—special charters, general charters, classified charters, optional charters, and home rule charters. *Special charters* arose shortly after independence when the legislatures enacted different charters for each city. As a result, the patterns of city governance had very little uniformity, and the legislatures were more deeply involved in city governance than many people desired.

In reaction, states began enacting a *general charter* for cities that provided uniform patterns of governance but also imposed a straitjacket on city governing structures. A city of a few thousand people need not be governed in the same way as a city of a million. Consequently, the *classified charter* was established to separate cities by population size. Cities of the largest class have the greatest grants of authority.

A number of states provide an *optional charter,* which allows cities within the same population classification to choose among a number of optional kinds of government.

Most reformers prefer the *home rule charter,* which allows the residents of a city to choose whatever form of government they want. Such a charter is drafted by a local charter commission and submitted for voter approval through referendum.

Division of Local Government Responsibilities

As Table 7-2 shows, there is some overlap in the functions served by the different local governments. But there also is some specialization. Counties (outside of New England) bear the biggest burden for human and social services, yet they handle very little in the way of redevelopment activities. Cities have the biggest burden for public safety in urban areas and for the physical maintenance of the urban infrastructure (streets, sewers, water supply, and park space). School districts have the biggest burden for public education. And other special districts share with cities the main burden of redevelopment activity and physical maintenance.

◇ THE ORGANIZATION OF COUNTIES AND CITIES

Counties

Counties are governed by legislative bodies that usually bear the name **county board of supervisors** or **county board of commissioners.** More than 70 percent of these county legislators are elected from districts, with the balance being chosen in countywide, at-large elections.[6] County boards tend to be very weak and fragmented.[7]

Although some of the most important public services—such as welfare, public health, sheriff's patrol, county jail—are delivered by county governments, these governments are generally the most fragmented of all major local governments. The executive power is typically divided among several agencies, which report individually to the county board rather than to a chief executive. This gives the agencies considerable independence, especially the larger departments, such as welfare and highway maintenance. Many of the smaller agencies, such as tax assessors and bureaus of vital statistics, are dominated by local political factions and are hotbeds of patronage employment. These factions effectively resist and oppose centralized administrative control. Some department heads, such as sheriffs, are often elected directly, giving them an independent political base and making them even more insulated from the county board. In Texas, for example, independently elected county officials include the sheriff, county attorney, county clerk, tax assessor, treasurer, auditor, and county surveyor.[8]

In order to reform these executive weaknesses of traditional county government, reformers have posed three alternatives—the county administrator, the county manager, and the elected county executive. The county administrator is

Table 7-2 DIVISION OF LOCAL GOVERNMENT RESPONSIBILITIES

Expenditures for all Services in the Category by Type of Local Government: 1986–87
(in Billions)

General Category of Local Service	County	Municipality	Township	Special District	School District	Total
Human and social services (welfare, hospitals, public health, corrections)	$34.6 (60.2%)	$15.2 (26.4%)	$0.3 (0.6%)	$7.4 (12.8%)	$0 (0%)	$57.5 (100.0%)
Physical maintenance (highways and streets, sewerage, water supply, parks and recreation, libraries, natural resources)	$15.4 (22.0%)	$38.6 (55.2%)	$4.0 (5.7%)	$11.9 (17.1%)	$0 (0%)	$69.9 (100.0%)
Other traditional city government services (police protection, fire protection, sanitation)	$7.7 (20.2%)	$27.2 (70.9%)	$2.3 (6.1%)	$1.1 (2.8%)	$0 (0%)	$38.3 (100.0%)
Redevelopment activities (transit, housing and community development, airports)	$2.4 (9.6%)	$9.1 (35.7%)	$0.2 (0.7%)	$13.8 (54.0%)	$0 (0%)	$25.5 (100.0%)
Education	$14.0 (8.4%)	$13.4 (8.0%)	$3.9 (2.3%)	$0.3 (0.2%)	$135.6 (81.1%)	$167.2 (100.0%)

Source: Bureau of the Census, *Census of Governments, 1987,* Vol. 4 *Government Finances,* No. 1 *Public School Systems,* No. 2 *Special Districts,* No. 3 *County Governments,* No. 4 *Municipal and Township Governments* (Washington, D.C.: U.S. Government Printing Office, 1990), Table 1 in all cases.

the most popular form and has been adopted by about 29 percent of all coun ties.[9] The administrator, hired directly by the county board, helps the board set the budget and tries to coordinate operations of the various departments.

The county manager form of government is somewhat more powerful than the county administrator. Like the administrators, the county managers are hired by their county boards and help set the budgets. Additionally, they have broad budgetary and supervisory control over the county agencies. Only about 6 percent of all counties have a county manager. The most prominent is Dade County (Miami), Florida.

The elected county executive is similar to the strong-mayor form of city gov- ernment, which will be discussed. As an elected official, the county executive has more political influence to deal with administrative agencies and with the county board. Only about 6 percent[10] of all counties have adopted the elected county executive. The largest is Milwaukee, Wisconsin.

Finally, to facilitate the modernization of counties, many reformers push for the adoption of county home rule charters, especially in the populous metropol- itan areas. Like municipal home rule, county home rule charters let county resi- dents choose the form of county government they want. By the mid-1990s, 117 counties had adopted home rule charters.[11]

Municipalities

Municipal government can be described as reformed or unreformed. The re- formed municipal government has a city council characterized by several fea- tures of the early twentieth-century progressive reform movement, especially nonpartisan and at-large elections and lack of direct control over the city admin- istrative departments. Reform-style cities are also more likely to have city man- ager or commission forms of government. Unreformed cities, by contrast, are characterized by partisan elections, ward elections, and considerable interven- tion of council members in the internal affairs of the departments. Council mem- bers put pressure on the departments to hire their relatives or political support- ers, and they interfere with departments by demanding special services and favors for the neighborhoods in their own districts.

Over time, the progressive movement to reform city government structure has been resoundingly successful. Seventy-three percent of all cities elect their council members through nonpartisan elections, and 60 percent also rely on at-large elec- tions.[12] Whether a city uses these reformed structures has an important policy im- pact. Probably because of their partisan and neighborhood basis, unreformed coun- cils respond more effectively to political divisions within the city than do reformed councils. The unreformed councils tend to tax more and spend more money on city services than do reformed councils.[13] And, as we shall see in Chapter 8, whether a city council is elected at-large or from wards has emerged as a major issue for the equal representation of minority groups, especially blacks and Hispanics.

The Commission   The commission form of government was created in Galve- ston, Texas, after a tidal wave in 1900 killed 5,000 people. This disaster required

Figure 7-1 MANAGER AND COMMISSION FORMS OF GOVERNMENT

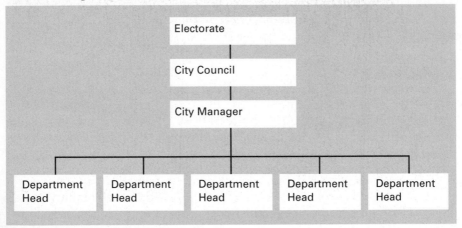

In the commission form of city government, each city council member (commissioner) is also a department head. In the council–manager form, executive and legislative functions are separated. The council theoretically sets policy, whereas the manager theoretically confines himself or herself to administering the city. In practice, as the text discusses, the manager is indeed political.

emergency action that the weak-mayor form of government was unable to provide, so a commission of prestigious businesspeople was appointed to run the city during the emergency. This commission carried out its task so effectively, the leading citizens got a charter change that permanently installed the commission form of government.

Commission government unites executive and legislative functions in the same people. Each commissioner is the head of a city department, as shown in Figure 7-1. Although this form of government apportioned out responsibility clearly enough to take decisive action during the Galveston tidal wave disaster, it had some inherent defects when installed on a permanent basis. As department heads, the commissioners tend to defend the interests of their particular departments during the city council meetings. Budget sessions turn into contests in which alliances are established and the department heads left out of the alliance are given budgetary leftovers. Since neither a chief executive nor a legislative body is independent of the existing departments, the commissioners tend to be unreceptive to new spending needs outside of their limited responsibilities. Under this system, executive leadership is thwarted. Although the commission form of government spread rapidly in the early 1900s, the defects of the system began to appear and it swiftly lost favor. Today only 3 percent of all cities still maintain the system, and only two cities of more than 250,000 still keep it (Tulsa, Oklahoma, and Portland, Oregon).

City Manager　The second and most lasting reform-style government is the **city manager,** or the *council-manager,* which is generally conceded to have been created in Staunton, Virginia, in 1908. Where the commission form unites the legislative and administrative functions, the city manager form separates them. It also tries to separate politics from administration. Reformers viewed the city council as the legislative and political body. It is engaged in the politics of campaigning, lobbying with the state legislature, establishing political support for the city government, and adopting overall city policies. The manager is hired by and serves at the pleasure of the city council. The manager's job is to administer the policies established by the council and to take charge of all personnel matters, budget preparation, and other administrative details.

　In practice, does the manager form of government really remove politics from administration? Hardly at all! To be sure, managers are supposed to be nonpolitical, in the sense of staying out of election campaigns and seeking to protect the city administration from partisan politics, campaign pressures, and patronage.[14] However, in the more commonly understood definition of politics as including the process of policymaking, city managers are definitely political.[15] Furthermore, a survey in the 1980s found that up to a third of managers helped council members get re-elected.[16] They make most of the policy proposals that city councils adopt.[17] They spend nearly a third of their time on policymaking and a fifth of their time on political activities such as trying to influence state legislators and other elected officials and showing up at community meetings where local issues are debated.[18] Furthermore, a study of 448 city managers in 1983 found that they had a strong tendency not only to identify themselves in ideological terms (24 percent as liberals and 45 percent as conservatives) but to pursue local policies that reflected their own ideological orientation.[19]

　Given these sharply defined political involvements, it is not surprising that city managers find it necessary to align themselves with members of the dominant coalition of their city councils. When the council majority changes, the manager either realigns his or her loyalties or faces dismissal by the council.

　The city manager role works best in medium-sized cities, especially suburbs, where the populations are less heterogeneous and less divided politically than they are in large cities. As Table 7-3 shows, a majority of all cities in the 25,000 to 250,000 range have the manager form of government. Only 5 of the cities over 500,000 popu-

Table 7-3 FREQUENCY OF LOCAL GOVERNMENT FORMS

Form of Government (Number and Percent)

Population Group	All Cities	Mayor-Council	Council-Manager	Commission	Town Meeting*
Over 1,000,000	8	6 (75%)	2 (25%)	0 (0%)	0 (0%)
500,000 to 1,000,000	16	13 (81%)	3 (19%)	0 (0%)	0 (0%)
250,000 to 499,999	39	16 (41%)	22 (56%)	1 (3%)	0 (0%)
25,000 to 249,999	1137	407 (36%)	681 (60%)	22 (2%)	27 (2%)
10,000 to 24,999	1602	676 (42%)	751 (47%)	52 (4%)	123 (8%)
2,500 to 9,999	3792	2192 (58%)	1240 (33%)	73 (2%)	287 (8%)
Total (all cities over 2,500)	6594	3310 (50%)	2699 (41%)	148 (2%)	437 (7%)

*Includes representative town meeting

Note: The mayor-council form of government is most popular in very large and very small cities. The council-manager form is most popular in medium-sized cities. The commission form continues to lose popularity.

Source: Calculated from International City and County Management Association *The Municipal Year Book 1993* (Washington, D.C.: International City and County Management Association, 1993), Table 2, p. xi.

lation have a city manager. In these large cities, the political divisions often become too acrimonious to be handled smoothly by a manager appointed by a council that is likely to reflect the political divisions of the city. This could be seen in San Diego, where a city manager form presided smoothly over a city growth period during the 1950s and 1960s. By 1970, San Diego had grown to nearly 700,000 people. Severe opposition arose to the ethos of unrestricted growth, and the city manager proved unable to negotiate effectively between the city's pro-growth and no-growth political factions. This led to the emergence of Mayor Pete Wilson in the 1970s, who gradually strengthened the mayor's office, weakened the city manager, built a strong electoral coalition, and successfully balanced the city's competing pro-growth and no-growth factions.[20] Another city where growing political divisiveness undermined the city manager system was Saint Petersburg, Florida, which in 1993 scrapped its council–manager government in favor of a strong mayor system.[21]

It is a fair question to ask if San Diego and Saint Petersburg are pioneering a move away from the city manager system in large and medium-sized cities. The city manager plan is based on the assumption that policy can be established by a cohesive city council. But the growing social, political, and economic divisiveness of big and midsized cities make a cohesive council difficult to achieve.

Mayors   Table 7-3 reveals that the mayor form of executive is most popular in large cities and small towns. The major difference between the city manager and the mayor is that the mayor is elected and the manager is appointed by the council. This gives the mayors an independent base of political support and strengthens their hand in dealing with the council.

Two types of mayor—the weak mayor and the strong—are illustrated in Figure 7-2. The **weak mayor** resulted from the traditional American distrust of strong executives. Because of this distrust, city departments were set up independent of each other and of the mayor. Often the department heads were directly elected by the people and were given political patronage jobs to hand out. The weak mayor has little appointive power and very limited budget-making powers, and often cannot veto measures of the city council. In most instances, the weak mayor is not even elected by the public but is instead picked by the city council from among its members. The **strong mayor,** by contrast, is elected by the public, has broad appointive powers, presides over council meetings, sets the council's agenda, has strong budget-making powers, and has a veto. In large cities the mayor often has a chief administrative officer or a deputy mayor who runs the day-to-day operations of the city departments and leaves the mayor free to deal with the larger areas of policy and leadership.

◇ THE EVOLUTION OF REFORM-STYLE CITY POLITICS

The evolution of reform-style local government forms, such as county manager, city manager, and strong mayor-councils, was a direct product of the **progressive political reform movement** of the early twentieth century. This movement sought to replace boss-dominated, machine-style politics with a style of politics that reformers hoped would be less corrupt and less partisan in nature.

**Figure 7-2   STRONG AND WEAK-MAYOR FORMS
OF GOVERNMENT**

Weak-Mayor Government

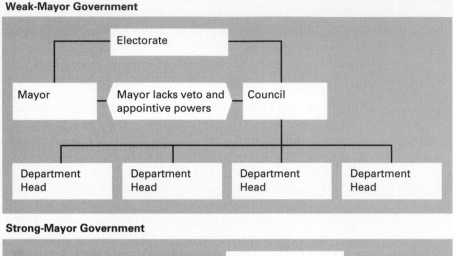

Strong-Mayor Government

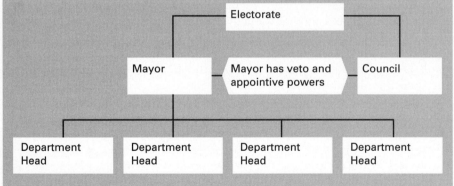

Under the weak-mayor form of government, the mayor has neither a veto over the council nor the power to appoint department heads. Under the strong-mayor form, the mayor is given both of these powers.

Machine-Style Urban Politics

Political machine refers to a state or local political party that has organized itself so strongly that it dominates politics in its region. The political machine differs from just any political party, however, in several respects. The machine is led by a single boss or a unified central committee. The organization controls the nominations to public office. The machine leaders are often of working-class or lower-class social origins. They usually do not hold public office. The machine's workers are kept loyal through material rewards (such as patronage jobs) and nonideological psychic rewards (such as fellowship and ethnic recognition). Finally, the machine controls extensive patronage.[22]

Machine politics had an ethnic basis. The rise and decline of machine politics coincided with the massive immigration of Europeans to American cities between 1840 and 1930. During those 90 years, 37 million people migrated to the United States from Europe. A majority of the 37 million immigrants came from only five nationality groups—Germans, Irish, Italians, Poles, and Russians.

As the number of immigrants increased, the political parties—notably the Democratic party—began nominating European ethnic minorities to run for office in the hope that these ethnic candidates would attract other immigrant voters. This development has been called the politics of recognition,[23] and through it the Democratic party began to secure the voting loyalties of the European ethnics.

The machines also provided assistance to lower-class immigrants. This assistance was granted on an individual basis to people who could be expected to support the machine's candidates. This had the effect of creating a large body of supporters for the machine. In the nineteenth century, Tammany Hall's district leader George Washington Plunkitt bragged that whenever a family in his district was burned out of its home, he showed up on the scene to provide lodging and assistance.[24] When young people got into trouble with the courts and the police, the machine politicians like Plunkitt often acted as mediators. The machines also found city jobs for their supporters, the so-called patronage jobs. To keep these patronage jobs, city workers were expected to work for the party during election campaigns, to contribute money to the parties, and to promote the party's welfare.

These political services to the immigrants not only helped keep the machines in power, but they also facilitated the upward-social mobility of the immigrants and their children. Although the extent of this upward mobility can be questioned,[25] it is beyond question that many ambitious immigrants turned to the machine for opportunities when they perceived other doors were closed. Boston's famous machine politician, James Michael Curley, said, "I chose politics because prospects of ever getting anywhere elsewhere seemed remote."[26] And Chicago's legendary machine boss, Richard J. Daley, echoed similar sentiments.[27]

The oldest and most famous machine is New York City's Tammany Hall, founded in 1789 as a social club. It became politicized under the Irish, who used it as a central device for controlling the district bosses. A district boss was a machine leader responsible for getting out the vote for the machine in his district (sometimes called ward) of the city. The leader of Tammany Hall controlled New York's elections, patronage, and treasury. From the end of the Civil War until the early 1900s, New York City was intermittently controlled by a succession of Tammany Hall leaders—William Marcy "Boss" Tweed, Charles F. Murphy, and Richard Croker.

Boss Tweed is probably the most famous of all the bosses. He started his career as a foreman for the fire department and worked up through alderman, congressman, and finally the leader of Tammany Hall. As boss of Tammany Hall, he exerted considerable influence over government contracts, franchises, licensing, and construction activity. He stole millions from the city treasury and finally was arrested. He died in prison.[28]

For the most part, machine politics is largely a relic of the past, existing today in scattered locations and seldom dominating a region's style of politics as

Tammany Hall did a century ago. The most important machine today is Chicago's, which was dominated from 1955 to 1976 by the legendary Mayor Richard J. Daley and which has been splintered by struggles for control ever since.[29] The heart of the Chicago machine is the Cook County Central Committee, which is made up of one committeeperson from each of the city's fifty wards plus the suburban municipalities. As both mayor of the city and chairperson of the county central committee, Daley was able to control the two most powerful tools of the machine—Democratic party nominations for elective office and patronage jobs. Patronage jobs are ones that are given out on the basis of political connections.

A key strategy for the machine's success was the so-called balanced ticket. The ticket referred to the slate of nominees endorsed by the Democratic party, and the slate was said to be balanced when the city's largest ethnic groups were represented among the nominees. One machine historian wrote in 1975:

> Every ethnic, racial, religious, and economic group is entitled to have some representation on the ticket. Thus, in Chicago, the mayor's job has been an Irish job since 1933. The city clerk's job belongs to the Poles. The city treasurer can be a Jew, a Bohemian, or a black. On the county ticket, the county assessor, the state's attorney, and the county clerk must usually be Irish, but the county treasurer, the county superintendent of public schools, or the sheriff can be a member of one of the other ethnic or racial groups. A judicial slate is made up of three or four Irishmen, two or three Jews, two or three Poles, several blacks, a Lithuanian, a German, a Scandinavian, several Bohemians, and several Italians.[30]

These ethnically balanced tickets worked well to represent most ethnic groups as long as the European ethnics predominated in the city's population. But by the 1980s, European ethnics had become a distinct minority. Today, blacks and Hispanics account for nearly 60 percent of the city's population, and both minority groupings want a greater share of the machine's benefits.

After Daley's death in 1976, the machine was rent by persistent infighting and racial conflict. With the election of a black, Harold Washington, to the mayor's office in 1983 and his re-election in 1987, the machine was widely viewed as having been dealt a death blow. Washington had campaigned for mayor on a platform of reform, pledging that he would dance on the grave of patronage and open up the political process to those who had previously been left out. In practice, reform under Washington meant using affirmative action hiring procedures to increase the number of black and Hispanic employees in city government.[31] In this respect, Washington did not abolish the machine so much as he sought to take command of it and use it to advance the minority populations of the city. He seemed well on the road to achieving that goal when he died of a heart attack late in 1987. His death opened once again a bitter struggle between the various political factions in the city to achieve dominance over the machine.

In 1989, the black electorate split between two candidates, black voter turnout declined, Hispanic voters dropped out of the coalition that Washington had forged six years earlier, and the mayor's office was reclaimed by the machine's heir apparent, Richard J. Daley, Jr., the son of the city's late boss.[32] In the

1990s, however, the Chicago machine is a pale imitation of the powerful institution it once was. Though thousands of patronage jobs still exist in Chicago, one of the mainstays of machine politics, bitter divisions among the city's political factions, along with the technological and sociological pressures on political parties discussed in Chapter 6 (p.132), are likely to continue eroding the relevance of Chicago's machine to the mainstream of American political life.

Who Benefited from Machine Politics?

The biases of the political machines are obvious. First, they were biased against ideological or programmatic politics. The machine politicians had no ideologies; they had no plans to end poverty, provide housing, improve education, or end discrimination. Rather, they dealt in the concrete transactions of trading favors for services.

Second, the machines also were biased in favor of the lower- and working-class immigrants who secured patronage jobs and political positions. In the process of controlling city government, the machines helped integrate the European immigrants into American society, find them employment, get them into the political system, and get them registered to vote. Sociologist Robert Merton referred to these functions as the *latent functions* of the machines. He distinguished them from the machine's *manifest function* of gaining control of the government.[33] As shown by the Chicago example, however, these latent functions did not work very well for later migrants to the cities, such as blacks and Hispanics.

The Progressive Reform Movement

To the upper class and the upper-middle class, it was intolerable to have city government controlled by machine politicians who catered to the lower-class immigrants. Historian Samuel P. Hays has documented very painstakingly that the initiative for progressive reform in the early twentieth century came primarily from the cities' top business leaders and upper-class elite.[34]

These business people-reformers sought to make direct financial gains by overthrowing the corrupt machine politicians. But they also had philosophical reasons for displacing the machine politicians. Historian Richard Hofstadter contrasted the political vision of the typical reformer with the vision of the typical machine politician. The immigrant politician viewed politics in personal terms. Government was "the actions of particular powers. Political relations were not governed by abstract principles; they were profoundly personal."[35] In contrast, the upper-middle-class reformers looked upon politics as "the arena for the realization of moral principles of broad applications—and even, as in the case of temperance and vice crusades—for the correction of private habits."[36]

The Mechanics of Reform

The political reformers devised several mechanisms to make it more difficult for the machines to operate. The most prominent reform mechanisms were the merit system of public employment, the direct primary, at-large elections, non-partisan elections, the short ballot, and the city manager and commission forms of government. No one single measure destroyed the machines, and some machine organizations showed a tenacious ability to persist despite the reforms. The reformers hoped that the combination of reforms would have a detrimental effect on the machines.

The Merit System   If the machine bosses relied on patronage to keep themselves in power, then the obvious antidote was **civil service** and the **merit system.** From the point of view of reformers, it was inconceivable that partisanship should have anything to do with the delivery of public services. The machine politicians, however, thought that partisanship had a great deal to do with delivery of services. Tammany Hall district leader George Washington Plunkitt once remarked that civil service is the "curse of the nation. . . . Parties can't hold together if their workers don't get the offices when they win."[37]

The Direct Primary   The convention system of nominations favored the political machines. Because the bosses controlled the selection of delegates to the conventions, they easily controlled the nominations for public office. The reformers' cure was a system wherein nominations were made directly by the voters in a **direct primary** election, thus weakening the political bosses' influence.

At-Large Elections   Election from wards enabled ward leaders and council members to provide enough services and close personal contact with their constituents to control their votes. The reformers' rejoinder was **at-large elections,** in which a candidate runs in the city as a whole rather than from a specific district. They hoped that at-large elections would force the voters to adopt a citywide vision of how the government was supposed to operate. With elections conducted at-large, reformers hoped the ward politicians would find it more difficult to give people favors in exchange for their votes.

Nonpartisan Elections   Partisan elections also benefited the bosses. The likely reform was **nonpartisan elections.** With the party designation removed from the ballot, the machine's choices for office would be much less obvious and other endorsing organizations, such as good-government leagues, newspapers, and interest groups, would presumably gain influence.

The Short Ballot   The bosses promoted weak mayors who had no control over city agencies and bureaucracies, many of which were headed by elected officials. Because the department heads and elected officials competed with each other and depended on the machine to keep them in office, it was easy for the boss to control them and, in turn, the city government. The obvious antidotes were the **short ballot** and either the city-manager or the commission form of government. The short ballot has the voters elect only those few offices that set overall policy—preferably just the mayor and the city council. It is distinguished from the long ballot, in which a large number of purely administrative and nonpolicymaking positions are elective. The more names on the ballot, the more individual voters have to rely on recommendations of endorsing organizations. As the best-organized endorsing organization, the political machine has the most influence under the long ballot. By substituting a short ballot, the voter is better able to focus attention on the candidates.

Reformed City Government   Finally, the city-manager and commission forms of government provided professional administration for city functions, thereby weakening machine influence. These reforms do not always cause machines to die, but where all the reform mechanisms went into effect, machines found it difficult to survive.

The Bias of Progressive Reform

If political machines were biased in favor of white, working- and lower-class ethnics, reform politics also had their biases. They made it easier for upper- and upper-middle-class people to gain influence in city politics. Correspondingly, low-status voters lost influence. Nonpartisan elections, for example, produce council members of higher socioeconomic status than do partisan elections.[38] And reform-style politics generally makes it harder for city government to be responsive to majority demands in the city. One study found that local officials in cities with partisan elections were much more likely to agree with a majority of city residents about the city's problems than were officials in cities with nonpartisan elections.[39] These findings suggest that reform-style politics makes it harder for the leaders of the city to be responsive to peoples' concerns and interests.

A major reason for this lies in the types of people recruited to city council positions in reformed cities. Very few of them look on the city council as a stepping-stone to building a political career. Rather, they are characterized by an attitude that Kenneth Prewitt calls **volunteerism.** Prewitt interviewed more than 300 city council members in the Oakland–San Francisco Bay area and found that they perceived themselves as volunteers serving on city councils as a civic duty. For the most part, they were not interested in higher office and not greatly concerned about re-election. For this reason, they felt free to make their own decisions on matters that came before the city councils rather than paying great attention to citizens' opinions.[40]

Council members in other cities may not be quite as voluntaristic in their attitudes as the council members that Prewitt surveyed in the San Francisco area, but few council members in most cities seem to face strong competitive pressures to keep them responsive to city residents. A study of thirty-seven Texas communities in the 1980s found little competition in local elections. Nearly three-fourths of council members and more than two-thirds of school board members sought re-election. Of the council members seeking re-election, 74 percent achieved that goal, and the comparable figure among school board members was 78 percent.[41]

The legacy of progressive reform for today's city is mixed. Early in the twentieth century, machine politics had been a mechanism, however imperfect, for representing the interests of the lower classes in city government. But because the machines tended to become financially corrupt and to foster a personalized style of politics that did not cope well with contemporary urban problems, they have probably outlived their usefulness. The reform style politics that tends to replace machines, however, has had a pervasive bias against representing the interests of the lower classes and lower-income neighborhoods.

Recent Reforms

To counter this trend, there have been a number of attempts in recent years to make city governments more effective and more accountable to the citizenry. As a result of the Community Development Block Grant program (see Chapter 3), for example, many cities set up neighborhood councils and city advisory committees to give residents a voice in the spending of the community development block grant funds. New York, Boston, and some other cities experimented with little city halls, which were neighborhood offices that served as an outreach arm for the mayor. But many of these were disbanded in the budget-retrenchment years of the early 1980s. In 1973, Detroit established an **ombudsman** office, which is an independent office responsible for handling citizen complaints about city government services. Its ability to improve services varies, not surprisingly, with the intractability of the problems involved. It is easier, for example, for the ombudsman to get trees trimmed and storm sewers unclogged than to resolve problems associated with abandoned buildings in poor neighborhoods.[42] Finally, as cable television becomes widespread, another device aimed at improving ties between citizen and local government may be the televised city council meeting. Not enough is yet known to determine whether this development will have a positive or negative impact. A study of such televised meetings in Kansas found that, despite a tendency for members to play to the cameras, televising the meetings increased the feedback council members got from city residents, and the viewers were disproportionately people of lower socioeconomic status.[43]

◇ THE METROPOLITAN CHALLENGE

The official designation of a metropolitan region in the United States is the **metropolitan statistical area (MSA),** which consists of any county containing a city or contiguous cities of 50,000 people plus the surrounding counties that are economically integrated into the central county. Areas lacking a central city of 50,000 can also qualify if their built-up, urbanized area contains 100,000 people. Because the MSA is defined by counties, most MSAs contain substantial rural areas as well as urbanized areas. The extreme case of this is found in the San Bernardino–Riverside (California) MSA, where the sparsely populated rural areas cover a huge space that vastly exceeds the urbanized areas around the cities of San Bernardino and Riverside.

There are more than 300 MSAs, and they contain three-fourths of Americans. The typical metropolitan area is a patchwork of community identities and governing institutions. In no metropolitan area is there a central political authority that can speak for the metropolis as a whole. The mayor is the most visible spokesperson for the city, and the governor the most visible spokesperson for the state. But the intermediate metropolitan level has no highly visible spokesperson. Lack of such a visible spokesperson makes it almost impossible to create a sizable metropolitan constituency with any interest in metropolitan problems. The lack of such a constituency makes it hard for government to tackle metropolitanwide problems.

A typical MSA is built up around a central city, sprawls over into two or more counties, and embraces dozens of municipalities, school districts, and special districts. Some of the most serious problems (air pollution, crime control, housing, education, transportation, racial discrimination) lap over into all of these governmental jurisdictions. Because of this fact, the past forty years have seen many attempts to create governmental structures that could deal with metropolitanwide problems with the same authority that mayors and city councils deal with individual city problems.

The Hopes for Metropolitan Government

Following World War II (1941–1945), many metropolitan areas appeared headed for trouble because of the lack of metropolitanwide institutions to cope with metropolitanwide problems. The rapid suburbanization of this period led to numerous problems, especially local governments' inability to provide the normally expected urban services in the suburban fringes. Central city water and sewer lines, for example, were usually not extended into the new suburban subdivisions, and homeowners often had to rely on private wells and backyard septic tanks. As populations grew, this combination led to inevitable pollution of wells.

Compounding the task of resolving these service problems was the fact that by 1945 no metropolis in the nation possessed a governmental mechanism for coping on a coordinated, areawide basis with such problems as air pollution, sewage disposal, water supply, solid waste disposal, mass transit, and public health, which were beyond the abilities of any individual community to solve. Instead, the responsibility was divided among literally hundreds of governments. The New York City region had 1,400 different local governments; Chicago had 1,100. Little thought was given to coordinating the policies of these many units, which led to overlapping of responsibilities, intergovernmental conflicts, and important gaps in service.

From the viewpoint of political reformers, the great hope for coping with problems of this sort was to scrap the existing system of governance and create a single general-purpose authority at the metropolitan level. Two strategies evolved for doing this.

City–County Consolidation   The ideal strategy was to develop one acting government, normally achieved by **city–county consolidation** of the central city with the surrounding county. A single countywide council would replace the previous city council and county board of commissioners, and the city and county service departments would be merged. This synthesis would prevent the formation of new municipalities in the suburbs and reduce the need for more special districts. Prominent successes in city–county consolidation occurred in Nashville–Davidson County, Tennessee (1962), Jacksonville–Duvall County, Florida (1967), and Indianapolis–Marion County, Indiana (1969).[44]

The Two-Tier Government Strategy   A second strategy for metropolitan reform was the development of **two-tier government**.[45] Local units would perform the governmental functions best suited for localities, and a regional authority would handle the broader functions, such as sanitation, transportation, and regional planning. The inspiration for this strategy came from Canada, where federative forms of metropolitan government were established in Toronto, Ontario, and Winnipeg, Manitoba.[46] A variation of this approach was achieved in Miami–Dade County, Florida, in 1957. The county government was reorganized that year and given expanded regional service responsibilities for transportation, sewage, water supply, and land-use planning. The existing twenty-six municipalities continued to provide such local services as police patrolling and zoning.

The Great Hopes Dashed

Despite these great hopes for major surgery on the metropolitan governmental body, proposals for metropolitan government failed about 75 percent of the time that they were submitted to the electorate for a vote.[47] And with the few exceptions just noted, most of the successes occurred in relatively small metropolitan areas, where the problems were least serious.

Several reasons have been given for the failure of metropolitan reform. First, many reform proposals encountered severe resistance from suburban voters, who viewed the reform as an attempt by central city politicians to grab their tax base, schools, amenities, and above all their autonomy.[48] Second, resistance also tended to come from many local political elites, who foresaw a loss in their own influence if the reforms were approved.[49] Since the establishment of a centralized regional government intentionally reduces the influence of leaders in suburban municipalities, special districts, and isolated county offices, their opposition was probably unavoidable.

A final reason for the failure of metropolitan reform is that in most metropolitan areas, central-city and suburban voters have appeared relatively satisfied with their existing governmental arrangements. The proponents of reform often phrased their definitions of the problems in such abstract terms as "inefficiency" and "overlapping functions," which had little meaning to the average voter. They often failed to demonstrate convincingly that reorganization would mean better services or lower taxes. By contrast, when voters did have a high level of dissatisfaction with public services (as in Jacksonville, Miami, and Nashville), and the reformers campaigned on the basis of those dissatisfactions, people often voted for the reforms.

Annexation as an Approach to Metropolitan Governance

Perhaps the simplest way to achieve metropolitan governance is to let the central city expand by annexing land beyond the central city boundary. In this way metropolitan growth would be gradually contained within the central city. This, in fact, was what typically happened during the nineteenth century. But early in the twentieth century, many state legislatures began requiring that annexations be approved by dual referendums of the voters both within the city doing the annexation and within the area to be annexed. In the Northeast and Midwest, suburbanites often voted against annexation in order to keep their distance from the large immigrant populations whom they blamed for the vice and corruption of central city politics.[50] As a result, by the 1930s, the central cities of the Northeast and Midwest were mostly encircled by a ring of suburbs. Attempts by central cities to annex noncontiguous land beyond the ring of suburbs were generally frowned upon by the courts. Following World War II, many states relaxed their annexation restrictions and a new phase of annexation took place, especially in the South and West.

One of the leaders in this trend was Texas, which passed legislation in 1963 that made it easier for central cities to grow through annexation.[51] By taking advantage of this legislation, Houston and San Antonio were able to keep growing and to capture a portion of the growing suburban tax base. Most northern and midwestern cities, by contrast, were increasingly surrounded by incorporated suburbs. If San Antonio had been restricted to its 1950 boundaries, as were most northern big cities, it never would have grown to its present size of nearly a million people. The growth of Houston through annexation was even more dramatic. Forty-eight percent of the Houston MSA population is contained in the central city, a feat accomplished by no other metropolitan area of comparable size.

This practice of growth through annexation worked well for Texas cities until the 1970s and 1980s, when it came under attack from blacks and Hispanics who charged that annexation diluted their influence on the city government. By the 1980s, antiexpansion groups in both cities gained considerable influence, and the prospects for future growth through annexation appear to be limited.

Groping for a New Regionalism

Despite the defeat of metropolitan-reform proposals, the problems of metropolitan America did not go away. In many ways, they worsened. In response, urbanists around the nation began groping for a new type of regional approach to urban problems. The earliest of these new regional approaches were metropolitan planning agencies and councils of governments. A **metropolitan planning agency** seeks to develop long-range plans for regional land use and also to develop plans for the rational extension of major public services (such as roads, public transit, sewers) into the growing suburban fringes. A **council of governments (COGs)** is a metropolitanwide organization composed of representatives from the counties and larger municipalities. With metropolitan plans drawn up and councils of government as forums for intergovernmental cooperation, it was hoped that metropolitan areas would come to grips with their growing problems on a voluntary regional basis. COGs expanded rapidly during the 1960s as a consequence of federal funds for planning and requirements that local-government grant applications for federal aid be reviewed by a COG-like metropolitan agency to see if they were consistent with their area's metropolitan plans. For the most part, however, COGs were a major disappointment, having failed to solve any major problems.[52] When federal funds dried up in the 1980s, many COGs disappeared.

Despite the disappointment with COGs, two dynamic attempts to convert metropolitan planning into a metropolitan governing system emerged in Minneapolis–St. Paul, Minnesota, and Portland, Oregon. Minnesota created a Metropolitan Council in 1967 to handle metropolitan planning and policy formulation for the Minneapolis–St. Paul metropolitan area. Over the next twenty-five years, the Metropolitan Council forced suburbs to take their share of subsidized housing, developed a plan to contain suburban growth largely inside an area demarcated by a *metropolitan urban services area* line (called the MUSA line), and achieved policy control over the metropolitan commissions in charge of airports, transit, and waste control. The Metropolitan Council also used its influence to create a system of regional parks, veto plans for an expensive rapid rail transit system, create a metropolitanwide system for sharing an all-new commercial real estate tax base, and drafted a "regional blueprint" that addressed the region's growing disparities between affluent, outlying suburbs and central city-inner suburban core areas that is absorbing the bulk of the region's poverty and social problems associated with poverty.[53] These were spectacular achievements. Prior to this time, no metropolitan institution in the nation had even come close to building such a record. But the Metropolitan Council's very achievements generated opposition from affluent suburbs that wanted to keep their distance from the social problems of the inner city and that viewed the tax-sharing program as an unwarranted grab at their lucrative property tax base. The Metropolitan Council suffered severe political handicaps in confronting this opposition because the council members were appointed by the governor and thus had no independent political base to support them in their goals. After a series of crises, the Metropolitan Council was reorganized in 1994 and its powers expanded. But it remains an appointive, rather than an elective, body and the jury is still out on whether the Metropolitan Council will be able to reclaim leadership over the metropolitan issues.[54]

Although the new regionalism in Minnesota ran into troubles, Portland barged ahead with far-reaching experiments. Its most famous accomplishments were a light rail line linking the downtown with key suburban locations and the establishment of a metropolitan growth boundary in 1979 that successfully contained most of the suburban development over the next sixteen years. In 1995, Portland Metro also adopted a 2040 Growth Plan prescribing in considerable detail how it expects to handle future growth over the next four decades.[55] Given that the state of Oregon has backed up Portland Metro's efforts with substantial enabling legislation, the 2040 Growth Plan is by far the nation's most ambitious attempt yet to gain control over suburban sprawl.

◇ SOCIAL CHANGE AND LOCAL GOVERNMENT

MSAs comprise about 20 percent of the land mass of the United States, but they house 80 percent of the American population. As recently as 1970, MSAs covered barely 11 percent of the land mass and housed about two-thirds of the population. The social changes of the past quarter century have not been kind to the ability of local governments to cope with this metropolitanization process. With a few exceptions—mostly newer, smaller, metropolises of the West—the typical metropolitan area is careening down a path toward severe social and economic segregation. Suburban development has rarely created cohesive communities analogous to the small towns that the suburbs were originally designed to imitate. Instead, the typical pattern is for low-density sprawling development tracts that make their residents overdependent on automobiles and cheap gasoline for getting around. While suburban sprawl proceeds unabated, central cities and inner suburbs have absorbed the bulk of the nation's minority population and the poverty population. Most of the nation's large cities steadily lose population each time a census is conducted. Not only has there been a mass exodus of middle-income people out of the central cities, but by and large the jobs have followed them. While most central cities have seen their minority and poverty populations growing over the past quarter century, they have experienced negligible job growth. The most dynamic job growth has occurred near the interstate highway connections in what has been called the suburban "Edge City."[56] Public transit connections to these edge-city employment centers are almost universally inadequate, which further limits the job prospects for much of the inner city poor population. As the gap widens between central city and suburban incomes, one more point of resentment is found for the nation's growing intercultural and interracial animosities.

How well organized are local governments for dealing with these disparities and animosities?

Not very!

David Rusk, former mayor of Albuquerque, New Mexico, argues that most central cities lack what he calls **elasticity,** the ability to use annexation or consolidation to tap into the financial resources generated by metropolitan growth. In terms of a central city's economic and social viability, he believes that a city drops beyond the point of no return once it loses 20 percent of its population, once its minority population exceeds 30 percent of the total, and once the average income of city families falls to less than 70 percent of the average suburban family income.[57] Rusk argues further than the surrounding suburbs will cease to prosper if their core areas continue to disintegrate beyond the point of no return. He came to this conclusion after finding that family incomes in both central cities and the suburbs is greatest in MSAs with the greatest elasticity, and it is lowest in the MSAs with the lowest elasticity. For this reason, Rusk thinks that it is in the best interests of the suburbs to cooperate in shoring up the economic vitality of their central cities; the health of the suburbs depends on the health of the central city.

Whether suburban health depends on central city health as much as Rusk believes it does is an issue that is hotly debated by urban scholars. But even if Rusk is only partially correct, he raises an issue that should be of concern to every suburbanite as well as every central city resident. Unfortunately, the typical metropolitan area is not very well organized to deal with the problem because its governmental structure consists of agencies that have overlapping and fragmented powers. Annexation is the most direct way to increase elasticity, but annexation is a trend that peaked in the 1980s. Even where it was extensively practiced, as in San Antonio and Houston, there is resistance to expanding it today. This leaves the New Regionalism models of Portland and Minneapolis–St. Paul as the next best hopes for coping with contemporary social changes on the local level.

◇ CONCLUSION

In this chapter, we have examined the major governing institutions at the community level. It is important to stress that none of these institutional forms are politically neutral. The reformed structures of city government (commission, city manager, at-large elections, nonpartisan elections) were promoted by upper-class elites who wanted to get control over city government out of the hands of machine politicians and the lower-status European ethnics to whom the machines were responsive. The more recent attempts at metropolitan reform have often been defeated because many citizens and entrenched local elites see them as curbing the power of existing political elites and strengthening the power and authority of elites who might not be very accessible.

It is important to stress that most cities and metropolitan areas today present serious problems in governability. Many, if not most, urban leaders lack the authority and effective power to cope comprehensively with urban problems. The governability problem is especially acute at the metropolitan level, where metropolitan problems have persisted despite the lack of progress in metropolitan reorganization. In the absence of effective metropolitanwide institutions, power and authority over some problems (such as pollution control and transportation) have drifted to the federal- and state-level agencies, while power and authority over other problems (such as land use and racial integration) have proved elusive.

SUMMARY

1. There are more than 80,000 local governments (counties, municipalities, school districts, special districts, towns, and townships) in the United States. The number continues to grow as special districts proliferate.

2. The most important distinction to make about local governments is that some are reformed and some are unreformed. Reformed counties have a county manager or an elected county executive. Unreformed counties have no chief executive power, and numerous county agencies report independently to a board of supervisors or commissioners. Reformed city governments are characterized by city-manager or strong-mayor forms of executive, the at-large city council, and nonpartisan elections.

3. The sprawling metropolis presents serious governmental challenges. Through the 1970s, political reformers had great hopes for metropolitan reform, such as city–county consolidation or two-tier metropolitan government. Such proposals were rejected by the voters about 75 percent of the time, however, and reformers have been forced to be content with less extensive incremental reforms, such as metropolitan planning and councils of government. Two attempts to create a new regionalism paradigm are taking place in Minneapolis–St. Paul and Portland, Oregon.

4. The typical metropolis is not well organized to cope with contemporary social change. These changes are exacerbated by growing economic disparities between affluent, growing outer suburbs and less affluent central cities and inner suburbs. Most cities lack the elasticity to tap the resources of metropolitan growth.

KEY TERMS

At-large election   A city council election in which a candidate runs in the city as a whole rather than from a specific district.

City–county consolidation   A metropolitan reform strategy in which the city and its surrounding county are merged into a single government.

City manager   A city chief executive who is a professional administrator picked by the city council and serves at the pleasure of the council.

Civil service   A form of recruitment for government jobs in which people are hired on the basis of merit, as measured by their performance on competitive examinations.

Commission government   A form of city government in which the council members (commissioners) also serve as the city's executives.

Council of government (COG)   A metropolitanwide agency composed of representatives from counties and larger municipalities.

County   The general-purpose local government that is the basic geographic subdivision of the state. Used throughout the country, except for New England.

County board of commissioners   See *County board of supervisors.*

County board of supervisors   The legislative body for the county in states where towns and governmental units have representatives on the board. Called *board of commissioners* in counties where the representatives come from districts or are elected at-large instead of coming from existing governmental units.

Dillon's Rule   The principle that city government powers must be interpreted very narrowly.

Direct primary   A means of nominating a party's candidates for office. The nominees are chosen directly by the voters at the ballot box.

Elasticity   A term invented by David Rusk that refers to a city's ability to use annexation or consolidation to top the financial resources of suburban growth.

Merit system (employment)   A recruitment method for government jobs that hires and promotes people on the basis of their training and competence to perform specific jobs. See *Civil service.*

Metropolitan planning   The attempt to develop long-range plans for land use and the extension of urban services throughout the metropolis.

Metropolitan statistical area (MSA)   The official U.S. government definition of a metropolitan area. Prior to 1983, the term used was *standard metropolitan statistical area (SMSA)*.

Municipality   A city government.

Nonpartisan election   An election in which the party affiliation of the candidates is not printed on the ballot.

Ombudsman   An office established to follow up on citizen complaints about government services and to get the complaints resolved.

Progressive political reform movement   An early-twentieth-century political movement that sought to replace boss-dominated machine-style politics with a less corrupt and less partisan form of politics.

School district   A government that runs a school system.

Short ballot   An election in which only a few offices are contested.

Special district   A government that performs only a single function, such as a waste control commission.

Strong mayor   A mayor who has power to appoint the city department heads and the authority to play a strong role relative to the city council.

Town   A general-purpose form of local government especially prominent in New England.

Township   A form of local government in rural areas, prominent in the Midwest.

Two-tier government   A metropolitan reform strategy that divides public services into those to be performed by a metropolitanwide central government and those to be performed by local governments.

Volunteerism   An ethic common among city council members by which they are serving as volunteers doing a civic duty rather than as professional politicians building a career.

Weak mayor   A mayor who cannot appoint the city department heads or play a strong role relative to the city council.

REFERENCES

1. See Stanley Scott and John Corzine, *Special Districts in the San Francisco Bay Area: Some Problems and Issues* (Berkeley, Calif.: Institute of Governmental Studies, 1964).

2. Virginia Marion, *Special Districts, Special Purposes: Fringe Governments and Urban Problems in the Houston Area* (College Station, Tex.: Texas A & M University Press, 1984). Also see Advisory Commission on Intergovernmental Relations, *The Problems of Special Districts in America*, Report A-22 (Washington, D.C.: U.S. Government Printing Office, 1964); and Advisory Commission on Intergovernmental Relations, *Regional Decision Making: New Strategies for Substate Districts* (Washington, D.C.: U.S. Government Printing Office, 1973), Ch. 2.

3. Russell W. Maddox and Robert F. Fuquay, *State and Local Government*, 4th ed. (New York: Van Nostrand, 1981), p. 333.

4. Two students of New England local government argue that, even today, residents in places where town meetings exist are more knowledgable about local government affairs than are residents in places without the town meeting. See William Doyle and Josephine F. Milburn, "Citizen Participation in New England Politics: Town Meetings, Political Parties, and Interest Groups," *New England Politics*, Josephine F. Milburn and Victoria Schuck, eds. (Cambridge, Mass.: Schenkman, 1981), pp. 36–37.

5. John F. Dillon, *Commentaries on the Law of Municipal Corporations*, 5th ed. (Boston: Little, Brown and Co., 1911), Vol. I, sec. 237.

6. Beverly A. Cigler, "County Governance in the 1990s," *State and Local Government Review* 27, no. 1 (Winter 1995): 57.
7. Ibid.
8. Eugene W. Jones, Joe E. Ericson, Lyle C. Brown, and Robert S. Trotter, Jr., *Practicing Texas Politics*, 5th ed. (Boston: Houghton Mifflin, 1983), p. 233.
9. These data are derived from Advisory Commission on Intergovernmental Relations, *Profile of County Governments: An Information Report*, Report M-72 (Washington, D.C.: U.S. Government Printing Office, 1972), p. 13, and Advisory Commission on Intergovernmental Relations, *For a More Perfect Union: County Reform*, Report M-61 (Washington, D.C.: U.S. Government Printing Office, 1971).
10. Tanis J. Salant, "County Governments: An Overview," *Intergovernmental Perspectives* 17, no. 1 (Winter 1991): 9.
11. Ibid., p. 6.
12. Tari Renner, "Municipal Election Processes: The Impact of Minority Representation," *Baseline Data Report* 19 (November–December 1987).
13. Robert L. Lineberry and Edmund P. Fowler, "Reformism and Public Policies in American Cities," *American Political Science Review* 61, no. 3 (September 1967): 701–716; Terry N. Clark, "Community Structure, Decision Making, Budget Expenditures and Urban Renewal in 51 American Communities," *American Sociological Review* 33, no. 4 (August 1968): 576–593.
14. See H. G. Pope, "Is the Manager a Political Leader? No," *Public Management* 34 (February 1962).
15. See Gladys Kammerer, "Is the Manager a Political Leader? Yes," *Public Management* 34 (February 1962).
16. Roy E. Green, *The Profession of Local Government Management: Management Expertise and the American Community* (New York: Praeger, 1989), p. 106. This survey, however, included county managers and Council of Government directors as well as city managers, so it is not conclusive that city managers were as active in campaigns as were the other types of managers.
17. One survey of more than 1,700 cities found that 94 percent of city managers sought to set the policy agenda for their city councils. Robert J. Huntley and Robert J. McDonald, "Urban Managers: Managerial Styles and Social Roles," *Municipal Yearbook, 1975* (Washington, D.C.: International City Management Association, 1975), pp. 149–159.
18. Clifford J. Wirth and Michael L. Vasu, "Ideology and Decision Making for American City Managers," *Urban Affairs Quarterly* 22, no. 3 (March 1987): 454–474.
19. David N. Ammons and Chaldean Newell, "City Managers Don't Make Policy: A Lie; 'Let's Face It,'" *National Civic Review* 77, no. 2 (March–April 1988): 124–132. Also see their "Role Emphases of City Managers and Other Municipal Executives," *Public Administration Review* 47, no. 3 (May–June 1987): 246–253.
20. Glen Sparrow, "The Emerging Chief Executive: The San Diego Experience," *National Civic Review* 74, no. 11 (December 1985): 538–547.
21. Ron Gurwitt, "The Lure of the Strong Mayor," *Governing* (July 1993): 36–41.
22. The first four points are taken from Fred I. Greenstein, "The Changing Pattern of Urban Party Politics," *Annals of the American Academy of Political and Social Science* 353 (May 1964): 3.
23. Raymond E. Wolfinger, *The Politics of Progress* (Englewood Cliffs, N.J.: Prentice-Hall, 1974), p. 69.
24. *Plunkitt of Tammany Hall*, recorded by William L. Riordan (New York: Dutton, 1963), pp. 46, 53.

25. Steven P. Erie, *Rainbow's End: Irish-Americans and the Dilemmas of Urban Machine Politics, 1840–1985* (Berkeley, Calif.: University of California Press, 1988).
26. Alfred Steinberg, *The Bosses* (New York: New American Library, 1972), p. 134.
27. Mike Royko, *Boss: Richard J. Daley of Chicago* (New York: Dutton, 1971).
28. For background on Tammany Hall, see Gustavus Myers, *The History of Tammany Hall* (New York: Boni and Liveright, 1917). On Boss Tweed, see Seymour Mandelbaum, *Boss Tweed's New York* (New York: Wiley, 1955) and Harold Zink, *City Bosses in the United States* (Durham, N.C.: Duke University Press, 1930).
29. There are several background works on Daley. For a polemical treatment, see Royko, *Boss.* A critical but much less polemical account that gives considerable insight to Chicago politics is given by Milton Rakove, *Don't Make No Waves—Don't Back No Losers: An Insider's Analysis of the Daley Machine* (Bloomington: Indiana University Press, 1975).
30. Rakove, *Don't Make No Waves,* p. 96.
31. See Paul M. Green, "Making the City Work: Machine Politics and Mayoral Reform," a paper presented at the 1987 meeting of the American Political Science Association, Chicago, September 1987.
32. *The New York Times,* April 5, 1989, p. 12; April 6, 1989, p. 1.
33. Robert K. Merton, *Social Theory and Social Structures* (Glencoe, Ill.: Free Press, 1957), pp. 78–82.
34. Samuel P. Hays, "The Politics of Reform in Municipal Government in the Progressive Era," *Pacific Northwest Quarterly* 55 (October 1964): 157–166.
35. Richard Hofstadter, *The Age of Reform: From Bryan to F.D.R.* (New York: Knopf, 1935), p. 181.
36. Ibid.
37. Riordan, *Plunkitt of Tammany Hall,* pp. 11, 13.
38. Carol A. Cassel, "Social Background Characteristics of Nonpartisan City Council Members: A Research Note," *Western Political Quarterly* 38, no. 3 (September 1985): 493–501.
39. Susan Blackall Hansen, "Participation, Political Structure, and Concurrence," *American Political Science Review* 69, no. 4 (December 1975): 1181–1199.
40. Kenneth Prewitt, "Political Ambitions, Volunteerism, and Electoral Accountability," *American Political Science Review* 67, no. 4 (December 1973): 1288–1307.
41. Norman R. Luttbeg, *Comparing the States and Communities: Politics, Government, and Policy in the United States* (New York: HarperCollins, 1992), pp. 206–207.
42. Lynn W. Bachelor, "The Impact of the Detroit Ombudsman on Neighborhood Service Delivery," a paper presented at the 1983 meeting of the Midwest Political Science Association, Chicago, April 1983.
43. Elaine B. Sharp and Allen Cigler, "The Impact of Televising City Council Meetings," a paper presented at the 1983 meeting of the Midwest Political Science Association, Chicago, April 1983.
44. See Daniel R. Grant, "Urban and Suburban Nashville: A Case Study in Metropolitanism," *Journal of Politics* 17, no. 1 (February 1955): 82–99; Brett W. Hawkins, *Nashville Metro: The Politics of City-County Consolidation* (Nashville, Tenn.: Vanderbilt University Press, 1966).
45. See Committee for Economic Development, *Reshaping Governments in Metropolitan Areas* (New York: Committee for Economic Development, 1970).
46. See Advisory Commission on Intergovernmental Relations, *A Look to the North: Canadian Regional Experience,* vol. 5 of *Substate Regionalism and the Federal System* (Washington, D.C.: U.S. Government Printing Office, 1973), Chs. 3, 6.

47. Vincent L. Marando, "City-County Consolidation: Reform, Regionalism, Referenda, and Requiem," *Western Political Quarterly* 32, no. 4 (December 1979): 409–422.

48. Sharon P. Krefetz and Alan B. Sharof, "City-County Merger Attempts: The Role of Political Factors," *National Civic Review* 66, no. 4 (April 1977): 178.

49. Thomas A. Henderson and Walter A. Rosenbaum, "Prospects for Consolidation of Local Governments: The Role of Local Elites in Electoral Outcomes," *American Journal of Political Science* 17, no. 4 (November 1973): 695–720.

50. See Kenneth T. Jackson, "Metropolitan Government Versus Suburban Autonomy: Politics on the Crabgrass Frontier," in *Cities in American History,* Kenneth T. Jackson and Stanley K. Schultz, eds. (New York: Knopf, 1972), pp. 442–446.

51. Stuart A. MacCorkle, *Municipal Annexation in Texas* (Austin: Institute of Public Affairs, University of Texas, 1965), pp. 28–36; Arnold Fleischman, "The Politics of Annexation: A Preliminary Assessment of Competing Paradigms," *Social Science Quarterly* 67, no. 1 (March 1987): 128–142.

52. Melvin B. Mogulof, *Five Metropolitan Governments* (Washington, D.C.: Urban Institute, 1973).

53. John J. Harrigan and William C. Johnson, *Governing the Twin Cities Region: The Metropolitan Council in Comparative Perspective* (Minneapolis: University of Minnesota Press, 1978); William C. Johnson and John J. Harrigan, "Political Stress and Metropolitan Governance: The Twin Cities Experience," *State and Local Government Review* 19, no. 3 (Fall 1987): 108–113.

54. John J. Harrigan, "Minneapolis–St. Paul: Structuring Metropolitan Government," in *Regional Politics in a Post-City Age,* eds. H. V. Savitch and Ronald K. Vogel. *Urban Affairs Annual Reviews,* v. 45 (Thousand Oaks, Calif.: Sage Publications, 1996).

55. Carl Abbot, *Historical Development of the Metropolitan Service District* (Portland: Portland Metro, 1992); Carl Abbot, *Portland* (Lincoln: University of Nebraska Press, 1983); Portland Metro, *Concepts for Growth* (Portland: Portland Metro, June 1994).

56. Joel Garreaux, *Edge City: Life on the New Frontier* (New York: Anchor Books, 1992).

57. David Rusk, *Cities Without Suburbs* (Baltimore: Johns Hopkins University Press/Woodrow Wilson Center, 1995).

THE DYNAMICS OF COMMUNITY POLITICS

Chapter Preview

Having examined the institutions of local government in the previous chapter, in this chapter we go on to explore the dynamics of community politics today. Discussed in turn are:

1. Competing theories for explaining who runs community politics.
2. Who governs in the age of urban restructuring.
3. Urban mayors and the quest for community leadership.
4. Urban mayors and the politics of ethnic change.
5. The challenge of the urban political economy.

Let us begin with an examination of a classic passage in the literature of community power studies—the X family.

◇ INTRODUCTION

What can citizens do to influence public policy and affect the way public services are delivered to them? Some pessimists think that most people can do very little, and that power is concentrated in a very small, closely knit group of elites who dominate the lives of the rest of the people in their communities. This viewpoint was articulated sixty years ago by a Middletown resident complaining about the extent to which his life was dominated by Middletown's most prominent family, the X family.

> If I'm out of work I go to the X plant; if I need money I go to the X bank, and if they don't like me I don't get it; my children go to the X college; when I get sick I go to the X hospital; I buy a building lot or house in an X subdivision; my wife goes downtown to buy clothes at the X department store; if my dog strays away he is put in the X pound; I buy X milk; I drink X beer, vote for X political parties, and get help from X charities; my boy goes to the X Y.M.C.A. and my girl to their Y.W.C.A.; I listen to the

word of God in X-subsidized churches; if I'm a Mason I go to the X Masonic Temple; I read the news from the X morning newspaper; and, if I am rich enough, I travel via the X airport.[1]

Is this pessimistic view of elite dominance of community life accurate? Was it ever accurate? And whether or not it is accurate, what roles do interest groups, citizens, and political parties play in American communities? Are individual citizens gaining or losing influence over the public services that affect their lives? What are the dynamics of community politics?

To answer these questions, we must approach them from four different perspectives. First, we must examine two opposing theories about the way power is distributed in American communities. Second, we must explore the application of these theories to the contemporary scene in which economic change and international competition have undermined the economic security of many, if not most, American cities. Third, we must look at the big-city mayor as the catalyst for urban political change. And finally, we must examine the mayor's role in adapting city politics to the two most forceful pressures on cities today: (1) the racial and ethnic cleavages that characterize most big cities and (2) the challenge of economic competition.

◇ THEORIES OF COMMUNITY POWER

Who really runs American communities? Some people think that community power resides in a core of wealthy persons who secretly control all key decisions. Others think that power is widely dispersed among a variety of interested groupings that participate democratically in running the community. These two schools of thought are the *elitist* and the *pluralist* theories of community power. In either theory, power can be defined as the ability of groups or individuals to influence what a government does.[2]

The Elitist Theory of Community Power

The elitist theory was developed by a small group of early-twentieth-century European sociologists who viewed society as ruled by a relatively small group of leaders referred to as elites.[3] This view influenced American sociologists and anthropologists, who began conducting community studies during the 1920s and 1930s[4] and who often found that their communities were dominated by a small business elite. One of the most famous of these studies focused on Middletown (Muncie, Indiana) and its dominance by the X family, described earlier.

Perhaps the most influential of the early elitist studies was Floyd Hunter's book *Community Power Structure*.[5] Hunter concluded that community politics in Regional City (Atlanta, Georgia) in the early 1950s was controlled by a small, closely knit group of elites. These elites were predominantly the people who ran the major business and economic institutions. They manipulated government officials to give the top elite what it wanted. Further, power was viewed as cumulative in that the individual elite person who got power in the economic sphere also began to accumulate power in the social and political spheres. Political decisions flowed from the elite down to ordinary citizens. Because he viewed Atlanta's power structure as a stratified pyramid, Hunter's theory is called **elitist theory** or **stratificationist theory.**

Hunter came to these conclusions using a research method called the **reputational approach.** He began by asking, "Who runs Regional City?" To identify the leadership, he compiled lists of prominent leaders in civic affairs, business, and society. He then selected a panel of knowledgeable people to examine the lists and identify the most influential individuals and organizations. From these selections Hunter identified forty individuals who, he said, constituted the top power structure in Regional City. Most of these forty served on the boards of directors of the same corporations and belonged to the same social clubs. Beneath these top forty leaders were dozens of other important but less prominent persons whom Hunter called *understructure personnel.* They carried out the will and the instructions of the top power structure.

Hunter contended that this elite power structure initiated most of the development that occurred in Regional City and that it successfully kept most projects it disliked from appearing on the decision-making agendas of the local governments.[6] Enterprising newspaper or journal writers lost their jobs when they disagreed with the power structure. Social welfare professionals carefully avoided raising issues that might violate the interests of the power structure. Hunter pictured the governor, the U.S. senators, the key state legislators, the party leaders, and most other officials as subordinated to the top power structure.

This elitist theory rapidly came under criticism,[7] particularly from political scientists who objected to Hunter's conclusion that the political structures were subservient to the economic institutions. Hunter's critics also objected to his assumptions about power and his methods of researching power. By asking knowledgeable observers to identify the most influential leaders, said Hunter's critics, he had not really measured the exercise of power. He had merely measured the reputation for power.[8] To make a valid measurement of power, they argued, one would have to analyze the actual decisions through which power was in fact exercised.

The Pluralist Theory of Community Power

The first major attempt to measure power through a **decision-making approach** was Robert Dahl's study of New Haven, Connecticut, and was reported in his book *Who Governs?*[9] This and several other decision-making studies that followed spelled out the principles of **pluralist theory.**[10] Rather than believing that power is stratified, pluralists believe that a plurality of power centers exists in a city—labor unions, political parties, banks, manufacturing plants, churches, school systems, and government agencies. These power centers compete with each other democratically, and public policy emerges out of their competition. Each of these power centers is powerful only within particular functional areas. Pluralists also reject the elitist implication that some permanent, vague power-holder controls situations from behind the scenes. Rather, power exists only when it is exercised through specific decisions by specific individuals. Finally, pluralists reject the elitist's belief that power is cumulative.

Dahl deliberately set out to test the hypothesis that New Haven was governed by the kind of economic and social elite that Hunter had discovered in Atlanta. He isolated thirty-four important decisions in the three functional areas of urban renewal, education, and the selection of party nominees for mayor during the 1940s and 1950s. Contrary to Hunter's findings, Dahl discovered that in New Haven *no significant overlap* occurred between the economic and social elites, that these elites had little influence on the decisions he studied, and that power in New Haven was *noncumulative*—that is, power in one functional area did not lead to power in other functional areas.

In the three issue areas that concerned him, Dahl conducted extended interviews with forty-six top decision makers. He found very few instances in which an individual person was involved in more than one major decision, let alone more than one issue area. The exception to this was the mayor of New Haven, Richard C. Lee. Lee was a supreme political tactician at bargaining with leaders of all the functional power centers in New Haven plus some others in federal and state agencies that ran programs in the city. Through his bargaining skill, he successfully started and carried out the kinds of programs he thought the city needed to grow and prosper. Dahl perceived Mayor Lee as occupying the critical position in what Dahl referred to as an "executive-centered coalition" of a plurality of interest groups in New Haven. Because this view sees power as noncumulative and dispersed among several power centers, Dahl's theories about community power are called *pluralist* theories.

Early Refinements of the Two Models of Community Power

Following the publication of the initial studies by Hunter and Dahl, increasingly sophisticated research methods were used to examine every conceivable subtlety of these two models[11] (see Table 8-1 for a summary). Three issues, in particular, kept recurring in these studies: the role of business, the importance of nondecisions, and the great variety of power relationships that exist.

The Role of Business   Subsequent research has tended to dispel the picture of top businesspeople operating as a cohesive clique and dominating city public affairs, the picture that Hunter presented of the businesspeople in Atlanta. However, it is conceivable that Hunter's observations of Atlanta were accurate for that period, and that businesspeople did indeed dominate the city's politics during the early 1950s. Hunter's findings of business dominance is consistent with the overwhelming majority of early anthropological and sociological community studies, such as that of the X family in Middletown cited earlier. Many other cities in addition to Muncie and Atlanta seem to have had a particular business elite that dominated local affairs. United States Steel Corporation planned and built Gary, Indiana, and exercised considerable influence over its government. The Mellon family had disproportionate influence in Pittsburgh. One-company mining towns often stayed under the control of their patrons for

Table 8-1 KEY TENETS OF THE PLURALIST AND STRATIFICATIONIST THEORIES

Issue	Pluralist Tenet	Stratificationist Tenet
Locus of political power	In individual action and individual competence	In positions of economic and institutional leadership
Structure of power	Divided among competing power centers	Stratified in pyramid form
Nature of power	Not cumulative. Power in one area does not necessarily lead to power in a different area	Cumulative. Power in one area tends to lead to power in different areas as well
Most common approach to identifying powerholders	Decision-making analysis	Reputational analysis
Exercise of power	Through decisions only	Through decisions and nondecisions
Role of business community	The business community is only one of many competing power centers. The great diversity of business interests makes it impossible to speak of *the* business-community interest	Business is the dominant interest in the community. Despite its diversity, there is considerable unity on issues important to top business leaders

decades. And even today the Anaconda Corporation exerts extensive power over Butte, Montana.

Despite these examples of business dominance, it is a mistake to think in terms of *a* unified business community. Any large metropolis is bound to have several business communities that compete with each other as much as they co-operate. For example, when Philadelphia first proposed an urban renewal program in the 1950s, the business community was split on the idea. The idea drew strong support from those portions of the business community that were locally oriented and stood to benefit from a rejuvenated downtown: law firms, local retailers, and banks. Businesses that were engaged in manufacturing for a nation-wide market, however, as well as national retailers and the Chamber of Commerce, either had little interest in the plan or opposed it outright. An officer of one manufacturing corporation said:

> It makes little difference to us what happens in the city. We do not have our homes here; we have no large plants located within the city limits; we have only an office

building that we can close at any time that conditions within the city become too oppressive.[12]

This division of the business community in Philadelphia is common in most metropolises. In the years that have passed since the first community power studies were conducted, most sectors of the economy have come to be increasingly dominated by national corporations rather than local companies. This means that business leadership in a community is often bifurcated between a local elite of retailers who are very much interested in local affairs and the managers of the national corporations whose careers and interests impel them to pay more attention to the internal affairs of their corporation than to local politics.[13]

The business sector is not only divided between the owners of local businesses and the managers of national corporations; it is also divided into several functional categories. Few businesspeople exhibit much interest in public issues that lie beyond their functional sphere. Thus urban renewal agencies routinely seek out the advice and collaboration of real estate brokers and the financial community, whereas other kinds of businesspeople—such as retail merchants, automobile dealers, and shopping center owners—are often quite uninterested. Utilities seek to promote a city's population, income, and employment, whereas railroads often display little interest in city politics.[14] Because of this divergence of interests, the business community is not nearly as cohesive in its approach to local politics as the Hunter portrayal suggests. It is highly competitive. And the resources that businesspeople have to influence public affairs depend on the functional area involved, the issue, the interests of the businesspeople, and the unity with which they can act.

The Importance of Nondecisions If subsequent research on the role of businesspeople in city politics tended to dispel the stratificationist notion that they manipulate public affairs as one cohesive, well-organized bloc, it also found flaws in the decision-making approach to analyzing community power. Political scientists Peter Bachrach and Morton S. Baratz charged that the concentration on actual decisions ignores "the fact that power may be, and often is, exercised by confining the scope of decision-making to relatively 'safe' issues."

> Of course power is exercised when A participates in the making of decision that affect B. But power is also exercised when A devotes his energies to creating or reinforcing social and political values and institutional practices that limit the scope of the political process to public consideration of only those issues which are comparatively innocuous to A. To the extent that A succeeds in doing this, B is prevented, for all practical purposes, from bringing to the fore any issues that might in their resolution be seriously detrimental to A's set of preferences.[15]

Such an exercise of power is referred to as coming to **nondecisions.** This is a form of "preemptive power" according to Clarence Stone.[16] Only certain kinds of questions are put on the agendas of decision-making agencies. Other kinds of questions are never put on those agendas and hence never reach the point where decisions about them can be made.

Furthermore, some people have fewer resources for waging political battles than do others. The people with few resources usually lose these battles, and they quite often are the poorest people in the city. Many issues stay in the realm of nondecisions because these people lack either the resources or the will to fight for them. In the words of Clarence Stone, "Because people have no taste for waging costly battles they are sure to lose, much goes uncontested."[17]

Although pluralists have expressed doubts about the usefulness of the concept of nondecisions, pertinent examples have been cited in the literature on local politics.[18] In his study of New Haven, for example, Robert Dahl paid very little attention to the black community because it did not figure in the major decisions he analyzed. Even the urban renewal decisions, which deeply touched the lives of large numbers of New Haven blacks, were made without much input from the local black community. When a riot broke out in New Haven in 1967, some people began to ask why decisions had not been made on questions the blacks themselves apparently considered important.[19] The answer seems to be that the blacks did not constitute a strong enough interest group to have their demands placed on the decision-making agenda. The needs and demands of people who do not have the backing of strong interest groups and powerful civic leaders are likely to remain in the realm of nondecisions.

The Variety of Power Relationships Finally, pluralists pointed out that power is structured differently in different communities, and the structures change over time. Atlanta of the 1990s is vastly different not only from the New Haven that Dahl studied but even from the Atlanta that Hunter studied in the early 1950s. For one thing, it has a black majority today compared to only a black minority at the time of Hunter's analysis. Atlanta has had black mayors for the past two decades, an accomplishment that would have been impossible if the city's power structure were still the same as the one described by Hunter.

Highly stratified power structures are most likely to be found where city leaders share a consensus on the role of government and where power is not shared extensively with the mass of the people. Highly stratified power structures are also most likely to be found in isolated communities dominated by a single industry, in small homogeneous communities, and in the South.[20] Pluralist power structures are most likely to be found in metropolitan areas, communities with a heterogeneous population, and communities with a diversity of economic foundations and social cleavages.

◇ WHO GOVERNS IN THE AGE OF URBAN RESTRUCTURING?

By the end of the 1970s, these three statements reasonably summarized the dispute over community power. The role of business is a great deal more complex than the elitists had portrayed it. But the existence of nondecisions give business a larger role than pluralists generally admitted. And the structure of power relationships varies greatly from place to place and from time to time.

While these debates over community power were raging, the cities themselves were undergoing a dramatic restructuring that neither elitists nor pluralists could explain very well. Especially prominent were the eruption of riots during the 1960s, the staggering economic decline of many cities, widespread fiscal stress in the late 1970s, a changing global economic restructuring that wreaked havoc on many old manufacturing cities, and more than anything the impressive downtown and economic redevelopment schemes that blossomed across the land. In terms of their ethnic base, their economic base, and their physical appearance, American cities in the last third of the twentieth century experienced one of the greatest restructurings that had occurred to any system of cities in history.

If the stratificationists were correct that a small group of business elites controlled the cities for their own benefit, why would they have collaborated with the economic disinvestment that has been so disastrous for so many cities? And why did so many of the economic redevelopment schemes appear to originate not in company board rooms but in city halls? If the pluralists were correct in their optimistic view that a plurality of interest groups governed the city through competition and coalitions, then how do we explain the fact that the huge central-city underclass is almost always left out of the governing coalition? And how do we explain the fact that the economic redevelopment schemes have had so little payoff at the neighborhood level, where the rank-and-file members of the supposedly powerful interest groups lived?

These questions are very difficult to answer within the framework of early elitist or pluralist theories. But just as nature cannot tolerate a vacuum, the human mind cannot tolerate unexplainable facts. So it is not surprising that new theories emerged to answer the perplexing question of who governs in the current age of urban restructuring. As cities struggle to cope with the task of urban restructuring, who has the most influence? How is it exerted? And who benefits?

Dominance by Global Capital

One troubling set of answers came out of neo-Marxist schools of thought. In their view, as cities grapple with the challenge of urban restructuring, cities literally respond to the dictates of the global capital markets. It is the market that governs. The city needs investment capital to prosper, and this fact puts city officials at the mercy of the global markets that control the investment of capital around the world. Cities must compete with each other to attract capital investments, and a fundamental problem facing many American cities (especially old manufacturing centers such as Detroit or Gary, Indiana) is that they simply are no longer competitive in the global market place. The evolution of capitalism has made the traditional American city obsolete.[21]

From this viewpoint the old industrial cities like Gary and Detroit were formed a century ago when labor-intensive industrial manufacturing required large numbers of unskilled laborers to be assembled in concentrated areas. It was the job of the city to provide the sewers, streets, and other infrastructure that would enable this concentration of laborers to take place. For today's automated, capital-intensive factory, however, large concentrations of workers are no longer needed. Automation and computers enable machines and robots to perform almost any repetitive mechanical task more efficiently and cheaply than human laborers.

Not only is today's factory capital intensive rather than labor intensive, but also capital is mobile; corporations can move the production facilities out of troublesome spots into more receptive locations. Cities, by contrast, are stationary; you cannot move Detroit to the sunbelt. Detroit, in fact, has been suffering from the outflight of capital for years, as corporations closed down plants in the city and built new ones in the suburbs, in the sunbelt, or overseas. Between 1960 and 1976, Detroit lost 200,000 jobs, about 30 percent of all the jobs that had existed only 16 years earlier, in 1960.[22]

When General Motors in the late 1970s decided to invest $40 billion to build new automobile production plants, there were probably 100 places around the globe in addition to Detroit where GM could have profitably made the investments in new plants. The juxtaposition of the stationary city with highly mobile investment capital put Detroit and every other city at a disadvantage in dealing with GM. Nowhere was this seen more clearly than in Detroit's bid to get the site for GM's new Cadillac plant in 1980 and 1981. GM adopted an uncompromising take-it-or-leave-it attitude on the site specifications for the new plant. To produce the site, the city had to destroy a neighborhood (Poletown), suffer severe attacks on its public image as a result of that destruction, and spend over $200 million to turn the site over to GM. There is no realistic projection under which increased city revenues and tax base could recapture that $200 million within the next two decades.[23]

Growth-Machine Theory

To a second school of thought about urban restructuring, the most important force is what sociologist Harvey Molotch called "a growth machine."[24] Molotch argues that local elites with substantial local land holdings dominate community policymaking and that these leaders' common interest lies in promoting growth. Growth will make their land more valuable. To secure their investment, these local land-based elites dominate local government and seek to co-opt local political leaders by bringing them into the pro-growth machine.

Growth-machine theory differs from global capital theory in at least two key respects. First, the goal of the growth machine is not to *maximize profit* from selling goods and services in a national market, as is the goal of the corporation. Rather, the goal of the growth machine is to *maximize rental return* through renting space to the businesses and people who will use the facilities built by the growth machine.[25] In this sense, from the viewpoint of the growth-machine advocates in Detroit, the possibility that the city might never recover the $200 million it invested in the Poletown site was less bothersome than the prospects of nothing being built on the site. Second, due to its interests in land use rather than maximizing profit, the growth machine is not composed of the national upper class or even the leaders of the national corporations. Instead, the elites of the growth machine are local real estate owners, bankers, developers, construction unions, and central-city newspapers whose circulations and advertising revenues will expand with growth in the metropolis.

In dealing with the growth machine, city government plays two conflicting roles. First, it must support the growth machine's promotion of economic growth and redevelopment, on the grounds that growth will bring in the jobs for city residents and will make land in the region more valuable. Second, since it represents people in local neighborhoods, city government often finds itself playing an intermediary role in the conflicts that arise when neighborhood residents oppose particular redevelopment projects.

Cities as a Unitary Interest

In contrast to the neo-Marxist and growth-machine interpretations of urban decline and redevelopment is Paul Peterson's concept of *unitary interest*, spelled out in his highly influential 1981 book *City Limits*.[26] The heart of Peterson's theory focuses on the role that city governments can effectively play in the local political economy. Peterson placed great emphasis on the role of investment capital in determining the fate of cities. Cities are in competition with each other to capture as much investment capital as they can. A city also has export industries (automobiles in Detroit, computer hardware and software in Silicon Valley, health services in Cleveland) that provide a lot of jobs and bring money into the city. The business leaders of the city, political leaders, and ordinary residents have a *unitary interest* in protecting those export industries and helping attract new investment capital that will help them expand in the future. Thus it is not a "growth machine" that impels the mayor to pursue downtown redevelopment. It is simply a mutual recognition of the best interests of all the city's residents.

This argument provides a powerful justification for the economic redevelopment activities of most cities. But, like the other theories, it too has been criticized.[27] The key interests of business leaders diverge sharply from those of political leaders. Although political leaders may care most about maximizing the city's export industries, the self-interest of most corporate leaders necessarily lies in maximizing the profits of their particular corporations, and in most instances this goal is divorced from the well-being of the cities in which the corporation resides. Finally, neighborhood residents might or might not benefit from downtown redevelopment. In fact, one could make a powerful argument that strengthening neighborhoods is a more important unitary interest of a city than is downtown redevelopment. If crime rates are low, the middle class is not moving out, city services are good, and schools are excellent, then a city will be a very attractive location for many kinds of businesses. This is precisely the situation in many suburban cities. But simply redeveloping the central-city downtown or putting in an automobile production plant will not necessarily pull in the middle class, improve the schools, reduce the crime rates, or make the neighborhoods better places in which to live.

Different Regimes for Different Cities

One of the strongest critics of the idea of a unitary interest has been Clarence Stone, who argues that each city has a dominant coalition of interests who create an "Urban Regime."[28] The urban regime consists of a working relationship between three power clusters in cities: (1) a pro-growth business elite, (2) the elected city government leaders and their top appointees, and (3) city residents and the variety of neighborhood groups, labor union locals, political party organizations, and other political groups to which the residents belong. The mayor is elected to office by the residents. But once in office, the mayor and other top political leaders can gain very few additional rewards from the city voters or their representative groups. Instead it is the business elite and to a lesser extent other institutional elites who control access to most of the things that most reasonable mayors are likely to want (a thriving city economy, a successful administration, prestige, respect, and possibly postmayoral employment at a high salary). Ordinary voters can give a mayor none of these things.

Because they control access to the goals that most reasonable mayors seek, business and institutional elites exercise *systemic power* over the city government.[29] Their exercise of power will seldom be overt, but the mayor will psychically identify with the top institutional elite rather than with the masses. The mayor will anticipate the reactions of the elite to mayoral initiatives before the initiatives are taken. And it makes little difference if the mayor is black, white, male, female, Democrat, or Republican. Mayors and high public officials generally "find themselves rewarded for cooperating with upper-strata interests and unrewarded or even penalized for cooperating with lower-strata interests."[30]

No better example of Stone's analysis could be found than Dennis Kucinich, the mayor of Cleveland from 1977 to 1979. Kucinich got himself embroiled in a disastrous fight with the city's banks and the privately owned electric power company, Cleveland Electric Illuminating Company (CIE). CIE was putting pressure on the city-owned electric power company, Muny Light, with the intent of purchasing Muny Light and taking over its assets. Kucinich had won his 1977 mayoral election by opposing the takeover of Muny Light, which (due in part to pressure from CIE) had piled up big losses in prior years and was being partially subsidized by the City of Cleveland. The city itself was heavily in debt to local banks, and the banks pressured Kucinich to sell off Muny Light assets as a condition to lending the city any more money. As the conflict became rancorous, Kucinich at one point called the bankers "blood-sucking vampires," while the bankers in turn referred to the mayor as the "little canker downtown." In this bitter environment, the banks refused to roll over the city's debt, the city defaulted on its loan payments, and Kucinich was discredited and lost his reelection bid in 1979.[31] His successor, George Voinovich, was much more cooperative with the business community, presided over considerable downtown redevelopment, enjoyed considerable respect as mayor, and held the office for a decade.

What is at work in most cities, according to Stone's analysis, is a regime of systemic power. There is no unitary interest binding the masses, the mayor, and the business elite. Rather, successful elected officials subtly and almost invisibly align themselves with the upper-strata interests of the area and keep themselves in power by convincing a majority of the average voters that all this will benefit them in the long run.

What is important, in Stone's analysis, is to determine what sort of regime dominates in a given metropolis. The *entrepreneurial* or *corporate* regime is devoted primarily to downtown development policy, and in towns with corporate regimes, mayors will not have much success reorienting the city's priorities toward serving its neighborhoods or its disadvantaged residents. Cities with a *pro-*

gressive regime, however, provide greater leeway for the mayor to expand services and shift priorities to neighborhoods. In Boston, for example, Mayor Raymond Flynn (1983–) was able to follow several redistributive policies. He instituted a "linkage" program that required large developers to contribute to trust fund ($70 million raised by 1987) that the city uses for housing and job-training purposes. Flynn also curbed the conversion of apartments into condominiums and required large residential development projects to earmark 10 percent of their space for low- and moderate-income renters.[32]

The Pluralist Rebuttal

In the last analysis, it may be that there are just too many kinds of cities in the United States and the urban restructuring that has been going on since the 1950s may be too complex for any single theory to explain who governs the city. What is true of one city might not apply to a different one. Clarence Stone's analysis of the mayor's dependence on growth-oriented business elites for the success of his or her administration is probably accurate for Atlanta and other cities with a corporate-dominated urban regime. Lawrence, Kansas, by contrast, has a strong tradition of citizen activism, and local residents for more than a decade successfully prevented the construction of a downtown shopping mall dearly wanted by the city's local business leaders.[33] The growth machine there was clearly not dominant.

Not only does the nature of the urban regime differ from place to place, but different theories lead us to focus on different aspects of the same event. This is why different observers can look at the same political event and react with completely incompatible conclusions. The case of Detroit's Poletown (see p. 190) serves as a good example. From growth machine and global capital perspectives, Poletown is an unfortunate instance of Detroit's political leaders knuckling under to the demands of a *Fortune* 500, multinational corporation. From the viewpoint of unitary interest theory, things worked out pretty well because everybody in the city had an interest in having the city secure the jobs that would be required to build and operate the Cadillac plant in Poletown. But Bryan D. Jones and Lynn W. Bachelor look at the same facts and see something akin to old-fashioned pluralism.[34] First, they find no unitary interest between Detroit's or any city's business elite and the top political leaders. General Motors faced considerable competition from foreign automobile manufacturers, and GM's chief aim was to locate its new Cadillac production plant in a place that would contribute to the goal of successful competition. This put GM's primary interest at odds with Mayor Coleman Young, whose primary interest was not GM's profits but increasing the level of economic activity within the city of Detroit. In this sense, the mayor's job is akin to "making water run uphill; attracting capital where it would not normally flow . . . [getting] . . . businessmen to do things that they would not do on their own."[35]

Although this situation clearly put GM in a privileged bargaining position in dealing with Mayor Young, Young was by no means powerless. Indeed, the only reason GM even considered the Poletown site in the first place was because Young had vocally badgered GM chairman Thomas Murphy about previous location decisions that had excluded Detroit.

In summary, Jones and Bachelor view the destruction of Poletown not as an example of either big capital trampling on the rights of a minority or a mayor systematically deferring to upper-strata interests rather than to lower-class needs. Instead, they view Poletown as an example of a democratically elected mayor, supported by the overwhelming majority of the city's residents, engaging in extremely effective political leadership to bring the city a very important economic resource it would not otherwise have had.

In sum, a rich variety of research has emerged in recent years seeking to explain the role of city government in the local political economy. Global capital theorists see the city as helpless in the face of world economic realities. Growth-machine theorists and regime theorists focus on a local, land-based elite and its relations with the local political system. Peterson's unitary interest theory focuses on the proper role for city government to play in handling urban problems and on the very real limits confronting those governments. And pluralists generally tend to reaffirm city government's independence in these conflicts, asserting that it is not simply a passive actor playing out a predetermined role.

◇ MAYORS AND THE QUEST FOR LEADERSHIP

Whatever the nature of the forces that are restructuring cities today, city leaders must respond in ways that help the city prosper. The political leader who is best positioned to lead that response is usually the central-city mayor.

The Changing Urban Setting for Mayoral Leadership

Being mayor of a sizable city is one of America's impossible jobs.[36] It is "fun and exciting, but there's no future in it," said Boston's legendary mayor James Curley.[37] There is no future in it because, with a few notable exceptions (such as Pete Wilson of San Diego, Federico Pena of Denver, Henry Cisneros of San Antonio, or Richard Lugar of Indianapolis), most mayors do not move up to higher elective or appointive office. And it is an impossible job because the mayor is held responsible for solving the city's many problems while he or she is seldom given the resources to make a noticeable dent on those problems.

In large part as a result of the Progressive Reform movement, the devices for accumulating political power have been weakened. The mayor's formal powers are sharply restricted by the state constitution, the legislature, and the city charter. Many of the most important governing functions in cities are carried out, not by the city government, but by other governments. Public health and welfare are usually administered by the counties; public transit, sewers, and airports are under the control of metropolitan agencies; and schools are usually run by independent school districts. Even within the city government, the mayor usually faces strong resistance from city council members who increasingly have their own agendas to push and are not too inclined to defer to the mayor.[38] Many council members would be happier with the chief executive power vested in a city manager rather than a mayor.[39] The city manager by definition is supposed to implement the council's goals, but the mayor is likely to have goals of his or

Table 8-2 PRECONDITIONS FOR MAYORAL LEADERSHIP

Governmental, or Formal, Preconditions

1. Sufficient financial resources with which a mayor can launch innovative social programs.
2. City jurisdiction in the vital program areas of education, housing, redevelopment, and job training.
3. Mayoral jurisdiction within the city government in those policy areas.
4. A salary sufficiently high that the mayor can work full time at the office.
5. Sufficient staff support for the mayor, such as policy planning, speech writing, intergovernmental relations, political work.

Extragovernmental, or Informal, Preconditions

6. Ready vehicles for publicity, such as friendly newspapers and television stations.
7. Politically oriented groups, including a political party, that the mayor can mobilize to help achieve particular goals.

Source: Adapted from Jeffrey L. Pressman, "The Preconditions for Mayoral Leadership," *American Political Science Review* 66, no. 2 (June 1972): 512–513, 522.

her own. In addition to stronger city council members, there has been a growth in interest groups, neighborhood groups, ideological groups, and ethnic groups that all want a say in how the city conducts its business.

In the face of these pressures on the mayor, two things must happen for mayors to exercise strong leadership. First, mayors must be given the legal and political resources to do their jobs.[40] Table 8-2 outlines seven such resources. The first five are legal or formal preconditions. Without sufficient jurisdiction, money, and staff, the mayor faces an uphill battle to implement his or her objectives. The last two items in Table 8-2 are informal or political preconditions.

Second, in addition to having the objective preconditions for power, an effective mayor must have a subjective vision of what needs to be done and how to do it. John P. Kotter and Paul R. Lawrence analyzed the subjective vision factor in terms of the mayor's ability to impose his or her own style on the city.[41] They analyzed the leadership styles of mayors in twenty different cities and isolated five variables that were critical to mayoral strength: setting a decision-making agenda, controlling the mayors' time, expanding their political alliances to attract new supporters, building a large staff to whom they could delegate appropriate supporters, building a large staff to whom they could delegate appropriate responsibilities, and gaining political control over the city government. If we juxtapose the objective preconditions with the subjective vision dimension, we derive four major types of leadership: the ceremonial mayor, the caretaker mayor, the crusader mayor, and the program entrepreneur. These are shown in Figure 8-1.

Types of Mayoral Leadership

The Ceremonial Mayor   The person with little subjective vision occupying an office that has few preconditions is very likely to follow the style that Kotter and

Figure 8-1   STYLES OF MAYORAL LEADERSHIP

Subjective Vision for Mayoral Leadership

	0	1	2	3	4	5
Exhibits none of the five qualities (left) / Exhibits all of the five qualities (right)						

Possesses none — 1, 2

Objective Preconditions for Mayoral Leadership — 3, 4

5 Caretaker Mayor

Possesses all seven preconditions — 6, 7

	(left quadrant)	(right quadrant)
top	Ceremonial Mayor	Crusader Mayor
bottom	Caretaker Mayor	Strong Mayor or Program Entrepreneur

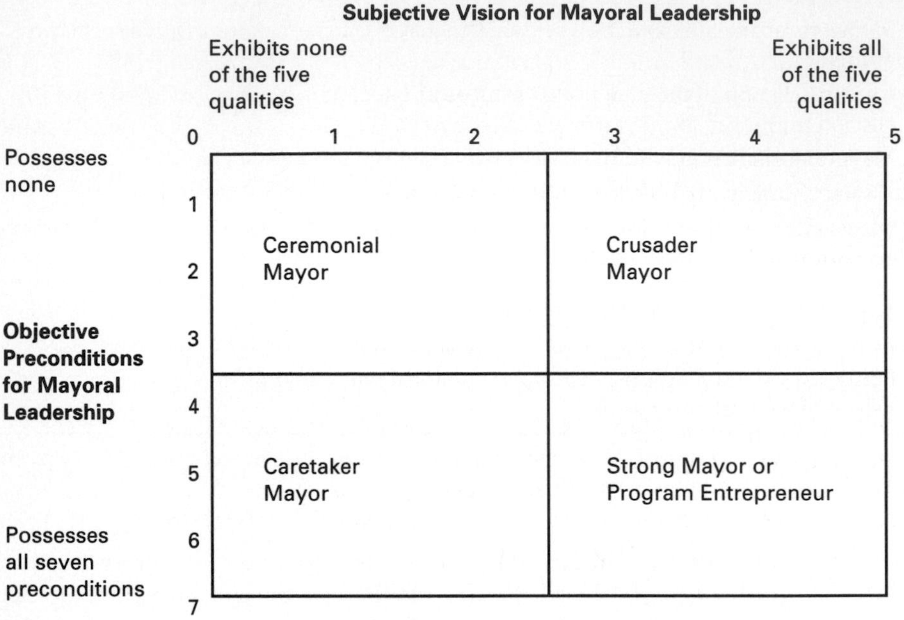

By juxtaposing the objective preconditions with the subjective vision for mayoral leadership, we can identify four major styles of mayoral leadership.

Sources: This figure was composed by juxtaposing criteria developed in Jeffrey L. Pressman, "The Preconditions for Mayoral Leadership," *American Political Science Review* 66, no. 2 (June 1972): 511–24; John P. Kotter and Paul R. Lawrence, *Mayors in Action: Five Approaches to Urban Governance* (New York: Wiley, 1974), Ch. 7; and Douglas Yates, *The Ungovernable City* (Cambridge, Mass.: M.I.T. Press, 1977), p. 165.

Lawrence call the **ceremonial mayor.** These mayors make little effort to set a decision-making agenda for dealing with city problems. They have no broad goals to be accomplished; rather, they deal with problems individually. They have a modest staff and do not try to build new political alliances to contend with city problems; they rely instead on past friendships and personal appeals. In coping with mayoral tasks, the ceremonial mayor attempts to tackle all the tasks individually rather than delegate authority to others. As an example of a ceremonial mayor, Kotter and Lawrence point to Walton H. Bachrach of Cincinnati (1963–1967). They write of Bachrach:

> Walt was a very personable guy and just about everybody loved him. He'd walk down a crowded street and say hello to nearly everyone—by their first name.
>
> As mayor he spent nearly all of his time in ceremonial activities. He gave speeches at banquets, he welcomed conventions, he cut ribbons at all types of openings, he gave out keys to the city, and so on. He really looked the part and he played it with grace and dignity.[42]

The Caretaker Mayor   The mayor with limited subjective vision who occupies an office that has several of the preconditions is likely to be a **caretaker mayor.** Like the ceremonial mayors, the caretaker mayors also do not set an agenda of goals to be accomplished. They, too, deal with problems individually. They do make more of an effort than the ceremonial mayors to build political alliances, to surround themselves with a loyal staff, and to delegate authority to others, especially to the established bureaucracies.

The prototype of a caretaker mayor was Ralph Locher of Cleveland (1962–1967). Locher dealt with city problems with an unsystematic approach. He let his own daily agenda be dictated by other people who placed demands on him and by regular office routines such as opening the mail and dictating letters. There is no evidence that Locher attempted to establish goals for some of Cleveland's broader social problems. He was simply a caretaker for the city. Locher himself said:

> You know, I suppose it could be said that Burke [another mayor] and I were custodial mayors. We tried to keep the city clean and swept and policed. Some say that wasn't enough. Let me just say this about that complaint. You can't nurture flowers and good thoughts and ideals when you're living in a rat-infested squalor and your city services aren't being done.[43]

The Crusader Mayor   The **crusader mayor** has the subjective vision for strong leadership to a high degree but occupies an office that lacks several preconditions for strong leadership.[44] The crusader style emerges when the mayor's office is occupied by a very active, imaginative, and ambitious personality who has a very weak political power base. Douglas Yates points to former New York City Mayor John Lindsay as a crusader. Lacking the political strength to control the city bureaucracies and dominate the government, Lindsay adopted a crusading, symbolic style of leadership. During the riots of the 1960s, he went into the streets in the riot-torn sections and urged people to return to their homes. He traveled often to Washington to testify before congressional committees and to serve as a spokesperson for the nation's urban problems. He engaged in political battles with New York State Governor Nelson Rockefeller. Despite the battles, the conflicts, and the publicity, however, it is hard to identify Lindsay with very many significant accomplishments.

The Program Entrepreneur   The **program entrepreneurs** are the most ambitious of all the mayoralty types, and the offices they hold necessarily possess several of the objective preconditions. Their agenda is much more detailed. They have not only broad goals but even a list of objectives or priorities to be covered. Only a small portion of their daily work schedule is spent reacting to events. The rest is spent on activities tied to short- and long-range objectives. The program entrepreneurs skillfully build political alliances and surround themselves with a substantial staff.

The prime example of the program entrepreneur is Richard Lee of New Haven. Lee built a solid alliance around the large interest groups in the city—the city bureaucracy, federal renewal agencies, the city council, the business community, organized labor, the Democratic party, and Yale University. Much of the basis for Lee's success was his strong political support in New Haven's Democratic party. With this backing, he was assured of renomination and reelection, thus giving him a long tenure as mayor. The long-term mayor has advantages in dealing with the bureaucracy that the short-term mayor does not have. It is easier for bureaucratic officials to oppose or ignore the wishes of the short-term mayor because he or she might not be around very long. One of Lee's first goals on becoming mayor was to establish control over city departments and bureaucracies.[45] He was able to maintain control over New Haven's urban renewal projects, a feat not performed by mayors in other cities, such as Newark and New York.[46] At the center of what Robert Dahl called an executive-centered coalition, Lee was able to line up business leaders, university leaders, union leaders, and other civic leaders behind his redevelopment goals.[47]

The Prospects for Mayoral Leadership

Whatever the leadership type, few mayors today have enough formal authority and informal power to run their cities with a free hand, as did, for example, Chicago's legendary mayor, Richard J. Daley (1957–1976). In contrast to Daley, most mayors today lack the powerful support that Daley enjoyed from business organizations, unions, and his political party. In addition, they face assertive city councils, cantankerous neighborhood organizations, and a smattering of ideological and single-issue groups that might not support the mayor's agenda.

This type of environment puts a premium on mayors with a facilitative leadership style of compromising, keeping in touch with city council members, and courting a wide array of potential supporters. Philadelphia's Ed Rendell and Los Angeles's Richard Riordan have been pointed to as practitioners of this new facilitator style of mayoral leadership. They were both adept at building cooperative working relationships rather than adversarial relationships with their city councils.[48] If Rendell and Riordan are the prime examples of the new, facilitator mayor, however, this new mayor might not be as liberal as have been most big-city mayors of the past thirty years. Both mayors made significant cuts in their city budgets, prevailed over the objectives of the public employee unions, and privatized some city services. And Riordan, a Republican, captured the vote of significant numbers of Latinos and Jews who had previously been viewed as solidly Democratic.[49]

◇ MAYORS AND THE CHALLENGE OF SOCIAL CONFLICT

Mayors are not immune to the great social conflicts sweeping American society today. Most cities are more racially diverse than they have ever been. As recently as the 1960s, city politics was composed essentially of the clash between different European nationalities. Today, the clash is not only between European nationalities but also between African Americans, Hispanics, American Indians, and Asians. Furthermore, none of these ethnic groupings is itself homogenous. The label *Hispanics*, for example, applies to the three largest groups—

Mexicans, Puerto Ricans, and Cubans—but it also includes migrants from the five Central American nations plus the fourteen South American nations. Asians are even more diverse than Hispanics, hailing from China, Japan, Korea, India, Vietnam, and dozens of other nations. As the people in each of these groupings become politically active, they contribute a new vibrancy to the tone of city politics.

The Minority Mayor

The growth of minority populations has, quite naturally, made the minority mayor an increasingly common phenomenon. Minority mayors have included African Americans such as Wilson Goode (Philadelphia), Tom Bradley (Los Angeles), and Coleman Young (Detroit); Hispanics such as Federico Pena (Denver) and Xavier Suarez (Miami); and women such as Kathy Whitmire (Houston), Maureen O'Connor (San Diego), and Annette Strauss (Dallas). Minneapolis's Sharon Sayles Belton was both female and black.

Minority mayors may confront problems and opportunities that white male mayors do not face. The minority mayor is much more likely than the white mayor to confront a problem of conflicting constituencies.[50] To get elected, the earliest black mayors usually relied heavily upon an overwhelming vote from black neighborhoods plus a small minority of white liberals.[51] Providing these margins of victory, black voters had some reason to expect favorable policies from the black mayors they elected. However, to initiate the economic development activities that are needed to increase employment for the cities' minority populations, the black mayors also have to cultivate a constituency of upper- and upper-middle-class whites who have the economic power to put economic development programs into action. The more that minority mayors cater to their minority election constituencies, the more problems they create with their economic development constituencies, and vice versa. Some of the more recent minority mayors have been able to build broader coalitions and thus might be less vulnerable to these conflicting constituencies. Sharon Sayles Belton, for example, won a majority of the Minneapolis white vote in her 1994 victory, and Cleveland's Michael White won a majority of the white vote in 1989 in a race that featured two black candidates. White was the less militant of the two.[52]

If divided constituencies bring minority mayors special problems, these mayors also have special opportunities to increase employment and business prospects for the minority populations. Studies of black mayors have shown that they indeed increased the number of blacks employed by city government.[53] Similar studies of female mayors also found that they increased the number of women holding city jobs.[54]

The Bipolar City

Whatever the race or cultural background of the mayor, central cities almost universally face a growing *urban underclass* that is disproportionately black, Hispanic, American Indian, and Asian. There is a growing fear that for the first time in American history just such a permanent class of impoverished people, segregated within the confines of the central cities, is emerging, without realistic hope of achieving much, if any, upward social mobility. As Table 8-3 shows, the average level of income and education for Puerto Ricans, Mexican Americans, and blacks is far below that of the rest of the population.

The concentration of impoverished people in central cities has several important political and economic consequences. Because of their impoverishment, they put a strain on many urban services: public schools, public health agencies, social welfare agencies, and public housing agencies. Their neighborhoods attract a disproportionate share of drug peddling, prostitution, and violent crime, and this puts a strain most obviously on police services but, more important, on the social organizations of the neighborhoods themselves.

When individual residents of these neighborhoods, white or minority, take a good-paying job, they face a difficult choice—the **exit option** or the **voice option** to use Albert Hirschman's term.[55] If they choose to exit the problems of the inner city and move to better neighborhoods or the suburbs, they take their spending power with them and this leaves the inner city slightly poorer as a result. To maintain homes, to pay for public services, to support supermarkets and other amenities in the cities requires people with steady incomes. If they choose the voice option of staying in the older neighborhoods and fighting to improve them, they have a very constructive role to play. Poor neighborhoods rely heavily on residents who are just a little more affluent than the average, just a little better educated than the average, and just a little feistier than the average to put pressure on the city to pay attention to neighborhood problems.[56]

Unfortunately for cities, the exit option is usually the more attractive one for upwardly mobile people. This depletes the city's supply of people with sufficient spending power to pay for public services and to keep their own neighborhoods in good repair. When too many upwardly mobile people exert their exit option, the city becomes increasingly bifurcated between the very rich and the very poor. The bipolar city emerges: a large underclass on the one hand and a small upper class on the other, without the stabilizing influence of the working and middle classes.[57] This is already the reality for some of America's oldest and most distressed cities, such as Atlantic City, New Jersey. And given present trends, it is the likely future for a great many other cities as well.

For big-city mayors, the central task confronting them in trying to forestall this bipolar situation is to create conditions under which upwardly mobile people (whites and minorities) will choose the voice option rather than the exit option. There are essentially two ways to do this. First, recognizing the interracial frictions that underlie the exit option, the mayor must construct a political coalition that crosses racial and ethnic lines. Second, the mayor must promote economic development policies that create jobs in the city and provide taxes to support the badly needed public services.

Striving for a Rainbow Coalition

If low-income whites, Hispanics, blacks, American Indians, and Asians could form an electoral coalition capable of swinging election results, they would be-

Table 8-3 ECONOMIC STATUS OF URBAN MINORITIES: 1994

Characteristic	Mexican American	Puerto Rican	Hispanic Total	White	Asian	Black
Education						
Percentage who completed four years of high school (among those twenty-five years old or older)	46.2	59.8	53.1	34.5	24.5	36.2
Percentage who completed four years of college (among those twenty-five years or older)	5.9	8.0	9.0	22.9	41.2	12.9
Income Median family income	$23,714	$20,301	$23,915	$39,308	$44,456	$21,549
Unemployment Rate	8.6	9.6	8.0	5.3	6.5	11.9
Percent of Persons Below the Poverty Level	30.1	36.5	29.3	12.2	15.3	33.1
Age Percent of persons under age fifteen	32.3	31.0	29.6	21.6	23.5	28.9

Source: Bureau of the Census, *Statistical Abstract of the United States: 1995* (Washington, D.C.: U.S. Government Printing Office, 1995), pp. 48–51.

come a formidable force for redistributing income in their favor. The most prominent spokesperson for this movement is Jesse Jackson, who in his 1984 and 1988 presidential campaigns coined the term *rainbow coalition*. Just as the rainbow's natural beauty lies in the spectrum of colors it presents, the political rainbow coalition would embrace a spectrum of people of different colors: whites, browns, reds, yellows, and blacks.

Scholars have devoted considerable energy to the question of why a cross-nationality electoral coalition did not emerge among lower-class European immigrants in the late nineteenth and early twentieth centuries. Ethnic divisions, religious divisions, the hope of upward social mobility, workplace-oriented unions (as distinct from a class-oriented labor movement), nonideological machine politics, and repression of ideological movements by the law, the police, and various national guards all conspired in the past to prevent the emergence of institutions that would enable the urban lower classes to advance their political and economic self-interests. Has anything changed from the past that might permit the emergence of something akin to Jesse Jackson's rainbow coalition in the 1990s?

Let us analyze this question first from the viewpoint of the central-city black leader seeking to put together a multiethnic electoral coalition capable of winning office. The most logical allies would seem to be lower-class whites, since they face many of the same economic problems faced by lower-class blacks (inadequate housing, poor schools, need for social services, and need for more jobs). The tendency of lower-class blacks and lower-class whites to form a united constituency has not been analyzed thoroughly, but one study of voting patterns in the South between 1960 and 1977 suggests that such alliances are very difficult to forge. In partisan elections, lower-income whites had a strong tendency to support the same candidates as those supported by blacks—as long as the candidates were white. But this support dissipated when the candidate was black or when elections were nonpartisan.[58]

A more successful voting alliance for blacks has been with upper-middle-class white liberals. In Berkeley, California, for example, a sizable black middle class coalesced with liberal academic whites to get black representation on the city council.[59] The most successful citywide black candidates have held the loyalty of a small minority of whites while getting an extraordinary turnout of blacks. This was true of Harold Washington's victories in Chicago, as we have seen, as well as of most other big-city black mayors.

A third possible voting alliance for blacks is with Hispanics. An important example of a black–Hispanic coalition emerged in Chicago, where Mayor Harold Washington won an estimated 57 percent of the Hispanic vote in 1987[60] and relied on Hispanic support to gain control of the city council.[61] But in most cities, blacks and Hispanics do not seem to coalesce very easily. Houston mayor Kathy Whitmire was supported by a majority of blacks in her 1983 election but opposed by a majority of Mexican Americans. Former New York mayor Edward Koch often enjoyed warm support from Puerto Rican leaders but frequently had hostile relations with blacks in the city. A number of California cities have both black and Hispanic populations, and in a few of these cities, such as Sacramento, black–Hispanic coalitions did emerge. But the preeminent analysis of minority-group politics in northern California describes black–Hispanic alliances as difficult to achieve.[62] Across the continent, in Miami, black–Cuban relations are openly hostile.[63]

If black leaders face innumerable problems in building a rainbow coalition, can the same be said of Hispanic leaders? On the face of it, urban Hispanics could logically ally themselves with several other disadvantaged groups in the city—principally American Indians, blacks, and lower-class whites. F. Chris Garcia and Rudolph O. de la Garza think that racial and cultural differences preclude a successful coalition with lower-class whites.[64] They do point out, however, that some successful alliances have been made with American Indians and blacks. As we discussed earlier, however, several pitfalls hinder black–Hispanic alliances, even though both groups suffer from similar economic and discriminatory handicaps. Ironically, the most successful political alliances have been with upper- and upper-middle-class whites, who provided considerable financing and support for the United Farm Workers' struggle with the Teamsters Union and various agricultural landowners in California.

As with blacks, historic Hispanic allegiance (except for the Cubans) has been to the Democratic party, although to a much smaller degree. About 58 percent of Hispanics in a 1986 *New York Times* poll identified themselves as Democrats.[65] Some critics think this Democratic inclination has been a blind allegiance that is not always in the best interests of Hispanics.[66] These critics would play Democrats and Republicans against each other by giving Hispanic support to the party that offered the most benefits or by supporting a Hispanic-based third party.

Finally, there are important partisan and ideological differences that would have to be bridged to create a successful rainbow coalition in the 1990s. Based on surveys conducted by the National Opinion Research Center, blacks and non-Cuban Hispanics are ten times as likely to call themselves Democrats as they are to identify as Republicans, but among American Indians that ratio drops to three to one, and among Asians it is less than two to one. In terms of ideology, blacks stand alone as the most liberal of the ethnic groups, with American Indians being the most conservative and Asians being the most split between liberals and conservatives. Finally, there are also important differences among these groups on specific issues of public policy. Asians and Indians are much more likely than blacks or Hispanics, for example, to take the conservative position of saying that too much money is being spent on welfare. On social issues, such as abortion, however, Asians are much more likely to support freedom of choice than are members of the other three groups.[67]

If partisanship, ideological beliefs, and issue positions make a difference in terms of who joins a political coalition (and they usually do make a difference), there appear to be significant obstacles to the formation of a rainbow coalition. This does not mean that such a coalition is foredoomed. Particular mayors in specific circumstances will be able to forge such coalitions in their cities. But before such a broad political movement sweeping urban America could emerge, there would have to be a revolution in people's ability to see themselves as sharing similar economic conditions rather than as being separated by obvious racial conditions.

Social Conflict and Political Change

In summary, contemporary urban changes are moving toward an economically polarized city that has varying degrees of social conflict between the different ethnic groupings who live in the city. The key political leader is the big-city mayor who must put together a governing coalition among the city's competing ethnic, economic, and ideological groups. Minority mayors are well positioned for this task because they can usually count on a huge majority of their own ethnic constituency plus a clustering of votes among other minorities and white liberals. When these mayors take office, however, they face the choice of using race-based policies such as affirmative action that appeal to their ethnic constituencies or universalistic, race-neutral polices that will enable them to claim to be mayor of "all the people." Scholars are divided on which of these approaches is most appropriate.[68] Successful minority mayors, however, are usually able to strike a balance between these competing pressures.

The "You Decide" exercise on p. 205 gives you a chance to wrestle with an important issue and social change.

◇ MAYORAL LEADERSHIP AND THE URBAN POLITICAL ECONOMY

The name of the game for urban mayors in recent years has been economic development. The typical mayor's success has been measured largely by the amount of economic development attracted during his or her administration. A number of development tools exist. Although these will be examined in detail in Chapter 17, we will briefly discuss them here. They can be categorized as either direct subsidies or indirect tax subsidies.

Direct Subsidies

Direct subsidies for economic development have been encouraged in great measure by federal programs, beginning with the urban renewal programs of the 1950s, which for the first time provided federal funds for cities to clear blighted neighborhoods and provide for new commercial and residential development projects in their place. A critical change occurred with the Housing and Community Development Act of 1974, which established a **Community Development Block Grant** (CDBG) for urban redevelopment and for the first time permitted the mayor's office to take direct charge of redevelopment activities. More than any other single piece of legislation, this act concentrated mayors' attentions on economic development. They used the CDBG grants as seed money to entice private developers into the central cities. As a consequence, most cities have undergone a boom in the construction of downtown office buildings and retail shopping facilities. Most cities have also used their CDBG funds to redevelop local historic sites and to "gentrify" some of their historic neighborhoods. During the Reagan-Bush presidencies (1981–1992), federal funds for urban development shriveled.

YOU DECIDE

Should You Seek to Curb Immigration?

You are the chief speech writer for a big-city mayor who is being pressured to take a position on federal legislation that would restrict immigration. Your city receives substantial immigration, as reflected by its ethnic composition: 45 percent white, 25 percent black, 20 percent Mexican American, 8 percent Asian (mostly poor refugees from Southeast Asia), and 2 percent American Indian. Furthermore, your city has seen a significant outflow of jobs, and the city's unemployment rates are persistently above the national average.

On one side of the argument are powerful reasons to support an open-door policy on immigration:

Your city has historically been a beacon for immigrants seeking upward mobility. Most of your white population are descendents from early twentieth-century immigrants.

Church leaders argue that the city has a moral obligation to keep its doors open to immigrants.

Hispanic and Asian leaders are vocal in their opposition to restricting immigration.

Business leaders in the state complain that they need the immigrants to take the low-wage, physical jobs that unemployed and underemployed natives will not take.

Economists have demonstrated that immigrants put less of a burden on the city's welfare services than do the native residents of the city.

If you come out strongly for restrictions, you will be clearly painted as a racist with no sympathies for immigrant cultures.

On the other side of the argument are some compelling reasons to support restrictions on immigration:

Because of its limited economic prospects, new immigrants are unlikely to find lucrative job opportunities in your city.

Because unemployment rates are particularly high among existing peoples of color in your city, immigration will exacerbate the competition for already scarce jobs.

There is danger that the increased job competition brought on by immigration will spill over into interethnic conflicts that you would like to see the city avoid.

In contrast to the rhetoric of Hispanic and Asian leaders, public opinion polls show that Hispanic and Asian residents are divided on the issue of curbing immigration.

If you oppose restrictions, and the economic situation of your city worsens, the mayor will be blamed for not having taken a stand to reduce the competition for jobs when he could have done so.

As the mayor's chief speech writer, your job is to draft his official statement on the proposed legislation restricting immigration. Do you:

A. _____ Explicitly oppose the legislation?
B. _____ Explicitly endorse the legislation?
C. _____ Attempt to work out a compromise law that will put some curbs on immigration but not enough that will repel the opponents.

Explain the reasons for your choice. If your choice is C, what compromise would you endorse?

Indirect Tax Subsidies

As federal funds for economic development dwindled under the Reagan administration, urban redevelopers were more than able to make up the shortfall by relying on tax subsidies that were made available by the states and by the federal government. The most obvious tax subsidy is for a city simply to give a firm a property tax abatement (that is, forgive the tax) if the firm locates or expands within the city. Most popular was probably the IDRB, or Industrial Development Revenue Bond (see Chapter 4), under which a city helped a company raise investment capital at lower interest rates by using the city's tax-exempt municipal bonding authority. Linked with the use of IDRBs were tax increment financing plans, under which the increased property taxes from a development project would be used to pay off the city's investment rather than going into the city treasury. Finally, because the Reagan administration in 1981 dramatically reduced the number of years over which investors could depreciate their investments in real estate, tax-sheltered investments in central-city office buildings, condominiums, and renovation projects became the rage during the first half of the 1980s.

Looking to the Future

Imaginative and aggressive mayors were able to centralize much of the planning for these economic development activities in their own offices. This helped the mayor of the last fifteen years acquire a stature that the office did not have in the 1950s and 1960s. Whether the mayor's new stature will continue, however, is unknown. The prospects for continued direct federal subsidies do not look very bright, and revisions of the federal income tax code have reduced the attractiveness of IDRBs and real estate tax shelters. Furthermore, there has arisen a glut of central-city office buildings in much of the country that is likely to require a period of slow growth or no growth so that demand for office space can catch up with the supply. Finally, criticism of the government-sponsored redevelopment activity of the 1980s maintains that it did not really address the severe social and economic problems of the older central cities and the poor residents of the central cities.[69] We will examine these criticisms in Chapter 17.

SUMMARY

1. Two competing theories of community power are the elitist, or stratificationist, theory and the pluralist theory. These theories were traced to early research conducted in Atlanta, Georgia, and New Haven, Connecticut. More recent community power research has modified the early elitist interpretations of the business community's role in community power, has attributed greater importance to the concept of nondecisions, has shown that a variety of community power relationships exist, and has found that community power relationships can change over time. In the 1990s, the community power debate has been enriched by neo-Marxist theory, growth-machine theory, unitary interest theory, systemic-power theory, and a pluralist counterattack.

2. Regardless of one's interpretation of community power, a major fact of life in contemporary community politics has been the emergence of functional fiefdoms. As the political machines weakened and as new urban programs such as public housing, ur-

ban renewal, airport construction, and metropolitan freeway construction emerged, the functionally organized bureaucracies became powerful. Popularly elected city councils, mayors, and school boards were weakened in their ability to control urban bureaucracies.

3. The major office for providing executive leadership to cope with diverse power centers, the functional fiefdoms, and the federal government is that of the central-city mayor. Getting mayors who are strong requires giving mayors the objective legal and political resources needed to do their jobs and getting mayors who have a subjective vision of what needs to be done in the city and how to do it.

4. The prospects for a rainbow coalition of lower-income people in urban America do not seem great. Minority mayors usually have to craft an electoral coalition that bridges minority populations and white liberals.

5. Strong mayors in the 1980s have built their records principally on guiding economic development activities in the cities. Whether this process can continue at its recent pace is doubtful.

KEY TERMS

Caretaker mayor A mayor with more initiative than the ceremonial mayor, but one who fails to set an agenda of goals to be accomplished.

Ceremonial mayor A mayor who tackles problems individually and devotes much time and effort to ceremonial and symbolic acts.

Community Development Block Grant Formula grant created in 1974 by consolidating several urban-related categorical grants.

Crusader mayor An active and aggressive mayor who lacks many of the preconditions for strong mayoral leadership.

Decision-making approach The approach to analyzing community power that relies on identifying the people who actually make decisions that exert power in the community.

Elitist theory The theory of community power that sees communities as being dominated by a top elite composed principally of major business leaders.

Exit option The option of exiting the city's problems by moving to the suburbs or using the private marketplace to purchase services that are normally public services.

Nondecision The exercise of power by keeping an item off the decision-making agenda of a governmental body.

Pluralist theory The theory of community power that sees communities as being run through the competition of a variety of power centers.

Program entrepreneur A dynamic governor or mayor who sets an agenda of goals to be accomplished and builds alliances with the interests needed to reach the goals.

Reputational approach The approach to analyzing community power that relies on asking a panel of judges to indicate the most powerful people and institutions.

Stratificationist theory See *Elitist theory.*

Voice Option The option of staying in the city and fighting to improve the quality of life there.

REFERENCES

1. Robert S. Lynd and Helen M. Lynd, *Middletown in Transition* (New York: Harcourt, Brace, 1937), p. 74.
2. See Robert A. Dahl, *Modern Political Analysis,* 2nd ed. (Englewood Cliffs, N.J.: Prentice-Hall, 1970), pp. 19–25, 32–34.

3. See especially Gaetano Mosca, *The Ruling Class,* trans. Hannah Kahn (New York: Mc-Graw-Hill, 1939); Roberto Michels, *Political Parties: A Sociological Study of the Oligarchical Tendencies of Modern Democracy,* trans. Eden Paul and Cedar Paul (New York: Free Press, 1962).

4. For a survey of these early studies, see Nelson Polsby, *Community Power and Political Theory* (New Haven, Conn.: Yale University Press, 1963).

5. Floyd Hunter, *Community Power Structure* (Chapel Hill: University of North Carolina Press, 1953).

6. Earlier editions of this book asserted that the power elite "vetoed" projects it disliked. But a recent analysis by Clarence Stone argues persuasively that elite control in Atlanta was really much more subtle. The word *veto* suggests a command and control form of influence. But, argues Stone, Hunter was really describing a preemptive form of influence by which elites controlled the decision-making agenda. See his "Toward An Urban-Regimes Paradigm," *Urban Politics and Urban Policy Section Newsletter* 1, no. 2 (Spring 1987): 7 and *Regime Politics: Governing Atlanta, 1946–1988* (Lawrence, Kan.: University Press of Kansas, 1989).

7. See Polsby, *Community Power and Political Theory;* Herbert Kaufman and Victor Jones, "The Mystery of Power," *Administrative Science Quarterly* 14 (Summer 1954): 2–5; Raymond Wolfinger, "Reputation and Reality in the Study of Community Power," *American Sociological Review* 25 (October 1960): 636–644; Robert A. Dahl, "A Critique of the Ruling Elite Model," *American Political Science Review* 52 (June 1958): 463–469.

8. See Polsby, *Community Power and Political Theory,* pp. 45–56.

9. Robert Dahl, *Who Governs? Democracy and Power in an American City* (New Haven, Conn.: Yale University Press, 1966).

10. See Wallace S. Sayre and Herbert Kaufman, *Governing New York City* (New York: Russell Sage Foundation, 1960); Robert V. Presthus, *Men at the Top: A Study in Community Power* (Ithaca, N.Y.: Cornell University Press, 1964); Aaron Wildavsky, *Leadership in a Small Town* (Totowa, N.J.: Bedminster Press, 1964); Frank J. Munger, *Decisions in Syracuse* (Bloomington: Indiana University Press, 1961); Linton C. Freeman et al., *Metropolitan Decision-Making* (Syracuse, N.Y.: Syracuse University Press, 1962).

11. See, for example, Delbert C. Miller, "Decision-Making Cliques in Community Power Structures: A Comparative Study of an American and an English City," *American Journal of Sociology* 64 (November 1958): 299–310; William H. Form and William V. D'Antonio, "Integration and Cleavage Among Community Influentials in Two Border Cities," *American Sociological Review* 24 (December 1959): 804–814; Robert E. Agger, Daniel Goldrich, and Bert Swanson, *The Rulers and the Ruled: Political Power and Impotence in American Communities* (New York: Wiley, 1964); John Walton, "Discipline, Method, and Community Power: A Note on the Sociology of Knowledge," *American Sociological Review* 31, no. 5 (October 1966): 684–689.

12. Nancy Klemiewski, "Local Business Leaders and Urban Policy: A Case Study," *Insurgent Sociologist* 14, no. 1 (Winter 1987): 47.

13. Robert D. Schulze, "The Bifurcation of Power in a Satellite City," in *Community Political Systems,* Morris Janowitz, ed. (New York: The Free Press, 1961).

14. Edward C. Banfield and James Q. Wilson, *City Politics* (New York: Vintage Books, 1963), pp. 261–276.

15. Peter Bachrach and Morton S. Baratz, "The Two Faces of Power," *American Political Science Review* 56, no. 4 (December 1962): 948.

16. Clarence N. Stone, "Systemic Power in Community Decision Making: A Restatement of Stratification Theory," *American Political Science Review* 74, no. 4 (December 1980): 978–990.

17. Clarence N. Stone, "Social Stratification, Non Decision Making, and the Study of Community Power," *American Politics Quarterly* 10, no. 3 (July 1982): 293.

18. On the methods of researching nondecisions, see Matthew Crenson, *The Unpolitics of Air Pollution: A Study of Non-Decision-Making in the Cities* (Baltimore: Johns Hopkins Press, 1971). Raymond Wolfinger finds the concept of nondecisions so fraught with methodological problems that he thinks it is unresearchable. See his "Non-decisions and the Study of Local Politics," *American Political Science Review* 65, no. 4 (December 1974): 1063–1080. Frederick W. Frey takes a more optimistic viewpoint. See his "Comment: On Issues and Non-issues in the Study of Community Power," *American Political Science Review* 65, no. 4 (December 1971): 1081–1101. Other criticisms of nondecisions can be found in Geoffrey Debnam, "Nondecisions and Power: The Two Faces of Bachrach and Baratz," *American Political Science Review* 69, no. 3 (September 1975): 889–899; and Richard Merelman, "On the Neo-Elitist Critique of Community Power," *American Political Science Review* 62, no. 2 (June 1968): 451–460.

19. For example, see Bernard Asbell, "Dick Lee Discovers How Much Is Not Enough," *The New York Times Magazine,* September 3, 1967, p. 6.

20. Delbert C. Miller, "Industry and Community Power Structures," *American Sociological Review* 23 (February 1958): 9–15.

21. Richard Child Hill, "Fiscal Collapse and Political Struggle in Decaying Central Cities in the United States," in *Marxism and the Metropolis,* William K. Tabb and Larry Sawyers, eds. (New York: Oxford University Press, 1978), pp. 213–240.

22. See Richard Child Hill, "Crisis in the Motor City: The Politics of Economic Development in Detroit," in *Restructuring the City: The Political Economy of Urban Redevelopment,* Susan Fainstein et al., ed. (New York: Longman, 1983), pp. 98–102.

23. Several projections are analyzed in David Fasenfest, "Community Politics and Urban Redevelopment: Poletown, Detroit, and General Motors," *Urban Affairs Quarterly* 22, no. 1 (September 1986): 114.

24. Harvey Molotch, "The City as a Growth Machine: Toward a Political Economy of Place," *American Journal of Sociology* 82 (September 1976): 309–332.

25. G. William Domhoff, "The Growth Machine and the Power Elite: A Challenge to Pluralists and Marxists Alike," in *Community Power: Directions for Future Research,* Robert J. Waste, ed. (Beverly Hills, Calif.: SAGE Publications, 1986), p. 57.

26. Paul E. Peterson *City Limits* (Chicago: University of Chicago Press, 1981).

27. See, for example, Domhoff, "The Growth Machine and the Power Elite," p. 70.

28. Clarence N. Stone, "Summing Up: Urban Regimes, Development Policy, and Political Arrangements," in *The Politics of Urban Development,* Clarence N. Stone and Heywood Sanders, eds. (Lawrence: University Press of Kansas, 1987):

29. Clarence N. Stone, "Systemic Power in Community Decision Making: A Restatement of Stratification Theory," *American Political Science Review* 74, no. 4 (December 1980): 978–990.

30. Ibid., p. 987.

31. The specific quotes can be found in Alberta M. Sbragia, "The 1970s: A Decade of Change in Local Government Finance," in *The Municipal Money Chase: The Politics of Local Government Finance,* Alberta M. Sbragia, ed. (Boulder, Colo.: Westview Press, 1983), p. 83; and Todd Swanstrom, "Urban Populism, Fiscal Crisis, and the New Political Economy," in *Cities in Stress: A New Look at the Urban Crisis,* vol. 30 Urban Affairs Annual Reviews, M. Gottdiener, ed. (Beverly Hills, Calif.: SAGE Publications, 1986), p. 90. For more background, see Todd F. Swanstrom, *The Crisis of Growth Politics: Cleveland, Kucinich, and the Challenge of Urban Populism* (Philadelphia: Temple University Press, 1985).

32. Alan Digaetano, "Urban Political Regime Formation: A Study in Contrast," *Journal of Urban Affairs* 11, no. 3 (1989): 269.

33. Paul D. Schumacher, *Critical Pluralism, Democratic Performance, and Community Power* (Lawrence: University Press of Kansas, 1990).

34. Bryan D. Jones and Lynn W. Bachelor with Carter Wilson, *The Sustaining Hand: Community Leadership and Corporate Power* (Lawrence: University Press of Kansas, 1986).

35. Ibid., pp. 206, 212.

36. James H. Svara, "Institutional Power and Mayoral Leadership," *State and Local Government Review* 27, no. 1 (Winter 1995): 71–83.

37. Robert S. Lorch, *State and Local Politics: The Great Entanglement* (Englewood Cliffs, N.J.: Prentice-Hall, 1995), p. 275. Original source: John T. Galvin, *Twelve Mayors of Boston 1900–1970* (Boston: Boston Public Library, 1970).

38. Timothy Bledsoe, *Careers in City Politics* (Pittsburgh: University of Pittsburgh Press, 1993) and Alan Ehrenhalt, *The United States of Ambition* (New York: Random House, 1991). These two studies suggest that council members may be moving away from the belief in volunteerism (as described in Chapter 6, p. 123) and toward a belief in the city council as a stepping stone to higher office.

39. Svara, "Institutional Power and Mayoral Leadership," pp. 77–78.

40. This was one of the conclusions of the so-called Winter Commission. National Commission on State and Local Public Services, *Hard Truths/Tough Choices: An Agenda for State and Local Reform* (Albany: Nelson A. Rockefeller Institute of Government, State University of New York, 1993).

41. In addition to the three styles mentioned in the text, they identified two other styles: the personality individualist and the executive. For a discussion of these, see John P. Kotter and Paul R. Lawrence, *Mayors in Action: Five Approaches to Urban Governance* (New York: Wiley, 1974), Ch. 7.

42. Ibid., p. 107.

43. Ibid., p. 111.

44. Douglas Yates, *The Ungovernable City* (Cambridge, Mass.: M.I.T. Press, 1977), p. 165.

45. Allan R. Talbot, *The Mayor's Game: Richard Lee of New Haven and the Politics of Change* (New York: Harper & Row, 1967), p. 29.

46. Jewell Bellush and Murray Hausknecht, "Entrepreneurs and Urban Renewal: The New Men of Power," *Journal of the American Institute of Planners* 32, no. 5 (September 1966): 289–297.

47. Dahl, *Who Governs?* pp. 200–214.

48. Svara, "Institutional Power and Mayoral Leadership," pp. 79–81.

49. *The Washington Post National Weekly Edition,* June 21–27, 1993, p. 23; March 28–April 3, 1994, p. 9.

50. Peter K. Eisinger, "Black Mayors and the Politics of Racial Advancement," in *Culture, Ethnicity, and Identity,* William C. McReady, ed. (New York: Academic Press, 1983), p. 106.

51. In Ernest N. Morial's first election as mayor of New Orleans, in 1977, he received only 19 percent of the white vote but 95 percent of the black vote. In Richard Arrington's first election as mayor of Birmingham, in 1979, he won less than 15 percent of the white vote. Philadelphia's Wilson Goode won about 20 percent of the white vote in his 1983 victory. Chicago's Harold Washington won few white votes but an estimated 95 percent of the black vote in his 1983 victory. In his 1987 re-election, Washington expanded his vote in white neighborhoods but still received only a small minority of white votes. See John J. Harrigan, *Political Change in the Metropolis,* 4th ed. (Glenview, Ill.: Scott, Foresman, 1989), p. 144.

52. Terrance D. Lumpkins, "From Stokes to White: Assessing a Lack of Political Power in Cleveland, 1965–1994," a paper presented at the 1995 meeting of the American Political Science Association. Chicago, Ill.: September 1995.

53. Eisinger, "Black Mayors and the Politics of Racial Advancement," pp. 95–109.

54. Grace Hall Saltzstein, "Female Mayors and Women in Municipal Jobs," *American Journal of Political Science* 30, no. 1 (February 1986): 128–139.

55. Albert O. Hirschman, *Exit, Voice, and Loyalty: Responses to Decline in Firms, Organizations, and States* (Cambridge, Mass.: Harvard University Press, 1970).

56. See especially Matthew A. Crenson's *Neighborhood Politics* (Cambridge, Mass.: Harvard University Press, 1983).

57. George Sternlieb and James W. Hughes, "The Uncertain Future of the Central City," *Urban Affairs Quarterly* 18, no. 4 (June 1983): 455–472.

58. Richard Murray and Arnold Vedlitz, "Racial Voting Patterns in the South: An Analysis of Major Elections from 1960 to 1977 in Five Cities," *Annals of the American Academy of Political and Social Science* 439 (September 1978): 29–39.

59. Rufus P. Browning, Dale Rogers Marshall, and David H. Tabb, *Protest Is Not Enough: The Struggle of Blacks and Hispanics for Equality in Urban Politics* (Berkeley: University of California Press, 1984), pp. 46–53.

60. *The New York Times*, April 9, 1987, p. 11.

61. Paul Green, "The Message from the 26th Ward," *Comparative State Politics Newsletter* 7, no. 4 (August 1986): 16.

62. Browning, Marshall, and Tabb, *Protest Is Not Enough*, pp. 121–124.

63. Joan Didion, "Miami: 'La Lucha,'" *The New York Times Review of Books* 34, no. 10 (June 11, 1987): 15, and David Rieff, "The Second Havana," *The New Yorker* 63 (May 1987): 65–83.

64. F. Chris Garcia and Rudolph O. de la Garza, *The Chicano Political Experience: Three Perspectives* (North Scituate, Mass.: Duxbury Press, 1977), pp. 36–37.

65. *The New York Times*, July 18, 1986, p. 6. The percentage of Mexican-Americans and Puerto Ricans identifying themselves as Democrats is probably much higher, however, since this poll included Cubans, who overwhelmingly tend to be Republican.

66. See Mark R. Levy and Michael S. Kramer, *The Ethnic Factor: How America's Minorities Decide Elections* (New York: Simon and Schuster, 1973), p. 83.

67. The data reported here was cumulated from the General Social Surveys conducted by the National Opinion Research Center from 1973 to 1985. For details, see Harrigan, *Political Change in the Metropolis*, 4th ed. pp. 145–146.

68. Fainstein et al., *Restructuring the City*, Ch. 7.

69. In defense of universalistic politics, see Theda Skocpol, "Sustainable Social Policy: Fighting Poverty without Poverty Programs," *The American Prospect*, no. 2 (Summer 1990): 58–70. In defense of race-based policies, see Donald L. De Marco and George C. Galster, "Pro-Integrative Policy: Theory and Practice," *Journal of Urban Affairs* 15, no. 2 (1993): 141–160.

9

STATE LEGISLATURES AND PUBLIC POLICY

Chapter Preview

This chapter examines the role of state legislatures in establishing and overseeing public policy. We shall discuss in turn:

1. The three main functions performed by state legislatures.
2. The structure of state legislatures, with an eye to the impact of organizational patterns on policymaking.
3. Legislative processes, including the bill-passing sequence.
4. The impact of legislative reform movements on state legislatures over the past two decades.

Let us begin by looking at legislative functions.

◇ INTRODUCTION

The state legislatures are crucial bodies for setting public policies. Each session of each legislature finds it enacting many policies that deeply affect our lives. Legislatures raise or do not raise our taxes. They appropriate money for various purposes, such as higher education, highway maintenance, and public health. They pass laws in attempts to deal with various social issues, such as drunk driving, wildlife preservation, and minority rights. As they go about the task of trying to carry out these difficult responsibilities, they get resoundingly criticized. James Bryce, the great English observer of American politics, once commented that "the state legislatures are not high-toned bodies."[1]

Many people today would agree with this understated criticism and perhaps express it even more vehemently.[2] Whether the state legislatures still deserve their disrepute is a topic we will examine in this chapter. We will do that by asking four broad questions. First, what do legislatures do? (That is, what are their functions?) Second, how are legislatures organized to carry out their functions? (How are they structured?) Third, what roles do individual legislators play in legislative policymaking? (What are the legislative processes?) Fourth, can legislative performance be improved? (Have the reforms of recent years been effective?) Finally, when we ask these four questions of state legislatures, we must also ask what effects structure, process, and reform have on the kinds of public policies enacted.

◇ LEGISLATIVE FUNCTIONS

Legislatures authorize the building of roads, set taxes and budgets, help constituents, and oversee state agencies, among many other things. In trying to categorize what legislatures do, three functions stand out—policymaking, legislative oversight, and representation.

Public Policymaking

One of the most important tasks of legislatures is to establish public policies. They do this in a variety of ways. When the state legislature appropriates money for the state budget, determines which taxes will be used to raise money, or passes special educational programs that are mandatory for local school districts, it obviously establishes a statewide policy that affects many people in numerous ways.

Conventional wisdom holds that the governor initiates policy and the legislature reacts to the governor's agenda.[3] Today, however, this conventional wisdom is no longer true. Legislators are just as apt as the governor to try to set the state's policymaking agenda.[4] Legislatures are distinct from other policymaking bodies such as the governor, courts, executive agencies, and local governments in that the legislatures are the critical arenas for debating proposed policies and determining which ones shall have the force of law.

Legislative Oversight

The legislature establishes policies and programs, but that does not necessarily mean that those programs will be implemented the way that the legislature intended. To take one example, an important social change of the past twenty years requiring a public policy response has been the dramatic reliance on child-care facilities for working mothers and single parents. To ensure the safety and well-being of children in day-care homes and day-care centers, most states passed laws providing for the licensing of such establishments. Inevitably, such laws delegate to state welfare departments the responsibility for drawing up the specific rules concerning the number of children per center, the number of staff workers per child, the amount of space per child, and similar requirements. If the rules are too rigid, day-care providers will complain to their legislators, and the legislators will come under pressure to seek to get the rules relaxed. Or if a child is badly maimed or abused in one of these centers and the incident becomes widely publicized through television and other media, the legislators will come under pressure to tighten up the rules. To deal with these types of situations, legislatures have adopted a variety of techniques for conducting **legislative oversight.**

Sunset Legislation   One oversight technique is the **sunset law** (discussed more fully in Chapter 11), which attacks the possibility that some programs and agencies outlive their usefulness. To combat this, legislatures establish a specific life span for an agency (usually six or seven years). At the end of that period, the sun goes down on the agency, and it dies unless it can convince the legislature that it is still needed.

Assessments of sunset legislation as an oversight mechanism have been mixed. The most comprehensive study of sunset laws found that more than 1,500 agencies in all sunset states had been reviewed over a five-year period (1976–1981), resulting in the termination of only 300 agencies and modifications in the procedures of 300 others. The vast majority were recreated without change.[5] Many legislators complain that the sunset review process is too time consuming. Thirty-six states adopted sunset review after it was begun in Colorado in 1976, but disillusionment with the process led twelve of those states to drop it.[6]

Legislative Veto   Perhaps the most direct approach for overseeing situations like the administration of day-care licensing is the **legislative veto,** which allows one or both houses of the legislature to veto a rule within a specified period (usually thirty to ninety days) and prevent it from taking effect. By the early 1980s, twenty-nine states had provided for a legislative veto,[7] and thirteen others had established some other procedure for reviewing administrative rules.[8]

Unfortunately for the advocates of the legislative veto, however, it has run into trouble with the courts. In 1983, the U.S. Supreme Court struck down a congressional veto as violating the separation of powers principle of the federal Constitution.[9] At the state level, the legislative veto was also struck down in five states,[10] although one of them (Connecticut) reinstituted the legislative veto through a constitutional amendment.[11] Today, reliance on the legislative veto is on the decline,[12] and states are replacing it with the creation of administrative commissions that have power to reject proposed rules.[13]

Casework   **Casework** or constituency service is the practice of individual legislators following up on constituent complaints about their contacts with administrative agencies. If there is a persistent pattern of complaints, casework can be an effective oversight tool for legislators to learn about the shortcomings of specific programs. By and large, however, casework as an oversight tool tends to be haphazard. It is much more widely practiced in some states than in others; legislatures with more staff are able to handle more casework.[14] Depending on the state, the individual legislator receives anywhere from a half dozen to two dozen casework requests per week.[15] Some legislators view the handling of constituent complaints as a plus for their career aspirations and solicit casework by setting aside office hours when constituents can call in with their complaints.

Other Oversight Techniques   In addition to sunset legislation, review of administrative rules, and casework, legislatures also have other oversight mechanisms. Legislative committees review administrative agencies and can conduct investigations of administrators in special situations. Finally, there is the legislative audit (or postaudit) under which a legislative auditing body makes studies of selected agencies to see how programs are working and whether the agencies are complying with legislative intent. Today, about two-thirds of the states have postaudit provisions.[16]

Representation and Contemporary Social Conflict

The third major legislative function, and the one causing immense social conflict today is representing the people in government. In America, this is done through the **apportionment** of seats in the legislature. Each legislature must be reapportioned every ten years, and the fundamental representation issue is this: In a society where increasing numbers of people form groups and demand that their group be represented in government, do we apportion our legislatures to represent those groups or to represent individual citizens on the basis of one-person, one-vote regardless of group differences? This question has bedeviled legislatures for the past decade and promises to do so again when the legislatures reapportion after the year 2000 census.

One-Person, One-Vote (or Geographic) Representation   The legislatures are divided into geographic districts that are ideally supposed to be equal in population (one person, one vote), contiguous (no part of the district geographically separated from the rest), and compact. State legislatures began failing the one-person, one-vote test as the U.S. population shifted from a huge rural majority in 1900 to a huge urban majority later in the century. Several states stopped redistricting their legislatures to reflect population shifts, and by the 1960s, metropolitan areas were grossly underrepresented in every state except Wisconsin and Massachusetts.[17] The federal courts had stayed on the sidelines as this was taking place.[18] Then in the 1960s, the U.S. Supreme Court moved vigorously to enforce the principle of equal representation by forcing the states to reapportion their legislatures on the basis of one person, one vote.[19] The one-person, one-vote principle was subsequently applied to congressional districts and to local general-purpose governments.[20]

Looking back on these decisions thirty years later, it is clear that they had far-reaching consequences.[21] After reapportionment, legislatures became much more attentive to the problems of metropolitan areas,[22] and the states assumed more active roles in dealing with problems such as air pollution, housing, and sewerage treatment.[23] Reapportionment also helped increase black representation, and it led to the allocation of more state financial aid to local governments, especially those in metropolitan areas.[24] Reapportionment increased suburban representation more than central-city representation. In a partisan sense, Democrats seemed to benefit most in the North, whereas Republicans made gains in the South.[25] The most long-standing impact of reapportionment may well have been that the influx of suburban, minority, younger, and more heterogeneous legislators led to important reforms of the legislatures themselves and made them more capable of confronting today's problems.

Partisan Gerrymandering   It is important to recognize that legislative seats can be perfectly apportioned on a one-person, one-vote basis and still leave groups of people feeling underrepresented. This can be accomplished through the **gerrymander,** the practice of mapping legislative boundaries into odd shapes so that one party's voters are overconcentrated in a few districts, thus allowing the other party to win a majority of the legislative seats. A Republican-dominated 1981 Indiana reapportionment, for example, concentrated Democratic districts in Indianapolis while splitting the Democratic vote in Fort Wayne. The Democrats cried foul when they subsequently won only 43 percent of Indiana's House seats, even though they had won 52 percent of the vote in House races throughout the state. In California, Republicans called foul after Democrats redrew that state's legislative boundaries to their own advantage. In 1986, the U.S. Supreme Court ruled in the Indiana case that gerrymandering cases will be considered justiciable.[26] Despite this ruling, neither Indiana nor California[27] was ordered by the courts to undo their gerrymandered legislative districts. And the Supreme Court has subsequently seemed to lose its enthusiasm for venturing into issues of partisan redistricting.[28]

How extensive is partisan gerrymandering? Probably not as extensive as commonly thought. Despite some highly publicized exceptions like Indiana and California in the 1980s, recent redistrictings seem to have reduced greatly the amount of partisan bias in representation.[29] Is partisan gerrymandering unfair? If one was a weak Democrat Indianan who frequently voted a split ticket, was she truly denied representation just because that state's 1980s reapportionment put her in a Republican district? Probably not to any serious degree seems to be the answer of political scientist Mark Rush. As the party loyalty of voters continues to weaken (see Chapter 6) and split ticket voting increases, it becomes ever-more difficult to argue that partisan gerrymandering denies representational opportunity to any significant portion of the population.[30]

Racial Gerrymandering   The same, however, cannot be said of racial gerrymandering. People feel strongly about their ethnic and cultural identities. The Supreme Court has held consistently that districts cannot be drawn deliberately to exclude minorities. The most egregious case was probably that of Tuskegee, Alabama, which in the 1950s changed the city boundaries from a square to a twenty-eight-sided polygon that wove in and around black neighborhoods, keeping enough blacks out of the city that they could not elect a majority of the city council. This action was so flagrantly intended to dilute black representation that the Supreme Court invalidated it in 1960.[31]

The Court was less venturesome, however, in striking down electoral arrangements that had a discriminatory impact even though they had not been established with an intent to discriminate. At issue was the system of at-large elections of city council members, which was thought by many observers to dilute the voting strength of blacks and Hispanics. Mobile, Alabama, for example, had never elected a single black person to its three-member, at-large city council, even though blacks by the 1970s accounted for nearly 40 percent of the population. When this was challenged as discriminatory, the U.S. Supreme Court refused to strike down Mobile's at-large elections, because there was no evidence that the designers of the system in 1911 had intended it to dilute black representation.[32]

This ruling infuriated Democrats in Congress, and they retaliated with the 1982 amendments to the Voting Rights Act. Under this legislation, an election system is illegal if it results in diluting minority representation, even when there had never been an intent to discriminate. In 1986, the Supreme Court relied on this law to strike down a multimember system for electing state legislators in North Carolina that had diluted black representation.[33] The Court spelled out three principles for states to follow when conducting future reapportionments. A racial or language minority group must be given its own legislative or congressional district if:

- The minority population is large enough and compact enough to be a majority of the population within a district
- It is a politically cohesive group
- The surrounding majority of white voters vote often enough as a bloc that they can usually defeat minority candidates

For the 1990 reapportionments, this decision obliged mapmakers to create a number of **majority–minority districts.** The results were some strange-looking districts (see Figure 9-1) that clearly violated the compactness principle and

Figure 9-1   GERRYMANDERS: OLD AND NEW

One result of the battles over reapportionment in the 1990s has been the creation of some legislative and congressional districts whose shapes are strikingly evocative of the original gerrymander. Illinois's 4th congressional district in 1992 was designed to create a district for Chicago's Hispanic population. Puerto Ricans were heavily concentrated in its northern portion of the district and Mexican Americans in the southern portion.

Sources: Chicago's 4th district courtesy of U.S. Congress, Illinois 4th District Office.

barely met the contiguity principle. The Supreme Court ordered lower federal courts to determine the legality of a bizarrely shaped North Carolina district,[34] and that action encouraged a flurry of suits challenging the legality of other majority–minority districts.

What was the impact of majority–minority districting? As intended, its major impact was a dramatic increase in black and Hispanic representation.[35] It also aided Republicans. By packing large numbers of minority Democrats into a majority–minority district and siphoning off white Democrats into surrounding suburban districts where they would be outnumbered by Republicans, race-based districting gave southern Republicans four additional seats in Congress in 1992 and made Republicans competitive in several other districts.[36]

In recent years, however, the Supreme Court has been backing away from majority–minority districts if the minority population is geographically dispersed. The Court struck down two such congressional districts in Georgia in 1995, thus forcing a redrawing of that state's congressional districts. Despite the dissolution of the two majority-black districts, the two black representatives won re-election in 1996 in districts that were by then majority-white.

Social Change and Categorical Representation   The conflict over majority–minority districts opened up a Pandora's box of representational issues. A growing minority of people is pushing to have people represented by group categories in addition to, or perhaps even instead of, representation by geographic district on a one-person, one-vote basis.[37] If blacks and Hispanics can have districts carved out for them, what other categories of people might be found to be grossly underrepresented in legislatures and thus deserving of special representative schemes?

In terms of categorical representation, legislators are most representative of their constituents on the *birthright characteristics* of race, religion, and ethnicity and are becoming more so all the time. Nevertheless, some people have a smaller share of legislators than their percent of the population. Despite improvements in representation, only 7 percent of state legislators are black (compared to about 12 percent of the overall population), another 2 percent Hispanic (compared to 9 percent of the population), and about 21 percent women. Legislators tend to be well grounded in their communities, having lived there longer than the average constituent and having been engaged in community life. They are more educated than the general population and are much more likely to have professional or managerial occupations. Contrary to popular beliefs, legislatures are not dominated by lawyers. Only about 16 percent of legislators are attorneys and 10 percent are business owners.[38]

Obviously, the upper-middle sectors of the population are much better represented in the legislatures than are the lower sectors. It is also probable that sharply defined ideological positions are less represented than are those in the ideological mainstream.

We are not likely to bring about a significant increase in representation of left wing or right wing ideologies without altering our two-party electoral system and the single-member district legislature. If we were to adopt multimember districts, however, it would be possible to broaden the spectrum of ideas and interests with representation in the legislature. An environmentally oriented Green party, for example, might win a seat in a multimember district that it is unable to win in a single-member district. Judging from the politics of Italy and Israel and other places with proportional representation and multiparty systems, what a state gained in broadened representation might well be undone in terms of increased political instability.

Perceptual Representation   In addition to representation by geographic district and by social category, representation can also refer to the *perceptions* legislators have about their representational role. The classic presentation of perceptual representation was made by Edmund Burke, the great British theorist, who distinguished between the trustee role and the delegate role. Burke advocated the **trustee** role, in which the legislators vote according to their own best judgment and not according to the wishes of their constituents. In the **delegate** role, by contrast, the legislators vote according to their constituents' wishes. Legislators sometimes balance the two roles, voting as a trustee on issues that generate little public interest or emotion but voting as a delegate on issues that enflame their constituents. Such legislators are said to play the **politico** role. A study of state legislators in Ohio, New Jersey, Tennessee, and California found that almost two-thirds indicated a trustee orientation, about 14 percent a delegate orientation, and about 23 percent a politico orientation.[39]

This overwhelming preference of legislators to function as trustees rather than as delegates seems to fit a broader set of values held by the public. Researchers in Iowa asked the legislators, a sample of the general public, and a sample of other political influentials who the legislators *should* be most attentive to as they decide how to vote in the legislature. Six possible sources for attentiveness were given—the legislator's conscience, the state, the legislator's district, the political party, the governor, and special interest groups. The results, given in Table 9-1, show very little difference between the three samples. Before you look at Table 9-1, however, it might be useful to do the "You Decide" exercise on page 221 to sort out your own views on this issue.

◇ LEGISLATIVE STRUCTURE: HOW ORGANIZATION AFFECTS POLICYMAKING

The fifty states are very similar in their legislative organization. All but Nebraska are bicameral, or have two houses. All but Nebraska and the one-party states of the South organize themselves around political party caucuses. And all fifty states rely heavily on committees to do most of their work. Of these three structural features, bicameralism has the least effect on policy formulation.

Bicameralism

Bicameralism developed during the colonial period, when the house was looked on as the body of the people and the senate as the body of the governor. After the

YOU DECIDE

Legislators: Trustees or Delegates?

When your legislator votes on major issues such as abortion or taxing and spending, do you want him or her voting as a trustee or as a delegate? If you want your legislator to vote as a delegate, to which constituency group do you want the legislator to be accountable: an interest group, the governor, the political party, or the district that he or she represents?

You can use the table shown here to rank various representational styles from the one you most prefer (number 1) to the one you least prefer (number 6).

Trustee Roles

Vote one's conscience   _____

Vote what's best for the state   _____

Delegate Roles

Vote as an interest group directs   _____

Vote as the governor directs   _____

Vote as the political party directs   _____

Vote what is best for one's district   _____

After indicating your own priorities, turn to Table 9-1, on p. 221, which shows how different samples of Iowans responded to a similar question.

Revolution in 1776, the state senates served mainly to represent wealthy people with property, who feared that the popularly dominated lower houses would redistribute the wealth. By the early nineteenth century, all the states were bicameral. Only Nebraska reverted to the unicameral form, doing so in 1934.

Unicameralism has worked well in Nebraska, and legislative reformers have urged it upon other states. Reformers argue that elimination of one of the two houses would make the legislature operate more efficiently and effectively. It would eliminate the need for conference committees and increase the prestige of the body. In contrast, the supporters of bicameralism say that the two-house legislature helps preserve the traditional principle of checks and balances and impedes the hasty passage of poorly conceived bills by slowing down the legislative process. Whatever its merits, unicameralism is not popular with either legislators or the voters. When put on the ballot, unicameral proposals have been invariably voted down.

The Responsible-Party Model of Centralizing Influence

The **responsible-party model** has been very popular with many reform-minded political scientists, who feel it is the best way to make the legislature accountable to the voters.[40] They allude to the British Parliament as the ideal responsible-

Table 9-1 EXPECTATIONS ABOUT PERCEPTIVE REPRESENTATION

"Which Should a Legislator Be Most Attentive to in Deciding How to Vote?"

Iowa Legislators	Sample of Iowa Political Influentials	Representative Sample of Iowa Voters
1. Conscience	1. Conscience	1. Conscience
2. State	2. State	2. District
3. District	3. District	3. State
4. Party	4. Party	4. Party
5. Governor	5. Governor	5. Governor
6. Group	6. Group	6. Group

Note: There was great similarity between the expectations of voters, legislators, and the political influentials about whose opinions a legislator should represent. Conscience, state, and district scored high; political parties, interest groups, and governors scored low.

Source: Ronald D. Hedlund, "Perceptions of Decisional Referents in Legislative Decision Making," *American Journal of Political Science* 19, no. 3 (August 1975): 538. Reprinted by permission.

party system. Voters in England elect either the Conservative or the Labor party to office. The winning party controls both the executive and legislative branches of government and enacts its own policies. When the voters become dissatisfied with the government's performance, they can vote the governing party out of office. No American state has a responsible-party system comparable to that in Great Britain, but the states vary widely on their degree of party strength and the ability of the parties to provide leadership in the legislature.

Party Leadership   The key feature of party organization of the legislature is the attempt to provide for leadership through the *centralization of influence* in a few party leaders. The dominant party leader in the lower house is the **speaker of the house,** who is the presiding officer and is chosen from the majority party (or the majority coalition in one-party states). The speaker's powers vary from state to state, but speakers typically have the authority to assign bills to committee, to recognize house members who desire to speak on the floor, to influence committee assignments of the members, to determine the house calendars, and to control the ebb and flow of legislative business on the floor. In order to restrain the potential power of the speaker, ten states limit how long any single person may serve as speaker. In some cases, Florida, for example, speakers are limited to a single two-year term.[41]

Immediately subordinate to the speaker are the **majority leader** (or floor leader) and assistant majority leaders (or whips), whose task is to line up floor votes for party-supported bills. The same job is performed for the minority party by the **minority leader** and the assistant minority leaders. From time to time, all the legislators of a party gather in a meeting called the party **caucus,** where they set goals and plan legislative strategies. At these meetings, the party determines who will hold the leadership positions, what bills will demand party discipline, and who will prevail in the recurring battles between opposing factions within the party.

It is up to the speakers and majority leaders to get their members to vote the party position on the most important bills. There are trends in place that both aid and hinder the leaders in this task. Helping the speakers in their quest to provide leadership has been the emergence of the speaker as a campaign fund raiser. Ohio Speaker of the House Vernal Riffe, for example, doled out $2.7 million in 1990 legislative races.[42] California's Assembly Speaker Willie Brown was so successful at raising campaign funds in the 1980s that he provided up to half the funding for Democrats running in open seat elections and he regularly provided about a third of the funds for Democrats running in marginal districts.[43] Party leaders also have other means to persuade fellow legislators to follow party discipline on crucial votes. They influence committee assignments, office space, staff, and other perquisites that affect the job of a legislator.

There are countervailing trends, however, that are slowly eroding the ability of legislative party leaders to dominate their houses.[44] Most of these trends stem from the weakening of the political parties in general. There are very few states anymore where one political party controls all three institutions of state government (the House, the Senate, and the governorship). Strong leadership is also being eroded by the movement to limit the number of terms that a legislator can hold office.

Do Strong Competitive Parties Make Any Difference? In American political theory, two-party competition is expected to result in responsible parties that present alternative policy programs to the voters. As the two parties compete for votes, the competition forces the parties to be more responsive to the voters' wishes. In contrast, the absence of party competition is believed to lead to political factionalism built around personalities and temporary issues. The factions are not permanent, and they fail to translate voter preferences into public policy.[45]

Do strong, competitive parties in fact lead to more policies that the voters want? Although the results of voluminous studies are not conclusive, four generalizations have emerged.

First, insofar as spending policies are concerned, states dominated by one party spend less money per capita than do the more competitive, two-party states. But the one-party states also tend to be poorer than the competitive states. And elaborate statistical tests indicate that it is their impoverishment, not their lack of interparty competitiveness, that leads these states to spend less money per capita.[46]

Second, there are, however, certain conditions under which party competitiveness leads to more liberal spending policies. This is most likely to occur in states where the competitiveness is highly volatile and the majority has a realistic chance of losing its control over state government.[47]

Third, on nonexpenditure measures, competition seems to make legislatures more responsive to demands. Wayne Francis found that the competitive states were more likely to take action on issues before the legislature than were the noncompetitive states.[48]

HIGHLIGHT

The Tools of Legislative Leadership

In an era of weak party loyalty, senate and house leaders use informal methods of persuasion to maintain party discipline. One tactic is to help out other legislators as much as you can and only rarely pressure them to reciprocate by voting with you. But make sure they understand that when their cooperation is really needed, failure to go along with you will put them in a very weak position to ask favors in the future.

One senate leader was described:

> If you need a state trooper to give you a ride somewhere, he'll get it for you. If you need a bill killed in committee, he'll help you kill it. He'll do favor after favor and won't ask anything in return. But when he needs you to vote with him, and he doesn't ask often, he'll just say, 'I need you on this one.' And you may be voting against your mother when you vote with O'Keefe, but you'll go ahead and vote with him anyway.

Source: Alan Rosenthal, *Governors & Legislatures: Contending Powers* (Washington, D.C.: Congressional Quarterly Press, 1990), p. 83.

Fourth, outside the South, when Democrats control the legislature, they often enact different kinds of policies than the Republicans enact when they have control. Civil rights laws, for example, were much more likely to be passed under Democratic control than under Republican control.[49]

In sum, strong competitive parties can make a difference in the kind of policies a state adopts. This is most likely to happen when the competition is very close and very volatile. Outside the South, Democrats appear to be more liberal than Republicans. The parties have a much stronger impact on nonbudgetary policy areas than they do in budget areas, however. For budgetary policy, two-party competition is probably less significant than the level of affluence of a state. The affluent states spend more because they have more money to spend.

Committee Organization as a Decentralizing Force

In contrast to party organization, which centralizes political influence in the hands of party leaders, committee organization *decentralizes political influence* to the chairpersons of the various committees that study legislative proposals called bills. The typical legislature will consider 3,000 or 4,000 measures each biennium (New York considered more than 3,000 in 1993–1994).[50] To provide a division of labor capable of processing this massive amount of work, committees are created. Committees receive bills, conduct hearings, change the substance of bills, and vote to approve or disapprove them. There is usually a **standing committee** for each major area of legislation, such as taxes, agriculture, education, or transportation.

In addition to standing committees, **select committees** are created on a temporary basis to study important issues that do not fit readily into the workload of the standing committees. Another type of committee is the **joint committee,** which is composed of members of both houses. Connecticut, Maine, and Massachusetts rely heavily on joint standing committees.[51] The advantage of such an arrangement is that it precludes the necessity of a bill's being examined separately by senate and house committees. Finally, a special type of joint committee is the **conference committee,** which is created to resolve the differences between house- and senate-passed versions of a bill.

◇ LEGISLATIVE PROCESS: HOW LEGISLATORS MAKE POLICY

Before an idea, no matter how brilliant, can be turned into public law, it must work its way through the legislative maze. Some of the procedures for doing this are very formal; others are very informal. Legislators play a variety of roles in this process, and they follow several unofficial and unwritten rules that govern legislative behavior.

Passing a Law

A simplified model of a bill's passage is shown in Figure 9-2. The bill may originally be conceived by a legislator, a lobbyist, a state agency, the governor's staff, a citizen group, or an interested citizen. But it can only be formally introduced by a house or senate member, who is called the bill's author. The bill's first reading* occurs when the clerk announces the bill's number and title to the full house or senate.

After introduction, the bill is referred to a committee. It is very important to the author that the bill be sent to a friendly committee. If it is referred to a hostile committee in a state with strong committees, it may be given an unfavorable recommendation or simply **pigeonholed.** An important bill will be sent to a subcommittee that will conduct public hearings, invite all interested parties to testify, and amend the bill. In states with effective **sunshine laws,** all official committee action is taken publicly in open meetings, records are kept of votes on amendments, and tape recordings of the debate are made available to reporters and the public.

After a bill is reported out of committee, it is put on a **calendar** to await its second reading and floor debate. Debate quite often occurs in a committee of the whole, which is simply the whole house meeting under the less formal committee rules. These allow a smaller **quorum** and make it easier to amend bills. Since the committee of the whole is where the full chamber makes its most serious amendments, the votes in committee of the whole indicate a legislator's intent much more than do the votes on final passage of bills.

---

*It is called a reading because the clerks originally read the bills aloud to the full chamber. Although this requirement is still demanded by some state constitutions, bills are never read aloud anymore.

Figure 9-2 STEPS IN THE PASSAGE OF A BILL

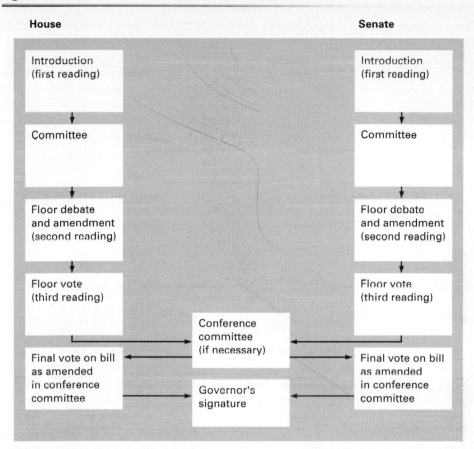

House

Senate

Introduction
(first reading)

Committee

Floor debate
and amendment
(second reading)

Floor vote
(third reading)

Final vote on bill
as amended
in conference
committee

Conference
committee
(if necessary)

Governor's
signature

Introduction
(first reading)

Committee

Floor debate
and amendment
(second reading)

Floor vote
(third reading)

Final vote on bill
as amended
in conference
committee

Before being enacted into law, a bill must go through several steps in the legislative maze. Probably 60 percent or more of bills do not get enacted into law.

Finally, after floor debate and amendment, the bill comes back for final passage as amended. This is the third reading. Most states require roll call votes on the passage of the bill and provide electronic voting devices that flash a green light for an *aye* vote and a red light for a *nay* vote, and automatically record the votes. When roll call votes are not used, or to determine unanimous consent, voice vote may be used.

When the house-passed version of a bill differs from the senate-passed version, the first house will usually accept the amendments made by a second house. If not, a joint conference committee is appointed by the speaker of the house and the president of the senate to resolve the differences. The conference committee has an equal number of senators and representatives. The house and senate must approve or reject the conference committee report without amendment.

Once the chambers pass a single version of a bill, it is printed in final form (called *enrollment*) and sent to the governor for signature. At this stage, the governor has three choices. If the governor signs the bill, it becomes law. If the governor neither signs nor vetoes it, it becomes law without his or her signature. If the governor vetoes the bill, it does not become law unless the veto is overridden by the legislature. This seldom happens, in part because some states require a two-thirds majority vote in each house to override a veto and in part because many vetoes are made at the close of the legislative session, when the legislators are no longer present to conduct an override vote. To cope with this, more and more states are providing for special override sessions to give the house and senate a chance to override vetoes made after the regular session ends. Finally, some states provide for a pocket veto. If a bill comes to a governor at the close of a session and it is not signed or vetoed within a specified number of days (usually five to fifteen), it does not become law, and the governor is said to have exercised a **pocket veto.**

How Legislators Are Influenced to Vote

Perhaps the most important aspect of the informal legislative process concerns how legislators are influenced to vote on specific public policies. In our earlier discussion of representation, we asked whether the legislator *should* be a trustee or a delegate. In reality, the pressures on legislators are much more complex than this. They consult and are influenced by a wide variety of sources, ranging from fellow legislators to individual constituents. One survey asked state legislators to identify the sources they consulted most frequently when they decided how to vote. They tended to rely much more heavily on advice they got from fellow legislators than they did on advice from sources outside the legislature such as the governor or constituents.[52] The only extralegislative sources that ranked high were lobbyists.

This finding about the influence of lobbyists was reinforced by a study of lobbyists registered in Iowa. It found that interest group lobbyists were more active than other actors. They took positions on 61 percent of the bills before the legislature, compared to 35 percent for the governor and only 26 percent for the house majority caucus. Further, on 84 percent of the bills, there was no conflict among lobbyists. When they came into conflict with the governor or the house majority caucus, however, the interest groups were more likely than the others to lose.[53] Finally, legislators are also affected by their own ideological leanings. A study of voting in the Connecticut and North Carolina legislatures found that a liberal or conservative orientation of legislators had a greater impact on their vote than did their partisanship or the economic characteristics of the districts they represented.[54]

◇ LEGISLATIVE REFORM: IMPROVING LEGISLATIVE PERFORMANCE

As legislatures have gone about their tasks of making public policy, they have been heavily criticized for the way they conduct the public's business. The American Political Science Association's Committee on American Legislatures, for example, charged back in 1954 that "the state legislatures are poorly equipped to serve as policymaking agencies in . . . America."[55] Today, some four decades later, that charge no longer rings true. State legislatures are now a "leading source of policy innovations."[56] The legislatures have revamped themselves extensively in the intervening forty years, but they still face numerous problems. We need to examine the agenda for legislative reform in the states, the accomplishment of reform, and the consequences of that reform.

The Agenda for Legislative Reform

Since midcentury, several prestigious organizations joined the call for reforming state legislatures.[57] The most ambitious such calls came in a 1971 book, *The Sometimes Governments*,[58] that ranked the fifty states on an index of legislative reform and outlined dozens of specific steps that legislatures should take in order to make themselves more accountable to the voters and more responsible in carrying out their job. The goal of reform was to professionalize the legislatures, and professionalization was to be achieved through the following five-point agenda.

1. *Legislatures should meet full time and offer decent pay.* There should be more full-time legislatures capable of holding longer sessions in order to conduct the public business. Part-time legislatures, it was argued, inevitably make it harder for salary earners to give up their incomes in order to serve. Low salaries perpetuate the dominance in legislatures of lawyers, farmers, and the small number of business owners who can afford to absent themselves from their primary occupations for three or four months at a time in order to serve in the legislatures.

2. *Legislatures should have better staff and research capability.* Without adequate staff and research capabilities, legislatures are unduly dependent on the information provided by interest groups, state agencies, and other interested parties. Legislative committees and individual legislators need staff assistance, especially to draft bills, analyze bills that legislators do not have time to read thoroughly, analyze the governor's budget proposals, and evaluate programs being administered by state agencies.

3. *Constitutional restrictions on state legislatures should be removed.* In particular, reformers seek to remove constitutional provisions that set legislative pay, limit the length of sessions, and put restrictions on state budget-making powers. Of especial concern are the many *earmarked funds* in state constitutions that hamper legislative flexibility to set spending policies for the state.

4. *Legislative ethics should be improved.* By its nature, raising campaign funds indebts some legislators to vested interests. Many legislators have hidden conflicts of interest. They receive benefits from organizations that in turn benefit from policies supported by those very legislators. Accordingly, reformers seek extensive campaign finance reform that will disclose campaign contributors to public light, put limits on campaign contributions, provide public funds for legislative campaigns, and put tough restrictions on legislative lobbyists.

5. *Legislatures should be smaller in size.* Just how large a legislature should be cannot be determined. Minnesota—with 67 members—has the largest state

senate, and New Hampshire—with 400 members—has the largest house. The Committee for Economic Development recommends that state legislatures be no larger than 100 members. Reformers feel that a smaller legislature would enhance its prestige, make it possible to offer higher salaries, and enable more highly qualified people to run for office. Reducing the size would necessarily force the legislatures to restructure the committees and make it easier to pinpoint responsibility.

Accomplishing Legislative Reform

Considerable progress has been made toward these reformist goals. All states adopted some of the reforms, and some states adopted a substantial majority of them. The most extensive progress has been made on the structural and procedural items spelled out in goals 1, 2, and 3. The least progress has come on goals 4 and 5.

On goal 1, nine legislatures have, for all practical purposes, become full-time bodies and another thirty-four meet annually.[59] As legislative sessions have lengthened, legislative pay has also gone up. The median annual salary in 1994 was only about $15,000, but many states supplement the base pay with per diem allowances that easily enable a legislator to earn $30,000 or more. Although no one will get rich on such incomes, legislative salaries are now high enough that dedicated, frugal people can devote full time to their legislative tasks, even in the states without full-time bodies. Almost one-fourth of state legislators now make this a full-time job.[60] On goal 2, there has been a dramatic increase in legislative staff in the past twenty years. Today the 50 state legislatures collectively employ 33,000 people during the sessions (see Table 9-2).

The net impact of legislative reform has been to turn the most professionalized legislatures into dynamic institutions that now play a significant policy innovation role.[61] The Oregon legislature, for example, took the lead in overhauling federally assisted health-care programs so that half a million uninsured people would be covered. Michigan totally revamped its school financing system to eliminate the "savage inequalities" (discussed in Chapter 1). Colorado and Florida passed tough bans on children possessing guns. California's air pollution control plan set the model for the federal government's Clean Air Act Amendments in 1993.[62] And Wisconsin in 1996 restructured its welfare programs. Since some of these innovations leaned in a liberal direction and others in a conservative direction, no one is pleased with them all, obviously. What is beyond dispute, however, is the policy leadership exhibited by the state legislatures in the past few years.

The Unintended Consequences of Legislative Reform

However innovative the legislatures have become, they are not getting much credit for accomplishments. This in no small measure is because of some unintended consequences that have accompanied reform.

First, legislative professionalization may have inhibited progress on the goal of improving legislative ethics. As legislatures spend increasing amounts of

Table 9-2   PROFESSIONALIZATION LEVELS OF THE STATE LEGISLATURES

1 New York	13 Florida	26 Louisiana	39 Georgia
2 Michigan	New Jersey	27 Oregon	40 West Virginia
3 California	15 Arizona	28 South Carolina	41 Idaho
4 Massachusetts	Oklahoma	29 Virginia	42 Montana
5 Pennsylvania	17 Connecticut	30 Maine	43 Arkansas
6 Ohio	18 Washington	31 Mississippi	44 Kentucky
7 Alaska	19 Iowa	Nevada	45 New Mexico
8 Illinois	20 Texas	33 Alabama	46 South Dakota
9 Colorado	21 Maryland	34 Kansas	47 Utah
10 Missouri	22 North Carolina	35 Rhode Island	48 North Dakota
11 Hawaii	23 Minnesota	36 Vermont	49 Wyoming
12 Wisconsin	24 Delaware	37 Indiana	50 New Hampshire
	25 Nebraska	38 Tennessee	

Note: This index of professionalization is based on the salary, staff, and time spent in session.

Source: Peverill Squire, "Legislative Professionalization and Membership Diversity in State Legislatures," *Legislative Studies Quarterly* 17, no. 1 (February 1992): 72. Copyright © 1992 Comparative Legislative Research Center. Reprinted by permission.

money on a wide range of public programs, they inevitably attract a larger number of interest groups and lobbyists who make campaign contributions, attend their fund-raisers, hold out the possibility of lucrative job opportunities, and sometimes offer outright bribes.[63]

A second unintended consequence in the minds of some observers has been that legislative professionalism gives more political help to the Democrats than to the Republicans. As the legislatures become full-time jobs, they are less attractive to people with lucrative careers of their own than they are to people without their own full-time careers. Since Republicans on average have better nonpolitical career opportunities than do the Democrats, highly qualified Republicans are less likely to make careers out of the legislature.[64] There is nothing wrong, of course, with any Democrat making a full-time job out of the legislature, but it is not surprising that Republicans and Independents would look skeptically at an institution that puts them at a disadvantage. When the issue of limiting legislative terms of office was put before voters in California, it was supported by more than two-thirds of people who identified themselves as strong Republicans and nearly three-fifths of Independents, compared to less than half of the strong Democrats.[65]

If legislators who are students, retired, or housewives are included in the count, about one-fourth of all legislators are full-time today. Increasing numbers of them are also staying in the job for longer periods. As recently as the 1960s, about 40 percent of all legislators would be serving their first term. That percentage has steadily dropped. In 1992, after a legislative redistricting that should have dramatically increased the number of first-timers, the number actually dropped to 30 percent.[66] If the legislature is one's only career, one becomes preoccupied with maintaining himself or herself in office.[67] The more that legislators become careerists with no outside occupation to fall back on, the more pressure they feel to preserve their seats in the state capitol.

The Term Limitation Movement

The trend toward legislative careerism has obviously not set well with the public. By 1995, twenty-one states had reacted to careerism by adopting legislative term limits, twenty of them through the initiative process described in Chapter 6.[68] The most restrictive limits are in Arkansas, California, Michigan, and Oregon, which put a six-year limit on representatives and an eight-year limit on senators.

Is the idea of term limits a good one? On the positive side, proponents argue that term limits will ensure a constant infusion of new blood and new ideas into the legislatures, will reduce the advantages that incumbents have in elections, will create a healthy competition for other political offices, and will nip legislative careerism in the bud.[69]

Most scholars, however, are negative. Their arguments fall into one of two camps. In the first camp are those who think that the fear of careerism has been overdone. They point out that most legislators voluntarily retire after a few terms even without term limits. One study of six states over an eighteen-year period found that less than 3 percent of legislators remained in office the entire

Taken to its logical extreme, the movement to limit terms is ultimately destructive of the legislature.

Source: C. P. Houston from *The Houston Chronicle,* 1992.

eighteen years.[70] Another study looked at all fifty states over twelve years and found that barely one-fourth of representatives and one-third of senators who were first elected in 1979 were still in office twelve years later in 1990.[71] For these reasons, the twelve-year term limits imposed by Colorado and Oklahoma would have no effect on most legislative careers.

A second camp of observers, however, think that term limits will lead to some dangerous unintended consequences. Term limits will impede the growth of leadership in legislatures. It takes a few years' experience for legislators to familiarize themselves with the goals and tactics of other political actors such as lobbyists, legislative staff, and executive branch officials who have been around for a long time. Under California's six-year limit, just when these legislators reach the point where they have accumulated the experience and knowledge to become effective leaders they will be forced to retire. This will necessarily increase the strength and influence of other political actors such as the bureaucracy, interest groups, paid legislative staff, and the governor.[72]

Are these dire predictions about term limits coming to pass? We do not know for certain, yet, since it was only in 1998 that the first class of legislators were forced out of office by term limits. However, early indications suggest that both the advocates and opponents of term limits can claim vindication. Proponents note that mere existence of term limits has speeded up voluntary retirements and thus put a curb on careerism.[73] Opponents point to California as evidence that the negative predictions are starting to materialize. The California Assembly's long-time, flamboyant Speaker Willie Brown was forced from office in 1988, opening the probability of a leadership vacuum and a decline in party discipline.[74] As the magic date of term limits taking effect approached (1998), California's centralized leadership began losing its ability to control the legislatures. The first class to be forced out were unceremoniously called "terminals." And as the leadership began to lose influence over the legislature, lobbyists gained influence, writing speeches for legislators and, in some instances, even drafting legislation.[75]

The Overall Effect of Legislative Reform

Despite its unintended consequences and its limited impact on the direction of public policy, legislative reform, on balance, has been a positive development. Legislatures are generally much more capable institutions than they were a quarter century ago and have a much greater independent ability to impose their own wills on the policymaking process. If from time to time they do not seem to measure up to their new capabilities, that is probably a reflection of the limitations of structural reform to deal with political divisions. As a political body, a legislature will necessarily mirror its state's political divisions. And the direction of public policy that flows from such a legislature is more likely to depend on which political interests are dominant than on the elegance of the legislature's structural reform.

SUMMARY

1. The legislative functions discussed in this chapter are public policymaking, legislative oversight, and representation.

2. A major legislative representation conflict involves reapportionment. In the 1960s, the Supreme Court demanded apportionment according to the one-person, one-vote principle. However, instituting that principle did not eliminate partisan gerrymandering, did not make the legislature economically representative of the population, and did not affect the legislators' tendencies to think of themselves as trustees rather than as delegates.

3. Several patterns were observed in the organization of state legislatures. All legislatures but one are bicameral. The two organizing devices are the political parties, which tend to centralize influence, and the committee systems, which tend to decentralize influence. Although state legislative committee systems have typically been much weaker than the congressional committee system, very little development of strong and responsible parties has occurred to strengthen ties between the legislature and the voters.

4. The legislative process seems to put a premium on delay, caution, and checks so that powerful political minorities are able to block bills that threaten them. Throughout the 1950s and 1960s, this phenomenon gave the state legislatures a noninnovative image in the face of pressing social changes.
5. Partially in order to restore the autonomy of state legislatures, the legislative reform movement accelerated in the late 1960s and the 1970s. Although the reforms improved the internal procedures of the legislatures, scholars have been able to find few consistent patterns in policies that resulted from legislative reform. The most recent move for legislative reform has been to impose limits on the number of times that legislators may serve.

KEY TERMS

Apportionment The division of legislative seats among the population. *Malapportionment* refers to a very unequal division of legislative seats. *Reapportionment* refers to the act of apportioning the seats once again to make their division more equal.

Calendar A list of bills that have been acted on by committee and are waiting for debate or final vote. There are specific types of calendars with a wide variety of names for the specific stages of floor consideration of bills.

Casework The practice of helping constituents handle their problems with government agencies. So called because each constituent's problem becomes a "case" to be solved.

Caucus A group of legislative members who meet jointly to push a legislative program. Usually refers to a party caucus such as the House Republican caucus or the Senate Democratic caucus.

Conference committee A temporary joint legislative committee created to work out a compromise when the house-passed version of a bill differs from the senate-passed version.

Delegate The representation role in which legislators vote as their constituents with rather than voting their own consciences.

Gerrymander The practice of drawing legislative district boundaries with the intent of discriminating against some group of people.

Joint committee A committee composed of members of the house and senate.

Legislative oversight The legislature's responsibility to see that the executive branch implements laws as the legislature intended them to be implemented.

Legislative veto A device whereby the legislature can reverse an action of the governor or executive agencies by passing a resolution (the legislative veto) opposing the action within a short period after its announcement (usually thirty to ninety days).

Majority–minority district A legislative district deliberately created so that it would elect a minority representative.

Majority leader The majority-party leader responsible for managing legislation on the floor of the legislature.

Minority leader The minority-party leader responsible for managing legislation on the floor of the legislature.

Pigeonholing The act of filing a bill for the record but never taking it up for consideration.

Pocket veto The governor's act of killing a bill he or she has received after the close of a legislative session simply by not signing it within the required number of days (usually five to fifteen).

Politico The representation role in which legislators sometimes vote their consciences and other times vote as their constituents wish.

Quorum The number of members needed to be present for the legislature to conduct its business. A usual quorum is a majority of the members.

Responsible-party model A model of parliamentary control similar to that in Britain in which voters elect a party to power and the individual legislators are accountable to the party, which in turn is accountable to the voters. When voters become displeased with the party's performance, they can vote it out of power.

Select committee A temporary legislative committee that is responsible for legislation that has surfaced in a particular legislative session but that is not expected to recur permanently.

Speaker of the house The key party leader, who presides over the lower house of the state legislatures.

Standing committee A permanent legislative committee that is responsible for legislation in each subject area that recurs in every legislative session, such as education or transportation.

Sunset law A law requiring programs to terminate in a given number of years unless they are reauthorized by the legislature. This forces the legislature to reevaluate the purposes and operations of the sunset agencies and programs.

Sunshine law Legislation requiring that all government business, including legislative business, be open to the public.

Trustee The representation role in which the legislators vote their consciences rather than as their constituents wish.

REFERENCES

1. James Bryce, *The American Commonwealth,* vol. 2 (New York: Macmillan, 1906).
2. This extent of people's disapproval of state legislatures seems to vary from time to time. In a 1979 survey, the National Conference on State Legislatures found that only 31 percent of the people approved of their legislature. By 1989, this had gone up to 61 percent. Rich Jones, "The State Legislatures" in *The Book of the States: 1990–91* (Lexington, Ky.: Council of State Governments, 1990), p. 115.
3. Sarah McCally Morehouse, for example, wrote that "few major state undertakings get off the ground without [the governor's] initiative." See her *State Politics, Parties and Policy* (New York: Holt, Rinehart & Winston, 1980), p. 243.
4. Alan Rosenthal, *Governors & Legislatures: Contending Powers* (Washington, D.C.: Congressional Quarterly Press, 1990), p. 119.
5. *The Status of Sunset in the States: A Common Cause Report* (Washington, D.C.: Common Cause, 1982).
6. *The Book of the States: 1990–91* (Lexington, Ky.: Council of State Governments, 1990), p. 466. Six states repealed their sunset laws, and six others left the laws on the books but ceased doing the review process.
7. Thad L. Beyle, "Governors and Legislatures," *The Book of the States: 1984–85* (Lexington, Ky.: Council of State Governments, 1984), pp. 42–43.
8. James R. Bowers, "An Overview of Rules Review in Illinois," *Comparative State Politics Newsletter* 9, no. 6 (December 1988): 18.
9. *Chadha* v. *Immigration and Naturalization Service* 103 U.S. 2764.
10. Rosenthal, "Legislative Oversight and the Balance of Power in State Government," pp. 90–98.

11. Rosenthal, *Governors & Legislatures*, p. 184.
12. Ibid., p. 184.
13. Lanny Proffer, "Legislative Veto Alternatives," *State Legislatures* 10, no. 1 (January 1984): 23–25.
14. Alan Rosenthal, "The Legislative Institution—In Transition and at Risk," *The State of the States*, 2nd ed. (Washington, D.C.: Congressional Quarterly Press, 1993), p. 129; Richard Elling, "The Utility of State Legislative Casework as a Means of Oversight," *Legislative Studies Quarterly* 4, no. 3 (1979): 353–380.
15. Patricia K. Freeman and Lilliard E. Richardson, Jr., "Casework in State Legislatures," *State and Local Government Review* 26, no. 1 (Winter 1994): 21–26.
16. Alan Rosenthal, "Legislative Oversight and the Balance of Power in State Government," *State Government* 56, no. 3 (1983): 90–98.
17. Gordon E. Baker, *The Reapportionment Revolution: Representation, Political Power and the Supreme Court* (New York: Random House, 1966).
18. *Colegrove* v. *Green*, 328 U.S. 549 (1946).
19. In *Baker* v. *Carr*, 369 U.S. 186 (1962), the Supreme Court agreed to hear reapportionment cases for lower houses of state legislatures, which eventually forced reapportionment upon the lower houses. In *Reynolds* v. *Sims*, 377 U.S. 533 (1964), the Supreme Court extended the one-person, one-vote principle to state senates.
20. *Wesberry* v. *Sanders*, 367 U.S. 1 (1964) was the congressional case.
21. The earliest research on reapportionment had not found a significant impact. Its effects became clear only as time went on. See Herbert Jacob, "The Consequences of Malapportionment: A Note of Caution," *Social Forces* 63 (1964): 261; Thomas R. Dye, *Politics, Economics, and the Public: Outcomes in the American States* (Chicago: Rand McNally, 1966), p. 273; David Derge, "Metropolitan and Outstate Alignments in the Illinois and Missouri Legislative Delegations," *American Political Science Review* 53 (1958): 1051–1065; Thomas A. Flinn, "The Outline of Ohio Politics," *Western Political Quarterly* 13 (September 1960): 712–721. On the delayed impact of reapportionment, see Yong Hyo Cho and H. George Frederickson, "The Effects of Reapportionment: Subtle, Selected, Limited," *National Civic Review* 63, no. 7 (July 1974): 357–362.
22. Michael C. Le May, "The States and Urban Areas: A Comparative Assessment," *National Civic Review* 61, no. 11 (December 1972): 542–548.
23. Ibid.
24. Paul N. Ylvisaker, "The Growing Role of State Governments in Local Affairs," *State Government* 51 (Summer 1968): 150–156.
25. See Timothy O'Rourke, *The Impact of Reapportionment* (New Brunswick, N.J.: Transaction Books, 1980).
26. *Davis* v. *Bandemer*, 106 S.Ct. 2797 (1986). Also see Malcom E. Jewell, "What Hath *Baker* v. *Car* Wrought?" *Comparative State Politics Newsletter* 9, no. 5 (October 1988): 3–15; and Robert X. Browning, "Partisan Gerrymandering: From *Baker* v. *Carr* to *Davis* v. *Bandemer*," *Comparative State Politics Newsletter* 9, no. 5 (October 1988): 25–38.
27. *Badham* v. *Eu*, 109 S.Ct. 34 (1989).
28. *Voinovich* v. *Quilter*, S.Ct. (1993).
29. Andrew Gelman and Gary King, "Enhancing Democracy Through Legislative Redistricting," *American Political Science Review* 88, no. 3 (September 1994): 541–558.
30. Mark E. Rush, *Does Redistricting Make a Difference?: Partisan Representation and Electoral Behavior* (Baltimore, Md.: Johns Hopkins University Press, 1993).
31. *Gomillion* v. *Lightfoot*, 81 S.Ct. 125 (1960).
32. *City of Mobile* v. *Bolden*, 446 U.S. 55 (1980).

33. *Thornburg* v. *Gingles,* 106 S.Ct. 2752 (1986).
34. *Shaw* v. *Reno,* 113 S.Ct. 2816 (1993).
35. Black representatives in Congress increased from 25 to 40, while Hispanic representatives increased from 11 to 17; black representatives in state legislatures increased from 448 to 521, and Hispanic representatives increased from 140 to 182. U.S. Bureau of the Census, *Statistical Abstract of the United States, 1995* (Washington, D.C.: U.S. Government Printing Office, 1995), pp. 281, 287.
36. Kevin A. Hill, "Does the Creation of Majority Black Districts Aid Republicans? An Analysis of the 1992 Congressional Elections in Eight Southern States," *The Journal of Politics* 57, no. 2 (May 1995): 384–401.
37. See, for example, Lani Guinier, "Don't Scapegoat the Gerrymander," *The New York Times Magazine* (January 8, 1995): 36–37 and *The Tyranny of the Majority: Fundamental Fairness in Representative Democracy* (New York: Free Press, 1994).
38. Rich Jones, *The Book of the States: 1994–1995* (Lexington, Ky.: Council of State Governments, 1994), 100.
39. Heinz Eulau et al., "The Role of the Representative," *American Political Science Review* 53, no. 3 (September 1959): 742–756.
40. "Toward a More Responsible Two-Party System," *American Political Science Review* 44 (September 1950): supplement.
41. Bill Moss, "Rotation: One Chance for the Brass Ring," *State Legislatures* 20, no. 7 (July 1994): 21.
42. David C. Saffell, "Happy Birthday, Speaker Riffe," *Comparative State Politics* 12, no. 4 (August 1991): 16–18.
43. Richard Clucas, "Legislative Leadership and Campaign Support in California," *Legislative Studies Quarterly* 17, no. 2 (May 1992): 276–277.
44. Alan Rosenthal, "Challenges to Legislative Leadership," *Journal of State Government* 60, no. 6 (November–December 1987): 265–269. Also see his "A Vanishing Breed," *State Legislatures* 15, no. 10 (November–December 1989): 30–34.
45. See V. O. Key, *Southern Politics* (New York: Vintage Books, 1949), Ch. 14.
46. Dye, *Politics, Economics, and the Public: Outcomes in the American States,* 258. In analyzing similar data somewhat differently, political scientist John H. Fenton came to the opposite conclusion. See John H. Fenton, "Two-Party Competition: Does It Make a Difference?" in *People and Parties in Politics,* John H. Fenton, ed. (Glenview, Ill.: Scott, Foresman, 1966). Also see John H. Fenton and Donald W. Chamberlayne, "The Literature Dealing with the Relationships Between Political Process, Socio-Economic Conditions and Public Policies in the American States, A Bibliographic Essay," *Polity* 1, no. 3 (Spring 1969): 388–404. Finally, Virginia Gray analyzed competitiveness over time rather than at a single point in time as Dye had done. She discovered that party competition had a significant impact on changes in policy outcomes over time. Virginia Gray, "Models of Comparative State Politics: A Comparison of Cross-Sectional and Time Series Analyses," *American Journal of Political Science* 20, no. 2 (May 1976): 235–256.
47. Gray, "Models of Comparative State Politics." Gerald C. Wright, Jr., "Interparty Competition and State Social Welfare Policy: When a Difference Makes a Difference," *Journal of Politics* 37, no. 3 (August 1975): 796–803.
48. See Wayne L. Francis, *Legislative Issues in the Fifty States: A Comparative Analysis* (Chicago: Rand McNally, 1967).
49. Robert S. Erikson, "Relationship Between Party Control and Civil Rights Legislation in the American States," *Western Political Quarterly* 24, no. 1 (March 1971): 178–182.

50. *The Book of the States. 1994–1995* (Lexington, Ky.: Council of State Governments, 1994), 149.

51. George Goodwin, Jr., "State Legislatures of New England," *New England Politics*, Josephine F. Milburn and Victoria Shuck, eds. (Cambridge, Mass.: Schenkman, 1981), pp. 117–118.

52. Eric Uslaner and Ronald Weber, *Patterns of Decision Making in State Legislatures* (New York: Praeger Publishers, 1977).

53. Charles W. Wiggins and William P. Browne, "Interest Groups and Public Policy Within a State Legislative Setting," *Polity* 14, no. 3 (Spring 1982): 548–558.

54. Robert M. Entman, "The Impact of Ideology on Legislative Behavior and Public Policy in the States," *Journal of Politics* 45, no. 1 (February 1983): 163–182.

55. Belle Zeller, ed., *American State Legislatures: Report of the Committee on American Legislatures of the American Political Science Association* (New York: Crowell, 1954), p. 2.

56. Jones, *The Book of the States. 1994–1995*, p. 99.

57. The most prestigious of these were the Advisory Commission on Intergovernmental Relations, the Council of State Governments, the Eagleton Institute of Rutgers University, the Committee for Economic Development, and the Citizens Conference on State Legislatures.

58. The Citizens Conference on State Legislatures, *The Sometimes Governments: A Critical Study of the 50 American Legislatures* (New York: Bantam Books, 1971).

59. Jones, *The Book of the States: 1994–1995*, pp. 99, 101.

60. Ibid., p. 100.

61. See William T. Pound, "Legislatures: Our Dynamic Institutions," *State Legislatures* 19, no. 1 (January 1993): 22–25.

62. Karen Hansen, "Our Beleaguered Institution," *State Legislatures* 20, no. 1 (January 1994): 12–17.

63. Ibid.

64. Morris P. Fiorina, "Divided Government in the American States: A Byproduct of Legislative Professionalism?" *American Political Science Review* 88, no. 2 (June 1994): 304–316.

65. Todd Donovan and Joseph R. Snipp, "Support for Legislative Term Limitations in California: Group Representation, Partisanship, and Campaign Influence," *The Journal of Politics* 56, no. 2 (May 1994): 496.

66. Calculated from *The Book of the States: 1994–1995*, p. 115.

67. See especially Alan Rosenthal, "The Legislative Institution: Transformed and at Risk," in *The State of the States*, Carl E. Van Horn, ed. (Washington, D.C.: Congressional Quarterly Press, 1989), pp. 69–101.

68. Jack Treadway, "Adoption of Term Limits for State Legislators: An Update," *Comparative State Politics* 16, no. 3 (June 1995): 1–3.

69. A good summary of the pros and cons of term limits is offered by Karl T. Kurtz, "Limiting Terms—What's in Store?" *State Legislatures* 18, no. 1 (January 1992): 32–34. For an excellent background on the term limitation movement, see Stuart Rothenberg, "How Term Limits Became a National Phenomenon," *State Legislatures* 18, no. 1 (January 1992): 35–40.

70. Norman R. Luttbeg, "Legislative Careers in Six States: Are Some Legislatures More Likely to Be Responsive?" *Legislative Studies Quarterly* 17, no. 1 (February 1992): 49–68.

71. Gary F. Moncrief, Joel A. Thompson, Michael Haddon, and Robert Hoyer, "For Whom the Bell Tolls: Term Limits and State Legislatures," *Legislative Studies Quarterly* 17, no. 1 (February 1992): 37–47.

72. Cal Ledbetter, Jr., "Limiting Legislative Terms Is a Bad Idea," *National Civic Review* 80, no. 3 (Summer 1991): 243–247.
73. Claude R. Marx, "Limit Terms, and They Go Home," *Investors Business Daily,* March 13, 1996, p. 1.
74. Chris Fastnow, "Willie Brown's Successor: or What Happens to Party Discipline After Term Limits?" a paper presented at the annual meeting of the Midwest Political Science Association. Chicago, Ill.: April 1996.
75. Douglas Foster, "The Lame-Duck State," *State Legislatures* 20, no. 7 (July 1994): 32–42.

10

GOVERNORS AND THE CHALLENGE OF EXECUTIVE LEADERSHIP

Chapter Preview

This chapter examines the role of state governors in providing public policy leadership. We shall discuss in turn:

1. The demand for strong executive leadership.
2. The reformers' goal of increasing the formal powers of governors.
3. Governors' leadership styles.
4. Governors' careers.
5. Other state executives.
6. The impact of strong governors on public policy.
7. Governors and the political economy of states.

Let us begin with a glimpse at some fascinating governors.

◇ INTRODUCTION

In most states, the governor is the most visible politician, and over the years governors have been some of the most interesting people in American politics. Woodrow Wilson, Franklin Roosevelt, Jimmy Carter, Ronald Reagan, and Bill Clinton used the governor's office as a springboard to the presidency.

Many others sought to do so but failed. Huey Long, calling himself the "Kingfish," established a virtual dictatorship in Louisiana (1928–1931), went on to the U.S. Senate, then was gunned down by an assassin as he plotted a challenge to the incumbent president, Franklin Roosevelt. Jerry Brown of California (1975–1983) chose to live in a small apartment rather than in California's governor's mansion, which he derided as a Taj Mahal, drove a simple Plymouth

239

rather than being chauferred in a state limousine, and urged the people of California to follow his example of a simpler lifestyle. He then went on an African safari with pop singer Linda Ronstadt. Scorned by some as "Governor Moonbeam" but idealized by others, Brown at the age of thirty-eight won upset victories in five out of six presidential primaries in 1976 and was re-elected governor in 1978 by 1.3 million votes. Seemingly with no place to go but up, Brown made one disastrous mistake in 1981 that ended his career. When an infestation of the Mediterranean fruit fly threatened to destroy California's agricultural industry in 1981, Brown vacillated on allowing aerial spraying of the crops. California's agribusiness recovered, but Brown did not; the next year he was resoundingly defeated in a bid for the U.S. Senate.[1]

A springboard to national fame may be the most dazzling thing about the governorship today, but there is much more to the office than that. Governors have the opportunity to provide policy leadership in their states. They are often expected to make sure the state bureaucracy does its job responsibly, to cope with crises as they arise, and to preside over a strong state economy.

This chapter examines executive power at the state level of government. It looks first at the effects of the political reform movement on the changing expectations about executive leadership. Second, it discusses leadership exercised by governors and other state executives. Third, it examines the importance of career patterns on gubernatorial leadership. Fourth, it asks whether strong executive leadership has any significant consequences for the public policies adopted and for the way in which public benefits are distributed. Finally, it explores the importance of the political economy to governors today, as well as the role of governors in dealing with issues of political economy and social conflict.

◇ THE DEMAND FOR STRONG EXECUTIVES

Executive Representation

Our expectations of the state and local executives have evolved through three historical stages. First, from the 1830s until about 1900 there was a demand for what Herbert Kaufman called **executive representation.**[2] This demand was based on the belief that the executive branch should represent people just as the legislature does. Its origins were in **Jacksonian democracy,** the concept of the **spoils system,** and the direct election of large numbers of administrative officials through the **long ballot,** so called because of its long list of elective executive offices. Voters choose not only governors and mayors but other statewide administrators, clerks, and many local officials not engaged in broad policymaking.

Philosophically, the demand for executive representation was supported by two arguments. First, it was thought that the long ballot would make the bureaucracy conform to the wishes of the people. To a limited degree, the long ballot, when tied to the nineteenth century urban political machines, may have helped accomplish this. As the immigrants began to dominate the urban population, they voted their fellow immigrants into office. These officeholders, in turn, lured their immigrant supporters to work in the public bureaucracies, including fire and police departments.

The second argument for executive representation was based on the separation of powers. Early American political philosophers—especially James Madison—taught that the concentration of power is dangerous.[3] They advocated dividing power among many hands. At the state and local levels, the number of elective executive offices was expanded. This change limited the power of governors and mayors to act as chief executives responsible for the overall direction of the executive branch.

The system of executive representation and the machine politics that was closely associated with it, however, soon led to widespread abuses—graft, corruption of law enforcement agencies, undemocratic politics, and inefficient government. These things soon came under attack by the progressive political reformers of the late nineteenth and early twentieth centuries.

Neutral Competence

As the nineteenth century ended, reformers demanded the removal of partisanship from public services. They wanted services to be performed competently and in a politically neutral fashion. The demand for **neutral competence** is reflected most obviously in the merit systems of employment. In 1883, the United States Civil Service System was established. In the same year, New York passed a civil service act, and Massachusetts passed one the following year. Today, all the states use some variation of a merit system for hiring, promoting, and firing state employees. (For greater elaboration, see Chapter 11.)

The administration of public services was another area in which reformers sought neutral competence. As the concept of neutral competence became popular, service delivery agencies were increasingly insulated from political interference by the governor or the legislators. This was particularly the case in public education. Requirements for teacher certification, systems of tenure for teachers, and state education boards composed of citizen members were instituted to protect the education delivery system from political interference. The governor's influence was increasingly restricted to the overall level of funding that the states would provide to local schools.

As demands for more government services grew during the twentieth century, the new services were increasingly provided by government institutions independent of governors, legislatures, mayors, and city councils. This led to a proliferation of independent agencies, special districts, licensing boards, and regulatory agencies, each of which had its own constituency and few of which were under the policy control of the governor and the legislature. As the concept of neutral competence was put into practice, it led to a governmental structure characterized by weak governors, executive authority fragmented among a number of independent agencies, duplication of services, overlapping responsibilities, a lack of coordination, unconcern for overall state policy, and unaccountability to the voters.

Executive Leadership

By midtwentieth century, those deficiencies of neutral competence stimulated a demand for **executive leadership.** Critics wanted the chief executive's office to be strengthened so that it would exercise policy control over the delivery of services. These critics believed that meeting the service needs of the growing populations and establishing modern public policies to deal with these problems required strong governors and strong mayors who could control their bureaucracies. They wanted to counter the excessive fragmentation of authority that occurred as a result of both the executive-representation and neutral-competence philosophies. Control of administrative functions would be integrated and concentrated in the hands of a governor or mayor who would be chief executive in fact as well as in name.

As the movement for executive leadership picked up momentum, the governor's office grew in stature and began attracting higher-quality candidates. At midtwentieth century, the typical governor was more likely to be a "good-time Charlie" than a dynamic manager of government. The last two decades, in contrast, have seen the emergence of a "new breed" of governors who, in Larry Sabato's words, were "better educated than ever, and more thoroughly trained for the specific responsibilities of the governorship."[4]

◇ EXECUTIVE LEADERSHIP AT THE STATE LEVEL: MAKING GOVERNORS STRONGER

From the preceding discussion, we see that the general trend in state government has been to strengthen the governor in order to provide effective leadership. Governors exercise this leadership most visibly by carrying out the roles outlined in Table 10-1. As chief legislator, chief administrator, leader of public opinion, and so on, the governor primarily provides leadership in the formulation, adoption, and execution of public policies in the state.

The Governor's Role in Policymaking

More than anyone else, the governor sets the agenda for public policy decision making, coordinates the formulating of policy, and oversees its implementation.

Setting the agenda for policymaking is critical. The legislators can only pass bills that are put on their agenda. Ideas that are never drafted into bills or that fail to gain enough support to merit serious discussion in key committees do not get put on the decision-making agenda. The governor can shape this decision-making agenda by defining his or her own priorities and sending proposals to the legislature.

The strong governor also coordinates the formulating of state policies. His or her support is sought for the legislative proposals that are made by state agencies, relevant interest groups, the governor's party, and the governor's staff. Since governors have several bargaining tools, such as the threat of a veto, their legislative requests are seriously considered by the legislators. This is especially

Table 10-1 GOVERNORS' ROLES

Chief of State

Performs ceremonial functions. Represents the state in Washington, D.C., and in intergovernmental organizations such as the National Governors' Association.

Legislative Agenda Setting

Sends legislative proposals and budget proposals to the legislature. Gives an annual state-of-the-state message. Lobbies and bargains with legislators for passage of legislative proposals. Has veto power (except in North Carolina).

Chief Administrator

Appoints officials to many state agencies, regulatory commissions, and advisory boards. Requires state administrators to report on their activities. Prepares the state budget.

Military Chief

Is commander-in-chief of the state national guard. The national guard is often called out to keep peace and order during national disasters and civil disturbances.

Chief of Party

In two-party states, the governor is usually the most prominent party leader, especially if the governor's party also controls the legislature. In one-party states, the governor usually leads only one of the major factions within the party. As chief of party, the governor can seldom control local nominations for the legislature or control statewide nominations. However, by judicious use of patronage and campaign assistance, the governor can use these assets to build support for the party and in turn get legislators to support his or her legislative program.

Leader of Public Opinion

Makes public appearances, holds interviews and press conferences, and corresponds with residents. Tries to build support for himself or herself and his or her program. Takes part in activities, such as planting trees on Arbor Day, that give symbolic support for causes the governor favors.

Ultimate Judge

Has power to grant pardons. May commute sentences. May grant paroles. May grant a reprieve that postpones the execution of a sentence. Has power of rendition that enables the governor to return a fugitive from justice to a state asking for the fugitive's return.

Crisis Manager

When a natural disaster occurs or some other crisis erupts, the governor is often expected to organize a state response and resolve the problem.

---

true of budget requests. Because of their crucial position in the law-making process, strong governors can propose a legislative program and a budget and be fairly certain of getting much of what they want enacted into law. After the policies are established by the legislature and enacted into law, the strong governor is expected to oversee how well the state administrative agencies are carrying them out. If an agency falls under heavy public criticism for the way it implements the law, the governor is expected to bring that agency into line.

Table 10-2   STATES CATEGORIZED BY THE FORMAL POWERS OF THEIR GOVERNORS

Weakest	Moderately Weak	Moderately Strong	Strongest
North Carolina	Alabama	Alaska	Hawaii
South Carolina	California	Arizona	Iowa
Vermont	Colorado	Arkansas	Maryland
	Florida	Connecticut	New Jersey
	Georgia	Delaware	New York
	Idaho	Illinois	Ohio
	Indiana	Kansas	Pennsylvania
	Maine	Kentucky	Tennessee
	Massachusetts	Louisiana	West Virginia
	Mississippi	Michigan	
	Nevada	Minnesota	
	New Hampshire	Missouri	
	Oklahoma	Montana	
	Texas	Nebraska	
	Virginia	New Mexico	
	Washington	North Dakota	
	Wyoming	Oregon	
		Rhode Island	
		South Dakota	
		Utah	
		Wisconsin	

Source: Adapted from Thad Beyle, "Governors: The Middlemen and Women in Our Political System," *Politics in the American States: A Comparative Analysis,* 6th ed. (Washington, D.C.: CQ Press, 1996), p. 237.

Some Governors Are Stronger Than Others   Despite the expectations that the governor will play a strong policy role, many governors lack the legal authority to provide that leadership. Thad Beyle constructed an index of formal powers of governors.[5] The index has six measures of gubernatorial strength: (1) tenure potential (whether the governor can succeed himself or herself, and the length of the governor's term), (2) appointive powers (how many policymaking state officials are appointed by the governor), (3) budget powers (how much influence the governor has over the state budget), (4) veto powers (the conditions under which he or she can veto bills), (5) party support (how strongly the governor's party controls the legislature), and (6) extent of competing elected executives (how many separately elected executives the governor faces). By these criteria, as Table 10-2 shows, nine states are judged to have the most powerful governors, whereas North Carolina, South Carolina, and Vermont are ranked among the weakest.

Challenges to Gubernatorial Leadership

Leading the Legislature   The success of contemporary governors is measured most visibly by how much of their agenda gets passed by the legislature. Through their budget message, their state-of-the-state address, and other messages, the governors set the agenda for legislative action. Their most dramatic legislative tool is probably the **veto.** All states except North Carolina give the governor the right to veto. Forty-three states additionally give the governor an **item veto** over appropriations bills; that is, they can veto specific appropriations without vetoing the total package. Nine states allow governors to reduce amounts appropriated. Montana and Illinois grant their governor an **amendatory veto:** the governor can add money to appropriations made by the legislature.

There has been a great deal of interest in the item veto in recent years, primarily because Presidents Reagan, Bush, and Clinton sought an item veto on the grounds that it would enable them to impose fiscal restraint on the federal budget. Like governors with the item veto, presidents could then delete pork barrel items that legislators sneak into appropriations bills in order to do favors for constituents and contributors. Researchers who have studied the governor's use of the item veto, however, find that it has little, if any, impact on holding down state expenditures.[6] Most of the evidence suggests that governors employ the item veto primarily for political purposes of gaining the upper hand over legislatures.[7]

The most flamboyant example of the politically motivated item veto was probably Wisconsin governor Tommy Thompson's use of 290 item vetoes in 1987. Wisconsin law goes far beyond any other state's item veto by giving the governor a so-called partial veto that enables the governor not only to delete dollar amounts from appropriations but to delete words, punctuation marks, and even individual letters from bills. In one of his partial vetoes, Governor Thompson crossed out selected letters and words of a juvenile detention bill in such a way that he changed to ten days a forty-eight-hour limit on how long juveniles could be detained in county jails without charges. Although in keeping with that governor's punitive law-and-order philosophy, this action completely violated the legislative intent of the bill. The Legislature sued, but the Wisconsin Supreme Court and the federal courts upheld the governor.[8] Wisconsin voters then reacted by approving a constitutional amendment that put a limit on the partial veto that would prevent the governor from scratching out specific letters (it was dubbed the "pick-a-letter veto").[9]

Thompson's 290 vetoes were extraordinary, however, because few governors would issue that many vetoes.[10] But when they do, the vetoes are rarely overridden. Overrides usually require a two-thirds vote in each house. Although overrides are becoming more frequent than in the past, they are still rare, happening less than 10 percent of the time.[11]

Because vetoes are so rarely overridden, the threat of a veto is a powerful tool that governors use to shape legislation. This is especially the case in states with an executive amendment provision. Under this provision, the governor returns a bill to the legislature and suggests that it be changed.[12] If the legislature rejects the changes, the governor is still free to veto the entire bill. If it accepts the amendment, then the governor has shaped the legislation as intended without resorting to an outright veto.

If the legislative session ends with the governor's program still unpassed, most governors have authority to call a special session of the legislature. The governor can usually control the agenda for these special sessions, and this gives him or her a powerful tool for coaxing action out of the legislature. However, the tactic can also backfire. Texas governor James E. Ferguson called a special session in 1917 only to have the legislature impeach him and remove him from office.[13]

Of all the weapons in the governor's political arsenal, probably none is more important than the backing of a strong political party that has a commanding majority in the legislature.[14] Too large a majority, however, can be too much of a good thing. When the majority goes beyond 70 percent, intraparty factionalism tends to erupt. Massachusetts Governor Michael Dukakis's strongest opposition often came from his fellow Democrats in the legislature rather than from the Republicans. Said Dukakis, "When you've got majorities of four to one in the legislature—I'm sure you recognize that it is by no means an unmitigated blessing—you've got conservative Democrats, you've got liberal Democrats, you've got moderate Democrats, you've got suburban Democrats, you've got rural Democrats, and you don't have any Republicans."[15] Nevertheless, having his or her party in control of the legislature is usually key to the governor's ability to dominate a state.

Despite their powerful tools for leadership, there is reason to believe that governors are losing ground to the legislatures in their perennial battles to dominate state politics.[16] Governors' powers have increased over the past two decades, but so have legislatures' capacities to deal with the governor. The improved legislative staffs have especially helped put the legislatures on a more even footing with the governor.

Running the Bureaucracy   As chief executive, governors are expected to run the state's administrative agencies. But they face several obstacles in this quest. First, they are confronted by several other state officers, such as the lieutenant governor, the attorney general, the treasurer, and the auditor, who in most states have been elected to office in their own right, some belonging to the governor's party and others belonging to the opposition (see Table 10-3).

A second obstacle to strong administrative leadership is the autonomy of most individual departments. Some of the most important state departments are administered by a separately elected head or by an independent board or commission. Education is perhaps the most pertinent example. Table 10-3 shows that heads of education departments are separately elected in sixteen states. Moreover, in forty-nine states the state department of education is under a state board of education that often appoints the state superintendent of education and establishes statewide education policies. With the interposition of such a board between the governor and the department itself, educational administration is well protected from gubernatorial interference. To be sure, the governor can also be a leading force for innovative educational programs, as exemplified in the 1980s

Tablo 10-3 STATEWIDE ELECTED EXECUTIVES

Office	Number of States in Which Elective
Governor	50
Lieutenant Governor	42
Attorney General	43
Treasurer	37
Secretary of State	36
Education Department Head	16
Agricultural Department Head	13
Comptroller	13
State Board of Education	12
Insurance Commission Head	9
Public Utilities Commission	7
Auditor	5

Number of Offices	Number of States With That Many Elective Offices
10 or more	1
8–9	8
5–7	?9
3–4	6
1–2	6
	50

Source: The Book of the States: 1996–97 (Lexington, Ky.: Council of State Governments, 1996), pp. 35–39.

by Tennessee governor Lamar Alexander[17] (see Chapter 14). But by and large, the governor has little to say about administrative matters such as personnel, curriculum, and the organization of public instruction.

The third obstacle to strong administrative leadership is the relationship that exists between state agencies and private enterprise. All states have licensing boards that control admission to the professions, administrative agencies that run programs, and regulatory agencies that oversee such functions as pollution control, health-care facilities, and utility rates. It is often charged that the regulatory agencies serve the interests of the industries they are supposed to regulate rather than serving the interests of the public.[18] And the licensing boards tend to be peopled by representatives from the sectors they are supposed to oversee. This close relationship between state agencies and specific private sector interests creates an obstacle for gubernatorial leadership because the private groups often come to the support of agencies when governors try to control them or lead them in new policy directions.

To strengthen the governor's administrative powers, reformers have sought to remove the three administrative obstacles just discussed, by:

1. Eliminating separately elected state executives
2. Allowing the governor to appoint a cabinet of department heads
3. Reducing the number of independent state agencies
4. Centralizing the budget-making process in the governor's office
5. Removing boards and commissions from direct administrative roles

All these reforms have been implemented in many states, some in all states. But the effect has *not* been to give the governor undisputed control over the executive. Glenn Abney and Thomas P. Lauth surveyed state agency heads and reported that a majority of them (53 percent) felt the legislature exerted more influence over them than did the governor.[19] For most governors, successful administrative leadership probably lies less in controlling administrative details than it does in carving out a limited number of policy initiatives, selecting competent agency heads who agree with those policy initiatives, securing a budget that reflects the policy priorities, and avoiding embarrassments in the few staff agencies directly under the governor's authority (usually Planning and Finance).

Strengthening the Governor, in Practice

In practice, the governor has a number of sources of strength in his or her attempts to exert policy leadership. Some of these (such as budgeting) result from increasing the governorship's formal powers, and some (such as public relations and political party) result from personal characteristics and political factors.

Budgeting as a Source of Strength   Budgeting helps the governor control the state administration. (The budgeting process will be discussed in detail in Chapter 11.) The normal budgeting practice is for executive agencies to submit their budget requests to a budget office or a finance commissioner who works closely with the governor. The governor determines overall spending guidelines and tries to establish priorities on how funds are divided among the various programs and agencies. He or she then submits the budget to the legislature, where the governor is expected to fight for its passage.

By establishing overall spending limits and by setting priorities, the governor can exert significant influence on policies and on agencies' procedures for implementing them. Most governors enjoy strong budget powers, but they gain much more policy-making influence from these powers, obviously, when there is a surplus of state revenues and they can pump new funds into their high-priority programs than they do when there is a revenue deficit and their high-priority programs can only be funded by decreasing the funding of some other program.

The Governor's Staff as a Source of Strength   Choosing an effective staff is the governor's cardinal task.[20] Poorly chosen staff members can give the governor a bad image, make poor suggestions on administrative appointments, alienate key legislators, and fail to accomplish important tasks. Governors' staffs have expanded dramatically in recent years, from an average of 4.6 persons in 1957 to 7.3 percent in 1967 to 48 percent in 1989.[21] Nearly 40 percent of staff members are women or minorities.[22] Staff members are needed to serve as media coordinator, administrative aide, personal secretary, legislative liaison, budget analyst, and policy analyst.

Public Relations as a Source of Strength   As political parties have weakened and as television has become increasingly important, public relations have become a source of gubernatorial strength. For one thing, the governor needs to project a positive public image if he or she hopes to get re-elected.[23] Governors also use public relations to create popular support for their legislative programs, thus increasing chances of getting those programs passed by the legislature. So important are public relations that governors seldom pass up an opportunity to appear before television cameras.

The Intergovernmental System as a Source of Strength   The governor's influence has also been enhanced by the growth of intergovernmental relations since the 1960s.[24] Governors now spend a fair share of their time lobbying for more federal aid, overseeing much of the program planning that is required by federal programs,[25] and acting together with other governors in the National Governors Association (NGA). At a minimum, taking a leading role in these activities brings the governor good publicity that can work to his or her advantage at home.

Political Party as a Source of Strength   Finally, the political party is a potential source of strength for governors although in many states it is an increasingly limited asset. A survey of fifteen governors who left office in the mid-1970s found that they made little use of the political party. They did not turn to the party as a source of either ideas for public policy or appointments to public office.[26] Nevertheless, few governors can afford to alienate their political parties. If for no other reason, governors are usually more successful if their political party controls the legislature. Governors are likely to feel that they can deal better with the federal government if their party controls the White House, and they might need party support to get renominated and re-elected.[27]

◇ EXERCISING LEADERSHIP: GOVERNORS' STYLES

In addition to formal powers, such as the veto power and the power of appointment, the successful governor needs effective leadership qualities. Without these all the formal powers may still not produce a strong governor.[28] The importance of leadership qualities was seen in an ambitious study by Larry Sabato, who compared 312 governors between 1950 and 1975 according to their hard work, competence, dedication, and ability to meet the needs of their states. He judged 117 (about a third) of them to be outstanding.[29] When those outstanding governors were compared to the nonoutstanding governors by several criteria (including their education and experience, the formal powers that their states gave to the office, and the degree of interparty competition in their states), there was only a slight tendency for states with substantial formal governor's powers (see Table 10-2) to produce outstanding governors. The strongest relationship found was that the outstanding governors were usually younger than the nonoutstanding governors. But youth as a factor may be "largely a proxy measure for personal dynamism and ambition."[30]

In short, the leadership style of governors is just as important in determining their success as is the formal power of their office. Little has been written about the style of governors' leadership. But at least four styles can be identified: the demagogue, the policy entrepreneur, the frustrated warrior, and the caretaker.

The Demagogue

The preeminent **demagogue** was undoubtedly Huey Long of Louisiana (1928–1931).[31] Long called himself "the Kingfish," established a virtual dictatorship in Louisiana, manipulated the state judges so they would interpret the constitution to fit his political ambitions, siphoned untold amounts of the state's money into his own political organization, and trampled unmercifully on opponents who dared to challenge him. His term did not lack substantive accomplishments, however. He provided free textbooks for the public schools for the first time in the state's history, broadened public higher education, established the state's basic highway structure, and engaged in well-publicized fights with the state utilities to lower their rates.

Huey Long's greatest success was in manipulating public relations in order to give symbolic gratification to his lower-class supporters. He proudly called for a nationwide "Share Our Wealth" plan that would prohibit anyone from earning more than $1 million a year. He appeared prominently before news cameras at the sidelines of Louisiana State University football games. He showed his disdain for the upper class by greeting a foreign dignitary while dressed in his pajamas. And he proudly showed his affinity with poor farmers by pulling off his shoe in the middle of a speech and displaying that, like them, he still had holes in his socks. As a reward for these antics, the people of Louisiana repeatedly returned him and his political machine's candidates to power. Long ended up in the U.S. Senate after a bitter struggle in which he had the state courts rule that he could not be succeeded by the lieutenant governor even though that succession was clearly specified in the constitution. Long was by this time enjoying considerable national popularity. He had his eye on the 1936 presidential campaign when his career was ended by an assassin.

The Policy Entrepreneur

The **policy entrepreneur** was the most popular style of governor during the 1960s and early 1970s, when governments were broadly expanding their public service programs. Nelson Rockefeller of New York (1959–1973) is one of the best examples.[32] Rockefeller proposed programs for housing, highways, higher education, elementary and secondary education, and a host of other services. The

HIGHLIGHT

Conditions of the Governor's Office

Legal Qualifications

The governor must be a citizen, and in some states must have been a citizen for a minimum number of years. Most states require the governor to have been a state resident for a minimum number of years. Most states also require a minimum age of thirty although thirty-one states have a minimum age of only eighteen.

Terms of Office

All states but three have a four-year term of office. Those three (New Hampshire, Rhode Island, Vermont) have a two-year term of office but put no limit on the number of terms a governor may serve. Twenty states have a four-year term with no limit on re-election. Twenty-six states have a four-year term with a limit of two consecutive terms.

Compensation

The range of governors' salaries is from $55,800 in Montana to $130,000 in New York. The median is about $80,000. Forty-six states also provide the governor with a mansion, and most states provide an expense allowance.

Succession

Forty-two states provide for a lieutenant governor to succeed to the office when it becomes vacant. The others provide for either the secretary of state or the president of the senate to succeed.

Removal

All states but Oregon have an impeachment process, but only five governors have been removed through impeachment since 1900. Thirteen states provide for a recall, but only one governor, Lynn J. Frazier of North Dakota, has been removed by recall (in 1921). Few states have a workable provision for removing governors in cases of physical or mental disability.

---

policy entrepreneur's style of leadership works best during times of economic expansion when there are growing revenues to fund new programs that seek to address a state's problems.

Unfortunately for ambitious governors, however, the 1990s have not been times of dramatic economic expansion, and most states have found their revenue sources to be constricting rather than growing. What is needed for this new environment, according to David Osborne, is a new twist to gubernatorial entrepreneurism that will enable the state to create new policies without establishing new bureaucracies to carry out them out.[33] States can do this through public–private partnerships designed to achieve public goals without expanding the public sector itself.

Recent governors who have been praised for this style of leadership include Bill Clinton of Arkansas (1979–1981; 1983–1993) and Republican Richard Thornburgh of Pennsylvania (1976–1986). Thornburgh, for example, set up several job development initiatives, facilitated economic development research, and provided public funds for venture capital to help new businesses get started.[34]

This new "governing paradigm" of policy entrepreneurism works with Republican governors (Thornburgh) as well as Democratic ones (Clinton), and it is difficult to categorize such governors in the traditional liberal or conservative camps. They emphasize greater government action than would traditional Republican conservatives. But they also seek less expansion of the government bureaucracy than would be the case with traditional Democratic liberals. One of the hallmarks of the new policy entrepreneurism is using the political arena to define public goals but using the private sector as much as possible to implement those goals. According to David Osborne we need policy entrepreneurs of this sort to "reinvent government" so that governments can respond to the challenges they face.[35]

The Frustrated Warrior

A frustrated warrior is in essence a governor who has sought to be a policy entrepreneur but has been unsuccessful. For many reasons, the frustrated warrior is unable to get his or her programs adopted, and he or she ends the governorship in frustration. New York's Averell Harriman (1955–1959) and Hugh Carey (1975–1979) were frustrated warriors. They, like Nelson Rockefeller, faced a Republican-dominated legislature. Furthermore, personality differences made it difficult for them to deal effectively with the Republican legislative leaders.[36]

The Caretaker

A fourth style of govenor is the **caretaker.** Caretakers may be either Democrats or Republicans, but they are usually conservative. They are not demagogues, nor do they push for programs. They see the job largely as one of maintaining the state in operation but not using the state's power to achieve any social goals. Caretakers often have lieutenant governors who succeeded to the governorship but were unable to win election in their own right. Elected governors who become caretakers usually do so during times of governmental retrenchment, such as the 1980s.

◇ GOVERNORS' CAREERS

What does it take to become governor? There seem to be two important criteria—developing the appropriate backgrund and choosing the appropriate campaign strategy. To meet the background requirements, the most likely candidates are men between forty and forty-five years of age who share the dominant ethnic and religious backgrounds of their states. Asians do well in Hawaii, for example, Hispanics in Florida, Italians in New York, and Scandanavians in Minnesota. The most notable exception to this principle took place in 1989 when predominantly white Virginia elected the nation's first black governor since Reconstruction, Douglas Wilder. Women are enjoying increasing success in their campaigns for the office, as the "Highlight" on p. 254 shows. Nevertheless, only two of the current governors (1997) are women (Christine Whitman, R, N.J., and Jeanne Shaheen D, N.H.). Important background characteristics also include education and occupation, since governors by and large enjoy a higher socioeconomic status than the average citizen in their states. Most governors are lawyers.[37] And as the "Highlight" on minority and women governors suggests, the successful aspirant usually has a background of accomplishment in politics, business, civic affairs, or professional life. These accomplishments provide a certain credibility for the candidate.

Although not essential, it helps one's quest for the governor's mansion to have held prior public office; more than 90 percent of governors held some other public office before being elected governor.[38] However, there is no point in starting at the bottom and working your way up through the political ladder if you can develop a campaign strategy that will bring you enough public visibility and popular support to start at the top. This is what Ronald Reagan did to win and hold the governorship of California (1967–1975). Well known as a movie star, president of the Screen Actors Guild, and host of a popular television series, Reagan gained political visibility through his work for Barry Goldwater's ill-fated conservative bid for the presidency in 1964. Capitalizing on this visibility, Reagan sought and won the California governorship in 1966.

Today's best example of this approach is probably Christine Todd Whitman, who won New Jersey's governorship despite never having held prior public office. She attained prominence in 1992 when she came within an eyelash of beating New Jersey's U.S. Senator Bill Bradley in his re-election bid that year. Having done so unexpectedly well with her antigovernment, antitax campaign against Bradley, she obviously had tapped a deep wave of discontent among New Jerseyians. In 1993, she waged the same type of campaign against incumbent governor, Democrat James Florio and captured the governorship by promising to cut the state's income tax.

Finally, if you want to become governor, you will need plenty of money. Whitman spent nearly $10 million on her 1993 New Jersey campaign.[39] In smaller states, obviously, it will cost less. All gubernatorial candidates together spent less than $3 million in New Hamsphire in 1992.[40]

Governors' future career prospects are also important to their political influence. A governor eligible for re-election can get more cooperation from recalcitrant legislators and bureaucrats than can a lame duck governor whose influence is going to disappear in a few months. The governor cannot seek re-election indefinitely, however, since forty states put limits (usually two four-year terms) on how long a governor can serve. Even lame duck governors can enhance their influence, however, if they have bright prospects for going on to the U.S. Senate, a future cabinet position, or the White House. "The lure of following a national leader to Washington can bring action out of legislators and administrators."[41]

HIGHLIGHT

Minority and Female Governors in the 1990s

Women

Vermont: Madeleine Kunin (1985–1991)
Party affiliation: Democrat
Age at election: 51
Background: immigrant refugee from fascist Italy in the 1930s; newspaper and TV reporter
Political experience: state legislator 1973–1979; lieutenant governor 1979–1983; unsuccessful gubernatorial candidate 1983.

Arizona: Rose Moffard (1988–1991)
Party affiliation: Democrat
Age on assuming governorship: 65
Background: state employee since 1943
Political experience: secretary of state 1977–1988. Assumed the governorship in 1988 when the incumbent was impeached and removed from office.

Nebraska: Kay Orr (1987–1991)
Party affiliation: Republican
Age on assuming governorship: 47
Political experience: state treasurer 1981–1987; governor's chief of staff.

Oregon: Barbara Roberts (1991–1995)
Party affiliation: Democrat
Age at election: 53
Background: citizen activist for autistic children
Political experience: state legislator 1981–1985; secretary of state.

Texas: Ann Richards (1991–1995)
Party affiliation: Democrat
Age at election: 58
Background: political activist; public official.
Political experience: state treasurer 1983–1991

Kansas: Joan Finney (1991–1995)
Party affiliation: Democrat
Age at election: 65
Background: political activist; public official.
Political experience: state treasurer 1975–1991

New Hampshire: Jeanne Shaheen (1997–)
Party affiliation: Democrat
Age at election: 49
Background: school teacher, business owner; political campaign manager
Political experience: state senator 1991–1996

New Jersey: Christine Todd Whitman (1993–)
Party affiliation: Republican
Background: nearly won election to U.S. Senate in 1992
Political experience: elected local official and former president of the New Jersey Board of Public Utilities

Minorities

Virginia: Douglas Wilder (1989–1993)
Party affiliation: Democrat
Age at election: 57
Background: lawyer
Political experience: state senator 1969–1985; lieutenant governor 1986–1989

Florida: Bob Martinez (1987–1991)
Party affiliation: Republican
Age at election: 52
Background: teacher; businessperson.
Political experience: mayor of Tampa, 1979–1986.

Hawaii: John Waihee III (1989–1993)
Party affiliation: Democrat
Age at election: 44
Background: lawyer; public official.
Political experience: lieutenant governor, 1982–1986.

Most governors, however, do not go on to the Senate or to cabinet positions. Some governors are forcibly removed by impeachment, as the "Highlight" shows. Although highly publicized, impeachments are rare events. Out of more than 2,000 people who have ever served as governors probably fewer than a dozen have been removed through impeachment. Also highly publicized but still rare is the governor who ends his or her career in prison for having broken the law while in office. This happened to Arkansas Governor Jim Guy Tucker in 1996 who profited from illegal real estate transactions and West Virginia's Arch A. Moore, Jr. who was convicted in 1989 of extortion, tax fraud, and obstruction of justice. Again, it must be stressed that conviction for illegal shenanigans is rare in the governor's mansion. Most governors serve honorably and return to private business or to their private careers.

◇ OTHER STATE EXECUTIVES

In their efforts to provide leadership, governors face competition from several other state-level executives, some of whom have no allegiance to the governor, and some of whom are elected directly by the people. This is in sharp contrast to the federal government where all the top-ranked executive officials are appointed by the president, thus facilitating at least nominal loyalty to the president. Few governors enjoy this luxury. Most governors confront several statewide officials beyond the governor's appointive or dismissal powers, and this creates the near certainty that some of those officials will be from the opposition political party or from incompatible political ideologies. The most important of these are the lieutenant governor, the attorney general, the secretary of state, the auditor, the treasurer, and a number of independent executive boards and commissions.

Lieutenant Governor

The office of **lieutenant governor** exists in forty-two states, but in only twenty-three are the governor and lieutenant governor elected jointly as a team. The lieutenant governor succeeds the governor if the office becomes vacant, casts tie-breaking votes in twenty-six states, and in thirty-one states serves as acting governor while the governor is temporarily out of the state. Like that of vice president of the United States, the office of lieutenant governor can be a frustrating position with little authority. Lieutenant governors are often appointed to lead various advisory boards, but they seldom get a very visible role. Hence, many lieutenant governors do little more than wait for the governor's office to become vacant. Because of this fact, many critics have argued that the position is useless and ought to be abolished. In the states where the office does not exist, a line of succession has been established in which either the president of the senate or some other elected state official succeeds the governor. The main exception to this principle of weak lieutenant governors is Texas, where the lieutenant governor is one of the most powerful leaders in the state.

HIGHLIGHT

Removal by Impeachment: Arizona Style

On April 4, 1988, Governor Evan Mecham (R, Ariz.) became the fifth governor in the twentieth century to lose office through the impeachment process. Even before completing a single year in office, Mecham found himself the target of a recall petition drive that had collected more than 300,000 signatures, a grand jury criminal indictment that charged he failed to report a $350,000 campaign loan, and an impeachment movement that was growing in the Arizona legislature. How anyone could generate such drastic measures against himself in such a short period is fascinating. From the beginning, Mecham had courted the dislike of liberal groups when he cancelled the state's Martin Luther King holiday, referred to blacks as "pickaninnies," made remarks that infuriated feminists and gays, and derided his adversaries as radicals. These indiscretions might have been sufficient to start the recall drive, but the impeachment movement would have bogged down had not more serious charges surfaced.

In February 1988, the Republican-controlled house of representatives voted to impeach the governor on three charges. Impeachment Article I charged that Mecham sought to block investigation of a death threat that one of his close appointees had made against a former Mecham aide for testifying before the grand jury looking into Mecham's campaign finances. Article II charged Mecham with failing to report a $350,000 campaign loan. And Article III charged him with illegally taking $80,000 from a state fund and loaning it to his Pontiac car dealership in Phoenix. Two months after these impeachment charges were voted, the Republican-controlled senate voted by a two-thirds majority to convict Mecham of making the illegal loan and blocking the death threat investigation. The senate dropped the campaign loan charge because it had become subject to a court trial. With Mecham removed from office, the Arizona Supreme Court ruled that the recall election was unnecessary and cancelled it, thus allowing the acting governor, Rose Mofford, to fill out the remainder of Mecham's term of office. Mecham was partially vindicated the following June when a court acquitted him of the charge of concealing the campaign loan.

The Mecham saga did not end at this point, however. Mecham still had strong support from fundamentalist Christians and from Mormons in the state. With these forces behind him, he led opposition to the key legislators who had voted for his impeachment. In fall 1988, eleven of those legislators were defeated in their re-election efforts, including the speaker of the house of representatives and the president of the senate. Mecham launched a campaign to regain the governorship in 1990, but he was decisively beaten in the Republican primary election that year.

Sources: Dan Harris, "The Arizona Impeachment," *State Legislatures* 14, no. 6 (July 1988): 18–23; "Mecham's Revenge on Arizona Legislators," *State Legislatures* 14, no. 10 (November–December 1988): 13.

Attorney General

In most states, the **attorney general** is the second most important statewide office. The attorney general is the official legal adviser to the state and the state's chief prosecutor. After legislation is passed, administrators may ask the attorney general for a legal opinion on the meaning of the law on points where the intent of the law is unclear. Although the attorney general's opinion is not legally binding and could be overturned by the courts, public officials normally will be reluctant to oppose the attorney general's ruling.

Besides giving legal opinions, the attorney general—as state prosecutor—has considerable influence on policy. An attorney general who takes an interest in prosecuting consumer protection cases, for example, can make a significant impact on the lives of consumers. The same may be true of other areas of public concern such as nursing home facilities, health insurance provision, corrections systems, and drug and other criminal prosecutions.

By using their prosecution powers aggressively, attorneys general are well positioned to create a popular image that can serve as a springboard to higher office. The two most historic examples of this are Governors Robert M. La Follette of Wisconsin and Thomas E. Dewey of New York. Both prosecuted vice and organized crime to gain the prominence that eventually enabled them to get elected governor.[42]

Secretary of State

The third major statewide office is the **secretary of state.** This office is found in all states except Hawaii, and it is elective in thirty-six states. Typically, the secretary of state keeps the state archives, supervises elections, compiles election statistics, publishes a *Blue Book* on state government organization, and often serves on state commissions and advisory boards. In some states, the secretary of state issues automobile and drivers' licenses and issues certificates of incorporation. In recent years, the office has sometimes been used as a springboard for a run at the governorship.[43]

Auditor

Two tasks of auditing need to be accomplished in state government—a preaudit and a postaudit. The preaudit authorizes payment of state funds, ensures that funds have been appropriated by the legislature, and makes certain that there is a sufficient balance in the appropriate state account. The preaudit is conducted by a person, technically called a comptroller, who certifies that funds are available before the state treasurer writes a check.

The postaudit occurs after the expenditure of funds and is made to ensure that the funds were spent in accord with the intent of state law. Because the postaudit provides considerable potential to investigate officials at both the state and local levels, public administration specialists normally think that an **auditor** should be accountable to the legislature rather than to the governor or the executive branch. In practice, the preaudit and postaudit functions are usually combined in the same office located in the executive branch. An activist auditor can play an important policy role by shedding light on how public policies were in fact carried out.[44]

Treasurer

Treasurers are custodians of the state's funds. They determine which banks will be the depositories for the state monies, and they authorize the checks that pay for state obligations. Although their duties are largely clerical, they can have a policy impact by, for example, refusing to deposit state money in banks that redline or that fail to take part in central-city redevelopment. Thirty-eight states have elected treasurers, but modern public administration theory suggests that appointed treasurers are preferable to elected ones.

Administrative Boards and Commissions

Finally, governors also face political competition from independent boards and commissions. Virtually every state, for example, has a state board of education that is responsible for setting state educational policy. A forceful governor determined to reform state education can usually, but not always, convince the state board to support his or her efforts, especially if those efforts will give more money to the schools. But not infrequently, the state board will resist too much gubernatorial encroachment. The board was created in the first place to protect the schools from political influence by governors and legislators, and what may seem like sound policy to the governor can easily seem like political meddling to the board members. In sixteen states, the boards of education are elective, which gives them even greater independence from the governor. In addition to boards of education, states frequently have utilities commissions that determine how much you will pay for electricity and telephone usage, state regents who determine what your tuition and graduation requirements will be (if you attend a public university), insurance commissions who set your automobile and health insurance rates, and welfare boards that oversee welfare. How independent one wants these boards to be is in part a reflection of the demands for executive representation, neutral competence, or executive leadership discussed at the beginning of this chapter.

◇ GOVERNORS AND PUBLIC CONFLICT

How do governors fit in with the two broad questions of public policy conflict that we have been discussing?—contemporary social change and the political economy. More than any other public official, the governor occupies the hot seat on both of these issues.

Governors and Social Conflict

How gubernatorial leadership affects contemporary social conflicts can be illustrated by two governors on opposite coasts—Pete Wilson of California and Christine Todd Whitman of New Jersey. California is home to one of the nation's festering issues of social conflict, affirmative action. Republican Governor Pete Wilson played a key and controversial role in California's handling of this conflict. One of the focal points for affirmative action conflict arose at the University of California, which, by anybody's reckoning, has for the past quarter century made a good-faith effort to increase its number of minority and female students.

Since some of its campuses are among the most prestigious campuses in the nation, the traditional admissions criteria were highly competitive. The university adopted what for all practical purposes was a form of "race norming" the admissions criteria so that black and Hispanic candidates competed only with each other. Over time, this practice made it much more difficult for white or Asian students to gain admission than it did for blacks or Hispanics. At the UCLA Law School, for example, whereas 38 percent of blacks, Latinos, and Native Americans were admitted with LSAT scores below 38, only 2 percent of whites and Asians with such scores were admitted. The average LSAT score for minority students was in the bottom 2 percent of other students. At the University's San Diego Medical School, affirmative action applicants constituted only 13 percent of the applicant pool but 32 percent of the students accepted in 1993. The average MCAT scores of the affirmative action candidates was in the bottom 1 percent of the rest of the pool.[45]

Governors do not usually involve themselves in their universities' admissions criteria. For one thing, it is a political mine field in which opinions are shifting, different people have different opinions on what the term *affirmative action* means, and there are probably more votes to be lost than gained. Although polling data show substantial public support for making special efforts to recruit minorities, there is overwhelming opposition to the types of quotas and racial preferences in admissions that the University of California seemed to be following.[46] When Wilson ran for governor in 1994, he declared his opposition to the university's affirmative action program and, in 1995, successfully pressed the University Board of Regents to drop the program.

Wilson also made the difference in getting a California Civil Rights Initiative placed on the ballot in 1996. This initiative amended the California constitution so as to ban both discrimination and preferential treatment on the basis of race, gender, or national origins. When it looked as though this effort was going to die for lack of sufficient signatures, Wilson threw his support as governor behind the effort, and it did indeed appear on the ballot in November 1996 when Californians adopted it.

Across the continent in New Jersey, Governor Christine Todd Whitman took a totally different approach to a different issue of social conflict—the savage inequalities of public school funding that we have touched on periodically in this book (pp. 80–81). She was elected governor in 1993 by blaming her opponent, Democrat James Florio, for the state's huge income tax increase that Florio had endorsed as a means of complying with New Jersey court orders to reduce school funding inequalities in the state. Whitman promised a 30 percent income tax reduction in the campaign and, true to her word, pushed that reduction through the legislature once she was in office. This action knocked out one of the key sources for pumping more funds into the state's poorest school districts. By 1995, New Jersey was collecting $1.2 billion less in income taxes than it would have collected without her tax cuts, thus forcing local governments to choose between cutting services and increasing their own property taxes.[47]

There is no lack of critics to both Wilson's approach to social conflict in California and Whitman's approach in New Jersey. Even nonpartisan observers worry what these two approaches will do to black recruitment for California universities and the level of funding for New Jersey's poorest school districts. But the electoral success of these two governors shows how difficult it is to grapple with contemporary social conflicts today.

Governors and Political Economy

If social conflict puts today's governor on the hot seat, so does the political economy. What happens in a state's economy is vitally important to the incumbent governor. If a significant part of the state's economy suffers from a prolonged recession, several repercussions are possible, none of them pleasant for the incumbent governor. Increasing unemployment caused by recession will reduce state tax collections, forcing the governor to call for budget cuts and tax increases. These actions do not necessarily cost governors a chance at re-election. But they do seem to lose votes when they raise taxes—especially for income tax and sales tax increases.[48] Out of the 389 governors seeking re-election from 1950 to 1980, 35.6 percent of those who raised or sought to raise taxes lost their re-election bids, compared to only 20.7 percent of those who did not raise taxes.[49]

Governors also seem to pay a price from a general deterioration in the state's economy, even if the governor is not forced to raise taxes. Recessions mean that more people file for unemployment compensation and welfare benefits, and this risks overloading the state's capacity to provide those benefits, which will reflect poorly on the governor's leadership. Even if these things do not happen, many people demonstrate their economic frustrations by voting against the incumbents, regardless of whether the incumbents have any real power to combat the economic conditions.[50] As the most visible of incumbents, the governors feel pressure to do something about their states' economies.

What makes the governor's job difficult in dealing with the state economy is that the American economy has been undergoing a revolution in recent decades. Older, manufacturing sectors of the economy (especially those based in the Northeast and Midwest) have not kept pace with the nation's economic growth and during the 1980s were badly damaged by foreign competition. The newer, service sectors of the economy have led the nation's economic growth. This has been a boon to the South and Southwest. Energy-producing states of the West, after experiencing explosive growth in the 1970s, were decimated by the oil glut and falling energy prices in the mid-1980s. Most of them had at least partially recovered by the 1990s.

No state is untouched by these changes. Economic life today is characterized by intense competition among states to attract new economic development, to keep businesses they already have, and to position themselves for an increasingly global economy. At the center of this competition is the governor. As the most visible political leader, the governor is expected to do something about the state's economic conditions.

A Premium on Strong Leaders

In the last analysis, strength of gubernatorial leadership makes a great deal of difference in how a governor responds to social conflict and political economy.

Strong governors have greater freedom to grapple with these issues than do weak governors. But even strong governors pay a cost if they stray too far from what public opinion will tolerate.

The consensus of informed opinion is that a strong governor is critical if the states are to meet the challenges they face today.[51] Since the federal government abdicated much of its responsibility for domestic initiatives during the 1980s and 1990s, states increasingly became the "laboratories of democracy" to fill that void. The task has essentially been twofold: to foster economic growth in the state and to guide that growth so that the poor as well as the rich get some benefit from it. This is a daunting task because it often means raising state taxes, cutting services, or redistributing public funds from one set of programs to another.[52] It is to the governor, more than anyone else, that people look for leadership on these tasks. States with strong governors are in a much better position to confront the economic challenges of the 1990s than are the states with weak governors. When New Jersey's James Florio, for example, began losing his popular support, the effort to reduce that state's savage school funding inequalities became a major casualty.

The poorer half of the population has the most to lose from weak governors because they are the people most in need of strong leadership on behalf of social welfare policies. Sarah Morehouse writes, "It takes organization to put forward and pass a sustained program in behalf of the needy. Disorganization can obstruct such a program. A fragmented executive may be a holding operation, a bastion of the status quo."[53]

To conclude this examination of governors and policy conflict, three generalizations are warranted. First, the formal powers of the governor do make a difference. It is easier for a person to be a dynamic governor if that position has been given substantial amounts of those formal powers. Second, leadership qualities also make a difference. Formal powers alone will not make a dynamic and forceful governor if the governor lacks the personal drive and skill to lead successfully. Third, formal powers alone will not lead to liberal state policies. But if we accept the arguments of Sarah Morehouse, liberal governors are unlikely to overcome the forces of the status quo unless those governors do have substantial formal powers.

SUMMARY

1. Although the substance of voters' demands on governors changes over time, the one persistent demand that stays constant is that governors be strong leaders.
2. The demand for strong executive leadership has evolved through three historical stages revolving around the progressive reform movement.
3. The governors' main sources of leadership strength are legislative powers, administrative powers, budget powers, public relations powers, the capabilities and resources of their personal staffs, and influence that they derive from their new roles as federal systems officers.
4. The governor's ability to lead depends in part on the gubernatorial style he or she adopts. There are four main styles: the demagogue, the policy entrepreneur, the frustrated warrior, and the caretaker.

5. Governors political influence is enhanced by their career record and prospects. Governors who win office with large victory margins carry more influence than governors who just squeak by. Governors with good prospects for re-election or moving on to higher office carry more influence than lame duck governors.

6. The governors' political influence is frequently challenged by other statewide-elected executives such as the lieutenant governor, attorney general, secretary of state, treasurer, auditor, and independent administrative boards.

7. Governors occupy the hot seat today in dealing with issues of social change and political economy. Governors with strong powers and strong political support are in a better position to deal with these issues than are weak governors.

KEY TERMS

Amendatory veto   Power of the governor in some states to add sums to appropriations bills.

Attorney general   The chief law enforcement officer of a state.

Auditor   The state officer responsible for ascertaining that funds are spent properly and legally.

Caretaker   A gubernatorial style in which the governor maintains the operations of the office but rarely pushes for new legislation, new programs, or new authority.

Demagogue   A political leader who builds his or her political support by enflaming people's passions over emotional political issues. A gubernatorial style practiced by Governor Huey Long of Louisiana (1928–1931).

Executive leadership   The demand that the chief executives in governmental jurisdictions (principally governors and mayors) exercise considerable authority over other executives.

Executive representation   The demand that people be represented in the executive branch by elected executives just as they are represented in the legislative branch by elected legislators.

Item veto   Power of the governor in some states to veto specific provisions of appropriations bills without vetoing the entire bill.

Jacksonian democracy   A governing concept attributed to the period of President Andrew Jackson (1829–1837) that government should rule for the benefit of the common people.

Lieutenant governor   A statewide officer who succeeds the governor if the governor leaves the governorship.

Long ballot   An election ballot containing many offices to be filled by election.

Neutral competence   The demand that public services should be provided competently and in a politically neutral fashion.

Policy entrepreneur   A dynamic governor or mayor who sets an agenda of goals to be accomplished and builds alliances with the interests needed to reach the goals.

Secretary of state   A statewide office responsible for administering the state election system, publishing a legislative manual, and conducting various clerical duties.

Spoils system   A patronage theory of public hiring that the winning candidates in elections should be able to find jobs for their supporters in the public bureaucracies. "To the victors go the spoils" was the slogan of this theory.

Treasurer   The state officer responsible for custody of state funds and for writing the checks that pay state obligations.

Veto   Power of a governor to negate a bill passed by the legislature and prevent it from becoming law.

REFERENCES

1. On Huey Long, see T. Harry Williams, *Huey Long* (New York: Bantam Books, 1970); Alan Sindler, *Huey Long's Louisiana: State Politics 1920–1952* (Baltimore: Johns Hopkins Press, 1956). On Jerry Brown, see Terry Christensen and Larry N. Gerston, *The California Connection: Politics in the Golden State* (Boston: Little, Brown and Co., 1984), pp. 103–106, 114–115.

2. These three stages were articulated by Herbert Kaufman in "Emerging Conflicts in the Doctrines of Public Administration," *American Political Science Review* 50 (1956): 1057.

3. See especially *Federalist Papers* no. 10 and no. 51.

4. Larry Sabato, *Goodbye to Good-time Charlie: The American Governor Transformed*, 2nd ed. (Washington, D.C.: Congressional Quarterly Press, 1983), p. 52.

5. Just how to make the best measurement of the formal power of governors has been a subject of intense debate among political scientists. An up-to-date version of the most widely used index of gubernatorial power is that of Keith J. Mueller, "Explaining Variation and Change in Gubernatorial Powers, 1960–1982," *Western Political Quarterly* 38, no. 3 (September 1985): 424–431. Mueller used essentially the same index to compare governors' powers from 1960 to 1982 and concluded that governors had become more powerful. The index was resoundingly criticized by Nelson C. Dometrius as inherently flawed because it took no account of recent gubernatorial innovations such as the team election of governors and lieutenant governors, amendatory vetoes, and staff size. See his "Changing Gubernatorial Power: The Measure vs. Reality," *Western Political Quarterly* 40, no. 2 (June 1987): 318–328. Finally, Robert Jay Dilger compiled an index comprising measures such as staff support, control over a cabinet, access to travel funds and compensation. See his "A Comparative Analysis of Gubernatorial Enabling Resources," *State and Local Government Review* 27, no. 2 (Spring 1995): 118–126. The index used for Table 10-2 has the advantages of being recent and including the political variable of party control in the legislature.

6. A study of the line item veto in Texas found that it did not give the governor any improvement in control over the budget. Pat Thompson and Steven R. Boyd, "Use of the Item Veto in Texas, 1940–1990," *State and Local Government Review* 26, no. 1 (Winter 1994): 38–45. This finding was consistent with earlier studies. See David C. Nice, "The Item Veto and Expenditures Restraint," *Journal of Politics* 50, no. 2 (May 1988): 482–502 and B. Abrams and W. Dougan, "The Effects of Constitutional Restraints on Government Spending," *Public Choice* 49, no. 2 (1986): 101–116. One study, however, did find that the item veto produces a minor reduction in state expenditures when the governorship and legislatures are controlled by opposite parties. See James Alm and Mark Evers, "The Line Item Veto and State Expenditures," *Public Choice* 68 (1991): 1–15.

7. Glen Abney and Thomas P. Lauth, "The Line-Item Veto in the States," *Public Administration Review* 45, no. 3 (May–June 1985): 372–377. Abney and Lauth came to this conclusion after surveying the legislative budget officers in the fifty states.

8. See "Legislators Fight Item Veto in Wisconsin," *State Legislatures* 14, no. 8 (September 1988): 9. Also see Tony Hutchison, "Legislating via Veto," *State Legislatures* 15, no. 1 (January 1989): 20–24.

9. Michael H. McCabe, "Wisconsin's 'Quirky' Veto Power," *State Government News* 34, no. 8 (August 1991): 11–14.

10. In the 1990–1991 sessions, governors in the fifty states vetoed about 2,337 out of 74,229 bills, about 3 percent. Forty percent were vetoed in only three states: California, Maryland, and Illinois. *The Book of the States: 1992–93* (Lexington, Ky.: Council of State Governments, 1992), pp. 183–188.

11. On the increasing frequency of overrides, see Charles W. Wiggins, "Executive Vetoes and Legislative Overrides in the American States," *Journal of Politics* 42, no. 4 (November 1986): 1110–1112. In California, the legislature failed to override even a single governor's veto from 1946 to 1974; in New York, from 1877 to 1976; in Texas, from 1941 to 1979. See Noel J. Stowe, *California Government: The Challenge of Change* (Beverly Hills, Calif.: Glencoe Press, 1975), p. 138; Eugene J. Gleason and Joseph Zimmerman, "The Strong Governorship: Status and Problems, New York," *Public Administration Review* 36, no. 1 (January–February 1976): 92–95; Clifton McCleskey et al., *The Government and Politics of Texas,* 7th ed. (Boston: Little, Brown and Co., 1982), p. 176. In the 1990–1991 legislative sessions there were 206 overrides of 2,333 vetoes. *The Book of the States: 1992–93* (Lexington, Ky.: Council of State Governments, 1992), pp. 183–188.

12. E. Lee Bernick, "Special Sessions: What Manner of Gubernatorial Power," *State and Local Government Review* 26, no. 2 (Spring 1994): 79–88.

13. On the executive amendment provision, see Coleman Ransone, Jr., *The Office of Governor in the United States* (Tuscaloosa: University of Alabama Press, 1956), pp. 182–184.

14. Alan Rosenthal, "Legislative Oversight and the Balance of Power in State Government," *State Government* 56, no. 3 (1983): 90–98.

15. Thad Beyle, "Governors: The Middlemen and Women in Our Political System," in *Politics in the American States: A Comparative Analysis,* 6th ed. Virginia Gray and Henry Jacob, eds. (Washington, D.C.: CQ Press, 1996), p. 241.

16. Rosenthal, "Legislative Oversight and the Balance of Power in State Government."

17. Steven Williams, "Alexander's Master Teacher Program Fails in Tennessee," *Comparative State Politics Newsletter* 4, no. 3 (May 1983): 11–12; "Master Teacher Program Update," 4, no. 6 (December 1983): 21; and "The First Year of Merit Pay for Tennessee Teachers," 6, no. 5 (October 1985): 33.

18. See Louis M. Kohlmeier, Jr., *The Regulators: Watchdog Agencies and the Public Interest* (New York: Harper & Row, 1969).

19. Glenn Abney and Thomas P. Lauth, "The Governor as Chief Administrator," *Public Administration Review* 43, no. 1 (January–February 1983): 40–49. This was the same result as Deil S. Wright had found when he conducted a similar survey two decades earlier. See Deil S. Wright, "Executive Leadership in State Administration," *Midwest Journal of Political Science* 11, no. 1 (February 1967): 1–26.

20. Norton Long, "After the Voting Is Over," *Midwest Journal of Political Science* 6, no. 2 (May 1963): 183–200.

21. See Donald P. Sprengel, *Gubernatorial Staffs: Functional and Political Profiles* (Iowa City: Institute of Public Affairs, University of Iowa, 1969), pp. 34–52; *The Book of the States: 1988–89* (Lexington, Ky.: Council of State Governments, 1988), p. 38.

22. Thad Beyle, "The Governors, 1988–89," *The Book of the States: 1990–91* (Lexington, Ky.: Council of State Governments, 1990), p. 55.

23. Patrick J. Kenney and Tom W. Rice, "Popularity and the Vote: The Gubernatorial Case," *American Politics Quarterly* 11, no. 2 (April 1983): 237–242. Kenney and Rice examined nineteen gubernatorial elections in four states where polling organizations periodically track governors' popularity (California, Iowa, Minnesota, and New Jersey). In fifteen of the nineteen elections, the governors lost their re-election bids if their final pre-election popularity ratings dropped below 48 percent.

24. See Deil S. Wright, "Governors, Grants, and the Intergovernmental System," in *The American Governor in Behavioral Perspective,* Thad Beyle and J. Oliver Williams, eds. (New York: Harper & Row, 1972), pp. 187–193.

25. See Thad L. Beyle and Deil S. Wright, "The Governor, Planning, and Governmental Activity," in Beyle and Williams, *The American Governor in Behavioral Perspective,* pp. 193–205.

26. Lynn Muchmore and Thad L. Beyle, "The Governor as Party Leader," *State Government* 53, no. 3 (Summer 1980): 121–124.

27. Sarah M. Morehouse, "Money versus Party Effort: Nominating the Governor," *American Journal of Political Science* 34, no. 3 (August 1990): 706–724. Morehouse conducted an elaborate statistical comparison of money spent in gubernatorial campaigns in states where the parties endorsed gubernatorial nominees (strong party states) and states where parties do not endorse (weak party states).

28. Lee Sigelman and Nelson C. Dometrius demonstrate that for the governor to exercise effective influence over state agencies, for example, the governor's formal powers need to be bolstered by informal sources of influence (especially the ability to win election by a substantial margin and the ability of his or her party to control the legislature). See their "Governors as Chief Administrators: The Linkage Between Formal Powers and Informal Influence," *American Politics Quarterly* 16, no. 2 (April 1988): 157–171.

29. Larry Sabato, *Goodbye to Good-Time Charlie: The American Governor Transformed, 1950–1975*, 1st ed. (Lexington, Mass.: Lexington Books, 1978), pp. 50–56.

30. Lee Sigelman and Roland Smith, "Personal, Office, and State Characteristics as Predictors of Gubernatorial Performance," *Journal of Politics* 43, no. 1 (February 1981): 169–180. Quote on p. 180.

31. The preeminent biography of Huey Long is T. Harry Williams's *Huey Long*. Also see Alan Sindler, *Huey Long's Louisiana: State Politics 1920–1952*. Also see Long's autobiography, *Every Man a King: The Autobiography of Huey Long* (New Orleans: National Book Co., 1933), and the political novel based on the life of Huey Long by Robert Penn Warren, *All the King's Men* (New York: Bantam Books, 1968).

32. See Alan G. Hevesi, *Legislative Politics in New York State: A Comparative Analysis* (New York: Praeger, 1975).

33. David E. Osborne, *Laboratories of Democracy* (Boston: Harvard Business School Press, 1988).

34. Ibid., pp. 48–70.

35. David E. Osborne and Ted Gaebler, *Reinventing Government: How the Entrepreneurial Spirit Is Transforming the Public Sector* (Reading, Mass.: Addison-Wesley, 1992).

36. Hevesie, *Legislative Politics in New York State.*

37. Sarah McCally Morehouse, "The Governor as Political Leader," in *Politics in the American States: A Comparative Analysis*, 3rd ed. Herbert Jacob and Kenneth N. Vines, eds. (Boston: Little, Brown and Co., 1977), p. 204. Of the 156 governors during the 1960s, 92 were attorneys and 32 were businesspersons.

38. Of 995 governors from 1870 to 1950, 90 percent had held prior public office. See Joseph A. Schlesinger, *How They Became Governors* (East Lansing: Michigan State University, Governmental Research Bureau, 1957), p. 11. Since 1970, only 8 percent of governors have had no prior elective experience. See Thad C. Beyle, "Governors: The Middlemen and Women in Our Political System," *Politics in the American States: A Comparative Analysis*, 6th ed. Virginia Gray and Henry Jacob, eds. (Washington, D.C.: CQ Press, 1996), p. 212.

39. Thad C. Beyle, "The 1993 Gubernatorial Elections: Dollars and Votes," *Comparative State Politics* 15, no. 5 (October 1994): 39.

40. Thad C. Beyle, "The 1992 Gubernatorial Elections," *Comparative State Politics* 15, no. 1 (February 1994): 30.

41. Morehouse, "The Governor as Political Leader," pp. 201–202.

42. On La Follette, see Robert S. Maxwell, *La Follette and the Rise of the Progressives in Wisconsin* (Madison: State Historical Society of Wisconsin, 1956). On Dewey's use of the prosecution power to become governor, see Warren Moscow, *Politics in the Empire*

State (New York: Knopf, 1948), pp. 29–32. Dewey, however, was not the attorney general; he was a special prosecutor appointed to prosecute organized crime figures.

43. This was the case for California Governor Jerry Brown (1975–1983) and Oregon Governor Barbara Roberts (1991–1995). Arizona Governor Rose Mofford (1988–1991) ascended from secretary of state to the governorship when Governor Evan Mecham was impeached. Minnesota Secretary of State Joan Growe used the office as a launching pad for an unsuccessful bid for the U.S. Senate in 1986.

44. Edward M. Wheat, "The Activist Auditor: A New Player in State and Local Politics," *Public Administration Review* 15, no. 5 (September–October 1991): 385–391.

45. Data reported in *The American Prospect* and *Investors Business Daily,* July 24, 1995, p. A2.

46. For example, a 1995 CNN/*USA Today* poll showed that 59 percent of people who expressed opposition to affirmative action nevertheless favored special efforts to recruit minorities. And 56 percent of those who expressed support for affirmative action, opposed favoring a minority over an equally qualified white applicant. See Jim Norman, "America's Verdict on Affirmative Action Is Decidedly Mixed," *The Public Perspective* (June–July 1995): 49.

47. Frank Lally, "If You Really Want Better Government Today, The Buck Stops with You," *Money,* May 1995, p. 10.

48. Susan L. Kone and Richard F. Winters, "Taxes and Voting: Electoral Retribution in the American States," *The Journal of Politics* 55, no. 1 (February 1993): 22–40.

49. Theodore J. Eismeier, "Votes and Taxes: The Political Economy of the American Governorship," *Polity* 15, no. 3 (Spring 1983): 368–379. In a study of governors seeking re-election over the thirty-year period from 1950 to 1980, Eismeier compared those who raised or proposed to raise taxes with those who did not. He found that 35.6 percent of the tax raisers lost their bids for re-election compared to only 20.9 percent of those who did not raise taxes.

50. The impact of economic conditions on the governor's re-election prospects is a contested issue. John Chubb analyzed this relationship for the years 1940 through 1982 and concluded that citizens do not hold their governors accountable for economic conditions. See his "Institutions, the Economy, and the Dynamics of State Elections," *American Political Science Review* 82, no. 1 (March 1988): 133–154. By contrast, analyses of gubernatorial elections from 1986 to 1990 found that governors lose votes when their states' voters perceive troubles in the state economy or in their personal finances. On the 1986 elections, see Richard G. Niemi, Harold W. Stanley, and Ronald J. Vogel, "State Economies and State Taxes: Do Voters Hold Governors Accountable?" *American Journal of Political Science* 39, no. 4 (November 1995): 936–957. On the 1990 elections, see Randall W. Partin, "Economic Conditions and Gubernatorial Elections: Is the State Executive Held Accountable?" *American Politics Quarterly* 23, no. 1 (January 1995): 81–95. Also, a survey of Louisiana voters in 1988 found that the state's economic conditions played a strong role in whether people approved or disapproved of the governor. See Susan E. Howell and James M. Vanderleeuw, "Economic Effects on State Governors," *American Politics Quarterly* 18, no. 2 (April 1990): 158–168.

51. This was the opinion of the National Commission on State and Local Public Service, popularly called the Winter Commission after its chair, former Mississippi governor William Winter. For an assessment of the commission's recommendations, see Frank J. Thompson, "Executive Leadership as an Enduring Institutional Issue," *State and Local Government Review* 27, no. 1 (Winter 1995): 7–17.

52. See Thad Beyle, ed., *Governors and Hard Times* (Washington: CQ Press, 1992), pp. 8–12.

53. Morehouse, "The Governor as Political Leader," p. 225.

11

ADMINISTRATORS AND THE IMPLEMENTATION OF POLICY

Chapter Preview

This chapter examines the role of state and local administrators in carrying out the policies and implementing the programs established by political leaders. The main topics we will explore are:

1. Perennial tensions between administrators and executives.
2. Public approaches to personnel practices.
3. Administrative reorganization as an approach to state government reform.
4. Budgeting and the attempts to reform budgeting as a device for improving executive management.
5. Reform alternatives for improving executive management.
6. The political economy and government productivity.

Let us begin our examination of state and local administration with a look at a typical attitude that many people have toward their public servants.

◇ INTRODUCTION

The great whipping boy of American politics is the public bureaucracy. The cartoon on p. 269 sums up many people's feelings about government bureaucracies on all levels. In the popular image, the typical bureaucrat's response to a legislative or gubernatorial order for full speed ahead is to fudge, shuffle, hedge, obfuscate, and so on.

When Jerry Brown became governor of California in 1975, he declared war on that state's bureaucracy. One of his first acts was symbolic, a ban on issuing briefcases to state employees. The paperwork generated by bureaucrats simply multiplied to fill the briefcases, said the governor, and the paperwork itself is written in a jargon that is incomprehensible to the outsider.[1] Brown eliminated one regulatory agency, reduced the size of three others, and cut the volume of the state's records by 51,500 cubic feet. But he lost the war. Although he wiped out one regulatory agency, he created three others. Although he eliminated 109 staff positions, he created 443. Midway through his first term, Brown admitted that he was losing.[2] And midway through his second term, the state had 18 percent more employees than it had when Brown was first elected governor.[3]

This chapter looks at the major facets of public administration that cause concern to elected officials such as Governor Brown. It examines first a basic tension between executives and administrators that causes executives such as Governor Brown to attack the administrators in the first place and to concede defeat in the second place. The chapter then focuses on three mechanisms that have been or are being created to enable the elected executives and legislative policymakers to control the administrators. These are personnel practices, reorganization, and budgeting. Next, the chapter will discuss a number of new management devices that have been experimented with since the mid-1960s. Finally, the chapter will explore the political economy and its relation to government productivity.

◇ TENSION BETWEEN ADMINISTRATORS AND EXECUTIVES

In theory, the legislators write the laws and the governors execute them. In practice, the legislators and governors combine to write the laws, and the laws are implemented by numerous state and local government administrative agencies. (In the following discussion, we will use the word *executives* to mean the persons who are either elected or appointed through the political process to head public agencies. By *administrators* we mean the permanent, career employees of public agencies.) The job of the executive is to ensure that the administrative agencies implement the law in the way the governor and legislators intended. Governors and legislators, faced with electoral pressures, may demand changes in agency procedures. Administrators defend their routines by actively trying to influence the formulation of policies. The net result is considerable tension and conflict between the governor and major executives and the public agency administrators.

This tension between executives and administrators is kept alive by several other factors. First, the administrators are permanent employees, whereas the executives are temporary. The average term of executives is only 5.6 years for big-city mayors and barely 4 years for governors. But top civil service employees remain until they retire or resign, which gives them a longer-range perspective on the services provided by their agencies. If a governor's policy proposals challenge strongly held agency privileges, the civil servants can often stall the demanded changes until the governor is replaced.

A second source of tension is that administrators are professionals in government, whereas the executives are not. The executives, who typically look on

Source: MacNelly, © 1977. Reprinted with permission: Tribune Media Services.

themselves as citizen-officials responsible for overseeing the activities of the professionals, are skeptical of the supposedly professional expertise of the administrators.[4] Technical expertise is necessary in the case of highway engineering, for example. But decisions on the location of roads and freeway interchanges, the awarding of construction contracts, and the choice of urban neighborhoods to be torn up by freeways are primarily political decisions. In making such decisions, executives have to weigh the demands of professional standards against the vocal demands of angry citizens.

A third source of tension is that the professional administrators have much more detailed knowledge about government programs than do the citizen-executives. Administrators are deeply embedded in a significant communications network involving other professionals at the federal, state, and local levels of government. In fact, the professional administrators often either initiate or review new policy ideas that the executives put forward to the public.

◇ MANAGING PERSONNEL FOR BETTER POLICY IMPLEMENTATION

A major management problem lies in directing the daily activities of the fifteen million people who work for state and local governments. Most of these employees, as shown in Table 11-1, work in education, health, and police protection. Nearly three-fourths of them work at the local level. How are these fifteen

Table 11-1 STATE AND LOCAL GOVERNMENT EMPLOYMENT: 1992

Function	Number (in Thousands)	Percentage
Education	8,225	52%
Health and hospitals	1,544	10
Police protection	770	5
Highways	561	4
Public welfare	496	3
Financial administration	355	2
Fire protection	344	2
All other functions	3,403	22
Total	15,698	100%

Source: Bureau of the Census, *Statistical Abstract of the United States: 1975* (Washington, D.C.: U.S. Government Printing Office, 1995), p. 322.

million people to be hired, promoted, or fired? Should it be on the basis of favoritism or of merit? Should special preferences be given for racial minorities and females? Should salaries be determined by executive decision or by collective bargaining? What kind of pension systems should these employees have? And how should those pensions be funded? These questions involve billions of dollars in taxes and go to the heart of the struggle over who should control state and local government.

The Patronage System of Employment

The **patronage** system, or the spoils system, is a recruitment method that gives government jobs to political supporters of the winning candidates. Traditional patronage was the main public employment system until late in the nineteenth century. Until recently, it flourished best in cities such as Chicago and New York, which have a tradition of machine politics.[5] But most elected executives today find traditional patronage difficult to administer. A new administration that fired large numbers of workers to make way for political appointees would in most places suffer a severe public relations setback.

The critical blows to traditional patronage started in 1939 when the Hatch Act made it illegal for federal employees to engage in partisan political activity. This prohibition was later extended to cover state and local employees who administered federally funded programs.[6] In 1970, the Intergovernmental Personnel Act provided grants to train administrators, to improve state civil service systems, and to prohibit partisanship in hiring practices if federal funds were involved. The most dramatic restrictions on traditional patronage have come from the U.S. Supreme Court, which has ruled consistently since 1976 that politically motivated dismissals could only be made among policy-making officials and could not touch rank-and-file employees.[7] The most recent and far-reaching case, *Rutan* v.

Republican Party of Illinois,[8] involved former Illinois Governor James R. Thompson, who had his personnel office review job and promotion applications to ensure that the applicants had voted in the Republican party primary or had contributed money or work to the party. These court decisions will not eliminate patronage employment, but over time they will certainly reduce the number of patronage-type jobs that are available in state and local government.

The Merit System of Employment

The **merit system,** or the **civil service system,** is a recruitment method that hires and promotes employees on the basis of their training and competence to perform specific jobs. Once employees are given civil service status, they are protected from arbitrary removal.

One gets civil service status by passing a test. A job description is drawn up for each civil service position. The position is classified at a specific level and assigned a pay range. Promotion to higher positions is achieved by competition, with the promotion ideally going to the candidate whose experience, qualifications, training, and test scores best fit the responsibilities of the job.

The first state civil service system was established in New York in 1883. Since then it has spread to all states[9] and to most large cities.[10] Most of these state and local civil service systems were established after 1939, in response to federal laws and court decisions that prohibited patronage systems in federally funded programs.

Criticisms of Civil Service   As merit systems of employment gradually replaced patronage systems, the quality of the state and local government workforce improved accordingly. But critics charge today that civil service systems are inherently outdated nineteenth-century institutions that eventually led to severe management problems of their own.[11] For one thing they conflict with the demand for executive leadership. High-ranking administrators with civil service protection sometimes drag their heels implementing policy changes sought by newly elected governors. From the administrators' viewpoint, agency policies have worked well for years, and it would be chaotic and intrusive if each new governor were to overhaul them each time political winds blew in a new direction. From the critics' viewpoint, however, the whole purpose of the democratic process is to keep administrators and policies in tune with political realities. Critics also charge that civil service rules make it difficult to fire incompetent workers. One study found that less than 2 percent of state and local employees are dismissed from their jobs each year.[12] What is the appropriate percent of public employees who deserve to be fired each year? That is hard to know. But there is little doubt that cumbersome personnel rules do hamper effective personnel management.

Another popular criticism of civil service is that it pays too well in comparison to the private sector. Critics note that public employees on average enjoy higher salaries than do private sector workers on average.[13] Such figures are often misleading, however, because the public workforce has a higher percent of professional employees than does the private workforce. The best estimates are that the public employees at the lower levels enjoy higher pay than their private sector counterparts. But midlevel, professional, and upper-level employees do better in the private sector.[14]

Civil Service Reform Given these criticisms, it is not surprising that movements to reform civil service have emerged in recent years. Two approaches to civil service reform can be identified. The most common approach is probably that pioneered by Wisconsin. Wisconsin's Civil Service Reform Law of 1977 increased the number of top-level political appointments that the governor can make and located the personnel management department directly in the governor's cabinet. The general goal was to enhance the governor's influence over state agencies, to increase the number of high-level political appointees, and to make it easier to dismiss poorly performing employees.[15]

A different tack to civil service reform is to set up a senior executive service tier of the civil service system. Under such a system, which now operates in a dozen states, several hundred of the top-ranking civil servants are given senior executive status, which allows the governor to move them around from agency to agency as needed. If they do not perform well, the governor can replace them with other senior executives.

In both of these approaches, the common goal is to make the bureaucracy more responsive to the democratic process. Both approaches seek to do this by making the top-ranking civil servants more accountable to the governor.

Collective Bargaining

Another trend that has made a big impact on state and local personnel practices is **collective bargaining.** This is the process by which a group of employees (called the bargaining unit) negotiates a master contract that stipulates conditions of employment, grievance procedures, salary schedules, fringe benefits, and seniority provisions. Collective bargaining among public employees made very little progress until the 1970s. During that decade, strikes of teachers, police officers, and other public employees led to state laws that permit employees to bargain collectively and in many states to strike under certain circumstances. Today, most states permit some form of collective bargaining for public employees, and some states even give them the right to strike.

The foremost public employee union is the **American Federation of State, County, and Municipal Employees (AFSCME),** which by 1993 had 1.2 million members. Forty-five percent of all government workers are represented by unions, with the greatest unionization occurring among firefighters, sanitation workers, and teachers.[16]

The provision of collective bargaining that causes the most conflict with civil service is the seniority provision. Civil service rules usually provide for advancement on the basis of merit and performance, but collective bargaining contracts usually provide for advancement on the basis of seniority. If an engineering position becomes available, civil service rules usually call for a supervisor to hire from among the three or four most qualified applicants as judged by the civil service office. Collective bargaining rules demand that the qualified person with the most seniority in the agency be given the position. In this example, two important principles are in conflict. No one would argue against promoting the most competent person to a position. But from the union's viewpoint, what looks like merit to the supervisor may look like cronyism or favoritism to other workers. Furthermore, the need to maintain morale and a high-quality work-force requires that some considerations be given to seniority. A highly competent person who could not look forward to advancement as he or she gained experience in the agency would soon look elsewhere for employment. Merit and seniority might not be incompatible in principle, but striking a proper balance between them is a tricky task.[17]

◇ SOCIAL CONFLICT IN THE PUBLIC WORKFORCE

The public workforce has been a central arena for the social conflicts of the past two decades. Regardless of whether the personnel system was one of patronage, civil service, or collective bargaining, racial minorities and women did not historically fare well in the public bureaucracies. As minority and women's groups gained political clout, they demanded greater representation in the public workforce.

Pressure for a Representative Bureaucracy

The federal government has followed two policies that aimed to address these complaints. The first, stemming from the Civil Rights Act of 1964, was to promote **equal employment opportunities.** Federal grants and loans for programs administered by state and local governments could be denied unless the recipient government hired its employees without regard to race, sex, religion, or country of origin. This equal employment opportunity principle was written into the 1970 Intergovernmental Personnel Act.

By itself, however, equal opportunity did not produce equality of results. The percent of women and minorities in top government positions lagged far behind the percent of men and whites, which led feminists to complain of a "glass ceiling" that kept them and minorities out of top positions.[18] To remedy this and gain equality of results, federal law adopted the practice of **affirmative action.** Each state and local agency receiving federal funds must have an affirmative action plan for increasing the employment of legally "protected classes" of people (mainly women and minorities) who had suffered from discrimination in the past. These affirmative action plans ranged from making diligent efforts to recruit more women and minorities to setting up what amounted to numerical quotas that would make a state's public workforce representative of the ethnic or gender composition of its labor pool.

How successful have the affirmative action programs been? Table 11-2 tells much of the story. At least for women, the glass ceiling of the past looks pretty porous today. Women now occupy nearly a third of the top-level administrative positions shown in Table 11-2 and, equally important, they hold a majority of professional-level jobs from which future top administrators will be appointed. Given their rapid rates of increase, they will soon dominate the two highest paid levels of employment. Minorities are well represented at all levels except the top administrator level, and their share of jobs at the middle and higher levels is increasing rapidly. Blacks have much greater penetration in government employment than do Hispanics. Although white males occupy a majority of the top administrator positions, their share of these jobs will slowly erode over time since many of them are approaching retirement age, and they are not being recruited into these positions as fast as women and minorities. The biggest winners in this competition for jobs appear to be white females, as Table 11-2 shows. The biggest losers are white males. Evidence does not show a systematic pattern of promoting minorities and women over better qualified white males,[19] but many white males charge that affirmative action has become "reverse discrimination" designed to reduce their numbers in the public workforce.

It is also important to note that the racial and gender distribution of jobs differs greatly from state to state. In Connecticut, women accounted for 27 percent of all appointed state assistant department heads and 19 percent of all department heads.[20] This is probably much higher than most states. In sum, affirmative action has enjoyed considerable success.

Underlying the concern over the success of women and minorities in state government employment is the concept of **representative bureaucracy.** This is an old concept that, as we saw in Chapter 10, surfaced during the period of Jacksonian Democracy (1829–1837) and reached its zenith in the heyday of machine politics (1870–1930), when the European immigrants demanded that they have representatives in the public bureaucracies as well as in the state legislatures and city councils. As executive representation under the political machines degenerated into political favoritism and patronage, civil service practices and merit systems of employment were promoted to create a fairer system of hiring and dismissing public employees. The contemporary move to affirmative action is in some ways reminiscent of the motives of the European immigrants a century ago. The immigrants then and minorities and women today wanted jobs and hoped that getting some of their own people into the bureaucracies would ensure them better treatment by the bureaucracies.

Affirmative Action Under Fire

The goal of affirmative action frequently finds itself in conflict with the other two principles of personnel management today (merit and collective bargaining). At least in principle, affirmative action's goal of promoting people on the basis of gender and ethnic origin conflicts with the civil service notion of promoting people on the basis of merit. In practice, the most volatile conflicts have taken place between affirmative action and collective bargaining. Usu-

Table 11-2 STATE AND LOCAL GOVERNMENT JOBS BY AFFIRMATIVE ACTION CATEGORIES: 1993*

Category	Median** Salary (1993)	Percentage of These Jobs Held in 1993 by				Change in This Group's Share of Jobs 1981–1993			
		Women	Minorities	White Males	White Females	Women	Minorities	White Males	White Females
High-pay positions									
Official/administrative	$47,200	31.5%	15.4%	58.3%	26.7%	22.5%	25.6%	-10.6%	18.1%
Professional	$37,800	51.3%	23.5%	37.3%	39.3%	15.2%	46.2%	-20.0%	5.3%
Medium-pay positions									
Protective service	$31,400	14.2%	25.3%	64.0%	10.6%	43.3%	70.4%	-16.6%	25.8%
Technician	$30,400	41.9%	25.2%	43.5%	31.4%	1.6%	29.0%	-8.1%	-5.6%
Skilled craft	$28,500	4.3%	24.3%	72.4%	3.3%	16.5%	29.7%	-7.4%	8.5%
Low-pay positions									
Service/maintenance	$23,100	21.8%	43.8%	43.9%	12.3%	10.1%	12.5%	-10.1%	1.4%
Office/clerical	$22,700	87.1%	32.0%	8.8%	59.2%	-1.0%	32.0%	-3.8%	-11.1%
Paraprofessional	$22,600	72.2%	39.4%	16.8%	43.7%	2.0%	12.7%	-12.2%	-4.9%
All employees	$30,600	43.9%	28.6%	18.9%	6.8%	6.4%	24.2%	-11.4%	-1.3%

*Data does not include public education.

**Median salary is for non-Hispanic white males.

Salary for administrators is an estimate.

Data for white males and white females are estimates.

Source: U.S. Bureau of the Census, *Statistical Abstract of the United States: 1995* (Washington, D. C.: U.S. Government Printing Office, 1995), p. 323; 1984, p. 305.

ally these conflicts center on the concept of seniority rights, which, as we saw, is a hallowed principle in collective bargaining. Seniority provides loyal workers with employment stability and protects them from arbitrary dismissals as they move up the pay scale and reach a point where employers could save some money by firing highly paid senior workers and replacing them with newer workers who are paid less. Of course, as the female and minority share of the public workforce gains tenure, seniority provisions will work in their favor. But in the fiscally stringent environment of the 1980s and 1990s, the last-hired, first-fired principle of seniority distinctly threatened to undermine affirmative action attempts to increase minority employment in government.

When Boston, for example, was forced by fiscal stress in the early 1980s to lay off firefighters and police officers, the city was operating under both a federal court order that prevented it from laying off blacks and a state law that obliged it to protect seniority rights when conducting layoffs. The city gave priority to its affirmative action plan, and layed off several whites who had more seniority than blacks who were not laid-off. The laid-off workers sued to get their jobs back, and the stage seemed to be set for the Supreme Court to make a ruling on the conflict between affirmative action and seniority rights. The need for such a ruling was forestalled, however, when the state of Massachusetts passed a law rehiring the laid-off whites.[21]

In 1986, the Supreme Court upheld an affirmative action plan in Cleveland that gave black and Hispanic firefighters promotion preference over whites. But in two other cases in the 1980s, the Court seriously backed away from supporting affirmative action. In a Memphis, Tennessee, case, the Supreme Court ruled that black firefighters could be protected from layoff by affirmative action only if they could show that they individually had been subjected to discrimination.[22] In 1989, in a case involving the Birmingham, Alabama, fire department, the Supreme Court allowed white firefighters to challenge an eight-year-old affirmative action plan designed to increase the hiring and promotion of minorities.[23] The Court seemed to be saying that whites who had been hired since the plan's inception could not have been guilty of prior discrimination and hence they should not be bound by agreements to undo prior discrimination.

The net impact of these decisions, and some related decisions involving the business world, was to put the burden of proof on the employee to show that he or she had been individually subjected to racial discrimination.[24] In 1991, Congress amended the Civil Rights Act so that the burden of proof would henceforth be on employers to show that any racial imbalances in their workforce did not result from discrimination. In 1994, Republicans gained control of the U.S. Congress and threatened to dismantle much of the affirmative action legal edifice, but to date they have not done so. Even if they were to do so, such actions would involve only the federal affirmative action effort. Several states by now have invested considerable effort and resources to promote female and minority recruitment into the public workforce, and it seems unlikely that they would make a wholesale reversal of this practice. The exception seems to be California, which passed an initiative in 1996 to repeal all the state's affirmative action pro-

YOU DECIDE

Taking a Stab at Comparable Worth

Listed below in alphabetical order are several jobs that had to be classified according to Washington State's comparable worth guidelines. Assume that you are a member of the task force responsible for giving these jobs a rating that can be transformed into a pay scale. In doing this task, comparable worth consultants typically consider criteria such as: educational and training requirements for the job, difficulty of the job, danger in the job, experience levels needed for the job, complexity of the job, accountability of the job holder, problem solving skills needed for the job, and overall working conditions.

Rank the following six jobs with number 1 being the job that you think should have the highest rating and number 6 the job you think should have the lowest rating.

Job	Rank
Civil engineer	
Fisheries patrol officer	
Jail Guard	
Secretary with shorthand duties	
Teacher's aide	
Truck Driver	

To compare your rankings with those of the State of Washington, see the box on p.278.

grams. A federal judge ruled that this initiative was illegal under federal law, and the U.S. Supreme Court will eventually decide the issue.

Comparable Worth

Even though women are advancing into the higher-level public jobs, they average barely 79 percent of men's pay, only a slight improvement over the 74 percent that they had averaged twenty years earlier.[25] Table 11-2 suggests one of the reasons for this disparity. Women dominate in low-paid fields such as paraprofessionals whose average earnings per year are $500 less than those of the male-dominated maintenance jobs and $6,000 less than those of the male-dominated skilled trades jobs. **Comparable worth** advocates argued that many low-paid, female-dominated jobs actually required greater skills, training, and personal danger than did many higher-paid, male-dominated jobs. These advocates demanded that comparable worth consultants rank all jobs in an organization by various criteria and that the pay schedules for female dominated jobs be raised when inequities are discovered.[26] The female-dominated job of librarian, for example, requires extensive training and skills, but it is poorly paid, and comparable worth argues that its pay should be upgraded accordingly.

Opponents of comparable worth argue that pay differences for different jobs reflect the differing economic values of the jobs as determined by supply and de-

HIGHLIGHT

Comparable Worth: How Jobs Compare

Washington State ranked the six jobs shown on p. 277 as follows:

Job	Rank
Civil engineer	2
Fisheries patrol officer	1
Jail guard	4
Secretary with shorthand duties	3
Teacher's aide	5
Truck driver	6

Source: Calculated from Peter T. Kilborn, "Wage Gap Between Sexes Is Cut in Test, but at a Price," *The New York Times,* May 31, 1990, p. 1.

mand and the marketplace. Accordingly, they argue, women who wish to earn more money should seek jobs that pay more. From this viewpoint, if poorly paid librarians want more money, it would be better public policy for them to shift careers into a better-paying job than it would to upgrade the pay for all librarians, which would encourage even more women to prepare for a field in which the supply of workers is already oversaturated and job openings are scarce.[27]

Comparable worth came to national prominence in 1983 when federal courts ordered the state of Washington to spend nearly half a billion dollars making pay equity adjustments for 62,000 workers. Much of this went to boost the wages of low-income female workers. Between 1986 and 1990, for example, secretarial workers saw a 28 percent increase in their pay.

Despite its achievements, Washington's comparable worth plan also produced some unintended consequences that complicated the personnel problems of the state. In contrast to the 28 percent pay increase for secretaries, the male-dominated field of transportation engineers saw only an 11 percent increase.[28] Not surprisingly, as their pay increases fell behind both inflation and the pay increases that were occurring in the private sector, many highly skilled employees resigned their government jobs to take better-paying positions in the business world. By 1990, male representation in the Washington civil service slipped from 50 to 47 percent. With its pay scales lagging behind the private sector, the state soon experienced labor shortages in some critical skilled occupations. To cover those shortages, the state offered special pay raises for psychiatrists and pharmacists. But that seemed inconsistent with the state's original comparable worth plan because those pay increases necessarily increased the pay gaps that comparable worth had sought to reduce.

Notwithstanding its implementation problems, comparable worth in Washington is generally viewed as a success, especially by the American Federation of State, County, and Municipal Employees (AFSCME), which sponsored the original suit leading to comparable worth. AFSCME chapters in other states took a cue from Washington and began pressing for comparable worth studies in their areas. By 1990, twenty states had adjusted pay schedules to eliminate sexual or racial bias.[29]

Sexual Harassment

Another major personnel issue is that of sexual harassment. As women workers gained in numbers and influence, they became much better positioned to challenge long-standing practices of sexual harassment on the job. This issue caught the nation's attention in an unprecedented way in 1991 when the confirmation hearings for Supreme Court justice nominee Clarence Thomas were rocked by accusations that Thomas had repeatedly harassed a female employee with unwanted sexually oriented comments and attentions. Whether Thomas was guilty of the charges was not proved, but there is no doubt that millions of women had experienced equal or worse treatment on the job, and Thomas's confirmation galvanized their anger at that treatment.

Sexual harassment practices include, among other things, unwanted sexual advances, sexually offensive jokes, demeaning comments about women, or any other behavior that reduces a person's stature solely because of gender. Although sexual harassment is illegal under the 1964 Civil Rights Act, it is nevertheless widespread.

Most states and communities have adopted policies that both define and prohibit sexual harassment. Most state and local governments have also instituted training programs to bring an end to sexually harassing behaviors.

◇ REORGANIZING AND REENGINEERING BUREAUCRACY

There is a strong feeling that political executives at both the state and local levels could do a better job of managing the public bureaucracies and implementing public policies if the bureaucracies were better organized. "Reinventing government" has become a popular phrase in the 1990s,[30] as political reformers sought innovative ways to make government acceptable in an era of growing distrust of the public sector.

The Administrative Reorganization Movement

The reinventing government movement is the latest in a long history of administrative reforms. As early as 1910, President William Howard Taft established the Commission on Economy and Efficiency to recommend improvements in the federal government. The first major state reorganization occurred in 1917 in Illinois under Governor Frank D. Lowden, who consolidated more than a hundred independent agencies, boards, and commissions into nine departments. Following the lead of Illinois, more than over a dozen states made some effort at reorganization over the next decade.

A second stimulus to state reorganization was the publication in 1949 of the report of the National Commission on the Organization of the Executive Branch of the Government, known as the Hoover Commission, after its chairman, Herbert Hoover. In the next few years, thirty-five states formed so-called **Little Hoover Commissions** to study reorganization. These commissions generally argued for a hierarchical form of state government structure to be built on the following six principles:[31]

1. Concentrate authority and responsibility in the governor.
2. Consolidate the many separate agencies into a small number of departments so that all agencies working in similar service areas will be grouped under the same functional department.
3. Eliminate boards for purely administrative work.
4. Coordinate staff and other administrative services.
5. Provide an independent audit.
6. Provide a governor's cabinet.

The immediate response to these recommendations was mixed,[32] but they grew increasingly popular as time went on. Between 1965 and 1991, twenty-six states underwent major administrative reorganizations that incorporated one or more of these six principles.[33] In the early 1990s, the well-publicized Winter Commission endorsed continued administrative reform at the state level with particular emphasis on reorganizations that would strengthen the governor's authority over the bureaucracy.[34]

Assessing Reorganization: Some Caveats

No conclusive studies have assessed the impact of the reorganization of state government on the kinds of policies adopted and on the delivery of services. Reformers assume that more public services can be delivered at a lower per-capita cost if state administrative activities are coordinated so that all independent agencies performing related activities are consolidated into one large department.[35] In practice, the cost savings are usually small, and lumping many small agencies into one superagency sometimes simply creates a large "garbage can" agency that is internally unmanageable.[36] One study found that reorganized states do not necessarily provide equal services for fewer dollars than unreorganized states.[37] Another study seeking to discover efficiences in reorganized states compared the performance of departments headed by a single executive (favored by reformers) with departments headed by boards or commissions (disapproved by reformers). Not only did the study fail to find that single-head departments consistently outperformed multihead departments, but the multihead departments had some advantages lacking in the single-head departments. Multihead commissions improve representation in the bureaucratic process, and they absorb public criticisms when things go poorly in the department.[38]

Other Approaches for Improving Administrative Performance

In addition to executive reorganization, administrative reformers have introduced a number of other devices to improve administrative performance.

Program Evaluation   One approach to improving administrative performance is **program evaluation.** Governments cannot make rational policy choices unless they can evaluate whether their programs attain their objectives. Without evaluation, they cannot know which programs are successful, which administrative practices work, and even which groups of employees are competent.[39] By the mid-1980s, forty-three states had adopted some form of program evaluation.[40] The methods of program evaluation run the gamut from highly sophisticated cost–benefit analyses to public opinion surveys to unsystematic anecdotal descriptions.

One of the most interesting evaluation projects in recent years was a national survey of the population, called *Bureaucratic Encounters,* seeking to measure how well people evaluated public bureaucracies. Based on a national sample, the study found that well over a majority of the population (58 percent) had used government services provided at the federal, state, and local levels. These included employment services, welfare services, and health services. People tended to give higher evaluations to the agency they encountered than to government agencies in general. For example, 71 percent of the people said that the agency they contacted had solved their personal problem satisfactorily, and 79 percent felt that they had been treated fairly. When the same people were asked to evaluate government offices generally, however, only 30 percent thought that the agencies could take care of problems, and only 42 percent thought that government offices treated people fairly.[41] These findings suggest that although government bureaucracies perform satisfactorily for their specific clients, they have serious image problems among the general population.

Management by Objectives (MBO)   Under **management by objectives** (MBO), each agency director stipulates his or her objectives for the upcoming year.[42] Once the agency head's objectives are defined, the bureau chiefs propose their objectives, which will be consistent with the director's. The subordinates of the bureau chiefs then define their objectives for the year in relation to those of the bureau chief. Theoretically, all the employees of a given department work to attain a common set of objectives for the department as a whole. Throughout the year, supervisors evaluate their subordinates' progress toward the objectives. In systems that provide merit pay, MBO can be tied to pay increases for employees so that employees who exceed their objectives get the best pay raises. Although MBO rarely works this neatly in practice, evaluation studies suggest that MBO does bring productivity gains when implemented properly.[43]

Total Quality Management (TQM)   The latest buzzword in the administrative reform movement is total quality management (TQM). Like many other public management innovations, TQM was borrowed from private industry and seeks to instill a performance-based ethos in government. Just as a private business must focus on performance that meets the needs of its customers to be profitable, TQM argues that public agencies must treat the public as customers and satisfy those customer needs if it hopes to gain and keep the public's confidence. Focusing on the public as a customer, thus, is the key to TQM, and accomplishing this goal requires the following attitudinal and behavioral adjustments in public agencies:[44]

Empowering employees to participation in decentralized agency teams that make important decisions about the planning and implementation of agency services

Basing agency decisions on the systematic analysis of data and facts about the agency's services, and how those services are provided

Seeking continual improvement in the quality of services as the agency's customers evaluate that quality

By 1994, some component of TQM had been adopted in forty states.[45]

◇ BUDGETING AS A DEVICE FOR IMPROVING EXECUTIVE MANAGEMENT

Budgeting is the most important weapon that governors and legislatures have for imposing policy control over their administrators. To the extent that they control the budget, governors can influence the overall level of expenditures, and they can decide which public services will get the largest share of the budgetary pie. The executive's ability to wield this leverage, however, depends on the extent to which a state has moved from traditional budgeting practices to newer approaches such as program budgeting and zero-base budgeting.

Traditional Budgeting

Incrementalism   Traditional budgetmaking is an incremental process.[46] An *increment* is simply a small step, and an *incremental process* is a process that moves in one direction in small steps. Budgeting is an incremental process because most agencies get a budget increase each year that makes the budget slightly larger than the previous year's. Only under extraordinary circumstances, such as the creation of a new agency or the introduction of a new federal program, does a department or agency get a substantial increase that greatly exceeds the overall budget increase. **Incrementalism** produces stability in the budgeting system. Since each agency knows it will get a slight increase each year, it also knows that it will not get cut back sharply or cut out entirely.

The Budget Timeline   The incremental process fits well into the traditional budget timeline. State agency heads make initial budget requests that far exceed their expectations. This allows the governor and the budget director to cut the requests without harming any of the agency's programs. The governor leaves the total requests high enough so that the legislature can make more cuts without damaging the governor's priorities. Finally, the legislature makes cuts that leave the agency an amount slightly larger than the previous year's budget.[47] In this way, both the governor and the legislature can tell tax-conscious citizens how much money they cut. And the program administrators can count on getting just about as much money as they really had expected.

Line-Item Budgeting   **Line-item budgeting** refers to the way that budget authorizations are listed. For example, the budget for a bureau of vocational rehabilitation might authorize expenditures for the line items of salaries, postage, mailing expenses, supplies, telephone expenses, travel, in-service training for employees, and contracted services. Although these line items enable the bureau chief to keep track of the bureau's expenditures, they do not enable him or her to compare how the bureau's money is being divided among its various programs. Nor do they allow the department head to compare how money is apportioned on a program basis. At no point do the budget director, the governor, or the legislative appropriations committees tie the line-item budget requests to actual programs in any comprehensive way. Since many services are delivered by more than one agency, the budget review process is to a considerable extent divorced from the actual operation of programs.

Earmarking Revenues   Earmarked revenues, as noted in Chapter 2, are revenues dedicated to a specific state program. Earmarking has been extremely popular with the expansion of lotteries in the 1980s, with a large share of lottery revenues typically earmarked for education or some other specific purpose. States vary widely in the extent to which they use earmarking, ranging from Rhode Island which earmarks only 5 percent of its budget to Alabama which earmarks 89 percent.[48] The argument for earmarking is that it puts some continuity in funding for specific programs and limits the ability of the governor to shift money out of those programs for his or her pet short-term projects.[49] From the budgeter's point of view, however, earmarking is a nuisance. It increases the difficulty that governors and legislators have in responding to the changing needs of changing times.

Budgeting Innovations

Because of these limitations on traditional budgeting, public administration specialists began seeking ways to make budgeting more rational and more responsive to policy leaders. The most important such innovations were program budgeting and zero-base budgeting.

Program Budgeting   In the early 1960s the U.S. Department of Defense introduced a new concept called **planning program budgeting (PPB)**. The concept quickly spread to other departments and then to the states. PPB was an extremely complicated budgeting device that attempted to eliminate the separation between program planning and budget planning that was inherent to the line-item budget. Instead of organizing the budget by traditional line items, PPB organized a budget by programs. Agencies were obliged by PPB to define each activity's objectives and to indicate how the budget amounts related to the objectives, how to accomplish the objectives in alternative ways, and whether the objectives were being accomplished. This procedure involved a **cost–benefit analysis** of programs. If five different programs operated by three different agencies deal with the education of retarded children, PPB enables the policymakers to compare the results of these programs in terms of the costs involved and the benefits received. In theory, at least, policymakers could then choose the program that brought the most benefits to the largest number of retarded children at the lowest cost.

Tying all these elements of PPB together turned out to be such an enormously complicated task that the federal government eventually abandoned it.

And in most states the elaborate PPB process never got off the ground.[50] Less elaborate attempts to institute cost-benefit planning and to draw up budgets in a program format did take hold, however. By the mid-1980s, thirty-seven states were using some form of program budgeting.[51]

Zero-Base Budgeting   As PPB began to wither, budget reformers turned their attention to **zero-base budgeting** (ZBB). Under ZBB, each agency is forced to justify its own budget from a base of zero dollars as though it were just starting to operate for the first time. In practice, department heads would be ordered to prepare budgets for different performance levels, such as 105 percent of the previous year's budget, 100 percent, and 95 percent. By examining what the department heads put in and take out at the various performance levels, governors and mayors get a good picture of what is important and what is peripheral to the running of their governments. ZBB was adopted in twenty states by the mid-1980s, but a number of them dropped it after experimenting with it for a few years.[52]

Performance Budgeting   Today, elements of these earlier budgetary innovations survive in the concept of performance budgeting. This approach gives budget increases to agencies that perform well and small increases or even decreases to agencies that perform poorly. In principle, this is a sound idea. In practice, however, it has some inherent problems. One of the problems is coming up with an objective measure of performance. Another problem concerns what to do about an underperforming agency if that agency happens to be a critical one. If a city's fire department were to underperform this year, could the mayor and city council realistically cut its budget for the following year and run the risk of major property damage when the underbudgeted department's ability to respond became even worse? Probably not.

◇ POLITICAL ECONOMY AND REENGINEERING FOR GREATER PRODUCTIVITY

As public resources become scarcer and as public confidence in government stays low, there is a growing demand for increasing the productivity of public employees. This demand is reflected in most of the reform measures examined earlier. In the 1990s, a new twist was put on the productivity demand with David Osborne's notion that we can reengineer government so that it does the "steering" of the ship of state instead of the "rowing."[53] By this the advocates of governmental reengineering mean that government should set the policy goals for society, but should spin off the implementation of these goals to the private sector. Perhaps the lynchpin of reengineering was the principle of privatization.

Privatization of Public Services

One of the hottest concepts in state and local administration since 1980 has been **privatization,** the use of private organizations to produce certain public services. Governments responsible for a given service are increasingly contracting out to private companies to produce the service for the government. The government then becomes an overseer of the service rather than a producer of it.

Privatization receives a substantial boost from a body of research comparing the cost of public service delivery with private delivery of similar services. It was found, for example, that it cost New York City garbage collectors $39.71 to collect a ton of garbage, whereas private garbage companies in adjacent suburbs could collect the same amount of refuse for only $17.28.[54] In Chicago, the city spent $1.23 to read a single water meter, but a private firm in Indianapolis was able to do the same job for 27½c.[55] To the extent that public services generally could be produced more cheaply by private companies, governments had a tremendous incentive to contract out as many services as feasible.

Scottsdale, Arizona, gained nationwide publicity when it contracted out all its fire protection services to a private company.[56] Other jurisdictions followed suit, contracting out a variety of services, from residential treatment centers for delinquent children to jails. At the local level, the services most often contracted out are refuse collection, streetlight operation, vehicle towing, hospital management, solid-waste disposal, street repair, and traffic signal maintenance. Twenty-five percent of all cities contract out those services.[57]

Is privatization always cheaper than government production of public services? No. Phoenix, Arizona, in the early 1980s began a competitive bidding procedure for handling garbage collection. At first, the private contractors underbid the city's Sanitation Department. Within a few years, however, the Sanitation Department reduced its costs by one-third and began recapturing some of the contracts it had lost.[58]

Even when privatization is cheaper, is it better than government-produced public services? Not necessarily. But the answer to this question generally reflects one's values. Much of the advantage that private contractors have over public agencies is simply the cost of the labor force. Phoenix's Department of Sanitation, for example, paid its workers $6–$7 per hour, compared to the minimum wage of $3.35 per hour that was being paid by private contractors.[59] A study of privatization in the Los Angeles area found that lower costs of privately produced services were attributed in large part to labor costs. The private contractors hired younger workers at lower pay, gave them less vacation time, and often offered no pension benefits.[60]

One of the most controversial area of privatization today is that of corrections. Seventeen states have laws that permit some of their jails, prisons, and other corrections facilities to be run by private companies. However, less than 2 percent of all inmates are held in private facilities.[61] If this number can be expanded, it will provide a lucrative business opportunity for corrections entrepreneurs. Proponents claim that they can save taxpayers up to 15 percent of the cost of housing prisoners. But critics counter that the private prisons are usually given the healthiest and easiest prisoners to manage, so their costs are unrealistically low. Critics also bristle at the idea of the state contracting out the authority to punish and detain people to profitmaking entrepreneurs.[62]

Whether privatization is *better* than government production of services in these circumstances depends in great measure on what value one ascribes to maintaining a stable labor force and what value one places on the idea of paying a livable wage to workers who provide public services. Because privatization touches so painfully on the basic question of moral values, much of the debate over privatization is highly polemical. Many of its strongest supporters are not only antiunion with little respect for ordinary workers but they are also antigovernment, viewing privatization primarily as a means to reduce the role of government in modern society.[63] Its strongest opponents are the labor unions, which take a very uncompromising attitude toward it.[64]

For the citizens trying to make up their own minds about privatization, it is useful to separate the polemics from the reasonable arguments. Some public services, such as garbage collection and water-meter reading, might be produced better by private companies under some circumstances than by government agencies. For some other public services, such as prison administration and licensing of day-care centers, the reverse is probably true. A survey of eighty-two cities in 1995 found that food services, janitorial services, and major construction projects were the activities most frequently contracted out, whereas street sweeping, jail food service, and bill collection were the least likely to be contracted out.[65]

In deciding whether to privatize a service, public officials should resist making cost efficiency the sole criterion. Charles T. Goodsell recommends a number of other criteria as well. In privatizing a service, government agencies should not give up control over the service. They should not let their own permanent workforce be undermined by privatization. The desire to produce services more cheaply should not lead them to compromise the goals of the services themselves. They should not privatize so many functions that the government itself loses its vital force for achieving public goals. And they should be careful about awarding contracts to entrepreneurs with strong political connections.[66] If these conditions are met and there are no hidden costs, then it probably makes sense to privatize a particular public service. If these conditions are not met, then officials might be well advised not to privatize the service.

Assessment

It has become imperative for state and local governments to improve their productivity. There is more at stake than simply reducing the cost of public services, however. The effective delivery of urban services makes a significant difference in the quality of our lives and the ability of private-sector institutions to function. If the potholes in our streets are not filled, our lives are less comfortable. If the police do not respond to our calls, our lives are less secure. For public managers in the 1990s, how do they ensure that the most appropriate agencies deliver the right services most effectively to the target people on time? And how do they meet the demands of cost-conscious groups that all these services be delivered at the lowest possible cost per unit of service?

SUMMARY

1. A basic tension exists between career administrators and policy-level executives, such as governors and their appointed department heads.
2. With fifteen million state and local employees, personnel management has become an awesome governmental task. Traditional patronage systems of recruitment have given way to more modern civil service personnel management practices.
3. Public bureaucracies have become key battle grounds in the social conflicts of recent years. At issue is the concept of group representation in the executive branch. Key issues are affirmative action and comparable worth.
4. State and local governments have traditionally been organized in a fragmented and ineffective manner. In order to modernize their governments, twenty-six states reorganized their executive branches between 1965 and 1991. The goals of these reorganizations are to concentrate more authority in the governor, to create a hierarchical form of organization, and to consolidate hundreds of scattered agencies into a limited number of departments that would be directly accountable to the governor.
5. A major device for improving the governor's or the mayor's ability to manage administrative departments is the budget. Budgeting at the state level has become the task of a budget director, who is usually tied closely to the governor. At the local level, budgeting is less centralized. It is most centralized in city-manager and strong-mayor systems and least centralized in weak-mayor, commission, and traditional county governments. The desire to use budgeting control over the executive branch has led to a series of budget innovations such as PPB, ZBB, and performance budgeting.
6. In the 1990s, the movement for reengineering government provided support for privatization as a means of increasing the productivity of public employees.

KEY TERMS

Affirmative action The principle that special preference should be given to minorities and women in hiring for public jobs. The objective of affirmative action is to make up for past discrimination against women and minorities.

American Federation of State, County, and Municipal Employees (AFSCME) The largest state and local government employees union.

Civil service system A form of recruitment for government jobs in which people are hired on the basis of their performance on competitive examinations or merit.

Collective bargaining The process of workers banding together and bargaining as a unit with their employer over wages and job conditions.

Comparable worth The principle that jobs of equal skill requirements should receive equal pay.

Cost–benefit analysis A budgeting procedure that weighs the costs of different programs against the benefits to be derived from them so that officials can select the programs that achieve agency goals at the lowest cost–benefit ratio.

Earmarked revenues Revenues raised from specific sources (such as gasoline taxes) that can be spent only for related purposes (such as transportation).

Equal employment opportunity The practice of giving equal opportunity to all job applicants, regardless of race or religion.

Incrementalism A budgeting process in which budgets increase annually at about the rate of inflation.

Line-item budgeting A form of budgeting in which budgets are organized by specific expenditures unrelated to specific programs.

Little Hoover Commission   A type of commission appointed in the 1950s to study the organization of state government and make recommendations for improvement. About thirty-five states formed such commissions.

Management by objectives (MBO)   A procedure in which managers and supervisors set annual objectives that are consistent with agency goals. Their performance is then measured by their ability to attain their objectives.

Merit system (employment)   A recruitment method for government that hires and promotes people on the basis of their training and competence to perform specific jobs. See *Civil service system.*

Patronage   A recruitment method for government jobs in which people are hired as a reward for their political support of the winning candidates.

Planning program budgeting   A form of budgeting organized around programs rather than line items and planned out two or three years into the future.

Privatization   The practice of governmental contracting with private firms to provide public systems.

Program evaluation   A procedure for determining if programs meet their objectives. There are three different approaches to program evaluation.

Representative bureaucracy   The concept that different ethnic and categorical groups should be represented in the public bureaucracy in proportion to their percentage of the overall population.

Zero-base budgeting   A budgeting procedure in which agencies must set various performance levels and indicate which services will be reduced as budget levels are reduced. This enables officials to set priorities on different services and programs.

REFERENCES

1. *The New York Times,* July 12, 1977, p. 12.
2. Ibid.
3. Calculated from *The Book of the States: 1982–83* (Lexington, Ky.: Council of State Governments, 1982), p. 341, and *The Book of the States: 1976–77,* p. 155.
4. Ira Sharkansky, "State Administrators in the Policy Process," in *Politics in the American States: A Comparative Analysis,* 2nd ed., Herbert Jacob and Kenneth N. Vines, eds. (Boston: Little, Brown and Co., 1971), p. 238.
5. Martin Tolchin and Susan Tolchin, *To the Victor: Political Patronage from the Clubhouse to the White House* (New York: Vintage Books, 1972), Chs. 2 and 4.
6. See *Oklahoma* v. *U.S. Civil Service Commission,* 330 U.S. 127 (1947).
7. *Elrod* v. *Burns,* 427 U.S. 347 (1976). In subsequent cases, the Supreme Court upheld the principle established in this case but allowed some exceptions. In *Branti* v. *Finkel* (1980), the Court allowed a public employee to be fired for political reasons if the employer could demonstrate that the employee's political beliefs in fact interfered with the performance of his or her duties. In *Connick* v. *Myers* (1983), the Court allowed governments to fire public employees who complained about their supervisors and their working conditions. But in 1990, the Court outlawed patronage employment in the state of Illinois. *Rutan* v. *Republican Party of Illinois* 110 S.Ct. 2729 (1990).
8. *Rutan* v. *Republican Party of Illinois* 110 S.Ct. 2729 (1990).
9. *The Book of the States: 1982–83* (Lexington, Ky.: Council of State Governments, 1982), pp. 312–313.
10. An official of the Bureau of Intergovernmental Personnel Program of the United States Civil Service Commission cites a survey that indicates that 95 percent of all local employees are covered by some form of merit system. Whether all those systems

are free of political influence, however, is debatable. See Andrew W. Boesel, "Local Personnel Management: Organized Problems and Operating Practices," *Municipal Yearbook: 1974* (Washington, D.C.: International City Management Association, 1974), pp. 92–93.

11. This was the testimony of David Osborne before the Winter Commission on State Government Organization. See Steven D. Gold, "The Compensation Conundrum," *State Legislatures* 18, no. 9 (September 1992): 21.

12. Richard C. Elling, "Bureaucracy: Maligned Yet Essential," *Politics in the American States: A Comparative Analysis*, 6th ed., Virginia Gray and Herbert Jacob, eds. (Washington, D.C.: CQ Press, 1995), p. 300.

13. According to U.S. government data, average annual wages and salaries for private workers totaled $29,367 in 1993, compared to a median salary of $30,800 for state and local employees. *Statistical Abstract of the United States: 1995*, pp. 323, 431.

14. Elling, "Bureaucracy: Maligned Yet Essential," p. 300.

15. Dennis L. Dresang, "The Politics of Civil Service Reform: Lessons from Wisconsin," a paper presented at the 1978 meeting of the Midwest Political Science Association, Chicago, April, 1978.

16. United States Bureau of the Census, *Statistical Abstract of the United States: 1995* (Washington, D.C.: U.S. Government Printing Office, 1995), p. 443.

17. Joel Douglas, "State Civil Service and Collective Bargaining: Systems in Conflict," *Public Administration Review* 52, no. 1 (January–February 1992): 162–169.

18. Mary E. Guy, "Three Steps Forward, Two Steps Backward: The States and Women's Integration into Public Management," *Public Administration Review* 53, no. 4 (July–August 1993): 285–291.

19. Angela Bullard and Deil Wright, "Circumventing the Glass Ceiling: Women Executives in American State Governments," *Public Administration Review* 53, (1993): 189–220.

20. Catherine M. Havens and Lynne M. Healy, "Do Women Make a Difference?" *Journal of State Government* 64, no. 2 (April–June 1991): 63–67.

21. *Boston Firefighters Union* v. *Boston Chapter, NAACP* 103 S.Ct. 2076 (1983).

22. *Memphis* v. *Stotts* 467 U.S. 561 (1984).

23. *Martin* v. *Wilks* 109 S.Ct. 2180 (1989).

24. *Ward's Cove Packing Co., Inc.* v. *Antonio* 109 S.Ct. 2115 (1989).

25. *Statistical Abstract of the United States: 1995*, p. 323; *Statistical Abstract of the United States: 1984*, p. 305.

26. See Elaine Soreson, *Comparable Worth: Is It a Worth Policy?* (Princeton: Princeton University Press, 1994).

27. See Steven Rhoads, *Incomparable Worth: Pay Equity Meets the Market* (Cambridge: Cambridge University Press, 1993), p. 110.

28. Peter T. Kilborn, "Wage Gap Between Sexes Is Cut in Test, but at a Price," *The New York Times*, May 31, 1990, p. 1.

29. Elling, "Bureaucracy: Maligned Yet Essential," p. 303.

30. David Osborne and Ted Gaebler, *Reinventing Government: How the Entrepreneurial Spirit Is Transforming the Public Sector* (New York: Penguin Books, 1993).

31. The original outlining of these six principles is usually attributed to A. E. Buck, *The Reorganization of State Governments in the United States* (New York: Columbia University Press, 1938), pp. 14–28. These provisions were also reiterated in an influential document of the Committee for Economic Development, *Modernizing State Government* (New York: Committee for Economic Development, 1967), pp. 49–60.

32. Karl A. Bosworth, "The Politics of Management Improvement in the States," *American Political Science Review* 47, no. 1 (March 1953): 84–99.

33. James Conant, "Executive Branch Reorganization in the States, 1965–1991," *The Book of the States* (Lexington, Ky.: Council of State Governments, 1992–1993).

34. Frank J. Thompson, "Executive Leadership as an Enduring Institutional Issue," *State and Local Government Review* 27, no. 1 (Winter 1995): 7–17.

35. York Willbern, "Administrative Organization," in *The 50 States and Their Local Governments*, James W. Fesler, ed. (New York: Knopf, 1967), pp. 341–342.

36. Elling, "Bureaucracy: Maligned Yet Essential," p. 294.

37. See Kenneth J. Meier, "Executive Reorganization of Government: Impact on Employment and Expenditures," *American Journal of Political Science* 24, no. 3 (August 1980): 396–412.

38. Charles T. Goodsell, "Collegial State Administration: Design for Today?" *Western Political Quarterly* 34, no. 3 (September 1981): 447–466.

39. See Carol H. Weiss, *Evaluation Research: Methods of Assessing Program Effectiveness* (Englewood Cliffs, N.J.: Prentice-Hall, 1972).

40. Stanley B. Botner, "The Use of Budgeting/Management Tools by State Governments," *Public Administration Review* 45, no. 2 (September/October 1985): 618.

41. Daniel Katz, et al., *Bureaucratic Encounters: A Pilot Study in the Evaulation of Government Services* (Ann Arbor, Mich.: Institute for Social Research, 1975), pp. 120, 182.

42. On MBO, see Jong Jun, "Introduction: Management by Objectives in the Public Sector," *Public Administration Review* 36, no. 1 (January–February 1976): 1–4; Frank Sherwood and William Page, "MBO and Public Management," *Public Administration Review* 36, no. 1 (January–February 1976): 5–11.

43. Robert Rodgers and John E. Hunter, "A Foundation of Good Management Practice in Government: Management by Objectives," *Public Administration Review* 52, no. 1 (January/February 1992): 27–37.

44. Evan Berman, "Implementing TQM in State Governments: A Survey of Recent Progress," *State and Local Government Review* 26, no. 1 (Winter 1994): 46–53.

45. "TQM Rings Cash Registers for States," *State Trends*, a publication of The Council of State Governments 1, no. 2 (February/March 1995): 2.

46. There are two different versions of incrementalism. The *rational incremental* version argues that the largest increments go to the agencies that run programs consistent with the short-term political interests of the legislators who approve the budget. See Charles E. Lindblom, "Decision Making in Taxation Expenditures," in National Bureau of Economic Research, *Public Finances: Needs, Sources and Utilization* (Princeton, N.J.: Princeton University Press, 1961), pp. 295–329. In contrast, the *role-constrained* model of incrementalism argues that the budget increments get determined by individual actors playing out predetermined roles. It is essentially this model that is described in the text. See Thomas J. Anton, "Roles and Symbols in the Determination of State Expenditures," *Midwest Journal of Political Science* 11, no. 1 (February 1967): 27–43.

47. Anton, "Roles and Symbols," pp. 27–40. Anton's model was derived from a study of the budgeting process in Illinois.

48. Ronald K. Snell, "The Trouble with Earmarking," *State Legislatures* 17, no. 2 (February 1991): 35.

49. Jim Rosepepe and Christopher Zimmerman, "The Case for Earmarking," *State Legislatures* 17, no. 9 (September 1991): 22–24.

50. Aaron Wildavsky says of PPB, "I have not been able to find a single example of successful implementation of PPB," and he makes specific reference to attempts at zero-base budgeting in the U.S. Department of Agriculture. See Wildavsky, *The Politics of the Budgetary Process*, 2nd ed. (Boston: Little, Brown, 1974), pp. 195, 200. Also see John

A. Worthley, "PPB: Dead or Alive?" *Public Administration Review* 34, no. 4 (July–August 1974): 393.

51. Stanley B. Botner, "The Use of Budgeting/Management Tools by State Governments," *Public Administration Review* 45, no. 2 (September/October 1985): 618.

52. ZBB was tried and then dropped in Pima County (Phoenix), Arizona, as well as in the State of Montana. See Keith J. Mueller, "Can Hungry Bureaucrats Be Forced to Diet? Zero-Base Budgets in Local Government," a paper presented at the annual meeting of the Midwest Political Science Association, Chicago, April 1980; and John S. Fitzpatrick, "Montana's Experiment with Zero-Base Budgeting," *Government* 53, no. 1 (Winter 1980): 17–21. One successful experiment with ZBB occurred in New Jersey. See Michael J. Scheiring, "Zero-Base Budgeting in New Jersey," *State Government* 49, no. 3 (Summer 1976): 174–179.

53. David E. Osborne and Ted Gaebler, *Reinventing Government: How the Entrepreneurial Spirit Is Transforming the Public Sector* (Reading, Mass.: Addison-Wesley, 1992).

54. E. S. Savas, "Municipal Monopolies Versus Competition," in *Improving the Quality of Urban Management*, vol. 8, *Urban Affairs Annual Reviews*, Willis D. Hawley and David Rogers, eds. (Beverly Hills, Calif.: SAGE Publications, 1974), p. 483.

55. Robert L. Lineberry, *Equality and Urban Policy: The Distribution of Urban Services*, vol. 39, SAGE Library of Social Research (Beverly Hills, Calif.: SAGE Publications, 1977), p. 167.

56. On Scottsdale, see Edward C. Hayes, "In Pursuit of Productivity: Management Innovation in Scottsdale," *National Civic Review* 73, no. 6 (June 1984): 273–277.

57. Data from a 1985 survey by the International City Management Assoc. Reported in *The New York Times*, May 28, 1985, p. 9.

58. *The New York Times*, April 26, 1988, p. 34.

59. Ibid.

60. Eileen Brettler Berenyi and Barbara J. Stevens, "Does Privatization Work? A Study of the Delivery of Eight Local Services," *State and Local Government Review* 20, no. 1 (Winter 1988): 11–20.

61. Donna Hunzeker, "Private Cells, Public Prisoners," *State Legislatures* 17, no. 11 (November 1991): 24–26.

62. Ibid.

63. See especially, E. S. Savas, *Privatizing the Public Sector* (Chatham, N.J.: Chatham House Publishers, 1982).

64. Linda Lampkin, "Contracting Out: Public Employees' Group Contends the Practice Has Serious Shortcomings," *American City & County* 99, no. 2 (February 1984): 49–50.

65. *The New York Times*, March 2, 1995, p. A-8.

66. Charles T. Goodsell, "Perspective on 'Privatization:' In Defense of Bureaucracy," *State Government News* 29, no. 6 (July 1986): 20–21.

12

COURTS, CRIME, AND CORRECTIONS IN AMERICAN STATES

Chapter Preview

One of the most important concerns of state and local government is the courts and their handling of crime. In this chapter, we will survey this topic by examining, in turn:

1. How the courts play important roles establishing and implementing public policy.
2. The decentralized nature of court organization and court procedures.
3. How politics is inherently embedded in the judicial process in American states.
4. How crime and its handling put state courts at the forefront of this aspect of social conflict.
5. The importance of political values in setting and carrying out criminal justice policies.

Let us begin by looking at three of the most publicized cases in recent history.

◇ INTRODUCTION

The last several years have been hard on the public image of state courts. A few highly publicized criminal cases left many citizens shaking their heads in ways that seemed to exacerbate rather than ease the great social conflicts that we have been considering in this book. Consider, for example, three cases from California, a state whose court system had up to this time been one of the best regarded in the nation. In 1996, O. J. Simpson was acquitted of murdering his ex-wife. The evidence against Simpson was strong, but not strong enough to convince the jury, which deliberated for a mere two hours before rendering its verdict.

Whether or not Simpson committed the murder, the public's opinion of the case was fascinating, to say the least. Three-fourths of whites surveyed thought that he was guilty, whereas two-thirds of blacks thought that he was innocent.[1]

At least in the Simpson case, there were no eyewitnesses to the crime, and honest people could differ about the interpretation of ambiguous evidence, but in two other cases, the criminal deed had been stored on videotape. In 1993, a predominantly nonblack jury acquitted four white police officers of using excessive force when arresting Rodney King, a black man who had led them on a high-speed chase through Los Angeles. This acquittal astonished most people because network television had broadcast scenes of the officers raining more than eighty blows on King with their nightsticks while King lay prostrate on the ground. African Americans were outraged at the acquittal, and Los Angeles erupted in one of the nation's worst urban riots. During the course of that riot, a black man, Damian Williams, was also recorded on videotape picking up a concrete block and throwing it into the skull of a white driver who had been pulled out of his truck and was laying helpless on the ground. When brought to trial, Williams was acquitted of attempted murder by a predominantly black jury.[2] One juror told the media that she had voted for acquittal because she felt that Williams had just gotten caught up in the spirit of the riot and just happened to be in the wrong place at the wrong time,[3] suggesting that evidence was a less compelling argument to her than ethnic solidarity.

Were these cases aberrations? Are the courts generally more competent than this at rendering justice? Or have we become a nation so splintered by ethnic and ideological antagonisms that justice is impossible?

In addition to the questions about the ability of courts to render justice in criminal cases, state and local courts have been attacked for their handling of some highly publicized civil cases. A tort award of nearly a million dollars for being burned by a spilt cup of coffee. Generous malpractice awards against physicians that united the medical and insurance industries in an effort to put a cap on such judgments. Court involvement in the administrative affairs of schools and prisons. Politically divisive decisions on issues such as abortion and school desegregation. Court decisions in New Jersey forcing the state to adopt an income tax in order to reduce the funding disparities among the state's school districts.

Whatever one thinks of the merits of these decisions, it is clear that state and local courts today are in the forefront of the great social conflicts that confront the nation. The judicial branch is no longer the "least dangerous" branch of government, as Alexander Hamilton called it 200 years ago.[4] In this chapter, we will discuss five major facets of state court systems: (1) public policy and the courts, (2) the organization of court systems, (3) the role of politics in American courts, (4) crime and the legal system in America, and (5) political values as they affect the criminal justice system. Although we will focus heavily on crime and criminal justice to illustrate the courts at work, it is important to note that the bulk of court time and resources is probably spent with civil cases.

◇ PUBLIC POLICY AND THE COURTS

State and local courts play three major roles in the creation and implementation of public policy. First, the courts resolve legal disputes. Second, they help set many public policies. And third, they get intimately involved in the administration of some of these policies.

Resolving Legal Disputes and Administering Justice

The primary role of the courts is to resolve legal disputes. These may be disputes of **civil law** or of **criminal law.** In civil cases, one individual or group sues another, and the court's job is to settle the dispute and determine whether damages will be awarded. Typical civil cases involve divorce, settlement of estates, and malpractice suits. In criminal cases, the government prosecutes an individual for violating a law. The court is called on to determine whether the accused person is guilty and, if guilty, to apply a jail sentence, fine, or other punishment prescribed by state law. A serious crime such as murder, arson, or theft of large amounts of money is called a **felony.** A lesser crime is called a **misdemeanor.** Although criminal cases usually get more media attention, the overwhelming majority of cases handled in court are civil cases.

Setting Public Policy

As they go about their primary business of resolving disputes, state courts often establish public policies. They do this mainly by interpreting the law and by determining whether a law is constitutional (**judicial review**). When a state supreme court declares a law unconstitutional, that law becomes unenforceable, and the court establishes a new policy. When judges engage in extensive policy-making that overturns policies of legislatures or governors, the judges are sometimes said to be practicing **judicial activism;** and when they limit themselves to narrow interpretations of the law that do not challenge legislative or gubernatorial policy, they are said to exercise **judicial restraint.** Whether judges should exercise activism or restraint is a highly controversial issue that is seldom separated from the purposes for which judicial activism is used. Conservatives object when judicial activism is used for liberal purposes but not when it is used for conservative purposes. Liberals object to conservative judicial activism but not to liberal activism.

The judicial review role of the state courts is carried out primarily by the state supreme courts. The lower courts are limited to applying the law. Most cases are simply applications of previous decisions, referred to as *precedents.* Lower state courts can nevertheless make an impact on public policy by issuing declaratory judgments, injunctions, and cease-and-desist orders. A **declaratory judgment** is a legally binding court order, and anyone who disobeys it is liable for a fine or a jail sentence. The **injunction** and the **cease-and-desist order** are court orders to stop some particular action. Such court orders can be used to set public policy. For example, courts that consistently use these powers to stop strikes or to permit nonunion workers to take the jobs of striking workers are clearly setting a legal policy that is pro-management and antiunion.

Distributive or Redistributive Policies? The most frequent conflict between liberal values and conservative values in court occurs when judges must choose between a **distributive policy** and a **redistributive policy.** Throughout most of American history, state and local court policies have been distributive; that is, they have followed a conservative pattern of reinforcing the existing distribution of wealth and influence. But in the New Jersey school finance case (see pp. 80–81), the court's aim was clearly redistributive. The state supreme court forced the state to adopt an income tax that would take money from people in well-to-do areas of the state and redistribute it to poor school districts.

Perhaps nowhere have recent redistributive decisions of state courts been more controversial than in those cases in which the courts have sympathized with plaintiffs against doctors in malpractice suits, against manufacturing corporations in product liability suits, and against insurance companies in a variety of personal injury and liability suits. These types of suits for damages fall under a category of common law called *torts.* In the wake of some highly publicized tort cases that awarded extremely lucrative settlements for the plaintiffs, insurance companies raised malpractice rates and liability rates. Physicians, in particular, reacted by threatening to withhold services because they did not want to pay the high malpractice rates. And in state after state, the 1980s saw vicious battles between trial lawyers, doctors, insurance companies, and manufacturers, as state legislatures sought to limit the amount of damages that courts could award to plaintiffs in such tort cases.[5]

Administration of Public Services

Another controversial area of judicial activism has been court administration of public services. This has sometimes happened when a court found a public service to be operating in violation of constitutional principles. The Alabama prison system, for example, was found by federal courts to be so overcrowded and so brutal in its living conditions that the court took over the entire prison system in the 1980s and held control of it until a series of prison reforms were adopted.[6]

◇ COURT ORGANIZATION AND PROCEDURE

A dual court system exists in the United States—the federal court system and the state court systems. But there is a fair amount of overlap in their jurisdictions, for crimes such as kidnapping, sale of illegal narcotics, and robbery of federally insured banks violate both state and federal laws. For such crimes, a person could be prosecuted in either the state or the federal courts, depending on a number of factors, although most such prosecutions occur in state courts. In the Rodney King incident cited earlier, the four police officers who beat King were prosecuted at both levels. First they were acquitted under California law. Then they were convicted in a federal court for violating King's civil rights not to be abused by public officials. The judgment of the state courts is final and cannot be

Figure 12-1 STRUCTURE OF A TYPICAL COURT SYSTEM

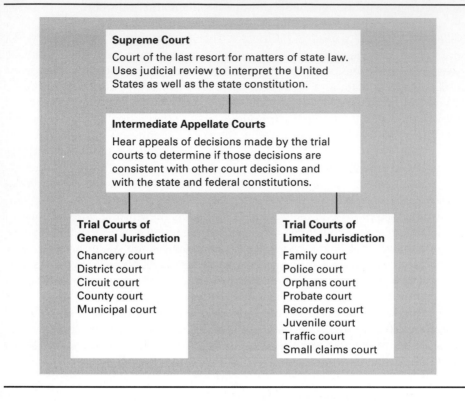

Supreme Court

Court of the last resort for matters of state law. Uses judicial review to interpret the United States as well as the state constitution.

Intermediate Appellate Courts

Hear appeals of decisions made by the trial courts to determine if those decisions are consistent with other court decisions and with the state and federal constitutions.

Trial Courts of General Jurisdiction

Chancery court
District court
Circuit court
County court
Municipal court

Trial Courts of Limited Jurisdiction

Family court
Police court
Orphans court
Probate court
Recorders court
Juvenile court
Traffic court
Small claims court

appealed to the U.S. Supreme Court unless the case involves a *federal question*—a violation of either federal law or the U.S. Constitution.

A Decentralized Court System

In Figure 12-1 the organization of a typical state court system looks hierarchically structured. At the top is the court of last resort, usually called a supreme court.* It hears appeals from the trial courts. Forty states have created intermediate appellate courts under the supreme court to reduce the work loads of the supreme courts. Like the U.S. Supreme Court, these courts primarily hear appeals only to determine if proper judicial procedures were followed in the trial court or to make an interpretation of the law or the constitution. With the task for making such decisions removed from the supreme courts, the supreme courts can generally do a more thorough job of focusing on the most important constitutional and legal problems.[7]

At the bottom of the organization chart are the trial courts, where the parties present their testimony, facts are investigated, and a judicial decision is made.

---

*Two states—Maryland and New York—simply call the court of last resort the court of appeals. Confusing matters somewhat, New York uses the term *supreme court* to refer to its trial courts of general jurisdiction. Texas and Oklahoma have two supreme courts, one for civil cases and the other for criminal cases.

For trial courts of general jurisdiction, the state is divided into districts, and thus these courts are usually called district courts, county courts, municipal courts, or sometimes circuit courts or chancery courts. All major criminal and civil cases are tried in these courts.

For minor criminal cases such as misdemeanors, for civil cases involving relatively small sums of money, or for specialized problems such as traffic tickets and divorces, courts of limited jurisdiction are used. Small claims courts, for example, deal with civil cases in which the amount of damages is small and the parties can present their testimony in person without the expense of hiring a lawyer.[8] Another option for resolving civil disputes is alternative dispute resolution under which a neutral third party meets with the disputants and helps mediate a solution to their disagreement.

Keeping Judges Honest

Public faith in the court system depends as much as anything on ensuring that judges act ethically and competently, and adhere to professional standards. There is little to restrain a judge from vindictive or unprofessional behavior while on the bench, and every state has its own examples of this. In the famous "Greylord" scandal, four Chicago judges and a court clerk were convicted of bribery and corruption for fixing cases.[9] A Rhode Island chief justice resigned in 1986 under threat of impeachment for his ties with organized crime.[10] And a Wisconsin judge was recalled in 1977 for statements offensive to women in his handling of a sexual abuse case (see "Highlight," p. 298).

But recall, impeachment, and criminal prosecution are not systematic ways of holding judges accountable. To provide systematic restraints, all the states have created judicial-performance commissions to investigate charges of judicial impropriety. These commissions allow any citizen to make a complaint about improper judicial behavior. Most of these complaints focus not on corruption or bribery but on slow decisions or improper courtroom behavior, such as appearing on the **Bench** (another term for *court*) smelling of alcohol and using abusive, sexist, or racist language. In a recent year (1987), the American Judicature Society counted 5,827 complaints made to judicial performance commissions. Ninety-two percent of these were dismissed as frivolous (usually filed by some one who disliked a judge's decision), 126 judges were censured for their behavior, and 21 were removed from office.[11] Considering that there are 17,000 judges in the country and that any person can bring a complaint against a judge for any reason, these numbers suggest that the average person appearing in court stands a fairly decent chance of being treated in a professional and acceptable manner.

◇ POLITICS IN AMERICAN COURTS

Politics can enter the judicial process in various ways, three of which are of specific importance. First, the selection of judges is itself a political act. Second, judicial decisions are influenced by the political and socioeconomic backgrounds of the judges. Last, the courts become the focus of interest group activity.

HIGHLIGHT

How Should Judges Be Removed?

Unless they severely violate deeply felt community values, judges can normally serve for as long as they want or until they reach their state's mandatory retirement age. Judge Archie Simonson blatantly affronted community values in Madison, Wisconsin. In 1977, two black youths, aged fourteen and fifteen, were charged with sexually assaulting a sixteen-year-old white girl in a Madison high school. A third teenage boy became a state's witness and was not charged. Judge Simonson sent the fourteen-year-old boy to a group home in Milwaukee but released the fifteen-year-old to the custody of his parents. The prosecuting attorney argued that the fifteen-year-old should also be placed in a group home. Judge Simonson replied that Madison was a sexually permissive community and suggested that the youth had been reacting normally in committing the sexual assault. When asked to apologize for these remarks, Simonson refused. Feminist groups in Madison collected enough petition signatures to set up a special recall election. The election was held in September 1977, and Judge Simonson was replaced by Moira Krueger, a specialist in juvenile law. This was the first time in thirty-five years that a judge anywhere in the United States had been recalled.

Source: *The New York Times,* September 8, 9, 11, 1977.

Selecting Judges

Five selection methods exist, as Table 12-1 shows, and all five are political. Political party interests benefit most from partisan elections of judges or from direct appointments by the governor or the legislature. Under these methods, party supporters and contributors with many years' service to the party, legislators, or the governor can be rewarded with nominations or appointments to the bench. In states with strong political machines, such as New York and Pennsylvania, the judges can be called on to contribute a portion of their salaries to political campaigns. If politically sensitive issues come before these courts, the party in power can hope that the judges will look out for the party's vital interests. Not surprisingly, judges with political party connections in those states benefiting from party selection resist proposals for a merit plan of selection.[12] Most judges, however, prefer a merit plan of selection or, as a second choice, election on a nonpartisan ballot.[13]

Judicial reformers strive for nonpartisan elections or, better yet from their viewpoint, **merit plans** of selection. Since the first merit plan was put into practice in Missouri in 1930, such plans are known as **Missouri Plans.** Under such plans a nominating commission suggests a list of three nominees to the governor, who must select the judge from among those three. The nominating commission usually includes a governor-appointed citizen member, a judge, and representatives of the bar association. The bar association is a formal organization of lawyers that sets standards for admitting lawyers to practice and ethical codes that govern the lawyers' conduct. Under the merit plan, bar associations usually dominate the selection of nominees sent to the governor. After appointment by the governor, the judge stays in office for a year and then must stand

Table 12.1   METHODS OF SELECTING JUDGES FOR APPELLATE AND MAJOR TRIAL COURTS

Much Party Influence and Little Bar Influence		Little Party Influence and Much Bar Influence	
Partisan Election	**Appointment**	**Nonpartisan Election**	**Merit Plan**
Alabama	*By governor*	Georgia	Alaska
Arkansas	Delaware	Idaho	Arizona
Illinois	Hawaii	Kentucky	California
Mississippi	Maine	Louisiana	Colorado
New York	Massachusetts	Michigan	Florida
North Carolina	New Hampshire	Minnesota	Indiana
Pennsylvania	New Jersey	Montana	Iowa
Tennessee	Vermont	Nevada	Kansas
Texas		North Dakota	Maryland
West Virginia	*By legislature*	Ohio	Missouri
	Connecticut	Oregon	Nebraska
	Rhode Island	Washington	New Mexico
	South Carolina	Wisconsin	Oklahoma
	Virginia		South Dakota
			Utah
			Wyoming

Source: Calculated from *The Book of the States: 1992–93* (Lexington, Ky.: Council of State Governments, 1992), pp. 233–235.

unopposed in a retention election on the merits of his or her record in office. Needless to say, very few judges lose their elections for retention.[14] Unlike federal judges who hold their positions for life, most state judges serve terms of six to eight years. Only three states have life tenure for judges.

Does Merit Selection Make Any Difference?   Notwithstanding its merits, the merit plan does not remove politics from the judicial selection process. Missouri, the birthplace of the merit plan, was rocked by a scandal in 1985 that involved overt partisan manipulation of its merit plan of selection. One Supreme Court appointment went to an allegedly poorly qualified governor's aide, and two other Supreme Court appointments were apparently engineered by the Republican State Party chairperson.[15]

The most controversial example of the inherent political nature of judicial selection was that of California Chief Justice Rose Bird. Appointed by Governor Jerry Brown in 1977, she narrowly won her first retention election in 1978. In her 1986 re-election bid, she faced a $7 million conservative Republican campaign to unseat her because of her opposition to the death penalty. Two other supreme court justices went down to defeat with Bird in November 1986, thus enabling conservative Governor George Deukmejian, an outspoken Bird foe, to appoint a new, conservative majority to the court.[16] Whereas the court under Bird's chief justiceship upheld only 4 out of 68 death penalty cases it reviewed, in the next 4 years the court upheld 84 out of the 109 death penalties it reviewed.[17]

Not only did the merit plan fail to remove politics from judicial selection, it also failed to meet reformers' expectations that it would produce judges from more relevant legal backgrounds and prestigious law schools. A study of 324 state supreme court justices from the 50 states in 1980–1981 found that the merit plan had no advantage over other selection methods in getting judges from prestigious law schools or judges with relevant legal experience. The study did find, however, that merit plans had some biases of their own. The states with merit plans systematically had fewer Catholics or Jews on their supreme courts than did states with other selection methods.[18] Blacks, by contrast, fared better when their initial move to a judgeship was by appointment rather than by election.[19] Judges are often elected from multijudge districts that can put black candidates at a disadvantage just as at-large city council districts often put black candidates at a disadvantage. These types of judicial elections have been increasingly struck down by federal courts,[20] and as a result there should be an increasing number of black judges in the future.

Reformers also expected that since appointed judges do not have to gain popular support, merit plan judges would be more apt than elected judges to support upper-class economic interests and be tougher on criminal defendants. However, a study of the highest appellate courts in the fifty states found that the method of selecting judges had no significant impact on the kinds of decisions made. Elected judges were just as likely as appointed judges to espouse upper-class economic interests or to favor the prosecution rather than the criminal defendant.[21] Judges are not immune to electoral considerations, however. A study of southern supreme court justices found that elected justices were sometimes swayed by constituent opinion in death penalty cases if it looked as if the justice faced a tough re-election battle.[22]

The Policy Influence of Judges' Backgrounds

Studies of judicial decisions have consistently found a relationship between the backgrounds of judges and the kinds of decisions they make. In workers' compensation cases, for example, Catholic or Democratic judges are much more likely than are Protestant or Republican judges to hand down decisions that favor workers over employers. In criminal cases, Catholic or Democratic judges are much more likely than Protestant or Republican judges to rule in favor of defendants rather than plaintiffs.[23]

Although the patterns vary from state to state,[24] significant partisan differences were found on fifteen different kinds of cases, ranging from unemployment compensation to the governmental regulation of business. You are much better off in front of a Democratic or Catholic judge if you are a tenant being sued by a landlord, a consumer seeking damages for shoddy merchandise bought under misleading sales tactics, a person injured in an automobile accident, or a government tax lawyer seeking to collect more taxes from a taxpayer. Conversely, you are much better off in front of a Republican or Protestant judge if you are the landlord, the merchant being sued for unfair sales tactics, the insurance company being sued in the automobile case, or the taxpayer being sued for more taxes by the government.

Do the racial and gender background of judges also make a difference in their decisions? Apparently so. But not always in the direction that one would expect. A study of judicial decisions over a ten-year period in a major metropolitan area found that black judges were more likely than white ones to send defendants to prison, but they also tended to hand out shorter sentences than did the white judges. Moreover, black judges sent black defendants and white defendants to prison in about equal proportions, whereas white judges sent a higher percentage of black defendants to prison than white defendants.[25] Another study found that female judges in one metropolitan area were more likely than male judges to send women defendants to prison.[26]

These relationships between judges' backgrounds and court decisions do not mean that justice is impossible and that judges are arbitrary. But the relationships do demonstrate quite clearly that judges are human and that their decisions reflect the values they have acquired over a lifetime, in part as a result of their religious, political, and racial backgrounds.

Pressure Group Influence

Pressure group activities are more subtle in the judicial arena than in the legislature or administrative agencies. Although lobbyists can contribute to judges' reelection campaigns, they cannot use business luncheons, cocktail parties, or other entertainments to influence judicial opinions. They also have to be more restrained and formal in presenting information they hope will sway judges' opinions. They are restricted largely to two major tactics: initiating litigation and presenting **amicus curiae** (or "friend of the court") briefs in cases filed by other contestants.

Political interests used both of these tactics to try to influence the courts in the New Jersey school finance case that we examined earlier (pp. 80–81). As an eleven-year-old child from a middle-class family, Kenneth Robinson had neither the financial resources nor the legal knowledge to wage what would be a six-year legal battle to reform New Jersey's system of school finance. He was carefully recruited to file the suit by the mayor of Jersey City and his legal adviser. Once the suit was filed, several interest groups—including local chapters of the National Association for the Advancement of Colored People (NAACP) and the American Civil Liberties Union (ACLU)—filed amicus curiae briefs in which they provided the court with strong arguments and much data to support the striking down of New Jersey's reliance on local property taxes to finance public education.[27]

Probably the most important outside influence on state courts is the state attorney general who frequently files lawsuits in the state courts. Attorneys general win about two-thirds of the cases they litigate before their supreme courts. This is a much higher batting average than any other category of litigant.[28]

◇ COURTS AND SOCIAL CONFLICT: COPING WITH CRIME

Courts, like other governing institutions, are obliged to deal with the great social conflicts of our time. One of the most important arenas of social conflicts for the court system is crime. To explore the courts' handling of crime and the social conflicts surrounding it, we need to eaxmine (1) the different kinds of crime and trends in crime, (2) how the courts process criminal cases, and (3) how different political values influence law enforcement and correctional policies.

Crime

Because different kinds of crime have different degrees of impact on society, it is useful to detail the important distinctions among them.

Index Crime　Index crime refers to the crimes listed annually in the Uniform Crime Reports of the Federal Bureau of Investigation (FBI). These are all the crimes reported each year by police departments. They are divided into two major categories—crimes against property (larceny of $50 or more, burglary, auto theft) and crimes against persons (assault, forcible rape, robbery, murder). *Assault, auto theft, rape,* and *murder* are self-explanatory. *Robbery* is stealing someone's property through the threat or use of force. *Burglary* is the act of entering a building unlawfully to commit a felony or a theft. In robbery, the thief directly threatens the victim or forces him or her to hand over a purse, wallet, or some other valuable. In burglary, usually no direct confrontation occurs between thief and victim. More than twelve million index crimes are reported by the police each year.

　　Because index crime refers only to reported crimes, the Uniform Crime Reports index has been subjected to considerable criticism.[29] Since much crime goes unreported,[30] the Uniform Crime Reports index greatly understates the amount of actual crime, especially rapes and assaults. Police departments are widely known to distort their reports for political purposes—to get a bigger budget, to respond to newspaper criticisms, or to cover up administrative problems.[31] For all these reasons, the FBI has been studying ways to improve the Uniform Crime Reports.[32] **White-collar crimes** (embezzlement, fraud, and commercial theft, for example) are not included in the FBI index. The President's Commission on Law Enforcement and the Administration of Justice argued that white-collar crime was just as costly to society, if not more so, than index crime.[33]

Organized Crime　The FBI crime index also does not provide a sufficient accounting of *organized crime.* The index does not indicate how much crime is attributable to organized criminal elements and how much of it is done by isolated individuals or gangs.

　　U.S. government reports during the 1960s argued that in the United States a national confederation exists of twenty-four criminal organizations or families called La Cosa Nostra or the Mafia.[34] These families are located in the big cities of the Northeast, the Great Lakes states, the South, and the Southwest. They control prostitution, narcotics, and gambling activities—especially gambling on major league sports such as football and horse racing. The 24 families comprise about 5,000 men who, these reports say, are all Italian. This "Italian organization in fact controls all but an insignificant proportion of the organized-crime activities in the United States" and may involve as many as 100,000 people.[35]

This official version of organized crime has been criticized as too romantic,[36] and too inclined to assume a business organization structure of crime,[37] and too inclined to associate organized crime with Italian communities.[38] Actually, many ethnic groups have contributed heavily to organized crime, and a path of ethnic succession has been traced.[39] Until the 1920s, it was dominated by Irish, Jews, and Germans.[40] Italian dominance came later and appears to have peaked in the 1960s. Much of the lower-class narcotics and numbers-racket activities in minority neighborhoods has been taken over by blacks, Latinos, and Asians.[41] Italian spokespersons have vigorously objected to linking their nationality to the Mafia, and whatever dominance Italians may have had in organized crime at one time was shattered, perhaps irreversibly, by a number of successful trials in the 1980s, culminating in the 1986 conviction of the top Cosa Nostra leadership in the country.

The most devastating impact of organized crime in the 1990s is its distribution of illegal drugs—especially crack and cocaine. The leaders of these distribution networks are primarily Cubans, Colombians, and Nicaraguan contra leaders instead of Italians. The widespread use of drugs is disastrous for the social fabric of many inner cities, leading to violent street crime. One study found that one-half to three-quarters of men arrested for serious crime in twelve cities in 1988 tested positive for drugs in their blood.[42] Despite a succession of "drug czars" in Washington and a dramatic stiffening of penalties for drug use and drug trafficking, criminal justice experts do not at this point see any realistic way either to reduce drug use or to neutralize the new Latino-based organized crime groups that are becoming so powerful.[43]

Crime Trends   As Figure 12-2 shows, the growth of crime was explosive in the 1970s but has slowed dramatically in the 1990s. Some cities saw spectacular reductions in crime rates. New York City, for example, experienced a 14 percent drop in overall crime rates between 1994 and 1995, and saw its murder rates drop by 25 percent.[44] Do not expect this lull in the crime trend to last much longer, however. Much of the trend's decline was due to the aging of the baby boomer generation that was born between 1945 and 1964. Since most crime is committed by people in their late teens and early twenties, a crime rate drop-off was inevitable as the huge baby boomer generation moved into middle age. A new surge in the late-teen to early-twenties age cohort is expected by the turn of the century, however, and this age cohort already experiences very high rates of violent crime,[45] so the current drop in crime rates probably will not continue.

Crime and the Courts   In examining the court's role in crime policy, it is very important to keep in mind that the criminal justice process is only one of the many factors that influence crime, and the courts do not have control over these

Figure 12-2   THE CRIME EXPLOSION

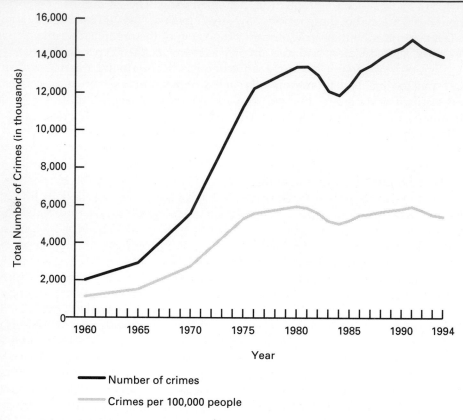

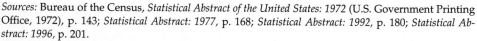

━━━━ Number of crimes

░░░░ Crimes per 100,000 people

Sources: Bureau of the Census, *Statistical Abstract of the United States: 1972* (U.S. Government Printing Office, 1972), p. 143; *Statistical Abstract: 1977*, p. 168; *Statistical Abstract: 1992*, p. 180; *Statistical Abstract: 1996*, p. 201.

other factors. Demographic change, as we saw, is a prime variable over which the courts have no control, as are growing inequalities in wealth distribution, laws passed by legislatures, and implementation of those laws by administrators. Finally, courts do not control society's values toward crime. Some criminologists argue that crime exploded in the 1970s because society became more tolerant of criminal deviant behavior than that it was a generation earlier.[46]

The Jury System   There are two types of juries—the grand jury and the trial jury. The **grand jury** is an official panel of citizens who investigate a crime and determine whether there is enough evidence to warrant filing charges. If a grand jury finds sufficient evidence, it reports a *true bill,* or indictment. Few states require indictment by grand jury. A majority of states gives the prosecutor some discretion in calling a grand jury. Prosecutors file most of the criminal charges.

They rely on the grand jury only for cases that are extremely sensitive, such as those involving public officials or organized crime.

Trial juries can be used in either civil cases or criminal cases. In civil cases the trial jury decides which party deserves to be awarded damages and sometimes sets the amounts. In criminal cases, the trial jury's role is to determine whether a defendant is guilty. Traditionally, conviction requires a unanimous verdict of twelve jurors persuaded "beyond a reasonable doubt" that the defenant is guilty. And it was probably this reasonable doubt concept that came into play in the famous jury decisions we noted earlier. If you are a juror, regardless of your feelings about the defendant's race or whether your intuition tells you he or she committed the act, if you have a "reasonable doubt" about his or her guilt in the specific charge before you, then you are duty bound under American law to vote for acquittal. Because of this standard, it often is very difficult to obtain unanimity among twelve jurors. In reaction, some states have relaxed this requirement. Louisiana permits convictions on a vote of only nine of the twelve jurors. Florida now permits six-member juries instead of the traditional twelve. As jury size gets smaller, the chances of a hung jury decrease. Relying on this experience, the Supreme Court in 1978 refused to approve five-person juries.[47] Arizona plans to allow jurors to take notes and to send questions to witnesses. And several states are cutting back exemptions from jury service usually given to professionals.[48] The hope is that these reforms will help produce juries better qualified to weigh evidence and follow complicated logical arguments.

Money and Criminal Justice A second area highlighted by the O. J. Simpson trial is the role of money. A complicated trial can easily involve court fees, lawyers' fees, fees for investigators and court recorders, costs for getting witnesses to testify, and expenses for specialists such as accountants, psychiatrists, scientists, and jury selection consultants. Without a multimillion dollar fortune, Simpson never could have mounted his high-priced defense. If a person cannot afford a lawyer, the state is obliged to provide one (usually called a public defender),[49] but the quality of these court-appointed lawyers varies from state to state.[50] Certainly, no public defender could have mounted the defense that Simpson's lawyers mounted. In civil cases, the federal government established the Legal Services Corporation to provide lawyers for poor people.[51]

Bail is a sum of money an accused person must deposit with the court to ensure that he or she will show up for trial. People without money must borrow from a bail bondsperson at a very high interest rate or stay in jail until their case comes to trial. For persons acquitted of the charges against them, the time spent in jail awaiting trial is a travesty of justice. A study in Baltimore found that 38 percent of felony defendants were kept in jail right up to the moment of their trial,[52] greatly compounding their difficulty in finding witnesses and taking other actions that might help their defense. As a consequence of experiences like this, the 1970s and 1980s saw a number of programs to release suspects without bail—on their own recognizance—if the suspects were reputable people with a job and stable residential history. Kentucky's experience with this and other pretrial release programs was so successful that it abolished all commercial bail bondspersons.[53]

By the 1990s, criticism was being raised about pretrial release programs in the conservative press. One such criticism cited a U.S. Justice Department study in the seventy-five largest counties that found that one-third of defendants in serious felony cases were released without bail. About one-fourth of these failed to turn up for their trials, and about one-tenth of them committed another felony while out on pretrial release. Defendants who had been released on bail were much more likely to show up for their trial and much less likely to commit crimes while out on bail.[54]

Plea Bargaining   A third target of criticism is the practice of **plea bargaining**. The prosecutor may have several possible charges on which to prosecute the defendant, but the evidence on the most serious charge may not be strong enough to win a conviction. So the prosecutor may offer to drop the most serious charge if the defendant will plead guilty to a lesser charge. From the defendant's point of view, the certainty of a short sentence for the lesser charge might be preferable to risking a conviction and a possibly long sentence on the serious charge. The defendant and the prosecutor thus bargain with each other until they reach an agreement about the plea that the defendant will make. Hence the term *plea bargaining*. Plea bargaining is so popular that probably no more than 20 percent of all persons charged with a felony go to trial.[55] The overwhelming majority plead guilty to a lesser charge.

Plea bargaining has both its opponents and its defenders. Opponents of plea bargaining view the compromises made as inherently contrary to the ideal of impartial justice. The bargaining inevitably leads to different punishment levels for the same crime. Defenders of plea bargaining point out that criminal courts would be intolerably overloaded with cases if plea bargaining were eliminated. In this view, the overloaded courts and the long delays in getting to trial would provoke much more injustice than does plea bargaining. These arguments appear to be persuasive to state legislators, who have chosen not to abolish plea bargaining, and to the American Bar Association, which would prefer to see the practice refined and improved.[56]

Minimum Standards of Justice   Attaining a high quality of justice also depends on the substantive decisions that judges make and the tactics that police use to get evidence. The idea of justice would be a sham, for example, if court standards were so lax that police were permitted to torture their suspects in order to gain confessions or if court standards were so rigid that nobody ever got convicted.

Between these extremes has been a wide variety of minimum standards of justice in the fifty states. Although some disparities may be acceptable, the U.S. Supreme Court has ruled that most of the provisions of the Fourth, Fifth, Sixth, and Fourteenth Amendments to the U.S. Constitution should be applied with consistency in all the states. The application of these federal provisions to the states is called the *incorporation* of the **Bill of Rights**.

Although the Supreme Court never stated that the establishment of minimum standards of justice was its goal, its decisions have effectively accomplished this. Table 12-2 outlines the major Supreme Court cases addressing the question of minimum standards of justice. Probably the most controversial cases have been those involving the exclusionary rule, the Miranda rule, and the death penalty.

The **exclusionary rule** states that illegally seized evidence may not be used against a defendant in a trial. The rule was first applied to the states in *Mapp* v. *Ohio*.[57] Cleveland police officers had asked to search the home of Dollree Mapp for a suspect in a bombing. When she refused to let them enter, they forcibly broke in and searched the house. They did not find the suspect they claimed to be seeking, but they did find pornographic materials that were illegal under an Ohio statute. The police confiscated the materials and prosecuted Ms. Mapp for violating the pornography law. In court the police could not produce a search warrant entitling them to search the Mapp home, thus making the search illegal. Mapp had been convicted on the basis of the evidence, but the Supreme Court overturned the conviction on the grounds that the illegally seized evidence should have been excluded from the trial.

The **Miranda rule** was established in *Miranda* v. *Arizona*.[58] In that case, the Supreme Court ruled that police must advise a suspect of the right to speak to a lawyer before interrogation. At issue was Miranda's conviction for rape. Miranda had confessed while being questioned by the police; however, Miranda had not asked to see an attorney. The Supreme Court overturned his conviction and issued very specific rules prescribing that police must inform suspects of their constitutional rights to remain silent and to see an attorney. As a result of this case, police officers began carrying so-called Miranda cards. These cards spelled out the suspect's constitutional rights to remain silent and to see a lawyer. On arresting a suspect, the police officer would read the card out loud to the suspect.

Relaxing the Minimum Standards   In recent years, the exclusionary rule and the Miranda rule have been relaxed somewhat. The Supreme Court upheld the conviction of a man who had given police incriminating evidence before he had a chance to see his attorney. Thomas Innis had been picked up by police on suspicion of murder and was being transported by police officers in a police car. When the car passed a home for retarded children near the scene of the crime, one of the officers began speculating aloud that one of the retarded children might find the gun used in the murder and get injured or injure someone else. Innis then led the officers to the gun, and it was used as evidence in his trial. Although his lawyers later asked to have the gun excluded as evidence because it violated both the Miranda rule and the exclusionary rule, the evidence was not excluded, Innis was convicted, and the Supreme Court upheld his conviction.[59]

In the 1980s, the Supreme court permitted a "good-faith exception" that would allow illegally seized evidence to be used in court if the police officer involved believed in good faith that the seizure was legal.[60]

A third area where the setting of minimum standards has generated controversial court decisions involves the death penalty. In 1972, the Supreme Court struck down the death penalty as arbitrary and capricious.[61] In reaction to that decision, several states rewrote their death penalty laws in order to make them less arbitrary, and most of these have been upheld. Thirty-six states now have

Table 12-2   SETTING MINIMUM STANDARDS OF JUSTICE: INCORPORATING THE BILL OF RIGHTS INTO STATE CRIMINAL LAW

Expanding the Minimum Standards		Relaxing the Minimum Standards	
1957	If a suspect is not taken before a judge as soon as possible after arrest, any unnecessary delay will make it impossible to admit into court any confession made prior to being brought before the judge. *Mallory* v. *United States*	1971	If a suspect during a legal interrogation contradicts any voluntary statements made prior to seeing a lawyer, those prior statements may be used as a basis for further questioning. *Harris* v. *New York*
1961	If a person's constitutional rights have been violated by a police officer, that person may sue the police officer in federal court. *Monroe* v. *Pape*	1972	A unanimous jury verdict is not necessarily required for a verdict of guilty in felony cases. Nine of twelve jurors is sufficient if permitted by state law. *Johnson* v. *Louisiana*
1961	Evidence collected in an "unreasonable" search and seizure may not be used against a person in court. Established guidelines for obtaining evidence and conducting searches. *Mapp* v. *Ohio*	1976	The death penalty *may* be imposed if the legislation establishing it and the judicial sentencing procedures provide safeguards against arbitrariness and capriciousness. *Gregg* v. *Georgia*
1963	Free legal counsel must be provided in felony cases for defendants who cannot afford to hire a lawyer. *Gideon* v. *Wainwright*	1976	States may not impose a mandatory death penalty. *Woodson* v. *North Carolina*
1964	A person is not required to testify against himself or herself. *Mallory* v. *Hogan*	1980	Exclusionary rule relaxed in a case where a prisoner may have been tricked into providing incriminating evidence without benefit of a lawyer. Being transported in a pa-

death penalty laws but two-thirds of the executions since the reintroduction of the death penalty in 1976 took place in just four states (Florida, Georgia, Louisiana, and Texas).[62] About three-fourths of the American public support the death penalty.[63] And, as we saw earlier, California Chief Justice Rose Bird lost her retention election in 1986 in large part because of her opposition to capital punishment.

◇ POLITICAL VALUES AND CONFLICTS OVER CRIMINAL JUSTICE POLICY

How we deal with social problems depends in great measure on how we think about them, what we think causes them, and how we think they might best be solved (if, indeed, we think they can be solved). This is as true of crime as of all social problems.

Table 12.2 *(continued)*

Expanding the Minimum Standards	Relaxing the Minimum Standards
1964 If police obtain a confession from a suspect before letting him or her see an attorney, that confession cannot be used in court. *Escobedo v. Illinois*	trol car past a school for handicapped children, Thomas Innis overheard a police officer express hope that the murder weapon not be found by one of the children. Innis led the officer to the spot where he had left the weapon, and it was used as evidence against him. *Rhode Island v. Innis*
1966 A suspect must be warned of the rights to be represented by a lawyer and to remain silent. If such warning is not given, no information provided by the suspect may be used against the suspect in court. *Miranda v. Arizona*	
	1984 Good-faith exception to the exclusionary rule permitted. *United States v. Leon;* and *Massachusetts v. Sheppard*
1967 The right to free counsel is guaranteed to juveniles being tried in juvenile court. *In Re Gault*	1987 Death penalty expanded so it could apply to accomplices in murder cases even though they did not kill or plan to kill. *Tison v. Arizona*
1972 In any case for which a jail sentence might be imposed, free legal counsel must be provided for defendants who cannot afford to hire a lawyer. *Argersinger v. Hamlin*	1987 Death penalty expanded by rejection of the contention that the death penalty is racially discriminatory because of the statistical fact that blacks who murder whites get the death sentence more often than blacks who murder blacks. *McCleskey v. Kemp*
1972 The death penalty was struck down as unconstitutional because it was applied capriciously and arbitrarily. *Furman v. Georgia*	

Approaches to Coping with Crime

As we noted in Chapter 1, political ideologies can be visualized along a liberal–conservative, left–right continuum. Although the percentage of people at either extreme is very small, it is useful to describe the ideologies in their extreme versions, for this gives us criteria for evaluating what political leaders tell us. It also enables us to examine our own attitudes about crime in connection with ideological positions. To what extent do our beliefs on crime and punishment reflect leftist philosophies? Rightist philosophies? Are our beliefs consistent with our underlying set of values about society? Once we draw these connections between our beliefs and values and ideological positions, we are in a good position to evaluate campaign promises of candidates and anticrime bills put before the legislatures. The liberal and conservative ideological positions on crime and punishment are summarized in Table 12-3.

The View from the Right—The Criminal Is Depraved The traditional extreme conservative views crime as a moral or psychic defect in the individual person.

Table 12-3   OVERVIEW OF THEORIES OF CRIME AND PUNISHMENT

	Liberal	Conservative
Major cause of crime	Social injustice	Individual defects
View of the criminal offender	Can be rehabilitated	Probably cannot be rehabilitated
View of punishment	No useful function	Deters others from committing crime
View of prisons	Reduce to the minimum needed to incarcerate dangerous criminals; prefer community corrections	Prisons preferred over community corrections
View of police	Skeptical	Positive
Preferred policy solutions	Make educational, employment, and social reforms to reduce the stimuli to crime	Make punishment more severe, and increase the likelihood of getting caught and being punished

Crime is an irrational deviation from social norms that exhort us not to kill, steal, rape, and so on. The criminal is diseased, and there is not much hope for a cure. This conservative has a strong concern for social order and emphasizes the government's role in preserving social order and preventing violence. In reaction to the Supreme Court decisions protecting the rights of criminal suspects, such as *Miranda* v. *Arizona* (see p. 307), a typical conservative might point out that society also has the right to be protected from violent crimes.

The traditional conservative policy for crime logically follows. If crime is a moral defect, the criminal must be punished for the transgression. Most criminals cannot be rehabilitated; thus, the punishment must be both harsh and certain to deter others from committing the same crimes. Consistent with their concern for social order, conservatives view the police favorably as the keepers of order. They favor increasing the size of police forces; giving the police sophisticated hardware such as helicopters, computers, Mace, and lethal weapons; and experimenting with crime-prevention tactics. They see a need for prisons to house habitual criminals who are too dangerous to be returned to society, where they can prey on innocent victims.[64]

The View from the Left—Crime Is Rooted in Social Injustice   In contrast to conservatives who think crime is caused by defects in the individual person, liberals trace the causes of crime to social injustice (see cartoon on p. 312). Most index crimes are committed by poor people against other poor people living in poor neighborhoods. The liberal views this as evidence that poverty, economic deprivation, and lower-class social conditions are the main causes of crime.

These conditions alienate criminally disposed persons from society and make them unreceptive to middle-class social values. At the extreme left, the radical carries this argument one step further: Crimes for money are rational—the insecurity and competitiveness of capitalist societies naturally lead people at all class levels to commit crimes in order to acquire the material goods they want.

Just as the conservative policy responses of force and punishment are consistent with conservative beliefs on the causes of crime, so are leftist policy responses consistent with leftist beliefs. At the extreme left, the radical believes that crime will wither away in the just society. The radical argues that "we cannot realistically expect to 'solve' the problem of crime in the United States without first effecting a fundamental redistribution of power in our society."[65] At the moderate left, the liberal aims at two things—rehabilitating the criminal offender and improving the social conditions that breed crime.

The left views the police much more negatively than does the right. Radicals view the police as instruments of class oppression, the means by which the upper classes maintain the lower classes in their place. The moderate liberal notes that police officers have frequently been hostile toward racial minorities and lower-class white communities. Rather than giving the police more lethal weapons to deal with criminals, moderate liberals seek to sensitize the police to these communities' needs and to increase the number of minority police officers.

The moderate liberal also supports reform efforts to overhaul the criminal justice system. This includes professionalizing police departments and implementing court reforms such as bail reform and the uniform court system. Reform also emphasizes rehabilitation programs that train offenders in marketable job skills and reorient their value systems so they can function better in society.[66]

Critique of the Rational Economist: Crime Pays   Until the late 1960s, most social science research on crime and punishment was conducted by sociologists, social psychologists, and criminologists. Because they found criminal behavior directly related to social class, their findings have generally supported the leftist rather than the rightist philosophy of crime. Further, the main thrust of psychological counseling and behavior modification experiments supported the notion that rehabilitation is possible.

Conservative criminologists got some significant research support from economists, who began to take an interest in crime in the 1960s. In 1968, a seminal article by Gary Becker outlined the basis of the rational economic conservative theory.[67] Like the traditional conservative, the rational economist attributes crime to individual free choice. Rather than assuming that the individual criminal is ill or morally depraved, the rational economist asks whether the criminal act is a rational thing to do. That is, does crime pay? Does the criminal earn more money at crime than would be possible at a legitimate occupation?

These researchers first note that the risk of arrest for any specific crime is small. In Pennsylvania the chances of going to prison for a specific act of burglary were less than twenty-nine to one in the early 1970s. Even of those convicted of burglary, only 58 percent went to prison.[68] In Chicago in the same period, the chance of imprisonment for any specific offense was less than three out of a thousand, and for a juvenile it was less than two out of a thousand.[69]

This cartoon captures the essence of the liberal and conservative approaches to crime. Liberals see crime as rooted in social problems and want to cut off the problem at its roots by attacking social problems. Conservatives see crime as individual deviancy and seek to imprison the criminals.

Source: Jerry Fearing, *St. Paul Pioneer Press*, February 1994, p. 14.

Although the risk of imprisonment is negligible for any specific offense, the person who habitually commits crime will end up in prison. However, the stays in prison will probably be short.

The economists then note that a good burglar can earn more money at burglary than at most legitimate occupations for which he or she might qualify. The average burglar lacks the skills to make much money at legitimate jobs. A study of all imprisoned burglars from Norfolk, Virginia, found that they averaged $1.55 per hour in wages at legitimate jobs in 1966 and only worked for 30 weeks. When researchers divided the total amount of jailed burglars' income from their burglaries and subtracted the amount of income lost during the average thirteen months they spent in prison for their crimes, they found that the burglar got almost three times as much income from their burglaries as they could have earned legitimately.[70]

A similar study of burglaries in Chicago in 1969 calculated an average net return of $36.70 per burglary. If a juvenile worked at burglary at the rate of one burglary a day for five days a week, and if the time spent in jail for those crimes is regarded as unemployment, the juvenile still made two and one-half times as much income from working as a burglar than could have been earned working forty hours a week legitimately.[71] An early-1970s study of Pennsylvania burglars led to conflicting interpretations. One economist, using one set of assumptions, found that each burglary brought its perpetrator a net loss of $197 over what could have been earned legitimately. But another economist, using different assumptions, discovered a profit of $15 per burglary.[72]

The message of the rational economists is clear: If you are a low-wage, unskilled laborer who suffers periodic bouts of unemployment, and if you do not mind the risk of spending twenty to thirty months in prison now and then, you would be much better off to go into burglary than into virtually any legitimate occupation for which you could qualify. Burglary pays. To the rational economist, the only sensible policy response to combat burglary is to make punishment so certain, so extreme, and so unpleasant that crime will no longer pay. In this view, punishment deters crime.[73]

Correctional Policy 1: Rehabilitation   Nowhere is the impact of these diverse viewpoints more dramatically seen than in recent trends in corrections philosophy. Until the 1930s, the dominant views of corrections were primarily punishment and deterrence. Most felt that criminals could not be rehabilitated. From the 1930s to the 1970s, the concept of rehabilitation came into greater favor. With the tools of modern psychology, counseling, and the teaching of marketable skills in prison, it was hoped that prisoners could be rehabilitated to rejoin society in a productive capacity.

As time went on, however, it became apparent that the correctional institutions did not rehabilitate many criminals. Many released inmates ended up back in prison once again. This is called **recidivism**. About two-thirds of all persons arrested for felonies had previously served time in prison.[74] To some observers, these high rates of recidivism suggested that the prisons were training young offenders to become better criminals instead of rehabilitating them.

In most instances, rehabilitation was not taken seriously. Only a fifth of all corrections personnel work in rehabilitation or in treatment.[75] Many vocational programs teach skills that are unmarketable. For example, many vocational programs teach barbering; yet in most communities, felons may not become barbers.[76]

Nobody really knows which rehabilitation programs might cut down recidivism. Robert Martinson surveyed 231 experimental studies of juvenile and adult offenders of both sexes. The experiments included vocational training for inmates, individual counseling, transforming the atmosphere of the prison to be less custodial and more rehabilitative, the use of drugs and surgery, manipulating the length of the sentence, and moving the inmates to community-based facilities. In each study, the experimental group in the rehabilitation program was compared to a control group in a regular prison population. After this intensely thorough review of all these experiments, Martinson came to the conclusion that "with few and isolated exceptions, the rehabilitative efforts that have been reported so far have no appreciable effect on recidivism."[77] Some isolated programs seem to hold some promise, but Martinson's overall conclusion was pessimistic.

Correctional Policy 2: Getting Tough   Although later research put some qualifications on Martinson's findings,[78] the overall impact of his pessimistic conclusions was to support those who wanted to scrap rehabilitation approaches in favor of "getting tough" approaches.[79] Getting tough is exemplified by two popular ideas in the 1980s and 1990s—determinate or mandatory sentences and a three-strikes-and-you're-out approach to sentencing.

Determinate or mandatory sentencing was a reaction to indeterminate sentencing under which a judge might sentence a felon to a sentence of perhaps five to twenty years. Felons who take part in rehabilitation programs and convince their parole boards that they are good risks can often get released after only a few years of their sentence. Under **determinate sentencing,** the judge must give a sentence for a fixed number of years, regardless of the inmate's participation in rehabilitation programs. Furthermore, in giving their sentences, the judges must usually adhere to a set of sentencing guidelines based on severity of the crime and the conviction history of the felon. The theory behind this approach is that mandatory punishment and determinate sentencing will influence criminals to commit fewer felonies.[80] The result has been a general trend toward increasing the length of prison sentences, making parole more difficult to get, and setting minimum sentences for certain crimes, such as those involving drugs.[81]

The 1990s have also seen sharp growth in the prison population. The total number of persons in prison in the 50 states rose from 176,000 in 1970 to 448,000 in 1985 and to 835,000 in 1993.[82] The growing incarceration rates also stimulated a boom in new prison construction. At an estimated construction cost of $125,000 per cell and an annual operating cost of $20,000 per inmate, the politics of getting tough was not cheap.[83]

Correctional Policy: An Assessment   Have the new get-tough policies worked? Rehabilitationists charge that they have been counterproductive, have not reduced crime, and have put many people into prison who were no real threat to society.[84] Defenders of the get-tough policy, by contrast, maintain that the new policies are working. They point to high recidivism rates as evidence that most prisoners are in fact repeat offenders who threaten society.[85] And studies of New Jersey and Wisconsin inmates in the 1990s found that the average inmate had participated in an average of twelve crimes in the year preceding his or her incarceration. Even including the enormous expenses of prisons, the cost of keeping these people locked up for a year was less to society than the cost of the crimes they had committed while on the streets for a year.[86] The authors of the study concluded that prison works for probably three-fourths of all offenders, but the other one-fourth would be more appropriately sentenced to a nonprison supervised facility.

In addition to mandatory sentencing, several states adopted a three strikes and-you're-out law in the early 1990s. California's version, for example, called for a minimum twenty-five-year sentence for a third conviction for a violent or serious crime. This led to a number of anomalies such as the man who received a twenty-five-year sentence because his third felony was stealing a slice of pizza, another whose third conviction was for stealing $80 of blue jeans, and a cocaine addict who was convicted of possessing thirteen ounces of the drug. In 1994, the California Supreme Court overturned the three-strikes law and permitted judges to make exceptions to it at their discretion.[87]

Policing as a Crime Control Approach

The 1990s have also seen some evidence that improved policing practices reduce crime. John Dilulio calls for more community policing patrols. This is an approach that gets police officers out of their squad cars into neighborhoods. The hope here is to turn policing from a confrontational cops-and-robbers game to a cooperative cops-and-citizens game.[88] New York City also attributed much of its 1990's crime drop to better policing strategies. These put a heavy emphasis on quality-of-life offenses such as low-level drug dealing and street prostitution, on the assumption that tolerance of low-level crimes such as these leads to fear and disorder that create the atmosphere for major crime. New York City also increased pay for police officers, attacked crime strategically, strove for accountability, and decentralized authority to precinct commanders.[89] Houston saw a big drop in crime rates in the 1990s, but credited it not to community-based policing but to an expansion in police force, better pay, and a get-tough policy on crime.[90]

Political Economy and the Privatization of Prisons

If determinate sentencing was the corrections fad of the 1970s, the contemporary fad is privatization. This can take various forms, the most controversial of which is the contracting out of the operation of prisons themselves. In fact, the contracting out of prison operations was a common practice in America in the nineteenth century. Contracting firms would make a profit by hiring out convicts to work in mines, on farms, and in other labor-intensive industries. There were so

YOU DECIDE

Public Policy for Crime

Assume that you have just been hired as the chief criminal justice adviser to the mayor of your city. The mayor wants to make a serious attempt to reduce crime and has called on you to outline policy alternatives. To do this, you must use your general knowledge about crime and corrections and create practical policy proposals. As you go through this exercise for the mayor, several things become apparent.

First, you must determine whether the mayor seriously wants to reduce crime or whether the real goal is to make symbolic gestures that will gain newspaper publicity and voter support. If the goal is symbolic gestures, then the mayor will respond favorably to proposals for crackdowns on vice or juggling police crime reports to show crime reductions on paper. A crackdown on prostitutes for a few months combined with arresting an occasional male customer may get the mayor publicity, but it will have little effect on actual crime.

Second, as you try to assess the practical consequences of the liberal and conservative philosophical positions, you will note that both positions help us understand crime, but neither has a monopoly on the truth. At least two generalizations seem warranted by empirical social science research. First, research by the rational economists and by Robert Martinson provides impressive (although inconclusive) evidence that liberals have emphasized rehabilitation too much and have not paid enough attention to the fact that some crime does pay. At the same time, other research findings, that most of the index crimes are committed by people low on the socioeconomic ladder, impressively suggest that the conservative position does not pay enough attention to the impact social injustices have on crime rates.

Unfortunately for the mayor, he or she does not exert much influence over either of these things. Questions of punishment rates and determinate versus indeterminate sentencing are in the hands of legislators, not mayors. Sentences, convictions, paroles, and rehabilitation programs are the domain of the courts and corrections departments, neither of which are under the mayor. Finally, issues of social justice and providing a livable income for all the city's residents are not controlled by the mayor either.

---

many scandals, abuses, and slaverylike conditions of work that these systems were gradually abandoned in the twentieth century, however. Today's privately run prisons are a far cry from these nineteenth-century enterprises. The largest firm, Corrections Corporation of America, is an institution well respected within the correctional community and has all its facilities accredited by the American Correctional Association. By 1989, it was running eleven correctional facilities in four states and for the Immigration and Naturalization Service.[91]

In favor of privatizing prisons are the arguments that it might be cheaper and that many state prisons are so inhumane and incapable of rehabilitating inmates that private industry ought to be given an opportunity to see if it can do better. On the negative side, many in the legal profession argue, privatization of prisons would necessarily create a strong interest group lobbying for more frequent and longer prison sentences (because more money could be made that way). Finally, privatization of prisons raises a fundamental issue about constitutional governance. Under a constitutional democracy, only the state has the au-

What the mayor can do, however, is to use the visibility of the mayor's office to lobby for appropriate legislation and to drum up public opinion on behalf of his or her criminal justice goals.

Third, you can recommend utilizing the mayor's ability to propose law enforcement strategies to the city's police department. Even if the mayor does not immediately oversee the police, the police will respond to political pressures created by the mayor. A local criminal justice crime reduction commission can survey law enforcement strategies that have been successful in other cities and investigate their appropriateness for your city. Crime attack strategies, community service strategies, or police deployment strategies may be appropriate in your city. Once these are identified, the mayor is in an influential position to get the police department to adopt some of them.

Fourth, the mayor can urge reforms in the state and county corrections agencies. It may take courageous intervention by the mayor to get certain neighborhoods to accept community-based facilities. The mayor's support for reforms in sentencing, parole boards, juvenile justice, and the administration of state prisons may be instrumental in getting such reforms adopted by the legislature.

Fifth, the mayor must take a strong role in raising money for these experiments and reforms. The mayor's staff clearly needs a grants person who can get federal funds for projects. An active mayor testifying before the legislative appropriations committees will get more funds for the projects than a passive mayor who neglects to testify.

In taking this swift look at what a mayoral aide might suggest that the mayor do about crime and corrections, three broad generalizations are evident. First, the strategies the mayor adopts will reflect the mayor's personal philosophical perspectives on crime and his or her assessment of the prevailing attitudes among the city's voters. Second, since responsibilities for dealing with crime are spread out among all levels and agencies of government, any comprehensive attack on crime is obviously an intergovernmental enterprise. Third, because crime is disproportionately concentrated in central cities, the central-city mayor has a unique opportunity to exercise leadership and influence to solve problems.

---

thority to deprive people of their liberty and to run their lives while they have been brought into custody. How much of this authority can be legitimately delegated to private corporations without violating this fundamental principle of government and without rupturing the bonds of constitutional accountability?[92] The balance of the 1990s will determine how these questions are answered.

SUMMARY

1. Courts in America resolve legal disputes, help set many public policies, and become intimately involved in the administration of some policies.
2. A dual court system exists in the United States: a single federal court system and fifty separate state systems. The state and local court systems are typically decentralized and not integrated.
3. Politics enter the judicial process in several ways: through the selection of judges, the dispensing of patronage, the political nature of some judicial decisions, the socioeconomic backgrounds of judges, and the activities of interest groups.

4. Crime presents an important example of courts confronting today's social conflicts. Crime rates mushroomed between 1960 and 1980 then declined in the 1990s. Experts have no consensus on how crime can best be combated. The conservative orientation attributes crime to defects in the individual and looks to prison as a means of punishment and deterrence. The liberal orientation attributes crime to social injustices and looks to prisons as a place where criminals can be rehabilitated.

5. Empirical social research does not provide unequivocal support for either of these two orientations. Research by the rational economists supports the conservative view by finding that much crime is more profitable than legitimate work and by suggesting a punitive approach to corrections. Punitive approaches adopted in the 1980s led to problems of their own, principally serious prison overcrowding.

6. Courts play a major role in dealing with crime. Considerable criticism has been aimed in recent years at the jury system, the role of money in justice, plea bargaining, and the attempts of some courts to establish minimum standards of justice.

KEY TERMS

Amicus curiae   Friend of the court. Refers to a third party permitted to file a brief arguing on behalf of one of the two parties involved in a suit.

Bench   A court.

Bill of Rights   The first ten amendments to the Constitution of the United States.

Cease-and-desist order   A court order to a person to stop carrying out a particular act.

Civil law   That portion of law that deals with conflicts between individuals and groups rather than with official legislation.

Criminal law   Law that deals with the violation of legislative statutes.

Declaratory judgment   A legally binding court order.

Determinate sentencing   The practice of sentencing inmates to very specific prison terms rather than giving a sentence with a wide range of possible time in prison, adjusted to the inmate's behavior in prison.

Distributive policy   A policy that allocates benefits to citizens but does not upset the prevailing distributions of wealth and influence. Also called *distributive services.*

Exclusionary rule   The rule that prohibits illegal evidence from being used in a trial.

Felony   A major crime.

Grand jury   A group of citizens empaneled to examine a particular situation and determine whether enough evidence exists to indict somebody for a crime.

Index crime   The seven types of crime listed annually in the FBI's Uniform Crime Reports.

Injunction   A court order prohibiting a person from carrying out a particular act.

Judicial activism   Judges' practice of using judicial review to impose their own beliefs on the law and to overrule policies set by legislators and executives.

Judicial restraint   Judges' practice of making limited use of judicial review and generally refraining from overruling the policies set by legislators and executives.

Judicial review   The power of courts to determine the constitutionality of acts of other government actors.

Jury (trial)   A group of citizens selected to determine the innocence or guilt of a person being tried.

Merit plan   A plan for judicial selection on the basis of qualification for office. See *Missouri Plan.*

Miranda rule   The rule that police officers must warn suspects of their constitutional rights to remain silent and to be represented by an attorney before they question the suspect.

Misdemeanor A lesser crime, which usually brings a limited fine or short jail sentence.

Missouri Plan A merit plan for judicial selection under which a nominating commission suggests a list of three nominees to the governor, who makes the appointment from one of the three.

Plea bargaining Offering a defendant the chance to plead guilty on a lesser charge in exchange for not being prosecuted on the more serious charge.

Recidivism The act of returning to prison after once having been released.

Redistributive policy A policy that takes wealth or income from one class of citizens and gives it to another class.

White-collar crime Crimes such as embezzlement, fraud, and commercial theft.

REFERENCES

1. *Newsweek,* October 16, 1995, p. 39.
2. *The New York Times,* October 21, 1993, p. A-1.
3. *The Washington Post National Weekly,* November 2, 1993, p. 15.
4. Hamilton was talking about the federal courts, not the state courts. See *Federalist 84.*
5. Lawrence Baum, "State Supreme Courts: Activism and Accountability," in *The State of the States,* Carl E. Van Horn, ed. (Washington, D.C.: Congressional Quarterly Press, 1989), pp. 116–121.
6. Larry W. Yackle, *Reform and Regret: The Story of Federal Judicial Involvement in the Alabama Prison System* (New York: Oxford University Press, 1989).
7. Herbert Jacob, "Courts," in *Politics in the American States,* 4th ed., Virginia Gray, Herbert Jacob, and Kenneth N. Vines, eds. (Boston: Little, Brown and Co., 1983), p. 226.
8. See Alfred Steinberg, "The Small Claims Court: A Consumer's Forgotten Forum," *National Civic Review* 63 (June 1974): 289; John H. Weiss, "Justice Without Lawyers: Transforming Small Claims Courts," *Working Papers for a New Society* 2, no. 3 (Fall 1974): 45–54.
9. See *The New York Times,* December 19, 1984, p. 10; May 31, 1984, p. 11; March 16, 1984, p. 8; December 15, 1983, p. 1. Also see James Tuohy and Rob Warren, *Greylord: Justice Chicago Style* (New York: Putnam, 1989).
10. See *The New York Times,* May 29, 1986, p. 7.
11. Harry P. Stumpf and John H. Culver, *The Politics of State Courts* (New York: Longman, 1992), p. 52.
12. On New York, see *The New York Times,* October 23, 1985, p. 22; on Pennsylvania, see *The New York Times,* January 4, 1984, p. 8.
13. A survey of 562 judges in 49 states found that 48.7 percent of trial court judges preferred the merit plan, and 24.3 percent preferred nonpartisan elections. Only 10.7 percent preferred partisan elections, and 7.8 percent appointment by the governor. The comparable percentages for appellate judges were 56.2, 16, 9.2, and 11. John M. Sheb II, "State Appellate Judges' Attitudes Toward Court Reform: Results of a National Survey," *State and Local Government Review* 22, no. 1 (Winter 1990): 18.
14. In Illinois, out of 1,864 retention elections held between 1964 (when retention elections began) and 1984, only 22 trial judges lost. Herbert Jacob, "Courts: The Least Visible Branch," in *Politics in the American States: A Comparative Analysis,* p. 267.
15. Kenyon D. Bunch and Gregory Casey, "Political Controversy on Missouri's Supreme Court: The Case of Merit vs. Politics," *State and Local Government Review* 22, no. 1 (Winter 1990): 5–16.
16. See *The New York Times,* March 20, 1985, p. 10; January 17, 1986, p. 23; *Washington Post National Weekly Edition,* November 11, 1985, p. 12; *Minneapolis Star and Tribune,* November 6, 1986, p. 15a.

17. Stumpf and Culver, *The Politics of State Courts*, p. 50.
18. Craig F. Emmert and Henry R. Glick, "The Selection of State Supreme Court Justices," *American Politics Quarterly* 16, no. 4 (October 1988): 445–465. The inability of merit plans to produce judges from prestigious law schools and judges with the most relevant legal experience was also found in earlier studies of California, Iowa, and Missouri. See Richard A. Watson and Rondal G. Downing, *The Politics of Bench and Bar: Judicial Selection Under the Missouri Non-Partisan Court Plan* (New York: Wiley, 1969), pp. 338–339. For research on California and Iowa, see Larry L. Berg et al., "The Consequences of Judicial Reform," *Western Political Quarterly* 28, no. 2 (June 1975): 263–280.
19. Barbara Luck Graham, "Do Judicial Selection Systems Matter? A Study of Black Representation on State Courts," *American Politics Quarterly* 18, no. 3 (July 1990): 316–336.
20. Ibid., p. 331.
21. Burton M. Atkins and Henry R. Glick, "Formal Judicial Recruitment and State Supreme Court Decisions," *American Politics Quarterly* 2, no. 4 (October 1974): 427–429.
22. Melinda Gann Hall, "Electoral Politics and Strategic Voting in State Supreme Courts," *Journal of Politics* 54, no. 2 (May 1992):
23. See Stuart Nagel, "Political Party Affiliation and Judges' Decisions," *American Political Science Review* 55, no. 4 (December 1961): 851–943; Nagel, "Ethnic Affiliation and Judicial Propensities," *Journal of Politics* 24 (1962): 92–110; Sidney Ulmer, "The Political Variable in the Michigan Supreme Court," *Journal of Political Law* 11 (1963): 552–562.
24. In the Wisconsin Supreme Court, political party background did not have an independent effect on justices' voting records. David W. Adamy, "The Party Variable in Judges' Voting: Conceptual Notes and a Case Study," *American Political Science Review* 63, no. 1 (March 1969): 57–73. But a study of Michigan justices found that when party background is consistent with other background factors, such as religious denomination and social status, there is a cumulative effect on justices' voting behavior. Malcolm M. Feeley, "Another Look at the Party Variable in Judicial Decision Making: An Analysis of the Michigan Supreme Court," *Polity* 4, no. 1 (Autumn 1971): 91–104.
25. Susan Welch, Michael Combs, and John Gruhl, "Do Black Judges Make a Difference?" *American Journal of Political Science* 32, no. 1 (February 1988): 126–136.
26. John Gruhl, Cassia Spohn, and Susan Welch, "Women as Policymakers: The Case of Trial Judges," *The American Journal of Political Science* 25, no. 2 (May 1981): 308–322.
27. Lehne, *The Quest for Justice*, pp. 28, 34.
28. This was the conclusion of James Brent who analyzed the litigation of attorneys general in twelve states in the 1980s. See his "State Attorneys General Before Their State Courts of Last Resort: A Research Note," *Comparative State Politics* 17, no. 2 (March 1996): 16–30.
29. See Wesley G. Skogan, "The Validity of Official Crime Statistics: An Empirical Investigation," *Social Science Quarterly* 55 (June 1974): 25–38. Skogan compared reported crime in ten cities with crime discovered through survey research. Although reported crime apparently understated the actual level of crime, Skogan found a high correlation between the two methods of measuring crime rates. He concluded that reported crime rates do have valid uses.
30. A Department of Justice study in the mid-1980s concluded that two-thirds of crimes go unreported. *Minneapolis Star and Tribune*, December 2, 1985, p. 13-A.
31. Arthur Niederhoffer, *Behind the Shield: The Police in Urban Society* (Garden City, N.Y.: Anchor Books, 1967), pp. 14–16.

32. *The New York Times*, November 19, 1984, p. 13.

33. President's Commission on Law Enforcement and the Administration of Justice, *The Challenge of Crime in a Free Society: A Report* (Washington, D.C.: U.S. Government Printing Office, 1967), pp. 155–159.

34. The governmental viewpoint is fairly well summarized in two documents by the President's Commission on Law Enforcement and the Administration of Justice, *The Challenge of Crime in a Free Society*, Ch. 7; the Commission's Task Force on Organized Crime, *Task Force Report: Organized Crime* (Washington, D.C.: U.S. Government Printing Office, 1967). The testimony of former FBI Director J. Edgar Hoover has been widely used in promoting the notion of the dominance of the Mafia over all organized crime in this country. See Hoover's testimony in U.S. Congress, Senate, Permanent Subcommittee on Investigation of the Senate Committee on Governmental Operations, *Organized Crime and Illicit Traffic in Narcotics*, 89th Cong., 1st sess., 1965, S. Rep. 72. See also U.S. Congress, House, Appropriations Subcommittee of the House Committee on Appropriations, testimony of J. Edgar Hoover, *Hearings Before the Subcommittee of Departments of State, Justice, and Commerce, the Judiciary and Related Agencies*, 89th Cong., 2nd sess., 1966, H. Rep. 273.

35. Ralph Salerno and John S. M. Tompkins, *The Civic Confederation: Cosa Nostra and Allied Operations in Organized Crime* (Garden City, N.Y.: Doubleday, 1969), p. 89.

36. Gordon Hawkins, "God and the Mafia," *Public Interest*, no. 14 (Winter 1969): 24–51.

37. See Ramsey Clark, *Crime in America* (New York: Simon & Schuster, 1970), p. 73; Andrew F. Rolle, *The Immigrant Upraised* (Norman: University of Oklahoma Press, 1968), p. 106.

38. Francis A. J. Ianni, "The Mafia and the Web of Kinship," *Public Interest*, no. 22 (Winter 1971): 78–100; Francis A. J. Ianni and Elizabeth Reuss-Ianni, *A Family Business: Kinship and Social Control in Organized Crime* (New York: Mentor, 1973).

39. See Ianni, "The Mafia and the Web of Kinship," p. 97; Daniel Bell, *The End of Ideology: On the Exhaustion of Political Ideas in the Fifties* (Glencoe, Ill.: Free Press, 1960), pp. 128–136.

40. For some interesting accounts of Irish, Jewish, and German organized crime before the 1920s, see Herbert Asbury, *The Gangs of New York: An Informal History of the Underworld* (New York: Capricorn Books, 1970, originally published 1927).

41. See Ianni, "The Mafia and the Web of Kinship," p. 97; Salerno and Tompkins, *The Civic Confederation*, p. 376; Francis A. J. Ianni, "New Mafia: Black, Hispanic and Italian Styles," *Society* 11, no. 3 (March–April 1974): 26–39.

42. *The New York Times*, January 22, 1988, p. 1.

43. See Jerome H. Skolnick, "Seven Crack Dilemmas in Search of an Answer," *The New York Times*, May 22, 1989, p. 21.

44. *The New York Times*, May 6, 1996, p. 1.

45. *The New York Times*, September 8, 1995, p. 6.

46. James Q. Wilson, "Crime and American Culture," *Public Interest*, no. 70 (Winter 1983): 22–48.

47. The Supreme Court cases that upheld these developments were *Johnson* v. *Louisiana*, 406 U.S. 356 (1972); *Williams* v. *Florida*, 399 U.S. 78 (1970); *Ballew* v. *Georgia* 435 U.S. 223 (1978).

48. *The New York Times*, November 4, 1995, p. 7.

49. *Argersinger* v. *Hamlin*, 407 U.S. 25 (1972).

50. See Christopher E. Smith, *Courts and the Poor* (Chicago: Nelson-Hall Publishers, 1991), 29.

51. See Susan E. Lawrence, *The Poor in Court: The Legal Services Program and Supreme Court Decisions Making* (Princeton, N.J.: Princeton University Press, 1990).

52. Smith, *Courts and the Poor,* p. 24.

53. Ibid., p. 25; also see Julian M. Carroll, "Pretrial Release: The Kentucky Program," *State Government* 49, no. 3 (Summer 1976): 187–189.

54. See *The Wall Street Journal,* July 9, 1996, p. 15.

55. H. Ted Rubin, *The Courts: Fulcrum of the Justice System* (Pacific Palisades, Calif.: Goodyear, 1976), pp. 26, 37.

56. See Herbert Jacob, *Justice in America: Courts, Lawyers, and the Judicial Process,* 2nd ed. (Boston: Little, Brown and Co., 1972), pp. 171–172. On the American Bar Association, see Rubin, *The Courts: Fulcrum of the Justice System,* p. 26. On legislators' attitudes, see Mike Kennensohn and Winifred Lyday, "Legislators and Criminal Justice Reform," *State Goverment* 48, no. 2 (Spring 1975): 122–127.

57. *Mapp* v. *Ohio,* 367 U.S. 643 (1961).

58. *Miranda* v. *Arizona,* 384 U.S. 436 (1966).

59. *Rhode Island* v. *Innis,* 446 U.S. 291 (1980).

60. *United States* v. *Leon,* 104 S.Ct. 3405 (1984) permitted searches with an invalid search warrant. *Massachusetts* v. *Sheppard,* 104 S.Ct. 3424 (1984) permitted the use of a warrant that did not specify the materials to be seized.

61. *Furman* v. *Georgia,* 408 U.S. 238 (1972).

62. *The New York Times,* April 21, 1992, p. 7.

63. A Gallup Poll in 1985 found 72 percent favoring the death penalty. See *Gallup Report* nos. 232 and 233 (January–February 1985): 4.

64. See David M. Gordon, ed., *Problems in Political Economy: An Urban Perspective,* 2nd ed. (Lexington, Mass.: D.C. Heath, 1977), p. 356.

65. Ibid., p. 359.

66. Ibid.

67. Gary Becker, "Crime and Punishment: An Economic Approach," *Journal of Politial Economy* 76, no. 2 (March–April 1968): 169–217.

68. Michael Sesnowitz, "The Returns to Burglary," *Western Economic Journal* 10, no. 4 (December 1972): 477–481.

69. Gregory Krohm, "The Pecuniary Incentives of Property Crime," in *The Economics of Crime and Punishment,* Simon Rottenberg, ed. (Washington, D.C.: American Enterprise Institute for Public Policy Research, 1973), p. 33.

70. William E. Cobb, "Theft and the Two Hypotheses," in Rottenberg, *The Economics of Crime and Punishment,* pp. 19–30.

71. Krohm, "The Pecuniary Incentives of Property Crime," pp. 31–34. Adult burglars, however, fared better only if their *in-kind* earnings in jail (that is, free food, clothing, and lodging) were added to the benefits they derived from burglary.

72. For the net loss argument, see Sesnowitz, "The Returns to Burglary." For the net profit argument, see Gregory C. Krohm, "An Alternative View of the Returns to Burglary," *Western Economic Journal* 11, no. 3 (September 1973): 364–367.

73. Gordon Tullock, "Does Punishment Deter Crime?" *Public Interest* no. 36 (Summer 1974): 103–111.

74. The U.S. Department of Justice studied the criminal records of 16,000 persons released from prison in 11 states in 1983. Within three years, 62 percent of them were arrested once again on felony or serious misdemeanor charges. Reported in *St. Paul Pioneer Press and Dispatch,* April 3, 1989, p. B-1.

75. Alan E. Bent and Ralph A. Rossum, *Police, Criminal Justice, and the Community* (New York: Harper & Row, 1976), p. 156.

76. Ibid.

77. Robert Martinson, "What Works? Questions and Answers About Prison Reform," *Public Interest* no 35 (Spring 1974): 25.

78. James Q. Wilson, "'What Works?' Revisited: New Findings in Criminal Rehabilitation," *Public Interest,* no. 61 (Fall 1980): 3–18. These later studies showed that some offenders were indeed amenable to rehabilitation, whereas others were not, and they suggest that different approaches should be taken to the two different types of offenders. Also, studies in Utah and Illinois showed that strict supervision of youthful offenders decreased the frequency with which they were subsequently rearrested.

79. Ibid., Tullock, "Does Punishment Deter Crime?"

80. On determinate and indeterminate sentencing, see Suzanne de Lesseps, "Reappraisal of Prison Policy," *Editorial Research Reports,* March 12, 1976, p. 189.

81. See *The New York Times,* December 13, 1985, p. 1.

82. James Austin, "Too Many Prisoners," *State Legislatures* 12, no. 5 (May–June 1986): 12–19. *Statistical Abstract of the United States: 1995,* p. 217.

83. Julie Lays, "The Complex Case of Costly Corrections," *State Legislatures* 12, no. 5 (May–June 1986): 20–24.

84. See, for example, Lois G. Forer, *A Rage to Punish: The Unintended Consequences of Mandatory Sentencing* (New York: W. W. Norton, 1994).

85. Michael K. Block and Steve J. Twist, "Lessons from the Eighties: Incarceration Works," *Commonsense: A Republican Journal of Thought* 1, no. 2 (Spring 1994): 73–83.

86. Anne Morrison Piehl and John J. Dilulio, Jr., "'Does Prison Pay?' Revisited: Returning to the Crime Scene," *The Brookings Review* 13, no. 1 (Winter 1995): 21–25.

87. *Los Angeles Times,* June 21, 1996, p. 1.

88. John J. Dilulio, Jr., "A Limited War on Crime That We Can Win," *The Brookings Review* 10, no. 4 (Fall 1992): 6–11.

89. William J. Bratton, "How to Win the War Against Crime," *The New York Times,* April 5, 1996, p. 15. Bratton was the New York City police commissioner who was credited with much of the city's crime reduction.

90. *St. Paul Pioneer Press,* June 1, 1994, p. 4.

91. *The New York Times,* March 17, 1989.

92. See John J. Dilulio, Jr., "What's Wrong with Private Prisons," *Public Interest,* no. 92 (Summer 1988): 66–83.

POVERTY AND SOCIAL WELFARE POLICIES

Chapter Preview

Few phenomena are more of a challenge to the widely held American value of upward social mobility than the continued existence of widespread poverty. And few public policy areas evoke as much emotion as trying to determine what to do about poverty in America. This chapter explores these issues by examining:

1. Poverty as a social problem.
2. The importance of conservative, liberal, and radical values to understanding poverty policy.
3. The roles of federal, state, and local governments in carrying out social welfare policy.
4. The major social welfare programs.
5. Health-care policies.
6. The attempts to reform social welfare policy since the 1960s.
7. The interrelationship between social welfare policy, social conflict, and political economy of states.

Let us begin by looking at three individual poor people and how they became poor.

◇ INTRODUCTION

America, we are taught, is the land of opportunity. Immigrants arrived, worked hard, saved their money, and saw their children move up a rung on the social ladder. **Horatio Alger** grew rich writing stories about boys who climbed to the top of the social ladder in a single lifetime. This message was so popular that his books sold more than twenty million copies.[1] And there were plenty of real-life examples to sustain this Horatio Alger myth. The ingenious Thomas Edison rose from telegraph boy to become the nation's foremost inventor. Andrew Carnegie, an impoverished immigrant, became the nation's foremost steel magnate. Even in our own day, the dynamic American economy has provided unmatched opportunities to reach the top. Between 1970 and 1980 the number of people earning $1 million or more in income quadrupled.[2]

Upward **social mobility** may be common in America, but many people, for whatever reasons, fail to partake of it. Ed Criado was eighty-seven years old when Studs Terkel interviewed him for his book *Division Street: America.* He had worked at a skilled trade as a tool and die maker only to end, if not in poverty, certainly in a very precarious financial situation.

> Now when I retired, I had in the neighborhood of eight thousand dollars in the bank. Well, I thought, that's gonna keep me, I'm seventy-seven. I probably won't live another five, six years. Well, you know that's dwindled down to six hundred dollars in ten years. Between the sickness that I had, and her [his wife's] illness. It's absolutely out of order.[3]

If Ed Criado was retired poor, Lucy Jefferson, fifty-two, was working poor. She was a physical therapy aide in a Chicago hospital but did not make enough money to rent a decent apartment in the private housing market. She lived with her two children in a subsidized public housing project in a black section of the city. Too proud to accept public assistance, she managed to squeak by on the margins of poverty—seeing a movie every two or three months, buying only sale meats at the supermarket, pinching pennies from paycheck to paycheck, and terribly worried about her son, who was doing poorly in one of the city's poorest schools. Lucy was not destitute, but she also was not upwardly mobile.[4]

Tally Jackson and his friends experienced a type of poverty entirely different from that of Ed Criado and Lucy Jefferson. Tally exemplifies what is called the urban underclass. He was a cement finisher in his thirties who hung out on a street corner in Washington, D.C., with about twenty other male unskilled laborers. They worked fairly steadily, but they never earned enough to provide their families with the luxury goods they saw advertised on television. They were broken men. They drifted in and out of marriages, lost all confidence in their ability to lead the middle-class lifestyle to which they aspired, stole from their employers to make up for their low wages, had numerous brushes with the law, and lost all hope that their future would be any better than their present.[5]

As Figure 13-1 shows, the percent of people in poverty goes up during periods of recession and down in times of economic expansion. But the total number of people in poverty today, 38 million in the mid-1990s was one-and-half times greater than it was two decades earlier in the middle 1970s. This persistent upward growth over the past two decades is a challenge to the relevance of the Horatio Alger myth for contemporary America and raises several questions. What is poverty? Why does it exist? Who is poor? Do different kinds of poverty require different kinds of public policies?

In 1996, the federal government devolved an enormous share of its poverty and welfare policies to the states. How effectively will states deal with poverty and welfare policy in the light of their new responsibilities?

These questions will occupy this chapter. We will first examine poverty as a social problem. Second we will look at conflicting views on the causes of poverty

Figure 13-1 NUMBER AND PERCENT OF PEOPLE IN POVERTY

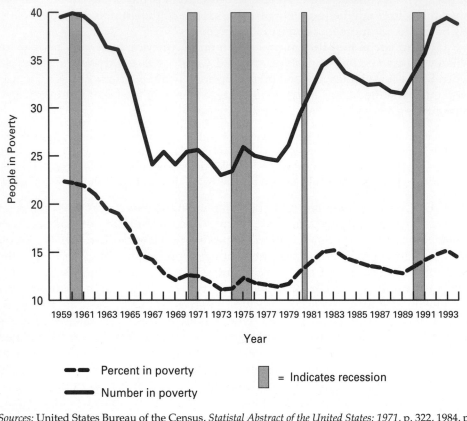

Sources: United States Bureau of the Census, *Statistal Abstract of the United States: 1971*, p. 322, 1984, p. 471, 1996, p. 472.

and the ways to deal with it. Third, we will differentiate between the roles played by the federal, state, and local levels of government in setting and implementing social welfare policies. Fourth, we will outline the major welfare programs that operate at the state and local levels. Fifth, because health-care programs are the single most expensive area of social welfare expenditures, we will examine them in greater detail than the other programs. Sixth, we will discuss attempts over the last thirty years to reform social welfare programs. Finally, we will look at the re-lationship between social welfare policy, social conflict, and political economy.

◇ POVERTY AS A SOCIAL PROBLEM

What Is Poverty?

Poverty can be defined in two ways. The first definition is **absolute deprivation,** and the second is **relative deprivation.** Both of these definitions are somewhat

Table 13-1 THE POVERTY LEVEL: 1990 AND PREVIOUS YEARS

The 1990 Poverty Level for Different-Size Nonfarm Families		The Poverty Level in Selected Years for a Four-Person, Nonfarm Family	
Size of Family	Average Poverty Line	Year	Average Poverty Line
		1992	$14,335
1 person	$7,143	1991	13,924
2 persons	9,137	1990	13,359
3 persons	11,186	1989	12,675
4 persons	14,335	1988	12,092
5 persons	16,592	1987	11,611
6 persons	19,137	1985	10,989
7 persons	21,594	1980	8,414

Source: U.S. Bureau of the Census, *Current Population Reports,* Series P-60, no. 185, *Poverty in the United States* (Washington, D.C.: U.S. Government Printing Office, 1993), p. A-8.

arbitrary and judgmental. And as will become apparent, one's definition of poverty affects the policies one favors. Calling poverty absolute deprivation leads to one policy approach; calling it relative deprivation often leads to other policy approaches.

Poverty as Absolute Deprivation   In absolute terms, poverty can be defined as the minimum subsistence income needed to survive without deprivation. Anybody below that income level is judged to live in poverty. Based on the assumption that poor families spend one-third of their income on food, the U.S. Social Security Administration sets an official **poverty line** at three times the amount of income needed to eat according to a modest food plan.*

The official poverty level is adjusted each year to compensate for inflation. Table 13-1 lists the official poverty-level income by family size and by year. Because the poverty line is one of the criteria used to determine eligibility for federal programs, it is important that this line be set at a realistic level. However, some critics argue that the level is too low. Other critics argue that the assumptions behind the poverty line are no longer valid. One economist argues that the poverty line ought to be set at four times the economy food plan instead of three times.[6] At whatever level the poverty line is set, compensating for special circumstances of different families is impossible. Obviously, $14,335 will cause less deprivation for a family that owns its house than for a family still making rent or mortgage payments. It will cause less deprivation for a family in subsidized

*This modest food plan is actually the economy food plan prepared by the U.S. Department of Agriculture. The Department of Agriculture annually estimates the cost of buying food on an economy plan, a low-cost plan, a moderate plan, and a liberal plan. For a description of how the poverty line is calculated, see *Social Security Bulletin, Annual Statistical Supplement: 1991* (Washington, D.C.: U.S. Government Printing Office, 1991), pp. 321–323.

Table 13-2   PEOPLE LIKELY TO BE POOR

Characteristics			Percentage Below the Poverty Line, 1992
All Persons			**14.8**

Birthright Characteristics

Race

White			11.6
Black			33.3
Hispanic			29.3

Gender

Male			12.7
Female			16.3

Race and gender

White males	10.1	White females	13.0
Black males	29.3	Black females	36.8
Hispanic males	27.0	Hispanic females	31.6

Behavioral Characteristics

Education	High School Dropout	Some College	College Graduate
White males	17.3	4.6	2.5
Black males	31.5	11.3	5.4
Hispanic males	27.9	10.9	6.4
White females	26.1	7.0	2.7
Black females	52.3	18.0	5.8
Hispanic females	36.8	12.6	7.3

housing than for a family in nonsubsidized housing. If all government assistance programs, such as public housing, food stamps, and medical assistance, were counted in determining poverty status, the number of people considered to be living in poverty would be sharply reduced.[7] This fact obviously complicates the task of defining poverty, and its implications for government policy have stimulated considerable debate among social welfare policy specialists.

Poverty as Relative Deprivation   Partly because of the difficulty in making an absolute-deprivation definition of poverty, some critics prefer to define poverty relative to society's overall standard of living. According to this view, as the standard of living goes up, the poverty level should also rise. A majority of poor people today have conveniences that only a generation ago would have been considered luxuries—a television set, a refrigerator or freezer, an oven, hot water, access to a telephone, a private bath, and a flush toilet.[8]

Some writers have suggested that a realistic definition of poverty would draw the relative poverty line at 50 percent of the median income.[9] (The median income

Table 13 2 PEOPLE LIKELY TO BE POOR *(continued)*

Characteristics		Percentage Below the Poverty Line, 1992
All Persons		**14.8**
Work Experience		Worked Year Round Full Time
White males		2.6
Black males		3.8
Hispanic males		8.5
White females		2.7
Black females		6.6
Hispanic females		6.0
Marital Status	Unrelated Individuals	Persons in Married Couple Families
White males	15.6	6.7
Black males	30.3	17.4
Hispanic males	28.2	21.4
White females	22.8	6.7
Black females	41.8	19.1
Hispanic females	42.8	21.5
Children in Female-Headed Households, No Husband Present		
White		45.4
Black		67.1
Hispanic		65.7

Source: U.S. Bureau of the Census, *Current Population Reports,* Series P-60, no. 185 *Poverty in the United States* (Washington, D.C.: U.S. Government Printing Office, 1993), pp. 10, 14–15, 71–72, 84–87.

is the point at which half the people earn more and half earn less.) Since the median family income in 1989 was $34,213, poverty income by this measure would be $17,107. About 21 percent of the families lived on incomes below this amount.[10]

Despite the theoretical advantages of defining poverty in relative terms, the U.S. government continues to use its official definition based on a principle of absolute deprivation. That definition is important for determining eligibility for several federal social programs and for allotting several federal grants-in-aid to states and communities. Because of these reasons, this chapter also will rely on the official poverty definition in discussing trends in poverty.

Who Is Poor?

The incidence of poverty is deeply affected by two broad factors—birthright characteristics and behavioral characteristics (see Table 13-2). Birthright characteristics are the ones you are born with and over which you have no control. These include your gender, your ethnic background, and the cultural-class-religious milieu in which you grew up. Behavioral characteristics are the ones over which you do have some control. Although you do not have complete control over these things, your behavior influences greatly whether you become a high school dropout or a college graduate, an employed person or a full-time worker.

Table 13-2 shows starkly the impact of birthright characteristics. Poverty is higher among minorities than among whites, and it is higher among women than among men. But the table also shows that within each of these birthright categories poverty is greatly influenced by behavior. Take, for example, the two categories with the most amount of poverty (black females) and the least amount of poverty (white males). Among black females, the incidence of poverty is almost ten times as great for high school dropouts (52.3 percent) as it is for college graduates (5.8 percent). Among white males, the poverty rate is almost seven times as great for high school dropouts (17.2 percent) as it is for college graduates (2.5 percent). Regardless of one's race and gender, a person dramatically reduces the risk of poverty simply by completing as many years of formal education as possible. A similar pattern is true for two other characteristics influenced by our behavior, whether we work and whether we are married. For black females, the poverty rate drops to 6.6 percent for those working full time. And the poverty rate drops from 41.8 percent for unmarried black females living alone to 19.1 percent for black females who are married. For married, college-educated black females working full time, the poverty rate is miniscule.

None of us controls everything in our lives, and the path to a high school degree and full-time work is harder for most minorities than it is for most whites, but the message of Table 13-2 is clear. Economic disaster is least likely among those people who develop the personal behaviors than enable them to complete as much formal education as possible, work full time, and attract a marriage partner who exhibits similar behaviors.

The most disturbing statistics in Table 13-2 are those showing poverty rates among children, especially those in female-headed families. Recent decades have seen an explosion in divorce rates and in the percent of children born to unmarried mothers. By 1990, 23 percent of all births were to unmarried mothers: The rate was 17 percent for white mothers, 23 percent for Hispanics, 56 percent for blacks, and 67 percent for teenagers.[11] If these numbers continue rising, the number of children living in poverty is destined to continue rising as well. And this is especially foreboding for the future of America's social relations. Children raised in poverty confront a wall of disadvantage that becomes increasing difficult to scale as each year passes. Children born into poverty are more likely than others to be sickly at birth and to spend their infancies suffering from malnutrition and the physical and developmental deficiencies caused by malnutrition. They do worse in school. As they grow older, they suffer more unemployment, have more problems with drugs and alcohol, and spend more time in jail. Finally, poor children are more likely than others to become teenage parents, with all the attendant risks that they will raise another generation of children in poverty.

Kinds of Poverty

Permanently vs. Marginally Poor   In trying to decide what, if anything, should be done about poverty, it is important to distinguish between the *permanently poor,* as illustrated by Tally Jackson (p. 325), and the *temporarily* or *marginally poor.* One family may fall into poverty for a two- or three-year period immediately following a divorce, for example, but subsequently recover. During that two- or three-year period, the single parent may need job training, placement counseling, and direct financial assistance. Poverty, in this case, is a temporary status.

The Survey Research Center traced the economic fortunes of more than 5,000 families for a nine-year period and found that only about 3 percent had lived in poverty all nine years.[12] This suggests that only about seven million people live below the poverty line all the time.

However, the Survey Research Center study also found that poverty is much more widespread than suggested by the Census Bureau. Nearly a third of all American families fell into poverty at least once in the nine years. This means that as many as 90 million people live in a fairly precarious situation. Normally, they earn enough money to live comfortably, but they fall into poverty during various stages of their lives—when they are laid off work because of a recession, when they get divorced and have to divide their incomes between two homes, when they get fired or widowed or face a medical or financial disaster, when their pension fund goes broke, or, like Ed Criado, when they retire on a fixed-income pension that cannot keep pace with inflation.

These marginally poor do not get a proportionate share of the national income. They do not accumulate much savings. They have few assets other than their houses, and many do not own their homes. The overwhelming majority work as regularly as possible, but they are extremely vulnerable to technological change, social developments, and other events over which they have no control.

The Working Poor and the Nonworking Poor   Another important distinction is between the *working poor* and the *nonworking poor.* Nearly half of all poverty families are headed by somebody with a job.[13] However, their jobs are often part time and do not pay enough to keep them above the poverty level.

Tally and his friends worked. They were busboys, dishwashers, parking lot car jockeys, and unskilled construction laborers. However, those jobs did not protect them from poverty.

> The busboy or dishwasher who works hard becomes, simply, a hard-working busboy or dishwasher. Neither hard work nor perseverance can conceivably carry the janitor to a sitdown job in the office building he cleans up. And it is the apprentice who becomes the journeyman electrician, plumber, steam fitter, or bricklayer, not the common unskilled Negro laborer.
>
> Thus the job is not a stepping stone to something. It is a dead end. It promises to deliver no more tomorrow, next month, or next year than it does today.[14]

Figure 13-2 **TRENDS IN INCOME INEQUALITY 1929–1990: PERCENTAGE OF THE NATIONAL INCOME EARNED BY EACH OF THREE INCOME GROUPS**

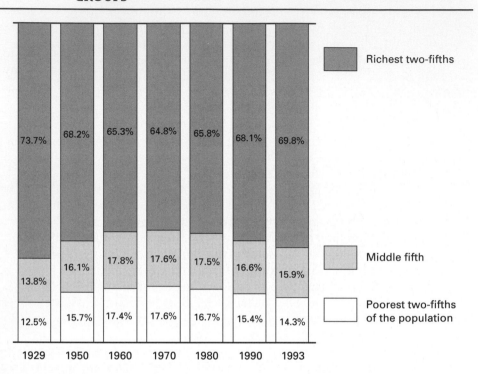

Sources: For 1970 thru 1988, Bureau of the Census, *Current Population Reports: Trends in Income by Selected Characteristics: 1947 to 1988* (Washington, D.C.: U. S. Government Printing Office, 1990), p. 9. For earlier data, *Statistical Abstract of the United States*, various years. For 1990, *Statistical Abstract: 1992*, p. 450. *Statistical Abstract, 1995*, p. 475.

As Figure 13-2 shows, the plight of people with average or below average incomes is getting worse today. The poorest two-fifths of Americans saw their share of the national income steadily grow from 12.5 percent in 1929 to 17.6 percent in 1970 and then decline slightly in 1980. Since then it has fallen dramatically to 14.3 percent. During the same period, the richest two-fifths of Americans saw their share of the national income decline until about 1970, and then rise until today, when it is higher than it has been since the 1930s.

Figure 13-2 clearly illustrates that income inequality in America is growing, with income shifting away from the 60 percent majority of Americans to the 40 percent who are the richest. Measured in real dollars, the poorest fifth of the population saw its income fall by 9.8 percent from an average $5,439 in 1979 to $5,107 in 1987. During the same period, the richest fifth of the population saw its real income grow by 15.6 percent to an average $68,775.[15] A way of viewing the same trend from a perspective closer to that of a middle-class college student would be to compare the average income of a well-paid corporation president to that of a typical middle-income professional person, a school teacher. In 1960, the average corporation chief executive earned thirty-eight times as much as the average school teacher. In 1987, the average president earned $2,025,485, or 72 times as much as the average school teacher.[16]

Why is this happening? There are many explanations, but analysts point to three overriding reasons. First, the transformation of the American economy from one based on manufacturing to one based on services eliminated 11.5 million well-paying manufacturing jobs from 1979 to 1984. Only 60 percent of those workers found new jobs during that period.[17] At least that many new jobs were created in the same period, but these were primarily lower-paying service jobs in such enterprises as restaurants, hotels, and hospitals.

A second reason for the growing inequalities stems from international competition. American workers now compete for jobs with ambitious and hardworking contemporaries all over the world. Most low-skilled production jobs today can be done just as competently and much more cheaply by someone in Mexico or Brazil or Indonesia or just about any country bent on boosting its economic growth.

A third reason for growing inequality in incomes can be traced to the changes in national tax and welfare policies in the 1980s. As will be discussed later in this chapter, these policies had the effect of reducing the incomes of low-income families while increasing the take-home pay of upper and upper-middle income families.

◇ POLITICAL VALUES AND POVERTY

Many perceptions exist about the causes of poverty and how it can best be dealt with. These perceptions can be placed along the leftist–rightist continuum. On the right side of the spectrum, conservatives look at the poverty data in Table 13-2 and draw one conclusion; liberals look at the same data and draw a different conclusion.

The View from the Right

Conservatives focus on the behavioral characteristics shown in Table 13-2. In their view, people are poor because of their individual shortcomings. The dynamic, capitalistic American economy provides millions of opportunities for self-advancement. The individual is master of his or her fate: If the individual is too lazy, too dumb, too unstable, or too sick to work, then that is the individual's own fault. Those people trapped in poverty are trapped there, according to one conservative analyst, "because they usually do not work." Only 9 percent of poor adults worked full time in 1987. Most people "responded to stagnant wages by working *more;* only the poor have worked *less.*"[18]

Conservatives tend to view poverty not only as an individual matter but also as inevitable. Life circumstances will always put some people into poverty, but the people with initiative will overcome their poverty. For this reason, the conservative is likely to attribute great significance to the difference between temporary and permanent poverty. Many people are temporarily thrown into poverty by external circumstances such as a divorce, but those people usually climb out of poverty.

More disturbing to the conservative, however, is the long-term poverty of what has come to be called the underclass. Some social critics argue that a **culture of poverty** exists among the underclass. These people become cynical about the social system. They fail not only to develop marketable job skills but to develop positive attitudes that would enable them to work eight hours daily and cause no trouble to their supervisors. Edward C. Banfield writes,

> Lower-class poverty . . . is "inwardly" caused [by psychological inability to provide for the future, and all that this inability implies . . .]. Extreme present orientedness, not lack of income or wealth, is the principal cause of poverty in the sense of "the culture of poverty." Most of those caught up in this culture are unable or unwilling to plan for the future, to sacrifice immediate gratifications in favor of future ones, or to accept the disciplines that are required in order to get and spend.[19]

In its most extreme form during the early twentieth century, the classic conservative explanation for poverty was **Social Darwinism.** Charles Darwin argued that natural evolution occurred through the survival of the fittest. Social Darwinists, such as Herbert Spencer,[20] applied that argument to the evolution of society. Poverty is a mechanism for the survival of the fittest in the social sphere. It weeds out the weakest members of the species, and the overall result is a healthier society.

The extreme conservative would carry this argument to its logical conclusion and deny that the government has any responsibility to combat poverty. Indeed, Charles Murray argues that government welfare programs have only made problems worse by sapping poor people of their initiative and making them dependent on the welfare system.[21] He further argues that technological change will make the poor even worse off in future years because he thinks that the poor lack the basic intelligence needed to function in the coming high-tech world.[22] The classic conservative believes that the best antipoverty policy is one of **laissez-faire,** a policy by which the government leaves the marketplace alone and does not intervene. And lest one thinks that these ideas disappeared with the nineteenth-century Social Darwinists, a 1987 book by two Heritage Foundation authors expressed distaste not only for government-sponsored welfare but for charity itself. They wrote that they "have always been troubled by the notions of welfare and charity. There is a seeming indignity to it all that chills the soul. It raises deep and difficult questions about the obligations of both the giver and the receiver of help."[23]

More moderate conservatives do favor some intervention in the marketplace and some programs to help people who have fallen into poverty. If the government must intervene, however, the conservative would usually prefer that the government give financial incentives to private industry to carry out government objectives.

Some conservatives emphasize the distinction between absolute poverty and relative deprivation. Edward C. Banfield, for example, argues that most poverty today is little more than a gap between poor people's limited capabilities and their inflated aspirations for an upper-middle-class lifestyle.[24]

The View from the Left

In contrast to the conservative emphasis on individualism, leftist theories stress that much poverty is structural and would still exist if everybody had a future-oriented value system.[25] This view prevails among liberal social scientists, journalists, and political leaders, who dominate liberal thought. Tracing their views back to the Great Depression of the 1930s and President Franklin Roosevelt's New Deal response to it, liberals point out that private enterprise cannot by itself produce enough jobs for everybody. Even during the late 1960s high tide of the greatest economic boom in history, the unemployment rate remained above 4 percent. The liberal policy approach for dealing with poverty reflects this belief in the structural causes of poverty. Government spending should stimulate economic growth so that full employment can be maintained, and specific government programs such as unemployment compensation should strive to protect people from recessions that occur in the business cycle. The conservative is pessimistic about individuals, but the liberal is optimistic. The liberal supports education programs, retraining programs, and job placement programs that give individuals an opportunity to take advantage of structural changes in the economy.

At the extreme left, radical thought argues that poverty is caused by major economic institutions and the small class of very wealthy people who control those institutions. Radicals believe those people share a consensus opinion that the prevailing class structure of the society must be maintained. This class structure requires a relatively small impoverished class, a fairly substantial class of marginal workers who can be moved into and out of employment as conditions dictate, and a fairly sizable group of upper-middle-class people who can serve as doctors, lawyers, professionals, supervisors, and other managers to run the major institutions of the society.

Neither liberals nor radicals deny the importance of individual traits for social mobility. Some gifted and ambitious people can work their way from the bottom to the top of the social ladder. Leftists stress, however, that unless the basic structure of society is changed, the pool of permanently and marginally poor people will continue to exist. Moreover, the class structure perpetuates itself over generations. Most poor people have parents who are poor, and twenty-five years from now most poor people will be the sons and daughters of today's poor people. Most rich people, interestingly, do not seem to have come from rich parents. A survey of the country's wealthiest 1 percent of the population found that only 10 percent said they inherited their wealth.[26]

In truth, there is support in Table 13-2 for both the conservative and the liberal view of poverty. The conservative's emphasis on individual behavior is supported by the fact that within each of the ethnic categories, poverty rates are lowest among those people who succeed in finding full-time jobs and those who get married and stay married. Poverty rates are also lowest among people who complete high school, achieve some post–high school education or training, and who behave in ways that make them attractive to employers. It is impossible to reject completely the conservative's belief that individual behavior has an effect on one's economic success or failure.

However, Table 13-2 also provides some support for the liberal's contention that poverty is caused by social structures. Within any of the marital or employment categories shown, poverty rates always end up being the highest among blacks and the lowest among whites. Having a full-time job is very likely to keep you out of poverty, but a fundamental problem of the 1990s is that increasing numbers of employers have been retrenching their full-time workforce. Furthermore, a huge portion of people in poverty are children under the age of eighteen who have no control over the marital or employment status of their parents.

To cope effectively with poverty, public policy must take into account both the behavioral and the structural factors that lead to poverty. There is a need both for educating poor children about behaviors that maximize their chances of escaping the poverty trap and also for public policies that provide economic opportunities.

◇ STATE, LOCAL, AND FEDERAL ROLES IN SOCIAL WELFARE POLICY

These theories of poverty have had a profound influence on the social welfare system that evolved in the United States. Prior to the depression of the 1930s, classic laissez-faire conservatism was the dominant theory of social welfare, and the government intervened minimally in the economy. The depression was such a monumental catastrophe, however, that laissez-faire was no longer a viable policy. The economy's total output of goods and services (the **gross national product,** or **GNP**) dropped 45 percent between 1929 and 1933 and did not get back to its 1929 level until 1941. By 1932, a quarter of the workforce was unemployed. Traditional systems of welfare, or relief, as they were called in those days, were overloaded with requests for help. These traditional relief systems were run and financed by local governments that were unable to cope with the depression.

In response to the disaster of the Great Depression, a social welfare system emerged that intricately involved all three levels of government. The federal role initially attempted to provide financial support for local governments to give traditional relief.

Federal Roles

In time, a completely new intergovernmental welfare system evolved. The federal government's role in this system now embraces four elements. First, through the grant-in-aid system, the federal government provides financial incentives to the states to run a variety of social welfare programs that will be described shortly.

Second, the federal government established minimum payment levels for the programs run by the states. Third, because the federal government provides financial incentives, it effectively plays the key role of deciding which poverty problems will be tackled and what programs will exist to tackle them. Fourth, in addition to setting up and financing programs for the states to run, the federal government directly operates a number of programs itself. Medicare, for example, is handled exclusively by the federal government.

State Roles

Whereas the federal government determines the overall structure of social welfare programs and minimum payment levels, the states implement most programs and set the policies that govern eligibility for program benefits and the ultimate benefit levels. Until it was revamped in 1996, the core of this intergovernmental approach to social policy was a relatively small federal program called **Aid for Families with Dependent Children (AFDC).** Congress wrote the program into the **Social Security Act of 1935** to provide financial relief for widows with dependent children. The federal government provided a minimal AFDC payment level. The state legislatures supplemented this amount, which led to wide differences in benefit levels since some states are more generous than others. In 1993, average monthly AFDC benefits ranged from $120 in Alabama to $568 in California. After the state legislature set policy for the benefit levels, implementation of the AFDC program was turned over to the state and local departments of human services. Starting in 1997, the state role in welfare policy was greatly expanded when Congress replaced AFDC with a block grant that gave states much wider leeway on how they spent their federal welfare grant monies.

Local Roles

Local departments of human services, which are usually found at the county level of government, are most often the agencies that run the welfare programs. People apply for welfare assistance at the local level. Local officials determine whether the applicant is eligible and what level of benefits the applicant will receive. If the applicant is female, the local welfare officials try to find the father of the children and force him to make child support payments. After going through all these steps to ensure the applicant's eligibility and to boost her outside sources of income, the local department begins to send monthly checks. Sometimes welfare officials find it difficult to set eligibility rules that are fair and equitable, as the "You Decide" exercise on pp. 338–339 shows.

Why Welfare Policies Differ Among the States

States differ greatly in the generosity of their welfare benefits. As we saw, California, with its average monthly AFDC payment of $568 in 1993 was more than four times as generous as Alabama, with its average payment of only $120. Why do states differ so much in their level of welfare benefits?

YOU DECIDE

A Dilemma in Welfare Eligibility

Deciding who should receive welfare under what conditions is very difficult and often arbitrary. Getting a fair judgment in some cases would tax the wisdom of Solomon. Such was the case of Wendy Sabot of Suffolk County, New York.

In July 1974, Ms. Sabot applied for AFDC. Although at that time she was receiving $350 per month in child support payments from her former husband, her rent alone was $300 monthly, leaving little for other necessities.

One AFDC eligibility rule requires that recipients have no other liquid assets. Ms. Sabot had no other liquid assets, but her children had accumulated $1,221 in savings. Ms. Sabot told reporters, "Some of it they had earned themselves—baby-sitting, washing cars, working a news-paper-delivery route—and the rest was gift money from birthdays and Christmas. I made the children deposit all of their gift money and half of what they earned in their accounts."

The Suffolk County Social Services Department told Ms. Sabot that she would not be eligible for welfare payments until she had either spent the children's savings or turned them over to the department. She asked the Legal Aid Society to help her appeal this decision but was turned down because very few poor people would benefit from her case. So she went to a law library and prepared a lawsuit. When the trial court ordered the Social Services Department to make her eligible for welfare, the department appealed the case to New York State's highest appellate court. Finally, three years later, in October 1977, the appellate court upheld Ms. Sabot. "The broad humanitarian purpose of the social services law," read the court's opinion, "does not contemplate that a person must be stripped bare, emotionally and economically."

Affluence as an Explanation   The main explanation for the disparities seems to be the level of affluence of the state. California can be more generous than Alabama in large part because California has a higher per-capita income than Alabama, and the cost of living is higher there. Although affluence partially explains the difference in benefit levels, it is not a completely satisfying explanation. California is four times as generous as Alabama, but it is not six times as rich. Other factors must be involved. One possibility is that political forces in some states lead them to choose higher benefit levels.

Politics as an Explanation   One popular **hypothesis** among political scientists has been that welfare benefits will be highest in the states where Democrats compete vigorously with Republicans for voter support and where voter turnout is high. The assumption behind this hypothesis is that the voters will choose the party that gives them the most benefits, causing the two parties to outbid each other. The higher the turnout and the greater the competitiveness, the more incentive the parties have to bid against each other for voter support. In states with little competition and low voter turnout, the dominant party has little fear of losing office and thus has no incentive to give the voters high benefit levels. This hypothesis is not supported by empirical data, however. Although highly competitive states and high voter-turnout states do give higher welfare benefits than one-party and low-turnout states, the competitive, high-turnout

The Sabot case presents some difficult dilemmas for welfare officials trying to determine eligibility rules. On the one hand many observers would agree with Ms. Sabot that it was "unreasonable" for the Social Services Department to take away the children's money before the family could get help. "It wasn't my money. It never was. . . . Taking away their money would have taken away their incentive. I don't want them to perpetuate the welfare system. I want them to be independent. I didn't want them to grow up to become welfare recipients and have children who were welfare recipients."

On the other hand, the same observers could probably sympathize with the Social Services Department commissioner that "it is questionable whether the public should be required to support this family at a subsistence level while it has $1,200 in the bank." The Sabot case opens the possibility that other AFDC applicants might transfer their own savings to their children's accounts in order to keep their cash reserves and still receive welfare payments.

The Sabot case gave the Suffolk County welfare officials the difficult task of writing a new set of regulations that would be more humanitarian and at the same time not susceptible to fraud.

If *you* were a public official responsible for this task, how would *you* approach this problem? How much in assets should a family be permitted and still be eligible for AFDC benefits? How would you guard against parents transferring their savings to their children in order to gain AFDC eligibility? And if children were to lose AFDC benefits when they saved money, how would you teach them the value of saving to acquire assets?

Source: *The New York Times,* October 14, 1977, p. 25. Quoted material copyright © 1977 by the New York Times Company. Reprinted by permission.

---

states are also the most affluent states. Although the influence of partisanship cannot be ignored, most statistical analyses have concluded that the level of affluence is much more significant for determining welfare benefits than is the degree of two-party competition or whether the state is controlled by Democrats rather than Republicans.[27]

More important than two-party competition and high voter turnout is the extent to which the working classes and lower classes have politically influential interest groups. The strength and militancy of labor unions do appear to have a significant impact on social welfare benefits. The political culture of states also helps explain the differences in welfare benefits. Governmental intervention in the economy, it will be recalled from Chapter 2, is favored much more in moralistic political cultures than it is in traditionalistic or individualistic cultures. Ranking states by the AFDC benefit levels they pay, all but three of the top twenty states have a moralistic strain in their political culture, whereas only four of the bottom twenty states have such a strain. Conversely, none of the top twenty states have a traditionalistic strain, but sixteen of the bottom twenty states have a traditionalistic strain.

In sum, state and local governments play a vital role not only in administering federal welfare programs but also in determining the generosity of the benefit levels. The most significant variables for determining the generosity of state welfare policies appear to be the level of affluence and the type of political culture in the state. Economic and political factors interact in rather complex ways to influence welfare policies.[28] But, in general, benefits are most generous in states that are affluent, that have strong labor unions, and that have a moralistic strain in their political culture. Benefit levels are the lowest in states that are poor, that lack strong labor unions, and that have a traditionalistic strain in their political culture. The generous states are found disproportionately in the Northeast, Midwest, and Pacific regions, and the least generous states tend to be in the South and Southwest sunbelt region.

◇ THE MAJOR SOCIAL WELFARE PROGRAMS

There is no agreement on what programs are included under the term *welfare.* Most of the debate over welfare reform in the 1990s focused on AFDC and food stamps, but Table 13-3 shows that these two programs account for a very small amount of the money that governments spend on assistance to individuals.[29] As Table 13-3 shows, social welfare programs provide three types of assistance: (1) social insurance transfer payments, (2) cash transfer payments that are not social insurance, and (3) in-kind assistance.

Social Insurance Transfer Payments

A **transfer payment** is a direct payment of money by the government to individuals. It is not a payment for purchasing goods or services, as are federal expenditures. Nor is it a payment to run a program, as are the services listed in Part 3 of Table 13-3. It is called a transfer payment because its net effect is simply to transfer money from the people who pay taxes to the people who receive the cash. Some transfer payments, such as OASDHI, are **social insurance.** That is, individuals make payments into a social insurance trust fund much as they would make payments into a private insurance policy. Later on they receive benefit payments when they become eligible. The three major social insurance programs—OASDHI, Medicare, and Unemployment Compensation—were established by the Social Security Act of 1935 and its later amendments.

Old Age, Survivors, Disability, and Health Insurance (OASDHI)   OASDHI is the granddaddy of social welfare programs. It was not only the first of the programs in Table 13-3, it is the largest. While working you make regular payroll contributions to the Social Security trust funds. When you retire, become disabled, or die, you or your beneficiaries receive a monthly payment just as would happen under a pension program or a life insurance plan. This is why it is called social insurance.

Social Security probably does more than any other program to reduce poverty in America. A 1988 Census Bureau study calculated that fifteen million people were lifted above the poverty line by their Social Security benefits. Without such benefits, the poverty rate would likely be six percentage points higher than it is.[30]

Social Security is currently undergoing a great debate that will affect your well-being enormously. Although the Social Security trust fund currently has as-

Table 13-3   APPROACHES TO SOCIAL WELFARE POLICY

Approach and Program	Major Recipients of the Assistance	Level of Government That Writes the Checks or Administers the Delivery of the Service	Federal Dollars Spent 1982 (in Billions)	Spent 1989	Budgeted 1993
1. Social insurance transfer payments					
a. Old Age Survivors Disability and Health Insurance (OASDHI)	Retired people and/or the survivors of workers who died; mostly nonworkers; all income categories	Federal	152.1	227.2	302.3
b. Medicare	The aged; all income categories; both the working and the nonworking poor	Federal	49.2	94.3	129.3
c. Unemployment compensation	Mostly the bottom 40 percent of the income recipients; workers who are temporarily unemployed	State	22.3 $223.6	14.1 $335.6	29.7 $461.3
2. Nonsocial insurance cash transfer payments					
a. Aid for Families with Dependent Children (AFDC)	The nonworking poor; the bottom 20 percent of the income recipients; mostly single, divorced, or widowed mothers and their children	State and county	7.5	11.2	15.3

Table 13-3 *(continued)*

Approach and Program	Major Recipients of the Assistance	Level of Government That Writes the Checks or Administers the Delivery of the Service	Federal Dollars Spent 1982 (in Billions)	Spent 1989	Budgeted 1993
b. Food stamps	The bottom 40 percent of the income recipients; both the working and the nonworking poor	Federal and county	11.0	13.7	22.7
c. Supplemental Security Income (SSI)	The aged, the blind, and the disabled; the nonworking poor; the bottom 20 percent of the income recipients	Federal	6.8	11.5	21.3
d. General public assistance (excluding AFDC and SSI)	The nonworking poor; the bottom 20 percent of the income earners; mostly destitute and homeless people who do not qualify for AFDC, SSI, or unemployment compensation	State and county	No federal funds $25.3	$36.4	$59.3
e. Earned income tax credit					$4.0
3. *In-kind assistance*					
a. Housing programs	Mostly the bottom 40 percent of the income recipients; both the working and the nonworking poor	Municipal or county housing authorities	8.0	14.7	21.8

Table 13-3 *(continued)*

Approach and Program	Major Recipients of the Assistance	Level of Government That Writes the Checks or Administers the Delivery of the Service	Federal Dollars Spent 1982 (in Billions)	Spent 1989	Budgeted 1993
b. Medicaid	The bottom 40 percent of the income recipients; both the working and the nonworking poor	State and county welfare departments	16.5	33.1	84.4
c. Other health programs	All income categories; mostly concentrating on the bottom 40 percent; people with special health problems; health care professionals	Federal, state, and county	10.2	14.2	22.1
d. Legal Services Program (LSP)	The bottom 40 percent of the income recipients; both the working and the nonworking poor	Federal	0.3	0.3	0.3
e. Employment programs	Middle 40 percent of the income recipients; the working poor who are unemployed	Federal, state, county, and municipal	4.1	4.1	5.9
f. Other social services (e.g., child day care, foster care, family planning, services for the mentally retarded)	The bottom 40 percent of the income recipients; both the working and the non-working poor; people with special needs and special problems	State, county, and municipal	5.0 / $44.1	7.4 / $73.8	12.7 / $147.2

Sources: For 1982, *Historical Tables: Budget of the United States Government, Fiscal Year 1990* (Washington, D.C.: U.S. Government Printing Office, 1989), pp. 228, 284. For 1989, *Budget of the United States Government, Fiscal Year 1991* (Washington, D.C.: U.S. Government Printing Office, 1990), pp. A319, A325, A1139 For 1993, *Budget of the United States Government, Fiscal Year 1993* (Washington, D.C.: U.S. Government Printing Office, 1992), Appendix 1, pp. 11–12, 110.

sests of $5 trillion, these assets will drop rapidly once the huge baby boomer generation starts retiring in the early twenty-first century. Conservative opponents of Social Security have seized on this projection to seek to discredit and destroy it.[31] In fact, the system can easily be saved with a combination of steps involving benefit reductions, reductions in indexation, and other reforms.[32]

Medicare   Persons over age sixty-five are eligible for Medicare. They pay a small monthly premium that entitles them to medical services. Doctors send their bills directly to the federal government for payment.

Unemployment Compensation   Unemployment compensation is a social insurance program. While you work, your employer makes regular contributions to an unemployment compensation trust fund; if you become unemployed, you can draw benefit checks for up to twenty-six weeks. Unemployment compensation was initiated by the Social Security Act of 1935. It is financed jointly by employers, the states, and the federal government, but it is administered by the individual states.

Transfer Payments That Are Not Social Insurance

In contrast to the social insurance programs, some other transfer payment programs, such as AFDC, are not social insurance. People can receive assistance from those programs when they meet the eligibility requirements and if they can pass a **means test,** that is, if their income or assets fall below a certain level. The main cash transfer payments of this type are AFDC, food stamps, SSI, and General Public Assistance.

Aid for Families with Dependent Children (AFDC)   Until its demise in 1996, AFDC was the most controversial transfer payment. It provided a direct monthly payment to single parents with dependent children. In 1993 AFDC payments averaged $377 per family. About fourteen million people received AFDC,[33] but the number fluctuates with economic conditions.

The AFDC program was controversial not only because of the sums of money involved but also because of a very negative stereotype ascribed to AFDC recipients. According to this stereotype, the typical recipient misspends AFDC checks on alcohol, gambling, and frivolities. Nevertheless, rigorous research has shown that AFDC recipients spend more of their income on food and housing and less on frivolities than do non-AFDC recipients.[34] Another stereotype is that the recipient is able-bodied enough to work but is simply ripping off the system by drawing AFDC checks. Federal investigations find that only a small minority of AFDC recipients are truly ineligible.[35] The overwhelming majority of people on the AFDC rolls are young children, and most of the rest are single or divorced women. Another stereotype is that the typical AFDC mother becomes permanently dependent on welfare. The fact is that 50 percent of AFDC recipients receive this benefit for four years or less. Thirty percent received AFDC for eight or more years.[36]

Food Stamps   Another controversial measure has been the **food stamps program,** which was started in 1961 as a pilot project and then established on a permanent basis in 1964. It is totally funded by the federal government but is administered by the federal Department of Agriculture jointly with the state and county departments of welfare.

Food stamps serve both the working and the nonworking poor. To qualify, the family income must be below a certain cutoff level. Eligible households receive a monthly allotment that is tied to the amount of money needed for the Agriculture Department's "thrifty food plan."[37] Food stamps were attacked strenuously by President Reagan, whose administration tightened eligibility requirements and sought to reduce the number of recipients. This produced a temporary drop in recipients, but the numbers inched upwards in the wake the 1990–1991 economic recession, and by the mid-1990s, twenty-seven million were receiving food stamps.[38] In its welfare reform act of 1996, Congress tightened the eligibility requirements once again.

Supplemental Security Income (SSI)   Supplemental Security Income (SSI) is a federal program that provides aid to the aged, the blind, and the permanently or totally disabled. The Social Security Administration sends a monthly SSI check to each recipient, and each state is permitted to supplement the federal payment. SSI is clearly a relief program, not a social insurance program. It is aimed exclusively at the nonworking poor.

General Public Assistance   The final transfer payment program is general public assistance (GPA), or general relief. This is administered and financed exclusively by state and local governments. Homeless and destitute persons who do not qualify for other public assistance programs can get general relief from their state and county welfare departments, although the amounts are very restricted in some states.

Earned Income Tax Credit (EITC)   Started in 1975 as a minor program to provide tax relief for the working poor, this program escalated to more than $20 billion by the mid-1990s. A four-person family is currently eligible for a maximum of up to $3,370, depending on their income. At about $12,000, the family would receive the entire $3,370. The amount received goes down as their earned income goes up, until the credit phases out entirely at about $27,000. If the family's income is so low that they do not owe any federal income tax, they receive the tax credit as a cash payment on top of whatever other refund they are entitled to. The EITC is not an easy benefit to receive. Not only must you file an income tax return, but you must understand that the program exists and fill out the required tax forms. Despite these difficulties, fifteen million families participate in the program.[39]

In-Kind Assistance Programs

In addition to transfer payments, the federal, state, and local governments have a wide range of specific services for the poorer part of the population. These are sometimes called **in-kind assistance,** because they provide assistance that has a cash value, even though it is not received in cash. Five of the most prominent social services are outlined in Table 13-3—public housing, health programs, Medicaid, legal services, and employment services. Housing and health will be discussed elsewhere in this chapter, so only the last two will be dealt with here.

Employment Programs   All states provide employment services through which they help people find jobs. In addition, a number of federal and state programs have existed over the years to provide training, job location services, and public jobs for teenagers. The most prominent of these is a program called JTPA (Jobs and Training Partnership Act).

Legal Services   One of the most controversial social services has been the **legal services program (LSP).** It was created in 1965 as part of the **War on Poverty.** Under this program, federally paid lawyers handle legal problems, such as divorce filings, disputes with landlords, and consumer complaints of individuals against government bureaucracies.

Other Social Services   In addition to the programs just discussed, state and local governments provide a wide variety of other social services, such as child day-care licensing, adoption, homemaker services for the elderly, and child-protection services. Federal involvement in these programs is traced to the 1975 Title XX amendment to the Social Security Act, which established a social services block grant.

◇ HEALTH-CARE POLICIES: THE INTERGOVERNMENTAL SYSTEM IN PRACTICE

State and local governments have traditionally maintained public health departments to curb communicable diseases and to promote the general public health. Additionally, counties in metropolitan areas have maintained large public hospitals where needy persons could go for emergency care.

Growing State and Local Government Role

In recent years, the state and local government role in health care has expanded far beyond traditional roles. In most instances, the state and local expansion occurred as a response to new federal programs. One of the first was the Hill-Burton Act of 1946, which provided funds for hospital construction. Later amendments to this act provided federal funds for rehabilitation facilities and nursing homes. Federal funds went to both public and private facilities.

As public and private health-care facilities expanded, the states saw themselves forced into a much stronger regulatory role. A major consequence of the Hill-Burton Act, for example, was the overbuilding of hospital capacity and bed space, thus contributing to the inflation of health-care costs. In order to gain better control over hospital construction costs, most states have passed certificate-of-need laws. These require any organization to get state certification that the new construction is actually needed before it can add to its hospital, nursing home, or clinic, or before it can buy expensive diagnostic equipment.

State and local governments are also heavily involved in the direct provision of health-care services to the poor. This role expanded dramatically after the passage of the Medicaid Act in 1965. Medicaid must not be confused with its partner, Medicare; the two are very different. **Medicare** is a health insurance program for elderly people of all income levels. **Medicaid** provides medical services for people who cannot afford health care on their own. All public assistance recipients (AFDC, SSI, GPA) are eligible for Medicaid, as are the aged who cannot afford the Medicare premiums. Under Medicaid, states are required to provide eight basic health services, and they may add up to seventeen other services if they choose. A cost-sharing formula is scaled to the state's per-capita income. More than thirty-three million people are now covered by Medicaid.[40]

Issues for the 1990s

As more and more government funds have gone to health care, a number of issues have surfaced that will plague governments at all levels well into the twenty-first century. First, the U.S. health-care system is extremely expensive. Health care adds up to more than $880 billion and consumes 14 percent of the gross domestic product, up from only 7.4 percent in 1970.[41] Second, an estimated thirty-seven million people currently lack health insurance coverage. Most of these are working people who earn too much money to qualify for Medicaid but whose jobs do not provide health insurance. Third, the difficulty of getting health insurance is also cited as one of the major factors keeping single mothers on welfare. Until 1997, AFDC recipients automatically qualified for Medicaid. But if they left AFDC to work in a job without health insurance they found themselves and their children without either health insurance or Medicaid.

Massachusetts in 1988 pioneered a plan that requires employers of more than five people to make health insurance available and to pay a portion of the premium. To help the employer skirt the paperwork costs of negotiating with insurance companies, the employer, under a so-called play or pay plan, can deposit the premium in a state trust fund that will purchase the coverage from private carriers.[42] This act was barely on the books, however, when a downturn in the New England economy left Massachusetts without the revenues to implement the plan. In 1991, a new governor, Republican William Weld, vetoed a bill designed to implement the plan and proposed instead his own plan, in which the play or pay principal was diluted.[43]

As Massachusetts' universal health plan was floundering, a comparable but less extensive plan was being implemented in Minnesota. Like the Massachusetts plan, the Minnesota plan requires employers to provide health coverage, but it eased the burden of doing so by creating a state-run insurance pool financed by a 2 percent tax on all medical services provided in the state. Persons who are uninsured can buy into the plan for a premium that is adjusted to their income level. To contain escalating costs, it set up a thirty-member commission to work with health-care providers and insurance companies in setting fee and payment guidelines.[44]

Another controversial area in which states are being forced to act is to determine who will have access to health care in a fiscal environment when not every person or every health problem can be covered. Today, access is determined by ability to pay. The more money you have and the more insurance you have, the more health care you can buy. Health insurance companies are moving to a concept called managed care, which tries to hold down medical costs by forgoing some expensive procedures and limiting access to others. This is accomplished by having primary care physicians and insurance company gatekeepers screen patients for specialized treatments. If your insurance company will not pay for a procedure you want, you will have to foot the bill or go without. Obviously, the less money you have, the more restrictive your care.

This situation raises important philosophical issues. In the real world, there are not enough health-care dollars to provide every service to every person who wants them. By what criteria should medical services be rationed? Should they be rationed by wealth, in which case the services go to the people with the most income and the best health insurance? Should they be rationed by some measure of social utility, in which case kidney transplants for a thirty-year-old person would probably have preference over the same procedure for a seventy-year-old person? And if they are rationed by social utility, who should be empowered to decide which procedures have the most social utility?

Oregon took a stab at these issues when it revamped how it spends its Medicaid dollars. The Oregon Health Services Commission spent four years studying more than 700 medical procedures and ranked them in priority. The top 583 procedures were approved for Medicaid funding, whereas the others were not. The net effect was to expand by more than 100,000 the number of people eligible for basic medical services but to preclude treatments for some other services. Some of the precluded services, such as medical therapy for AIDS patients believed to be in the last six months of life, have strong political constituencies that object to the plan.[45]

A National Health Insurance Plan?

Given the magnitude of these issues and the widely varying abilities of individual states to cope with them, should we have a national health insurance plan that would ensure everyone's right to some minimal level of health care? President Bill Clinton thought so and in 1993 proposed an ambitious overhaul of the nation's health services system. Clinton's plan aimed to reduce the number of people without health insurance and to expand the role of both the federal government and the states in providing a national system of managed care. The plan was narrowly defeated by Congress in 1994. And when conservative Republicans gained control of Congress later that year, national health insurance was quietly laid to rest.

Like the elevators in this cartoon, health care costs and health insurance continue to go up faster than economic growth rates.

Source: By Dan Foote for *Dallas Times-Herald*. Reprinted by permission of Texas International Features.

◇ REFORMING SOCIAL WELFARE

The American public exhibits a schizophrenic view of social welfare programs. National surveys find broad support for government aid to helpless people, but the word *welfare* is greeted with overwhelming hostility. A good example of this schizophrenic view was seen in a 1977 *New York Times*/CBS poll, which found that 58 percent of the people did not approve of government welfare programs.[46] Yet when asked if they would support a program to help poor people buy food at reduced prices, an implicit reference to the food stamps program, 81 percent of the people said yes. When asked if they would support financial aid for children in low-income, one-parent homes, an implicit reference to the AFDC program, 81 percent again said yes. And when asked if they would support paying health costs for poor people, an implicit reference to the Medicaid program, 82 percent said yes.

But there is more to welfare's poor image than simple confusion about the labels. For one thing, there is a perception of widespread "welfare cheating" that tarnishes the image of welfare recipients. When asked in 1994 whether most welfare recipients are genuinely needy or just taking advantage of the system, 69 percent of whites and 63 percent of blacks said that most people were taking advantage of the system.[47] In contrast to this perception, federal investigations reveal that only 5 to 8 percent of AFDC recipients have taken benefits to which they were not legally entitled.[48] Whatever the reality of welfare cheating, welfare recipients are an easy target for public officials currying popular support. President Ronald Reagan used the term *welfare queens* to convey an image of many recipients as too lazy to go out and find a job that would get them off the public dole.

Whatever the reasons for welfare's unpopular image, the fact of its unpopularity has provided continuing support over the years to reform the system. Four important approaches to welfare reform have been attempted over the past three decades.

The 1960s: War on Poverty

The Lyndon Johnson administration (1963–1969) did not really have a welfare reform plan; instead, Johnson proposed a war on poverty itself. Called the Great Society, the Johnson program brought about a massive expansion of social service funding and several new programs such as Medicare, Medicaid, and the legal services program. The keystone of the war on poverty was the **Economic Opportunity Act of 1965,** which created the Office of Economic Opportunity to conduct experiments in social services and to coordinate all the poverty-related efforts of the agencies of the federal government. In 1966, the model cities program was created to concentrate and coordinate federal programs in specific neighborhoods of 150 selected major cities. However, neither the model cities nor the economic opportunity programs were successful in coordinating the poverty efforts at either the federal or the local level.[49]

Perhaps the most significant impact was their requirement that the people affected by the programs participate in drawing up the program plans. In each locality receiving War-on-Poverty funds, a community action agency (CAA) was created to draft a community action plan for those communities. The net effect was to stimulate community organizing efforts in poor neighborhoods. In particular, the CAAs developed community leadership in black neighborhoods, provided jobs for poor and middle-class blacks, and organized residents of those neighborhoods to battle for better services from the city government, to vote, to combat absentee landlords, and to become politically active.

These social programs of the War on Poverty are under heavy criticism today, especially by some conservatives, who point out that poverty has not been eliminated and who argue that welfare efforts have trapped people in poverty by making them dependent on government aid.[50] Most analysts, however, while recognizing the failure to end poverty, credit the social programs of the 1960s with some important successes.[51] They put more economic resources into the hands of many poor people, and they were a major factor in cutting in half the percentage of people living in poverty.

The 1970s: Aborted Attempts at Income Maintenance

The second approach to welfare reform was **income maintenance,** the attempt to ensure that everybody in the country had a cash income above the subsistence level. This was the approach of Presidents Richard Nixon (1969–1974) and Jimmy Carter (1977–1981). Nixon called his proposal the **Family Assistance Plan (FAP)**. A four-person family with no income would receive $1,600. For each dollar the family earned, the government's payment would decrease by 50 cents. When the family's earnings reached $3,920, the government benefits would be phased out completely.

Although this was a truly revolutionary approach to welfare reform, it never became law. Liberals, who had previously pushed for income maintenance as the ideal tool for income redistribution, feared that FAP would phase out other major programs, such as food stamps.[52] They complained that Nixon's proposed benefit levels were too low and would reduce overall welfare benefit levels in most states.[53] Conservatives objected that FAP would reward poor families for not working. Social work professionals had no incentive to support FAP since it would reduce the need for AFDC caseworkers. Finally, there was no broad public support for the concept of income maintenance. A *New York Times*/CBS poll in 1977 found that 50 percent of the people opposed a guaranteed minimum income, and only 44 percent supported it.[54] Unable to build the political support needed for his plan, Nixon himself grew cool to it. A version of it twice passed the House of Representatives but died in the Senate.

When Jimmy Carter became president in 1977, he proposed a similar income maintenance plan to replace the existing AFDC, SSI, and food stamps programs. Carter's plan provided a mandatory work requirement for adults classified as able to work. To ensure an adequate supply of employment opportunities, he proposed an extensive expansion of public service jobs at the minimum wage. And to help out the working poor, he proposed a cash payment to supplement their wages. Under this plan, a family of four would receive a cash payment of $2,300 as long as its earned income was less than $3,800. For each dollar earned above that amount, the cash supplement would be reduced by 50 cents until it was completely phased out at $8,400. Thus, every four-person family in the country would be guaranteed a minimum income of $8,400, and there were strong work requirements in the program.

Carter's plan quickly ran into the same kind of opposition that had killed Nixon's family assistance plan earlier in the decade. The benefit levels were attacked as too high by the chairpersons of the House and Senate tax committees and too low by both the AFL-CIO and the Congressional Black Caucus.[55] The mandatory work provisions were criticized. The public service jobs at the minimum wage, it was said, would displace working people from jobs that would otherwise pay twice that amount for the same work. Labor leaders feared that this would give local governments an incentive to fire their regular employees and hire them back at the minimum wage with federal funds. Faced with this opposition, Congress again aborted the income maintenance approach and instead expanded the food stamps program.

The 1980s: From Welfare to Workfare

Following the failure of guaranteed income plans in the 1970s, welfare reform in the 1980s shifted toward the goals of reducing the welfare rolls and making welfare recipients work to earn their grants, if possible. This shift took place in three stages, culminating with a major change in AFDC regulations in 1988.

The Reagan Approach to Welfare Cuts   Picking up on the themes of conservative critics[56] (see p. 349), President Ronald Reagan (1981–1989) charged that welfare programs sapped people of their will to become self-supporting.[57] He also believed that plenty of jobs were available for people who truly wanted to work. Following on these beliefs, his approach to welfare was to force welfare recipients into the job market by reducing expenditures for most social service programs and by tightening up eligibility requirements for the programs. By these measures, less money would be available for welfare and fewer people would qualify for it. Reagan also pushed Congress to enact lucrative income tax cuts for upper- and middle-income people, and Congress on its own initiative in 1986 removed the lowest-income people from any income tax liability whatsoever.[58]

The hope of all this macroeconomic activity was, of course, that reduction in tax burdens combined with a booming economy would lift most people out of poverty and make welfare unnecessary. Unfortunately, economic growth in the 1980s did not bring about this happy state of affairs. As Figure 13-1 shows, there were more people in poverty at the end of Reagan's administration than there had been when he was elected (31.9 million in 1988 versus 29.3 million in 1980). When he left office in 1989, the percentage of people in poverty was still higher than it had been twenty years earlier.

State Initiatives at Workfare   While the federal government sought to reduce federal welfare benefits in the 1980s, states began to experiment with a number of approaches to moving people off of AFDC and into the workforce. What made these experiments different from previous attempts to force AFDC recipients into the job market was the recognition that welfare mothers can only be successful in the job market if certain conditions are met: There must be jobs available for them, they must have the skills and attitudes to win the jobs, they must have day-care help (which currently costs about $75–$100 per week per child), and they must have medical insurance to make up for their being taken off Medicaid.

The pioneers in seeking to meet these conditions are California's GAIN (Greater Avenues to Independence) plan and Massachusetts' ET (Employment and Training) plan. GAIN was passed in California through a fascinating political compromise between liberal Democrats (who agreed to the conservative demand for a mandatory work requirement) and conservative Republicans (who agreed to the liberal demand for putting up money for training and child-care expenses). The result was an elaborate program begun in 1985 that screens participants into appropriate training programs, creates "job clubs" to teach them how to find jobs, and gives them money for child care while they are in training and for their first year on the job.[59]

Whether workfare programs will reach these goals is still being studied. But preliminary reports have been cautiously optimistic about the ability to move AFDC recipients into decent-paying jobs under the proper conditions. In its first two and one-half years, Massachusetts' ET program claimed to have made a significant reduction in the state's AFDC caseload and to have moved a significant number of AFDC recipients into the workforce.[60] A San Diego workfare plan reported that its participants not only were more likely to get off welfare than were comparable nonworkfare AFDC recipients, but when they found jobs, those jobs paid higher wages than did jobs found by the non-workfare AFDC recipients.[61]

Federal Workfare Reflecting the growing belief that AFDC recipients should be working toward the goal of making themselves self-sufficient, Congress, on its own initiative, in 1988 passed an AFDC reform law that obliged the states to draw up training and employability plans for welfare recipients, required the states to improve collection of child support payments from noncustodial parents, and provided for up to one year of transitional Medicaid benefits while the welfare mother was moving into the workforce.

The 1990s: Behavior Modification

Despite the far-reaching nature of the 1988 reform act, it did not go far enough for welfare critics who focused increasingly on the responsibility of welfare recipients to develop attitudes and behaviors that would lead them out of welfare dependency. The problem of welfare dependency, says conservative analyst Lawrence Mead, is not the lack of economic opportunities; the problem is the lack of will to seize the opportunities that exist.[62]

Changing Public Opinion The growing conservative attack on welfare was accompanied by public opinion that seemed increasingly receptive to conservative-oriented welfare reforms. The Gallup Poll in 1995 found that 58 percent of the people favored moving mothers off welfare after two years, 62 percent favored a five-year time limit on welfare, and 78 percent favored no increased benefits if a mother had a child while on welfare.[63] When asked by a *Wall Street Journal*/NBC Poll whether the welfare system did more good than harm or vice versa, 72 percent of whites and 57 percent of blacks said that it did more harm.[64]

State Initiatives With a public opinion increasingly receptive to forcing welfare recipients to modify their attitudes and behavior, it is not surprising that the states began to act. One of the first states to use its welfare policies to modify the attitudes and behavior of welfare recipients was Wisconsin. Under Republican Governor Tommy G. Thompson, Wisconsin cut welfare grants for parents whose children missed too many school days, denied increased grants to AFDC mothers who had another child, encouraged teenage welfare mothers to get married, and reduced benefits to welfare recipients who moved into the state.[65] Called W-2, Wisconsin obliged mothers with children under twelve weeks to find work. And if they could not find private sector jobs, Wisconsin demanded that they work in subsidized community service jobs.

Several other states passed similar legislation designed to make the receiving of welfare assistance dependent upon the behavior of the welfare recipients. California approved AFDC benefits to teenage mothers only if they lived with their own parents. New Jersey sought to encourage welfare mothers to get married by allowing their benefits to continue after they got married (but only if the man was not the children's father). Ohio pays welfare recipients a bonus for good school attendance. Michigan eliminated general assistance benefits for able-bodied recipients.[66] By 1996, fourteen states had adopted some form of time limit that one could stay on welfare, twenty-three had adopted a work require-ment for welfare recipients, and nineteen had adopted a family cap that forbade increasing welfare benefits if another child was borne to a mother already on welfare. Thirty-three states had adopted at least one of these three measures.[67]

Federal Reform: 1996   In 1996, these piecemeal steps toward welfare reform cul-minated in the federal **Personal Responsibility and Assistance Act,** which pro-duced the most dramatic changes in federal welfare policy since the 1960s. This act:

- Replaced AFDC with a block grant program that would enable each state to design its own assistance plan for the poor
- Limited to two years the amount of time a family could stay on welfare at any one time
- Put a five-year lifetime limit on welfare for any one person
- Prohibited benefits to minor mothers unless they lived with an adult and were attending school
- Provided extra funds for states that reduced births to unmarried women
- Enacted stricter eligibility standards for SSI and food stamps
- Prohibited SSI and food stamp benefits to legal immigrants until they become citizens or work in the country for ten years

◇ WELFARE REFORM, SOCIAL CONFLICT, AND THE POLITICAL ECONOMY

What can we conclude about the welfare reforms of the 1990s? Are conservatives correct that the reforms will become a ticket to financial independence for people now allegedly trapped in a system of welfare dependency? Or are liberals correct that these reforms will throw millions of women and children into the streets and turn the nation's back on the plight of the needy? We will not know the an-swers to these questions for a number of years. But in the meantime, we can gain insight into the questions by looking at the relationships of welfare reform to our two theoretical concerns in this book—social conflict and political economy.

Welfare Reform and Social Conflict

The welfare reforms of 1996 are a great experiment in managing the dramatic so-cial changes of our time. These include rising divorce rates, huge jumps in the number of children being raised in poverty, and a dramatic worsening of the job prospects of the bottom half of the population. By replacing the keystone welfare program for single mothers (AFDC) with the Temporary Assistance of Needy Families Block Grant, the federal government has plunged into the unknown. And the plunge has pleased neither liberals nor conservatives. Liberal critics, as suggested by the cartoon on p. 355, charge that the federal government has

From the liberal critique, Congress abandoned its responsibilities to help the needy when it passed the 1996 Welfare Reform Act.

Source: By Keefe for the *Denver Post,* reprinted in *The Washington Post National Weekly,* August 12–18, 1996, p. 4.

turned its back on the nation's poor by terminating a sixty year federal guarantee of assistance to needy single mothers and their children. Conservatives fear that the reforms left so many hardship exemptions that some welfare recipients will avoid the two-year and five-year limits.[68]

At least in the short run, these reforms seem likely to worsen the social conflicts we have been examining. In part, this is because the reforms are a very important symbol of the federal government's abandoning its commitment to the needy. People fight over symbols, and the welfare reforms are a particular sore point for minority group leaders as well as some feminist organizations such as the National Organization of Women and children's advocates such as the Children's Defense Fund. There is no reason to think that they will take this symbolic defeat lying down.

In addition to the symbolic importance of the 1996 welfare reforms, there will be less government money going to the poor. With the welfare poor getting less government money at the same time that the working poor have been suffering from wage stagnation, class divisions are likely to sharpen. If the reforms work as intended, a flood of former welfare recipients into the workforce could intensify competition for scarce jobs and put downward pressure on wages. This is not likely to reduce social and class divisions.

Welfare Reform and Political Economy

The success of the welfare reforms will depend greatly on the political economy. Each state will be pressured to have lower welfare benefits than neighboring states for fear that high benefits might attract a flood of poor migrants. Critics fear that this will provoke a "race to the bottom" as each state seeks to become the one with the lowest benefit levels.

Another concern lies in the nature of the economic cycle. When the economy enters one of its periodic recessions, it is hard to see how there will be enough jobs available for all the current welfare recipients who will be forced into the workforce. Even when the economy is not in a recession, it has undergone profound changes over the past quarter century that limit the number of well-paying jobs. As noted in previous chapters, the major changes are twofold. First is the shift from an economy based on heavy, so-called smokestack industries (such as automobiles, steel, and rubber) to one based on services, communications, and high technology. The heavy industries required a huge unskilled labor force that became a formidable economic force once it unionized. But unskilled workers are at a severe disadvantage in the newer service-oriented economy.

A second change impinging the political economy is the growing challenge of foreign competition to American basic industry. This challenge has been most dramatic, perhaps, in the automobile industry, where foreign competition rose from a minimal share of the American automobile market to capturing nearly a third of it today. During the 1980s, these two developments provoked high unemployment in the Northeast and Midwest, where much of America's heavy industry was located.

As unemployment in these areas grew, the unemployed workers put a drain on the social service and welfare budgets of the affected states. Many displaced workers migrated to other regions, especially the sunbelt, in search of employment. But by the mid-1980s, the oil-rich states of the sunbelt (especially Texas, Oklahoma, and Louisiana) got badly hit by dropping oil prices, and they too found it difficult to meet all the commitments that had been made when revenues were rolling in. Texas, in particular, was hit hard. Along with declining oil revenues, real estate markets tumbled and tens of billions of dollars were lost in the savings and loan crisis that began in the late 1980s. The economic growth of the 1990s helped alleviate many of these problems for the political economies in most states. But the fundamental economic changes taking place seem likely to continue to threaten the economic status of blue-collar workers and the lower-middle-income groups. As we saw earlier, these groups are receiving a smaller share of the national income than they did a generation earlier. For these reasons, individual state and local governments are very likely to find their social welfare budgets squeezed very tightly for some years to come.

SUMMARY

1. The official U.S. poverty income line is based on the amount of money needed to purchase food on a modest food plan. The percentage of people below the poverty line declined from nearly 25 percent in 1960 to about 12 percent in the early 1970s. In the 1980s, it began to rise again.

2. Leftist and rightist theorists present conflicting views on the causes of poverty and the ways that government should deal with poverty.
3. The implementation of welfare policies is done on an intergovernmental basis, with complicated interactions among federal, state, and local governments. This decentralized process of implementation has led to differing benefit levels from one state to another and has made administering welfare policies rationally and efficiently very difficult.
4. Welfare benefit levels vary from state to state in part because of differences in affluence and levels of political competition, the militancy of the working and lower classes, and differences in political cultures.
5. The major social welfare programs can be grouped under three general headings: (1) social insurance transfer payments, (2) cash transfer payments that are not social insurance, and (3) in-kind assistance programs.
6. The most costly welfare policies are probably the health-care policies. A number of volatile health-care issues will confront the state governments in the 1990s, and the federal government will continue to be confronted with the question of creating a national health insurance system.
7. Despite the administrative deficiencies of existing welfare programs and despite popular dissatisfaction with the general concept of welfare, attempts to reform the welfare system by consolidating the categorical programs under an income maintenance plan and by nationalizing more of the program failed consistently during the 1970s. In 1996, AFDC was replaced with a welfare block grant, and severe restrictions were put on other social service programs such as food stamps and SSI.

KEY TERMS

Absolute deprivation   A definition of poverty that says that one is deprived of the necessities of life if one falls below a specific income line.

Aid for Families with Dependent Children (AFDC)   A federal program from 1935 to 1997 that provided cash assistance for single parents without income but with dependent children.

Culture of poverty   A term used to describe a combination of psychological traits among many people who are permanently poor. These traits include cynicism toward the social system, lack of hope for escape from their plight, inability to defer gratification, and inability to plan for the future.

Economic Opportunity Act of 1965   The fundamental legislation of President Johnson's War on Poverty. It created the Office of Economic Opportunity to conduct experiments in social services and to coordinate all the poverty-related efforts of the agencies of the federal government.

Family Assistance Plan (FAP)   An income maintenance proposal of the Nixon administration that did not pass Congress.

Food stamps program   A program that provides vouchers to low-income people to help them buy food.

Gross national product (GNP)   A nation's total output of goods and services.

Horatio Alger   An author who grew rich writing stories about boys who climbed to the top of the social ladder. "Horatio Alger myth" is synonymous with upward social mobility.

Hypothesis   A scientific term that refers to an educated guess about the factors that explain some phenomenon.

Income maintenance   An approach to social welfare that seeks to provide cash assistance that will maintain people's income above the poverty line.

In-kind assistance   Social programs, such as medical aid, that provide help that has a cash value, even though the help is not received in the form of cash.

Laissez-faire   The concept that government should leave the economy to the forces of the marketplace and should not seek to regulate the economy.

Legal services program (LSP)   A program that provides legal aid to poor people in civil cases but not in criminal cases.

Means test   A test that makes eligibility for benefits dependent on a person's ability to show need, usually by falling under a specified income level.

Medicaid   A program that provides medical assistance for people who cannot afford health care on their own.

Medicare   A government-run health insurance program for elderly people of all income levels.

OASDHI   Old Age, Survivors, Disability, and Health Insurance. The fundamental social insurance programs for retirement, disability, and Medicare set up under the Social Security Act.

Personal Responsibility and Assistance Act   The 1996 welfare reform law that replaced AFDC with a block start.

Poverty line   The federal government's official definition of poverty, based on the assumption that having less than three times the income needed to buy food on a modest food plan constitutes poverty.

Relative deprivation   A definition of poverty that says that a person can be considered poor only in relation to the rest of the people in a society.

Social Darwinism   An application to the social sphere of Darwin's theory of natural selection and survival of the fittest. Accordingly, Social Darwinists oppose social welfare policies.

Social insurance   A societal program in which one pays money into a government-sponsored trust fund and draws benefits from that fund later, when one becomes eligible.

Social mobility   Movement upward or downward in society's class structure.

Social Security Act of 1935   The original legislative authority for much of the social welfare programs existing today.

Transfer payment   A direct payment of government money to individuals.

War on Poverty   President Lyndon Johnson's Great Society approach to poverty. Johnson vastly expanded social service programs in the hopes of eliminating poverty.

REFERENCES

1. Robert E. Spiller et al., eds., *Literary History of the United States: Bibliography* (New York: Macmillan, 1974), p. 226.
2. Bureau of the Census, *Statistical Abstract of the United States: 1982–83* (Washington, D.C.: U.S. Government Printing Office, 1982), p. 256.
3. Studs Terkel, *Division Street: America* (New York: Avon Books, 1967), pp. 271–272.
4. Ibid., pp. 39–46.
5. Commentary on Tally Jackson is extracted from Elliot Liebow, *Tally's Corner* (Boston: Little, Brown and Co., 1967).
6. For critiques of the methods of drawing a poverty line, see Lee Rainwater, "Economic Inequality and the Credit Income Tax," *Working Papers for a New Society* 1, no. 1 (Spring 1973): 50–61; Michael Harrington, "The Betrayal of the Poor," *Atlantic* (January 1970): 71–72; Martin Rein, "Problems in the Definition and Mea-

surement of Poverty," *Poverty in America*, rev. ed., Louis Ferman et al., eds. (Ann Arbor: University of Michigan Press, 1968), pp. 123–125; Daniel M. Gordon, "Trends in Poverty," in *Problems in Political Economy: An Urban Perspective*, 2nd ed. (Lexington, Mass.: D.C. Heath, 1977), pp. 297–298. Also see Alan Haber, "Poverty Budgets: How Much Is Enough?" *Poverty and Human Resources Abstracts* 1, no. 3 (1966): 6.

7. Timothy M. Smeeding, *Alternative Methods for Valuing Selected In-Kind Transfer Benefits and Measuring Their Effects on Poverty* (Washington, D.C.: U.S. Bureau of the Census, 1982).

8. Thomas R. Dye, *Politics in States and Communities*, 3rd ed. (Englewood Cliffs, N.J.: Prentice Hall, 1977), p. 439.

9. For a review of this suggestion, see Gordon, "Trends in Poverty," pp. 299–300. Also see Victor R. Fuchs, "Redefining Poverty and Redistributing Income," *Public Interest*, no. 8 (Summer 1967): 91.

10. Bureau of the Census, *Current Population Reports: Trends in Income by Selected Characteristics: 1947 to 1988*, Series P-60, No. 167 (Washington, D.C.: U.S. Government Printing Office, April 1990), p. 14; *Statistical Abstract of the United States: 1991*, p. 454.

11. Data from the U.S. Census Bureau. Reported in *The New York Times*, December 4, 1991, p. A-11.

12. James N. Morgan et al., *Five Thousand American Families: Patterns of Economic Progress* (Ann Arbor: University of Michigan, Institute for Social Research, 1974).

13. Bureau of the Census, *Current Population Reports: Characteristics of the Population Below the Poverty Level: 1977*, Series P-60, no. 119 (Washington, D.C.: U.S. Government Printing Office, 1979), p. 4.

14. Liebow, *Tally's Corner*, p. 63.

15. The data is found in the United States Congress, House Ways and Means Committee, 1989 report on federal assistance programs. Reported in *The New York Times*, March 22, 1989, p. 1.

16. Leonard Silk, "Rich and Poor: The Gap Widens," *The New York Times*, May 12, 1989, p. 28. The data refers to the 708 highest-paid chief executives, not all corporation presidents.

17. From a study by the Congressional Office of Technology Assessment. See *The New York Times*, February 7, 1986, p. 1.

18. Lawrence M. Mead, "The New Politics of the New Poverty," *Public Interest*, no. 105 (Spring 1991): 107.

19. Edward C. Banfield, *The Unheavenly City* (Boston: Little, Brown and Co., 1970), pp. 125–126.

20. See Herbert Spencer, *Social Statics* (London: John Chapman, 1951).

21. Charles Murray, *Losing Ground* (New York: Basic Books, 1984), p. 9.

22. Charles Murray and Richard J. Herrnstein, *The Bell Curve: Intelligence and Class Struggle in American Life*. (New York: The Free Press, 1994).

23. Stuart Butler and Anna Kondratas, *Out of the Poverty Trap: A Conservative Strategy for Welfare Reform* (New York: The Free Press, 1987), p. 13.

24. Banfield, *The Unheavenly City*, p. 118.

25. A summary of ideological orientations to poverty is presented by David M. Gordon in his *Problems in Political Economy: An Urban Perspective*, 2nd ed. (Lexington, Mass.: D.C. Heath, 1977), pp. 272–281.

26. A survey conducted by U.S. Trust of people with greater than $200,000 in income or $3 million in assets. Reported in Gary Belsky, "Why Most of the Rich Will Get Richer," *Money* (May 1995): 135.

27. See especially Thomas R. Dye, *Politics, Economics and the Public* (Chicago: Rand Mc-Nally, 1966); Richard E. Dawson and James A. Robinson, "Interpreting Competition, Economic Variables and Welfare Policies in the American States," *Journal of Politics* 25, no. 2 (May 1963): 265–289; and Gary L. Tompkins, "A Causal Model of State Welfare Expenditures," *Journal of Politics* 37, no. 2 (May 1975): 392–416. These and more recent studies, however, are subject to important methodological criticism for often lacking coordination between the time periods in which they gather their data on policy results, party competition, and levels of affluence. See Harvey J. Tucker, "Interparty Competition in the American States: One More Time," *American Politics Quarterly* 10, no. 1 (January 1982): 93–116; and Harvey J. Tucker, "It's About Time: The Uses of Time in Cross-sectional State Policy Research," *American Journal of Political Science* 26, no. 1 (February 1982): 176–196.

28. An excellent review of the relative influence of economic and political variables on public policy is Jack Treadway, *Public Policy-Making in the American States* (New York: Praeger, 1985), pp. 131–176.

29. For an excellent summary of the major social welfare programs, see "Social Security Programs in the United States," *Social Security Bulletin* 49, no. 1 (January 1986): 5–61.

30. Based on 1986 data, the Bureau of the Census calculated that the percentage of people in poverty would have been 21.2 percent instead of the 14.9 percent that prevailed at the time. Reported in the *Minneapolis Star Tribune,* December 28, 1988, p. 3N.

31. For an articulate statement of this viewpoint, see Laurence J. Kotlikoff and Jeffery Sachs, "Privatizing Social Security: It's High Time to Privatize," *The Brookings Review* 15, no. 3 (Summer 1997): 16–22.

32. Henry J. Aaron, "Privatizing Social Security: A Bad Idea Whose Time Will Never Come," *The Brookings Review* 15, no. 3 (Summer 1997): 17–23.

33. *Statistical Abstract of the United States: 1996,* p. 388.

34. Teh-Wei Hu and Norman Knaub, "Effects of Cash and In-Kind Welfare Payments on Family Expenditures," *Policy Analysis* 2, no. 1 (Winter 1976): 81–82.

35. Office of Management and Budget, *Budget of the Government of the United States for FY 1978* (Washington, D.C.: U.S. Government Printing Office, 1977), p. 172. A 1987 study found that about 8 percent of AFDC funds were spent either on people who were ineligible or on overpayments. *The New York Times,* December 7, 1987, p. 17.

36. Kenneth T. Jost, "Welfare Reform," *CQ Researcher* 2, no. 14 (April 10, 1992): 320. Data from the House Ways and Means Committee.

37. *Congressional Quarterly Almanac, 1997,* pp. 458–462.

38. *Statistical Abstract of the United States: 1996,* p. 389.

39. Christopher Howard, "Happy Returns: How the Working Poor Get Tax Relief," *The American Prospect* No. 17 (Spring 1994): 46–52.

40. Henry J. Aaron, "End of an Era: The New Debate Over Health Care Financing," *Brookings Review* 14, no. 1 (Winter 1996): 350–357.

41. *Statistical Abstract of the United States: 1996,* p. 109.

42. *The New York Times,* April 26, 1988, p. 25; *Washington Post National Weekly,* May 9–15, 1988, p. 30.

43. Jerry Berger, "Prognosis Poor for Universal Health Care," *State Legislatures* 17, no. 6 (June 1991): 35–37.

44. *Minneapolis Star Tribune,* March 15, 1992, p. 1; April 11, 1992, p. 1.

45. See *The New York Times,* August 4, 1992, p. 6; August 5, 1992, p. 5.

46. *The New York Times,* August 3, 1977, p. 1.

47. *The Gallup Poll: Public Opinion, 1994* (Wilmington, Del.: Scholarly Resources, Inc., 1995), p. 85.

48. In 1977, the federal government estimated that 5.5 percent of AFDC recipients were ineligible. See Office of Management and Budget, *FY 1978 Budget*, p. 172. A decade later, a federal study estimated the number to be about 8 percent. See *The New York Times*, December 7, 1987, p. 17.

49. See James E. Anderson, "Coordinating the War on Poverty," *Policy Studies Journal* 2, no. 3 (Spring 1974): 174–178; and James L. Sundquist, *Making Federalism Work: A Study of Program Coordination at the Community Level* (Washington, D.C.: Brookings Institution, 1969).

50. See especially Butler and Kondratas, *Out of the Poverty Trap*, and Murray, *Losing Ground*.

51. See John E. Schwarz, *America's Hidden Success: A Reassessment of Twenty Years of Public Policy* (New York: Norton, 1983), especially pp. 57–59. Also see Sar A. Levitan and Robert Taggart, "Great Society Did Succeed," *Political Science Quarterly* 91 (Winter 1976–1977): 601–618.

52. Ellen Kelman, "Welfare Reform," *Dissent* 24 (Spring 1977): 126–128.

53. Lester C. Thurow, "The Political Economy of Income Redistribution Policies," *Annals of the American Academy of Political and Social Science* 409 (September 1973): 146–155.

54. *The New York Times*, August 3, 1977, p. 1.

55. See President Jimmy Carter's welfare reform message in *The New York Times*, August 7, 1977, pp. 1, 40. Also see *The New York Times*, September 16, 1977, pp. 4, 13; *The New York Times*, December 11, 1977, p. 43.

56. See especially Butler and Kondratas, *Out of the Poverty Trap*, and Murray, *Losing Ground*.

57. In his weekly radio address of February 15, 1986, Reagan blamed welfare programs for teenage pregnancies, family breakups, worsening poverty, and the creation of a permanent state of dependency among the poor. See *The New York Times*, February 16, 1986, p. 27a.

58. The Omnibus Tax Act of 1981 provided a 25 percent reduction in income tax rates staged over the next three years. The 1986 Tax Act reduced the number of rates to three: 15 percent on incomes under $29,750 (for married couples filing jointly), 28 percent on incomes from $29,751 to $71,900, and 33 percent on incomes from $71,900 to $149,250. Incomes over $149,250 were taxable at the 28 percent rate. This act effectively eliminated the income tax liability for any married couple with income under $6,200 and for any single person with income under $3,750.

59. David L. Kirk, "The California Work/Welfare Scheme," *Public Interest*, no. 83 (Spring 1986): 34–48.

60. Michael Wiseman, "Workfare and Welfare Reform," *Beyond Welfare: New Approaches to the Problem of Poverty in America*, Harrell R. Rodgers, Jr., ed. (Armonk, N.Y.: M. E. Sharpe, 1988), p. 30.

61. Judith M. Gueron, "State Welfare Employment Initiatives: Lessons from the 1980s," *Focus* (a newsletter of the University of Wisconsin Institute for Research on Poverty), 11, no. 1 (Spring 1988): 17–23.

62. Lawrence M. Mead, "Jobs Programs and Other Bromides," *The New York Times*, May 19, 1992, p. 18.

63. *The Gallup Poll: Public Opinion, 1995* (Wilmington, Del.: Scholarly Resources, Inc., 1996), pp. 28–32, 203–206.

64. *Public Perspective* 6, no. 4 (June–July 1995): 25.

65. Julie Kosterlitz, "Behavior Modification," *National Journal,* February 1, 1992, pp. 271–275.

66. *The New York Times,* October 7, 1991, p. 1.

67. *Washington Post National Weekly,* February 12–18, 1996, p. 29. Time limits were adopted by WA, MT, AZ, ND, SD, NE, MO, WI, IL, IN, FL, VA, DE, CT. Work requirements were adopted by OR, MT, WY, VT, CO, ND, SD, NE, OK, IA, MO, Wi, IL, IN MS, LA, SC, VA, MD, DL, CT, VT, HE. Family caps were adopted by CA, AZ, NE, KS, OK, AR, WI, IL, IN, MS, FL, GA, SC, NC, NC, VA, MD, DE, NJ, MA.

68. See *Investors Business Daily,* August 22, 1996, p. B-1.

14

EDUCATION

Chapter Preview

One of the most important services provided by state and local governments is public education. That service spends more tax dollars and employs more people than any other state or local policy area. Today, the public school systems are under widespread criticism. And as we move into the twenty-first century, much of education politics focuses on improving the quality of education. We will examine this phenomenon in this chapter by studying:

1. How state, local, and federal governments work together in providing public education.

2. How political values affect the role people think education should play in society.

3. How state and local governments cope with major educational problems today.

4. How state and local governments responded in the 1980s and 1990s to the demands for educational reform.

5. How education is linked to the political economies of states and communities.

Let us begin with a look at two people who made their way through the educational system, Edward Donohue and Herman the Pushout.

◇ INTRODUCTION

Public education in the United States has traditionally been viewed as the means by which people can learn skills and attitudes that will make them employable, enrich their lives, or help them move up socially. And there can be little doubt that education has done some of this for the average person. In 1993, the median annual income was $17,966 for high school dropouts, $28,700 for high school graduates, $35,000 for those with some college, and $87,686 for those with professional degrees.[1] One group of researchers tried to eliminate the potential influence of heredity on statistics such as these by studying the life earnings of identical twins and found that the twin with more education had better income than the twin with less education. The researchers concluded that each year of schooling adds 16 percent to a person's earnings over a lifetime.[2] Education also confers other benefits. Well-educated people tend to have better health habits than poorly educated people. They tend to know more about the world around them, and they tend to enjoy a wider variety of leisure activities.

Despite the importance of education for the individual's lifetime chances, a growing number of critics question whether the quality of American education is as good as it once was or whether it is good enough for America to keep up in an increasingly competitive and high-technology world. Knowledge of science is critical to high-technology, but an international science test for thirteen-year-olds found that American youngsters were outscored by children in twelve of the other fourteen countries where the test was administered.[3] Mathematics is also critical to high technology, but a mathematics proficiency test in 1993 found that American thirteen-year-olds were outperformed by children in ten out of the twelve countries where the test was administered. Among those outperforming the Americans were South Koreans, Hungarians, Israelis, Irish, Slovenians, and Spaniards.[4] A similar math test administered two years earlier had found similar results. American youngsters placed ninth out of ten countries studied.[5] However, a test of reading abilities found that the American youngsters did somewhat better, scoring fifth out of eleven countries studied.[6]

These results are not encouraging for America's future, and they have stimulated a succession of national reports on the state of education in America. The first and most seminal of these reports was *A Nation at Risk*, issued in 1983 by the **National Commission on Excellence in Education.** This report charged that, for the first time in American history, the average school graduate is less well educated than the average graduate a generation earlier, and that American students performed poorly in comparison to the students of other industrialized nations. "If an unfriendly foreign power had attempted to impose on America the mediocre educational performance that exists today," reported the commission, "we might well have viewed it as an act of war. As it stands, we have allowed this to happen to ourselves. . . . We have, in effect, been committing an act of unthinking, unilateral educational disarmament."[7] As a consequence of this report, education suddenly became an issue, both at the national level and in the states.

In this chapter, we will examine these educational concerns. We will first examine the disappearing tradition of local control over education and the conflicts growing out of the increasing state and federal responsibilities. Second, education will be viewed from the left and right philosophical perspectives. Third, the way governments cope with the main problems of education will be examined in detail. Fourth, we will explore developments in educational reform since the 1983 publication of *A Nation at Risk*. Last, we will discuss the role of education in our twin concerns of social conflict and the political economy.

"Thank you, Sir. I ain't never gonna forget today."

This cartoon captures well the public perception that too many school graduates have failed to learn basic intellectual skills, in this case the skill of speaking proper English.

Source: Schwadron. National Center to Improve Post-Secondary Teaching and Learning, *Update*, vol. 2, no. 1 (September 1988).

◇ STATE, LOCAL, AND FEDERAL ROLES IN EDUCATION

Local Roles

The basic unit governing public education is the local, independent school district. The main exceptions to this are in Alaska, Hawaii, and Maine, where all the schools (Hawaii) or some (Alaska and Maine) are run by the state. In a dozen states, some school systems are subordinated to local governments such as counties (Virginia and North Carolina, for example) or to cities (New York City and Chicago, for example). But 90 percent of all public school systems are **independent school districts** governed by locally elected **boards of education** that are independent of counties, cities, and other units of local government. The local school boards establish local school district policies, set the budget, and decide how much money to raise in property taxes.

In practice, the initiative in these matters usually is taken by the local superintendent of schools, not the school boards. The superintendent proposes policies and budgets to the board, sets the school board meeting agendas, and presents the board with a limited number of options. The board members, who are rarely professional educators, usually lack the educational expertise to become effective policy leaders. Instead, board members tend to involve themselves in small details of school operations and to lose their focus on the board's primary task—setting educational policy.[8]

Table 14-1 CENTRALIZATION OF PUBLIC SCHOOL FINANCE

	Percentage of Public School Expenditures Financed				
Level of Government	1960	1970	1980	1990	1993
Federal	4.4%	7.2%	9.2%	6.3%	7.1%
State	39.1	40.9	49.1	48.5	46.9
Local	56.5	51.9	41.7	45.3	46.0

Sources: Calculated from the Bureau of the Census, *Statistical Abstract of the United States: 1982–83* (Washington, D.C.: U.S. Government Printing Office, 1982), p. 154; *Statistical Abstract: 1991*, p. 149; *Statistical Abstract: 1996*, p. 156.

The Trend Toward Greater State Centralization

The existence of independent school districts gives the illusion of local control over schools. In fact, however, local control has eroded steadily over the past quarter century as the federal and state governments have gained influence in setting education policy. This trend is reflected in the decreasing role of local governments in financing public schools (see Table 14-1) and the declining number of local school districts themselves—from more than 127,000 in 1932 to 16,213 in 1987. Small, rural districts with only a few dozen high school students lacked the resources to finance modern laboratories, elaborate extracurricular activities, and the other expensive features of today's schools. Consequently, legislatures forced many small districts to consolidate.

The keystone of state educational policymaking is the **state education agency (SEA).** The SEA is composed of a state board of education, a chief state school officer the state calls a **commissioner** or **superintendent of education,** and a department of education. The state board of education adopts the overall educational policies for the state. It sets minimum high school graduation requirements. It legitimizes decisions made by the state department of education. It insulates the department from the governor, and, in half the states, it appoints the chief state school officer. Sixty percent of the state boards of education are appointed directly by the governor.

Although the SEAs historically exercised little influence on local school districts, their influence has grown in recent years. The local school districts, the governor, and the legislature look to the SEA to provide educational leadership—to initiate new ideas, to ask for money, to see that local districts carry out national and state policies, and to maintain a positive public image for public education. The SEA distributes state educational funds to local school districts, approves requests for categorical grants, and provides basic research and information to legislative committees that must deal with school problems. The more that other political actors look to the SEAs for educational leadership and services, the more important the SEAs become.[9]

Finally, governors and legislatures assumed increasing influence over educational policy in the 1980s. This resulted in great measure from the educational reform movement of that decade. As we will see later in the chapter, some of the

Table 14-2   FEDERAL AID TO EDUCATION LANDMARKS

1785	Northwest Ordinance. Reserved one section of each township in the Northwest Territory for the endowment of schools.
1862	The Morrill Act. Provided grants of federal land to set up land-grant colleges for agriculture and mechanical arts.
1917	The Smith-Hughes Act. Provided federal grants for vocational education at the precollegiate level.
1944	The Servicemen's Readjustment Act (GI Bill of Rights). Provided educational benefits to World War II veterans. Later expanded to include Korean, Cold War, and Vietnam veterans.
1946	National school lunch and milk programs. Provided for lunches and milk to be served in public and private schools.
1950	National Science Foundation (NSF) established. The NSF encouraged scientific research and the education of scientists.
1958	National Defense Education Act (NDEA). Provided grants for equipment, loans for college students, and fellowships for graduate students.
1965	Elementary and Secondary Education Act (ESEA). This act, plus its later amendments, set the framework for contemporary aid to education, including funds for compensatory education for children in poverty areas.
1965	National Endowments for the Arts and Humanities established (NEA and NEH). Established to stimulate the arts and humanities similar to the stimulus that NSF provided for science.
1965	Higher Education Act. This act, plus its later amendments, set the basic framework for federal aid to higher education including student financial assistance such as Upward Bound, scholarships, loans, and cooperative education.
1972	Basic Educational Opportunity Grant (later called Pell Grant) program started. Initiated federal assistance programs for college students.
1997	Initiated tax credits to finance part of the tuition for college.

most visible reforms in some states, such as testing teachers and tightening graduation requirements, were forced on local school districts by governors and legislatures over the initial objections of teacher organizations and other educator groups.

Federal Roles

The federal government historically played a small role in public education. It was not until 1965 that Congress passed a broad program of aid to all public school districts (see Table 14-2), and even today the federal government provides barely 6 percent of all public school funding.

The federal government's impact on public education, however, is far out of proportion to the small share of schooling that it funds. The federal influence comes largely from the federal mandates that we studied in Chapter 3. Through congressional and judicial mandates, the federal government has played a major role in public school desegregation, in seeking parity for male and female athletic programs, and in prodding local schools to offer **compensatory education** for disadvantaged children. The main instruments for this have been the 1965 **Elementary and Secondary Education Act** and the Head Start program, which was designed to give culturally deprived children some preschool preparation for the first grade. According to a 1980 study, these and other federal programs have been effective in improving the education of poor children.[10] In 1981, several educational grants were consolidated into a block grant under the **Education Consolidation and Improvement Act,** which reduced the amount of federal funds involved but increased the authority of states over how the funds would be spent.[11]

Postsecondary Public Education

At the postsecondary level, the most significant institutions are the state universities, the state college systems, the community college systems, the postsecondary vocational schools, and the private colleges. There is a clear pecking order among the public institutions. At the top of the pecking order are the central campuses of the state universities, which get the biggest share of the state higher education budget. They have the most affluent undergraduates. They generally pay their faculty higher salaries than are paid by other higher education facilities. They tend to be research-oriented institutions. And they get most of the grants awarded to higher education in the state for research, experimentation, and program implementation.

Less prestigious than the major campus of the state university is the state college system. These colleges often started as teachers' colleges early in the century but were expanded into extensive university systems to accommodate the boom of students during the 1950s and 1960s.

At the bottom of the pecking order are the two-year community colleges and the postsecondary vocational schools. On the average, they get the least money, have the poorest libraries, and give their instructors the heaviest teaching loads. A Brookings Institution study in 1981 charged that the community colleges have diluted academic rigor in their attempts to increase their budgets and enrollments. Only 10 percent of community college students graduated from the two-year programs, and fewer yet transferred to four-year programs at colleges and universities.[12]

For most of the past decade, higher education has been under attack. In 1986, the Carnegie Foundation called for more coherent undergraduate curricula, the scaling back of athletic programs, increased general education requirements, and a requirement that all undergraduates write and defend a senior thesis before graduating.[13] Also in 1986, former U.S. Secretary of Education William J. Bennett assailed the quality of higher education in the country. Bennett faulted the nation's colleges for not providing a moral grounding to their studies, for being too concerned over money, for being too liberal politically, and for not seeing to it systematically that their students achieved quality education.[14] A 1987 bestseller, *The Closing of the American Mind,*[15] took these criticisms one step further

and accused higher education of failing to place enough emphasis on the traditional culture of Western civilization and the liberal arts generally. And in 1991,
Dinesh D'Souza's *An Illiberal Education* charged that academic freedom and rigorous academic standards were being diluted by a mindless attempt to impose
liberal political views on the college campuses.[16] This attempt came to be called
political correctness. Political correctness proponents retaliated that this picture
is overdrawn and their only goal is to provide better academic treatment of op-
pressed minorities and women. As we will see (pp. 379–382), the net result was
to politicize and polarize some campuses to a greater degree than at any time
since the Vietnam War.

◇ POLITICAL VALUES AND PUBLIC EDUCATION

The View from the Right

Conservatives view public education as a force for promoting upward social
mobility and developing the human capital (skills, knowledge, attitudes) that
will improve overall economic productivity. For the hundreds of thousands of
young people who become high school dropouts and functional illiterates, however, public education has failed.

Conservatives view these failures partly as a failure of the individuals and
partly as a failure of the schools. Edward Banfield wrote, "There will be *some*
number of students who are simply not capable of doing high school work."[17]
That these individuals tend to be concentrated in the lower classes and the racial
minorities is attributed by some writers to a culture of poverty, which inhibits
the desire for achievement, self-improvement, and deferred gratification.[18] The
"lower-class person cannot as a rule be given much training," wrote Banfield,
"because he will not accept it."[19] Other writers have tried to relate poor educational achievement to genetic factors.[20] Some writers predict a hardening of socioeconomic divisions as low IQ people fail to acquire the knowledge and skills
needed to function in a high-tech world.[21]

Conservatives blame America's school problems on liberal educational
philosophies traced to John Dewey. Educational permissiveness has let the
schools drift away from the basics of education, which focus on reading, writing,
and mathematical skills. Conservatives also emphasize rigid discipline; in some
instances they favor giving schools the right to suspend or expel students identified as troublemakers. Many of these ideas found expression in the Report of the
National Commission on Educational Excellence mentioned earlier. Conservatives are very concerned about the ability of the educational system to provide a
competent workforce for American business.

The View from the Left

On the moderate left, the liberal shares with the conservative the assumption
that the purpose of education is to provide economic opportunity, assure upward social mobility, and produce skilled workers for the economy.[22] The liberal,

having an optimistic view of human nature, also views education as a force for human development, the expansion of minds. Unlike the conservative, the liberal views our educational shortcomings as failures of the school system, not the individual. To the liberal, the basic problems lie in segregated schools and in poor people's lack of control over their educational environment. Our problems could be solved if we would just spend enough money, teach white children to appreciate minority cultures, and eliminate the savage inequalities in school finance. The liberal also believes that, with the exception of the severely mentally retarded, everyone has the potential to acquire knowledge and develop employable skills. What prevents this development is that the school systems have never reformed themselves enough to cope with a broad range of students' cultural backgrounds. Many reform efforts of the Great Society were cut short before they were really given a chance.

The liberal advocates more reforms and more experimentation and often rejects the conservative emphasis on basic skills, rigid discipline, and rote learning. Much liberal support goes to such school reforms as open schools, programs that allow great permissiveness in the classroom, and programs to keep disruptive youngsters in the classroom rather than expelling them. The liberal seeks more desegregation and supports involuntary busing. The liberal also tends to support bilingual education and multicultural education, as we shall discuss shortly.

On the extreme left, the radical argues that public education fails to provide upward social mobility because it was never meant to do this for a great number of students. The radical argues that the public education system "screens potential workers through a sieve, sorting them according to their capacities to work persistently, to respond to incentives like wages, to conform to work requirements, and to defer gratification."[23] This sifting function can be seen most clearly in the system of formal credentials issued by the colleges and universities. People with professional degrees get sorted into upper-middle-class occupations like medicine and law. More typical middle-class occupations, such as public school teacher, social worker, accountant, computer programmer, and registered nurse, come disproportionately from the state college systems and from the less prestigious private colleges.

The radical contends that this sifting process also works below the college level. Graduates of high schools, technical schools, and trade union apprentice programs get sifted into occupations such as laboratory technician, hairdresser, dental assistant, and police officer. At the bottom of the occupational ladder are the high school dropouts, who become dishwashers, unskilled laborers, and public relief recipients. Radicals have also joined the efforts to reduce the emphasis of Western Civilization in the public school curriculum. (see pp. 379–382.)

At the heart of these differences over educational practice are conflicts over fundamental social values themselves. A survey of state educational policy leaders found that four fundamental values predominated.[24] These were: (1) quality (as exemplified by conflicts over making graduation requirements more rigid or lengthening the school year); (2) equity (as exemplified by conflicts over attempts to provide special programs for handicapped and disadvantaged youngsters); (3) efficiency (as exemplified by conflicts over holding down school costs in the face of potentially expensive reform measures); and (4) choice (as exemplified by conflicts over decentralization, giving local units more flexibility in providing educational services, and using a **voucher plan** to help parents send their children to private schools).

There are important inconsistencies in these values. Liberals and conservatives would agree, for example, on the value of quality education, but they might well part company on the tradeoffs between quality education and some of the other values. Liberals are likely to charge that the conservative emphasis on efficiency will reduce the quality of education. Conservatives in turn are likely to charge that the liberal emphasis on equity will divert resources from the goal of quality and make quality education more difficult to attain.

◇ EDUCATION AND SOCIAL CONFLICT

The social conflicts of the late twentieth century have not left public education untouched. Three areas in particular have felt the brunt of these conflicts—racial desegregation, equalization of school finance, and politicization of the curriculum.

Desegregation

De Jure Segregation   In 1954, the Supreme Court struck down school segregation as a violation of the equal protection clause of the U.S. Constitution. To understand the current struggle over desegregation, it is necessary to examine the evolution of constitutional law on the subject of segregated schools.

The equal-protection clause of the Fourteenth Amendment to the U.S. Constitution asserts that no state may deny any person the equal protection of the law. In a famous case in 1896, the Supreme Court set down the legal justification for segregation. The Court approved separate public facilities for blacks and whites as long as the separate facilities were equal. This was the famous **separate-but-equal doctrine.** Several states used this ruling to justify the establishment of separate school systems for whites and nonwhites, and in 1927 the Supreme Court specifically approved this practice.[25] By midtwentieth century, seventeen states plus the District of Columbia legally required segregated schools, and another four states permitted segregation at the local level.

Segregation consisted of a dual school system—one for white children and an entirely separate system for nonwhite children. Because this system was established by law, it is referred to as **de jure segregation.** The nonwhite system was never given as many resources as the white system, thus making a mockery of the provision that the separate systems be equal.

Black civil rights leaders, working through the National Association for the Advancement of Colored People (NAACP), spent the first half of the twentieth century attempting to get these dual systems declared unconstitutional. Their first victory came in 1938 in Missouri. The University of Missouri Law School refused to admit blacks even though the state had no separate law school for blacks. It attempted to meet the separate-but-equal requirement by offering scholarships to send blacks out of state to law school. The U.S. Supreme Court struck this down as unconstitutional.[26]

Ten years later, the University of Oklahoma was obliged to admit blacks to its law school.[27] The university did not treat its newly admitted black students equally with the white students, however. They were not allowed to use the cafeteria at the same time as the white students or to use the regular desks in the reading room of the library, and they were required to sit for classes in an anteroom adjoining the classroom, where they could not see the professor. This practice, too, the Supreme Court struck down as unconstitutional.[28] Texas attempted to meet the separate-but-equal requirement by building a separate law school for blacks, but the U.S. Supreme Court ruled that no such segregated school could possibly be equal to the University of Texas at Austin with its excellent library, its top-notch faculty, and the prestige that its law degree enjoyed among the state's attorneys.[29]

All these developments came to a climax in the famous 1954 *Brown* v. *Board of Education* decision, in which the Supreme Court unanimously struck down the dual school systems as violating the **equal-protection clause** of the U.S. Constitution.[30] The schools were ordered to desegregate with all deliberate speed. However, the desegregation that followed was much more deliberate than speedy, making slow progress in its first ten years.[31] In succeeding years, however, the pace of integration speeded up, and by the 1990s considerable progress had been made in desegregating the once legally segregated school systems of the South.

Outside the South, there were usually no laws requiring racial segregation in schools. Rather, the schools were segregated in fact because minorities lived in one part of the city while whites lived in another. This has been called **de facto segregation.**

Coping with de facto segregation is much harder than coping with de jure segregation. Although a variety of techniques have been attempted in the de facto-segregated cities to get black and white children into the same classrooms (magnet schools, voluntary transfers, open enrollment plans, paired schools), the most direct tactic was the involuntary busing of both black and white children to integrated schools. In *Swann* v. *Charlotte-Mecklenburg Board of Education* (1971),[32] the U.S. Supreme Court ruled that federal district courts may impose forced busing to desegregate if there is evidence that the segregation results from legal measures to alter school boundaries or to impose residential segregation.

Busing and White Flight   The Court's busing decisions were extremely unpopular. As Table 14-3 shows, an overwhelming majority of whites and other nonblacks opposed busing in 1972 although opposition declined over the next twenty years. Given these levels of opposition, it is not surprising that court-ordered busing was greeted with open resentment in several major cities. Since the school-age populations of many big cities were becoming overwhelmingly minority, however, there were limits as to how much desegregation could be achieved by busing within the central cities. In New York City, for example, the white population of public schools dropped from 68 percent in 1957 to 29 percent in 1977.[33] New York City's

Table 14-3 PERCENT OF PEOPLE OPPOSED TO BUSING FROM ONE SCHOOL
DISTRICT TO ANOTHER

	Whites	Blacks	Others
1972	84.6	37.2	83.3
1994	71.4	40.2	53.5

Source: James Allen Davis, *General Social Surveys, 1972–1994* [machine-readable data file]. Principal
investigator, James A. Davis; director and co-principal investigator, Tom W. Smith (Chicago: National Opinion Research Center, producer, 1994; Storrs, Conn.: Roper Public Opinion Research Center, University of Connecticut, distributor).

schools had not simply desegregated, they had resegregated. Nor is New York an
extreme example. By 1980, only three of the nation's twenty-five largest school districts had more white students than minority students.[34]

According to critics of busing, the movement from segregation to desegregation to resegregation stems in large part from **white flight.** White parents with
enough money could flee the whole problem of desegregation. If they did not
want to flee by actually moving to the suburbs, they could send their children to
private academies or parochial schools.

One of the most articulate spokespersons for the argument that busing pre-
cipitated white flight was Diane Ravitch, whose studies found that between
1973, when forced busing started in Boston, and 1975, the city lost more than a
third of its white pupils, while its minority population increased.[35] In Atlanta,
busing went into effect in 1972. Between then and 1975 the black share of school
enrollment increased from 56 to 87 percent. In Memphis, busing started in 1973,
and by 1976, the black share of enrollment increased from 50 to 70 percent.[36]

Not all white flight from central-city schools can be attributed to mandatory
busing since white enrollment also dropped off in cities that did not have com-
pulsory busing programs.[37] But white flight was much greater in places with the
mandatory busing plans. According to one respected pair of researchers, white
enrollment dropped an average of 25 percent between 1968 and 1991 in districts
with mandatory busing plans, compared to a drop of only 3 percent in districts
without such plans.[38]

Desegregation and Alternatives to Busing Mandatory busing, of course, is not
the only way to achieve desegregation, and evidence suggests that some other
alternatives are more effective. An analysis of desegregation in more than 600
school districts found that the most effective approach is a voluntary desegregation plan based on alternatives such as magnet schools and majority-to-minority
transfer programs. These transfer programs permit students to transfer from a
school in which their race is a majority to a different school where they will be a
minority. Voluntary plans such as these produced less white flight on average
than did the mandatory busing plans, and they produced more interracial exposure, as measured by the percent of white enrollment in the average black child's
school. The least successful desegregation tactics were controlled choice plans in

which parents have some choices in where to send their children, but the choices are limited to those that will increase rather than reduce racial balance in the schools. Controlled choice plans produced almost as much white flight as mandatory busing and accomplished less interracial exposure than the voluntary plans.[39]

Desegregation and the Suburbs   In retrospect, white flight was not anticipated very well by the advocates of mandatory busing, and it has led to problems that we as a nation have failed to cope with successfully.[40] It has left most large central cities such as Washington, D.C., Chicago, New York, and Atlanta with white school populations so small as to make meaningful central-city desegregation impossible.

Is it possible to enlist the suburbs of these and other central cities in the quest to desegregate the schools? The record to date is not very encouraging, at least it is not very encouraging for mandatory enlistment. The only places where mandatory desegregation could easily include the suburbs were those places where the school district boundaries followed county lines. And this phenomenon is limited primarily to the South and the border states.

In most instances, suburbs were exempted from forced busing. The Supreme Court, in the 1974 case *Millikin* v. *Bradley,* refused to extend busing to the Detroit suburbs because it could not be shown that the suburban school district boundaries had been drawn deliberately to exclude blacks.[41] In the absence of a suburban intent to segregate their schools, the Supreme Court seemed to be saying that racial homogeneity in the suburbs was an example of *de facto* segregation and beyond the court's authority to remedy.

Critics of the court reject this distinction between *de jure* segregation that the court can remedy and *de facto* segregation that is beyond the court's reach. In the critics' view, the concentration of racial minorities in the big cities is in reality de jure segregation because governments at all levels consistently supported racial segregation in housing. Federal loan programs had guaranteed many suburban mortgages. Federal and state highway programs had built the transportation network enabling suburbia to be built. And the states had sanctioned many exclusionary zoning and planning devices that protected suburbia from racial integration. These critics charged that the application of the intent-to-segregate principle should be broadened to include a whole range of government actions whose effect was to concentrate minorities in the central-city schools. From this viewpoint, there is no distinction between de jure and de facto segregation.

Some state courts have expressed sympathy with this view of the critics,[42] but the federal courts have consistently upheld the distinction between de facto and de jure segregation. For example, the U.S. Supreme Court relied upon the principle of official intent to segregate when it upheld busing plans in Columbus and Dayton, Ohio.[43] Where segregation appears to have resulted from de facto housing and demographic trends, however, the federal courts have not intervened. In a 1992 case, the Supreme Court said, "Racial balance is not to be achieved for its own sake. . . . the school district is under no duty to remedy the imbalance that is caused by demographic factors."[44]

Successful Suburban Experiments Where cross-district busing has been achieved, it has usually involved special circumstances. In Louisville, Kentucky, the central city and Jefferson County merged their two separate school systems in 1975 and initiated a countywide desegregation program. A federal court ordered that all schools in the county maintain between 14 and 18 percent minority enrollment. Although greeted by considerable white protest, this project was carried out successfully.[45]

In Delaware, the city of Wilmington was excluded from a 1968 statewide school district consolidation plan that changed the boundaries of all other school districts. Ruling that this exclusion had the effect of legally concentrating the black students in the Wilmington school district, thus constituting de jure segregation, the federal courts ordered busing between the suburban and central-city schools.[46]

Another cross-district experiment is taking place in St. Louis. In 1983, the city school district and twenty-two suburban districts began a voluntary busing agreement to increase the white population of St. Louis schools as well as the minority populations of the suburban schools. At the end of the first five-year phase, the plan was a modest success. About 12,000 children were bused across district lines each day, and minority enrollments reached the targeted level of at least 15 percent in all but two of the suburban districts. Suburban whites were less willing to have their children bused into St. Louis, however, and the state refused to put up money to fund all the original magnet schools that had been planned to attract suburban whites into the city schools. Indeed, by the end of the 1980s the state was looking for ways to rid itself of the burden of paying for the plan, which had cost an estimated $500 million during the previous five years.[47]

On balance, however, Missourians viewed the experience as successful. People in other parts of the country were attracted by the semivoluntary approach to the task of involving the suburbs in desegregation. As a result, some other metropolitan areas, especially Milwaukee, Wisconsin, and Minneapolis–St. Paul, Minnesota, began to experiment with voluntary approaches to desegregation beyond the central-city boundaries.

Judicial Backtracking In recent years, the federal courts have begun backing away from pressuring school systems into making desegregation agreements. In 1986, the Supreme Court allowed Norfolk, Virginia, to end its court-ordered busing plan even though that meant an increase in the number of children attending all-black schools.[48] The following year, federal courts returned control over the Boston schools to the local school board. From 1973 to 1987, the Boston schools had been run personally by federal court judge W. Arthur Garrity. He reacted to Boston's foot-dragging on desegregation by literally taking over the schools, imposing his own busing plan, and overseeing the day-to-day school operations down to the point of assigning teachers and approving specific budget items. After Garrity withdrew his control in 1987, the school board, on a racially divided vote, drew up a new attendance plan that would give both white and black parents unprecedented flexibility in choosing the schools for their children.[49]

Two years later, in 1989, the Supreme Court backed even further away from forced desegregation. It permitted Oklahoma City to end a court-ordered busing plan that had been in force since 1972.[50] A federal court had previously recognized the district as having put an end to its segregation, but the 1972 desegregation order nevertheless remained in force. Challenging the court order, the district cut back on crosstown busing in 1985 and made more use of neighborhood schools. As a result, eleven of the city's sixty-four elementary schools were left with enrollments that were 90 percent or more black. Parents of black children sued, and a federal district court ordered that the school system continue operating under the original desegregation order. In 1989, the Supreme Court overturned that judgment and freed the Oklahoma City schools from the court-imposed desegregation plan. Central to the Court's ruling was Oklahoma City's claim that its previously segregated school system had been made *unitary*. To be considered unitary, a school district had to meet three tests. First, it had to show that it had continuously complied with the court desegregation decree in good faith. Second, it had to have abandoned any intentional act of segregation. And third, it had to eliminate the vestiges of prior discriminatory conduct.

Three years later, in 1992, on similar grounds, the Supreme Court also allowed the De Kalb County, Georgia school system (suburban Atlanta) to end its desegregation plans.[51] These two cases are viewed as ominous by advocates of court-ordered desegregation. With Oklahoma City and De Kalb County as precedents, there might be many other school systems around the country that would seek to get out from under desegregation court orders by claiming that they too had been made unitary. In 1995, the Supreme Court ruled that enough progress had been made on desegregation goals in Kansas City that it permitted the state of Missouri to reduce its expenditures for magnet schools and other expenses associated with the Kansas City desegregation efforts.[52] This decision was viewed as a very important symbolic retreat on the Court's part because Kansas City had been the school district involved in the original, pathbreaking desegregation case of *Brown* v. *Board of Education* four decades earlier.

How Schools Are Financed

In addition to the growing racial bifurcation between predominantly white suburban schools and predominantly minority central-city schools, the central cities increasingly lack the money needed to cope with their much more complicated educational task. This imbalance in fiscal resources can be traced to the way in which public education is financed.

Table 14-1 showed that about 45 percent of the money for public schools comes from local governments, almost exclusively from the property tax, the traditional means for financing public education. In order to supplement local property taxes, the states have historically offered a **foundation aid program** that gives each school district a certain number of dollars for each pupil in the schools. The foundation aids frequently have an equalization formula so that more money goes to districts with many poor students and a small property-tax base.

Fiscal Disparities in School Finance   In places where a majority of school money comes from local property taxes, a small school district with an electric power plant, a large shopping center, or an industrial park will have abundant tax resources for public schools, whereas a neighboring district without these developments will be short on tax resources. The term for this uneven distribution of property tax resources is **fiscal disparities.** In some states, the disparities from one district to another lead to extreme differences in educational spending. In the late 1980s, the 100 poorest districts in Texas were able to spend barely 40 percent as much per child (less than $3,000 per year) as the 100 richest districts (over $7,000 per year).[53] The result, according to Jonathan Kozol, is a pervasive pattern of "savage inequalities" that trap the poorest and most disadvantaged children in the central city school districts that lack resources to provide them with effective schooling.[54]

Attempts at Finance Equalization   The problem of fiscal disparities came to a head in 1971 in the California court case of *Serrano* v. *Priest*.[55] Serrano lived in a school district that lacked substantial property tax resources and that consequently found it hard to spend as much on schools as nearby districts that had a better property tax base. Serrano sued the state of California for not providing equal educational opportunity for all children and all school districts in the state. The California Supreme Court agreed that the fiscal disparities inherent in the property tax financing of public education violated the state constitution and ordered California to find an alternative financing method.

No sooner had the California Supreme Court made this decision than parents in other states sought to get the principle applied nationwide under the equal protection clause of the U.S. Constitution. A San Antonio, Texas, case came before the Supreme Court for decision in 1973. However, in *San Antonio School District* v. *Rodriguez*, the U.S. Supreme Court refused to apply the Serrano principle under federal law. The Court agreed that the states relied too heavily on the property tax. However, the court held that there is no federally guaranteed right to equal education. The "ultimate solution must come from the lawmakers and from the democratic pressures of those who elect them."[56]

Since the *Rodriguez* case foreclosed the federal courts as an avenue for equalizing school finance, the battle shifted to state politics. Three general approaches emerged.

The first approach to finance equalization was to increase state funding for schools and allow local school districts to levy additional local property taxes on top of the state funds. The most explosive battle over this approach started in New Jersey in 1973 when the state's supreme court ordered the legislature to come up with a state income tax to equalize school finances.[57] The legislature, however, repeatedly refused to follow those directions, and in the summer of 1976, the supreme court reacted by closing all New Jersey public schools on the grounds that they were operating in violation of the state constitution. Faced with the prospect of school not being able to start the next September, the legislature relented and passed a state income tax that enabled the state to absorb a major share of school funding.

As a consequence of this new funding law, the state portion of school finances rose from 23.6 percent in 1975 to 33.8 percent in 1980. This helped reduce disparities in tax rates between school districts, but over the next ten years, the gap began to widen again. In the 1976–1977 school year, when the new income tax took effect, the top 5 percent of school districts spent 2.06 times as much money per pupil as the bottom 5 percent. By 1979–1980 that ratio had dropped to 1.79 times as much. But by 1989–1990, it was back up to 2.10 times as much.[58] Despite a massive state effort and an unpopular income tax, the schools were further apart on per-pupil spending than they had been when the issue had surfaced nearly twenty years earlier. In the light of this development, the New Jersey Supreme Court in 1990 ordered the state to bring the spending level of impoverished districts up to the level of the average suburb. New Jersey's Democratic Governor, Jim Florio, did just that with a plan that raised the income tax by $2.8 billion and earmarked $1.1 billion of it for the schools. Voter disenchantment with this solution was swift and harsh. The following year, voters dealt a resounding defeat to the Democrats by returning the Republicans to a majority in the legislature, and in 1993 Governor Florio was himself unseated by Republican challenger Christine Whitman who pledged to roll back the tax increases. Under Whitman, the $1.1 billion earmarked for schools was pared to $800 million. In 1994, the state supreme court once again ruled that the state needed to do more to reduce the disparities.[59]

How could it happen that state-level funding for New Jersey schools could increase dramatically from 1975 to 1989 and make no appreciable long-term dent in the problem of fiscal disparities? One answer seems to lie in the fact that the system intermeshed state funding with unlimited local funding. The receipt of state funding boosted overall spending in the affluent districts because those districts continued their high level of local property taxes after receiving their state aid. The poorer districts, however, tended to reduce their property taxes after receiving the state funds. Even though their overall funding went up, it continued falling behind that of the rich districts.[60]

The second approach to equalization relies solely on state funds. Hawaii has done this since achieving statehood, but Michigan presents the only example of a state moving to this method after having previously relied on property taxes for school funding. Like many states relying heavily on the property tax, Michigan was experiencing voter dissatisfaction, and in 1990, Republican John Engler won the governorship in part by promising to reduce property taxes. In 1993, the Democratic-controlled legislature passed a bill that would eliminate property taxes as a funding mechanism for schools, but they did not provide an alternative source of funds to make up for the dropoff in property tax receipts. They hoped to draw a governor's veto that would embarrass Engler by making it look as though he had reneged on his property tax cut pledge. Instead, Engler signed the bill into law, which threatened to leave the state's schools without any money. This self-inflicted crisis prodded the legislature to submit two funding proposals to Michigan voters in a referendum. The first option would increase the sales tax from 4 to 6 percent, and the second would make a comparable increase in the income tax. The voters chose the sales tax method, and in 1995–1996, Michigan schools were completely freed from their previous dependence on local property taxes.[61]

The third approach to reducing fiscal disparities occurred in Texas, which kept the property tax system but forced wealthy districts to share their property tax wealth with poor districts. In 1989, the Texas Supreme Court ordered the state to reduce the fiscal disparities in school finance. The legislature failed to act, and the court subsequently ordered all Texas public schools to close on June 1, 1993, if a new funding scheme was not in place by that date. Just a month before the deadline, voters rejected a funding proposal and thereby threw the state into a major crisis. To keep the schools open, the state now had to find a new funding scheme that would be acceptable to the state supreme court and still gain a majority vote among legislators whose constituents had just spoken loudly against equalization. The legislature accomplished this difficult feat just days before the deadline by coming up with a plan that would guarantee each school district $280,000 in property tax wealth per student. Wealthy school districts with more property tax wealth than this would have to give away some of their excess tax base so that it could be used to increase the tax base of poorer school districts.[62]

It is impossible to predict which of these three approaches to finance equalization will produce the best long-term results. Important philosophical positions underlie each approach. And it is difficult to gain universal support for equalization, in part because there is very little systematic evidence that equal funding in the absence of other reforms will make dramatic improvements in educational quality or student performance. Nevertheless, the overconcentration of minority and poor white children in so many grossly underperforming and inadequately funded inner-city schools does not bode well for the nation's future. This realization and the fact that more than thirty states face court challenges to their school funding systems will keep the equalization issue in the forefront of educational politics for many years to come.

Politicizing the Curriculum   Public schools are under great pressure today to use their curriculums for purposes of ideological indoctrination. These pressures have come from both the ideological right and the left. To the extent that schools have taught citizenship, democracy, and support for free enterprise, they have never been politically neutral in the broad sense of the term *politics*. But the last two decades have seen deliberate attempts to use the public schools to impose on children the narrow views of specific subgroups in society.

First in the 1980s came the objection of fundamentalist Christians to the teaching of evolutionary theory in biology classes. Under their influence the Arkansas and Louisiana legislatures passed laws requiring that equal time in biology classes be given to teaching creationist theories of the origins of human life. However, federal courts struck down this law as a violation of the constitutional separation of church and state.[63] By the mid-1980s fundamentalist Christians were making a broad assault on a variety of textbooks and other teaching materials that they claimed promoted "secular humanism," a vague concept that could be applied to many things. Some fundamentalists, for example, sought to have a story on Leonardo da Vinci removed from the schools because of its secular humanism.[64] A group in Tennessee initially got federal courts to exempt their children from public school reading classes that featured readings the parents opposed on religious grounds. In particular, the parents had objected to *The Diary of Anne Frank* because Anne Frank asserted that all religions were equal. A federal appeals court, however, overturned this ruling.[65] How these conflicts between fundamentalist Christians and the mainstream American culture will be worked out will be important issues for the 1990s.

A second area of curricular conflict stems from the demographic and sociological forces that are reshaping American society. America has been a great stewpot of many different subcultures, most of which have never fully melted into the common culture. Indeed the common culture itself continually evolves as each group makes its unique contribution. However, many African Americans and other minorities argue, with considerable justification, that their contributions to the development of American culture have been ignored by the public school curriculum.

To the extent that these demands want the social studies curriculum to include the historical accomplishments of African Americans, American Indians, Latin Americans, and women, they represent an emphasis on **cultural pluralism** that most scholars view as legitimate. Distinguished from cultural pluralism is what educational historian Diane Ravitch calls **ethnic particularism**.[66] This is the attempt of ethnic groups to use ethnic history, ethnic mathematics, and ethnic science to boost the self-esteem of children from these ethnic groups. The ethnic particularists condemn the idea of a common American culture as a racist "Eurocentrism" and seek instead to replace it with a curriculum that is organized around the achievements of a specific minority group. Thus, some black activists have adopted an extreme Afro-centrism that posits Africa as the mainspring of Western Civilization. Some Hispanic activists have adopted "Mayan mathematics." Some Indian activists teach that the Iroquois confederation was the main foundation for the American Constitution. And a New York State curricular task force proposal sought a history curriculum that ensured that children from Native American, Puerto Rican or Latino, Asian American, and African American cultures will have higher self-esteem and self-respect, whereas children from European cultures will have a less arrogant perspective of being part of the group that has "done it all."[67]

When the New York Board of Regents in 1990 adopted a somewhat diluted version of that report, it is not surprising that white Americans, like Professor Diane Ravitch, feared that the goal was for white children to emerge from the curriculum with less self-esteem and less self-respect. In this view, the multicultural curriculum borders on political indoctrination.

Especially criticized are the African-American Baseline Essays which were adopted in the Portland, Oregon, public schools in 1987 and which have had significant influence on multicultural teaching in public schools throughout the country. The eminent and liberal historian Arthur M. Schlesinger, Jr., charges the

Baseline series with being "bad history." Among the many examples of erroneous information that Schlesinger finds in the Baseline Essays is the following:

> The Baseline Essay on science and technology contains biographies of black American scientists, among them Charles R. Drew, who first developed the process for the preservation of blood plasma. In 1950 Drew, grievously injured in an automobile accident in North Carolina, lost quantities of blood. "Not one of several nearby white hospitals," according to the Baseline Essay, "would provide the blood transfusions he so desperately needed, and on the way to a hospital that treated Black people, he died." It is a hell of a story—the inventory of blood-plasma storage dead because racist whites denied him his own invention. Only it is not true. According to the biographical entry for Drew written by the eminent black scholar Rayford Logan of Howard for the *Dictionary of American Negro Biography*, "Conflicting versions to the contrary, Drew received prompt medical attention."[68]

Of course, it is possible for a curriculum to be responsive to cultural pluralism without deliberate distortions of history. And one presumes that the vast majority of teachers—whether black or not black, whether Afro-centrist or not Afro-centrist—make honest efforts to be honest and accurate in their teaching. But it is also impossible to deny that the public school curriculum has become highly politicized as it seeks to grapple with the wide variety of peoples that constitute American today.

At issue in the schools, as in society at large, is our vision of ourselves as a nation. To state this issue in the extreme, will the prevailing vision be that of cultural pluralists such as Diane Ravitch and Arthur M. Schlesinger who view the different subcultures as natural resources that contribute positively to the evolution of a common culture and a common society? Or will it be that of the ethnic particularists who reject any common ground among the various subcultures except for a mutual hostility between the various racial minorities and the 80 percent of the population that is of European extraction? Is there some common ground between the various ethnic groupings that will enable us to work together? Or are we destined to become, like Yugoslavia in the 1990s or Lebanon in the 1980s, isolated subcultures joined by mutual hatreds and incapable of cooperating on a common destiny?

A second area where multicultural issues affect education is in affirmative action—although the conflicts here have been more pronounced at the postsecondary level than at the public school level. The University of California at Berkeley presents an example of these conflicts at work. One of the nation's most prestigious campuses, Berkeley sought to admit more racial minorities and set up a de facto two-track admission process. This brought about an overrepresentation of blacks and Hispanics in comparison to whites and Asians. In the 1988–1989 school year, whites made up 70 percent of the pool of eligible applicants for admission, but they accounted for only about 40 percent of those accepted. Blacks made up 3 percent of the pool but 11 percent of the admittees, and Hispanics made up 7 percent of the pool but 19 percent of the admittees. At the minimum high school GPA required for admission, a black high school graduate stood a 70 percent chance for admission compared to a 9 percent chance for a white. More than 70 percent of eligible black applicants were admitted versus only about 25 to 30 percent of whites and Asians. Graduation rates were in the opposite order. Slightly more than 50 percent of blacks and Hispanics graduated after six years compared to more than three-fourths of Asians and whites.[69]

Critics looked at these data and concluded that Berkeley's affirmative action program was "outrageous."[70] Advocates point out that 85 percent of affirmative action admittees met Berkeley's minimum admission standards and that there are many socioeconomic reasons to explain the lower graduation rates of the affirmative action admittees. Further, there is a pressing social need for a diverse state like California to ensure that all categories of people have access to the state's flagship campus. Were academic merit the only criteria, admissions would be limited to the top 3 percent of high school graduates, and there would be very few blacks or Hispanics at the university.[71]

In 1996, California governor Pete Wilson persuaded the University of California Board of Trustees to end the school's affirmative action program. What type of admissions plan the university will come up with to replace it and how that plan will cope with the diversity issue is not yet clear.

◇ REFORMING PUBLIC EDUCATION

In the face of these developments and declining performance of public school graduates on various measures of educational quality,[72] tremendous pressures have built up in recent years for school reform. Reformers urge less free time in schools, more homework, more time spent in the classroom, more rigid graduation requirements, and minimal preparation standards for teachers.[73] The school reform movement received a very prestigious boost in 1983 when the National Commission on Excellence in Education proposed several measures to improve the schools—raising teachers' salaries, creating a cadre of master teachers, lengthening the school year, and raising requirements for graduation. Within a year, a half-dozen other prestigious commissions presented similar proposals.[74] The get-tough philosophy had struck the public schools.

School Reform and Its Implementation

Some of the proposed reforms proved easier to implement than others. Within two years of the 1983 publication of *A Nation at Risk*, forty-seven states had raised or proposed raising graduation requirements, forty-four had done so for testing students for minimum academic competencies, forty-nine had done so for raising teacher preparation standards, and thirty-four had done so for increasing the amount of instructional time.[75] By the end of the decade, every state had adopted at least one of the measures.

More difficult to implement were the proposals for dramatic increases in teachers' salaries and for merit pay for teachers. Tennessee presents an excellent case in point. Governor Lamar Alexander proposed a Master Teacher Program in 1983. Despite approval by a large majority of Tennesseans, the $200 million price tag was opposed by fiscal conservatives, the merit pay features were adamantly opposed by the Tennessee Education Association (TEA), and the program was defeated in the legislature. Alexander then took the initiative with an imaginative fight for his program. He appeared on national television and gave interviews to national magazines to promote it. He managed to enlist the American Federation of Teachers to criticize the TEA for its opposition. He ran television ads plugging the program and changed its title from "Master Teachers" to the "Better Schools Program."

Finally, in 1985, the Tennessee legislature raised the state sales tax to provide the money for one of the country's most extensive educational reform packages. The centerpiece of the proposal is a career-ladder provision under which teachers move up to the higher-paying ladder positions on the basis of their classroom competence rather than the number of graduate course credits they have accumulated.[76]

In addition to Tennessee's comprehensive reform, governors in other states also proved to be the catalysts needed for reform to pass. North Carolina Governor James B. Hunt promoted the North Carolina School of Science and Mathematics as a public school where gifted eleventh- and twelfth-graders could be taught by highly qualified teachers. Minnesota Governor Rudy Perpich pushed through the legislature an open-enrollment system that essentially allowed any child to attend any school in the state on a space-available basis.[77] Former Texas governor Mark White succeeded in getting an educational reform package that included competency testing for teachers and forcing high school football players to make passing grades if they wanted to stay on their teams.[78]

Finally, the renewed interest in school improvement was also backed up financially. Between the 1983 publication of *A Nation at Risk* and 1993, expenditures for public elementary and secondary education rose by 50 percent, compared to an inflation increase of only 45 percent.[79]

Assessing Educational Reform

Has all this commitment of money and energy to educational reform produced significant improvements in student achievement? Judging from the trends in SAT scores shown in Figure 14-1, the improvements appear to have been very modest. This is not surprising in the view of John E. Chubb and Terry M. Moe. They argue that the reforms themselves have failed to take into account what factors in fact lead to superior academic performance by students.[80] Chubb and Moe conducted a highly impressive survey of teachers and administrators in 342 schools, and they administered achievement tests to those schools' students at the end of their sophomore and senior years. Chubb and Moe found that differences in educational achievement were hardly affected at all by differences in teacher salaries, rigidity of curriculum, discipline, amount of homework, frequency of writing assignments, or most of the items found on the typical school reform agenda. Rather, the best- and worst-performing schools in their sample differed most substantially on two key variables. The first was organizational. The best-performing schools had clearer goals than the worst-performing schools; their staffs had more agreement on school priorities; they perceived the

Figure 14-1 TRENDS IN AVERAGE SAT SCORES

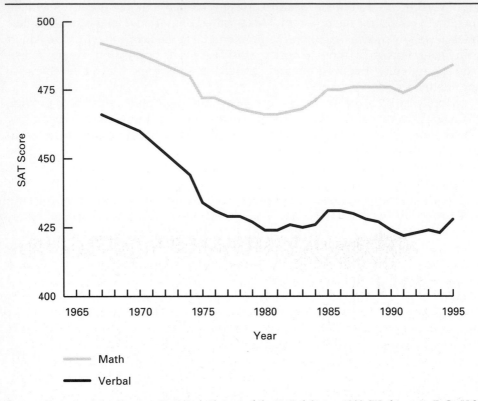

Math

Verbal

Sources: Bureau of the Census, *Statistical Abstract of the United States: 1980* (Washington, D.C.: U.S. Government Printing Office, 1980), p. 164; *Statistical Abstract: 1992*, p. 159; *Statistical Abstract: 1996*, p. 177.

school as having a mission; their principals had more teaching experience and were regarded by teachers as being more forceful leaders. The best-performing schools had more autonomy than the worst-performing schools. That is, they had more freedom to hire the teachers they wanted and to dismiss teachers who did not perform well. And they had more freedom to stress academic achievement and to place their best students in achievement-oriented tracks. For the students involved, the difference between attending a well-organized school and a poorly organized one was immense. According to Chubb, "All other things being equal, attending an effectively organized high school for four years is worth at least a full year of additional achievement over attendance at an ineffectively organized school."[81]

What makes Chubb and Moe pessimistic about the prospects for educational reform is that the typical public school lacks the autonomy they think is necessary for educational excellence to take place. Indeed, educational reform in the 1980s *reduced* school autonomy and *made it harder for schools to establish clear goals* by imposing, from the top down, numerous reforms and specific requirements. The net result is that teachers in individual schools have less independence in their classroom today than they had a decade ago, and that, according to Chubb and Moe, is counterproductive. Furthermore, the educational establishment of teachers groups, administrators' associations, and state education agencies have no incentive to extend more autonomy to individual principals and teachers.

The second factor Chubb and Moe found to be significant in determining student achievement was, not surprisingly, the socioeconomic background of the students themselves. The best-performing schools came disproportionately from better-educated and more affluent families. The reverse was true for the worst-performing schools. This finding is supported by an impressive body of comparative research at both the state level and the school-district level, which suggests that graduation rates and SAT scores are less influenced by increasing expenditures for public schools than they are by socioeconomic factors.[82] If this is the case, then instead of dramatically increasing school expenditures, a better approach to raising a state's average SAT scores might be to decrease the number of school children living in poverty and to increase the autonomy of local schools.

Happily, in light of the conclusions reached by Chubb and Moe, there seems to be a growing recognition of the need for more local autonomy in the attempt to improve educational performance. Chicago, in 1990, began an experiment with locally elected councils in each school that would have extraordinary authority to hire principals and oversee the school's operation.[83] Whether these movements toward local autonomy can counterbalance the general trend of reform to greater state control remains to be seen.

◇ EDUCATION AND THE POLITICAL ECONOMY

Historically, education has occupied a critical place in the American political economy. Through the public and private school systems, people were educated to play a variety of roles in an industrial and highly sophisticated society. Children received the educational basics they needed to become skilled workers, technicians, engineers, accountants, and professionals. Furthermore, education was assumed to play a great equalizer role in American democracy. So many millions of people enjoyed upward social mobility partially as a result of skills, knowledge, and credentials acquired at school that it became easy to believe that education was the answer to many social problems.

Today, many of these assumptions are being questioned. The National Commission on Educational Excellence performed a great service for educational reformers by complaining that the school systems are not preparing children well for the high-technology society those children will inherit. If the Commission's criticisms are accurate, important changes will have to be made in order for schools to carry out their traditional role of educating a work force to meet the nation's needs.

This cartoon by Mike Peters reflects the fear of many people that high technology will not provide much economic opportunity for average citizens, regardless of how good their education may be.

Source: Mike Peters, 1983. Reprinted by permission: Tribune Media Services.

Given these considerations, it is not surprising that much of the support for public school reform has come from the business community. Most of today's students will work for business corporations tomorrow, which gives those corporations an important interest in seeing that its recruits are literate and have the attitudes necessary to work eight-hour shifts. Business needs exist at least at two levels. First, keeping America competitive with the rest of the world requires highly skilled engineers, scientists, researchers, and technicians who can function comfortably in today's high-tech world. Hence the concern among businesspeople over literacy, the ability to write, the quality of scientific learning, and declining SAT scores. In all probability, however, the number of highly lucrative high-tech jobs is quite limited.

Second, a great many of the jobs created since 1980 have been very low-tech jobs—in restaurants, hotels, and other service establishments. What is needed for these jobs is not a highly skilled workforce but large numbers of people willing to work at repetitive tasks for long hours, day in and day out. This need is expected to be especially acute in the 1990s, when the number of young people entering the job market will be smaller than in the 1980s. Hence, many corporations are working closely with local school districts to acculturate teenagers into this kind of job environment.

Perhaps the most obvious link between public education and the political economy occurs with higher education. The link is especially strong between business corporations and the large research-oriented universities. Corporations benefit from the technical research done at those universities. And universities benefit from equipment donations, consulting contracts, and friendly ties with the corporations. From the point of view of state government, a well-functioning university system is a definite asset in attracting more industry.

SUMMARY

1. Local school districts have historically been the dominant unit of school governance. However, educational problems such as desegregation and financing could not be solved by small districts; thus, in recent years, policymaking and financing have been increasingly centralized at the state level, and the federal government has become more and more involved in public education. The federal government's greatest impact has been in the desegregation of public schools.

2. Theorists of the right view declining achievement and growing discipline problems as both failures of individual students and failures of the public school systems. They attribute the failures of the school systems to liberal educational philosophies that have led to permissiveness in the classroom, open schools, and poor discipline. Liberals attribute the failures of the school systems to inadequate implementation of and insufficient dedication to progressive educational programs. On the far left, radicals doubt that the public schools were ever meant to be major agents of upward social mobility for most students.

3. The impetus for desegregation has come mostly from the federal courts. The Supreme Court first struck down de jure segregation as unconstitutional. The courts have had less success in ending de facto segregation. The most volatile desegregation controversy has been over the use of forced busing to desegregate schools. By 1990, the federal government had retreated from imposing forced busing to bring about desegregation.

4. The main school finance problems stem from fiscal disparities in the distribution of property-tax resources. State governments supplement local school resources with foundation aids and categorical grants. There have been three approaches to equalizing school funding. The New Jersey approach was to increase the state share of funding while permitting local districts to gain revenue from a local property tax in addition to the state funds. The Michigan approach was to move to an exclusively state-funded system paid for by the state sales tax. And the Texas approach was to distribute some of the property tax base of the more affluent districts to the less affluent districts.

5. The culture wars of recent years have provoked intense conflict over the public school curriculum and over affirmative action admissions at the university level.

6. Public concern over declining scores on achievement tests as well as poor performance of American children in comparison to those in other nations has fueled the movement toward educational reform. The states have enacted numerous educational reform measures in recent years. But it is not clear whether these reforms will bring about any significant improvement in student learning.

KEY TERMS

Board of education   The governing board of a local school district.
Commissioner of education   See *Superintendent of schools.*

Compensatory education The tenet that disadvantaged children suffer from poor preparation for school and must be given special educational help to compensate for their backgrounds. See *Elementary and Secondary Education Act of 1965*.

Cultural pluralism An educational emphasis on including instruction on many cultural groups in American society. Does not reject the ideal of a mainstream, overall American culture.

De facto segregation Segregation that arises because of residential practices rather than because of laws requiring segregation. See *De jure segregation*.

De jure segregation Segregation that is imposed by law rather than by informal residential practices. See *De facto segregation*.

Education Consolidation and Improvement Act of 1981 A law that consolidated several educational categorical grant programs into a block grant, reduced the total funding for the programs involved, and increased state discretion in dispensing the funds.

Elementary and Secondary Education Act of 1965 The first extensive form of federal aid to public schools. Famous for its Title I compensatory-education provisions. See also *Compensatory education*.

Equal-protection clause The provision of the Fourteenth Amendment that forbids any state to deny persons in its jurisdiction the equal protection of the laws.

Establishment clause The Constitution's First Amendment provision that "Congress shall make no law respecting an establishment of religion."

Ethnic particularism A form of cultural pluralism that rejects a mainstream American culture as oppressively Euro-centric.

Fiscal disparities The situation in which neighboring governmental jurisdictions vary widely in their ability to raise revenue. One jurisdiction may have a substantial tax base, while a neighboring one has a meager tax base.

Foundation aid program A program of state aid for public schools under which the state provides a given number of dollars to each school district for the number of full-time pupils enrolled in that district.

Independent school district The basic governing unit for public schools.

National Commission on Excellence in Education A commission that reported in 1983 that the nation's school systems are failing to provide children with the quality of education they need in the contemporary world.

Separate-but-equal doctrine The principle established in *Plessy* v. *Ferguson* (1896) that segregated facilities do not violate the equal-protection clause as long as the separate facilities are equal.

State education agency (SEA) State educational policymaker, composed of the state board of education, the chief state school officer, and the department of education.

Superintendent of schools The chief executive officer for public schools. May be either a local or state superintendent. The state superintendent is sometimes called the *commissioner of education*.

Voucher plan (school) A proposal that would give parents vouchers to pay the cost of sending their children to the school of their choice.

White flight The theory that middle-class whites have in large numbers withdrawn their children from the central-city public schools in order to avoid school desegregation.

REFERENCES

1. United States Bureau of the Census, *Statistical Abstract of the United States: 1995* (Washington, D.C.: U.S. Government Printing Office, 1995), p. 470.

2. The study was conducted by Princeton economists Orley Ashenfelter and Alan Kreuger and was reported in *The New York Times*, August 19, 1992, p. 1.

3. *Newsweek*, February 17, 1992, p. 57.

4. *The Minneapolis Star Tribune*, December 2, 1993, p. 26A.

5. *The New York Times*, December 2, 1993, p. 26A.

6. Ibid.

7. National Commission on Excellence in Education, *A Nation at Risk: The Imperative for Educational Reform* (Washington, D.C.: U.S. Government Printing Office, 1983).

8. This was a major conclusion of a study by the Institute for Educational Leadership, "Governing Public Schools: New Times, New Requirements." Reported in *The New York Times*, October 28, 1992, p. A12.

9. See Burton Dean Friedman, *State Government and Education Management in the State Education Agency* (Chicago: Public Administration Service, 1971).

10. M. W. Kirst and R. Jung, "The Utility of a Longitudinal Approach in Assessing Implementation: A Thirteen-Year View of Title I, ESEA," *Educational Evaluation and Policy Analysis* 2 (1980): 17–34.

11. *The Book of the States: 1982–83* (Lexington, Ky.: Council of State Governments, 1982), p. 432.

12. Cited in *St. Paul Pioneer Press*, December 6, 1981, p. 16.

13. See *The New York Times*, October 10, 1986, p. 15.

14. For Bennett's speech, see *The New York Times*, October 11, 1986, p. 8.

15. Allan Bloom, *The Closing of the American Mind* (New York: Simon and Schuster, 1987).

16. Dinesh D'Souza, *An Illiberal Education* (New York: MacMillan, 1991).

17. Edward C. Banfield, *The Unheavenly City* (Boston: Little, Brown, 1970), p. 134.

18. This was especially the theme of Oscar Lewis. See his *La Vida* (New York: Random House, 1965). Also see Barbara E. Coward, Joe R. Feagin, and J. Allen Williams, Jr., "The Culture of Poverty Debate: Some Additional Data," *Social Problems* 21, no. 5 (June 1974): 621–633.

19. Banfield, *The Unheavenly City*, p. 139.

20. The proponents of this view are Arthur Jensen and William Shockley. See H. J. Eysenck, *The I.Q. Argument* (New York: Library Press, 1971). For a contemporary statement of it, see Michael Levin, "Implications of Race and Sex Differences for Contemporary Affirmative Action and the Concept of Discrimination," *The Journal of Social, Political and Economic Studies* 15, no. 2 (Summer 1990): 175–212.

21. See Charles Murray and Richard J. Herrnstein, *The Bell Curve: Intelligence and Class Structure in American Life* (New York: The Free Press, 1994).

22. See David M. Gordon, *Problems in Political Economy: An Urban Perspective*, 2nd ed. (Lexington, Mass.: D.C. Heath, 1977), pp. 108–112.

23. Ibid., p. 213.

24. D. Mitchell, C. Marshall, and Frederick M. Wirt, *Culture and Education Policy in the American States* (New York: Falmer), Ch. 4.

25. *Plessy* v. *Ferguson*, 163 U.S. 537 (1896). *Gong Lum* v. *Rice*, 275 U.S. 78 (1927).

26. *Missouri ex rel. Gaines* v. *Canada*, 305 U.S. 337 (1938).

27. *Sipuel* v. *Oklahoma*, 332 U.S. 631 (1948).

28. *McLaurin* v. *Oklahoma State Regents*, 339 U.S. 637 (1950).

29. *Sweatt* v. *Painter*, 339 U.S. 629 (1950).

30. *Brown* v. *Board of Educ.*, 347 U.S. 483 (1954).

31. Charles S. Bullock III and Harrell R. Rodgers, Jr., "Coercion to Compliance: Southern School Districts and School Desegregation Guidelines," *Journal of Politics* 38, no. 4 (November 1976): 987–1013.

32. *Swann* v. *Charlotte-Mecklenberg Board of Education,* 402 U.S. 1 (1971).

33. *The New York Times,* November 21, 1977, p. 57.

34. Gary Orfield, *Public School Desegregation in the United States: 1968–1980* (Washington, D.C.: Joint Center for Political Studies, 1983), p. 26.

35. Diane Ravitch, "The 'White Flight' Controversy," *Public Interest,* no. 51 (Spring 1978): 142.

36. Mary Costello, "Busing Reappraisal," *Editorial Research Reports,* December 26, 1975, pp. 945–964.

37. Christine H. Rossell, "School Desegregation and White Flight," *Political Science Quarterly* 90, no. 4 (Winter 1975–1976): 692. This was a very controversial article. It was criticized for its methods and policy suggestions by Diane Ravitch in her article, "The 'White Flight' Controversy," pp. 135–150. See also the exchange of views by Christine H. Rossell, Diane Ravitch, and David J. Armor, "Busing and 'White Flight,'" *Public Interest,* no. 53 (Fall 1978): 109–115.

38. See Christine H. Rossell and David J. Armor, "The Effectiveness of School Desegregation Plans, 1968–1991," *American Politics Quarterly* 24, no. 3 (July 1996): 289. Rossell and Armor have been two of the major researchers of desegregation efforts for the past two decades. This article is somewhat inconsistent with Rossell's earlier article "School Desegregation and White Flight" cited in footnote 37. It appears that the accumulation of evidence from her research over a twenty-year period has led her to a less benign view of mandatory busing today than she expressed in the earlier article.

39. Ibid., pp. 267–302.

40. Charles S. Bullock III, "School Desegregation After a Quarter Century," *Urban Affairs Quarterly* 18, no. 2 (December 1982): 295–296.

41. *Millikin* v. *Bradley,* 418 U.S. 717 (1974).

42. In 1996, the Connecticut Supreme Court obliterated the distinction between de jure and de facto segregation when it ordered the state to eliminate racial imbalances between the Hartford school systems, whose schools were 94 percent minority, and the surrounding suburban schools, which were overwhelmingly white, *The New York Times,* July 10, 1996, p. 13. Twenty-one years earlier, the California Supreme Court had made a similar ruling, but it was overturned by an amendment to the California Constitution that prohibited busing plans in excess of principles established by federal courts.

43. *Columbus Board of Education* v. *Penick,* 443 U.S. 449 (1979) and *Dayton Board of Education* v. *Brinkman,* 443 U.S. 526 (1979).

44. *Freeman* v. *Pitts* 498 U.S. 1081 (1992).

45. John B. McConahay, "Self-Interest Versus Racial Attitudes as Correlates of Anti-Busing Attitudes in Louisville: Is It the Buses or the Blacks?" *Journal of Politics* 44, no. 3 (August 1982): 692–720.

46. *The New York Times,* July 20, 1977, p. 10.

47. *The New York Times,* February 23, 1983, p. 1; March 10, 1983, p. 10; June 8, 1988, p. 23.

48. For background, see *The New York Times,* November 4, 1986, p. 1; *Newsweek,* November 17, 1986, p. 60.

49. *The New York Times,* December 28, 1988, p. 1; March 1, 1989, p. 8; *Minneapolis Star Tribune,* June 21, 1989, p. 6-A.

50. *Board of Education of Oklahoma City Public Schools* v. *Doswell,* January 23, 1989.

51. *Freeman* v. *Pitts* 498 U.S. 1081 (1992).

52. *Missouri* v. *Jenkins* 115 S.Ct. 2038 (1995).

53. *The New York Times,* October 3, 1989, p. 9.

54. Jonathan Kozol, *Savage Inequalities: Children in American Schools* (New York: Harper Perennial, 1992).

55. *Serrano* v. *Priest,* 3d 384 Calif. (1971).

56. *San Antonio School District* v. *Rodriguez* 4511 U.S. 59 (1973).

57. *Robinson* v *Cahill* 355 A.2d 129, 69 N.J. 1449 (1975). For an excellent background on the history of this case, see Richard Lehne, *The Quest for Justice: The Politics of School Finance Reform* (New York: Longman, 1978)

58. Michael Minton, "Why Efforts to Equalize School Funding Have Failed: A Political Economy Perspective," a paper presented to the Midwest Political Science Association, April 4–11, 1992, p. 30.

59. *The New York Times,* October 12, 1994, p. 15.

60. Minton, "Why Efforts to Equalize School Funding Have Failed."

61. *Time,* March 28, 1994, p. 38.

62. *The New York Times,* May 28, 1993, p. 7; June 1, 1993, p. 8; June 2, 1993, p. 9.

63. *The New York Times,* January 6, 1982, p. 1; June 20, 1987.

64. *The New York Times,* July 15, 1986, p. 8.

65. On the Tennessee case, see *The New York Times,* February 28, 1986, p. 11; October 25, 1986, p. 1; August 25, 1987, p. 1.

66. Diane Ravitch, "Multiculturalism: E Pluribus Plures," *The American Scholar* 59, no. 3 (Summer 1990): 337–354.

67. Quoted in Ibid., p. 351.

68. Arthur M. Schlesinger, Jr., *The Disuniting of America* (New York: Whittle Books, 1991), p. 43.

69. These data are taken from Lewis R. Jones, "Affirmative Action at Berkeley," *The American Prospect* No. 12 (Winter 1993): 154; and Jerome Karabel, "Berkeley and Beyond," *The American Prospect* No. 12 (Winter 1993): 157. Jones presents his data in a fairly antiaffirmative action manner, whereas Karabel presents his in a pro-affirmative action manner. Where the two differed on a piece of data, the text here leaned in the direction of using Karabel's data so as not to overstate the reverse discrimination aspects of the argument.

70. Lewis R. Jones, "Affirmative Action at Berkeley," p. 155.

71. Karen Paget, "Diversity at Berkeley: Demogoguery or Demography?" *The American Prospect* No. 8 (Spring 1992) 157. Jerome Karabel, "Berkeley and Beyond," *The American Prospect* No. 12 (Winter 1993): 156–160.

72. For example, on a cross-national science test, American thirteen-year-olds ranked behind those in twelve other societies, including Scotland, Slovenia, and the USSR. *Newsweek* February 17, 1992, p. 57. Another cross-national survey in 1992 found American school children ranked last in a comparison of nine nations in math, eighth out of nine in science, and fifth out of nine in geography. *The New York Times,* October 1, 1992, p. 10.

73. See Diane Ravitch, *The Troubled Crusade: American Education 1945–1980* (New York: Basic Books, 1983). Also see Deborah Meier's excellent critique in "Getting Tough in the Schools," *Dissent* (Winter 1984): 61–70.

74. Task Force on Education for Economic Growth, *Action for Excellence: A Comprehensive Plan to Improve Our Nation's Schools,* Education Commission of the States, June 1983; The National Science Board, *Educating Americans for the 21st Century,* 1983; The Twentieth Century Fund Task Force on Federal Elementary and Secondary Education Policy, *Making the Grade,* 1983; John I. Goodland, *A Place Called School: Prospects for the Future* (New York: McGraw-Hill, 1983); Ernest L. Boyer, *High School: A Report on Secondary Education in America* (New York: Harper & Row, 1983); Theodore R. Sizer, *Horace's Compromise—The Dilemma of the American High School* (Boston: Houston Mifflin, 1984).

75. D. Doyle and T. Hartle, *Excellence in Education* (Washington, D.C.: American Enterprise Institute, 1985), p. 18. Figures include the District of Columbia as though it were a state.

76. The history of Alexander's proposals have been traced by Steve D. Williams in a series of articles in the *Comparative State Politics Newsletter.* See "Alexander's Master Teacher Program Fails in Tennessee," 4, no. 3 (May 1983): 11–12; "Master Teacher Program Update," 4, no. 6 (December 1983): 21; "The First Year of Merit Pay for Tennessee Teachers," 6, no. 5 (October 1985): 33; and "The Politics of Merit Pay for Tennessee Teachers," 10, no. 5 (October 1989): 52–63.

77. Ross Corson, "Choice Ironies: Open Enrollment in Minnesota," *The American Prospect,* no. 3 (Fall 1990): 92–99.

78. L. McNeil, "The Politics of Texas School Reform," in W. Boyd and C. Kerchner, eds., *The Politics of Excellence and Choice in Education* (New York: Falmer, 1988). Also see Peter LeMann, "Texas: A Choice Without a Difference," *The Atlantic* 255, no. 5 (November 1985): 28.

79. Calculated from data in Bureau of the Census, *Statistical Abstract of the United States: 1995* (U.S. Government Printing Office, 1995), pp. 151, 492.

80. John E. Chubb and Terry M. Moe, "Politics, Markets, and the Organization of Schools," *American Political Science Review* 82, no. 4 (December 1988): 1065–1087, and *What Price Democracy? Politics, Markets, and American Schools* (Washington, D.C.: The Brookings Institution, 1988); John E. Chubb, "Why the Current Wave of School Reform Will Fail," *Public Interest* no. 90 (Winter, 1988): 28–49.

81. Chubb, "Why the Current Wave of School Reform Will Fail," p. 36.

82. See David R. Morgan and Sheila S. Watson, "Comparing Education Performance Among the American States," *State and Local Government Review* 19, no. 1 (Winter 1987): 15–20.

83. Joe Reed, "Grass Roots School Governance in Chicago," *National Civic Review* 80, no. 1 (Winter 1991): 41–45. David Moberg, "Can Democracy Save Chicago's Schools?" *The American Prospect,* no. 8 (Winter 1992): 98–108.

INFRASTRUCTURE POLICIES: TRANSPORTATION, HOUSING, AND COMMUNITY DEVELOPMENT

Chapter Preview

One of the most important roles of state and local governments is building and maintaining the physical infrastructure of modern society. In this chapter, we will examine three areas of infrastructure policy and analyze them from the perspective of political values and their social consequences. We will discuss in turn:

1. Transportation policy.
2. Housing policy.
3. Community development policy.
4. Political values and the social consequences of infrastructure policy.

Let us begin this examination with a short introduction to what is meant by infrastructure policy and why political values are significant to it.

◇ INTRODUCTION

One of the most important roles played by state and local governments is building, maintaining, and overseeing the physical infrastructure without which our modern society would not be possible. This chapter examines that part of the physical **infrastructure** that includes roads, transportation systems, housing, and community development projects. Some of this infrastructure, such as roads, is built by governments. Some, such as housing, is built by private entrepreneurs but is extensively regulated and subsidized by governments.

Chicagoans got a lesson in the importance of infrastructure in April 1992 when water from the Chicago River began pouring through a leak into a network of tunnels that carried power lines and telephone cables throughout the large downtown. Within hours, basements were flooded, merchandise was destroyed, people were trapped in elevators when the electricity went out, the nation's largest commodity exchange was temporarily put out of business, and most of the central business district was closed down. It took several days of pouring concrete into the river to close the leak. By the time life returned to normal, the damage had added up to billions of dollars. The whole disaster could have been averted if someone in city government had only followed up on early evidence that a hole was developing in the bottom of the river.[1]

In this chapter, we will examine the politics of infrastructure. On the face of it, transportation, housing, and infrastructure generally might seem to be technical matters better left to the engineers and city planners. In fact, however, these politics have sparked bitter conflicts across the nation over freeway location, downtown reconstruction, inner-city neighborhood deterioration, and suburban sprawl.

At the heart of these conflicts over infrastructure policy are conflicting values about the role of government, its costs and its benefits. If neighborhoods have to be torn up for government projects, can the burden be borne equally by all ethnic groups and social classes? Or do only certain ones pay the cost? Who benefits from infrastructure policies? Most infrastructure projects, without doubt, provide a public good. Everybody, for example, benefits from well-maintained streets. But do some groups of people benefit more than others? Finally, what impacts do infrastructure policies have on the social problems we examined in the two previous chapters? Is de facto racial segregation in most metropolises truly just a byproduct of the choices people make privately about where they want to live? Or did transportation, housing, and community development policies play a role in establishing the segregated metropolis?

We cannot answer all these questions in this chapter, but we will touch on many of them and try to provide a factual base for you to make your own judgments. We will examine transportation policy first, since the building of roads and transportation networks greatly influences where people are able to live and which communities will prosper. Second, we will examine housing and community development policies. Finally, we will examine the role of political values in these areas.

◇ TRANSPORTATION

Since the midtwentieth century, the American transportation system has been dominated by automobiles, trucks, and highways. Typically, most Americans get around by car. The widespread use and popularity of automobiles has given most Americans more mobility than any other people in history. This phenomenon has produced a number of positive results. The extent of our reliance on automobiles, however, has also led to an imbalance in the transportation system as other forms of transit have deteriorated. This imbalance has produced a number of negative consequences. Perhaps a third of the population is too old, too young, too disabled, or too poor to own and drive an automobile. Probably a fifth of all households do not own an automobile. This 20 to 33 percent of the population is unable to take advantage of the extensive mobility offered by automobiles, roads, and freeways. And the lack of balance between automobiles and other modes of transit has helped pollute the air and congest existing roadways.

These transportation conditions pose several important questions for state and local governments. First, how did automobiles, trucks, and highways become dominant in the transportation system? Why were railroads and mass-transit commuter systems allowed to deteriorate? Second, what prospects exist for public transit today? Third, what respective roles can states, communities, and the federal government play in bettering our transportation planning?

The Rise to Dominance of the Highway System

During the early twentieth century, the highway system and the railroad system competed to be the dominant means of transporting people around the country. As the road system grew extensive, the shortcomings of railroad passenger service became increasingly apparent. The railroads either would not or could not improve passenger service to the level of most European nations. As a result, they carried only a small fraction of the people carried by European railroads.[2] American passenger trains had severe drawbacks. For example, an analysis of railroad schedules during the 1910s found that a round trip from New Washington, Ohio, to the county seat of Bucyrus only fourteen miles away took nine hours and required a train change on both trips.[3]

Given this poor railroad service, it is not surprising that people preferred to travel by automobile once cars became reasonably priced. Especially in rural areas, cars met an economic need not fulfilled by any other system of transport.

The Federal Role in Highway Development   The federal government played an important role in the creation of the road system. In 1916, Congress created the Bureau of Public Roads, which was authorized to provide federal highway funds to the states on a fifty-fifty matching grant basis. To get federal funds, the states had to create state highway departments that would draw up highway construction plans and submit them to the Bureau of Public Roads for approval. To ensure that the state-built roads would tie together into a national system, the Bureau of Public Roads was empowered to establish construction standards and to see that the routes joined at state boundary lines.

In 1944, Congress passed a law calling for an extensive system of national highways, although money for it was not provided until the **Federal Aid Highway Act of 1956.** This act earmarked the revenues from a new 4-cents-per-gallon gasoline tax (increased to 14 cents by 1991) for the highway trust fund that was used to construct the **interstate highway system.** With a generous 90–10 matching formula, each state received $90 million in federal funds for each $10 million it put up. Today, the Highway Trust Fund turns over about $15 billion per year to the states for construction and maintenance of the 42,500-mile interstate highway system.[4]

Along with these generous matching grants have come a dozen so-called crossover mandates or sanctions, by which Congress imposes its will on the states. The most famous (or infamous, depending on one's viewpoint) was the 1984 requirement that each state raise its drinking age to twenty-one if it wished to continue receiving its full share of federal highway aid. Also, along with the huge amounts of money invested in highways came the creation of the so-called highway lobby, which has been a potent political force at both the state and national levels. As the cartoon on p. 397 illustrates, the highway lobby has effectively sought funds for highway construction while showing little sensitivity to related public needs.

The State Role in Highway Development   State governments have the main responsibility for actually constructing and maintaining the intercity highways. In addition to federal funds, they rely for this task primarily on gasoline taxes. To ensure that gas taxes would be earmarked for transportation purposes, most states enacted **antidiversion legislation** that prevented gas taxes from going into the general treasury.[5]

The most common purposes for which gas taxes were earmarked were highways, airports, state police, water transport, and boating. Few states designated gas tax revenue for public transit purposes.

The Consequences of Imbalanced Transportation   These developments in the highway system have had several important consequences for the lives of most Americans. First, because of the unprecedented mobility it gave people, the highway system helped disperse the metropolitan lifestyle throughout the countryside. The highways and the electronic communications systems of telephone, television, radio, satellite communications, fax machines, and computer modems now link the small town intimately to the metropolis. Possessing these communications links, many corporations increasingly construct new facilities in small towns beyond the fringes of the metropolis rather than in the heart of it.

The small town of the 1990s does not face the isolation that the same town might have faced a century earlier. The early-1900s characters of the novel *Main Street* were terribly isolated from the nearest metropolis, even though they were only a hundred miles away. Today, small-town residents can be just as urban by most criteria as the residents of the big city. They may have middle-class, managerial occupations in a state university, a branch office of a national corporation, or a local franchise outlet for a national retailing firm. The small-city residents may even have the best of both worlds. The residents of Tyler, Texas, can enjoy the advantages of Houston and Dallas and yet live a considerable distance away. They can drive to Houston in the morning in their

On a clear day you can see forever.

Source: Reprinted by permission from *Herblock's State of the Union* (New York: Simon & Schuster, 1972).

air-conditioned automobiles, shop at Neiman-Marcus or some other prominent department store, attend an afternoon ball game in the Astrodome, have dinner at any number of excellent restaurants, and be back home in Tyler in time to watch the 10:30 movie on television. Never before has this kind of mobility been possible.

This unprecedented mobility has permitted, paradoxically, both a *decentralization* and a *recentralization* of social activities. For Tyler, Texas, the automobile has spread the metropolitan lifestyle into the countryside. Until the 1920s, cities developed along streetcar lines,[6] but the combination of excellent roads and mass-produced automobiles permitted real estate developers to build subdivisions in suburban areas not served by streetcars or buses. Retail merchants began to abandon the congested central business districts for attractive, new suburban shopping centers that had plenty of parking space. In this way, the road network decentralized the metropolis.

A second consequence of the automobile age becomes apparent every time there is a petroleum shortage or a threat to our oil sources. The United States imports about 40 percent of the petroleum used to drive automobiles and heat buildings. This makes the new diffuse lifestyle extremely vulnerable to interruption of foreign supplies. In 1991, the United States fought the Persian Gulf War to protect its Middle East oil sources from falling under the control of a hostile regime in Iraq.

HIGHLIGHT

Traveling by Rail

The immense difficulty of using the railroad for local travel was documented by a vaudeville entertainer, Fred Allen, who wrote of his troubles in getting to various small towns and cities of the Midwest:

> There never seemed to be a direct way the actor could go from one date to another without changing trains once or twice during the night and spending endless hours at abandoned junctions waiting for connecting trains. One trip always annoyed me. Terre Haute and Evansville, both in Indiana, were a split week. The acts playing the Hippodrome Theater in Terre Haute for the first three days went to the Grant Theater in Evansville for the last three. If it had been possible to go directly from one town to the other, the trip could have been in three hours. It took the actors eight hours. Finishing at Terre Haute, they would leave there on the midnight train. After riding for an hour, they had to get off at some small town and wait four hours for a train to pick them up to ride the remaining two hours to Evansville. Most of the railroad stations were deserted at night. . . . Through the years, I have spent a hundred nights curled up in the dark, freezing railroad stations in the Kokomos, the Kenoshas, and the Kankakees, waiting for the Big Four, the Wabash, or C&A trains to pick me up and whisk me to the Danvilles, the Davenports, and the Decaturs.

Source: Fred Allen, *Much Ado About Me* (Boston: Little, Brown and Co., 1956), pp. 186–187.

A third consequence of the automobile age was the decline of the central cities of the Northeast and Midwest.[7] The freeways enabled retailers to abandon the central business district for the shopping centers in the suburbs, making it unnecessary for most people to venture into the old business districts except for an occasional excursion. The freeways built in the central cities tore up large numbers of homes and split up neighborhoods. In some cities, such as Los Angeles, Chicago, and Denver, they produced serious smog and air pollution. The third of the population that was too old, young, disabled, or poor to drive automobiles was increasingly compressed into central cities, where they had access to bus lines. The automobile did not by itself cause all this, but increasing reliance on the highways after 1945 was one of the important factors in the decline of the central cities.

A fourth problem that is increasingly serious is the cost of maintaining the road system. The highway trust fund, for its first thirty years, paid only for constructing the interstate system; maintenance costs were left to the states. As a consequence, the road systems have been poorly maintained in many places. Maintenance is an especially acute problem on the interstate highway system, which now allows heavy trucks weighing up to 80,000 pounds. The roads, however, were not designed to accommodate loads that heavy. One transportation study estimated that it would take 9,600 automobiles to do the amount of road damage caused by one 80,000-pound truck,[8] and the Congressional Budget Office estimated that taxes on trucks in this size range paid for only half of the wear and tear they added to the roadways.[9] To alleviate these problems, Congress in 1982, 1983, and 1991 increased the road taxes on trucks and increased the federal gasoline tax to 14 cents per gallon. Several states also raised their gasoline taxes. These measures are beginning to slow down the deterioration of the nation's roads. But 5,000 miles of the interstate system currently need replacement, a task that could cost up to $84 billion.[10]

The Uncertain World of Public Transportation

While automobile usage continues to climb, ridership on public transit declined steadily from the 1940s until 1972. It then rose for more than ten years and peaked in the mid-1980s at levels it had not seen since 1960. This renaissance in public transit in the 1970s and 1980s was due in no small measure to three factors: disenchantment with freeway construction in the early 1970s, new federal incentives for public transportation, and a new state government interest in public transit.

Disenchantment with Freeways Part of the public transit renaissance in the 1970s was due to a growing disenchantment with urban freeway systems. Whereas the state highway departments successfully overrode neighborhood objections to the metropolitan freeways during the 1950s and 1960s,[11] by the 1970s legal and political infighting had altered or terminated new free-way projects in Memphis,[12] Washington, D.C., Boston,[13] New York City, and several other cities. Among the most flamboyant of these battles was the one waged successfully by New Yorkers who, in 1985, brought an end to that city's so-called Westway project, a four-mile long highway redevelopment project slated to cost $15,782 *per inch.*[14]

Federal Incentives for Public Transit Equally important for the renaissance of public transit was a series of financial incentives starting in the 1960s. The first incentives were federal grants in aid for transit planning. In the *Urban Mass Transit Act of 1974,* Congress authorized an annual expenditure of roughly $2.2 billion through the end of the decade. Renewed in the 1980s and 1991, this act led to a total of about $89 billion in federal public transit spending up through the mid-1990s.[15] These funds helped subsidize operating expenses of transit systems as well as capital expenditures for construction and equipment. Also significant in this legislative history was the **Surface Transit Assistance Act of 1982** which earmarked, for the first time, some of the federal gasoline tax to public mass transit. It was primarily these earmarked funds that enabled mass transit to obtain federal funding during the 1980s when the Reagan and Bush administrations repeatedly proposed reducing mass transit subsidies and eliminating completely the subsidies for operating expenses for AMTRAK, the national railroad passenger line.

Despite the huge sums of money, subsidies for public transit are highly controversial. Opponents charge that transit systems and AMTRAK are like black holes in that they suck up huge amounts of money and never show a profit.[16]

Proponents charge that demands for profits and efficiency are misplaced. AM-TRAK, for example, saw its losses go down and its fiscal balance sheet improve in the late 1980s. But much of the financial improvement came at the cost of not buying replacement equipment for old equipment that was wearing out. The average age of locomotives increased from seven to eleven years. But failure to buy new engines in order to improve short-term financial reports has a long-term consequence of impairing operations. In AMTRAK's case, as the locomotives got older, the percent of long distance trains on time dropped from 78 to 54 percent.[17] As on-time performance drops, it is likely that passengers will get frustrated and abandon AMTRAK.

Europeans, by contrast, have consistently invested in modernizing train and transit facilities even though their passenger rail service also requires extensive government subsidies. The result is an elaborate system of intercity and intracity transit that is clean, fast, convenient, impressively punctual, and widely patronized by tens of millions of riders. With extensive public ridership, the Europeans save themselves a fortune in the cost of imported oil, and they make a major impact on holding down air pollution.

To get these advantages of public transit, however, it probably is not possible for public transit systems to run at a profit. Only about 44 percent of public transit revenues come from fares and advertising. The rest comes from state (47 percent) or federal (9 percent) subsidies.[18] Even at the peak of public transit ridership in the early twentieth century, transit operations lost money. In Boston, early transit operators built their streetcar systems primarily to transport people to real estate property they were developing on the fringes of the city. They not only lost money on their transit operations, they used their real estate profits to subsidize transit operations. Once the real estate was sold, they had no more incentives to subsidize the transit, and at that point they appealed to the city for financial aid. This occurred several times in Boston's history,[19] and the pattern was repeated throughout the United States. Schaeffer and Sclar write:

> The device was simple. A trolley line, charging low fares, was built beyond the city to marginal land, owned by the speculators. This land was then subdivided into building lots. The result was a manifold increase in the value of these real-estate holdings, which more than made up for operating trolley lines that were at best barely profitable. This connection between real estate profits and transit availability was thoroughly understood by the U.S. land speculators from coast to coast.[20]

An Increasing State Role   State and local governments have also been forced to consider increasing their own transit subsidies. Some states and communities, of course, were more able to meet these challenges than were others. On one extreme, transit systems in Chicago and Boston were so plagued with financial difficulties that they cut service, raised fares, and saw their riderships decline. At the other extreme, San Diego relied exclusively on state and local funds to build its famous light rail system, the famous Tijuana Trolley, and Dallas voters increased the sales tax to build a rapid rail system in their area.

Transit Options for the Nineties

In planning for effective public transit, each community must select the combination of transit vehicles that is most appropriate for its particular transit problems. Five major vehicle systems are available—expanded bus service, light rail systems, personal rapid transit (PRTs, or people movers), rapid rail systems, and commuter railroads.

Expanded Bus Service   Buses will remain the core of most transit systems. The greatest advantage of the bus is its flexibility. It can be driven any place where streets exist, and it can be used in a variety of ways. Many metropolitan areas now reserve special lanes on freeways for buses so that the buses can move faster than the automobile traffic. *Para transit* refers to small vans that cruise fixed routes and pick up and drop off passengers at any point. *Minibuses* or *stop-and-ride* buses have been used for shuttle purposes between central business shopping areas and outlying parking lots. *Dial-a-ride* is a system of small buses: when residents telephone, a minivan cruising in the neighborhood is dispatched to the resident's home to transport the resident to some point within the area serviced by the dial-a-ride.

In addition to flexibility, bus service has the lowest capital costs of any existing public transit system. *Capital costs* refer to the cost of building or purchasing a facility, and they are distinguished from *operating or maintenance costs*, which are the costs of running the facility once it is built.

The major disadvantage of buses is that they are labor intensive. Each bus, van, minibus, or other vehicle must have a driver. Drivers unionize. They bargain for higher wages, which increases the costs of operation. Bus operating expenses are also high for the large number of bus routes that do not attract enough passengers to pay for themselves.

Light Rail Systems   The light rail system is an updated version of the old streetcar. Streetcars are large, electrically powered vehicles that ride on tracks in the street. Most streetcar systems disappeared in the 1940s, when the transit companies changed to buses and paved over the streetcar rails. Between 1935 and 1970, the number of streetcar track miles declined from 25,000 to 762. In Los Angeles, which had an extensive streetcar system, the public transit company was purchased by a consortium owned by General Motors, Firestone, and Standard Oil, which tore up the tracks and replaced the streetcars with buses.[21]

In the 1980s, **light rail transit (LRT)** gained popularity. Unlike buses, light rail systems do not pollute the air and they are not vulnerable to petroleum shortages. They differ from the old-fashioned streetcar in that they can carry many more passengers (up to 500 in three linked cars) and they are more likely to run on separate railways than they are to run down the middle of busy streets, as did the old streetcars. The first LRT system began operating in 1981 when San Diego opened its Tijuana Trolley. Today, LRT operates in a dozen cities, and many other areas are exploring the option.

Most of these LRT systems have been very expensive to build and have disappointed their builders' goals of getting large numbers of automobile commuters to abandon their cars in favor of LRT. The two big exceptions to the general disappointment of LRT have been San Diego's 36-mile Tijuana Trolley system that carries 45,000 passengers per day and Portland's 15-mile system that carries 24,000 passengers per day.[22]

PRTs, or People Movers Personal rapid transit (PRT) is a proposal to have small cars running on a fixed rail system. Whereas subway cars and streetcars may carry up to 175 people, each PRT car would carry only six to ten people. Ideally, PRT lines could be constructed in a grid pattern with the lines no more than a mile apart, putting every resident of the city within walking distance of a PRT station. Because PRT cars are small, the fixed guideways needed for a PRT system would be much less costly than the fixed guideways needed for the subway or other rapid rail systems. Because the cars can be computer directed and need no driver, PRT's labor problems would be minimal.

Small-scale systems have been constructed and run successfully at some airports. The only attempts to establish a PRT or people mover system as a major element of city transit occurred in Morgantown, West Virginia (see p. 404), and Detroit, Michigan.[23]

Rapid Transit The fourth option for urban transportation is the traditional **rapid transit**—electrically driven trains that run in subways, on ground, or on elevated guideways. Such systems currently exist in ten U.S. cities. The major advantage of rapid transit is that it can move more passengers than any other mode of transit.

Rapid rail transit works best in areas with large populations, high densities, and large numbers of people commuting into the central business district (CBD) each day.[24] Unfortunately for rapid rail boosters, few metropolises meet these criteria. In the twenty-five largest urban areas in the 1980s, only 8.5 percent of workers commuted to jobs in the CBD. Nearly half (45.7 percent) commuted from homes in the suburbs to jobs in the suburbs.[25] And sprawling suburbs with low-density populations are not conducive to rapid rail transit.

Even in places with large numbers of people commuting to the CBD, such as San Francisco and Washington, D.C., rapid rail has had many problems. San Francisco's BART (Bay Area Rapid Transit), which opened in 1972, was the first rapid rail system to be built since the early 1900s. It has been heavily criticized for its initial cost overruns, its inability to run at a profit, and its failure to reduce traffic congestion in the San Francisco area.[26] In the smaller metropolitan areas, new rapid rail experiences have been even more disappointing. Miami's Metrorail has suffered from insufficient ridership—only one-fifth of original projections.[27]

Given all these considerations, it appears as though the smartest cities were the ones that resisted the temptation to use federal grants to build rapid rail, LRT, or people mover systems. But it is possible that history may judge otherwise. Few of the new systems have been operating for more than twenty years, and this may well be too short a time in which to evaluate such an expensive undertaking as an LRT. Conceivably, both New York and Chicago could have shown disappointing results only a few years after their subways first opened. Yet today those subway systems are invaluable, and in forty years, San Francisco

Bay Area residents, Atlantans, and Miamians may well be grateful for the wisdom of today's leaders in constructing their rail systems.

Multimodal Bus Rapid Transit   Finally, buses can be used on fixed guideways to gain the speed and passenger volume of LRT. Unlike LRT, however, these same vehicles can leave the fixed guideways to run as regular buses on city streets. Variations of this multimodal rapid transit have been used successfully in England, Germany, Brazil, and Australia. Because the fixed guideways are much cheaper to build than LRT or rapid rail and because the buses are cheaper to purchase than rail vehicles, a multimodal bus rapid transit can be built at a fraction of the cost of LRT.

The most elaborate system is probably the so-called O-Bahn in Adelaid, Australia, a city of about one million people with a low-density population similar to most American cities. Express buses on separate, fixed guideways connect the city of Adelaide to its suburbs. Once they enter the city, the buses leave the fixed guideway and cruise the city streets like regular buses. This gives the O-Bahn the high-speed, high-occupancy characteristics of LRT on the guideways combined with the flexibility of an ordinary bus on city streets. Although more expensive to build than simply adding more buses, the O-Bahn was built for one-half the cost of an LRT system, and it has proved immensely popular. It drew much higher ridership rates than projected, requiring the purchase of more buses than originally anticipated. The multimodal aspect of the system was one of the things that made the O-Bahn so popular. Because its vehicles could cruise the city streets to pick up passengers as well as speed along the fixed guideways, O-Bahn reduced the need for transfers between buses and for park-and-ride facilities. This dramatically decreased travel time compared to automobile commuters. The buses also can be equipped with both electric motors for traveling on the fixed guideway and diesel engines for driving the streets of the city or suburbs.[28]

A variation of bus rapid transit using fixed guideways was constructed in Curitiba, Brazil, a city of two million people. The government constructed the guideways and contracted out to private operators to run the buses along the guideways. The city paid the operators by the mile driven rather than by passengers carried, and this gave the operator a huge incentive to run as many bus miles as possible, which increased the passenger ridership. The Brazilians also used an imaginative set of incentives and design features that made the system very popular and resulted in a 25 percent reduction in the number of automobiles commuting into the city center each day.[29]

The Dubious Future of Public Transit

It is not clear whether mass transit can reverse its current decline and pick up with the renaissance it enjoyed in the 1970s. That renaissance was in great measure financed by nearly $100 billion in federal grants since 1970. Furthermore, the cause of mass transit has been hurt by grossly inflated projections of the benefits that would flow from LRTs, people movers, and rapid rail. When the benefits frequently fell short of these inflated projections, public mass transit itself

HIGHLIGHT

PRT in Morgantown

Morgantown, home of West Virginia University, was the scene of a daily traffic jam between the university's three campuses and the city's central business district. To relieve this congestion, the university requested a $13.5-million grant from the federal Department of Transportation (DOT) to construct a 3.6-mile, $18-million PRT system with six stops that would connect the university's parking lots, its three campuses, and downtown Morgantown. The 45 vehicles would be 6 feet wide by 15 feet long, would seat eight and take another twelve standing commuters. The chauffeurless cars were to be electrically driven at 30 miles per hour by a computer. The system runs on an elevated concrete guideway that on completion was to extend 5.4 miles. The riders signal for a car by placing their fare cards in a slot and pressing a designation button. This signals the computer to dispatch a car to the riders' station to take them to their destinations.

Early in the planning, Morgantown's PRT got caught in national politics. DOT decided it wanted to dedicate the Morgantown PRT guideway before the 1972 presidential election, but it did not yet know how heavy the cars would be. To accommodate the heaviest possible car, it built a much heavier and thus much costlier structure than the one originally anticipated. Planning and construction were rushed, the project manager was changed, designs were altered, inflation hit double digits, and the cost of the project quickly overran the original estimates.

When the first phase was completed, costs had reached $59.8 million. Rather than a 5.4-mile system reaching all three university campuses, it was only 2.2 miles long and reached only two campuses. Rather than six stations, the system had only three. At one point, when the development of vehicles was delayed, the university ran golf carts along the guideway.

The university complained that this abbreviated system did not meet its needs and threatened to tear it down at a cost to DOT of $7 million if DOT did not move into phase II, which would complete the original plans. Phase II was projected at the time to cost another $53.8 million. This would bring the total cost for the system to $113.6 million, nearly $100 million more than the original estimate of $18 million. DOT agreed to finish phase II, which would add two more stations and complete the 5.4 miles of guideways.

Despite its high start-up costs and the glitches surrounding its construction, Morgantown's PRT has run successfully since its maiden trip in 1975. It carries 16,000 riders a day and has generally operated free of serious problems. Despite running its cars at headways of only 15 seconds at times, the system has never suffered a collision.

Source: "Trouble in Mass Transit," *Consumer Reports* 40, no. 3 (March 1975): 190–195. *St. Paul Pioneer Press,* July 22, 1990, p. 179.

came under powerful attack by highly polemical writings that sought to turn opinion against mass transit.[30]

◇ HOUSING AND COMMUNITY DEVELOPMENT

A second area of infrastructure policy involves the framework for housing people and activities. In discussing these policy areas we need to examine: (1) the basic problems associated with housing and central-city deterioration; (2) the roles that states, communities, and the federal government play in housing and redevelopment policies; and (3) alternatives to present-day housing and community development programs.

The Basic Problems of Housing

The Homeless   The most visible housing problem is that of the homeless. Their numbers are estimated to be somewhere between 350,000 and 3 million, with the most likely number being somewhat more than half a million.[31] Never since the Great Depression of the 1930s have that many Americans lived without shelter. Why such a large number of homeless should exist today seems traceable to three explanations.

First is the argument that there simply is not enough low-income housing, and this forces some low-income people into homelessness. Advocates of homelessness point out that the Reagan years saw a sharp dropoff in the number of public housing units built each year from 16,000 when Reagan took office in 1981 to 2,000 per year in 1986 and 1987. The net result was that the national supply of low-income, publicly owned housing actually shrunk from 1,404,000 units in 1981 to 1,372,000 in 1987.[32]

Not a good argument, say Reagan's defenders, who offer a second explanation for homelessness. Although it is true that Reagan cut the budget for public housing, the total supply of public and private housing units grew by almost 20 percent during the 1980s, while the population grew only 10 percent. Additionally about 12 million housing units are vacant.[33] From this perspective, homelessness stems not from a lack in housing units but from the behavioral characteristics of the homeless people themselves.[34] The homeless, says Irving Welfeld, "are not like the rest of us."[35] Most of them have severe problems. A survey of California homeless, for example, found that 69 percent were abusers of either drugs or alcohol, and 77 percent suffered from either mental illness or substance abuse.[36]

A third reason for the growth of homelessness is traced to deinstitutionalization. Mental institutions housed half a million patients in 1963. By 1992, that number had dropped to about 125,000.[37] By these calculations, more than 300,000 institutionalized people had to find a place to live. For years, many of the people released from mental institutions drifted into single-room occupancy (SRO) hotels, but the gentrification process of the 1970s saw many SRO hotels torn down for condominiums and commercial buildings.[38]

By the 1990s, many cities were losing patience with the large numbers of homeless persons who drifted into their shelters and panhandled on the streets. Atlanta increased the number of arrests for loitering and public drunkenness, while New York City banned panhandling in the subways.[39]

What to do about the homeless is not self-evident. There is a growing belief that the problem requires more than just increasing the number of shelters. The McKinney Act of 1987 set up a number of programs that sought to provide medical care, mental health care, education, and job training for the homeless. Nevertheless, homelessness persists and is likely to persist unless the nation addresses the twin issues of "housing that is too expensive and incomes that are too low" to afford housing.[40]

Housing for Low- and Moderate-Income People   If the first basic housing problem is the homeless, the second is alleviating the difficulties facing low- and moderate-income people whose incomes are so low that they could easily become homeless without some form of public assistance. In 1989, 56 percent of poor people paid more than half of their income for shelter.[41] And the pressure on their budgets is likely to grow through the end of the 1990s because of a growing gap between the supply of low-income rental units and the demand for them. The number of low-income renters grew by 41 percent during the 1970s and 1980s, but the number of low-income rental units actually declined by 14 percent during the same period.[42]

For moderate-income families, whose goal most often is to own their home rather than to rent it, the perennial problem is cost. On the face of it, these people do not seem to be priced out of today's housing market. Almost two-thirds of American families own their own homes today, up from 44 percent in 1940.[43] However, many young, middle-class families are able to afford the down payment and monthly mortgage payments only if both spouses work. As Figure 15-1 shows, the cost of housing has dramatically outpaced inflation over the past quarter century.

There are several reasons for the escalation of new home prices, not the least of which is that the new single-family homes are seldom designed any more for the moderate-income household. They are designed for a much more upscale buyer than was the case twenty years ago.[44] In 1970, the average new house had 1,500 square feet of living space, only 34 percent of new houses had central air conditioning, and only 35 percent had a fireplace. By 1990, the average square footage had grown to 2,080, 76 percent of new houses had central air conditioning, and 66 percent had a fireplace.[45]

Although the moderate-income family has been priced out of the market for new single-family homes, they have a much better shot at getting a used home. Figure 15-1 shows that these houses have not exceeded the inflation rate as much as new homes have. Home mortgage rates have also moderated in recent years, which significantly reduces the cost of a mortgage loan. These rates averaged 14 percent in the early 1980s[46] but dropped below 7 percent by the mid-1990s. On a thirty-year fixed-rate mortgage, a drop of only two percentage points in the interest rates on a $75,000 mortgage reduces the monthly payment by $110. As mortgage rates dropped in the early 1990s, it was not only easier for first-time home buyers to make the purchase, but also those who had bought homes at the high 12–14 percent mortgage rates of the early 1980s could refinance. If used home prices remain stable and if mortgage rates remain low throughout the 1990s, moderate-income families will be given a huge boost in their quest for home ownership.

Racial Separation in Housing   Racial minorities find more obstacles in their search for decent housing than do whites of similar income levels. Only in 1948 did the Supreme Court hold that deed covenants that prohibited the sale of property to a noncaucasian were unenforceable in the courts. Federal Housing

Figure 15-1 MEDIAN COST OF SINGLE-FAMILY HOMES SOLD

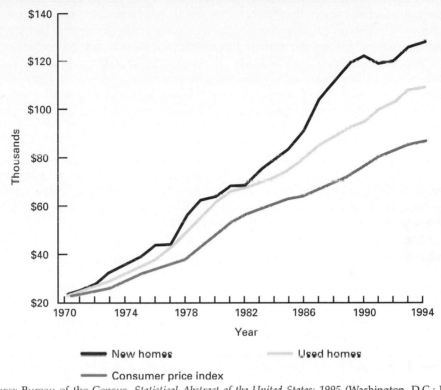

Source: Bureau of the Census, *Statistical Abstract of the United States: 1995* (Washington, D.C.: U.S. Government Printing Office, 1992), pp. 492, 730.

Administration (FHA) loans to nonwhites were prohibited as late as 1962. It was not until the Housing Act of 1968 that discrimination in the sale and rental of housing was made illegal.

This legislation expanded housing opportunities for many middle-income racial and cultural minorities. And racial separation is measurably less today than it was twenty years ago.[47] Nevertheless, separation and discrimination continue to exist. The most notorious case of officially sanctioned segregation occurred in Yonkers, New York, where the city's efforts to block the construction of public housing in white neighborhoods led a federal court to impose $100-per-day fines on the city until it approved the building of 1,000 units of low- and moderate-income housing. One hundred dollars does not sound like much, but the amounts doubled each day, and within twenty-five days would have reached $3 million per day. Faced with such a prospect, city officials finally relented and approved the project.[48] Despite this agreement, four years later, barely half of these units had been built.[49]

In the face of strong national legislation against racial discrimination in housing, how can it be that racial separation in housing is still the predominant pattern throughout the nation? Part of the racial separation can be attributed no doubt to whites freely choosing not to live among blacks and blacks freely choosing not to live among whites. But much of it also is due to exclusionary zoning practices in the richest suburbs. **Exclusionary zoning** exists when a suburb requires each house to have expensive amenities, such as a large lot, a garage, a paved driveway, and other costly building-code demands, plus prohibiting low-rent apartment buildings. The more such requirements, the more expensive it is to build housing in a community. An elite suburb, as shown by the "Highlight" on p. 410 can easily keep out low-income people this way. Since racial minorities disproportionately earn low incomes, minorities necessarily bear the biggest burden of exclusionary zoning. The motivation behind exclusionary zoning is clearly class based rather than race based, but the practice has racial consequences. By keeping out low-income people, a community can effectively keep out many blacks and other minorities.

Perhaps the most visible example of exclusionary housing takes place in **gated communities.** These are developments of $350,000 or higher homes that build walls around the developments and put up gates at the entry roads. Security measures are taken at the gates to ensure that unauthorized people cannot drive or walk into the gated development. The growing popularity of gated communities represents a significant break from previous social organization in American. In the past, only a small handful of people were rich enough to wall themselves off from the rest of society. But today, gated communities make it possible for the top 10 or 15 percent of income earners to wall themselves off. Because of their incomes and assets, these people tend to be among the most influential in society. By hiring their own security forces, sending their children to private schools, utilizing private recreational facilities, and opposing spending programs on these same services for the rest of society, they can literally wall themselves off from many of the problems that face the rest of society. Only a relatively few people live in this fashion today. If present trends continue, however, this will be a growing option for many doctors, lawyers, businesspersons, and other people in the upper-middle-income range. Nobody knows what the consequences would be for the social fabric of society if its most dynamic professional and business class were to wall itself off from the rest of society. But it is hard to believe that the consequences would be positive.

In 1975, New Jersey initiated a practice called **inclusionary zoning.** In that year, the New Jersey Supreme Court refused to allow Mount Laurel township to zone out low-income housing. Instead, it required every town to "include" low-income housing in their development plans. Hence the term *inclusionary zoning.* Implementation of inclusionary zoning has been plagued with difficulties, and in 1983 the court reaffirmed its decision that all communities must include low-income housing. In 1985, the New Jersey state legislature created a Council on Affordable Housing to determine how the principle would apply in each town and each development project.[50]

Minnesota tried to deal with exclusionary housing in 1995 by passing a Livable Communities Act. This law requires that some of the tax base created by expensive homes in the Minneapolis–St. Paul suburbs be used to construct moderate-income housing. Suburbs that refuse to construct moderate-income homes lose their excess tax base to other communities that take steps to provide housing for low- and moderate-income people.[51]

Deterioration of Central-City Neighborhoods   As gated communities spread over the past quarter century, many central-city neighborhoods deteriorated. The worst example was probably the South Bronx section of New York City from the mid-1970s to the mid-1980s, when 100,000 dwelling units were destroyed through arson, vandalism, and abandonment. What fifty years earlier had been a working-class, heavily Jewish community became by the 1980s a burned-out shell of a neighborhood dominated by crime, vandals, and gangs.[52]

No city faces the destruction unleashed on the South Bronx, but every city faces the general problem of deteriorating neighborhoods as middle-class residents move out to the suburbs and are replaced by people with less spending power, less ability to pay taxes, and less ability to maintain their residences.

The problem of declining neighborhoods is exacerbated by the practice called **red-lining.** Banks and insurance companies supposedly draw a red line around deteriorating neighborhoods, where it is a risky investment to make a mortgage loan or to insure a building. In Brooklyn, it was estimated in 1977 that 89 percent of the assets of mutual savings banks located in that city were invested in mortgages outside Brooklyn.[53] In fact, there is evidence to suggest that race is the main motive in red-lining. A study of the existence of commercial homeowners' insurance by zip code in Milwaukee found that the single strongest variable explaining the extent of commercially available home-owners' insurance was race. The zip codes with the most black residents had the lowest incidence of homeowners' insurance.[54]

When apartment owners are unable to get loans to improve their buildings, the more affluent tenants move out and are replaced by the less affluent. Homeowners lucky enough to get financing to sell their homes move to better neighborhoods. The red-lining practice accelerates the flight of the middle class to the suburbs. The in-coming low-income people have more problems, and the inevitable result is that those neighborhoods denied mortgage funds and homeowners' insurance continue to deteriorate. Because of these debilitating effects of red-lining, several states as well as Congress have passed laws seeking to discourage the practice.

Gentrification   Paradoxically, while some central-city neighborhoods are in decline and find it difficult to attract mortgage money, other neighborhoods have experienced **gentrification.** This has been characterized by upper-middle-income and professional people moving into old neighborhoods, refurbishing the houses there, and turning aged apartment buildings into condominiums. In most cities, the gentrifying neighborhoods are usually near the downtown area, are blessed with houses that have distinctive aesthetic qualities, and are often large enough to be converted into two- or three-unit condominiums. On the positive side, gentrification has led to neighborhood restoration, added to the urban

HIGHLIGHT

Keeping Minorities Out of Birmingham

Birmingham, Michigan, is an upper-income Detroit suburb with few blacks or other racial minorities among its 26,000 residents.

In fall 1977 Michigan's Housing Development Authority agreed to finance a 150-unit apartment complex for the elderly if Birmingham would in turn rehabilitate fifty existing houses for rental to low- and moderate-income families. Assuming that the low- and moderate-income families would be poor blacks, 4,600 Birmingham voters signed a petition urging the Birmingham Commission (the city council) to turn down this bargain.

When the city commission voted to approve the bargain, opponents began a petition drive to recall the six city commissioners who had voted for the plan. In April 1978 three of those city commissioners stood for reelection and were defeated by candidates who opposed the housing plan. Also on the ballot was a referendum on the housing plan itself. It was resoundingly defeated.

Source: *The New York Times*, April 12, 1978.

---

tax base, and attracted an upper-middle-income population. This in turn provides an economic base for restaurants and chic shopping facilities. However, gentrification, like most developments, has not been an unmitigated blessing. On the negative side, it has led to the **displacement** of lower-income people, usually racial minorities, who are driven out of the houses and apartments that are in the process of being gentrified.[55] This phenomenon occurs because the gentrification process drives up property values to the point where landlords can no longer charge cheap rents. As low-income people are displaced from their former homes, they are forced to rent newer ones in adjacent neighborhoods, usually at higher prices.

The Intergovernmental Connection in Coping with Housing Problems

Governmental initiatives to deal with these housing and community development problems began in the late nineteenth century at the local level. Social reformers attacked the spread of urban slum housing by enacting **building codes** that established minimum requirements for space, electricity, plumbing, and health matters such as garbage disposal. The first building codes were adopted in New York City in the 1860s after a cholera epidemic had spread through slum neighborhoods. By the early twentieth century most cities and states had adopted some form of housing regulations.[56]

In addition to building codes, cities also began enacting zoning regulations, which divide a community into zones restricted to specific uses. The **zoning codes** were largely designed to protect residential, middle-class, single-family-home neighborhoods from low-income apartments, industrial establishments, and other developments that were considered undesirable.

Finally, in response to the Great Depression of the 1930s, the federal government set up programs that the state and local governments were charged with implementing. This intergovernmental approach still characterizes housing and community development policymaking.

Helping Out the Middle Class—Mortgage Protection

The Federal Role   The Great Depression of the 1930s effectively destroyed the existing system of financing home purchases. The most common method to finance a home then was the so-called **balloon mortgage.** This required a down payment of 35 to 40 percent, and the life of the loan extended for ten to fifteen years. During those years, the home buyer made only interest payments and was required to pay off the entire principal with a single, so-called balloon payment at the end of the period. If the home buyer had not accumulated enough savings to make the final payment, the lending institution foreclosed the mortgage, sold the house, and used the proceeds of the sale to pay the balance of the loan and other bank charges.

The Great Depression set off a vicious cycle of events that destroyed this system. By 1932 nearly 25 percent of the workforce was unemployed. Those unemployed workers were unable to make their mortgage interest payments, thus depriving the banks, savings and loan associations, and credit unions of needed income. Lacking a national system of insured savings accounts, this declining income made it impossible for savings institutions to pay their depositors. In order to generate income, the lending institutions regularly foreclosed on mortgages that fell behind in interest payments. The supply of foreclosed homes vastly exceeded the demand for them, and home values dropped sharply. Unable to sell their foreclosed houses at a profit, unable to attract new depositors, and unable to pay existing depositors, many banks simply closed their doors. In 1930, 150,000 homes were foreclosed, and in 1933, more than 4,000 banks failed. These record levels have never been exceeded.[57]

The federal government responded by creating programs to insure mortgages and to insure people's savings deposits. By insuring mortgages against default, the federal government gave banks confidence to make more loans. And by insuring people's savings accounts, the government boosted people's confidence in the banking industry. The federal government also introduced the low down payment, long-term mortgage that helped average families secure home ownership.

State and Local Roles   These programs giving mortgage help for middle-class housing have been primarily a transaction between federal government agencies and private lending institutions. State and local governments play a regulatory role. They charter and regulate the lending institutions. They establish the building codes and zoning regulations to which the newly built FHA and VA homes must conform. Many states also have usury laws that limit the amount of interest that can be charged on loans. Finally, many states have active programs of their own to generate housing opportunities for middle- and moderate-income people.

Housing Programs for the Poor—Public Housing

The Federal Role   The Housing Act of 1937 provided for the Public Housing Administration (since 1965 a division of HUD) to contract with a local housing authority (LHA) to build apartment units that would be rented to low-income tenants at a subsidized rate. By 1974, when housing programs were overhauled, over 1.3 million housing units were rented by over five million families.[58] Most cities had long waiting lists of people applying to public housing projects.

Public housing was originally designed to provide housing assistance for middle- and working-class people who had been temporarily driven out of decent housing by the depression. Because very little housing was constructed from 1929 until the end of World War II, by 1945 an enormous housing shortage existed. During the next thirty years a housing construction boom took place largely in the suburbs and in the fast-growing cities of the South and Southwest. By the early 1960s, the supply of middle-class housing had caught up with the demand. Upwardly mobile tenants abandoned the public housing projects in the 1950s and 1960s. They were replaced by the poor, primarily by black migrants from the South and by Latinos.

State and Local Roles   Although initiated and overseen by the federal government, public housing was actually implemented by a local government agency, the local housing authority (LHA). The local city council establishes the LHA and approves its contract with the Public Housing Administration to build low-income apartments. Most LHAs were formed in the large central cities.[59] Once created, the LHA sold tax-exempt municipal bonds to raise the funds needed to buy land and build the projects. The LHA administers the project and retires the debt through the rent it collects from tenants. Since these rents are never high enough to let the project break even, the Public Housing Administration subsidizes the LHA for each low-income family in the project.

If success is measured by the demand for a product, then public housing has been very successful. Long waiting lists exist for most projects. Nevertheless, public housing has its problems and has been bitterly criticized. It increasingly concentrated low-income blacks in big-city ghettoes. In some places, public housing was used deliberately to relocate blacks from scattered locations throughout the cities to a few large ghettoes.[60] Some public housing projects concentrated large numbers of people with extensive social problems into the same residential area, leading to unsatisfactory living conditions for the majority of the residents of those projects. One of the worst of these was the Pruitt-Igoe project in St. Louis, which finally had to be closed.

Pruitt-Igoe was not typical of all public housing projects. Other cities followed different site patterns. In Dade County, Florida, public housing was located on 100 sites scattered throughout the county. In New York, Chicago, and St. Louis, it was commonly located in high-rise apartments.

HIGHLIGHT

The Death of Pruitt-Igoe

The most criticized of all public housing was probably the Pruitt-Igoe project in St. Louis, although it had received wide praise from architectural critics when it was built in the 1950s. It originally was built to house both blacks and whites, with the whites in the Igoe part and the blacks in the Pruitt part. After federal courts prohibited segregation in public housing, the two sections were integrated. The whites slowly moved out, and eventually the project became overwhelming black. The residents were continually harassed by teenage gangs that mugged and raped women. Broken windows went unrepaired, and glass scattered on the ground below went uncleared. Residents complained that the elevators were unsafe and were continually used for toilets. The laundry facilities were unsafe. One resident commented that although her apartment itself was much nicer than homes she had previously lived in, the surrounding environment was dirty, dangerous, and unsanitary.

So dangerous and unpleasant was the Pruitt-Igoe project, in fact, that people refused to live in it. Its 2,700 apartments never maintained high occupancy rates. And in 1972 the failure of this project was publicly admitted when the buildings were vacated and some of them torn down.

Sources: Lee Rainwater, "The Lessons of Pruitt-Igoe," *Public Interest* no. 8 (Summer 1967): 116–126; Eugene J. Meehan, *Public Housing Policy* (New Brunswick, N.J.: Rutgers University Press, 1975); and Nicholas J. Demarath, "St. Louis Public Housing Study Sets Off Community Development to Meet Social Needs," *Journal of Housing* 19 (October 15, 1962): 472–478.

Many of the public housing defects were attributed to the program's tendency to concentrate racial minorities, broken families, families subsisting on welfare, and recent migrants into the big cities. Concentrating people with several social problems together into large, high-rise buildings without supportive social services probably made social disorganization in the public housing projects inevitable. These problems are compounded by the poor upkeep maintenance that characterizes most projects.

Urban Renewal

Distinct from federally sponsored housing programs was the **urban renewal** program, which was created by a 1949 amendment to the Housing Act of 1937 and which allowed part of the housing money to be used for commercial development. The resulting program was called urban renewal.

The primary objective of urban renewal was to clear blighted areas and redevelop them with a mixture of commercial and residential establishments that would truly renew the old neighborhoods. Urban renewal was thus distinguished from public housing in that it focused on commercial redevelopment. Also in contrast to public housing, urban renewal developments were turned over to private entrepreneurs rather than owned by a government body, the local housing authority.

To qualify for urban renewal funds, a city had to create a local public agency (LPA), which was sometimes the same as the local housing authority. The LPA designated land to be cleared with urban renewal funds and submitted to the federal urban renewal agency a *workable program* for redevelopment.

When the local plan was approved, the federal urban renewal agency provided funds for the LPA to acquire the land, clear it, and reinstall the public facilities such as sewer and water lines. After this was completed, the LPA offered the land to redevelopers, who bought it at a much reduced price and erected their establishment on it. The federal government typically paid two-thirds of the LPA's net cost (acquisition, clearance, and upgrading costs less the price paid by the redeveloper), and the rest was made up through local bonds, cash, or other funds.

The residents and former merchants in the redevelopment area had to relocate to new areas. The LPA was obliged to give relocation assistance to the residents. But in fact this aid was seldom adequate,[61] and displacement of these residents became one of the biggest complaints against urban renewal.

In sum, the major impact of urban renewal was to redevelop the central business districts (CBDs) and other commercial areas of the major cities. Although urban renewal was instrumental in rebuilding many CBDs, it was resoundingly criticized from a variety of fronts. Community activists and architectural critics objected to it for destroying functioning communities.[62] Black leaders referred to urban renewal as Negro removal. Conservatives criticized it for using governmental authority to take property from one group of private citizens (the private homeowners and merchants) and turning it over to another (the redevelopers).[63]

Restructuring Housing and Renewal Programs

The 1974 Housing and Community Development Act   By the early 1970s, federal housing and urban renewal programs had come under resounding criticism. These criticisms came to a head under the presidency of Republican Richard Nixon (1969–1974) who wanted a program that would be cheaper and simpler to administer. After several years of political battles, Congress finally passed the **Housing and Community Development Act of 1974,** which set the structure of housing and community development programs that still exists today.

The community development provisions consolidated seven categorical grant programs, including urban renewal, into a community development block grant (CDBG) of $8.4 billion annually from 1975 to 1977. Successive renewals have kept it alive. Cities may use their community development funds for urban renewal purposes, more public housing, or other activities ranging from code enforcement to improving certain public services. Under a complicated formula, each community of over 50,000 is automatically entitled to a specific sum.

The housing portion of the 1974 Housing and Community Development Act created a rent supplement program called **Section 8.** Under Section 8, the local housing authority (HRA) provides rent assistance for tenants whose total family income is less than 80 percent of the median for the area. Tenants pay 30 percent of their income to the landlord. The LHA uses federal funds to pay the landlord the difference between that amount and a maximum allowable rent established by HUD.

Was the 1974 restructuring successful?

The answer seems to be both yes and no. On the positive side, the new programs clearly strengthened mayors in dealing with the LPAs and LHAs.[64] They also gave cities a great deal of flexibility in adapting the CDBG block grants to local needs. In St. Paul, Minnesota, a strong mayor exerted considerable influence to promote several large redevelopment projects and industrial parks. In four New England cities, by contrast, the mayors exerted very little influence, and CDGB funds were scattered to neighborhood projects throughout the cities.[65] In much of the South, as civil rights groups complained, compliance with CDBG requirements for citizen participation mostly ignored activists in poor communities.[66] But in Austin, Texas, poor neighborhoods were well represented.[67]

The Section 8 rent supplement program also had its successes. By guaranteeing landlords a fair rent, Section 8 encouraged thousands of developers to build apartments in the low- to moderate-income rental range. Section 8 rent supplements also made it possible to spread subsidized housing into white, middle-class neighborhoods. Although these neighborhoods had historically been willing to accept subsidized housing for the elderly, they usually balked at providing such units for poor families, and previous attempts at scattered-site public housing had failed. The Section 8 program was more successful than previous public housing at spreading subsidized housing into the suburbs.

Though Section 8 has simplified federal housing programs and has run fairly smoothly, it has not been free of problems.[68] For example, since Section 8 subsidizes the difference between actual rent and 30 percent of a tenant's income, this means that local housing markets in reality determine how much of a subsidy is paid under Section 8. In high-cost housing markets such as New York and San Francisco, this makes Section 8 a very expensive program.[69] In traditional public housing projects, the rental subsidies are not driven up so readily by the private housing market.

In addition to these problems with Section 8, the Department of Housing and Urban Development (HUD) was plagued with severe problems. During the 1980s, HUD lost as much as $4 billion due to fraud, influence peddling, political favoritism, poor supervision, and poor bookkeeping. Realtors who sold HUD properties fraudulently held onto escrow money that had been deposited with them. One such realtor was dubbed Robin Hud because she claimed to have given most of the $5 million she stole to the poor. Influence peddling and political favoritism are hardly strangers to Washington, but they reached new extremes in the 1980s when having connections with Republican insiders seemed to be the prime prerequisite for getting contracts for several HUD programs. Most notorious was former cabinet member James G. Watt, who served as consultant for housing contractors and once earned $300,000 in fees for six telephone calls made on behalf of his clients.[70] So badly was HUD's reputation scarred by the scandals that it is difficult to predict what effect they will have on Congress's willingness to delegate more housing authority to the agency.

Many of HUD's problems can be traced to irreconcilable differences between Democrats and Republicans over national housing policy. Democrats have tended to push for a **direct-production strategy** under which programs like Section 8 are used to construct new rental units for the poor. Republicans, on the other hand, tend to favor a **filter-down strategy** that lets the free market construct expensive new housing for the affluent. As affluent people move into the new housing, this sets off a chain reaction in which middle-income people buy the homes vacated by the affluent, and the lower-middle-income people buy the homes vacated by the middle-income people. As these lower-middle-income people move up, their units become available for renting to the poor. Republicans have also pushed fairly consistently for a **housing voucher plan** that gives eligible people a voucher to pay for a portion of their rent on any unit in the private market.[71]

Because of these perennial conflicts between Democrats and Republicans, national housing policy has fluctuated back and forth depending upon which party had the upper hand in Washington. With conservative Republican Ronald Reagan in the White House in the 1980s, Section 8 and CDBG funds suffered severe budget cuts. These were somewhat undone by the 1990 National Affordable Housing Act, which mollified congressional Democrats with an increase in Section 8 funding and mollified Republicans by creating a new program that encouraged the sale of public housing units to their tenants. When the Republicans took control of Congress in 1995, however, they pushed their approach by slicing HUD's budget 25 percent, with the bulk of the cuts coming in Section 8. They also built up pressure to eliminate HUD as a cabinet department and parcel out its major responsibilities to other federal agencies.

◇ POLITICAL VALUES AND THE SOCIAL CONSEQUENCES OF INFRASTRUCTURE POLICY

Infrastructure policies do not take place in a vacuum. They reflect political values of society at large. And they have important social consequences.

Political Values and Infrastructure Policy

The importance of political values to infrastructure policy is very clearly seen in relation to housing policies. The conservative perspective[72] seeks to minimize public-sector involvement in direct subsidy of housing as much as possible. Thus conservatives opposed the original Public Housing Act in 1937, and in 1949 they used their influence to involve the private sector in the Urban Renewal amendments to the Housing Act. They favor income tax deductions to help middle-class people pay for their mortgages.

Conservatives are reluctant to provide housing assistance to the poor for the same reasons that they are reluctant to provide welfare assistance in general to the poor. Poverty is seen as an individual defect rather than a product of the social structure. To the extent that conservatives support housing assistance to the poor, they tend to favor housing allowances or vouchers, as proposed by the Reagan and Bush administrations. From a philosophical point of view, vouchers have a decided advantage over public housing programs because they maximize freedom of choice. There is some contradiction in conservative thinking on vouchers, however. Philosophically, conservatives are sympathetic to the working poor and unsympathetic to those who will not work to support themselves. In practice, however, conservatives tend to put such stringent eligibility requirements on vouchers that the working poor are necessarily eliminated from participation.

In contrast to the conservative perspective, liberals prefer housing aid as in-kind assistance through direct-production strategies. Thus they are more favorable to the rental housing construction and rehabilitation components of Section 8 than they are to housing vouchers. Liberals fear that widespread use of housing vouchers will only drive up rents and effectively negate the impact of the aid. Liberals usually face an uphill battle for housing aid (as with other welfare aids) against majority political forces that want to provide only minimal welfare or housing assistance. This puts liberals in the position of having to make compromises that undermine the very programs they are trying to create. R. Allen Hays made this point succinctly when he wrote:

> Liberal politicians usually have to fight hard to get any sort of program put in place, no matter how limited in scope or design. Yet, the limits they must accept make the program vulnerable to valid criticisms from other liberal scholars, journalists, and policy advocates concerning its design, administrative procedures, comprehensiveness, or equity. . . . Such critiques may actually serve to undermine political support for existing programs, rather than generate pressures for expansion.[73]

In relation to transportation policy, liberal-conservative differences are not as marked as they are in housing and social welfare areas. Nonetheless, differences exist. Conservatives are more receptive to highway aid than they are to public transit aid. It is more consistent with their philosophy of freedom of choice. Public transit can take you only where the transit lines run, but automobiles can take you virtually anyplace you want to go. Furthermore, a highway construction in today's environment is likely to follow development rather than seek to channel it into predetermined sectors of the region. Conservatives also favor privatization of public transit systems by having them divest themselves of services that could be run profitably by private companies.

Liberals, since they also drive automobiles, do not reject highway aid. But they are much more sympathetic to public transit aid than are conservatives. Liberal ideology is also much more sympathetic to the notion that metropolitan development should be planned and coordinated. And they favor the use of public transit planning as a means to control and channel metropolitan growth. Liberals are skeptical of the current trend toward privatization of public transit systems. They fear that the most lucrative services will be spun off to private companies, and minimally subsidized public transit commissions will end up fighting uphill battles to get funds to run the unprofitable bus routes. Pointing out that probably a third of the population cannot get around without public transit, liberals would much prefer that all services be centralized in a metropolitan transit commission so that the profitable transit services could subsidize the unprofitable ones.

The Social Consequences of Infrastructure Policy

If infrastructure policy reflects ideological differences, it also has important social consequences for the social services discussed in Chapter 13. First, as seen from our review of transportation and housing policies, these policies over the past half-century played important roles in creating the racial residential patterns of de facto segregation. The great central cities, for example, might have kept expanding and never been ringed by independent suburban municipalities had it not been for a number of government policies and practices: federal highway aid, which helped build the suburbs; lax state municipal incorporation laws, which permitted suburban governments to form; and rigid annexation laws, which prevented central cities from expanding through annexation. Added to these were policies that enabled many suburbs to segregate: restrictive covenant clauses in deeds that prohibited the sale of such houses to noncaucasians and that were not struck down until 1948;[74] FHA regulations that financed much of suburbia but that prohibited mortgage loans to noncaucasians until 1962; local exclusionary zoning ordinances, which drove up the price of homes to the point where few minorities could afford them; deliberate attempts by some housing authorities to keep minorities out of housing projects in white neighborhoods or white suburbs; and deliberate attempts (as in the case of Birmingham, Michigan) to keep public housing out of specific suburbs. Some observers look at these facts and conclude that there is no such thing as de facto segregation (see Chapter 14), that government involvement at all levels was so extensive in building the segregated metropolis that most segregation is in fact de jure.

A second way in which infrastructure policies have social consequences is that they impede upward social mobility for the very poor. The housing displacement that results from urban renewal and highway construction usually forces the affected people into more expensive homes that take a larger share of their income. Redevelopment projects that replace mom-and-pop stores with shiny office buildings reduce entrepreneurial opportunities in poor neighborhoods. Policies promoting suburban sprawl transform the most dynamic economic areas many miles from poor residential neighborhoods. And policies that promoted the decline of public transit made it harder for poor people to get to locations where jobs are growing at the most rapid rate.

Of course, not all physical development policies hindered upward mobility. Public housing programs helped poor people meet their housing costs. In short, most of the infrastructure policies have a middle-class bias. The poor may have benefited from housing and transportation policies to some degree, but not nearly to the degree that the middle class has benefited.

SUMMARY

1. The basic transportation problem in America is lack of balance. Excessive reliance on the highway system has left a substantial minority of the population without mobility,

has made our transportation vulnerable to foreign supplies of fuel, and has created a maintenance problem that may be more costly than the original highway construction.

2. The 1970s saw what appeared to be a renaissance in public transit. Public transit ridership began to increase for the first time in a generation, and substantial federal aids were earmarked for transit purposes for the first time. By the 1980s, however, public transit ridership was no longer rising, and federal transit expenditures were no longer growing. States were forced to assume greater responsibility for financing public transit.

3. Urban transit options are most often discussed in terms of the kind of *vehicle* that should be used. The major options are expanded bus service, light rail systems, people movers, and the rapid rail systems. Multimodal use of buses as rapid transit has worked successfully in Australia, Brazil, and Europe.

4. Housing problems have led to the evolution of housing and community development programs that are intergovernmental in scope. Federal housing programs are implemented by local public housing authorities. Until 1974, urban renewal programs were administered by local public agencies, which had considerable autonomy from local mayors and city councils.

5. The 1974 Housing and Community Development Act completely restructured housing and renewal programs. It consolidated ten categorical grants into a single community development block grant. It gave the city councils greater control over the LPAs and LHAs. It gave local governments more discretion over the use of housing and community development funds. It required citizen participation in planning the use of community development funds. And it put the emphasis on rent supplements rather than on construction of more public housing projects.

6. After several years of housing policy stalemate during the Reagan presidency, Congress and President Bush enacted the 1990 National Affordable Housing Act. This act increased funding for traditional housing programs such as Section 8, and it initiated a Bush proposal to begin selling off public housing units to the tenants.

KEY TERMS

Antidiversion legislation   State laws that prohibit gasoline taxes and highway-use funds from being used for purposes not related to highways and automobiles or trucks.

Balloon mortgage   A mortgage plan in which one makes interest payments over the life of the mortgage but does not make any repayment of principal until the end of the mortgage, when the entire principal is due in a single, so-called balloon payment.

Building code   A municipal ordinance that establishes minimum requirements for space, electricity, plumbing, and health matters for residential buildings.

Direct-production strategy   The housing production strategy that focuses on providing housing assistance directly to low-income people.

Displacement   The phenomenon whereby low-income people are forced to move out of their homes by urban renewal agencies, by the gentrification process, or by freeway construction.

Exclusionary zoning   The practice by a municipality of putting expensive construction requirements in the local zoning plan and building code. This drives up the cost of new housing and thus excludes low-income people.

Federal Aid Highway Act of 1956   The act that established the federal gasoline tax that was earmarked for construction of the interstate highway system.

Filter-down strategy   A housing production strategy that focuses on constructing new housing for upper-middle-income people on the assumption that their old housing will "filter down" to the poor and moderate-income people.

Gated Communities   Exclusive upper-income housing developments surrounded by walls. Entrances are limited to a small number of security gates which can be used to keep out unauthorized people.

Gentrification   The process whereby upper-middle-income whites move into innercity neighborhoods and rehabilitate the homes there.

Housing and Community Development Act of 1974   The federal legislation that established the Section 8 housing program and the Community Development Block Grant program.

Housing voucher plan   A proposal of the Reagan administration to replace existing housing programs with a voucher plan in which poor people could receive government vouchers that would be redeemable for rent payments much in the same way that food stamps are redeemable for buying groceries.

Inclusionary zoning   The practice, as adopted in New Jersey, of requiring municipalities to include in their housing plans provisions for low-income people.

Infrastructure   The roads, buildings, sewers, water supply systems, and similar structures essential for an economy to operate.

Interstate highway system   The system of more than 40,000 miles of divided, limited-access highways that crisscross the United States.

Light rail transit (LRT)   A modern-day version of the streetcar. A large vehicle powered by overhead electric cables, run on tracks in city streets, and capable of carrying up to 200 passengers.

Rapid transit   The traditional big-city subway or elevated train systems that run large, electrically driven trains along fixed guideways that may be at ground level, elevated, or underground.

Red-lining   The practice of mortgage lenders and insurance firms not providing mortgages or home insurance in risky areas of cities. So called because the lending associations have supposedly drawn a red line around the affected areas.

Section 8   A housing program initiated by the Housing and Community Development Act of 1974. It provides for leased public housing by authorizing a local housing authority to pay a portion of poor people's rent directly to the landlord.

Surface Transit Assistance Act of 1982   A federal law that earmarked, through 1988, 1 cent of federal gasoline tax revenue for public transit.

Urban Mass Transit Act of 1974   The act that authorized the first extensive federal funding of mass transportation, including operating expenses as well as capital expenses.

Zoning code   A municipal ordinance that divides the city into different zones, with each zone being limited to specific kinds of structures. Some zones permit only single-family residences, others permit retail commercial buildings, others permit heavy industry.

REFERENCES

1. See *Time*, April 27, 1992, p. 139.
2. K. H. Schaeffer and Elliott Sclar write: "Even in their heydays around 1920 the U.S. railroads on a per-capita basis carried only a third of the passengers of the British and German railroads, or a fifth of the passengers of the Swiss system." *Access for All, Transportation and Urban Growth* (Baltimore: Penguin, 1975), pp. 41, 44.
3. Ibid., p. 44.
4. James J. Gosling, "Changing U.S. Transportation Policy and the States," *State and Local Government Review* 20, no. 2 (Spring 1988): 86.

5. Advisory Commission on Intergovernmental Relations, *Toward More Balanced Transportation: New Intergovernmental Proposals,* Report A-49 (Washington, D.C.: U.S. Government Printing Office, 1974), p. 218.

6. See Sam Bass Warner, Jr.'s analysis of Boston's growth in his *Streetcar Suburbs: The Process of Growth in Boston, 1870–1900* (Cambridge, Mass.: Harvard University Press, 1962).

7. On the costs of central-city expressways to the city's residents, see Anthony Downs, *Urban Problems and Prospects* (Chicago: Markham, 1970), Ch. 8.

8. Gosling, "Changing U.S. Transportation Policy and the States," p. 90. Also see *The New York Times,* February 4, 1983, p. 27.

9. Ralph Craft, "Shifting Gears: Federal Transportation Policy and the States," *State Legislatures* 8, no. 9 (October 1982): 13.

10. Wilfred Owen, "The View from 2020: Transportation in America's Future," *Brookings Review* no. 4 (Fall 1988): 10–14.

11. See Alan Altshuler, *The City Planning Process: A Political Analysis* (Ithaca, New York: Cornell University Press, 1965).

12. *Citizens to Preserve Overton Park, Inc.* v. *Volpe,* 401 U.S. 402 (1971).

13. See Lupo, Colcord, and Fowler, *Rites of Way.*

14. *Newsweek,* August 19, 1985, p. 28.

15. *Congressional Quarterly Almanac: 1991,* p. 137.

16. Paul N. Tramontozzi and Kenneth W. Chilton, *The Federal Free Ride: The Economics and Politics of U.S. Transit Policy* (St. Louis: Washington University Center for the Study of American Business, 1987), pp. 15–16.

17. David C. Nice, "Financial Performance of the Amtrak System," *Public Administration Review* 51, no. 2 (March–April 1991): 138–144.

18. Robert Beneson, "Mass Transit's Uncertain Future," *Editorial Research Reports* (June 21, 1985): 464.

19. Schaeffer and Sclar, *Access for All,* pp. 30, 39, 61–79, 97.

20. Ibid., p. 30.

21. See Jonathan Kwitny, "The Great Transportation Conspiracy," *Harper's* (February 1981): 14–21. Also see Schaeffer and Sclar, *Access for All,* p. 45; and Arnold W. Reitze, Jr., and Glenn L. Reitze, "Lau: Deus Ex Machina," *Environment* 16 (June 1974): 3–5. On streetcar track mileage, see *Transit Fact Book: 1970–71* (Washington, D.C.: American Public Transit Association, 1971), p. 12.

22. Eliza Carney, "A Desire Named Streetcar," *Governing* (February 1994): 36–39.

23. See *The New York Times,* November 23, 1984, p. 17; *Minneapolis Star and Tribune,* December 8, 1985, p. 32A.

24. See Advisory Commission on Intergovernmental Relations, *Toward More Balanced Transportation,* pp. 45–48.

25. Peter Gordon and Harry Richardson, "The Failure of Urban Mass Transit," *Public Interest,* no. 94 (Winter 1989): 77–86.

26. See Melvin M. Webber, "The BART Experience—What Have We Learned?" *Public Interest* no. 45 (Fall 1976): 79–108; and "Trouble in Mass Transit," *Consumer Reports* 40, no. 3 (March 1975): 190–195.

27. Miami Metrorail planners projected 117,000 to 202,000 daily trips. But when the first phase opened in 1986, ridership averaged only 33,000 trips daily. Tramontozzi and Chilton, *The Federal Free Ride,* pp. 15–16.

28. Director General of Transport, South Australia, *An Economic Evaluation of the Northeast Busway in Adelaide* (Adelaide, Australia: The Government of South Australia, December 1991) and "Mercedes Benze O-Bahn in Theory and Practice," a public rela-

tions brochure on the O-Bah system by its inventor, the Mercedes Benze Corporation. Available from Daimler-Benz AG; Pestfach 202 D-700 Stuttgart 60 ks, Germany.

29. Jonas Rabinovitch and Josef Leitman, "Urban Planning in Curitiba,"*Scientific America* (March 1996): 46–53.

30. See especially Gordon and Richardson, "The Failure of Mass Transit;" Tramontozzi and Chilton, *The Federal Free Ride;* and Webber, "The BART Experience."

31. The high estimate of 3 million was produced by homeless advocate Mitch Snyder's Communities for Creative Non-Violence. The low estimate of 250,000–350,000 was made in 1984 by the Department of Housing and Urban Development. Robert C. Ellickson, "The Homelessness Muddle," *Public Interest* no. 99 (Spring 1990): 52. The Census Bureau counted 459,209 homeless people on the night of March 20, 1990. Eileen Quigley, "The Homeless," *CQ Reporter* 2, no. 29 (August 7, 1992): 669. Several mayors and homeless advocacy groups criticized the Census Bureau over this count, claiming that it grossly undercounted the number of homeless. *The New York Times,* October 9, 1992, p. 13.

32. Bureau of the Census, *Statistical Abstract of the United States: 1989* (Washington, D.C.: U.S. Government Printing Office, 1989), p. 713.

33. Irving Welfeld, "Our Nonexistent Housing Crisis," *Public Interest* no. 101 (Fall 1990): 56.

34. Ibid., p. 57.

35. Ibid., p. 57.

36. Ellickson, "The Homelessness Muddle," p. 58.

37. Quigley, "The Homeless," p. 672.

38. Ibid., p. 670.

39. Ibid., p. 671.

40. Gordon Berlin and William McAllister, "Homelessness: Why Nothing Has Worked— And What Will," *The Brookings Review* 10, no. 4 (Fall 1992): 12–17.

41. Data from the Center for Budget and Policy and Priorities and the National Low-Income Housing Information Service. Reported in *The New York Times,* December 12, 1991, p. 1.

42. Ibid. p. 13.

43. *Statistical Abstract of the United States: 1995,* p. 736.

44. Welfeld, "Our Nonexistent Housing Crisis," p. 58

45. *Statistical Abstract of the United States: 1991,* p. 721.

46. Ibid., p. 508.

47. John E. Farley analyzed 1988 census data on St. Louis and concluded that a modest decrease in racial segregation had occurred since 1980. See his "Black-White Housing Segregation in the City of St. Louis, A 1988 Update," *Urban Affairs Quarterly* 26, no. 3 (March 1991): 442–450. Karl Taeuber calculated a segregation index for twenty-eight central cities and found a 9 percent decrease in racial separation between 1970 and 1980. See Karl Taeuber, *Racial Residential Segregation, 28 Cities, 1970–1980,* Working Paper 83–12 (Madison, Wisc.: Center for Demography and Ecology, University of Wisconsin, March 1983). A similar calculation for metropolitan areas rather than central cities found an 8 percent decrease in racial separation between 1960 and 1970. See Thomas L. Van Valey, Wade Clark Roof, and Jerome E. Wilcox, "Trends in Residential Segregation, 1960–1970," *American Journal of Sociology* 82, no. 14 (January 1977): 836.

48. *The New York Times,* August 4, 1988, p. 13; August 10, 1988, p. 12; August 11, 1988, p. 1; June 13, 1989, p. 22.

49. *The New York Times,* April 14, 1992, p. 18.
50. *The New York Times,* February 21, 1986, p. 35; February 24, 1986, p. 13. For background on Mount Laurel, see Alan Mallach, *Inclusionary Housing Programs: Policies and Practices* (New Brunswick, N.J.: Rutgers University Center for Urban Policy Research, 1984).
51. *Minnesota Journal* (April 18, 1995), p. 6.
52. Nathan Glazer, "The South-Bronx Story: An Extreme Case of Neighborhood Decline," *Policy Studies Journal* 16, no. 2 (Winter 1987): 269–276.
53. *The New York Times,* May 20, 1977, p. A-24.
54. Gregory D. Squires and William Velez, "Insurance Redlining and the Transformation of an Urban Metropolis," *Urban Affairs Quarterly* 23, no. 1 (September 1987): 63–83.
55. See Chester Hartman, Dennis Keating, and Richard L. Gates, with Steve Turner, *Displacement: How to Fight It* (Berkeley, Calif.: National Housing Project, 1982).
56. For a summary of these early developments, see Marian Lief Palley and Howard A. Palley, *Urban America and Public Policies* (Lexington, Mass.: D. C. Heath, 1977), pp. 161–164.
57. Even during the banking and real estate crisis of the 1980s, the largest number of foreclosures in a year was 100,000, the largest number of banks closed was 221, and the largest number of savings and loans turned over to the Resolution Trust Corporation was 318. *Statistical Abstract of the United States: 1991,* pp. 502, 505.
58. *Statistical Abstract of the United States: 1976,* pp. 742.
59. Larry Sawyers and Howard M. Wachtel, "Who Benefits from Federal Housing Policies?" in *Problems in Political Economy: An Urban Perspective,* 2nd ed., David M. Gordon, ed. (Lexington, Mass.: D. C. Heath, 1977), p. 484.
60. Theodore J. Lowi, *The End of Liberalism: Ideology, Policy and the Crisis of Public Authority* (New York: Norton, 1969), pp. 251–266.
61. See Chester W. Hartman, "A Rejoinder: Omissions in Evaluating Relocation Effectiveness Cited," *Journal of Housing* 23, no. 2 (February 1966): 88–89. Also see Herbert Gans, "The Failure of Urban Renewal: A Critique and Some Proposals," *Commentary* (April 1965): 29–37.
62. This in particular is the lament of Jane Jacobs, *The Death and Life of Great American Cities* (New York: Vintage Books, 1961).
63. See Martin Anderson, *The Federal Bulldozer* (Cambridge, Mass.: M.I.T. Press, 1964).
64. Raymond A. Rosenfeld, "Implementation of the Community Development Block Grant Program: Decentralization of Decision-making and Centralization of Responsibility," paper presented 1977 meeting of the Midwest Political Science Association, Chicago, April 1977.
65. Donald F. Kettl, "Can Cities Be Trusted? The Community Development Experience," *Political Science Quarterly* 94, no. 3 (Fall 1979): 437–452.
66. Raymond Brown with Ann Coil and Carol Rose, *A Time for Accounting: The Housing and Community Development Act in the South* (Atlanta: Southern Regional Council, 1976).
67. Ibid., pp. 86–87.
68. For criticisms of Section 8, see Irving Welfeld, "American Housing Policy: Perverse Programs by Prudent People," *Public Interest,* no. 48 (Summer 1977): 128–144.
69. Edgar O. Olsen, "Housing Programs and the Forgotten Taxpayers," *Public Interest* no. 66 (Winter 1982): 97–109.
70. See summaries of the HUD scandal in *Newsweek,* July 10, 1989, pp. 16–17; August 7, 1989, pp. 16–22; *The Washington Post National Weekly Edition,* June 5–11, 1989, p. 32; June 26–July 2, 1989, p. 31.

71. Housing vouchers are discussed favorably from several perspectives in Joseph Friedman and Daniel H. Wernberg, eds., *The Great Housing Experiment,* Urban Affairs Annual Reviews, Vol. 24 (Beverly Hills, Calif.: SAGE Publications, 1983). See especially the chapter by Ira S. Lowry, "The Supply Experiment." Also see Bernard J. Frieden, "Housing Allowances: An Experiment that Worked," *Public Interest,* no. 59 (Spring 1980): 15–35.
72. An excellent overview of ideology and policy can be found in R. Allen Hays, *The Federal Government and Urban Housing,* Ch. 2, "Ideological Context of Housing Policy."
73. Ibid., p. 33.
74. *Shelley* v. *Kramer,* 334 U.S. 1 (1948).

16

REGULATING THE ENVIRONMENT

Chapter Preview

In this chapter, we will explore the regulatory roles of state and local governments. We will examine in turn:

1. Pollution control and regulation of the environment.
2. The regulation of business and professions.
3. The reciprocal relationship between state and local governments and regulation on the one hand and the political economy of states on the other.
4. A cost–benefit approach to assessing regulatory politics.

Let us begin by asking *why* state and local governments exercise their regulatory roles.

◇ INTRODUCTION

State and local governments play major regulatory roles in our lives today. Among other things, government regulators force us to have our pets inoculated, send our children to certified schools, purchase automobile insurance if we wish to drive, and, in many states, submit our cars for annual inspections. In addition to restricting the behavior of individuals, state and local regulators impose a host of restrictions on business corporations. Regulators stipulate many provisions of health insurance and life insurance coverage, determine the conditions under which alcoholic beverages can be sold, and decide which corporations will be granted exclusive franchises to market electricity, cable television, and natural gas.

Why do governments intervene in our lives in these ways? Governments intervene when they are called on to correct for failures in the marketplace. In the mixed, public–private, capitalistic type of economy that exists in the United

States, most major goods and services are sold by private companies competing with each other in a market economy. According to traditional capitalistic theory, this competition ensures that goods and services will exist over a wide range of quality and prices. In theory, the public good is served through unrestrained competition in the marketplace. In the real world, however, the market-directed economy often fails to serve the public good, and government is called upon to correct for these market failures.

What kinds of market failures could justify governmental intervention and regulation? Economists have identified three types of market failures. First are those involving **externalities**—that is, costs that are not borne directly by the buyers or sellers of a particular product. Automobiles, for example, produce air pollution. Historically, the sales price of the car did not include any fee for cleaning up that air pollution. For this reason, automobile-produced air pollution could be viewed as a cost that was external to the cost of the car. If society wanted to deal with the externality of air pollution, it needed to give government an environmental regulatory role.

A second type of market failure involves **social goods.** A public recreational area or park, for example, is a social good. Its benefits are indivisible and nonexclusive in that everybody in the community can enjoy them without depriving anyone else of their use. Because private companies are in business to make profits, they have a very limited ability to provide free parks or other social goods for the general public. A community that wants a well-developed park system will necessarily have to purchase the park land publicly and create a public agency to develop and maintain the facilities.

A third type of market failure involves **merit goods.** Merit goods are those that society deems everyone deserves. In America today, merit goods include free public education, medical care by doctors and dentists who meet minimal professional standards, and the right to assume that foods and medicines sold in the marketplace are not contaminated. To ensure that the public receives these merit goods, governments either provide them directly (as in the case of schools) or regulate their provision by private entrepreneurs (as in the cases of medical care and food inspection).

Historically, government's regulatory role was much less extensive than it is today. State and local governments were the primary regulators, and the federal government played a less dominant role than it does today. Starting in the 1960s, however, the sheer volume of regulation expanded dramatically, and the federal government saw its regulatory responsibilities increase. As the federal government began playing a dominant regulatory role in areas (such as environmental protection) that had previously been considered state responsibilities, the whole topic of regulation itself came into question. By the 1980s proponents and opponents of regulation were debating whether the benefits of all this regulation outweighed the costs, and the Reagan and Bush administrations sought to devolve considerable regulatory responsibility to the states.

This chapter will examine two areas of public regulation—the environment and business. In examining these regulatory areas, we will pay particular attention to the intergovernmental politics involved, the question of cost–benefit analysis, and the implications for state and local political economics.

◇ ENVIRONMENTAL REGULATION

In the Love Canal neighborhood of Niagara Falls, New York, the air was so foul in 1978 that the mail carrier began wearing a gas mask. Radishes in backyard gardens turned coal black. Basements smelled like dead animals. Apparent congenital defects in the children vastly exceeded normal expectations: one child had an extra row of teeth, another a clubfoot; another was retarded. Miscarriages were exceedingly high in 1978, and during that summer five children were born with congenital defects.[1] Love Canal had been the dumping site for 21,800 tons of 200 different waste chemical compounds (eleven of which cause cancer) from 1947 to 1952. After the dumping ceased, the toxic wastes were covered with earth. Several years later, a real estate subdivision was built along the canal. In 1978, twenty-six years after the dumping ceased, a season of heavy rains brought the buried toxic chemicals to the surface. Getting complaints from neighborhood residents, government officials installed instruments to measure the air quality in local basements. The readings in many homes showed highly dangerous concentrations of eleven toxic chemicals, including two that were carcinogenic (that is, cancer causing). So dangerous was the environment along Love Canal that New York State provided money to help relocate thirty-seven families with children under the age of two. The local elementary school was closed for health reasons. Further research found other people endangered, and a complicated program of federal and state funding was set up to enable New York State to buy up the contaminated homes. Two hundred thirty-seven homes were eventually bought, bulldozed, along with the elementary school, into their basements, and covered with a mound of dirt that stands today as a visible reminder of the environmental abuse. Ten years after the incident, only about seventy houses in the general neighborhood were still inhabited. The rest were abandoned or boarded up, and 1,000 families had moved out.

Some critics believe that the dangers of Love Canal had been overblown. And in 1990, the Love Canal Revitalization Agency began selling the Love Canal houses that still existed to new buyers who believed that the hazardous wastes in the canal were by then safely contained. The agency then renamed the development Black Creek Village.[2]

Whether or not the specific instance of Love Canal was overblown, health hazards from toxic materials and environmental pollution are major concerns today. State and local governments have the primary responsibility for managing the environment. It was not until 1970 that the federal government entered in a big way into environmental management, intervening with its greater resources of money and its ability to set national standards that must be enforced at the state and local levels. The politics of this ecological management have become very intense.

The result of all these developments since 1970 is a wide range of public policy areas that interconnect: air and water pollution, solid and hazardous waste disposal, litter, the exhaustion of natural resources, water supply, nuclear energy, and so on. In order to present a sufficiently detailed discussion, this chapter is limited to three aspects of environmental management—air and water pollution control, hazardous-waste management, and energy regulation. In this examination, several questions arise. What steps have been taken at all levels of government to protect the environment? How does the intergovernmental system work? What policies have been established? How are they implemented? Have the policies and their implementation been effective? And, of course, are things getting better or worse? What are the trends?

A National Environmental Policy: New Tools for Environmental Management

The evolution of pollution-control policymaking has completely reversed the traditional relationship between the states and the national government. Historically, the states had primary responsibility for pollution control. During the 1950s and 1960s, however, the federal government became increasingly involved, and the intergovernmental mechanism began to resemble cooperative federalism rather than the traditional dual federalism model. A partnership existed between the state and federal governments in which the federal government assisted the states in defining their own policies and priorities. This system did not work effectively, however, and by the 1970s the mechanism had changed to the centrally directed federalism discussed in Chapter 3. A key step in this direction was the **Environmental Protection Act of 1970.**[3]

This act declared "a broad national policy for environmental protection."[4] It created the Environmental Protection Agency (EPA) to coordinate and oversee the federal government's wide-ranging activities in the field of environmental protection. It also established the Council on Environmental Quality (CEQ) within the executive office of the president to monitor progress in environmental quality and make annual recommendations to the president for improving it.

The National Environmental Protection Act also created the **Environmental Impact Statement (EIS).** Each federal agency is required to file with the CEQ a statement outlining the environmental impacts of any major construction project it plans to undertake. The EIS must outline adverse environmental effects of the project, alternatives to it, and its relation to maintaining and enhancing the long-term protection of the environment.[5]

Water Pollution Management

At the Federal Level: Setting National Policy   Today's water pollution management is traced to the **Water Pollution Control Act of 1972** (also called the **Clean Water Act**). This act and its amendments of 1977 and 1987 set the overall framework for water pollution management that still exists. Central to this system of management is a distinction the act drew between point-source and non-point-source pollution.

Point-source pollution refers to pollution that can be traced to a specific point of introduction into the water—hazardous wastes dumped in a river by a chemical company, for example, or untreated human waste discharged into a river by a city's sewers.

The act had two major provisions to deal with point-source pollution. First, it established the National Pollution Discharge Elimination System (NPDES). The NPDES requires any organization that discharges any waste products (called effluents) into a waterway to obtain a permit. National standards for discharges were established, and any discharge that exceeds those standards is not permitted. Second, the act also obliged municipal sewer systems to install secondary sewage treatment facilities. The Environmental Protection Agency (EPA) is responsible for administering the act, but it delegates its authority to the states. If a state or local government fails to set up a permit system or if its water-quality standards do not meet EPA criteria, the EPA can take over. Most states did act, and only a small minority preferred to have the EPA administer the program in their states. To assist the state and local governments in costly planning and sewer system construction, federal law provided billions of dollars in matching grants.

Nonpoint-source pollution in waterways is more difficult to manage because it comes from a variety of sources that cannot be traced to a specific point of entry. The most prominent example would be pesticides and fertilizers, which wash into lakes, streams, and underground aquifers when it rains. Northern states that salt their roads to prevent ice in the winter find that the salt flows into the waterways and pollutes them during the spring thaw. Air pollution ends up in the waterways when the rain cleans the air and washes the pollutants into streams and lakes. Thus, automobile emissions are a nonpoint source of water pollution.

Section 208 of the 1972 act provides funds for setting up agencies to develop an environmental management system. These so-called Section 208 agencies were set up throughout the country[6] and made responsible for developing regional plans to cope with all the varied nonpoint sources of pollution. This task has proved so overwhelming, however, that progress on this front has been disappointing, according to the Council on Environmental Quality.[7]

Whereas the 1972 Clean Water Act set the basic framework, subsequent legislation and amendments fine-tuned the system of water-quality control. The Safe Drinking Water Act of 1974 and its later amendments directed the EPA to set maximum allowable levels for certain chemical and bacteriological pollutants in the nation's water systems. The 1987 Water Quality Act sought to improve the ability of states to cope with nonpoint-source pollution and ground-water pollution.[8]

Today, this water-quality-control system is at a crossroads. More than $50 billion in federal and state funds have been spent since 1972 in constructing public sewer systems and waste treatment plants. The EPA estimates that constructing new waste treatment plants, or rehabilitating existing ones, plus making needed replacements of defective urban water supply and treatment facilities could cost another $134 billion by the end of the century.[9] The steps taken to date have halted the deterioration of the nation's water quality, but the budgetary squeeze on all levels of government raises questions about public willingness to continue existing high levels of investment in water-quality control. Finally, most pollution control efforts have focused on surface water (lakes and streams), but half of the nation's drinking supply comes from groundwater, which in many regions is endangered by toxic and chemical wastes that seep into underground water sources.[10]

At the State and Local Level: Cleaning Up the Willamette   Although the 1972 Water Pollution Control Act gave the Environmental Protection Agency primary authority to establish water-quality standards, the states were charged with implementing these standards and monitoring compliance. Perhaps one of the most successful examples of such cooperation was the cleaning up of the Willamette River in Oregon.

The Willamette is the twelfth longest river in the United States. It runs 150 miles from the western range of the Rocky Mountains to Portland, Oregon, where it joins the Columbia River. Nearly two million people, 70 percent of Oregon's population, live in the Willamette basin. Three sizable cities are located along the river—Eugene, Salem, and Portland.

Until 1950, every city along the river dumped untreated human wastes into it. The river also received the discharges of several highly polluting industries—especially lumber sawmills, paper mills, and vegetable-processing plants. During the summer, when the Willamette River is at low flow, tidal action and backflow of the Columbia River trap all the pollutants in the vicinity of Portland. These factors combined to make the Willamette one of the nation's most polluted rivers. During the 1920s, civic groups traced much of the pollution to the discharge of raw sewage into the river. Despite this identification of the problem, it was not until 1937 that the Oregon legislature finally required sewage treatment. However, that bill was vetoed by the governor because of the financial hardships it would have imposed on the municipalities that would have been forced to build their own treatment plants. Not until 1938 was the newly created state sanitary authority charged with developing and enforcing a statewide water-sanitation program.

The sanitary authority ran into a special problem with the paper mills, which objected to installing primary treatment facilities for their effluents. Some companies threatened to move to a friendlier state, but passage of the federal Clean Water Act of 1972 reduced the mills' ability to play states against each other and effectively strengthened Oregon in its own regulatory capacity.

As a result of these actions, the quality of the Willamette improved tremendously. For the first time, Chinook salmon moved upstream to spawn in the fall. Recreational use of the river also increased, and the state approved a greenway plan for developing a system of riverside parks and for preserving the river from real estate and commercial development.

The Council on Environmental Quality attributed Oregon's successful cleanup of the Willamette to four factors. First, the problems were identified early, and steady progress was made between the creation of the sanitary authority in 1939 and the availability of extensive federal support in the 1960s. Second, the cleanup efforts had broad popular support. Citizen organizations sparked the initial research into the river's condition in the 1920s and 1930s. And new, ecology-minded interest groups during the 1960s continued the pressure for improvement and for the greenway plan. Third, strong political leaders supported the cleanup. Finally, the growing federal role in the 1970s strengthened Oregon in dealing with the private paper mills. Additionally, federal grants-in-aid eased the financial burden on the municipalities.[11]

Air Pollution Control

At the Federal Level: Setting National Policies   The first federal air pollution law was enacted in 1955. Like the first water pollution efforts, it limited the federal government to providing support to state and local governments for research. The federal role was increased by the 1963 Clean Air Act, which established a $95 million grant-in-aid program to help states set and enforce air pollution standards. In 1965, Congress authorized emission standards for motor vehicles. The 1967 Air Quality Act divided the nation into 247 air-quality-control regions so that levels of air pollution could be monitored and cities could issue air pollution alerts when the air quality declined to dangerous levels. But it was not until the passage of the **Clean Air Act of 1970** that the federal government became the dominant partner in the battle to manage air pollution. This act set air-quality standards and obliged the states to draft **state implementation plans (SIPs)** for meeting the standards. The states may set higher standards than those set by EPA, but they cannot set lower standards.

Most states were unable to meet a 1977 deadline that Congress had imposed for meeting the air-quality standards, and Congress reacted by passing the **Clean Air Act Amendments of 1977.** These amendments tightened the air-quality standards, extended the deadlines for meeting them, and authorized the EPA to withhold federal highway and sewage treatment funds from states failing to meet the law's requirements.[12]

The 1977 amendments also provided that the act be renewed and upgraded every few years, but the Reagan administration (1981–1989) adamantly opposed efforts to strengthen the law.[13] In the meantime, serious acid rain problems were damaging forest and fish life, a huge hole was growing in the ozone layer, and the amount of toxic pollutants being emitted into the air also continued to grow. It was not until the **Clean Air Act Amendments of 1990** that Congress and the White House addressed these issues.[14] As the "Highlight" (p. 432) shows, this act took giant steps toward coping with these and other air pollution problems.

With the major air cleanup goals enacted into law by the 1990 Clean Air Act Amendments, the focus during the balance of the 1990s is likely to be on the implementation of the law's provisions rather than on the passage of new legislation. To date, the implementation record since 1990 has been mixed. On the positive side, EPA and its counterpart agencies in most states have begun moving on the implementation process. On the negative side, however, the Clean Air Act

HIGHLIGHT

Main Provisions of the Clean Air Act and Its Amendments

1. The EPA was required by the 1970 act to set **primary** and **secondary air-quality standards.** Primary standards aim at protecting public health, whereas secondary standards aim at protecting crops, vegetation, forests, animals, and other materials essential to the public welfare. The states were required to draft state implementation plans (SIPs) for EPA approval, proposing how they would meet the air-quality standards.
2. Emissions from automobiles were required to meet rigorous limits, beginning with the 1975 model year. The EPA was also required to set emission standards for stationary power plants.
3. The 1990 amendments would phase out and eventually halt the production of four major chemicals that lead to the destruction of the ozone layer (chlorofluorocarbons, carbon tetrachloride, methyl chloroform, hydrochlorofluorocarbon).
4. The 1990 amendments sought further reductions in automobile emissions by requiring auto manufacturers to improve emission control devices on cars and requiring gasoline companies to manufacture cleaner burning fuels.
5. The 1990 amendments attacked acid rain by reducing the emission from power plants and factories of two critical chemicals (sulfur dioxide and nitrogen oxide).
6. The 1990 amendments attacked urban smog by classifying cities into five nonattainment categories of ozone reduction and setting periodic timetables for meeting the reduction standards.
7. The 1990 amendments attacked toxic air pollutants. They listed 250 categories of hazardous pollutants and required companies to establish pollution control equipment that would reduce emission of these pollutants by up to 90 percent by the year 2003.
8. The 1990 act empowered citizen groups to sue the EPA or polluters for enforcement of the act.

Source: *Congressional Quarterly Almanac: 1975* (Washington, D.C.: Congressional Quarterly Press, 1975), p. 246; *Congressional Quarterly Almanac: 1991*, pp. 229–249.

---

came under attack from Republicans when they gained control of Congress in 1994. To mollify these critics, the EPA found it expedient to relax several implementation rules of the act. As a result, by 1996, only three of the fifty states were clearly on track to meet enforcement deadlines that had been established by the 1990 act.[15]

In sum, the 1970 Clean Air Act created an extremely complicated system of regulation that reflects the complexities of the federal system of government. Legislation at the national level is the driving force behind most air pollution control, but it is at the state and local levels of government where most of the air pollution control activities get carried out. States and localities have more than five times the number of personnel working in air pollution management as does the EPA and also take five times as many enforcement actions.[16] How the intergovernmental politics of this system work in practice is shown by Charles O. Jones's excellent study of cleaning up the air in Pittsburgh.

At the State and Local Level: Cleaning Up Pittsburgh As America's preeminent steel producing city, Pittsburgh was historically known for its dirty air. In 1862, Anthony Trollope called Pittsburgh "without exception, the blackest place I ever saw. The city itself is buried in a dense cloud."[17] Pittsburgh began passing smoke abatement ordinances as early as the 1860s, but these were seldom enforced. Either the corporations simply ignored them (as the railroads illegally continued burning the heavily polluting bituminous coal in their locomotives) or the courts ruled the ordinances invalid (as in the attempts to get emission standards for steel mills in 1895 and 1906). The first effective smoke abatement ordinance was not passed until 1941; because of the need to increase steel production during World War II, enforcement was delayed.

The first effective leadership in cleaning up Pittsburgh's air came after World War II from Richard King Mellon of Pittsburgh's influential Mellon family. He helped found the Allegheny Conference on Community Development (ACCD), which took the lead in redeveloping the city's central business district and in seeking industrial compliance to the smoke abatement ordinance. Mellon also used his personal influence to get the railroads to stop using the highly polluting bituminous coal in their locomotives. In 1947, the Pennsylvania Railroad opposed legislation that would give the county authority to prohibit bituminous-coal-burning locomotives. Legislative leaders found it impossible to round up the necessary votes for passage, so they appealed to Mellon.

> Mellon was a director of the railroad company and one of its principal stock-holders. He let its top management know that if the line failed to comply, or continued to block the new law, the companies he controlled would probably switch their freight haulage to other, competitive lines. Other customers of the railroad company took similar stands.
>
> In a matter of days, the smoke control bill passed through the legislature unamended. Soon the Pennsylvania line started replacing its old engines with diesel equipment.[18]

The key political leader for renewal and clean air was Pittsburgh Mayor David Lawrence. One of Lawrence's first acts as mayor was to set immediate deadlines for compliance with the 1941 smoke abatement ordinance. Lawrence worked hard during his long tenure as mayor (1941–1959) to establish a cooperative business and political alliance in the smoke-control struggle.

Because smoke crossed municipal boundaries, it was necessary to combat it on the county as well as the city level. Allegheny County appointed a Smoke Control Advisory Committee that was dominated by representatives of the major polluting industries and their labor unions. Thus the pollution-control system was, for all practical purposes, a system of self-regulation by the industries.

By the end of the 1950s, this cooperation between government and the polluting industries had achieved mixed results. Considerable progress had been made in clearing the air of dense smoke, but little had been done to eliminate less visible emissions such as particulates and gases.

The limitations of the cooperative approach were seen in the case of the U.S. Steel Corporation. In 1960, U.S. Steel agreed to a ten-year plan to install pollution collectors in order to reduce the emission of pollutants. The company discovered early in the ten-year period that the equipment to reduce pollution emissions was not working, but it did not report these findings to the advisory committee until it was too late for the company to meet its ten-year deadline.[19]

In the late 1960s, public concern over the environment rose sharply, and militant environmental groups formed around the nation. Given Pittsburgh's air pollution problems, environmentalists there cleverly named their organization GASP (Group Against Smog and Pollution). GASP had an extraordinary knack for getting favorable publicity and pulling off highly imaginative public relations stunts: awarding "Dirtie Gertie" prizes to polluting companies, selling cans of clean air, lobbying for improvements in regulations, and rounding up support for stronger air pollution regulations.

Militant environmentalists also succeeded in expanding the scope of the conflict beyond the closed doors of Allegheny County's industry-dominated advisory committee. In addition to attracting attention with their imaginative tactics, environmentalists looked to the federal government for stronger curbs on air pollution. These pressures led both the county and the state to draft stiffer regulations than had originally been anticipated.

The new regulations, adopted in the fall of 1969, replaced the industry-dominated advisory committee with a new Allegheny County Variance Board, whose members had few ties with the steel industry. For the first time the regulatory body had the authority to enforce its rules and regulations. The burden of proof was put on the companies. If a company could not meet the air-quality standards, then it had to either get a permit of noncompliance from the variance board or shut down.

The new regulatory system was tested almost immediately by the U.S. Steel Corporation's Clairton coke-producing plant. Coke is a processed form of coal that burns hotter than coal but produces less smoke. The final step in producing coke is to cool it by quenching it with water. As the water is poured over the coke, it releases several lethal chemicals—phenols, ammonia, cyanide, hydrogen sulfide, and chlorides. Under the regulations of Allegheny County, the state of Pennsylvania, and the federal Clean Air Act of 1970, U.S. Steel would have to remove 99 percent of these dangerous chemicals from the steam. The company asked for a variance on the grounds that it did not have the technology to remove 99 percent of the dangerous chemicals. The technology did exist for eliminating 90 percent of the pollutants, but U.S. Steel felt it could not justify expenditures to achieve an emission level that would still be illegal and would leave the company open to lawsuits.

Faced with this uncompromising attitude, the variance board denied the variance and recommended that the issue be transferred to courts that could deal directly with the legal ramifications of the case. The courts attempted to force the board and the corporation to work out a compromise. U.S. Steel was reluctant to accept the compromise devised at the local level because it might be rejected at the federal level. Under the 1970 Clean Air Act, the EPA had authority to veto any implementation plans that did not meet its own emission standards, and it refused to commit itself to any compromise.

In the fall of 1972, the court issued three consent decrees that would achieve a 90 percent reduction in sulfur emissions and would also set standards for other emissions. In exchange for U.S. Steel's agreement to these terms, local officials granted the company a ten-year immunity from being sued and being forced to install new equipment that might become available during the ten-year period.

Hazardous-Waste Management

A third major area of environmental concern lies in the disposal of the sixty million tons of hazardous and toxic waste that are produced each year. These range from low-level radioactive waste from medical testing and treatment facilities to the extremely toxic chemical wastes dumped into Love Canal over the years. The EPA has identified hundreds of dangerous toxic-waste sites around the nation. Cleaning them up and finding suitable locations for other hazardous wastes is a major environmental problem.

Federal and State Roles   As in other aspects of environmental protection, hazardous-waste management requires the cooperation of federal, state, and local levels of government. At the federal level, hazardous-waste management has followed a three-pronged pattern. First, to reduce the amount of new toxic substances reaching the environment, the **Toxic Substances Control Act of 1976** required the EPA to set up regulations for testing new chemical substances before they are marketed, authorized the EPA to ban any chemical it deemed unsafe, and prohibited the sale of the extremely toxic PCBs (polychlorinated biphenyls) not contained in enclosed systems. The second prong focused on cleaning up existing unsafe hazardous-waste sites and relied on a so-called **Superfund** created in 1980 to finance this task. The third prong stemmed from the **Resource Conservation and Recovery Act of 1976 (RCRA)** which set up a so-called cradle-to-grave process for controlling and disposing of hazardous wastes.

Superfund Cleanups   To clean up existing unsafe hazardous-waste sites, the Superfund was created by the Comprehensive Environmental Response Compensation and Liability Act in 1980 and reauthorized with a larger budget in 1986. The Superfund operates on a "polluters pay" principle under which seven-eights of Superfund's budget comes from a special tax on chemicals and oils that were believed to cause much hazardous waste. Additional cleanup costs are billed to specific companies and organizations that contributed to the waste site.[20]

In fact, Superfund has been a major disappointment. Despite the expenditure of $7.5 billion for hazardous-waste cleanup since 1981, only 64 of 1,200 sites on Superfund's list were completely cleaned up a decade later. This may not be as bad as it sounds since many sites can be made safe without a complete cleanup. This is done by containing the hazardous materials so that they do not spread and putting up signs to warn people to stay away from the site. But even giving the EPA credit for "containing" rather than completely cleaning up the sites, a huge portion of Superfund expenditures have gone to cover administrative costs and legal fees.[21] Under the "polluters pay" principle, potential violators have a powerful incentive to delay cleanup as long as possible through legal battles. In some instances, major polluters use these legal battles to pass off the cleanup costs to third parties, as shown in a Utica, New York case.

In an effort to clean up a site near Utica, New York, the EPA sued two companies—a cosmetics producer and manufacturer of metal components—who, in turn, sued more than 600 mostly small businesses and 41 towns and school districts. Among the defendants who settled the case—rather than battle a large corporation over liability percentages—was the owner of a tiny pizzeria. Although the exact nature of pizzeria's trash was not known, the attorney for the two large companies surmised that it might have included empty cleanser or insecticide cans containing trace amounts of toxins.[22]

The "polluters pay" principle has become a major issue in the struggle to reauthorize the Comprehensive Environmental Response Compensation and Liability Act that established the Superfund in 1980. The act's scheduled reauthorization in 1993 fell between the cracks of congressional Republicans who want to end the polluters pay principle and the Clinton White House that wants to retain that principle. In the absence of reauthorization, Superfund appropriations have not grown, and in 1996, the EPA announced that lack of money was forcing it to postpone cleanups at fifty-five sites.[23]

LULUs and NIMBY   If the cleanup of existing waste sites has been slow and plagued by difficulties, it is even more difficult to find *new* and safe waste sites for the tons of potentially dangerous wastes that are still being generated and discarded each year. These range from mercury flashlight batteries (that should *not* be thrown into your garbage can) to low-level radioactive wastes generated in hospitals to chemical byproducts in petrochemical factories. Disposal sites for these wastes are called LULUs (locally unwanted land uses), and the common approach to LULUs is the NIMBY syndrome (Not in My Back Yard).

The "Highlight" (p. 437) describing Arizona's confrontation over a LULU illustrates the NIMBY syndrome starkly. If a hazardous-waste facility cannot be placed on state-owned land in the middle of a sparsely populated desert, where can it be sited?

Local opposition to LULUs is not usually as volatile as the incident in Phoenix. One study of more than 66,000 statements in public hearings over the siting of radioactive waste sites in four states found that the persons giving testimony typically were fairly knowledgeable about the risk issues involved, phrased their testimony in unemotional terms, and had broader concerns than simply keeping the facility out of their back yard. Nevertheless, 88 percent of the testimony opposed the siting that was being proposed.[24]

Leaders of movements against LULUs deny, of course, that their activities are against the public good. Some are opposed not only to siting such facilities in their own back yard, but to siting them in anybody's back yard. From their viewpoint, there is something one-sided about an approach to hazardous waste that

NIMBY Confronts Arizona

Arizona was treated to the NIMBY problem when it was eventually forced by popular pressure to terminate plans for a hazardous waste incinerator and storage facility in a sparsely populated desert site 30 miles from Phoenix. Arizona bought the land from the federal government, conducted environmental impact studies that supported the project, approved transportation improvements for the site, signed a contract with an Arkansas company named ENSCO to build and operate the facility, and was in the process of constructing it when citizen opposition brought it to a halt in 1990. Opponents were especially upset that 90 percent of the waste was to be imported from other states.

Apparently under the leadership of Greenpeace activists, 400 people showed up at a May 7, 1990 public hearing at the disposal site to discuss the facility. The crowd exceeded the size of the meeting room, but officials refused to move the meeting outdoors to accommodate the number of people, and the crowd grew unruly. Sheriff's deputies responded by firing stun guns into the crowd and arresting 18 people, including a Greenpeace member. This incident galvanized public opinion against the project, and a follow-up public hearing in Phoenix drew 3,000 angry people, some of whom spat on the president of ENSCO, who had come to make his presentation.

Faced with what appeared to be overwhelming public opposition, Arizona lawmakers scuttled the plans for the site. But cancelling the plan did not come cheaply, since it cost $44 million to buy out the contract that the state had signed with ENSCO.

This still left the state with the problem of what to do with the 50,000 tons of toxic waste that are produced in the state each year. As a temporary expedient, Arizona joined a waste disposal agreement with other Western states.

Source: Don Harris, "Winning and Losing—A Hazardous Waste Standoff," *State Legislatures* 18, no. 1 (January 1992): 28–30.

focuses more on disposal sites than it does on cutting down the amount of such waste in the first place. More should be done to break down toxic materially chemically before it is shipped to disposal sites.[25]

Even conceding some merit to these arguments against disposal sites, the states are still faced with a major waste disposal problem. The U.S. Supreme Court has prohibited interstate bans on toxic waste shipments. Nevertheless, some new political creativity is needed to get beyond the NIMBY syndrome in dealing with this problem.[26]

Despite these difficulties with hazardous-waste regulation, it should not be concluded that the states are sitting on their hands. In fact, considerable policy has been established in the states to deal with the toxic materials. Not surprisingly, the most far-reaching policy has been set in states where the problem is most severe.[27] Californians, for example, passed an initiative measure in 1986 that requires businesses to warn consumers and the public of chemicals the companies use that post significant risk of cancer or birth defects. After the bill's passage, the state compiled a list of twenty-nine such chemicals, and companies are barred from discharging any significant amount of them into potential drinking water sources.[28]

◇ DOES THE POLLUTION CONTROL SYSTEM WORK?

Is the pollution control system actually cleaning up the nation's environment? The answer seems to be yes, but .... There is no doubt that the nation's air and water is cleaner than it was three decades ago when the environmental protection goals were first articulated. But some of the problems have turned out to be much more intractable than first thought, and new issues have arisen.

Much of the improvement in water quality can be attributed to the construction of sewage treatment plants and the National Pollution Discharge Elimination System effluent-discharge control system. One serious water pollution problem that is more difficult to cure, however, has been the presence of lead in drinking water in older cities served by lead pipes that were installed decades ago. In 1992, the EPA found excess lead levels in about 20 percent of the cities it examined. This does not mean that the average resident has unsafe drinking water, but it does mean that steps still need to be taken to keep the lead from reaching into the tap water.[29] Another persistent water pollution problem is contamination of the groundwater. As discussed earlier, the Section 208 planning process for dealing with groundwater has been much less successful than the pollution discharge elimination system that has worked for surface water.

Measurable improvements have also been made in air quality since the late 1960s.[30] In the mid-1980s, the Council on Environmental Quality (CEQ) reported a significant decline in the concentrations of five major air pollutants in cities (carbon monoxide, sulfur dioxide, lead, airborne particles, and ozone).[31] A decade later, the EPA reported that significant progress continues to be made on reducing concentrations of four out of the five major pollutants. The exception was ozone, which is the main ingredient of urban smog.[32]

The most intractable problems seem to be those arising from the production of toxic materials that are necessary for a highly technological society to function. We know, for example, that farmers with prolonged exposure to pesticides have abnormally high rates of cancer, but few people would be willing to ban the use of pesticides and bring about the major devastation to food production that would follow. Recall from Chapter 8 that California Governor Jerry Brown saw his political career plummet after he vacillated on the spraying of a pesticide to protect the state's crops from the Mediterranean fruit fly.

How we deal with these complicated problems is a very important issue in state politics. Some environmentalists demand that we turn our backs on high technology and return to a simpler lifestyle. The terms *sustainable agriculture* and *sustainable development* are associated with this idea. Others insist that there is a technological fix to our problems and we can achieve a clean environment without reducing our standards of living. Still others think that we should acknowledge that tradeoffs exist between our lifestyle and environmental quality. Inevitably, they think, we need to incorporate life quality measures (such as cancer rates and birth defect rates) in our understanding of living standards. From this viewpoint, each state needs not only a measure of its state economic product but a measure of its quality of life as well.

◇ SOCIAL CONFLICT AND THE ENVIRONMENT: ENVIRONMENTAL JUSTICE

These concerns over quality of life have put environmental protection in the middle of the social conflicts we have been discussing in this book. This happens in at least three ways: (1) charges of environmental racism, (2) land use policy, and (3) the interplay of environmental protection and the political economy.

Charges of Environmental Racism

It turns out that many of the nation's LULUs are found in very poor neighborhoods and neighborhoods of people of color. It might be that these people are less effective than middle-class people at using the NIMBY tactic to keep LULUs out of their neighborhoods. It might be that these neighborhoods are more amenable to LULUs because of lower property values and the lure of jobs.[33] Or it might be that the broader society simply has a callous disregard for the safety of its poor and minorities. Whatever the reason, the disproportionate siting of LULUs in poor and minority neighborhoods gave birth to the charge of environmental racism.

Environmental Racism at Prairie Island? A fascinating example of the intertwining of LULUs, NIMBY, and race took place in Minnesota in the early 1990s. About a fifth of the Minneapolis–St. Paul metropolitan area electricity is generated from a nuclear power plant operated by the Northern States Power Company (NSP) located along the Mississippi River immediately adjacent to the Prairie Island Indian Reservation, which is also the site of one of the area's most popular gambling casinos. By the mid-1990s, the plant was running out of underground storage space for its highly radioactive nuclear wastes and sought permission from the state legislature to store them in steel casks above ground until a disposal site could be agreed upon.

In the ensuing debate, supporters of the request were called "environmental racists" for wanting to store the fuel rods next to Indian reservation land. The tribal president expressed concern that the above-ground storage would be perilously close to the reservation's 160 residents and suggested instead that the fuels be stored in one of the area's richest suburbs, populated almost exclusively by whites. The tribe eventually agreed to a compromise under which it receives payments for use of the land and compensatory land in a nearby area of the county.

Environmentalist opponents to the bill formed a Minnesotans for Nuclear Responsibility (MNR) group that so outraged NSP that the company hinted it would stop selling MNR electricity under the favorable terms it sold electricity to other nonprofit groups in the state. MNR responded with newspaper ads suggesting that NSP was recklessly dumping radioactive waste into peoples' bath water. The fight came to a climax during the 1994 election season and spilled over into local party politics. Republican legislators predominantly supported the bill, but Democrats were torn between two powerful political forces in the state—organized labor that supported NSP and a loose coalition of environmentalists and liberal Democratic activists who supported the Minnesotans for Nuclear Responsibility. The Democrats were also put in the uncomfortable position of having to choose between a bill that would keep the electricity flowing to their constituents' homes but that could, at least in public relations terms, make them appear insensitive to the health and safety of Native Americans who lived next to the power plant. This was an especially sensitive issue for some Democrats because they had traditionally claimed that they were more inclusive than their Republican adversaries whom they usually painted as uncaring about the problems of the poor and minorities. Many Democrats now found themselves vulnerable to the same charge.

The chief Senate sponsor of the bill was subjected to death threats, and by the time the final vote was taken in the Senate, tempers were so enflamed that spectators were obliged to pass through metal detectors to ensure that nobody brought any weapons into the capitol building. The legislature finally agreed to allow NSP to store seventeen casks of the spent fuel above ground until the year 2004. If an alternative disposal site is not found by that time, the nuclear reactor must close down. In the meantime, NSP is obliged to provide financial support for windmills, biomass power, and other alternative forms of generating electricity.[34]

Transformational Politics   Also at issue in the Prairie Island dispute was what political scientist Betty H. Zisk calls **transformational politics**.[35] Had the debate over the storage casks been confined to the state's Public Utilities Commission where it started, it would, no doubt have been handled through the traditional political process that tends to use pragmatic tactics and seek incremental goals. Goals would have been incremental ones in the sense that the two sides would have bargained quietly over the number of casks to be stored and for how long. But the continued existence of the nuclear power plant would not have been called into question, and the moral integrity of NSP officials would not have been publicly attacked. Minnesotans for Nuclear Responsibility, however, followed a transformational politics approach that in reality was seeking a major change in the lifestyles of their fellow citizens. It was seeking not only to ban the storage of casks next to the Indian reservation but to shut down the plant, reduce energy consumption by Minnesotans, and force the power company to convert to allegedly "green" methods of generating electricity. Because the goals of transformational politics are about society's ultimate values, transformational activists feel justified in taking highly moralistic positions and branding their opponents as immoral (or environmentally racist as in the Prairie Island case). Because the transformational activists tended not to hold elective positions, they did not have to worry about whether they would be voted out of office in the next election or what would happen if the metropolitan area lost a quarter of its electricity supply. Hence they could reject the pragmatic and incremental goals associated with traditional politics as betrayals of moral principle.

Environmentalism and Civic Activism   It is impossible to know how extensive transformational politics are in the politics of environmentalism. But there can

be no doubt that protecting the environment has broad public support throughout the country, and millions of people back up their support with at least modest changes in their lifestyle. When asked about environmentalism in 1995, only
5 percent of people in a national survey said they were unsympathetic, and 54
percent considered themselves active environmentalists.[36] Almost 60 percent of
people say they always or often make a special effort to sort their waste for recy-
cling. About three-fourths of people say they use less heat or air conditioning in
order to conserve energy. About a fourth of the people belong to at least one environmental group, and more than a fourth had signed an environmental petition over the previous five years.

Social Conflict and Land Use Regulation

Next to the siting of LULUs, the most volatile issue in environmental politics
probably involves land use regulation. Especially in rapidly growing metropolitan areas, environmentalists argue that continued urban sprawl needs to be
brought under control. As metropolitan areas sprawl outward and house increasingly large numbers of people in low-density settlements, they pave over
countless acres of land, create a habitat excessively dependent on automobiles,
increase the nation's vulnerability to petroleum shortages, make public transit so
expensive as to be ineffective, drive up the cost of public infrastructure needed
to serve low-density populations, and lead to social arrangements that one
school of thought (the New Urbanists)[37] criticizes as sterile and dysfunctional.

To rein in uncontrolled sprawl, a number of interesting experiments have
been tried. Portland, Oregon, and Minneapolis–St. Paul, Minnesota, drew
growth boundary lines around their built-up areas and tried to contain most future growth within those boundaries.[38] California created a Coastal Zone Plan to
gain some influence over the sprawl of developments along the Pacific Coast.[39]
And Vermont literally gave the state authority to override local development initiatives if they challenged the state's development plan.[40]

These attempts to protect the environment from sprawl have come under
bitter attack in recent years by property rights advocates who challenge land use
regulations as a violation of the U.S. Constitution's Fifth Amendment protections against taking of property without just compensation. Legally, this is called
the taking issue. If a city requires a business to install a public bike path through
the business property as a precondition for being allowed to expand the size of
the business facility, has the company's property been "taken" without just compensation? Yes, ruled the U.S. Supreme Court in the case of Tigard City, Oregon.[41] This decision and a number of others in recent years[42] have sent shivers
down the spines of land use regulators. They have also encouraged a "property
rights movement" that seems to oppose almost any land use regulation for the
purpose of attaining environmental goals.[43]

Environment and the Political Economy

Finally, environmentalism engenders social conflict when it seems to be incompatible with economic growth. Growth advocates complain that environmental

restrictions hinder growth either because of excessive regulations or because they impose expenses that could otherwise be invested in job-creating enterprises. Environmentalists deny this and charge in return that unbridled development has "damage costs" that might well be greater than the costs of reducing environmental deterioration.

Sorting out these charges is not easy. There is no doubt to the assertion that the environmental gains of the past three decades have cost a significant amount of money. Some of these costs are quite visible. For example, the next new automobile you purchase would be a lot cheaper if it were not required to have a catalytic converter, a PCV valve, and other pollution control equipment. The costs of other environmental protection regulations are not so easy to identify, however.

Two big issues have grown out of the question of costs. First, do the benefits of environmental legislation exceed the costs? Second, who pays for the costs?

The Cost–Benefit Approach to Environmental Protection   Just as we can quantify some of the costs of environmental protection, we can also quantify some of the benefits. For example, if air quality were to revert to the level of 1970, it is estimated that the health bill for increased illnesses would total $40 to $100 billion per year.[44] By contrast the cost of implementing the Clean Air Act amendments of 1990 has been put at $20 billion per year.[45] If these figures are anywhere close to being accurate, the Clean Air Act seems to be worth the costs.

With some other environmental programs, however, the benefits of regulation are not so clear-cut. Under pressure from the Bush administration, the Office of Management and Budget (OMB) estimated cost–benefit figures for various regulatory rules involving health, safety, and environmental protection. The OMB released its results in the context of a grisly tradeoff. How much money are we willing to spend in order to prevent one's premature death? For example, consider the little lights along the floor of airliner cabins that will enable you to find your way to the exit in case the cabin blacks out or fills with smoke. For every premature death that will be averted, the OMB estimated that these lights cost $100,000. Considering that your airline ticket share of this cost is only a few pennies, you might well conclude that this expense is nevertheless a bargain. How much would you be willing to spend to prevent one child from dying in flammable pajamas? The OMB estimated the cost of banning flammable pajamas at $800,000 per death prevented. The ban on asbestos cost $110.7 million for each premature death averted. And the cost for banning the disposal of hazardous wastes in garbage landfills amounted to $4.19 billion for each premature death averted.[46]

One must accept the accuracy of these figures with a large grain of salt. They were compiled under political pressure to make the costs of regulation look inordinately expensive, and even under the best of circumstances, it would be difficult to be very precise about the costs of dying from asbestos exposure since the deaths do not occur until many years after the exposure first took place. Nevertheless, the idea of "costs per premature death averted" does illustrate for us the inevitable tradeoff that exists between the costs and benefits of environmental regulation.

Paying the Costs of Regulation   The second big political economy issue is, who pays for the costs? One way to approach this question is to determine whether the costs and benefits are disseminated throughout society or are concentrated on particular groups of people. James Q. Wilson identifies four patterns of regulatory politics, depending on how the costs and benefits are distributed.[47] First, *majoritarian politics* take place when both the costs and benefits are widely distributed. The benefits of safe drinking water, for example, are shared by the entire population, as are the costs.

A second pattern of regulatory politics, called *client politics*, emerges when the benefits of the policy are concentrated in a small group of people but the costs are spread widely. The regulation of utility rates for electricity, telephones, and natural gas serves as a good example. These rates are usually approved by public service commissions or public utility commissions. Utility companies regularly request rate increases that will concentrate profits in the company and its shareholders. Because the costs are so broadly spread among the general population, each person's share of the cost is so small that he or she will hesitate to invest time or energy opposing the rate increases. In a sense, the public utilities and other regulated industries can be seen as clients of the regulatory commissions. The regulatory commissions were created to protect consumer interests, but regulated industries themselves spend large sums of money in pressing their cases and lobbying before the commissions. Public utilities commissioners are often appointed by the governor, which means that the companies themselves have ample opportunity to influence the governor's appointment choices. In the Prairie Island dispute cited earlier, the issue of nuclear waste storage originated in the Public Utilities Commission. But the Minnesotans for Nuclear Responsibility distrusted the Public Utilities Commission, and they successfully shifted the arena of conflict from the client politics of the utilities to the state legislature.

A third type of regulatory politics, *entrepreneurial politics,* is best exemplified by the regulation of hazardous-waste disposal. Here the benefits are broadly diffused in that the policies aim to protect everyone from the ravages of toxic and hazardous wastes. Under Superfund legislation, however, the costs of regulation are narrowly concentrated on those companies that have to contribute fees to the federal Superfund and various state superfunds that have been established for hazardous-waste-site cleanups. The Prairie Island dispute eventually ended up as an issue of entrepreneurial politics because the costs eventually got shifted to NSP. NSP must find an alternative disposal site for the nuclear waste by the year 2004, or it will be forced by law to close down the reactor. Minnesotans for Nuclear Responsibility (MNR) became policy "entrepreneurs" who forced the conflict into the legislature. The difficult challenge for MNR, as for all entrepreneurial politics, is that a policy cycle exists in which issues eventually move out of the public limelight. When this happens, the entrepreneurial groups weaken or dissolve, and the regulations become routinized.

A final type of regulation, *interest group politics,* occurs when both the costs and benefits are concentrated on small groups. The most frequent case is labor–management relations. Because labor groups and business groups are continuing organizations in state politics, their conflict seems a permanent one, with the state regulatory bodies serving as both the forum for the conflict and the referees who apportion the benefits.

In sum, it is very difficult to determine precisely the costs and benefits of environmental policies. Involved is not only the obvious question of whether the costs outweigh the benefits, but also the question of who pays which costs and who gets what benefits. As we have seen, there are four patterns in the states—the majoritarian-politics pattern, the client-politics pattern, the entrepreneurial-politics pattern, and the interest-group-politics pattern. Business groups are most likely to dominate the client-politics pattern. Consumerists and environmentalists are most likely to dominate the entrepreneurial-politics pattern. But they find it difficult achieving permanent, effective regulation, because the entrepreneurial interest groups tend to weaken and dissolve, and the regulatory apparatus that was established tends to degenerate into the client-politics pattern. Unless the entrepreneurial groups can create permanent interest groups to look after their welfare during the politics of interest-group regulation, as organized labor does, they may not achieve many of their goals on a permanent basis.

SUMMARY

1. The Environmental Protection Act of 1970 declared "a broad national policy for environmental protection." It established the Environmental Protection Agency (EPA) and the Council on Environmental Quality (CEQ) and invented the environmental impact statement.

2. Water pollution management requires joint federal, state, and local action. The key federal legislation is the Water Pollution Control Act of 1972 and its later amendments, which set goals of making all the nation's water fishable and swimmable by 1983 and of eliminating all polluting discharges into the nation's waterways by 1985. To deal with point-source pollution, the act established the National Pollution Discharge Elimination System (NPDES). To deal with nonpoint-source pollution, the act established so-called Section 208 agencies, environmental planning agencies in 176 different regions of the country. The Section 208 agencies work through an intricate involvement of federal, state, and local interests.

3. One of the remarkable examples of successful water pollution cleanup occurred with the Willamette River in Oregon.

4. The key air pollution legislation at the federal level were the Clean Air Act amendments of 1970 and 1977. These directed the EPA to set primary and secondary air-quality standards. The states draft state implementation plans (SIPs) to indicate how they will meet the EPA standards. The Reagan administration sought to rewrite the Clean Air Act and soften its requirements, but that revision has not yet occurred.

5. A noteworthy example of air pollution cleanup took place in Pittsburgh. As examined in Charles O. Jones's study, Pittsburgh started with a system of voluntary partnership between government and business but ended with a system of mandatory compliance.

6. The federal role in hazardous-waste management stems primarily from three acts: the Toxic Substances Control Act of 1976, which requires EPA to provide for testing of new chemicals and banning of unsafe ones; the Resource Conservation and Recovery Act that established a cradle-to-grave process for hazardous wastes; and the Comprehensive Environmental Response Compensation and Liability Act of 1980, which established the so-called Superfund to finance the cleaning of abandoned

dump sites for toxic materials. Most of the responsibility for finding new disposal sites rests with the states.

7. The extent to which these environmental regulation measures work is hard to determine. The least progress has probably been made in managing hazardous wastes, and the most progress has probably been made in reducing air pollution. In water pollution control, substantial progress has occurred in reducing the discharge of pollutants into the lakes and streams. But much doubt remains about whether all cities can comply with requirements for sewage treatment plants. And little has been done to date to protect the quality of groundwater.

8. Environmental and social conflicts converge in at least three ways: charges of environmental racism, land use regulation versus property rights revolution, and trade-offs between environmental regulation and the political economy.

9. Regulatory policies at the state level fall into four categories: majoritarian-politics regulation, entrepreneurial-politics regulation, client-politics regulation, and interest-group-politics regulation.

KEY TERMS

Clean Air Act Amendments of 1977   Amendments that extended several deadlines for meeting the standards set in the 1970 Clean Air Act, stiffened standards, and gave the EPA increased authority to enforce them.

Clean Air Act Amendments of 1990   The first major attempt to combat acid rain and depletion of the ozone layer. The amendments also stiffened emissions control requirements for new automobiles and obliged oil companies to produce cleaner burning fuels.

Clean Air Act of 1970   The act that established the fundamental authority for the federal regulation of air quality.

Clean Water Act   See Water Pollution Control Act of 1972.

Environmental impact statement (EIS)   An assessment of the environmental impacts of a proposed development project. Required before the project can be approved. Applies to federal agencies and to some states.

Environmental Protection Act of 1970   The keystone of federal authority to regulate the environment. It established the Environmental Protection Agency and the Council on Environmental Quality and declared a broad national policy for environmental protection.

Externalities   Costs that are not borne directly by the buyers or sellers of a particular product. For example, the costs of cleaning up air pollution produced by automobiles are not included in the price of cars.

Merit goods   Goods that society judges all citizens should have as a matter of right.

Nonpoint-source pollution   Pollution whose specific point of entry into the water cannot be traced. Acid rain, which starts from smokestacks of coal-burning facilities and then disperses over a wide region and falls in the form of rain, is an example.

Point-source pollution   Pollution that is introduced into the water supply at a specific, identifiable point of entry, such as a storm sewer opening into a river.

Primary air-quality standards   Established by the 1970 Clean Air Act, these aim at protecting public health.

Resource Conservation and Recovery Act of 1976   This act set up a cradle-to-grave process for controlling and disposing of hazardous wastes.

Secondary air-quality standards   Set by the 1970 Clean Air Act, these aim at protecting crops, vegetation, forests, animals, and other materials essential to the public welfare.

Social goods   Goods whose benefits are nondivisible and nonexclusive. Their enjoyment by one person does not prevent their enjoyment by others.

State implementation plan (SIP)   A plan that states are required to draft to show how they will meet the primary and secondary air-quality standards set by the EPA.

Superfund   A federal fund set up to finance the cleanup of hazardous-waste sites.

The Taking Issue   The issue of whether land use regulations "take" peoples' property under the meaning of the Fifty Amendment's clause, "nor shall private property be taken for public use, without just compensation."

Toxic Substances Control Act of 1976   The act that gave the EPA authority to test new chemicals it considers unsafe and to prohibit sale of PCBs except in enclosed systems.

Transformational Politics   A form of politics that seeks to change the focus of politics from pragmatic give and take over specific issues to the uncompromising pursuit of ultimate social values.

Water Pollution Control Act of 1972 (Clean Water Act)   The keystone of federal environmental policy for water quality. Established the pollution discharge-elimination system and required municipalities to install secondary sewage treatment facilities.

REFERENCES

1. Andrew Danzo, "The Big Sleazy: Love Canal Ten Years Later," *The Washington Monthly* 28, no. 8 (September 1988): 11–18; *The New York Times*, September 28, 1988, p. 28; July 26, 1990, p. 1.
2. *The New York Times*, July 26, 1990, p. 1.
3. Dianah Bewar, "The National Environmental Policy Act," *Intergovernmental Perspective* 18, no. 3 (Summer 1992): 17–19.
4. Ibid.
5. See Thaddeus C. Trzyna, *Environmental Impact Requirements in the States: NEPA's Offspring* (Washington, D.C.: U.S. Environmental Protection Agency, Office of Research and Development, 1974), p. 19.
6. Ora Huth, "Managing the Bay Area's Environment: An Experiment in Collaborative Planning," *Public Affairs Report* 18, no. 2 (April 1977): 4 (Bulletin of the Institute of Governmental Studies; University of California, Berkeley).
7. Council on Environmental Quality, *Environmental Quality: The Eleventh Annual Report of the Council on Environmental Quality* (Washington, D.C.: U.S. Government Printing Office, 1980), p. 133.
8. Evan J. Ringquist, *Environmental Protection at the State Level: Politics and Progress in Controlling Pollution* (New York: M. E. Sharpe, 1993), 57–58.
9. John Grand, "Environmental Management: Emerging Issues," in *The Book of the States: 1984–85* (Lexington, Ky.: Council of State Governments, 1984), p. 451.
10. Zachary Smith, *The Environmental Policy Paradox*, 2nd ed. (Englewood Cliffs, N.J.: Prentice-Hall, 1995), p. 108.
11. This discussion is taken from the U.S. Council on Environmental Quality, *Environmental Quality Annual Report: 1973* (Washington, D.C. U.S. Government Printing Office, 1973), pp. 43–71.
12. *Congressional Quarterly Almanac: 1977*, p. 627.
13. See *Congressional Quarterly Almanac: 1989*, p. 665.
14. For background on the passage of this law, see Gary C. Bryner, *Blue Skies, Green Politics: The Clean Air Act of 1990* (Washington, D.C.: CQ Press, 1993).
15. Garr Lee, "The Clean Air Act Evaporates, One Program at a Time," *Washington Post National Weekly*, May 11–17, 1996, p. 11.
16. B. Dan Wood, "Federalism and Policy Responsiveness: The Clean Air Case," *Journal of Politics* 53, no. 3 (August 1991): 852.

17. Charles O. Jones, *Clean Air: The Policies and Politics of Pollution Control* (Pittsburgh: University of Pittsburgh Press, 1973), p. 21.
18. Jeanne Lowe, *Cities in a Race with Time: Progress and Poverty in America's Renewing Cities* (New York: Random House, 1968), p. 138.
19. Jones, *Clean Air*, pp. 97–98.
20. Marc K. Landy and Mary Hague, "Private Interests and Superfund," *Public Interest*, no. 108 (Summer 1992): 98–101.
21. *Washington Post National Weekly*, August 5–11, 1991, p. 10.
22. Landy and Hague, "Private Interests and Superfund," p. 100.
23. Gary Lee, "A Cleanup Operation Falls by the Wayside," *Washington Post National Weekly*, June 3–9, 1996, p. 33.
24. Michael E. Kraft and Bruce B. Clary, "Citizen Participation and the NIMBY Syndrome: Public Response to Radioactive Waste Disposal," *Western Political Quarterly* 44, no. 2 (June 1992): 299–327.
25. Michael Heiman, "From 'Not in My Backyard!' to 'Not in Anybody's Backyard!'" *APA Journal* 56, no. 3 (Summer 1990): 359 362.
26. Herbert Inhaber, "Of LULUs, NIMBYs, and NIMTOOs," *Public Interest*, no. 107 (Spring 1992): 52–64. (NIMTOO is "Not in My Term of Office.")
27. James P. Lester, James L. Franke, Ann O'M. Bowman and Kenneth W. Kramer, "Hazardous Wastes, Politics, and Public Policy: A Comparative State Analysis," *Western Political Quarterly* 36, no. 2 (June 1983): 257–283.
28. Robert K. Landers, "Living with Hazardous Wastes," *Editorial Research Reports* (July 19, 1988): 385.
29. Reported in *The New York Times*, October 21, 1992, p. A-15.
30. A slight improvement from 1969 to 1977 is indicated by the *National Wildlife* annual environmental-quality index. See "The 1982 Environmental Quality Index," *National Wildlife* 20, no. 2 (February March 1982): 32.
31. U.S. Council on Environmental Quality, *Environmental Quality Annual Report: 1983* (Washington, D.C.: U.S. Government Printing Office, 1984), pp. 18–19.
32. Reported in *The New York Times*, October 20, 1992, p. 17.
33. Robert D. Bullard, ed., *Confronting Environmental Racism: Voices from the Grassroots* (Boston: South End Press, 1993).
34. *St. Paul Pioneer Press*, February 6, 1994, p. 1; March 20, 1994, p. D-1; *Minneapolis Star Tribune*, March 31, 1994, p. 1-A; April 7, 1994, p. 16-A.
35. Betty H. Zisk, *The Politics of Transformation: Local Activism in the Peace and Environmental Movements* (Westport, Conn.: Praeger, 1992).
36. The source for these data and other data cited in this paragraph is a summary of public opinion polling on the issue and summarized in *The Public Perspective* (June–July 1996): 29.
37. See especially, James Howard Kunstler, "Home from Nowhere," *The Atlantic Monthly* (September 1996): 43–66.
38. John J. Harrigan, "Minneapolis–St. Paul: Structuring Metropolitan Government," in *Regional Politics in a Post-City Age*, eds. H. V. Savitch and Ronald K. Vogel, eds. *Urban Affairs Annual Reviews*, v. 45 (Thousand Oaks, Calif.: Sage Publications, 1996) and Carl Abbot, *Portland* (Lincoln: University of Nebraska Press, 1983).
39. Melvin B. Mogulof, *Saving the Coast: California's Experiment in Inter-Government Land Use Regulation* (Lexington, Mass.: Lexington Books, 1975).
40. Elizabeth H. Haskell and Victoria S. Price, *State Environmental Management* (New York: Praeger, 1973), pp. 173–194.
41. *Dolan v. City of Tigard* (1994).

42. *First English Evangelical Lutheran Church of Glendale* v. *County of Los Angeles,* 107 S.Ct. 2378 (1987); *Nollan* v. *California Coastal Commission,* 107 S.Ct. 3141 (1987).

43. See, for example, Bruce Yandle, "The Property Rights Revolution," *Madison Review* 1, no. 1 (Fall 1995): 26–32.

44. Jackie Cummins and Larry Morandi, "Now You See It, Now You Don't," *State Legislatures* 19, no. 10 (October 1993): 30–34.

45. Ibid.

46. Reported in *The New York Times,* March 24, 1993, p. C-19.

47. James Q. Wilson, ed., *The Politics of Regulation* (New York: Basic Books, 1980), pp. 367–372.

STATE AND COMMUNITY ECONOMIC DEVELOPMENT POLICIES

Chapter Preview

This chapter examines the politics of promoting economic development at the state and community levels. We will explore in turn:

1. How changes in the national economy and foreign competition have affected states and communities.

2. The economic development strategies that states and communities follow to improve their economic situation.

3. The political strategies that states and communities follow to influence economic development.

4. Important issues that are raised for state and community politics by the quest for economic development.

Economic development policies are important in easing the social divisions of the nation.

◇ INTRODUCTION

In February 1986, pop singer Bruce Springsteen returned to his hometown of Freehold, New Jersey, and gave an impromptu concert in support of local workers protesting the closing of 3M Corporation's audiotape manufacturing plant there. Able to produce the same tapes more cheaply in a more modern plant elsewhere, the 3M Corporation decided to close the Freehold plant, throwing 700 people out of work and dealing a heavy economic blow to the town as it awaited the shock of losing 700 regular paychecks. Freehold gained fleeting notoriety because of Springsteen's brief appearance. But with less media fanfare, similar plant closings—with their resulting local economic hardship—have been replayed regularly over the last several years, from communities as diverse as iron-mining towns in northern Minnesota to former energy-boom towns in Wyoming and even to the huge, bustling metropolis of Houston, which was hit hard in the mid-1980s by falling energy prices.[1]

If the plant being closed is a major player in the local economy, the state and community involved get doubly hit. First, the loss of a major employer brings economic and social havoc. As the town's income declines, mortgages fall into arrears, savings get depleted, local businesses close, alcohol abuse and family violence mount, and the town's physical appearance grows seedier as people become afraid to invest their scarce savings in maintenance and repair. For those seeking to move on to more prosperous areas of the country, houses become impossible to sell except at a small fraction of their former worth. A second adverse impact involves the state and community governments. Because of the economic decline, states and communities face a greater demand for welfare and social services to help the people who are displaced. But the state and community governments are less able to provide such services because their own revenue base declines with the local economy.

In contrast to Freehold, Spring Hill, Tennessee, enjoyed an unprecedented transformation in the 1980s from a sleepy hamlet to the growing site of a General Motors manufacturing plant for its new Saturn automobile. Unlike the unfortunate residents of Freehold, the residents of Spring Hill enjoyed the luxury of dollars being pumped into their economy, escalating property values, new stores and services, and an abundance of jobs and economic opportunities.

What, if anything, should governments do to cope with the dramatically changing economic conditions exemplified by Freehold and Spring Hill? To answer these questions and gain a broader insight into the dynamics of state and local political economies, we will examine four broad issues in this chapter. First, how does the changing American economy affect state and community politics? Second, what economic development strategies can states and communities pursue to protect themselves? Third, what political strategies can they follow? And fourth, what issues surface in the quest for economic development?

◇ THE CHANGING CLIMATE FOR STATE AND COMMUNITY ECONOMIES

To appreciate the causes of Freehold's problems and Spring Hill's good fortune, we must first examine three broad trends taking place in the American economy. First is the transformation from an industrial to a postindustrial economy. Second is the intensification of foreign competition. Third is the changing class structure of American society.

From Industrial to Postindustrial Economy

Economists distinguish among three sectors of the economy. The *primary sector* refers to extractive activities such as oil production, mining, timber production, and farming. The *secondary (industrial) sector* refers to manufacturing activities.

Table 17-1   CHANGES IN THE AMERICAN ECONOMY

Selected Aspects	Year	Percentage
International Interdependence		
1. Exports as a percentage of GDP	1970	4.2%
	1990	7.9
	2015	?
2. Imports as a percentage of GDP	1970	4.0%
	1990	9.0
	2015	?
Postindustrialization		
Growth of labor force employed in manufacturing and services as a percentage of growth of total civilian labor force, 1970–1994:		
Services		110.8%.
Manufacturing		−2.8%.
Total economy		56.4%.

Source: Bureau of the Census, *Statistical Abstract of the United States: 1995* (Washington, D.C.: U.S. Government Printing Office, 1995), pp. 416, 451, 814.

And the *tertiary sector* refers to a broad range of service activities, from retail trade to banking to hospital management. As Table 17-1 shows, while the total number of jobs in the overall economy has grown by 56 percent since 1990, there has been a decline in the number of manufacturing jobs. By contrast, the number of jobs in the service sector has more than doubled. The relative decline of industrial manufacturing and the relative growth of the service sector have led some social scientists to note that America has been shifting from an industrial base to a **postindustrial economy.**[2]

Within the manufacturing sector of the economy, dramatic changes are also occurring that have devastating impacts on places like Freehold. The most dynamic growth in the manufacturing sector has involved high-technology products such as computers, lasers, and sophisticated medical equipment. Those industries have been more competitive against foreign industries than have manufacturers of traditional products such as steel, automobiles, and television sets, which have been badly damaged by foreign competition and have lost heavily in their share of the market. The decline in manufacturing leveled off in the late 1980s, and manufacturers enjoyed a comeback.[3] Whether that comeback will be long-lasting will be discovered in the 1990s. Even if the comeback is permanent, manufacturing will not replace services as the dominant sector in the American economy.

Intensification of Foreign Competition

Part of the reason for the relative decline of the manufacturing sector can be traced to the intensification of foreign competition in the last quarter-century.

Table 17-1 shows that exports almost doubled their share of the gross domestic product (GDP) between 1970 and 1990, and that imports more than doubled their share. These percentages are likely to continue to grow in the future. A major step toward international interdependence came in 1992 when the United States, Mexico, and Canada signed the North American Free Trade Agreement (NAFTA). Through this pact, these three nations opened their borders more widely to increased trade and mobility of capital, thus increasing their exposure to economic interdependence.

On the positive side, this interdependence enriches the quality of American life by making a greater variety of imported goods and services available. Moreover, aggressive expansion of American exports opens up larger world markets to American companies, thus creating more jobs and income. In theory, the increased need to compete in both the import and export markets leads to better products at more reasonable prices.

On the negative side, many corporations and communities are poorly prepared to compete in international markets. Foreign nations have become increasingly successful in their abilities to manufacture and market high-quality consumer products such as automobiles and television sets. Much American manufacturing is done in outmoded plants (such as the 3M plant in Freehold), using old-fashioned production methods as compared with the highly automated plants in Japan with its extensive use of robots and other innovations. And industrializing third-world countries such as Brazil, Korea, and Taiwan have set up manufacturing plants that are able to hire workers at a tiny fraction of the wages paid in developed countries such as the United States and Japan. Apple Computer Corp., for example, now does most of its manufacturing in plants set up in third-world countries. Further complicating the problem for American communities is the fact that much of the foreign competition comes from countries with authoritarian governments that curb free labor unions, hold down wages for multinational corporations, and do not enforce environmental and safety standards that are prevalent in the United States. Additionally, the host governments often subsidize the export of their products to the United States (what American-based manufacturers call "dumping"). Despite huge transportation distances and costs involved, these and other factors combined in the 1970s and 1980s to give many imported products a distinct price advantage over comparable American goods.

Additionally, the relative advantage of American goods versus foreign goods varies directly with international exchange rates. When the value of the dollar rose in comparison to the Japanese yen and other foreign currencies in the early 1980s, imports became cheaper, American goods became more expensive abroad, and this was precisely the period of greatest devastation for American manufacturers. When the dollar began declining relative to foreign currencies in the mid-1980s, that decline propelled the comeback of American manufacturers by making it easier for them to export their products and by raising the prices of products imported to the United States. To complicate matters, although a strong dollar tends to be bad for American manufacturers, it helps other parts of

Like a ride on a kangaroo, the ups and downs of the American economy are greatly influenced by the ups and downs of the dollar in relation to foreign currencies.

Source: By Thompson, © 1989.

the American economy (major banks, for example). The net result is that the economic fortunes of communities across America are influenced by the actions of foreign bankers, foreign investors, foreign manufacturers, and foreign politics to a degree that is unprecedented.

The Changing Class Structure

As the American economy adapts to these technological and foreign challenges, that adaptation is provoking profound consequences in the social and political structures of towns such as Freehold and Spring Hill. Some economists flatly assert that the American middle class is shrinking, that the percentage of people earning middle-level incomes (defined as 75 to 125 percent of the median income) has decreased since 1970, while the number of lower- and upper-income families has increased.[4] Other economists deny that this is occurring.[5] The most detailed examination of the question is found in Frank Levy's *Dreams and Dollars,* which denies that there has been a significant shrinking of the middle class but presents considerable data to show that the living standards of most Americans have declined since 1973, with the lower- and middle-income classes suffering the worst declines.[6] A long period of corporate downsizing has helped produce what former Secretary of Labor Robert Reich called an "anxious class."[7] This refers to the millions of middle-level corporate workers threatened with losing their jobs in a corporate downsizing.

◇ STRATEGIES FOR ECONOMIC DEVELOPMENT

In the quest to promote jobs and attract industries, states and communities follow a number of strategies. Among the most important of these are public relations, promoting a positive business climate, creating incentives for business growth, and facilitating community development.

Public Relations

The most visible and inexpensive approach to economic development is public relations. Some states spend lavishly to promote their state as a good place for business. States with significant tourist advantages (such as Colorado and Florida) use public relations to attract tourist dollars. And states with extensive retirement communities, such as Arizona, use public relations to enhance their image as an attractive place to resettle. Retirees with their pension checks and tourists with their recreational dollars are just as effective a means of pumping money into a state and creating jobs as is a new manufacturing plant or a high-technology venture.

Promoting a Favorable Business Climate

Of key interest in many states is the **business climate** that will make the state attractive to the business community. What makes a positive business climate is not absolutely clear, however, because different types of businesses have different needs. The features that make a climate attractive to one type of business might be irrelevant to a different type. Traditional manufacturing firms, for example, tend to be very sensitive to labor costs and seek a business climate that discourages labor unions and holds down costs for workers' compensation and unemployment compensation. These concerns are less important to fast-growing companies in fields such as computer software or medical technology, and these companies need a business climate that facilitates venture capital and a highly educated workforce. Property taxes are a very important part of the business climate for companies with sprawling real estate holdings, but they are less crucial to firms that depend mostly on renting office space for their operations.

Taxing and Spending   Of the issues most involved in creating a favorable business climate, taxes and the level of government expenditures on public services are the most politically controversial. Many business organizations argue that the low-tax, low-spending states of the South and Southwest are more attractive to industry than are states with high taxes and high levels of public expenditures. According to this viewpoint, when firms decide to relocate or to expand they often go South or West in order to avoid the punitive tax structures of the Northeast and Midwest. But how true is this assumption?

Roy Bahl surveyed numerous studies of the impact of taxes on decisions to relocate from one state to another and concluded that although taxes do affect relocation within a metropolis, "the consensus of a great deal of such research would seem to be that taxes are not a major factor in interregional location."[8] State taxes represent a relatively small percentage of a firm's income, and most firms can save relatively little on taxes by moving from one state to the next.

The limited impact of taxes on locational decisions was also discovered by Roger W. Schmenner's study of location decisions by 410 of the *Fortune* 500 companies. Schmenner found that "tax and financial incentives have little influence on almost all plant location decisions." At best they are "tie breakers" when competing sites are otherwise equally desirable.[9]

Labor Costs   More important to the business climate than taxes are the costs of labor. At issue is whether or not a state's labor force is extensively unionized and whether unemployment compensation and workers' compensation benefits are high. Unemployment compensation is paid to laid-off workers for up to six months while they are between jobs. Workers' compensation awards payments to workers who suffer handicapping injuries on the job (for example, loss of an arm or a leg). Not surprisingly, workers' compensation, unemployment compensation, wages, and benefits tend to be higher in states with strong unions. Most southern and southwestern states have passed so-called **right-to-work laws** that prohibit the union shop. Most northeastern and midwestern states do permit the union shop.

Offsetting this factor, however, is the fact that many firms also want a labor force that is relatively well educated and has a reputation for reliable, hard work. For this reason, a state that reduced taxes by cutting back on public schools and higher education, which help produce quality workforces, may in the long run worsen its business climate rather than improve it. Mississippi, for example, scores high on the business climate criteria of low taxes, low spending, and antiunion legislation. But it also scores among the nation's lowest in educational levels, and for that reason Mississippi is not a very desirable location for corporations that require a well-trained or well-educated workforce.

Uncontrollable Factors   Finally, many locational criteria are not very directly under a state's control. Other things being equal, a moderate weather climate would be more attractive than an extreme climate. Access to low-cost energy was a major plus for Texas in attracting industry during the energy-conscious 1970s, for example. A region with a variety of first-class cultural, sports, and entertainment amenities would be more attractive than a state without such amenities. And perhaps most important, a region close to a firm's markets would be more attractive than a region far from a firm's markets.

Does Business Climate Make Any Difference? In sum, a state's business climate depends on many factors, and each state has its own peculiar combination of strengths and weaknesses. For example, South Dakota has little in the way of metropolitan cultural or entertainment amenities. Yet it has enjoyed a fair amount of success attracting the credit-card billing operations of major banks by relaxing limits on interest rates and by having no personal or corporate income tax.

Seldom discussed, however, is the question of how much difference the business climate actually makes in promoting a state's economy. If business climate were the single most important factor in economic development, then states like South Dakota and Mississippi would be among the highest in economic development, and states like New York and California would be underdeveloped. In fact, the high-spending, high-taxing states of the Northeast enjoyed better economic performance over the past decade than did most of the allegedly good business climate states.[10]

If theory says that corporations will move to states with the lowest taxes, then why is there not a stronger relationship between tax levels and economic development? In part it is because corporations are limited in their ability to relocate their facilities. Corporations continuously monitor their branch operations (deciding to open some new plants, expand some existing ones, and shut down others), but they do not commonly relocate entire facilities from one state or region to another. One of the most widely respected studies of the impact of corporate in- and out-migrations on jobs was David Birch's study of over two million firms in the early and middle 1970s. He found that such migrations had a negligible impact on the number of jobs a state gains or loses.[11]

Creating Incentives for Business Growth

Whatever the facts may be about the importance of company migrations from state to state, governors, mayors, and legislators find themselves pressured by political forces to provide an extensive array of incentives for business growth. The focus today is less on recruiting businesses to move in from other states than it is to help local businesses prosper.[12] Along these lines, twenty states in recent years have set up venture capital funds to help new businesses start up. Other states have offered tax credits to help corporations spin off new companies and help them get started. The most imaginative states have adopted an entrepreneurial attitude that helps "develop and create markets for private producers to exploit."[13] These states try to use existing resources to assist in technology transfers, to help small businesses, and to finance research and development for new products.[14]

Urban Enterprise Zones and Empowerment Zones

As part of their incentives for business, at least thirty-seven states established **urban enterprise zones** to entice firms to set up operations and employ local residents in blighted areas. Los Angeles, for example, established an enterprise zone covering Watts and the South Central area of the city that has been torn by riots, high crime, extreme poverty, and an outward migration of jobs. Employers who create jobs in the zone can receive wage credits on their state income taxes and reduced prices for public utilities such as electricity and gas. Other states, in addition to tax incentives, offer relaxed enforcement of environmental, health, and safety regulations for firms that expand in their urban enterprise zones.[15] Despite more than 3,000 urban enterprise zones across the nation, the results have been disappointing. In Watts, as in most of the other zones, it is hard to find a concrete example of a declining neighborhood being turned around because of an enterprise zone.[16] Advocates of the enterprise zone concept argue that this is because the federal government failed to join the program. According to this argument, the costs of federal taxes and federal regulations far outweigh those imposed by the states, and the absence of a federal tax and regulatory relief makes it impossible for enterprise zones to reach their full potential.

In 1994, the Clinton administration introduced a plan for *Empowerment Zones* that differed from the traditional enterprise zones in some key respects. In addition to tax breaks and regulatory relief, empowerment zones were eligible for a concentration of federal social service programs to promote community development, reduce crime, and "empower" residents with the skills, attitudes, and social resources needed to prosper in the world of work. Further, instead of the 3,000 urban enterprise zones scattered throughout the nation, there were to be only 9 empowerment zones (6 urban and 3 rural) in an attempt to target federal resources where they could do the most good. It was the targeting of resources and the inclusion of social services that distinguished empowerment zones from their enterprise zone cousins.[17]

Facilitating Community Development

Perhaps the most visible thing that states do to promote business growth is to facilitate strategies for economic development in local communities. Communities rely on states for legal authority and financial or tax authority to offer development packages. Working together, states and communities can offer a variety of specific incentives to companies to expand in place rather than move somewhere else.

Tax Abatement   Perhaps the most widespread local inducement to economic development is the **tax abatement**.[18] This is the tactic of forgiving a firm's property taxes for a number of years if it expands in a particular city. One of the most generous tax abatement programs exists in Missouri, which permits local governments to forgive real estate taxes on property improvements for up to twenty-five years.[19]

Federal Seed-Money Programs   Cities can also provide seed money for firms to locate within their boundaries. For example, suppose a firm wishes to expand in Bigtown, USA, but is hampered by lack of developable land. Using its powers of eminent domain, the city of Bigtown can force the owners of a desirable piece of land to sell the land to the local government, usually to a local development agency or a port authority. Purchasing and clearing such land is extremely expensive, but cities have many sources of financial aid for this purpose. From the federal government, there are Community Development Block Grant (CDBG) funds and Economic Development Administration funds to purchase and clear the land and lay groundwork for road and sewer installations. These expenditures can be viewed as seed money because they prepare the land and make it attractive for private developers and corporations to build on the new sites.

Industrial Development Revenue Bonds   A city can issue **Industrial Development Revenue Bonds** (IDRB) to raise money for a development project. The city in effect acts as an intermediary to help a company raise development money at a lower cost than if the company had to go directly to the market and sell its own bonds. Because the interest earned by municipal bonds is exempt from federal income tax (and usually state income tax in the issuing state), such bonds carry lower interest rates than corporate bonds. A city will entice a corporation to expand by issuing IDRBs, and the bonds will be paid off with revenues from the company's development project. Thus, for most corporations interest costs are reduced, and at no expense to the city, for the federal and state governments bear the entire cost in the form of lower income-tax revenues. Until 1987, IDRBs were the single most popular method of funding urban economic development. But Congress in 1986 put a cap on the total amount of IDRBs that each state is allowed.[20]

Tax-Increment Financing   Under **tax-increment financing** (TIF), a city declares a tax-increment financing district in the neighborhood it wants to develop. The city issues bonds to clear the land and entice a developer to build a commercial structure on the site. Because the new structure is usually more valuable than the former use of the land, it generates more property taxes. This increment, or increase, in generated property taxes is used to pay off the tax-increment financing bonds. Thus the new development does not bring new property taxes into the city's general revenue until *after* the TIF bonds are paid off, which will usually be fifteen or twenty years. But it is hoped that the development itself will create many new jobs for city residents and ultimately improve the city's fiscal picture.

Venture Capital   At least twenty states today have **venture capital** programs to invest start-up capital in new companies that have excellent prospects for growth.[21] The Sky Computer Co. of Lowell, Massachusetts, for example, badly needed capital in 1982 to market plug-in computer boards for scientific and engineering applications. The Massachusetts Technology Development Corporation (MTDC) then invested public funds in the company to help it get off the ground. Within three years, the company's workforce expanded from fifteen to eighty-five, and annual sales shot up to $10 million. By using its governmentally supplied venture capital for projects like this, MTDC has been able to increase the number of jobs in the state. Between 1979, when it was created, and 1984, the MTDC invested about $5.7 million of venture capital in 27 companies, which has added more than 1,000 jobs and $2 million a year in state income-tax collections.[22] By 1990, the MTDC had produced so many successful investments that it no longer depended on public funds.[23] In addition to public venture capital corporations like MTDC, three states (New York, New Jersey, and Michigan) allow public employee pension funds to invest in venture capital projects.[24] Although venture capital is extremely risky, the Massachusetts example shows that under the proper circumstances it can produce benefits far exceeding the costs.

Seeking Foreign Investment   Increasingly popular among governors is the tactic of enticing foreign corporations to build plants in their states. Japanese companies have been especially receptive to these initiatives because they view it as a means of avoiding trade wars with the United States. Nissan automobiles manufactured in Tennessee, for example, would not likely be subject to any trade restrictions imposed on Japanese imports. And the estimated 3,400 jobs created at Nissan's Tennessee plants[25] help defuse American complaints about foreign competition stealing jobs from American workers. The Commerce Department estimated in the early 1980s that 2.3 million jobs in the United States were a direct result of foreign investment, almost 20 percent of them in California and New York alone.[26] To make themselves look attractive to foreign investors, state governments compete vigorously with each other in offering most of the incentives described earlier plus paying for some direct costs such as land purchase, site improvements, and road construction.

Expanding Exports

State governments also exploit international interdependency by seeking to expand the export of products or services based in their states. During the 1980s, twenty-six states increased the number of state offices overseas, thirty states increased their budgets for export promotion, and thirty-one states increased the number of state employees working on export promotion. Although state exports did not appear to be boosted by setting up state offices overseas, there was a pickup in exports in those states that added agency staff for export promotion. Staff workers can perform very useful services for businesses that want to expand by lending a personal hand "to guide businesses on a one-to-one basis through the maze of problems they are likely to encounter" as they enter the export markets.[27]

Convention Centers and Sports Facilities

Perhaps the most visible symbols of government action to promote development are the numerous public subsidies for convention centers and major league sports facilities to capture the tourist and entertainment dollar. During the 1980s, more than 200 convention centers were built or expanded around the country, leading to a 60 percent increase in convention center floor space.[28] St. Louis, for example, in 1993 opened a $123 million expansion of its convention center that it hoped would reverse decades of decline in the city.[29] With its central geographic location and its distinctive cultural history, St. Louis officials believed that a contemporary convention center would catapult the city into the top rung of cities attracting conventions and trade shows. These activities bring enormous money into a city, bolster its image, and create few environmental costs.

State-of-the-art sports facilities have a similar appeal to cities, and they become a tourist attraction. If tourists come in to see a major league baseball game, they not only spend money at the ball park, they might eat in a local restaurant, spend the night at a local hotel, and shop at a local mall. Baltimore, for example, built the highly praised Camden Yards baseball stadium to keep the Orioles from moving to another location. Local boosters argue that the park as been well worth the $214 million in public funds that it cost because the number of out-of-towners who came to see the Orioles play doubled the year after Camden Yards Park opened, and city businesses raked in more than $200 million in retail sales.[30] Even if these estimates are grossly inflated, local stadium boosters in many other cities want to follow Baltimore's lead and construct their own state-of-the-art facilities. This puts enormous pressure on local elected officials to provide the facilities that will attract or retain a major league sports team. The chances are small that a central-city mayor will be booted out of office if he or she loses a team,[31] but few mayors would want to take that chance, and no one would want to be remembered in local history as the mayor who cost the city big league status.

Assessing Economic Developing Strategies

Cities and states are under so much economic and fiscal pressure that they have little choice but to take any reasonable action that seems likely to improve the local economy. However, before a city or state enters a public–private venture, a number of questions should be (but apparently seldom are) asked.

First, does the development project result in a *net* increase in jobs? Although development projects always generate new jobs, they also destroy jobs that existed on the site prior to the project. The city should also ask whether the people who lose jobs will find new ones in the city.

Second, does the project bring a *net* fiscal benefit to the area? Wellston, Ohio, for example, suddenly got 980 new jobs when Jeno's, Inc., decided to consolidate its $200-million-per-year pizza-making facilities in that city. To help Jeno's relocate to Wellston, the local county and the state of Ohio lent the firm more than $5 million at a very generous $1\frac{7}{8}$ percent interest rate. But once the new facility began operations, its waste products clogged the city sewage system with a mass of cheese, meat, and other ingredients the consistency of toothpaste and the color of tomato soup. When the EPA threatened to close down the plant as an environmental danger, Ohio had to give the firm $500,000 to find a way to clean up the wastes.[32] In the long run, Jeno's may be a net fiscal contributor to Wellston, the county, and the state. But in the short run, the location inducements appear to have been fairly costly.

Third, does a public–private redevelopment project actually generate new economic activity? Or does it just relocate activity that would have occurred anyway? Much of the redevelopment of the 1980s focused on central-city downtown areas. It is a fair guess that if the city governments had not acted, most of the investments would have been made anyway. They probably would not have been made downtown, but in the suburbs of the same metropolitan areas. Larger suburbs have learned that they, too, must compete for new development; so now they also are engaged in the game of offering a variety of tax or bond inducements to promote development. Many older regions probably had good reasons to redevelop their old, run-down central business districts. But from a broader perspective, one has to ask whether it any longer makes sense to have different communities in the same metropolitan area competing with one another by offering tax incentives for development projects that in all likelihood would occur somewhere in the same metropolitan area even without government inducement.

The same observation could be made about giving incentives to attract foreign investment. Japanese automobile companies had already decided by the early 1980s to build manufacturing plants in the United States; no incentives were needed to get that investment. But the keen economic competition among the states led to a number of bidding wars to see which state could offer the most advantages to the Japanese. Kentucky, for example, spent $150 million on land purchase, site improvements, road construction, and worker training in order to attract a Toyota plant that would employ about 3,000 workers, a cost of about $50,000 per worker.[33] Alabama spent $253 million to attract a Mercedes Benz sports utility vehicle assembly plant that would employ 1,500 people. Critics objected to the price tag of $170,000 per job created, but enthusiasts argued that the deal would put Alabama on the map as an industrial player and that the long-term benefits of the deal would outweight the costs.[34]

To find out just how influential state development policies are in promoting development that would *not* occur without state aid, political scientist Susan B. Hansen conducted a sophisticated regression analysis to measure the comparative impact of development policies and a variety of other economic and development forces, such as level of education, tax level, and extent of unionization. Her findings offer very little support for the proposition that economic development policies make a significant difference in job creation:

> Despite a few modest correlations, most state industrial development policies have had a minimal impact on state deviation from regional trends, at least for the short time periods considered here. Consider an example: Pennsylvania's Ben Franklin Partnership claims to have created over 200 firms since its inception in 1983, resulting in over 3,600 jobs. But compared to the work force in a state the size of Pennsylvania (over five million), the number unemployed (486,000 in late 1985), and the total number of new firms created in the state (17,000 in 1985 alone), the Partnership's effort appears to have had a marginal impact on the state's economy; several neighboring states are doing considerably better.[35]

It was partially concern over the effectiveness of federally subsidized development policies that prompted Congress in 1986 to restrict the amount of IDRBs that a city or state could issue in order to promote its own growth. With the federal government under great criticism for its own huge budget deficits, Congress became less willing to let the federal treasury underwrite a huge volume of development projects that might well have occurred without federal subsidies. The Reagan administration eliminated the UDAG program and pushed unsuccessfully to kill two other development subsidy programs, the CDBG program and the Economic Development Administration development grants.

Finally, in addition to their economic feasibility, economic development projects must also be judged for their political feasibility. Generally, public opinion supports state and local economic development efforts—but not always. Substantial tax incentives to lure new industries can sometimes draw the ire of existing businesses, which may feel they are not getting their share of tax breaks. And public opinion as well can sometimes oppose economic development efforts.

The most dramatic example of a situation where public opinion rejected economic development strategies took place in Rhode Island in 1984. A so-called Greenhouse Plan to nurture research and development for high-technology firms, to target subsidies at new industries, and to establish training programs for the local workforce was put together by an elite commission of representatives of government, big businesses, and organized labor. The Greenhouse Plan was to be financed by an increase in the state income tax, which would require a constitutional amendment before it could be applied.

Rhode Island desperately needed some sort of initiative to spur its economic growth. It had one of the slowest job-growth rates of any state in the nation. Despite this desperate need and despite an extensive public relations campaign by the state's government, business, and labor leaders to sell the Greenhouse Plan to the public, it was rejected by the voters by a huge four-to-one margin in June 1984. A postreferendum survey of Rhode Islanders found that a majority of people thought that the Greenhouse Plan would make no difference in their own lives, and a third of them thought they would be hurt by it in some way. Over 60 percent thought the main beneficiaries would be bankers and big business, and only 20 percent perceived the plan as beneficial to working people, low-income people, small-business owners, women, or minorities.[36] In sum, Rhode Island's Greenhouse Plan experience suggests that public support is very thin for economic development subsidies that will impose highly visible costs on taxpayers for benefits that will be narrowly distributed.

◇ POLITICAL COMBAT STRATEGIES

The economic development strategies just discussed are essentially positive, forward-looking strategies that seek to use public resources to promote private economic development. Sometimes the strategies do not work, however, and communities are obliged to follow more combative political strategies to protect themselves from the fallout of broken economic dreams.

Plant-Closing Legislation

States usually cannot prevent plants from closing, and most economists would probably maintain that in most instances they should not do so. From a national

economic perspective, it makes little sense to force a corporation to keep in exis
tence an inefficient plant that can be replaced by a new, more automated, more
efficient one. Protecting such inefficiencies, so the argument goes, will in the
long run only make American manufacturers less competitive in the world economy. Instead, we should encourage disinvestment from failing industries so that
those resources can be reinvested in more viable economic activities.[37]

Although states cannot prevent plant closings, they can pass legislation that
softens the blow to local communities.[38] Four states, in fact, have done so (Connecticut, Maine, Massachusetts, and Wisconsin). The most extensive legislation
is in Massachusetts, which encouraged companies to give ninety days' notice of
a plant closing so that the workers will have more time to plan and make the
necessary adaptations. The legislation also provides for an extra three months of
health insurance, unemployment compensation, and job retraining.[39] At a minimum, each state would seem to want to require the closing companies to provide severance pay and funds for retraining and job counseling. Many companies do provide severance benefits. But the results are not always as good as the
promises. U.S. Steel Corporation (now called USX Corp.) established a job counseling program for laid-off workers when it closed its Clairton mills outside
Pittsburgh. Despite the counseling and the motivational sessions, few workers
were able to find full-time jobs in the area. Heavily dependent on the now-
closed mills, the local economy simply was not strong enough to absorb all the
laid-off workers.[40]

In 1988, the federal government passed a worker notification law less stringent than the one in Massachusetts. Called WARN (Worker Adjustment and Retraining Notification Act) the federal law required companies to give 60 days advance notice of mass layoffs and plant closings for companies with at least 100
workers. Although WARN does not provide any federal funds for health insurance and retraining, earlier federal legislation required each state to set up a displaced workers unit (DWU), and the DWUs were responsible for providing key
services to dislocated workers.[41]

In practice, how much workers get in the form of outplacement services
seems to depend less on state or federal plant closing laws than it does on how
hard their unions fight against plant closings. A study of four plant closings in
northern Indiana found that the unions were not able to prevent any of the closings, but when they allied with community groups and political leaders they
were able to get more severance assistance for the laid-off workers.[42]

Buy the Plant and Run It   A far more daring strategy is for the local community
itself to purchase and operate the failing facility. Twenty-five states have passed
Employee stock ownership plan (ESOP) laws that provide financial aid and other
assistance to help employees purchase plants that are threatening to close. The
most prominent example of this was the purchase of the Weirton steel mill by the
workers and residents of Weirton, West Virginia. Few other communities, however, have been able to do this successfully. Formidable obstacles lie in their way.

The obstacles involved in purchasing a plant were demonstrated in
Youngstown, Ohio, in 1977. Religious leaders sought to purchase a factory of the

Youngstown Sheet and Tube Company, which announced it would close its Youngstown plant, putting 5,000 people out of work. One month after the announcement, a group of religious leaders led by Catholic Bishop James Malone formed an Ecumenical Coalition to find a way for the community and workers to buy the doomed plant. Barely had these plans been formed than opposition developed. The parent company of the steel plant (Lykes Corporation) opposed the sale for fear of creating a plant that would compete with its remaining steel mills in other parts of the country. Local leaders of the United Steel Workers (USW) did not support the plan because of their ambivalence about being put into a managerial role if the workers were to become part-owners of the mill. Putting a viable plan together took several months, during which the markets served by the now-closed Youngstown plant had turned to other suppliers, making it doubtful that the Youngstown mill could recapture the lost market share. Finally, banks refused to lend the coalition the $500 million needed to purchase the plant, unless the U.S. government would guarantee the loan. But that the U.S. government refused to do. In the face of these obstacles, the Ecumenical Coalition was unable to complete its purchase of the plant.[43]

Take the Plant to Court   One possibility for gaining concessions in a plant-closing situation would be to threaten court action. This is what Wisconsin Governor Tommy Thompson did when Chrysler Corporation announced in January 1988 that it planned to close its Kenosha plant at the end of the year. On the understanding that Chrysler would keep the plant open until 1992, the state of Wisconsin and the city of Kenosha had given Chrysler tens of millions of dollars in assistance plus air pollution credits that would absolve the plant from further pollution-control expenditures. Arguing that the company had broken a contract with the state, Governor Thompson threatened to sue Chrysler for $100 million if the company proceeded with its plans to close the plant.

The idea of suing a major corporation did not sit well with Wisconsin business leaders, however. They argued that such a suit would be bad for the state's business climate, and in the end the governor dropped the idea.

Although the threat of the suit did not prevent the plant closing, it may have increased the pressure on Chrysler to negotiate a settlement with the unions. This settlement provided for two years of health benefits and severance payments of $100 per week for two years. When put to a vote, the settlement was approved by 80 percent of the union members.[44]

◇ ISSUES IN THE SEARCH FOR ECONOMIC DEVELOPMENT

High Technology and the Quest for Its Holy Grail

In contrast to the decline of heavy industries (such as automobiles and steel) in the Midwest during the 1970s and early 1980s, there was a boom in high-technology industries, such as computer hardware, computer peripheral equipment, computer software applications, medical technology, and biotechnology. California's Silicon Valley and Boston's Route 128 symbolized this new boom as an un precedented number of high-technology companies were created and expanded in those two areas. Certain other areas, such as Austin, Texas, and Research Triangle, North Carolina, did almost as well. These places became the models that other communities tried to emulate. Why not use economic development packages such as those just discussed to create high-technology industrial parks? The logic of the argument was compelling. The economic development tools existed, and high-technology industry seemed to be much more insulated from foreign competition than were basic industries. The Japanese, Brazilians, and Koreans might be able to manufacture better automobiles more cheaply than could Detroit, but they were years behind the United States in high-technology research. So compelling was the argument for high tech that most states began to try to stimulate as much high tech as they could. Just as the computer age has spawned a new generation of computer wizards seeking to design this season's advanced computer, it has also created a new generation of community leaders seeking to turn their communities into next season's version of Silicon Valley.

But the quest for high technology is no more likely to produce economic salvation today than the quest for the Holy Grail produced salvation during the Middle Ages. There are two reasons for this. First, high technology in fact is no more immune to foreign competition and recession than is basic industry. Silicon Valley and Boston's Route 128, for example, suffered badly in the economic environment of the early 1990s, due in no small measure to a slowdown in global demand for computers as well as foreign competition in microchips and other computer products.

The second reason is that few communities have the combination of characteristics that facilitated the concentration of high-technology companies in places such as Silicon Valley, Boston, and Austin, Texas. Competitive industries are often located in small geographic clusters,[45] and the concentration of computer technology in places such as Silicon Valley, Boston, and Austin, Texas was no accident. These places all were located near major research universities. There already existed numerous high-technology industries that could supply the materials needed by the new and expanding high-tech firms. And the areas had a sophisticated workforce capable of making high-technology research productive and profitable. In short, some communities are more blessed than others.

If there is no future in basic industrial manufacturing, and if high technology is not in the future for most communities, then what activities can provide the growth that community leaders desire? The answer to this question, according to John Mollenkopf, is government jobs, third-sector institutions (for example, hospitals, universities, foundation headquarters), and advanced corporate services (such as legal work, accounting, computing, advertising, insurance, and investment banking).[46] The expansion of advanced corporate services has been especially important because cities with many such services become very attractive sites for corporate headquarters.

Mollenkopf argues that three types of cities are emerging today. First are the old, industrial cities, like Gary, Indiana, and Youngstown, Ohio. Despite dramatic changes in the national economy that have seen the industrial manufacturing sector decline relative to the service sector, these old cities have clung to their industrial economic bases. Gary and Youngstown are especially good examples because their basic industry (steel manufacturing) is heavily dependent on the fortunes of the automobile industry. As that industry suffered major setbacks in the 1970s and early 1980s, Gary, Youngstown, and many other old, industrial cities were economically shattered, although some industrial cities prospered during the late 1980s' resurgence of manufacturing.

In an entirely different situation are the newer service and administrative centers of the Southwest. Cities such as Phoenix and San Diego have attracted administrative and service corporations and high-technology industries that weathered the economic storms of the 1970s better than did the old, basic industries of the Midwest.

Finally, contends Mollenkopf, a third type of city has transformed its economy from old industry to banking and other advanced corporate services. Typical cities in this category are New York, Chicago, Philadelphia, Boston, and San Francisco. Although all have suffered significant population declines, they have maintained themselves as important locales for corporate headquarters and service-sector activities.

Counterproductive Competition

Although states have been trying to move away from the traditional competitive tactic of recruiting businesses from each other, they still hold expensive bidding wars to attract large installations. In 1991, for example, Indiana put up a $300 million package to win the bid for a United Airlines maintenance center. And in 1992, Minnesota pledged a package of $838 million to Northwest Airlines to get that company's maintenance facility.[47] At some point, these packages become counterproductive. If states such as Indiana and Minnesota in fact control hundreds of millions of dollars, there are probably more effective ways of stimulating economic growth than investing it all in a single site for a single company.

◇ SOCIAL CONFLICT AND THE COMPETITION FOR ECONOMIC DEVELOPMENT

Without doubt economic growth is essential for the nation to resolve its social conflicts. If growth rates are too slow or if economic growth turns negative, the competition intensifies between social groups to get their share of a relatively diminishing economic pie. If growth rates are dynamic, however, and inflation is held in check, there are more jobs for most people, and there is greater potential for the nation's many social groups to prosper together. To use the old rising tide metaphor, a rising tide lifts all the boats, and a growing economy helps everybody, or at least nearly everybody.

The problem, however, is that the use of government resources to promote economic development is not a neutral process. Because it helps some sets of interests and harms others, it is very important to the issues of social conflict that have concerned us throughout this book. This occurs in at least three ways.

First, despite the infusion of new money into community redevelopment projects, the economic benefits for the poor and minorities have been disappointing. As indicated earlier, central cities have experienced devastating losses in the number of jobs over the past two decades. Even in the sunbelt, where cities are still growing, population increases may have outpaced job increases, and most of the growth occurs on the expanding edge of the metropolis, not in the low-income residential neighborhoods.

Second, part of the reason for the lack of improvement in the cities' economies must be attributed to the biases inherent in the redevelopment process itself. One of the most commonly used redevelopment tools, the industrial development revenue bond (IDRB), for example, does not appear to be utilized to stimulate economically depressed regions, even though the rationale offered in the legislation establishing it usually names that as a prime objective. To examine how extensively IDRBs were aimed at depressed locations, Thomas A. Pascarella and Richard D. Raymond sought to see if high-unemployment areas in Ohio used IDRBs more than low-unemployment areas. They found no relationship.[48] IDRBs are now used in forty-seven states, and they are so popular they compose 70 percent of all municipal bond issues, whereas in 1970 they composed only 33 percent.[49] The most frequent use of IDRBs has been for the installation of pollution-control equipment, for the construction of hospitals, and for the construction of publicly subsidized housing. They also are often used to finance fast-food franchises, discount-store locations, and similar commercial facilities that have little developmental power. In short, the IDRB as often used has done little to generate permanent, well-paying jobs in poverty-stricken neighborhoods. In part because of these disappointments, Congress in 1986 limited the further issuance of IDRBs.

There are limits to what a city can raise money for, Paul Peterson has argued.[50] In Peterson's view, a city that tries to raise too much money for redistributive services for needy residents will drive out its middle-income residents to the less redistributive-oriented suburbs. Cities that focus on raising money for economic development are on a much sounder footing, according to Peterson.

Whether Peterson's view is accurate or not is impossible to prove. But most cities engaged in the redevelopment game today act as though it is accurate. That is, the most praised and successful redevelopment focused on economic activities in the mainstream of the nation's economy—primarily providing support and office space for service industries and retail commerce. Much also went into retaining or attracting manufacturing facilities and was especially helpful to industrializing efforts in the South and Southwest over the past decades. Urban redevelopment activities seem to be reinforcing the polarization of cities between the upper-middle class and the low-income classes while driving out the middle-income groups. Much public money has been spent supporting downtown development and gentrification projects. With the aid of public funds, many cities greatly overbuilt their hotel-room and office space capacity and were left with high vacancy rates when the commercial real estate market unraveled in the 1990s. In contrast to the billions of dollars that were thrown into the commercial real estate market and lost, no one has yet found the formula that would provide enough economic opportunities to make a permanent dent in the ranks of the urban poor. Small, owner-run retail establishments, which in the past assured the city of a substantial middle-class population, are squeezed out.

People find it very difficult to evaluate much of the urban redevelopment and gentrification activities of the past decade. Remembering the seedy and run-down appearance of many big-city downtown areas two decades ago, comparing them to the elaborate redevelopments in many of these same cities today, it is hard to say that the cities should not have initiated most of these projects. At the same time, however, many central-city residential neighborhoods have had trouble holding their own as their former middle-class occupants moved to the suburbs, and today they are increasingly occupied by people subsisting on marginal incomes. Many cities are moving toward a bipolar status, as George Sternlieb and James Hughes expressed it,[51] and urban redevelopment activities have not slowed that trend down—they may even have hastened it.

Accompanying these biases in the economic development process has been an abrogation of what Bennett Harrison and Barry Bluestone call the basic "social contract" that existed in America from about 1945 to the early 1970s.[52] Under this social contract, American business was assured of government policies to maintain national economic conditions conducive to corporate profitability. Business in turn agreed to cooperate with labor unions and support general overall improvements in living standards. By the late 1970s, however, inflation was squeezing corporate profits, foreign competition was intensifying, U.S. worker productivity was declining, and American business bailed out of the tacit social contract it had agreed to for a generation. By promoting economic development policies that exacerbate the bipolar city, that promote downtown redevelopment while neighborhoods continue declining, state and community leaders have in many cases contributed to the abrogation of the implied social contract.

SUMMARY

1. States and communities are today buffeted by dramatic changes in the national economy. Among the most important of these are (1) the transformation from an industrial to a postindustrial economy, (2) the intensification of foreign economic competition, and (3) the declining size of the middle-income groups in comparison to the upper-middle and lower-income groups.

2. To cope with these changes, states and communities have turned increasingly in the past decade to economic development strategies. These strategies include (1) public relations campaigns to attract tourists and industry, (2) promotion of a favorable business climate, (3) creation of business-growth incentives, and (4) the facilitation of community development. The most common community development approaches are tax abatements, the use of federal seed-money programs, industrial development revenue bonds, tax-increment financing, venture capital, and seeking foreign investment.

3. In assessing economic development strategies it is important to consider the negative consequences of these approaches as well as the positive ones.

4. To combat the out-migration of businesses, state and local governments have used plant closing legislation, strategies to facilitate the purchase of plants by the local communities, and the threat of legal action against firms that move out after receiving local subsidies.
5. Major issues in the search for economic development include questions over the quest for high-technology industries as a salvation to local economic problems, what to do about the competition that arises from variations among regional economies, and biases in the fight for economic development.
6. Although economic growth is essential to the task of alleviating the nation's social divisions, it is difficult to show that state economic development policies of the last two decades have contributed significantly to this goal.

KEY TERMS

Business climate   A term used by the business community to refer to the receptivity of a state to the business community. Although different ways of assessing the business climate exist, the business community usually prefers a business climate characterized by low taxes, low public expenditures, and limited state regulation.

Employee stock ownership plan   Also called **ESOP**. A plan to aid workers to find financing to take ownership of failing companies. Permits workers, unions, and their pension funds to buy stock in the company.

Industrial Development Revenue Bond   A tax-exempt municipal bond that a city sells to enable a local business or development project to obtain financing at below-market interest rates.

Postindustrial economy   The economy of contemporary America, which is increasingly being based on the provision of services rather than on industrial production.

Right-to-work law   Legislation that prohibits the union shop.

Tax abatement   The forgiving of local property taxes for a firm that dramatically expands a facility.

Tax-increment financing   A local development financing process under which the increases in property-tax revenue from a development project are reserved for a number of years to pay off the local government's subsidies or bonds issued for the project.

Urban enterprise zone   A blighted urban neighborhood that is designated as an enterprise zone where safety, health, and environmental restrictions would be eased and where companies would be offered generous incentives for locating facilities there.

Venture capital   Investment capital targeted for small start-up firms that have trouble raising investment funds through more conventional means.

REFERENCES

1. Between employment peaks from the late 1970s to 1984, eight northern Minnesota mining towns lost 7,340 jobs, a drop of 49 percent. *Minneapolis Tribune*, January 22, 1984, p. 8-A. On Wyoming boom towns, see *The New York Times*, March 12, 1985, p. 16. On Houston, see Robert H. Bork, Jr., "On the Waterfront: The Port of Houston," *Forbes*, December 17, 1984, pp. 108–116. Also see *The New York Times*, October 22, 1985, p. 1.
2. See John Kenneth Galbraith, *The New Industrial State* (Boston: Houghton Mifflin, 1967); and Daniel Bell, *The Coming of Post-industrial Society* (New York: Basic Books, 1973).

3. See Robert J. Samuelson, "Manufacturing Renaissance?" *Newsweek*, November 17, 1986, p. 72.

4. See especially Lester C. Thurow, "The Disappearance of the Middle Class," *The New York Times*, February 5, 1984, p. F-3. Thurow asserts that the percentage of people earning between 75 and 125 percent of the median income dropped from 28.2 percent in 1967 to 23.7 percent in 1982. At the same time there was an increase in both the percentage of people earning more than that level and the percentage earning less than that.

5. The argument against a shrinking middle class is well articulated by Marvin H. Kosters and Murray N. Ross, "A Shrinking Middle Class," *Public Interest* no. 90 (Winter 1988): 3–27.

6. Frank Levy, *Dollars and Dreams: The Changing American Income Distribution* (New York: Norton, 1988).

7. Robert B. Reich, "Toward a New Social Compact: The Role of Business," a speech to the National Alliance of Business. Dallas, Texas. September 27, 1994.

8. Roy Bahl, *The Impact of Local Tax Policy on Urban Economic Development* (Washington, D.C.: U.S. Department of Commerce; Economic Development Administration; Urban Consortium Information Bulletin, September 1980), p. 15.

9. Robert W. Schmenner, *Making Business Location Decisions* (Englewood Cliffs, N.J.: Prentice-Hall, 1982), pp. 50–51.

10. Bernard L. Weinstein and Harold T. Gross, "What Counts in the Race for Development," *State Legislatures* 14, no. 5 (May–June 1988): 22–24.

11. David L. Birch, *The Job Generation Process* (Cambridge, Mass.: M.I.T. Program on Neighborhoods and Regional Change, 1979), p. 21.

12. Dan Pilcher, "The Third Wave of Economic Development," *State Legislatures* 17, no. 11 (November 1991): 34–37. Pilcher describes recruiting businesses from other states as the first wave of development policy from the 1930s to the 1970s. The second wave, during the 1970s and 1980s, focused on developing local business incentives. A third wave in the 1990s focuses on long-term investments in education, workforce training, and public–private cooperation. Also see *The New York Times*, November 25, 1992, p. 1.

13. Peter Eisinger, *The Rise of the Entrepreneurial State* (Madison: University of Wisconsin Press, 1988), p. 9.

14. Delysa Burnier, "State Economic Development Policy: A Decade of Activity," *Public Administration Review* 51, no. 2 (March–April 1991): 171.

15. Robert Mier and Scott E. Gelzer, "State Enterprise Zones: The New Frontier?" *Urban Affairs Quarterly* 18, no. 1 (September 1982): 39–52.

16. William Fulton and Morris Newman, "The Strange Career of Enterprise Zones," *Governing* (March 1994): 32–34.

17. Ibid.

18. Bahl, *The Impact of Local Tax Policy*, pp. 8–9.

19. Ibid.

20. *Congressional Quarterly Weekly Report*, October 4, 1986, p. 2354.

21. Marianne C. Clarke, *Revitalizing State Economies* (Washington, D.C.: National Governors Association, 1986), pp. 5, 7, 19, 81–82.

22. Jane Carroll, "Economic Development Through Venture Capital," *State Legislatures* 11, no. 3 (March 1985): 24–25.

23. Margery Marzahn Ambrosius, "The Changing Nature of State Economic Development Policymaking," a paper presented to the Midwest Political Science Association. Chicago, Ill., April 1992.

24. *The New York Times,* June 23, 1986, pp. 1, 9.
25. See *The New York Times,* March 25, 1985, p. D-4.
26. Carol Steinbach and Neal R. Peirce, "Cities Are Setting Their Sights on International Trade and Investment," *National Journal,* April 28, 1984, pp. 818–822.
27. Richard Thomas Cupitt and Margaret Reid, "State Government International Business Promotion Programs and State Export of Manufacturers," *State and Local Government Review* 23, no. 3 (Fall 1991): 131.
28. David Laslo, "Convention Centers and the Urban Political Economy: The Case of St. Louis' Convention Center Expansion." A paper presented to the Midwest Political Science Association. Chicago, Ill., April 1996, p. 2.
29. Ibid., p. 14. The St. Louis population dropped by more than half from 856,000 in 1950 to 397,000 in 1990. During the same period, the number of jobs in the city dropped by 40 percent.
30. Carla Nielson, "Government at Bat," *State Government News* (June 1994): 6–10.
31. Timothy Krebs and Michael H. Walsh, "Mayors and Sports Franchises: The Electoral Consequences of Losing a Team." A paper presented to the Midwest Political Science Association. Chicago, Ill., April 1994. The authors identified twenty-six instances of cities losing a major league franchise from 1950 to 1990. In only seven of those cases did an incumbent mayor lose a re-election bid after the loss. In eight cases, the mayor's percent of the vote actually *increased* in the election following the loss of a team.
32. *St. Paul Pioneer Press,* March 13, 1983, p. A-11.
33. H. Brinton Milward and Heidi Hosbach Newman, "State Incentive Packages and the Industrial Location Decision," *The Politics of Industrial Recruitment,* Ernest J. Yanarella and William C. Green, eds. (New York: Greenwood Press, 1989), Tables 4–5.
34. Charles Mahtesian, "Romancing the Smokestack," *Governing* (November 1994): 36–40, Peter Behr, "Strategic Job Creation—or a Handout?" *Washington Post National Weekly,* August 28–September 3, 1995, p. 32.
35. Susan B. Hansen, "State Perspectives on Economic Development: Priorities and Outcomes," a paper presented at the 1986 meeting of the Midwest Political Science Association, Chicago, April 1986.
36. John Carroll, Mark Hyde, and William Hudson, "Economic Development Policy: Why Rhode Islanders Reject the Greenhouse Concept," *State Government* 58, no. 3 (Fall 1985): 110–112.
37. Lester Thurow, *The Zero Sum Society: Distribution and Possibilities for Economic Change* (New York: Penguin Books, 1980).
38. See especially Barry Bluestone and Bennett Harrison, *The Deindustrialization of America* (New York: Basic Books, 1982), pp. 8, 35, 63–66, 86–92.
39. Thomas J. Leary, "Deindustrialization, Plant Closing Laws, and the States," *State Government* 58, no. 3 (Fall 1985): 113–118; *The New York Times,* July 12, 1984, p. 7.
40. David Corn, "Dreams Gone to Rust: The Monongahela Valley Mourns for Steel," *Harper's* 273, no. 1636 (September 1986): 56–64.
41. John Portz, "WARN and the States: Implementation of the Federal Plant Closing Law," a paper presented at the 1992 meeting of the Midwest Political Science Association, Chicago, April 1992.
42. Bruce Nissen, "Union Battles Against Plant Closings: Case Study Evidence and Policy Implications," *Policy Studies Journal* 18, no. 2 (Winter 1989–1990): 382–395.
43. Terry F. Buss and F. Stevens Redburn, "Religious Leaders as Policy Advocates: The Youngstown Steel Mill Closing," *Policy Studies Journal* 11, no. 4 (June 1983): 640–647.

44. Thomas S. Moore and Gregory D. Squires, "Two Tales of a City: Economic Restructuring and Uneven Economic Development in a Former Company Town," *Journal of Urban Affairs* 13, no. 2 (1991): 159–173.

45. See Michael Porter, *The Competitive Advantage of Nations* (New York: The Free Press, 1990).

46. John H. Mollenkopf, *The Contested City* (Princeton, N.J.: Princeton University Press, 1983), pp. 31–36.

47. *Newsweek,* February 17, 1992, pp. 40–41. Financial problems forced the company to cancel the facility, so Minnesota's actual costs turned out to be substantially less than the $838 million pledged.

48. Thomas A. Pascarella and Richard D. Raymond, "Buying Bonds for Business: An Evaluation of the Industrial Revenue Bond Program," *Urban Affairs Quarterly* 18, no. 1 (September 1982): 73–89.

49. John E. Peterson, "The Municipal Bond Market: Recent Changes and Future Prospects," in *Financing State and Local Governments in the 1980s: Issues and Trends,* Norman Walzer and David L. Chicoine, eds. (Cambridge, Mass.: Oelgeschlager, Gunn & Hain, Publ., 1981), Ch. 7.

50. Paul E. Peterson, *City Limits* (Chicago: University of Chicago Press, 1981).

51. George Sternlieb and James W. Hughes, "The Uncertain Future of the Central City," *Urban Affairs Quarterly* 18, no. 4 (June 1983): 455–572.

52. Bennett Harrison and Barry Bluestone, *The Great U-Turn: Corporate Restructuring and the Polarizing of America* (New York: Basic Books, 1988).

CAREER PROSPECTS IN STATE AND LOCAL GOVERNMENT

What kind of career can you build for yourself in state and local government? Virtually any that you are likely to think of, if you wish to work in the public sector. From a stock clerk in a government purchasing office to a physician in a public hospital, more than 15 million state and local government employees work at nearly as many varied tasks as do employees in the private sector. To give you a better idea of state and local employment possibilities, we have outlined here several career categories in state and local politics. Where the data exists, estimates are given on employment outlooks through the 1990s, the type of work involved, and the educational and other requirements for the position. Following this list is a list of related occupations and career areas that are not normally thought of as public-sector occupations, even though many jobs in these areas are found in the public sector as well as the private sector. Unless otherwise noted, all data on salaries and employment opportunities are taken from the *Occupational Outlook Handbook: 1996–97* (Washington, D.C.: Bureau of Labor Statistics, 1996).

One useful way to test whether you might like a particular job is to take an internship in the area. This will enable you to gain college credit while exploring a career possibility.

◇ ADMINISTRATOR
(Chapters 7, 8, 11–17)

The term *administrator* refers to the highest level of permanent employee below the level of politically appointed executives. Administrators seek to ensure that all parts of their agency work together and carry out the policies set by elected or appointed political leaders. Although some agency administrators are brought in from outside sources, many work up through the agency ranks. Most administrators have training in a related professional occupation (engineering, for example, in the Transportation Department; social work in the Welfare Department). Increasingly, administrators bolster their professional experience by acquiring a master's degree in public administration. Salaries and benefits tend to be fairly generous, especially in large agencies. The position of administrator is not entry level. Opportunities for promotion to the administrative level will be limited by the currently slow growth rates of government and the existence of large numbers of managerial personnel competing for administrative jobs. Incomes vary widely by region and type of agency. City managers averaged $65,750 in 1994, while public elementary school principals averaged $58,600.

◇ BUDGET ANALYST

(Chapters 7, 8, 10–17)

Most large units of government have a budget specialist who helps prepare budget documents, sometimes controls the release of budgeted funds, and usually is one of the major financial advisers in the particular governmental unit. There were about 66,000 budget analysts in 1994—one-third of them in the public sector. Because analysts control agency spending, they find themselves in the thick of many political battles. Qualifications include a college degree and substantial training in, or at least understanding of, accounting practices. A master's degree in public administration, business, or accounting is desirable. Starting incomes were about $27,000 in 1993.

◇ CORRECTIONS OFFICER

(Chapter 12)

Corrections officers work as guards in jails, prisons, and other correctional facilities. The minimum education requirement is a high school diploma, although some college course work in criminology, psychology, and sociology is increasingly required. There were 310,000 corrections officers in 1994, most of them working for the public rather than the private sector. If the incarcerated population continues to rise as it has in recent decades, employment prospects in the corrections field will be expected to grow much faster than the average. Starting pay for corrections officers at the state level averaged $19,100 in 1994, but pay varies widely from region to region.

◇ COURT ADMINISTRATOR

(Chapter 12)

The increasing complexity of running the nation's courts has given rise to a relatively new position in public administration, that of court administrator. This professional organizes the calendar for courts, hires the personnel, and oversees the day-to-day administrative details of the court's operations. Although legal training is not a prerequisite, many court administrators are trained as lawyers before moving into administration. If judicial case-loads continue to rise as they have in recent decades and if the judicial reform movement keeps pressing for modernizing and professionalizing state and local court systems, it seems likely that the demand for court administrators will continue to grow.

◇ ECONOMIC DEVELOPER

(Chapter 17)

So intensive is the demand for people to spearhead and oversee economic development projects that many communities have begun hiring Certified Industrial and Economic Developers (CID/CED). Economic developers need an understanding of their local communities as well as training and experience in development financing tools, zoning processes, accounting, and marketing. Excellent communications skills are necessary. Certification for the CID/CED is handled by the American Economic Development Council, which demands five years of work experience in economic development plus appropriate course work.

Through 1986, more than 400 people held a CID/CED certification; about 15 percent of them were women. Employment is found throughout the country in a variety of private and public institutions such as banks, chambers of commerce, port authorities, and state government agencies. Because of the widespread perceived need for communities to do whatever is feasible and reasonable to attract industry, the demand for economic developers seems likely to continue growing over the near future. For more information, write: American Economic Development Council, Schiller Park, IL 60176.

◇ FIRE FIGHTER

Minimum educational qualification for a fire fighter is usually a high school diploma. Most fire fighting jobs are found at the municipal level. Employment tends to be stable, layoffs are infrequent, and fringe benefits are generous, especially in unionized states. The average income was $32,760 in 1994. Employment opportunities are expected to grow at a below average rate.

◇ FORESTER AND CONSERVATION SCIENTIST

(Chapter 16)

An important area of environmental protection involves forest management and conservation in order to protect the nation's forests, soils, and wildlife. Training qualifications usually include at least a bachelor's degree in forestry or range sciences. Employment opportunities are expected to grow as fast as the average.

There are about 40,000 such jobs today, about one-fifth of which are in state government, half in the federal government, and the balance in the private sector. The beginning federal government salary for foresters, range managers, and soil conservationists in 1995 was $21,100.

◇ HEALTH SERVICES MANAGER

(Chapter 13)

Health services managers are needed to run hospitals, nursing homes, health maintenance organizations, rehabilitation centers, urgent-care facilities, and the offices of doctors, dentists, and chiropractors. Because of the growing complexity of medical and health care provisions professional managers have been increasingly taking the responsibility for management of health care facilities out of the hands of medical personnel such as physicians and nurses, whose specialty is medical and health care treatment rather than management. Health services personnel range from executive directors in charge of an institution to internal managers to specialized staff. There were over 257,000 health care professionals employed in 1990, and those jobs are growing at a better-than-average rate.

Responsibilities of health care managers include budgeting, personnel administration, information management, marketing, strategic planning, systems analysis, and labor relations. Managers need a knowledge of management principles and most likely hold a master's degree in health administration (MHA), in business administration (MBA), or public administration (MPA) with a health services concentration. Salaries in 1994 ranged from $47,400 for nursing home CEOs to $165,000 for hospital CEOs.

◇ INSPECTOR, LICENSOR, AND COMPLIANCE OFFICER

(Chapters 7, 11–13, 16, 17)

A great many people are employed at all levels of government to carry out a variety of inspection, licensing, regulatory, and compliance functions, including health inspectors, consumer safety inspectors, food inspectors, environmental health inspectors, motor vehicle inspectors, traffic inspectors, occupational safety and health inspectors, wage-hour compliance inspectors, equal opportunity representatives, and building inspectors. About 157,000 inspectors and compliance officers were employed in 1994, about 34 percent of them at the state level, 18 percent at the local level, and the balance at the federal level or in private industry. Training and job requirements vary greatly because of the great diversity of functions. Employment growth is expected to be faster than average. Average earnings ranged from $31,280 for food inspectors to $62,970 for aviation safety inspectors in 1994.

◇ LEGAL ASSISTANT OR PARALEGAL
(Chapters 11, 12)

These professionals do much background investigatory work for the preparation of cases. They work in a variety of settings ranging from private law firms to community legal services agencies, where they help give legal aid to people of limited means. There were almost 90,000 paralegals in 1990. Job growth is expected to be much faster than average through the 1990s. Although earnings vary widely, the average salary was $31,700 in 1993.

◇ LEGISLATIVE AIDE
(Chapter 9)

Every legislature hires people to do a variety of specialized and professional tasks, ranging from policy research to putting into legal form the ideas for bills that legislators present. Some of these positions require legal training, some computer training, and others require training in accounting. For policy analysts, a master's degree in policy analysis, public affairs, or public administration is highly desirable. These analysts may work for committees, for a Democratic or Republican caucus, or even for a specific legislator. Beginning salaries vary greatly from state to state. Due to the increasing complexity of government in the United States, it seems likely that the number of legislative aide positions will continue to grow. One convenient way to test whether you would like to work as a legislative aide is to do an internship with your legislator or participate in some committee of the legislature.

◇ LIBRARIAN
(Chapters 11, 14)

As you inevitably discover when you begin working on your term papers, librarians play an extremely valuable role in helping to find resource materials that address important issues in our complicated society. There were about 149,000 librarians in 1990, with most of them working in the public sector. A Master of Library Science degree is required for most professional-level librarians. These jobs are expected to grow more slowly than average. Starting salaries for persons with a master's in library science averaged about $28,300 in 1994.

◇ LOBBYIST
(Chapters 3, 4, 5, 7–17)

Although no state has a lobbying industry as large as the one that deals with the federal government, lobbying at the state and local levels is important and most likely will continue to be so. There will be a continuing need for people who can effectively represent clients before state legislatures, city councils, and regulatory agencies. Lobbyists represent every conceivable sector of society, from welfare recipients to multinational corporations. Some lobbyists work for large organizations; others are self-employed persons who hire themselves out to clients. Effective lobbying requires excellent communications and interpersonal skills, intimate knowledge of the government agencies being lobbied, and a willingness to work long hours. Although there are no formal requirements for becoming a lobbyist, lawyers and former legislators have some distinct advantages over other people.

◇ MEDIATOR AND ARBITRATOR
(Chapters 5, 7, 11)

When labor–management negotiations reach an impasse, mediators are often hired to meet with each side, listen to their demands, and make suggestions that facilitate a compromise to which both can agree. Arbitrators do comparable kinds of work, but, unlike mediators, they are given the power to impose a solution on the two parties if a mediated agreement cannot be reached. Most states have a department of mediation or arbitration services that keeps a list of persons qualified to serve as mediators or arbitrators in contract disputes. Mediators usually have considerable experience in contract negotiations or a professional degree in personnel management or industrial relations. Arbitrators usually have a law degree.

◇ PERSONNEL AND LABOR RELATIONS
(Chapters 7, 11)

With more than 15 million employees, many of them unionized, state and local governments rely heavily on personnel officers and labor relations specialists. Personnel officers manage the procedures for hiring, promotion, and dismissal. Labor relations specialists help manage relations between government agencies and the collective bargaining agents of their employees. Related jobs include compensation analysts, employee-benefits managers, and training specialists. The goal behind these positions is to provide a competent and productive work force. Because of the diversity of these jobs, training and other requirements vary widely. For entry-level positions, undergraduate course work in personnel or labor relations is helpful, as is a degree or certificate in the field. In both the public and private sectors there were about 456,000 positions in 1990. Little growth is expected in public sector-personnel positions through the 1990s, but above average growth is expected in the private sector. Starting salaries in the public sector averaged above $17,000 in 1990, but there is considerable room for salary growth.

◇ POLICE WORK
(Chapters 7, 11, 12)

Police-related occupations include police officers, state highway patrols, detectives, and investigators. The ability to handle people is a prime prerequisite for these jobs. Qualifications include excellent physical condition and the ability to pass competitive written examinations. Although small communities require only a high school diploma for police officers, some college education and often a college degree is increasingly required in metropolitan areas. About 682,000 people worked in police occupations in 1994. Employment opportunities are expected to grow at an average rate. Salaries vary widely depending on the state and on the size of the community. The average salary for police officers was $34,000 in 1994.

◇ PUBLIC EDUCATION EMPLOYMENT
(Chapter 14)

The major professional occupations in public education are teachers, principals, and central-office administrators (i.e., superintendents, data processors, purchasing officers, and curriculum development specialists). There were about 393,000 education administrators in 1994 and 2.9 million teachers. These professionals bear the primary educational responsibility for preparing the next generation of American citizens to live in an increasingly competitive and complex world. To work effectively, these professionals need excellent communication and interpersonal skills.

Requirements for teaching positions include teacher certification and undergraduate course work in education. Principals, superintendents, and other high-level administrators also need several years' teaching experience, graduate training in school administration, and certification. Job outlook and salaries vary widely by state and region. Jobs for teachers are expected to have above-average growth. The average teacher's salary in 1995 was $36,900.

◇ PUBLIC RELATIONS SPECIALIST
(Chapters 5–7, 9–12)

Most large organizations, public or private, use public relations tactics to promote their image and maintain positive relations with the public. In government agencies, public relations is often the responsibility of offices of public information. These offices produce news releases, pamphlets, multimedia shows, and other materials designed to further the goals of their agencies. Major employment qualifications usually consist of a college degree plus public relations experience. A bachelor's or master's degree in journalism or public relations is helpful. Public relations professionals need highly developed writing and speaking skills as well as the ability to work with people. There were about 107,000 public relations jobs in 1994, a sizable percentage of them in the public sector. Employment opportunities are expected to grow more slowly than average. The average salary in 1994 was $23,000.

◇ RECREATION WORKER

(Chapter 11)

These workers organize leisure and recreational activities in a wide variety of settings, ranging from city recreation departments to wilderness areas. Although one can enter the field with less than a bachelor's degree, a college degree and some specialized training are usually required to move up to supervisory and managerial positions. There were 222,000 recreation workers in 1994, with about half of them in the public sector. Recreation worker jobs are expected to grow about at an average rate. While the median salary for all recreation workers is low (about $15,400 in 1994), those people in managerial and supervisory positions earn much more.

◇ SOCIAL WORKER

(Chapter 13)

Demand for social workers has been strong in recent decades because of several societal forces discussed in the text: the aging of the population; the existence of a large, impoverished subpopulation; the change of the population from predominantly rural to predominantly metropolitan; and the need to offer protection services for abused and neglected children, the handicapped, and the disabled. Effective social workers need a variety of important skills: communication skills, knowledge of principles of behavior, ability to work with people, and familiarity with relevant social legislation and administrative rules. The main training qualifications for social work are a bachelor's degree in the social sciences or social work (BSW) or, even more likely, a master's degree in social work (MSW).

There were about 557,000 social worker positions in 1994, with about 40 percent of them in state or local governments. Employment opportunities for social workers are expected to grow at a faster than average rate. Salaries vary widely from state to state and from the public to the private sector within states. The average MSW earned $30,000 in 1994.

◇ URBAN AND REGIONAL PLANNER

(Chapters 7, 8, 11, 15–17)

City planners, urban planners, and regional planners advise local and regional officials on decisions involving the growth and redevelopment of cities, suburbs, regions, metropolitan areas, and rural communities. Because planners are called on to make recommendations concerning land use, environmental issues, health issues, and economic development, planners must combine a broad knowledge of public issues with a technical ability to apply contemporary tools of statistical and policy analysis. Most planning jobs require a master's degree in urban or regional planning. Planners may also be certified by the American Institute of Certified Planners, a branch of the American Planning Association.

There were about 29,000 urban and regional planning positions in 1994. Employment opportunities for planners are expected to grow faster than average. Demand for them will obviously be greater in rapidly growing areas of the country, such as the South and Southwest, than in the more stable Northeast and Midwest. Median salaries for planners in 1994 were about $33,500 for those with less than five years of experience.

◇ RELATED OCCUPATIONS

The following occupations are not distinctly public service careers, since the majority of people working in them are employed in the private sector. Nevertheless, substantial numbers of these people also work in the public sector where their skills are needed.

Accountant and Auditor

These professionals prepare financial reports, analyze financial data, and provide the up-to-date financial data that governments need in order to make responsible decisions. Job requirements may include certification as a public accountant. Employment through the 1990s is expected to grow faster than average, and compensation can be very lucrative.

Lawyer

Given the complexity of life today, the large number of laws enacted by legislatures, and the even larger number of rules issued by regulatory and administrative agencies, lawyers continue to be employed widely by state and local governments in a variety of capacities. Minimum requirements are the LLB degree and in some instances passage of the state bar examination. Eighty percent of lawyers work in the private sector, and the majority of public-sector lawyers work at the local level. Lawyers also seem to have an edge working as lobbyists. And being a solo-practitioner lawyer is often considered a good starting place for a career in elective politics. Future employment demand for lawyers is difficult to gauge. There were about 735,000 lawyers in 1994. Because of the doubling in the number of law school graduates since 1970, some observers predict that the competition for law-related jobs will become increasingly keen. Other observers, however, predict that the demand for lawyers will continue to grow at an above-average rate. In 1994, beginning lawyers earned an average salary of $37,000.

Energy-Related Careers

If energy costs begin to rise in the 1990s, as many observers expect, there will be a need for educated people in many energy-related occupations. In the public sector, energy-related employment opportunities are likely to be found in federal agencies such as the Departments of Energy, Interior, Treasury, Commerce, Transportation, State, Agriculture, and Defense. State-level counterparts of some of these departments will also need energy-related workers.

Environment-Related Careers

Although the deregulation trends of the 1980s curbed spending for environmental protection, there is going to be no reduction in the need to protect the air, water, and atmosphere from further degradation. Accordingly, there will continue to be a need for people to serve in a variety of environmentally related occupations. Some of these include forester, range manager, recreationist, soil conservationist, soil scientist, wildlife conservationist, zoo keeper, landscape architect, urban planner, civil engineer, and biologist.

◇ GENERAL CONSIDERATIONS ON PUBLIC EMPLOYMENT PROSPECTS

Regional Considerations

Because job prospects are heavily influenced by population trends and business conditions, a person should be aware of these when planning a career. In general, it seems likely that professional-level jobs for college graduates will enjoy better growth in affluent areas rather than in poor areas and in fast-growing areas rather than in slow-growing areas. To give you an idea of where these conditions prevail, Table A-1 lists the 30 fastest growing metropolitan areas (1990–94). Column 1 shows the growth rate for each metropolitan area. Column 2 shows the median household income for the central city in each metropolitan area, and Column 3 shows the central city's poverty rate.

Table A-1   THE 30 FASTEST GROWING METROPOLITAN AREAS, 1990–1994

	Population Growth (1990–94)	Median Household Income (1989)	Percent of People in Poverty (1989)
Anchorage, AK	12.1%	43,946	7.1
Atlanta, GA	12.6	22,275	27.3
Austin, TX	13.9	25,414	17.9
Bakersfield, CA	11.8	32,154	15.0
Boise, ID	17.5	29,121	9.4
Brownsville, TX	15.2	15,890	43.9
Colorado Springs, CO	14.0	28,928	10.9
Daytona Beach, FL	10.3	18,631	22.5
Denver-Boulder, CO	10.6	25,106	17.1
El Paso, TX	12.4	23,460	25.3
Fort Pierce, FL	10.8	18,913	29.2
Fresno, CA	10.5	24,923	24.0
Brazoria, TX	10.3	34,418	10.4

Table A-1 *(continued)*

	Population Growth (1990–94)	Median Household Income (1989)	Percent of People in Poverty (1989)
Houston, TX	10.0	26,261	20.7
Kileen, TX	12.5	22,469	14.5
Las Vegas, NV	26.2	38,802	11.5
Riverside, CA	12.3	34,801	11.9
McAllen, TX	20.2	22,068	32.7
Melbourne, FL	11.2	25,893	12.8
Fort Lauderdale, FL	10.2	27,239	17.1
Orlando, FL	11.2	26,119	15.8
Phoenix, AZ	10.5	29,291	14.2
Portland, OR	10.5	25,592	14.5
Provo, UT	10.4	21,162	29.6
Raleigh, NC	12.4	32,451	11.8
Reno, NV	11.1	28,388	11.5
Bremerton, WA	16.2	22,610	18.1
Olympia, WA	16.1	27,785	13.0
Visalia, CA	10.0	29,463	17.6
West Palm Beach, FL	10.5	26,504	16.2
United States overall	4.7	28,906	12.8

As the table shows, the fastest growing areas are found exclusively in the South and the West. However, you do not want to migrate indiscriminately to the fastest-growing areas without thinking about the consequences. For example, Brownsville, Texas, and McAllen, Texas, are the sixth and second fastest growing areas, respectively, but they are also the first and second poorest areas. Unless some development is taking place that is not apparent on the surface, it seems unlikely that the their economies will be good hunting grounds for professional-level jobs. Of the 30 fastest growing metropolitan areas, 20 have median household incomes below the national average, and 21 have poverty rates above the national average.

◇ A SHORT BIBLIOGRAPHY FOR CAREER EXPLORATION

The Adams Jobs Almanac: 1994 (Holbrook, Mass.: Bob Adams, Inc., 1994).

Baxter, Neale, *Opportunities in State and Local Government Careers* (Lincolnwood, Ill.: NTC Publishing Group, 1993).

Cohn, Susan, *Green at Work* (Washington, D.C.: Island Press, 1992).

College Careers: Government and Political Science, Vocational Biographies (Sauk Centre, Minn., Vocational Biographies, Inc., 1991). With its handy sketches of specific people in public-related careers, this source book gives a nice introduction to what it might be like to work in a given career.

Farr, J. Michael, *America's Top Jobs for College Graduates* (Indianapolis, Ind.: JIST Works, Inc., 1994).

Fasulo, Michael and Paul Walker, *Careers in the Environment* (Lincolnwood, Ill.: VGM Career Horizons, 1995).

Krannich, Ronald L. and Caryl R. Krannich, *The Almanac of American Government Jobs and Careers* (Woodbridge, Va.: Impact Publications, 1990).

Krannich, Ronald L. and Caryl R. Krannich, *The Complete Guide to Public Employment* (Woodbridge, VA.: Impact Publications, 1991).

Krannich, Ronald L. and Caryl R. Krannich, *The Directory of Federal Jobs and Employers* (Manassas Park, Va.: Impact Publications, 1996).

Lauber, Daniel, *Government Job Finder,* 2nd ed. (Lanham, Md: National Book Network, 1994–95).

Lauber, Daniel, *Non-Profits Job Finder,* 3rd ed. (Lanham, Md: National Book Network, 1994).

Maze, Marilyn and Donald Mayal, *The Enchanced Guide for Occupational Exploration* (Indianapolis, Ind.: JIST Works, Inc., 1991).

Morgan, Dana and Robert Goldenkoff, *Federal Jobs: The Ultimate Guide,* 2nd ed. (New York: Macmillan General Reference, 1997).

Occupational Outlook Handbook: 1996–97 (Washington, D.C.: Bureau of Labor Statistics, 1996). This is an invaluable reference source for information on different occupations, the prospects for growth in the job area, and a feel for salary ranges.

Pitz, Mary Elizabeth, *Careers in Government* (Lincolnwood, Ill.: VGM Career Horizons, 1994).

Smith, Carter, *America's Fastest Growing Employers*, 2nd ed. (Holbrook, Mass.: Bob Adams, Inc., 1994).

Marcia P. Williams and Sue A. Cubbage, *The 1995 National Jobs Hotline Directory* (New York: McGraw-Hill, Inc., 1995).

NAME INDEX

Aaron, Henry J., 89n, 360n
Abbot, Carl, 181n
Abney, Glenn, 248, 263n, 264n
Abrams, 263n
Adamy, David, 320n
Adrian, Charles, 14n
Agger, Robert E., 208n
Aitkins, Burton, 320n
Albritton, Robert B., 15n
Alexander, Herbert E., 121n, 147n, 148n
Alexander, Lamar, 247, 382
Alger, Horato, 324, 357
Allen, Fred, 398
Alm, James, 362n
Ambrosius, Margery Marzahn, 470n
Ammons, David N., 179n
Anderson, James E., 361n
Anderson, Martin, 423n
Andrews, Edmund L, 88n
Anton, Thomas J., 290n
Armor, David J., 390n
Aronson, J. Richard, 89n
Arrington, Richard, 210n
Asbell, Bernard, 209n
Asbury, Herbert, 321n
Ashenfelter, Orley, 389n
Austin, James, 323n

Bachelor, Lynn, 180n, 193, 210n
Bachrach, Peter, 187, 208n
Bachrach, Walton H., 196
Bahl, Roy, 455, 470n
Baker, Gordon, 235n
Banfield, Edward C., 60n, 208n, 308n, 334, 359n, 369
Baratz, Joan C., 88n

Baratz, Morton S., 187, 208n
Barbash, Jack, 120n
Baum, Lawrence, 319n
Baxter, Neale, 483
Beck, Paul Allen, 148n
Becker, Gary, 311, 322n
Bell, Daniel, 469n
Bellush, Bernard, 119n
Bellush, Jewell, 119n, 210n
Belsky, Gary, 360n
Belton, Sharon Sayles, 199
Beneson, Robert, 521n
Bennett, William J., 368
Bent, Alan E., 322n
Berg, Larry, 320n
Berger, Jerry, 360n
Berlin, Gordon, 422n
Berman, Evan, 290n
Bernick, E. Lee, 264n
Bewar, Dianah, 446n
Beyle, Thad, 32n, 234n, 264n
Bibby, John F., 131, 148n
Birch, David, 470n
Bird, Rose, 299, 308
Bledwoe, Timothy, 210n
Block, Michael K., 323n
Bloom, Allan, 389n
Bluestone, Barry, 468, 471n, 472n
Boeckelman, Keith, 15n
Bosworth, Karl A., 289n
Botner, Stanley B., 290n, 291n
Bowers, James R., 234n
Bowman, Ann O'M., 15n, 447n
Boyd, Steven R., 263n
Boyd, W., 392n
Boyer, Ernest L., 391n

Boyte, Harry, 101, 119n
Bradley, Bill, 253
Bradley, Tom, 199
Brady, Henry F., 119n
Bratton, William, 323n
Brent, James, 320n
Brettler, Eileen, 291n
Brown, Jerry, 239, 267–268, 299, 438
Brown, Lyle C., 179n
Brown, Raymond, 423n
Brown, Robert D., 134, 149n
Brown, Willie, 133, 222, 232
Browne, William P., 121n
Browning, Robert X., 149n, 235n
Browning, Rufus P., 211
Bryce, James, 234n
Buck, A. E., 289n
Bullard, Angela, 289n
Bullard, Robert D., 447n
Bullock, Charles S., 389n, 390n
Bunch, Kenyon, 319n
Burke, Edmund, 219
Burnier, Delysa, 470n
Bush, George, 47, 204, 417
Buss, Terry F., 471n
Butler, Stuart, 359n

Caldeira, Gregory A., 149n
Calhoun, John C., 35
Calkins, Susannah E., 88n
Campbell, Angus, 118n
Carey, Hugh, 252
Carnegie, Andrew, 324
Carney, Eliza, 421n
Carroll, Jane, 470n
Carroll, John J., 32n, 471n
Carroll, Julian, 322n
Carter, Jimmy, 46, 239, 350–351, 361n
Casey, Gregory, 319n
Cashen, Henry C., 79n
Cassel, Carol A., 180n
Celis, William, 89n
Chamberlayne, Donald W., 236n
Chelf, Carl, 32n
Chicoine, David L., 472n
Chilton, Kenneth W., 421n
Cho, Yong Hyo, 235n
Christensen, Terry, 88n, 147n, 263n
Chubb, John E., 266n, 383, 392n
Cigler, Allen, 180n
Cigler, Beverly A., 179n

Cisneros, Henry, 194
Citrin, Jack, 88n
Clark, Terry N., 179n
Clarke, Marianne C., 470n
Clary, Bruce B., 447n
Clinton, Bill, 34, 239, 251, 348, 457
Clotfelter, Charles, 79n
Cloward, Richard, 142, 150n
Clucas, Richard, 236n
Cobb, William E., 322n
Cohn, Susan, 484
Coil, Ann, 423n
Combs, Michael, 320n
Conant, James, 290n
Conlan, Timothy J., 59n
Conway, M. Margaret, 119n
Cook, Philip, 79n
Corn, David, 471n
Corson, Ross, 392n
Corzine, John, 178n
Costello, Mary, 390n
Cotter, Cornelius P., 148n
Coward, Barbara E., 389n
Craft, Ralph, 421n
Crenson, Matthew, 209n, 211n
Criado, Ed, 325
Croker, Richard, 165
Cronin, Thomas E., 150n
Cropf, Robert A., 148n
Cubbage, Sue A., 484
Culver, John H., 121n, 150n, 319n
Cummins, Jackie, 448n
Cupitt, Richard Thomas, 471n
Curley, James Michael, 165, 194

D'Antonio, William V., 208n
D'Souza, Dinesh, 369, 389n
Dahl, Robert, 184–185, 188, 208n
Daley, Richard J., 132, 165–166
Daley, Richard J., Jr., 166–167
Danzo, Andrew, 446n
Darwin, Charles, 334
Davis, James Allan, 6, 93–94, 135, 373
de Lesseps, Suzanne, 323n
De Marco, Donald L., 211n
Dean, Gillian, 15n
Dearborn, Philip M., 60n
Debnam, Geoffrey, 209n
Demarath, Nicholas J., 413
Derge, David, 235n
Derthick, Martha, 60n

Dewey, John, 369
Didion, Joan, 211n
Digaetano, Alan, 210n
Dilger, Robert Jay, 263n
Dill, John C., 79n
Dilullo, John, 315, 323n
Dometrius, Nelson C., 263n, 264n
Domhoff, G. William, 209n
Dommel, Paul R., 60n
Donovan, Todd, 237n
Doolittle, Fred C., 60n
Dougan, W., 263n
Dow, Jay K., 121n
Downing, Rondal, 320n
Downs, Anthony, 96, 118n, 421n
Doyle, D., 392n
Doyle, William, 178n
Dran, Ellen B., 15n
Dresang, Dennis L., 289n
Drew, Charles R., 381
Dukakis, Michael, 246
Dunagin, Ralph, 84
Durenburger, David, 19
Dye, Thomas R., 60n, 119n, 121n, 137,
    147n, 359n, 360n

Edison, Thomas, 324
Edsell, Thomas B., 60n
Ehrenhalt, Alan, 210n
Eisinger, Peter K., 210n, 470n
Eismeier, Theodore, 266n
Elazar, Daniel, 7–11, 15n, 59n
Elkins, David, 90n
Ellickson, Robert C., 422
Elling, Richard, 235n, 289n
Emmert, Craig F., 310n
Endersby, James, 121n
Engler, John, 378
English, Arthur, 32n
Entman, Robert, 237n
Ericson, Joe E., 179n
Erie, Steven P., 180n
Erikson, Robert, 105, 119n, 137, 149n, 237n
Eulau, Heinz, 236n
Evers, Mark, 263n
Eysenck, H. J., 389n

Fainstein, Susan, 209n
Fairbanks, David, 155
Farley, John E., 422n
Farr, J. Michael, 484

Fasenfest, David, 209n
Fastnow, Chris, 238n
Fasula, Michael, 484
Feagin, Joe R., 389n
Fearing, Jerry, 54, 112, 312
Feeley, Jalcolm, 320n
Feigert, Frank B., 119n
Fenton, John, 15n, 236n
Ferguson, James E., 246
Ferman, Louis, 359n
Finney, Joan, 254
Fiorina, Morris P., 237n
Fitzpatrick, John S., 291n
Fleischman, Arnold, 181n
Flinn, Thomas A., 235n
Florio, James, 124, 253, 259, 378
Flynn, Raymond, 193
Foote, Dan, 349
Forer, Lois G., 343n
Form, William H., 208n
Foster, Douglas, 238n
Fowler, Edmund P., 179n
Francis, Wayne, 222, 236n
Franke, James L., 447n
Frederickson, George, 235n
Freeman, Linton C., 208n
Freeman, Patricia K., 235n
Frey, Fredrick W., 209n
Frieden, Bernard J., 424n
Friedman, Burton Dean, 389n
Friedman, Lawrence M., 32n
Friesema, H. Paul, 120n
Froman, Lewis A., 32n
Fuchs, Victor, 359n
Fulton, William, 470n
Fuquay, Robert F., 178n

Gaebler, Ted, 4, 8, 15n, 265n, 289n
Galbraith, John Kenneth, 469n
Galster, George C., 211n
Galvin, John T., 210n
Gann, Paul, 63
Garand, James C., 89n
Garcia, F.Chris, 203, 211n
Garreaux, Joel, 181n
Garrity, W. Arthur, 375
Garza, Rudolph O., de la, 203, 211n
Gates, Richard L., 423n
Gelman, Andrew, 235n
Gelzer, Scott E., 470n
Gerber, Elizabeth, 149n

Gerston, Larry N., 88n, 147n, 263n
Gianturco, Michael, 61n
Gibson, James L., 148n
Gingrich, Newt, 35, 36
Glasser, Mark L., 29, 33n
Glazer, Nathan, 423n
Gleason, Eugene J., 264n
Glick, Henry, 320n
Goertz, Margaret E., 89n
Gold, Steven D., 32n, 79n, 88n, 89n
Goldenkoff, Robert, 484
Goldrich, Daniel, 208n
Goldwater, Barry, 253
Goode, Wilson, 199, 210n
Goodland, John L., 391n
Goodsell, Charles T., 286, 290n, 291n
Goodwin, George, 237n
Gordon, Daniel M., 359n
Gordon, David, 322n, 389n
Gordon, Peter, 421n
Gosling, James J., 421n
Gottdiener, M., 209n
Graham, Barbara Luck, 320n
Grand, John, 446n
Grant, Daniel R., 180n
Gray, Virginia, 89n, 107, 114, 120n, 149n,
    236n, 264n
Green, Paul M., 180n, 211n
Green, Roy E., 179n
Greenberg, Pam, 79n
Greenstein, Fred I., 139, 150n, 179n
Gross, Harold T., 470n
Gruhl, John, 320n
Gueron, Judith M., 361n
Guinier, Lani, 236n
Gurwitt, Ron, 179n
Gurwitz, Aaron S., 61n
Guy, Mary E., 289n

Haber, Alan, 359n
Haddon, Michael, 238n
Hadley, Arthur T., 118n
Hadley, Charles D., 149n
Hagstrom, Jerry, 88n
Hague, Mary, 447n
Hall, Melinda Gann, 320n
Hamilton, Alexander, 37–38, 293
Hamilton, Howard, 139, 150n
Hamm, Keith E., 121n
Hansen, Susan Blackall, 89n, 180n, 461, 471n

Hansen, Karen, 237n
Hardy, Richard J., 60n
Harrigan, John J., 60n, 147n, 181n, 211n,
    447n
Harriman, Averell, 252
Harrington, Michael, 359n
Harris, Don, 256, 437
Harrison, Bennett, 468, 471n, 472n
Hartle, T., 392n
Hartman, Chester, 423n
Haskell, Elizabeth H., 447n
Hausknecht, Murray, 210n
Hawkins, Brett W., 180n
Hawkins, Gordon, 321n
Hawley, Willis D., 9
Hayden, Tom, 126
Hayes, Edward C., 291n
Hays, R. Allen, 417
Hays, Samuel P., 167, 180n
Hedlund, Ronald D., 148n, 220
Heiman, Michael, 447n
Henderson, Thomas A., 181n
Herblock, 397
Herrnstein, Richard J., 359n, 389n
Herzik, Eric B., 15n
Hevesi, Alan G., 265n
Hill, Gladwin, 150n
Hill, Kevin, 236n
Hill, Kim Quaile, 120n, 147n, 150n
Hill, Richard Child, 209n
Hinton–Andersson, Angela, 120n
Hirschman, Albert O., 100, 119n, 200, 211n
Hofferbert, Richard I., 149n
Hoffmann, Paul J., 149n
Hofstadter, Richard, 167, 180n
Holbrook, Thomas M., 131
Holbrook–Provow, Thomas M., 119n
Hoover, J. Edgar, 321n
Hopkins, Anne, 105, 120n
Houston, C. P., 46, 231
Howard, Christopher, 360n
Howell, Susan, 266n
Hoyer, Robert, 238n
Hrebenar, Ronald J., 107, 114, 120n, 121n
Hu, Teh–Wei, 360n
Huckshorn, Robert J., 148n
Hudson, William, 471n
Hughes, James W., 211n, 472n
Hunt, James, 383
Hunter, Floyd, 183–184, 188, 208n

Hunter, John E., 290n
Huntley, Robert J., 179n
Hunzeker, Donna, 291n
Hutchison, Tony, 263n
Huth, Ora, 446n
Hyde, Mark, 471n

Ianni, Francis A. J., 321n
Inhaber, Herbert, 447n

Jackson, Jesse, 202
Jackson, Kenneth T., 181n
Jackson, Tally, 325
Jacob, Herbert, 89n, 107, 114, 120n, 235n, 264n, 322n
Jacobs, Jane, 423n
Jarvis, Howard, 63
Jefferson, Lucy, 325
Jefferson, Thomas, 37–38
Jennings, M. Kent, 147n
Jensen, Arthur, 389n
Jewell, Malcolm E., 148n
Johnson, Charles A., 15n
Johnson, Gerald W., 119n
Johnson, Lyndon, 350
Johnson, William C., 181n
Jones, Bryan D., 193, 210n
Jones, Charles O., 432–433, 447n
Jones, Eugene W., 179n
Jones, Lewis R., 391
Jones, Rich, 234n, 236n
Jones, Victor, 208n
Jost, Kenneth T., 360n
Jun, Jong, 290n
Jung, R., 389n

Kammerer, Gladys, 179n
Kane, Susan J., 147n
Karabel, Jerome, 391n
Katz, Daniel, 290n
Kaufman, Herbert, 208n, 263n
Kearney, Richard C., 15n
Keating, Dennis, 423n
Keefe, Mike, 141, 355
Keefe, William J., 150n
Kelleher, Sean A., 32n
Kelman, Ellen, 361n
Kennensohn, Mike, 322n
Kenney, Patrick J., 264n
Kenworthy, Tom, 60n

Kerchner, C., 392n
Kettle, Donald F., 423n
Key, V. O., 136, 149n, 236n
Kilborn, Peter T., 289n
Kincaid, John, 29, 33n, 59n
King, Gary, 235n
King, James D., 120n
King, Martin Luther, 142
King, Rodney, 293, 295
Kirk, David L., 361n
Kirschten, Dick, 147n
Kirst, M. W., 389n
Klemiewski, Nancy, 208n
Knaub, Norman, 360n
Koch, Edward, 202
Kohlmeier, Louis M., 264n
Kondratas, Anna, 359n
Kone, Susan l., 266n
Kosaki, Richard H., 33n
Kosterlitz, Julie, 362n
Kosters, Marvin H., 470n
Kotlikoff, Laurence J., 360n
Kotter, John P., 195–196, 210n
Kozol, Jonathan, 4–5, 8, 15n, 390n
Kraft, Michael E., 447n
Kramer, Kenneth W., 447n
Kramer, Michael S., 211n
Krannich, Ronald L., 484
Krebs, Timothy, 471n
Krefetz, Sharon P., 181n
Kreuger, Alan, 389n
Kreuger, Moira, 298
Krohm, Gregory, 322n
Kucinich, Dennis, 192–193
Kunin, Madeleine, 254
Kunstler, James Howard, 447n
Kuttner, Robert, 89n
Kwitny, Jonathan, 421n

Lally, Frank, 266n
Lampkin, Linda, 291n
Landers, Robert K., 447n
Landry, Marc K., 447n
Lane, Robert, 118n
Laslo, David, 471n
Lauber, Daniel, 484
Lauth, Thomas P., 248, 263n, 264n
Lawrence, David, 433
Lawrence, Paul R., 195–196, 210n
Lawrence, Susan, 321n

Lays, Julie, 323n
Le May, Michael C., 235n
Leary, Thomas J., 471n
Ledbetter, Cal, 238n
Lee, Gary, 446n, 447n
Lee, Richard C., 185, 197
Lehne, Richard, 89n, 391n
Leighley, Jan E., 147n, 150n
LeMann, Peter, 392n
Lester, James P., 447n
Levitan, Sar A., 361n
Levy, Frank, 453–454, 470n
Levy, Mark R., 211n
Lewis, Oscar, 389n
Liebow, Elliot, 358n
Lieske, Joel, 16n
Lindblom, Charles E., 290n
Lindsay, John, 197
Lindsey, Robert, 88n
Lineberry, Robert L., 179n, 291n
Locher,Ralph, 197
Loew, Jeanne, 447n
Logan, Rayford, 381
Long, Huey, 239, 250
Long, Norton, 264n
Lorch,Robert S., 210n
Losi, Theodore J., 118n
Lowden, Frank D., 279
Lowery, David, 16n, 89n
Lowi, Theodore J., 423n
Lowry, Ira S., 424n
Lugar, Richard, 194
Lumpkins, Terrance, 211n
Luttbeg, Norman R., 120n, 180n, 237n
Lyday, Winifred, 322n
Lynd, Helen M., 208n
Lynd, Robert S., 208n
Lyons, E. J., "Squatty," 155

MacCorkle, Stuart A., 181n
Maddox, Russell W., 178n
Madison, James, 241
Magleby, David B., 150n
Mahtesian, Charles, 471n
Mallach, Alan, 423n
Malone, James, 463
Mandelbaum, Seymour, 180n
Marando, Vincent L., 181n
Marion, Virginia, 178n
Marshall, C., 389n

Marshall, Dale Rogers, 211n
Martin, Roscoe C., 14n
Martinez, Bob, 254
Martinson, Robert, 314, 322n
Marx, Claude R., 238n
Maxwell, James A., 89n
Maxwell, Robert, 265n
May, Janice C., 32n
Mayal, Donald, 484
Maze, Marilyn, 484
McAllister, William, 422n
McCabe, Michael H., 263n
McCleskey, Clifton, 264n
McClosky, Herbert, 149n
McConachie, Michael P., 60n
McConahay, John B., 390n
McDonald, Robert J., 179n
McIver, John P., 102, 119n
McNeil, L., 392n
McNulty, Michael F., 61n
McReady, William C., 210n
Mead, Lawrence, 353, 359n, 361n
Mecham, Evan, 256
Meehan, Eugene J., 413
Meier, Kenneth J., 290n
Melcher, James P., 148n
Meller, Norman, 33n
Mellon, Richard King, 433
Merelman, Richard, 209n
Merton, Robert K., 180n
Michels, Roberto, 113, 121n, 208n
Mier, Robert, 470n
Miewald, Robert D., 32n
Milbrath, Lester, 92, 94, 118n
Milburn, Josephine F., 178n, 237n
Miller, David Young, 15n
Miller, Delbert C., 208n, 209n
Miller, James Natha, 14n
Miller, Warren E., 120n
Milward, H. Brinton, 471n
Minton, Michael, 391n
Mitchell, D., 389n
Moberg, David, 392n
Moe, Terry M., 383, 392n
Mofford, Rose, 254, 256
Mogulof, Melvin B., 181n, 447n
Mollenkopf, John, 465, 472n
Molotch, Harvey, 190, 209n
Moncrief, Gary F., 238n
Moore, Thomas S., 472n

Moore, Arch A., 255
Morandi, Larry, 61n, 448n
Morehouse, Sarah McCally, 121n, 234n, 264n
Morgan, Dana, 484
Morgan, David R., 16n, 120n, 392n
Morgan, James N., 359n
Morial, Ernest N., 210n
Mosca, Gaetano, 208n
Moscow, Warren, 265n
Mosk, Stanley M., 33n
Moskowitz, Jay H., 88n
Moss, Bill, 236n
Muchmore, Lynn, 265n
Mueller, Keith J., 263n, 291n
Munger, Frank J., 208n
Munroe, Alan D., 119n
Murray, Charles, 334, 359n, 389n
Murphy, Charles F., 165
Murphy, Thomas, 193
Murray, Richard, 211n
Musgrave, Richard, 89n
Myers, Gustavus, 180n

Nader, Ralph, 109
Nagel, Stuart, 320n
Nagler, Jonathan, 150n
Nardulli, Peter F., 16n
Nathan, Richard P., 60n
Neal, R. Peirce, 88n
Neal, Tommy, 147n
Newell, Chaldean, 179n
Newman, Heidi Hosbach, 471n
Newman, Morris, 470n
Nice, David C., 15n, 32n, 89n, 263n, 421n
Nie, Norman, 118n
Niederhoffer, Arthur, 320n
Nielson, Carla, 471n
Niemi, Richard G., 266n
Nissen, Bruce, 471n
Nixon, Richard, 350, 414
Norman, Jim, 266n

O'Connor, Maureen, 199
O'Hara, Rosemary, 149n
O'Rourke, Timothy, 235n
Ogul, Morris S., 150n
Olsen, Edgar, 423n
Olson, David M., 148n

Ordeshook, Peter, 118n
Orfield, Gary, 390n
Orr, Kay, 254
Osborne, David E., 14n, 15n, 251, 252, 265n, 289n
Owen, Wilfred, 421n

Page, Benjamin I., 119n
Paget, Karen, 391n
Parks, Rosa, 142
Parrish, Thomas, 32n
Partin, Randall W., 147n, 266n
Pascarella, Thomas A., 467, 472n
Patterson, Samuel C., 149n
Paul, Cedar, 208n
Paul, Eden, 208n
Pedeliski, Theodore B., 121n
Peirce, Neal R., 471n
Pena, Federico, 194
Perlman, Ellen, 60n
Perpich, Rudy, 383
Peters, John G., 15n
Peters, Mike, 386
Peterson, John E., 472n
Peterson, Paul, 48, 60n, 191, 209n, 467, 472n
Piehl, Anne Morrison, 323n
Pierce, John C., 61n
Pilcher, Dan, 470n
Piven, Frances Fox, 142, 150n
Pitz, Mary Elizabeth, 484
Plunkitt, George Washington, 165, 168
Poe, Steven C., 119n
Polsby, Nelson, 208n
Pomper, Gerald, 147n
Pope, H. G., 179n
Popper, Frank J., 60n
Porter, Michael, 472n
Portz, John, 471n
Pound, William, 237n
Press, Charles, 14n
Pressman, Jeffrey L., 60n, 195–196
Pressman, Steven, 33n
Prewitt, Kenneth, 120n, 123, 147n, 169, 180n
Price, Charles M., 150n
Price, Victoria S., 447n
Proffer, Lanny, 235n
Putnam, Robert, 100, 119n
Pye, Lucian, 15n

Quigley, Eileen, 422n

Rainey, R. Lee, 15n
Rainwater, Lee, 359n, 413
Rakove, Milton, 180n
Ransone, Coleman, 14, 264n
Ravitch, Diane, 380, 390n, 391n
Raymond, Richard D., 467, 472n
Reagan, Ronald, 43, 45, 47, 53, 81, 204,
    239, 253, 352, 405–406, 416, 431, 462
Redburn, F. Stevens, 471n
Reed, Joe, 392n
Reich, Robert, 454, 470n
Reid, Margaret, 471n
Reitze, Glenn L., 421n
Renner, Tari, 179n
Reuss–Ianni, Elizabeth, 321n
Rhine, Stacy L, 119n
Rhoads, Steven, 289n
Rice, Tom W., 264n
Richards, Ann, 254
Richardson, Harry, 421n
Richardson, Lilliard E., 235n
Rieff, David, 211n
Riffe, Vernal, 222
Riker, William, 118n
Ringquist, Delbert J., 121n
Ringquist, Evan J., 446n
Riordan, William L., 179n
Roberts, Barbara, 254
Robin, Helena S., 120n
Robinson, James A., 149n, 360n
Rockefeller, Nelson, 197, 250
Rodgers, Harrell R., 389n
Rodgers, Robert, 290n
Rogers, David, 9
Romig, Candace, 120n
Ronstadt, Linda, 240
Roof, Wade Clark, 422n
Roosevelt, Franklin D., 36, 239, 335
Rose, Carol, 423n
Rosenbaum, Walter A., 181n
Rosenfeld, Raymond A., 423n
Rosenstone, 95, 97, 118n, 147n
Rosenthal, Alan, 234n, 235n, 236n, 237n
Rosenthal, Cindy Simon, 148n, 223, 264n
Rosepepe, Jim, 32n, 290n
Ross, Michael J., 121n
Ross, Murray N., 470n
Rossell, Christine H., 390n

Rossum, Ralph, 322n
Royko, Mike, 180n
Rubin, H. Ted, 322n
Rush, Mark, 216, 236n
Rusk, David, 181n

Sabato, Larry, 120n, 242, 263n, 265n
Sabot, Wendy, 338
Sachs, Jeffery, 360n
Saffell, David C., 236n
Salamon, Lester M., 119n
Salant, Tanis J., 179n
Salerno, Ralph, 321n
Saltzstein, GRace Hall, 211n
Samuelson, Robert J., 470n
Savage, Robert L., 15n
Savas, E. S., 9, 291n
Savitch, H. V., 181n
Sawyers, Larry, 209n, 423n
Sayre, Wallace S., 208n
Sbragia, Alberta M., 209n
Schaeffer, K. H., 400, 420n
Scheiring, Michael J., 291n
Schlesinger, Arthur M., Jr., 12, 16n,
    380–381, 391n
Schlesinger, Joseph, 124, 147n, 265n
Schlitz, Timothy D., 15n
Schlozmann, Kay Lehman, 119n
Schmenner, Roger W., 455, 470n
Schuck, Victoria, 178n
Schultz, Stanley K., 181n
Schulze, Robert D., 208n
Schumacher, Paul, 210n
Schwadron, Harvey, 365
Schwarz, John E., 361n
Sclar, Elliott, 400, 420n
Scott, Stanley, 178n
Sesnowitz, Michael, 322n
Shaffer, William R., 120n, 149n
Shaheen, Jeanne, 253–254
Shannon, John, 88n
Shapiro, Robert Y., 119n
Sharkansky, Ira, 15n, 288n
Sharof, Alan B., 181n
Sharp, Elaine B., 89n, 118n, 180n
Sheb, John M., 319n
Shockley, William, 389n
Shuck, Victoria, 236n
Sigel, Roberta S., 120n
Sigelman, Lee J., 16n, 264n

Silk, Leonard, 359n
Sills, David L., 15n
Simonson, Archie, 298
Simpson, O. J., 292–293
Sindler, Alan, 263n
Sizer, Theodore R., 391n
Skocpol, Theda, 211n
Skogan, Wesley, 320n
Skolnick, Jerome H., 321n
Smeeding, Timothy M., 359n
Smith, Carter, 484
Smith, Christopher, 321n
Smith, Roland, 265n
Smith, Tom W., 6, 93–94, 135
Smith, Zachary, 446n
Smookler, Helen W., 60n
Snell, Ronald K., 32n, 89n, 290n
Snipp, Joseph R., 237n
Sorauf, Frank J., 148n
Soreson, Elaine, 289n
Sparrow, Glen, 179n
Spencer, Herbert, 334, 359n
Spiller, Robert E., 358n
Spohn, Cassia, 320n
Sprengel, Donald P., 264n
Springsteen, Bruce, 449
Squire, Peverill, 229
Squires, Gregory D., 423n, 472n
Stanley, Harold, 149n, 266n
Steinbach, Carol, 471n
Steinberg, Alfred, 180n, 319n
Sternleib, George, 79n, 211n, 472n
Stevens, Barbara J., 291n
Stokes, Donald E., 120n
Stone, Clarence, 187–188, 191–193, 208n, 209n
Stowe, Noel, 264n
Strauss, Annette, 199
Stumpf, Harry, 319n
Sturm, Albert L., 32n
Suarez, Xavier, 199
Sundquist, James L., 361n
Svara, James H., 210n
Swanson, Bert, 208n
Swanson, Wayne R., 32n
Swanstrom, Todd, 209n, 210n
Syer, John C., 121n, 150n

Tabb, David H., 209n, 211n
Taeuber, Karl, 422n

Taft, William Howard, 279
Taggart, Robert, 361n
Talbot, Allan R., 210n
Terkel, Studs, 325, 358n
Thomas, Clarence, 278
Thomas, Clive S., 107, 114, 120n, 121n
Thompson, Frank J., 266n, 290n
Thompson, Joel A., 238n
Thompson, Pat, 263n
Thompson, Tommy G., 353, 464
Thoreau, Henry David, 140
Thornburgh, Richard, 252
Thurow, Lester C., 361n, 470n, 471n
Tolchin, Martin, 288n
Tolchin, Susan, 288n
Tompkins, Gary L., 360n
Tompkins, John S. M., 321n
Tramontozzi, Paul N., 421n
Treadway, Jack, 237n, 360n
Trollope, Anthony, 433
Trotter, Robert, 179n
Trzyna, Thaddeus C., 446n
Tucker, Harvey J., 121n, 360n
Tucker, Jim Guy, 255
Tullock, Gordon, 322n
Turk, William L., 148n
Turner, Steve, 423n
Tvedt, Sherry, 88n
Tweed, William Marcy "Boss," 165
Twist, Steve J., 323n

Ulmer, Sidney, 320n
Unruh, Jesse, 125
Uslaner, Eric, 120n, 147n, 237n

Van Evera, Stephen, 119n
Van Horn, Carl, 15n
Van Valey, Thomas L., 422n
Vanderleeuw, James, 266n
Vasu, Michael L., 179n
Vedlitz, Arnold, 211n
Velez, William, 423n
Verba, Sidney, 118n, 119n
Vines, Kenneth N., 89n
Vogel, Ronald J., 266n
Vogel, Ronald K., 181n
Voinovich, George, 192–193

Wachtel, Howard M., 423n
Wade, Larry L., 150n

Waihee, John, 254
Walker, David B., 60n
Walker, Paul, 484
Walsh, Michael H., 471n
Walton, Hanes, 150n
Walton, John, 208n
Walzer, Norman, 472n
Warner, Sam Bass, 421n
Washington, Harold, 166–167, 202, 210n
Waste, Robert J., 209n
Watson, Richard, 320n
Watson, Sheila S., 16n, 392n
Watt, James G., 415
Watts, Meredith W., 148n
Webber, Melvin M., 421n
Weber, Ronald E., 120n, 147n, 237n
Weinstein, Bernard L., 470n
Weiss, Carol H., 290n
Weiss, John H., 319n
Weissberg, Robert, 119n
Welch, Randy, 121n
Welch, Susan, 15n, 320n
Weld, William, 347
Welfeld, Irving, 405, 423n
Wernberg, Daniel H., 424n
Wheat, Edward M., 266n
White, Mark, 383
White, Michael, 199
Whitman, Christine Todd, 80, 253,
    258–259, 378
Whitmire, Kathy, 199, 202
Wiggins, Charles W., 121n, 148n, 237n, 264n
Wilcox, Jerome E., 422n
Wildavsky, Aaron B., 60n, 208n, 290n
Wilder, Douglas, 253–254
Willbern, York, 290n

Williams, Damian, 293
Williams, J. Allen, 389n
Williams, Marcia P., 484
Williams, Robert F., 33n
Williams, Steven, 264n
Williams, T. Harry, 263n
Wilson, Carter, 210n
Wilson, Pete, 194, 258–259, 382
Wilson, James Q., 208n, 321n, 323n, 443,
    448n
Wilson, Woodrow, 239
Winter, A. B., 32n
Winters, Richard F., 147n, 149n, 150n, 266n
Wirt, Frederick M., 389n
Wirth, Clifford J., 179n
Wolfinger, Raymond, 95, 97, 118n, 139,
    147n, 150n, 179n, 208n
Wood, B. Dan, 446n
Woodward, Gary C., 61n
Wright, Deil S., 59n, 264n
Wright, Gerald, 102, 119n, 134, 149n, 289n
Wyckoff, Mikel, 5n

Yackle, Larry W., 319n
Yandle, Bruce, 4348n
Yates, Douglas, 196–197, 210n
Ylvisaker, Paul N., 235n
Yomeyer, Neil, 89n
Young, Coleman, 193–194, 199

Zeigler, L. Harmon, 120n, 121n, 147n
Zeller, Belle, 237n
Zimmerman, Christopher, 32n, 290n
Zimmerman, Joseph, 264n
Zink, Harold, 180n
Zisk, Betty, 440, 447n

SUBJECT INDEX

Abortion, 125
Absolute deprivation, 326–328, 357
Accountant, 481
Administrative reorganization, 279–280
Administrator, 473
Advisory Commission on Intergovernmental Relations, 3, 32n, 44, 59n, 67, 69–70, 88n, 148n 178n, 179n, 180n, 237n, 421n
Affirmative action, 125, 258–259, 273–276, 287, 381–382
AFL-CIO, 107, 111, 113, 351
AFSCME, 83, 99, 108, 272, 278, 287
Aid for Families with Dependent Children, 45, 143, 337, 341–344, 357
Air pollution, 431–435
Air Quality Act, 431
Alabama, 10, 20, 22, 29, 52, 82, 103, 114, 131, 229, 244, 282, 299, 337–338, 461
Alaska, 10, 29, 52, 72–74, 82, 114, 131, 229, 244, 299, 365
Albuquerque, New Mexico, 175
American Civil Liberties Union, 301
American Federation of Teachers, 108, 383
American Judicature Society, 297
American Political Science Association, 226
Americans with Disabilities Act, 42
Amicus curiae, 301, 318
AMTRAK, 399–400
Anaconda Corporation, 186
Anchorage, Alaska, 482
Annexation, 173
Antidiversion legislation, 396, 419
Apple Computer Corp., 452
Apportionment, 215, 233
Arbitrator, 478
Argersinger v. *Hamlin*, 309, 321n

Arizona, 10, 29, 52, 54, 82, 103, 114, 131, 138, 140, 229, 244, 254, 299, 454
Arkansas, 10, 20, 27, 52, 82, 103, 114, 131, 229, 230, 244, 252, 255, 299, 379
Asians, 198, 202–204, 252, 259, 381–382
Atlanta, Georgia, 183, 373, 405, 482
Atlantic City, New Jersey, 79
At-large elections, 168, 177
Attentive constituents, 105, 117
Attorney General, 301
Auditor, 481
Audubon Society, 108
Austin, Texas, 415, 465, 482
Australia, 403

Badham v. *Eu*, 235n
Bail, 305
Baker v. *Carr*, 59n, 235n
Bakersfield, California, 482
Ballew v. *Georgia*, 321n
Balloon mortgage, 411, 419
Baltimore, Maryland, 305, 460
Bar association, 298
Barrington, Illinois, 92
Basic Educational Opportunity Grant, 367
Bench, 297, 318
Berkeley, California, 202
Bill of Rights, 28–29, 306, 318
Bipolar city, 199–203
Birmingham, Alabama, 276
Birmingham, Michigan, 410
Blacks
    affirmative action, 259, 274, 276, 381–382
    Afro-centrism, 380
    annexation and, 173
    Arizona, 256

Blacks *(continued)*
  coalitions, 202–204
  community power and, 188
  electoral success, 144
  employment success, 274
  as judges, 300–301
  Los Angeles riot, 293–294
  machine politics and, 166–167
  mayors, 198–200
  poverty rates, 329
  representation, 216–217
  school curriculum, 380–389
  school desegregation, 371–376
  urban renewal, 414
  voting, 96, 125
Blanket primary, 132, 146
Block grant, 40, 58
Board of Education, 365, 387
Board of Education of Oklahoma City Schools
      v. *Doswell,* 390n
Boise, Idaho, 482
Boston, 41, 56, 165, 194, 276, 373, 375,
      399–400, 466
Boston Firefighters Union v. *Boston Chapter,*
      NAACP, 289n
Boulder, Colorado, 48
Bowling alone, 101
Bracket creep, 81, 87
Brazil, 403, 452, 465
Brazoria, Texas, 482
Bremerton, Washington, 483
Brooklyn, New York, 409
Brown v. *Board of Education,* 59n, 372, 389n
Brownsville, Texas, 482
Budget analyst, 474
Budget retrenchment, 64, 87
Budgeting, 248, 281–284
Building codes, 410, 419
Bureau of Land Management, 53, 55
Bureau of Public Roads
Business, 106–107, 185–187, 454–456, 469
Busing, 372–373
Butte, Montana, 186
Bus transit, 401, 403

Calendar, 224, 233
California
  affirmative action, 17, 258–260, 381–382
  campaign finance, 125–127, 133
  closed primary, 131

  constitution, 20, 29–30
  courts, 299, 308
  crime, 315
  direct democracy, 138, 140
  economic development, 456
  education finance, 80, 377
  environment, 437
  fiscal federalism, 52
  gerrymander, 216
  governors, 244, 253, 267
  Hispanics, 203, 381
  ideology, 103
  initiative process, 63–64
  interest groups, 114
  land use regulation, 441
  legislature, 115, 228–230, 229
  political culture, 10
  political economy, 85
  political parties, 134
  Proposition 13, 62–64, 67
  social conflict, 258–260
  tax progressivity, 82
  welfare policy, 337–338, 352–353
Campaign finance, 125–128
Capital expenditures, 77, 87
Capital punishment, 105
Careers, 473–482
Caretaker executives, 196–197, 252, 262
Carnegie Foundation, 368
Casework, 214, 233
Casinos, 79
Categorical grant, 39–40, 58, 77, 87
Catholics, 8, 300
Caucus, 221
Cease-and-desist, 294, 318
Ceremonial mayor, 195–197, 207
Challenge primary, 130, 146
Chicago, Illinois,
  court politics, 297
  crime, 311, 313
  economic development, 466
  education, 365
  ethnic politics, 202
  flood, 394
  Hispanics, 217
  housing, 412
  local government, 171
  machine politics, 132, 165, 198
  patronage, 270, 285
  transit, 400

Child protection worker, 43
Christian fundamentalists, 379
Cincinnati, Ohio, 196
Circuit breaker, 71, 87
Citizens Conference on State Legislatures, 237n
Citizens for Tax Justice, 82
Citizens to Preserve Overton Park v. *Volpe*, 421n
City manager. *See* Council manager
City of Mobile v. *Bolden*, 236n
City-county consolidation, 171, 177
Civic duty, 95, 118
Civil law, 294, 318
Civil rights movement, 28, 141–142
Civil rights Act, 142, 143, 273, 276, 278
Civil service, 168, 177, 241, 271–272, 287
Civil War, 35–36, 133
Clean Air Act, 47, 228, 431–432, 442, 445
Clean Water Act, 428, 431–432, 445
Cleveland, Ohio, 191–193, 197, 276
Client politics, 443
Closed primary, 130, 146
Cold War, 2, 85
Colegrove v. *Green*, 235n
Collective bargaining, 107, 109, 143, 272, 276, 287
Colorado, 10, 17, 29, 52, 82, 103, 110, 114, 131, 138, 214, 228 229, 230, 244, 299, 454
Colorado Springs, Colorado, 482
Columbus Board of Education v. *Penick*, 390n
Columbus, Ohio, 374
Commerce clause, 28, 38, 58
Commission government, 159–161, 177
Commissioner of education, 366, 387
Committee for Economic Development, 32n, 180n, 228, 237n
Common Cause, 108, 110
Commonwealth Edison v. *Montana*, 60n, 89n
Community Development Block Grant, 204, 207, 458
Community power, 183–188
Compact theory, 35, 58
Comparable worth, 277–278, 287
Compensatory education, 368, 388
Competitive federalism, 48
Compliance officer, 476
Confederacy, 35
Congressional Black Caucus, 351

Connecticut, 10, 51, 52, 82, 103, 104, 114, 127, 131, 132, 134, 244, 274, 299
Connick v. *Myers*, 288n
Consensus model, 104
Conservation scientist, 475
Conservatism
   by state, 103
   crime and, 309–310
   direct democracy, 140
   educational policy, 369
   government finance, 67
   housing policy, 416–417
   judicial activism, 294
   on poverty, 333–335
Constitution (U.S.)
   bill of rights, 306, 318
   civil rights, 28, 96–97
   commerce clause, 28, 38
   delegated and reserved powers, 36–37, 39
   due process clause, 28
   equal-protection clause, 28, 371
   federalism, 36–39, 49
   Fifth Amendment, 441
   full faith and credit clause, 49
   interpretation, 30
   interstate compact, 49
   local governments in, 156
   national supremacy clause, 38, 58
   necessary and proper clause, 37–38, 59
   rendition clause, 49
   school desegregation, 371–376
   school finance, 377
   taking issue, 441
   Tenth Amendment, 39
Constitutions (state)
   amending, 25
   bills of rights, 28–30
   compared to U.S. constitution, 19
   conventions, 25–26, 31
   dedicated funds, 20, 31
   earmarked revenue, 20, 31
   fundamental law, 18, 31
   gateway amendment, 28, 31
   higher law tradition, 18, 23, 28
   judicial review, 31
   model constitution, 23, 31
   natural rights, 30
   positive law tradition, 19, 23
   problems, 19–23
   reform, 23–28

Constitutions (*continued*)
  revision commissions, 27–28, 31
  social change, 17–18, 28–30
  statutory law, 18, 31
  super legislation, 20, 31
Contract for America, 47
Cooperative federalism, 36, 39–42, 58
Correctional policy, 313–315
Corrections Corporation of America, 316
Corrections officer, 474
Cost-benefit analysis, 283, 287, 442–443
Council manager, 160–163, 177
Council of governments, 173, 177
Council on Environmental Quality, 61n,
    430, 438
Council on State Governments, 23, 108, 237n
Counties, 154, 157–159, 177
County government, 157–158, 177
Court administrator, 474
Courts
  constitutional provisions, 22
  crime and, 303–308
  interest groups and, 301
  judges' backgrounds, 300–301
  judicial selection, 298–300
  organization, 295–297
  politics and, 297–302
  public policy role, 294–295
Crime trends, 304
Criminal law, 294, 318
Crusader mayor, 196–197
Cubans, 199
Cultural pluralism, 380–381, 388
Culture of poverty, 334, 369
Curitiba, Brazil, 403

Dallas, Texas, 396
Davis v. *Bandemer*, 235n
Dayton Board of Education v. *Brinkman,* 390n
Dayton, Ohio, 374
Daytona Beach, Florida, 482
De facto segregation, 371, 388
De jure segregation, 371, 388
Decision-making analysis, 184, 207
Declaratory judgment, 294, 318
Dedicated funds, 20, 31
Delaware, 8, 10, 52, 73, 81, 82, 103, 114,
    131, 229, 244, 299
Delegated powers, 36–37, 58
Demagogues, 250, 262

Democratic Party
  education finance, 80–81, 378
  environment, 439
  ethnic base, 165
  gerrymander, 216
  Hispanics, 203
  housing policy, 416
  ideology, 9, 133, 137
  judges and, 300
  legislatures, 230
  machine politics, 165–167
  political broker role, 132
  regional strength, 133
  social base, 135
  voter turnout and, 125
  welfare policy, 338–339
Denver, Colorado, 194, 199, 482
Department of Agriculture, 327
Department of Housing and Urban
    Development, 415
Determinate sentencing, 314, 318
Detroit, Michigan, 55, 189–191, 193, 199,
    374, 402
Devolution, 45–46
Dillon's Rule, 48, 58, 156, 177
Direct action, 139–143, 146
Direct democracy, 138, 140, 146
Direct primary, 168, 177
Direct-production strategy, 416, 419
Displacement, 410, 419
Distributive policy, 295, 318
District elections, 123, 146
Dolan v. *City of Tigard,* 447n
Dual federalism, 36, 58
Due process clause, 28

Eagleton Institute, 237n
Earmarked revenues, 20, 31, 282, 287
Earned Income Tax Credit, 345
East St. Louis, Illinois, 4–5, 18
Economic developer, 475
Economic Opportunity Act of 1965, 350, 357
Edge City, 175
Education
  busing, 372–373
conservatism and, 369
curriculum, 379–382
desegregation, 371–376
federal role, 367
finance, 77–81, 376–379

ideological spectrum and, 371–382
liberalism and, 369–370
local roles, 365
political economy, 385–386
post-secondary, 368
reform, 382–385
state roles, 366
Education Consolidation and Improvement Act, 368, 388
Efficiency, 6, 8–9
El Paso, Texas, 482
Elasticity, 175, 177
Electioneering, 109, 117
Elections, 123–124, 125–127
Elementary and Secondary Education Act, 367, 368, 388
Elitist theory, 183–184, 207
Elrod v. *Burns*, 148n, 288n
Employee stock ownership plan, 463–464, 469
Employment, 270
Empowerment Zones, 457
Energy careers, 481
Energy crisis, 53, 58
England, 403
Entrepreneurial politics, 443
Enumerated powers, 36–37, 59
Environment, 425–444
Environmental Impact Statement, 428, 445
Environmental Protection Agency, 428, 429, 430, 435–436, 460
Environmental Protection Act, 428, 445
Environmental racism, 439
Equal opportunity, 273, 287
Equal-protection clause, 28, 58, 371–372
Escobedo v. *Illinois*, 309
Ethnic particularism, 380–381, 388
Evansville, Indiana, 398
Exclusionary zoning, 408, 419
Executive leadership, 242, 262, 271
Executive representation, 240, 262
Exit option, 100, 200, 207
Expenditure patterns, 2, 3, 65–67
Externalities, 87, 426, 445

Family Assistance Plan, 350, 358
Federal Aid Highway Act of 1956, 396, 419
Federalism
    competitive, 42–44, 47–48
    cooperative, 36, 39–42

creative, 42
definition of, 35, 58
delegated powers, 36–37
devolution, 45–46
division of powers, 36–38
dual, 36, 58
evolution of, 36–39
grants-in-aid, 39–40
interstate relations, 49–51
local governments in, 48–49
mandates, 41–42
New Federalism, 45–48
political economy, 55–57
poverty policy, 336–337
reserved powers, 36–37
Felony, 294, 318
Fifteenth Amendment, 96
Filter-down strategy, 416, 419
Fire fighter, 475
First English Evangelical Church v. *County of Los Angeles*, 448n
Fiscal disparities, 80, 87, 277, 288
Florida
    campaign finance, 127
    closed primary, 131
    constitution, 29
    courts, 299, 305, 308
    economic development, 454
    fiscal federalism, 52
    governors, 244, 253
    Hispanics, 253
    ideology, 103
    interest groups, 114
    interstate relations, 49
    legislature, 221, 228–229
    no income tax, 72
    political culture, 10
    tax progressivity, 82
Food stamps, 45, 143, 342, 345
Forester, 475
Formula grant, 40, 58
Fort Pierce, Florida, 482
Foundation aid program, 376, 388
Freedom of speech, 19
Freehold, New Jersey, 449n
Freeman v. *Pitts*, 390n
Fresno, California, 482
Frostbelt, 49–50, 58
Frustrated warriors, 252
Full-faith and credit clause, 49

Fundamental law, 18, 31
Furman v. *Georgia*, 309, 321n

Gallup Poll, 134, 139, 353
Galveston, Texas, 159–160
Gambling, 79
Garcia v. *San Antonio Metropolitan Transit Authority*, 59n
Gary, Indiana, 185, 189, 465
Gated communities, 408, 420
Gateway amendment, 28, 31
Gay rights, 17, 31, 109, 140, 144
General Motors, 190, 193, 450
General public assistance, 342, 345
General Revenue Sharing, 39, 58
General-obligation bond, 78, 87
Gentrification, 409, 420
Georgia, 10, 29, 52, 82, 103, 114, 131, 229, 244, 299, 308
Germans, 8, 165
Germany, 403
Gerrymander, 216, 233
GI Bill of Rights, 367
Gibbons v. *Ogden*, 59n
Gideon v. *Wainwright*, 308
Gladiators, 92, 99, 101, 118, 125
Global capital theory, 189–190
Gomillion v. *Lightfoot*, 119n, 236n
Governors
    administration and, 268–269
    budgeting, 248–249
    bureaucracy, 246–267
    career patterns, 252–255
    constitutional provisions, 22
    executive leadership, 242, 271
    legislatures, 245–246
    neutral competence, 241–242
    policy making role, 242–245
    political economy, 260–261
    public relations, 249
    social conflict, 258–260
    strengthening, 248–249
    styles, 249–252
    veto, 245, 262
Grand jury, 304, 318
Grandfather clause, 97
Grant-in-Aid, 39–40, 58
Great Britain, 220
Great Depression, 36, 38, 48, 335, 405, 411
Great Lakes, 9, 55, 56, 302

Great Society, 370
Gregg v. *Georgia*, 308
Greylord scandal, 297
Gross domestic product, 65, 85, 336, 357
Growth-machine theory, 190–191
Gun control, 105

Harris County, Texas, 155
Harris v. *New York*, 308
Hawaii, 10, 18, 27, 29, 52, 81–82, 114, 131, 229, 244, 252, 254, 299, 365
Hazardous wastes, 427–428, 435–437
Health services manager, 476
Higher Education Act, 367
Higher law tradition, 18
Highways, 395–398
Hill-Burton Act of 1946, 346
Hispanics
    affirmative action, 259, 274, 276, 381
    annexation and, 173
    coalitions, 202–204
    employment success, 274
    governors, 253–254
    machine politics and, 166–167
    mayors, 198–200
    poverty rates, 329
Home rule, 23, 157, 159
Hoover Commission, 279
Housing Act of 1937, 412–413, 416
Housing and Community Development Act of 1974, 204, 414–415, 420
Housing policy, 404–416
Housing voucher, 416, 420
Houston, Texas, 155, 173, 199, 202, 396, 483
Hypothesis, 338, 357

Idaho, 10, 29, 52, 82, 103, 104, 114, 131, 229, 244, 299
Ideological spectrum, 5–6, 14, 103, 333–336, 369
Ideology, 203
Illinois
    administration, 279
    constitution, 21, 26
    courts, 299
    fiscal federalism, 52
    governors, 244–245, 271
    ideology, 103
    interest groups, 114

legislature, 229
patronage, 271
political culture, 10
primary elections, 131
tax progressivity, 82
Immigrants, 167
Impeachment, 255–256, 297
In Re Gault, 309
In-kind assistance, 342–346, 358
Inclusionary zoning, 408, 420
Income inequalities, 331–333
Income maintenance, 350, 358
Income tax, 72–73
Incrementalism, 282, 287
Independent school districts, 365, 388
Index crime, 302, 304, 318
Indexation, 81, 87
Indiana, 10, 52, 82, 103, 114, 131, 137, 216, 229, 244, 299
Indianapolis, Indiana, 172, 194
Indians, 79, 198, 439–440
Individualistic culture, 7, 9–11, 14
Industrial development revenue bonds, 78, 87, 206, 458, 467, 469
Infrastructure, 394, 420
Initiative, 62, 138, 146
Injunction, 294, 318
Inspector, 476
Intensity problem, 105, 118
Interest groups, 105–116, 118, 443
Intergovernmental aid, 76
Intergovernmental Personnel Act, 270
Intergovernmental relations, 48, 58
International City Management Association, 108
Interstate commerce, 38
Interstate compact, 49, 56
Interstate Highway System, 21, 396, 420
Iowa, 10, 52, 64, 82, 103, 114, 131, 229, 244, 299
Iraq, 74
Irish, 165
Iron law of oligarchy, 113, 118
Issue-oriented politics, 9, 14
Italians, 165
Item veto, 245, 262

Jacksonian democracy, 240, 262, 274
Jacksonville, Florida, 172
Japanese, 465

Jobs-oriented politics, 9, 14
Johnson v. Louisiana, 308, 321n
Joint committee, 224–233
Judicial review, 18, 31, 294, 318
Jury system, 304–305, 318

Kansas, 10, 20, 52, 82, 103, 104, 131, 229, 244, 254, 299
Kenosha, Wisconsin, 464
Kentucky, 10, 25, 52, 82, 103, 104, 131, 229, 244, 299, 461
Kileen, Texas, 483
Korea, 452, 465
Kuwait, 74

Labor relations, 478
Laboratories of democracy, 6, 261
Laissez-faire, 334, 336, 358
Land issues, 51–53
Land Policy and Management Act, 52
Las Vegas, Nevada, 483
Lawrence, Kansas, 193
Lawyer, 481
League of Women Voters, 23
Lebanon, 381
Legal assistant, 477
Legal Services Corporation, 305, 343, 346, 358
Legislatures
audit, 215
bicameralism, 219–220
calendar, 224, 233
casework, 214, 233
committee organization, 223–224
constitutional provisions, 20–22
delegate role, 219, 221, 234
functions of, 213–219
gerrymanders, 216–217
governors and, 245–246
law passing process, 224–225
legislative veto, 214, 233
organization of, 219–224
oversight, 213
party organization, 220–223
pigeon hole, 224, 233
policy making, 224–226
political role, 219, 234
public opinion and, 104–105
quorum, 224, 233
reform, 226–232

Legislatures *(continued)*
  representation, 215–220
  responsible-party model, 220, 234
  term limitation, 230–231
  trustee role, 219, 221, 234
  veto, 226, 233
Liberalism
  blacks, 203
  crime and, 310–311
  direct democracy, 140
  educational policy, 369
  ethnicity and, 203–204
  government finance, 67
  housing policy, 417–418
  judicial activism, 294
  on poverty, 335–336
  by state, 103
Lieutenant governor, 255, 262
Light rail transit, 401–402, 420
Line-item budgeting, 282, 287
Literacy test, 97
Little Hoover Commissions, 279, 288
Lobbying, 110–111, 118
Lobbyist, 477
Local government
  charters, 156–157
  city manager, 161–162
  commission, 160–161
  community power theory, 182–188
  constitutional provisions, 23
  counties, 153, 155, 157–159
  general purpose, 154–157
  global capital, 189–190
  growth machine, 190–191
  machine politics, 164–167
  mayors, 194–198
  metropolitan challenge, 170–175
  municipalities, 153, 156, 158–163, 178
  political economy, 204–206
  Rainbow coalition, 200–204
  regime theory, 191–192
  school districts, 152–153, 158, 178
  single purpose, 152–154
  social conflict, 175–176, 198–204
  special districts, 152–153, 158, 178
  towns, 153–154, 178
  township, 153–154, 156, 158, 178
  types of, 153
  unitary interest, 191
Long ballot, 240, 262

Loose constructionist, 37
Los Angeles, California, 198–199, 285, 293–294, 456
Lotteries, 21, 79, 282
Louisiana, 10, 25, 29, 30, 52, 53, 103, 114, 131, 229, 239, 244, 299, 305, 308, 356, 379
Louisville, Kentucky, 375
Love Canal, 427
Lowell, Massachusetts, 458
LULU, 436–437, 441

Machine-style politics, 164–166
Madison, Wisconsin, 298
Maine, 10, 52, 82, 103, 114, 224, 229, 244, 299, 365, 463
Majoritarian politics, 443
Majority leader, 221, 233
Majority-minority districts, 217–218, 233
Mallory v. *United States,* 308
Management by objectives, 280–281, 288
Mandate, 41–42, 77
Mapp v. *Ohio,* 307, 308, 321n
Martin v. *Wilks,* 289n
Maryland, 10, 21, 27, 38, 52, 103, 114, 131, 229, 244, 299
Maryland v. *Louisiana,* 60n, 82, 89n
Massachusetts
  bill of rights, 29
  civil service, 241
  constitution,
  courts, 299
  direct democracy, 140
  economic development, 458–459, 463
  fiscal federalism, 52
  governors, 244, 246
  ideology, 103–104
  interest groups, 114
  legislature, 215, 224, 229
  political culture, 10
  primary elections, 131
  proposition 2 1/2, 64
  tax progressivity, 82
  welfare policy, 347–348, 352–353
Mayors, 163, 194–206
McAllen, Texas, 483
McCleskey v. *Kemp,* 309
McCulloch v. *Maryland,* 32n, 38, 59n
McKinney Act of 1987, 405
McLaurin v. *Oklahoma State Regents,* 389n
Means test, 344, 358

Mediator, 178
Medicaid, 45, 106, 143, 343, 347, 358
Medicare, 106, 143, 341, 344, 347, 358
Melbourne, Florida, 483
Mellon Family, 185
Melting pot metaphor, 12
Memphis, Tennessee, 276, 373, 399
Memphis v. *Stotts*, 289n
Merit good, 75, 87, 426, 445
Merit system, 168, 177, 271, 287, 298–299
Metropolitan planning, 173, 178
Metropolitan politics, 170–175
Metropolitan Statistical Area, 170, 178
Mexican-Americans, 199, 202–204
Miami, Florida, 140, 159, 172, 199, 203, 412
Michigan
    courts, 299
    economic development, 459
    education finance, 81, 378–379
    fiscal federalism, 52
    governors, 244, 254
    ideology, 103
    interest groups, 114
    legislature, 115, 229, 230
    political culture, 9–10
    primary elections, 131
    taxes, 64, 82
    welfare, 354
Middletown, 182–183
Midwest, 9, 49–51, 55, 85, 113, 123, 138, 156, 173, 260, 398, 398, 455
Millikin v. *Bradley*, 374, 390n
Milwaukee, Wisconsin, 159, 375, 409
Minneapolis, Minnesota, 174, 199, 375, 441
Minnesota, 9, 10, 26, 52, 82, 97, 103, 110, 114, 125, 130, 131, 227, 229, 244, 253, 299, 347, 408–409, 466
Minority leader, 221, 233
Miranda v. *Arizona*, 307, 309, 321n
Misdemeanor, 294, 318
Mississippi, 10, 20, 52, 73, 82, 103, 104, 114, 131, 229, 244, 299, 455
Missouri, 10, 49, 52, 82, 103, 110, 114, 127, 131, 133, 229, 244, 299, 371–372, 457
Missouri ex rel. Gaines v. *Canada*, 389n
Missouri Plan, 298, 319
Missouri v. *Jenkins*, 390n
Mobile, Alabama, 217
Model State Constitution, 23–24, 31

Monroo v. *Papo*, 308
Montana, 10, 29, 30, 52, 53, 73, 82, 103, 114, 131, 229, 244
Montana, 245, 299
Montgomery bus boycott, 141 142
Moralistic culture, 7, 9–11, 14
Morgantown, West Virginia, 402, 404
Morrill Act, 367
Motor Voter Bill, 97
Muncie, Indiana, 183
Municipalities, 153, 156–157, 159–160, 178

NAACP, 301, 371
Nashville, Tennessee, 172
National Affordable Housing Act of 1990, 416
National Association of County Officials, 108
National Commission on Excellence in Education, 364, 382, 385, 388, 389n
National Conference of State Legislatures, 108
National Defense Education Act, 367
National Education Association, 108
National Endowment for the Arts, 367
National Endowment for the Humanities, 367
National Governors Association, 59n, 108
National Labor Relations Board, 107, 142
National League of Cities, 108
National Municipal League, 23–24, 32n
National Opinion Research Center, 203
National Pollution Discharge Elimination System, 429, 438
National Science Foundation, 367
National supremacy clause, 38, 58
National Women's Political Caucus, 144
Natural rights, 30
Nebraska, 10, 52, 82, 103, 106, 114, 123, 131, 132, 219, 229, 244, 254, 299
Necessary and proper clause, 38, 59
Neo-Marxism, 189–190
Neutral competence, 241, 262
Nevada, 10, 51, 52, 82, 103, 114, 131, 229, 244, 299
New Deal, 36, 335
New England, 8, 154, 347, 415
New Federalism, 45–47, 59
New Hampshire, 10, 28, 29, 30, 52, 73, 82, 103, 114, 131, 138, 229, 244, 251, 253, 254, 299

New Haven, Connecticut, 184–185, 188, 197
New Jersey
  campaign finance, 127
  casinos, 79
  courts, 299
  crime, 315
  economic development, 459
  education finance, 80–81, 259, 377–378
  fiscal federalism, 52
  governors, 80, 124, 244, 253–254
  ideological parties, 133
  ideology, 103–104
  inclusionary zoning, 408, 420
  interest groups, 114
  legislature, 229
  political culture, 8, 10
  primary elections, 131
  social conflict, 258–260
  tax progressivity, 82
  taxes, 81, 124
  welfare, 353
New Mexico, 10, 27, 51, 52, 82, 103, 114,
    131, 244, 299
New York City
  crime, 303, 315
  economic development, 466
  education, 365
  ethnic politics, 202–204
  free-ways, 399
  homeless, 405
  housing, 212
  machine politics, 165, 270
  metropolitan challenge, 171
  public employees, 99, 285
  schools, 372–373
New York State
  civil service, 241, 271
  closed primary, 131
  constitution, 20, 27, 29–30
  courts, 298–299
  economic development, 456, 459
  fiscal federalism, 52
  governors, 241, 244, 253
  ideology, 103
  interest groups, 114
  Italians, 253
  legislature, 223, 229
  political culture, 8, 10
  tax progressivity, 82
Niagara Falls, New York, 427

NIMBY, 436–437
Nineteenth Amendment, 96, 125
Nominating convention, 130, 146
Nondecisions, 187–188, 207
Nonpartisan elections, 168, 177
Nonpartisan primary, 132, 146
Nonpoint-source pollution, 429, 444
Norfolk, Virginia, 313, 375
North American Free Trade Agreement, 452
North Carolina, 10, 29, 52, 82, 114, 131, 217,
    226, 229, 243, 244, 245, 299, 365, 383
North Central, 50, 103
North Dakota, 10, 27, 52, 82, 98, 103, 104,
    114, 123, 131, 138, 229, 244, 299
Northeast, 35, 50, 55, 85, 102, 113, 138, 173,
    260, 302, 398, 455
Northeast Coalition of Governors, 51
Northeast-Midwest Coalition of Congres-
    sional Members, 51
Northwest Ordinance, 367
Nullification Ordinances, 35

Oakland, California, 169
OASDHI, 340–341, 358
Office of Management and Budget, 442
Ohio, 10, 42, 52, 82, 103, 114, 131, 219, 222,
    229, 244, 299, 353
Oklahoma, 10, 52, 82, 85, 97, 103, 104, 114,
    131, 138, 229, 230, 244, 299, 356, 372
Oklahoma v. U.S. Civil Service Commission,
    288n
Olympia, Washington, 483
Ombudsman, 170, 178
One-person, one-vote, 215
Open primary, 132, 146
Open-ended reimbursement, 40, 59
Oregon, 10, 30, 52, 64, 73, 82, 97, 103, 111,
    114, 131, 138, 200, 228, 229, 230, 244,
    254, 348
Organized crime, 302–303
Organized labor, 98, 106–107, 339–340
Orlando, Florida, 483

Paralegal, 477
Patronage, 164–166, 270, 288
Pell Grant, 367
Pennsylvania
  closed primary, 131
  courts, 298, 299
  crime, 311, 313

fiscal federalism, 52
governors, 244, 252
ideology, 103
interest groups, 114
legislature, 229
political culture, 8, 10
tax progressivity, 82
Pennsylvania Railroad, 433
Personal Responsibility and Assistance
   Act of 1996, 354
Personnel officer, 478
Philadelphia, Pennsylvania, 186, 198, 199,
   466
Phoenix, Arizona, 436, 466, 483
Pigeon hole, 224, 233
Pittsburgh, Pennsylvania, 185, 433–434, 463
Planning program budgeting, 283, 288
Plant closing, 462–463
Plea bargaining, 306, 319
Plessy v. *Ferguson*, 389n
Pluralist theory, 184–185, 207
Pocket veto, 226, 233
Point-source pollution, 429, 444
Poles, 165
Poletown, 190, 193
Police, 479
Policy entrepreneurs, 250, 262
Political action committees, 109–110, 118,
   125
Political culture, 7–12, 14
Political economy
   corrections, 315–316
   definition, 4, 14
   education, 385–387
   environment, 441–443
   government finances, 84–87
   governors, 260
   intergovernmental relations and, 55–57
   mayoral leadership, 204–206
   reengineering government, 284–287
   welfare policy, 356
Political efficacy, 96, 118
Political participation, 92–102, 118
Political parties
   competition, 222–223
   constituencies, 133–135
   gerrymander, 216
   government, 135–136
   ideological parties, 133
   machine politics, 132, 146

nominating candidates, 130–131
organization, 127–133
partisan identification, 134
social base of partisanship, 135
states–controlled, 136
tripartite organization, 127, 147
two–party competition, 136–137
Politics of recognition, 165
Poll tax, 97
Port Authority of New York and New Jer-
   sey, 49
Portland, Oregon, 161, 174–175, 380, 402,
   430–431, 441, 483
Postindustrial economy, 451, 469
Poverty, 324–358, 326–328,
Prairie Island, Minnesota, 439–440
Preemptive legislation, 41
President's Commission on Law Enforce-
   ment, 321n
Primary election, 130, 146
Privatization, 284–285, 288, 315
Proactive accountability, 123, 146
Proctor & Gamble Co., 111
Program entrepreneur mayor, 196–198
Program evaluation, 280, 288
Progressive reform movement, 163–164,
   167–170, 178, 194
Progressive tax, 5, 68, 81, 82, 87
Project grant, 40, 59
Property tax, 69–72, 78, 80–81, 87
Proposition 13, 62–64, 67, 83, 87
Proposition 2 1/2, 64
Provo, Utah, 483
Pruitt-Igo, 412–413
Public Housing Authority, 412
Public interest groups, 108, 118
Public Interest Research Group, 108
Public opinion
   busing, 373
   definition, 102, 118
   direct democracy, 139
   ethnic attitudes, 203
   expenditures, 68
   ideological spectrum 6
   influence on policy, 104–105
   partisan identification, 134
   political ideology, 103
   political participation, 93
   public welfare, 349, 351, 353
   support for government, 44

Public opinion (*continued*)
  tax and spending, 67
  voter turnout, 94
  worst tax, 70
Public relations, 109, 118, 479
Puerto Ricans, 200

Quorum, 224, 234

Race norming, 44, 259
Rainbow Coalition, 200–203
Raleigh, North Carolina, 483
Rational activist model, 104
Recall, 138, 146, 297
Recidivism, 313, 319
Reconstruction Period, 133
Recreation worker, 480
Red-lining, 409, 420
Redistributive policy, 5, 13, 14, 295, 318
Reengineering government, 279–281
Referendum, 138, 146
Reform-style politics, 123, 146, 159
Regime theory, 191–193
Regional City, 183
Regional planner, 480
Regionalism, 49–51
Regressive tax, 5, 68, 81, 88
Regulation, 45–46, 425–444
Rehabilitation policy, 313–315
Relative deprivation, 326, 328–329, 358
Rendition, 49–51
Reno, Nevada, 483
Representative bureaucracy, 274, 288
Republican Party
  closed primaries, 132
  Contract for America, 34, 47
  control of Congress, 47
  education finance, 80–81, 378
  environment, 432, 439
  ethnic loyalities, 202
  gerrymander, 216
  housing policy, 416
  ideology and, 9, 130, 133, 137
  judges and, 300
  legislatures, 230
  political broker role, 132
  regional base, 113
  social base, 135
  soft money, 127
  Southern strength, 133

  voter turnout and, 125
Reputational analysis, 184, 207
Research Triangle, North Carolina, 465
Reserved powers, 36–37, 39, 59
Resource Conservation and Recovery Act
  of 1976, 435, 445
Responsible-party model, 220, 234
Retroactive accountability, 123, 147
Revenue bond, 78, 87
Revenue sources, 67–78
Revenue-anticipation note, 77, 87
Reynolds v. *Sims*, 235n
Rhode Island v. *Innis*, 309, 321n
Rhode Island, 10, 52, 82, 103, 114, 131, 138,
  229, 244, 251, 282, 297, 299, 462
Right-to-work law, 455, 469
Riverside, California, 483
Robinson v. *Cahill*, 80, 391n
Rodriguez v. *San Antonio School District*, 80,
  89n, 391n
Roe v. *Wade*, 59n
Role-playing model, 104
Roper Center for Public Opinion Re-
  search, 6, 93–94, 135
Rubber dollar ruling, 25
Russians, 165
Rutan v. *Republican Party of Illinois*, 148n,
  270, 288n

Sacramento, California, 202
Safe Drinking Water Act of 1974, 429
Sagebrush rebellion, 51–55, 59
Saint Petersburg, Florida, 163
Sales tax, 73–76, 87
San Antonio School District v. *Rodriguez*, 377
San Antonio, Texas, 80, 173, 194
San Bernardino, California, 170
San Diego, California, 163, 194, 199, 352,
  400–402, 466
San Francisco, California, 123, 169, 402, 466
Saturn plant, 450
Savage Inequalities, 4–5, 18, 228, 377, 390n
Scandinavians, 253
Scholastic aptitude test, 384
School districts, 152, 158, 178
School lunch program, 367
Scottsdale, Arizona, 285
Section 8, 414–415, 420
Secular humanism, 380
Select committee, 223, 234

Senior executive service, 272
Separate-but-equal doctrine, 371, 388
Serrano v. Priest, 80, 89n, 377, 391n
Severance tax, 53, 59, 73–74, 87
Sexual harassment, 278
Sharing model, 104
Shaw v. Reno, 236n
Shelley v. Kramer, 424n
Short ballot, 168, 178
Sierra Club, 108
Silicon Valley, 56, 191, 465
Single-purpose local government, 152–154
Sipuel v. Oklahoma State Regents, 389n
Smith v. Allwright, 119n
Smith-Hughes Act, 367
Social capital, 101
Social conflict
  balkanization, 12–13
  bureaucracy and, 275–278
  constitutions and, 17–18, 28–30
  courts and, 302–308
  economic development, 466–468
  education, 371–382
  elections and, 144–145
  environment, 439–442
  governors and, 258–260
  housing policy, 418
  Interstate Highway Systems and, 21
  land use regulation, 441
  legislature and, 215–219
  local politics, 175–176, 204
  transportation policy, 418
  welfare reform, 354–356
Social Darwinism, 334, 358
Social good, 75, 88, 426, 445
Social insurance, 340–341, 358
Social mobility, 325, 358
Social Security, 106, 337, 338, 340, 358
Social welfare policy, 234–358, 336–340
Social worker, 480
Soft money, 127, 133, 147
South
  annexations, 173
  civil rights movement, 28
  community development, 415
  community power and, 188
  compact theory, 35
  Democratic Party, 138
  economic development, 455
  elections, 123

growth patterns, 50, 55, 260
local government, 154
non-ideological parties, 134
organized crime, 302
political culture, 8, 11
public housing, 412
racial politics, 202–203
South Carolina, 10, 29, 35, 52, 82, 103, 114, 131, 229, 244, 299
South Dakota, 10, 52, 72, 82, 103, 114, 131, 229, 244, 299, 456
Southern Growth Politics Board, 51
Southwest, 11, 154, 260, 302, 412, 455, 466
Soviet Union, 2
Speaker of the house, 221, 234
Special districts, 152, 158, 178
Spectators, 92, 99, 101, 118
Spoils system, 240, 262, 270
Spring Hill, Tennessee, 450
St. Louis, Missouri, 412, 460
St. Paul, Minnesota, 140, 415
Standard Oil Corporation, 64
Standing committee, 223, 234
State education agency, 366, 388
State implementation plan, 431, 446
Statutory law, 18, 31
Staunton, Virginia, 161, 229
Stratificationist theory, 184, 207
Strict constructionist, 37
Strong mayor, 163–164, 178
Student Nonviolent Coordinating Committee, 140
Suburbs, 374–376
Sunbelt, 49–50, 59, 356
Sunset law, 214, 234
Super legislation, 20, 31
Superfund, 435, 446
Superintendent of education, 366, 387
Supplemental Security Income, 345
Supreme Court
  abortion, 41
  affirmative action, 276
  busing decisions, 363–372
  capital punishment, 307
  civil rights, 30
  criminal justice standards, 308–309
  environmental protection, 437
  equal representation, 41
  exclusionary rule, 307–308
  federalism, 38, 39, 41

Supreme Court *(continued)*
  freedom of speech, 19
  good faith exception, 307–308
  housing segregation, 406–407
  juries, 305
  legislative apportionment, 215
  legislative veto, 214
  patronage, 270–271
  primary elections, 132
  racial gerrymanders, 216–217
  representation, 216–217
  school desegregation, 41, 371–376
  severance tax, 53, 73–74
  taking issue, 441
  voting rights, 97
Surface Transit Assistance Act of 1982,
    399, 420
Survey Research Center, 331
Sustainable agriculture, 438
Sustainable development, 438
Swann v. *Charlotte-Mecklenburg Board of Ed-
    ucation*, 390n
Systemic power theory, 192

Taiwan, 452
Taking issue, 441, 446
Tammany Hall, 165
Tashjian v. *Republican Party of Connecticut,*
    148n
Tax abatement, 457, 469
Tax anticipation note, 77, 87
Tax base breadth, 74, 88
Tax burden, 68, 81–83, 88
Tax Foundation, 51, 52
Tax increment financing, 458, 469
Tax or expenditure limitation movement,
    64, 81, 88
Tax progressivity, 5
Teachers, 479
Tennessee, 10, 29, 52, 82, 103, 114, 131, 229,
    244, 247, 382, 459
Term limitation, 230
Terre Haute, Indiana, 398
Texas
  annexation law, 173
  campaign finance, 126–128
  courts, 299, 308
  economic development, 455
  education finance, 80, 379
  energy taxes, 53

  fiscal federalism, 52
  governors, 244, 246, 254
  ideology, 103
  interest groups, 114
  legislature, 229
  no income tax, 72
  political culture, 10
  political economy, 85
  primary elections, 131
  school segregation, 372
  soft money, 133
  tax progressivity, 82
  white primary, 97
Three M Corporation, 449
Tison v. *Arizona*, 309
Toledo, Ohio, 139
Toronto, Ontario, 172
Total quality management, 281
Town meeting, 163
Townships, 153–154, 156, 158, 178
Toxic Substances Control Act of 1976, 435,
    446
Traditionalistic culture, 8–11, 14
Transfer payments, 340–342, 358
Transformational politics, 440, 446
Transportation, 394–404
Tripartite organization, 127, 147
Trustee role, 219, 234
Tulsa, Oklahoma, 161
Tuskegee, Alabama, 216
Twenty-fourth Amendment, 97
Twenty-sixth Amendment, 96
Two-tier government, 172, 178
Tyler, Texas, 397–398

U.S. Steel Corporation, 185, 434–435, 463
Unemployment compensation, 143, 341, 344
Uniform Crime Reports, 302
Unitary government, 35
Unitary interest theory, 191
United Auto Workers, 107
United Farm Workers, 203
United States v. *Leon*, 309, 321n
United States v. *Sheppard*, 309, 321n
United States Conference of Mayors, 108
United Steel Workers, 107
Unreformed politics, 112, 147, 159
Urban enterprise zone, 46, 456, 469
Urban Mass Transit Act of 1974, 399
Urban planner, 480

Urban renewal, 413–414, 416, 420
Utah, 10, 27, 52, 82, 103, 114, 131, 134, 229, 244, 299
Utica, New York, 436

Venture capital, 458, 469
Vermont, 10, 52, 81, 82, 103, 104, 114, 131, 140, 229, 244, 251, 254, 299, 441
Veto, 245, 262
Virginia, 10, 29, 52, 82, 98, 103, 131, 244, 253–254, 299, 365
Visalia, California, 483
Voice option, 100, 200, 207
Voinovich v. *Quilter*, 235n
Volunteerism, 124, 147, 169
Voter turnout, 125
Voting Rights Act of 1965, 97–99, 118, 125, 142, 143
Voucher plan, 371, 388

War on Poverty, 346, 350, 358
Ward elections, 123, 147
Ward's Cove Packing Co., Inc. v. *Antonio*, 289n
Washington, D.C., 10, 29, 52, 72, 82, 103, 110, 114, 138, 229, 244, 277, 299, 325, 371, 399, 402
Water Pollution Control Act, 1972, 428, 446
Water Quality Act of 1987, 429
Watergate, 115, 125
Weak mayor, 163–164, 178
Welfare policy, 336–340
Welfare reform, 349–356
Wellston, Ohio, 460
Wesberry v. *Sanders*, 235n
West, 50, 123, 138, 173, 260
West Palm Beach, Florida, 483
West Virginia, 10, 52, 82, 98, 103, 114, 131, 229, 244, 255, 299
Weston, Illinois, 91
White flight, 373, 374, 388
White primary, 97
White-collar crime, 302, 304, 319
Willamette River, 430–431
Williams v. *Florida*, 321n
Wilmington, Delaware, 375

Winnipeg, Manitoba, 172
Winter Commission, 279
Wisconsin, 9, 10, 52, 82, 83, 103, 114, 131, 215, 228, 229, 244, 245, 272, 297, 298, 299, 315, 353, 463
Women
  affirmative action, 274
  comparable worth, 277–278, 287
  electoral success, 144
  employment success, 274
  governors, 253–254
  interest groups, 109
  as judges, 301
  mayors, 199
  National Women's Political Caucus, 144
  organized labor, 99
  participation, 99
  poverty rates, 329
  voting rights, 96
Woodson v. *North Carolina*, 308
Workers' compensation, 143
Workfare, 352–353
Wyoming, 10, 52, 72, 82, 97, 103, 111, 114, 131, 229, 244, 299

X Family, 182–183

Yale University, 197
Yonkers, New York, 407
You Decide
  budget cutting, 68
  campaign finance, 128–129
  comparable worth, 277
  constitutional circumvention, 26
  crime policy, 316
  efficiency in government, 8–9
  federalism, 37
  cmmigration, 205
  trustees or delegates, 221
  welfare eligibility, 338
Youngstown, Ohio, 463–465
Yugoslavia, 381

Zero-base budgeting, 284, 288
Zoning, 410, 420